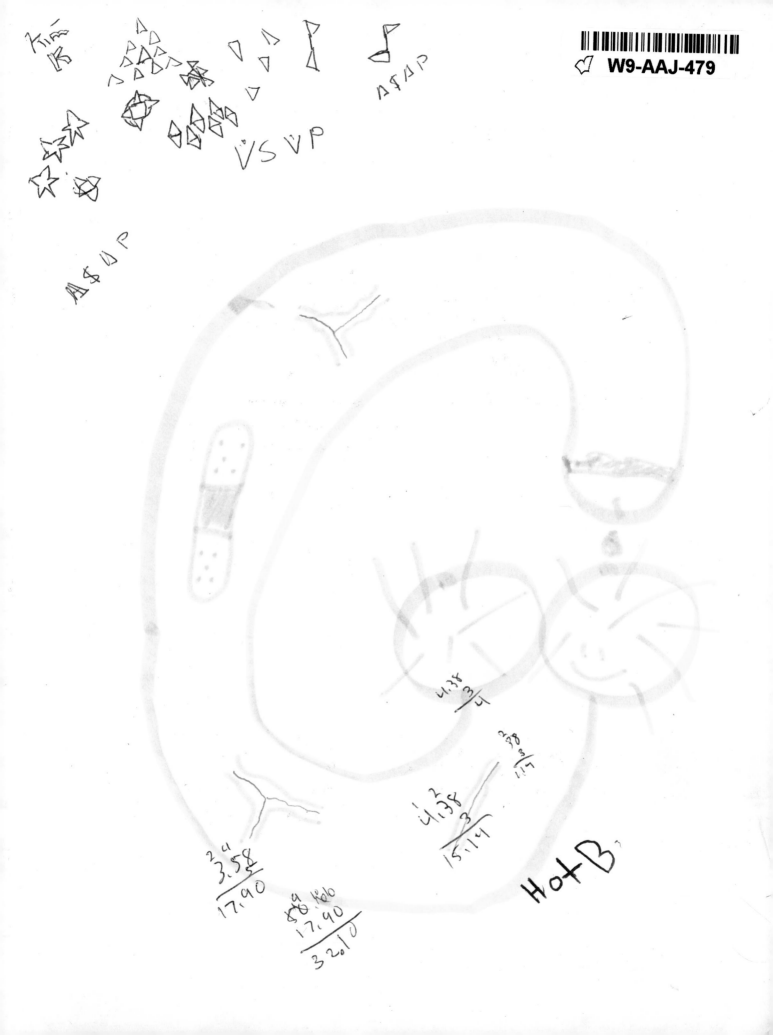

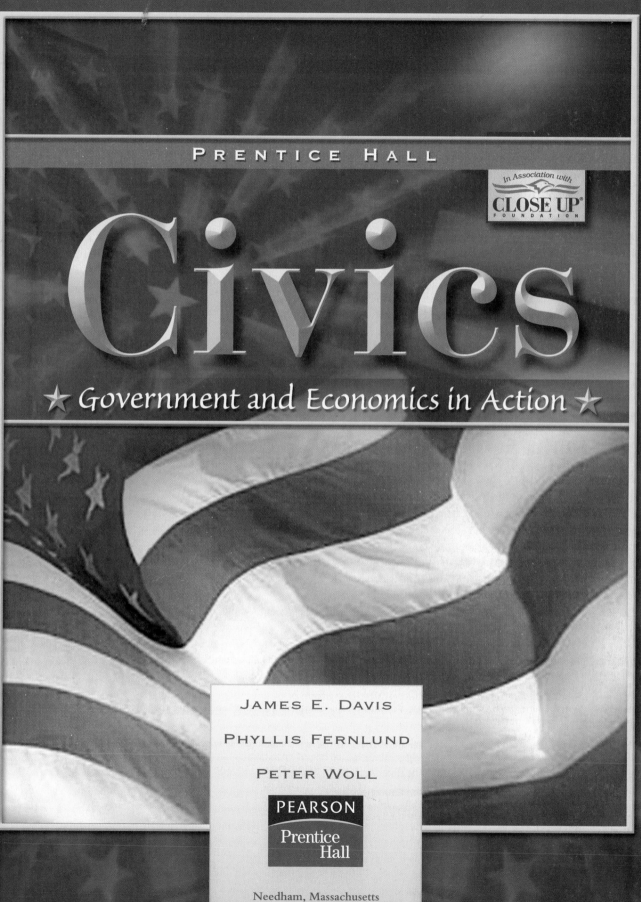

PRENTICE HALL

In Association with
CLOSE UP
FOUNDATION

Civics

★ Government and Economics in Action ★

JAMES E. DAVIS

PHYLLIS FERNLUND

PETER WOLL

PEARSON

Prentice
Hall

Needham, Massachusetts
Upper Saddle River, New Jersey

About the Authors

Senior Authors

James E. Davis

James Davis is Executive Director of the Social Science Education Consortium in Boulder, Colorado. He received his Ed.D. in social science education from the University of Colorado, Boulder. An active NCSS member for more than 30 years, and a former social studies teacher, he has developed curriculum materials and teacher resources for both elementary and secondary levels.

Phyllis Fernlund

Phyllis Fernlund is Dean of the School of Education at Sonoma State University. She received her B.A. and M.A. from the University of Illinois, Urbana, in the teaching of history and her Ph.D. in education from Northwestern University. A former high school social studies teacher, she has developed curriculum and professional development materials for K–12, business, and higher education.

Consulting Author

Peter Woll

Peter Woll is Professor of Politics at Brandeis University. He received his B.A. from Haverford College and his Ph.D. from Cornell University. His fields of specialization include American Government and Constitutional Law. Professor Woll has written 14 books, including *American Government: Reading and Cases* (2004) and *American Government: Competition and Compromise* (2001).

About the Close Up Foundation

The Close Up Foundation is the nation's leading civic education organization. Since 1971, Close Up has been a leader in the social sciences field, reaching millions of students, educators, and other adults. The Foundation's mission of informed participation in government and democracy drives its experiential civic education programs in Washington, D.C., for students and teachers, as well as its television programs on C-SPAN and its award-winning publications and videos. Close Up's work represents a multidimensional approach to citizenship education by increasing community involvement and civic literacy—one student, one citizen, at a time.

ISBN 0-13-181640-3
1 2 3 4 5 6 7 8 9 10   07 06 05 04

Program Reviewers

Content Consultants

Jeffrey J. Blaga, Ph.D.
Chair, Social Studies Department
William Horlick High School
Racine, Wisconsin

John R. Doyle
Administrative Director, Division
of Social Sciences
Miami-Dade County Public
Schools
Miami, Florida

Rita Geiger
Former Director of Social
Studies and Foreign Language
Norman Public Schools
Norman, Oklahoma

Betty M. Holland
Jefferson County Public Schools
Birmingham, Alabama

Thomas Ilgen
Jones Professor of Political
Science
Pitzer College
Claremont, California

Anne B. Langner
Central Baldwin Middle School
Robertsdale, Alabama

John P. Lunstrom
Professor Emeritus of Education
Florida State University
Tallahassee, Florida

Jack C. Morgan
Professor Emeritus
University of Louisville
Louisville, Kentucky

Chuck Schierloh
Social Studies Coordinator
Lima City Schools
Lima, Ohio

Dr. Donald Schwartz
California State University at
Long Beach
Long Beach, California

Heather Watkins
Social Studies Lead Teacher
South Oldham High School
Crestwood, Kentucky

Program Advisers

Michal Howden
Social Studies Consultant
Zionsville, Indiana

Joseph Wieczorek
Social Studies Consultant
Baltimore, Maryland

Service Learning Consultant

Maria Elena Keenan
Educational Specialist
Miami-Dade County Public
Schools
Miami, Florida

Reading Consultants

Kevin Feldman
K-12 Literacy Specialist
Sonoma County Office of
Education
Santa Rosa, California

Kate Kinsella
Adolescent Literacy Specialist
San Francisco State University
San Francisco, California

Block Scheduling Consultant

Barbara Slater Stern
Associate Professor
James Madison University
Harrisonburg, Virginia

Law and Government Consultant

Gregory I. Massing
Assistant District Attorney
Salem, Massachusetts

Economics Consultants

Arthur O'Sullivan
Professor of Economics
Oregon State University
Corvallis, Oregon
Author, *Economics:
Principles in Action*

Steven M. Sheffrin
Dean, Division of Social Sciences
University of California at Davis
Davis, California
Author, *Economics:
Principles in Action*

Contents

Target Reading Skills . . . . **.xvii**

Reading and Writing Handbook . . . . **.xviii**

UNIT 1 ⭐

Foundations of Citizenship . . . . **xxiv**

CHAPTER 1 **A Portrait of Americans** . . . . **.2**

   1 Who Americans Are 4

     Citizenship Skills: How to Volunteer . . . . **.9**

   2 America: A Cultural Mosaic 10

   3 The Values That Unite Us 18

   Review and Assessment 25

CHAPTER 2 **American Society and Its Values** . . . . **.28**

   1 Groups and Institutions 30

   2 Society's Training Grounds 34

     Debating the Issues: School Vouchers . . . . **.40**

   3 The Economy 41

   4 Government: Meeting Society's Needs 45

   Review and Assessment 51

CHAPTER 3 **The Meaning of Citizenship** . . . . **.54**

   1 What It Means to Be a Citizen 56

   2 The Rights, Duties, and Responsibilities of Citizens 59

     Citizenship Skills: How to Interview for a Job . . . . . **.68**

   3 Citizenship and Our Other Roles in Society 69

   Review and Assessment 77

UNIT 2 ⭐

Creating a Lasting Government 80

CHAPTER 4 America's Political Heritage 82

   1 The Colonial Experience 84

   2 Roots of American Government 91

   3 Moving Toward Nationhood 95

    Debating the Issues: Nation-Building 102

   Review and Assessment 103

   The Declaration of Independence 106

CHAPTER 5 Creating the Constitution 110

   1 The Constitutional Convention .112

    Citizenship Skills: How to Analyze
    Public Documents 119

   2 The Struggle for Ratification 120

   3 The Supreme Law of the Land .124

   Review and Assessment 133

   The Constitution of the United States 136

CHAPTER 6 The Bill of Rights 158

   1 Adding the Bill of Rights 160

   2 Protections in the Bill of Rights .163

   3 Interpreting the Bill of Rights 172

    Debating the Issues: Faith-Based
    Providers of Social Services 180

   Review and Assessment 181

CHAPTER 7 Our Enduring Constitution 184

   1 Changing the Law of the Land .186

   2 A Flexible Framework 196

    Debating the Issues: English as the Nation's
    Official Language 204

   Review and Assessment 205

Contents

UNIT 3
The Federal Government 208

CHAPTER 8   **The Legislative Branch** **210**

1 The Members of Congress 212

2 The Powers of Congress 218
    Debating the Issues: Government
    Regulation of the Internet **222**

3 How Congress Is Organized 223

4 Following a Bill in Congress 229

Review and Assessment 235

CHAPTER 9   **The Executive Branch** **238**

1 The Roles of the President 240
    Citizenship Skills: How to Conduct a Survey **248**

2 The Organization of the Executive Branch 249

3 Presidents and Power 255

Review and Assessment 261

CHAPTER 10   **The Judicial Branch** **264**

1 The Role of the Federal Courts 266

2 The Organization of the Federal Courts 271

3 The Supreme Court 276
    Debating the Issues: Term Limits **286**

Review and Assessment 287

UNIT 4

State and Local Government 290

CHAPTER 11 **State Government** 292

    1 Federalism: One Nation and Fifty States 294

    2 State Legislatures 298

    **Citizenship Skills: How to Write a Letter
to the Editor** 304

    3 The State Executive Branch 305

    4 State Courts 310

    Review and Assessment 315

CHAPTER 12 **Local Government** 318

    1 Types of Local Government 320

    2 Local Government Services and Revenue 327

    **Debating the Issues: Social Services
for Illegal Immigrants** 335

    3 Conflict and Cooperation Between Governments 336

    Review and Assessment 343

Contents

UNIT 5 ★
Foundations of Economics 346

CHAPTER 13   **What Is an Economy?** **348**

     1 Why Societies Have Economies 350

     2 Basic Economic Decisions 358

       **Citizenship Skills: How to Analyze
       an Editorial** **362**

     3 Three Types of Economies 363

     Review and Assessment 371

CHAPTER 14   **Basics of Our Economic System** **374**

     1 The Principles of Our Market Economy 376

     2 The Role of Businesses in the American Economy 382

       **Debating the Issues: Genetically
       Modified Foods** **387**

     3 Labor in the American Economy .388

     Review and Assessment 397

CHAPTER 15   **Our Economy and You** **400**

     1 Managing Your Money 402

       Citizenship Skills: How to Be a Wise Consumer . . .**408**

     2 Spending and Saving 409

     3 Careers: Planning for the Future .416

     Review and Assessment 423

UNIT 6

Government and the Economy 426

CHAPTER 16 **Government's Role in Our Economy** . . .**428**

1 Government Intervention in the Economy 430
**Debating the Issues: Stricter Regulations
on Corporate Practices** **435**
2 Government's Efforts to Solve
Economic Problems 436
3 Managing the Economy 443
Review and Assessment 451

CHAPTER 17 **Money and Banking** **454**

1 Money 456
2 Our Banking System 460
**Citizenship Skills: How to Write a Letter
to a Public Official** **468**
3 The Federal Reserve System 469
Review and Assessment 477

CHAPTER 18 **Public Finance** **480**

1 Government and Economic Goals 482
2 Paying for Government 491
3 Government Policy and Spending 497
Debating the Issues: Tax Cuts **504**
Review and Assessment 505

Contents

UNIT 7 ★

The American Legal System 508

CHAPTER 19 Laws and Our Society 510

1 Why We Have Laws 512
**Citizenship Skills: How to Analyze
Television News Programs** **517**
2. Where Our Laws Come From 518
3 Kinds of Laws 524
Review and Assessment 531

CHAPTER 20 Criminal and Juvenile Justice 534

1 Crime in American Society 536
2 The Criminal Justice System 542
3 The Juvenile Justice System 552
**Debating the Issues: Trying Juveniles
as Adults** **556**
Review and Assessment 557

CHAPTER 21 Civil Justice 560

1 The Role of Civil Law 562
**Citizenship Skills: How to Analyze a
News Article** **568**
2 Civil Procedure 569
3 Choices in Civil Justice 574
Review and Assessment 583

UNIT 8 ★

People Make a Difference 586

CHAPTER 22   **Political Parties in Our Democracy 588**
    1 The Role of Political Parties 590
    2 Our Two-Party System 595
     Debating the Issues: Campaign Contributions 604
    3 Choosing Candidates 605
    Review and Assessment 611

CHAPTER 23   **Voting and Elections 614**
    1 Being a Voter 616
    2 How Candidates and Groups Try to Influence
      Your Vote 622
     Citizenship Skills: How to Conduct an Interview . .630
    3 Campaigning for Office 631
    Review and Assessment 639

UNIT 9 ★

The United States and the World . . .642

CHAPTER 24   **American Foreign Policy 644**
    1 What Is Foreign Policy? 646
    2 Making Foreign Policy 651
     Debating the Issues: Promoting
     Democracy and Human Rights Overseas 656
    3 Foreign Policy in Action 657
    Review and Assessment 667

CHAPTER 25   **One Nation Among Many 670**
    1 The Nations of the World 672
     Citizenship Skills: How to Express Your Views 678
    2 Relations Between and Within Nations 679
    3 The Challenge of Interdependence 686
    Review and Assessment 693

Reference Section 696

Special Features

 Skills for Life

Interpreting Graphs 26
Identifying Points of View .50
Transferring Information 76
Analyzing Political Cartoons 90
Analyzing Primary Sources 132
Identifying Causes and Effects 171
Analyzing Photographs 195
Sequencing 234
Drawing Inferences 260
Evaluating the Validity of Internet Sources 275
Comparing Maps Over Time 314
Distinguishing Facts and Opinions 342
Synthesizing Information 370
Identifying Historical Trends 396
Determining Relevance 422
Evaluating Long-term Effects 450
Solving Problems 476
Recognizing Propaganda 490
Summarizing 530
Identifying Bias 541
Finding Main Ideas and Supporting Details 582
Comparing and Contrasting 610
Making Decisions 638
Predicting Consequences 666
Determining Patterns and Distributions of Maps 692

 Citizenship Skills

How to Volunteer 9
How to Interview for a Job 68
How to Analyze Public Documents 119
How to Conduct a Survey 248
How to Write a Letter to the Editor 304
How to Analyze an Editorial 362
How to Be a Wise Consumer 408
How to Write a Letter to a Public Official 468
How to Analyze Television News Programs 517
How to Analyze a News Article 568
How to Conduct an Interview 630
How to Express Your Views 678

 Debating the Issues

Should the Federal Government Give Parents
    Vouchers for Private School Tuition? 40
Should the United States Lead Nation-Building
    Efforts Around the World? 102
Should the Government Fund Faith-Based
    Providers of Social Services? 180
Should English Be the Nation's Official Language? . .204
Should the Government Regulate the Internet
    to Protect Users' Privacy? 222
Should the Government Set Term Limits For
    Supreme Court Justices? 286
Should the Government Provide Social Services
    to Illegal Immigrants? .335
Should Genetically Modified Foods Be Labeled? . . .387
Should the Government Impose Stricter
    Regulations on U.S. Corporate Practices? 435
Can Tax Cuts Stimulate Economic Growth? 504
Should the U.S. Court System Try Juveniles
    as Adults? 556
Should Further Limits Be Placed on Campaign
    Contributions? 604
Should U.S. Foreign Policy Focus on Promoting
    Democracy and Human Rights Overseas? 656

Students Make a Difference

Joey Peña 7
Khandi Johnson 63
Clem Wood 177
Christopher Elmore 202
Sarah Keister 230
Laquanda Leaven 256
Emily Meade 301
Ryan Melville 330
Michael Arriaga 368
Naudereh Noori 389
Marc Mallegni 441
Heather Thompkins 502
Laurel Olson 553
Melinda Sebastian 575
Matthew R. Greenfield 593
Nathaniel Weixel 633
Cassandra Katsiaficas 661
Jessica Rimington 690

Civics and Economics

The Bureau of Labor Statistics 5
The Cost of Raising Children 33
Young Volunteers 74
The Press 88
The Census 129
Department of the Interior 167
Income Gap Between Men and Women 199
Fair Labor Standards Act .217
Office of Management and Budget 251
Supreme Court Decisions 279
State Budgets 309
Love Park 337
Agriculture 352
State and Local Incentives to Business 377
The Health Insurance Industry 414
Labor Unions 432
Women and Small Businesses 464
Income Tax 486
Prison Population Rise and Cost 525
The Justice System 545
Asbestos 578
Fundraising 607
Campaigns and Money .634
World Trade 654
Doctors Without Borders 684

Focus on the Supreme Court

Korematsu v. *United States* (1944) 60
Grutter v. *Bollinger* (2003) 200
United States v. *Nixon* (1974) 282
Reno v. *Condon* (2000) 312
Goldberg v. *Kelly* (1970) 404
Eldred v. *Ashcroft* (2003) 439
Gideon v. *Wainwright* (1963) 544
Bush v. *Gore* (2000) 620
Crosby v. *National Foreign Trade Council* (2000) 683

Citizen Profiles

Mickey Leland 14
Michele Foreman 39
John Dickinson 100
James Madison 114
Carol Mosley-Braun 219
Louis Brandeis 272
Shirley Franklin 340
Michael Dell 359
Andrea Jung 385
Upton Sinclair 438
Alice Rivlin 474
Alan Greenspan 498
Thurgood Marshall 554
Mark Hanna 600
Madeleine Albright 664

Primary Sources

Colin Powell 67
James S. Ayars 176
Susan B. Anthony 191
Robert Reich 257
Linda Chavez 296
Occupational Outlook Handbook 420
Code of Hammurabi 521
Borel v. *Fiberboard Paper Products* 571
Ronald Reagan 632
Kofi Annan 689

Links to History

Ellis and Angel Islands 16
Slavery in America 117
American Armed Conflicts 244
Local Government 322
Labor Unions 390
Banking in America 470
Civil Law 570
Major Third-Party Presidential Campaigns 597
The Cold War 681

Special Features

Law and the Real World

The Patriot Act 49
The Death Penalty 169
Violent Video Games 268
High School Exit Exams 328
Lemon Laws 410
Taxing Your Internet Purchases 493
Student Survey 520
18-Year-Olds and the Vote .617
Democracies Around the World 676

ANALYZING Political Cartoons

Bill of Rights 22
Funding for Education 47
"Don't Blame Me!" 65
Taxation Without Representation 96
Ratifying the Constitution .121
Terrorism and the Bill of Rights 166
Museum of the Unconstitutional 190
Legislators in Congress 226
Congressional Inaction 246
An Overworked Court 277
Redistricting 299
Tammany Hall 325
Command Economy 365
Union and Management 392
Household Budgets 412
Business Monopolies 437
Corporate Mergers 465
Tax Legislation 495
Copyright Software 514
Internal Revenue Service 538
Inheritance 565
Political Party Symbols 606
Last Minute Campaign Stop 627
"You're to Blame" 653
Security Council 688

Maps

Immigration to the United States, 1900-2000 12
World Empires circa 1770 86
Slave States and Free States, 1854 189
Federal Court Circuits 273
State Constitutions 296
Federal Reserve Districts 471
The NATO Alliance 494
Comparison of Selected Nations 674

Graphs, Charts, Tables, and Diagrams

American Work Force 6
Immigration to the United States 12
United States Population by Group, 2000 15
The American Dream 25
Five Social Institutions 32
Families with Children Under 18 35
Religious Affiliation in the United States 36
Occupations and Education .38
American Economic Freedom 42
The Naturalization Process 57
Citizenship and You 62
The Seven Social Roles 70
Influences on Behavior 71
A Nation of Volunteers 73
Sources of American Government Concepts 93
From the Articles of Confederation to
   the Constitution 116
Sharing the Power 127
Checks and Balances 130
Formal Amendment Process 161
The Bill of Rights 164
Amendments 11-27 187
Amendments to the Constitution 192
Representation in Congress 216
Powers of Congress 220
The Growth of Congress 224
How a Bill Becomes a Law .227
Profile of Minimum Wage Earners, 2002 231
Roles of the President 242
Vice Presidents Who Succeeded to the Presidency . . .250
Executive Departments 252
The Federal Court System 270
How a Case Can Be Appealed to the
   Supreme Court 280

Number of Supreme Court Nominations for
Each President 284
How the States Spend Their Money, 2001 302
The Duties and Powers of the Governor 306
Mayor-Council Plans 324
Local Government Spending vs. Revenue,
2000-2001 333
Relations Among Governments: The No
Child Left Behind Act .338
The Want-Satisfaction Chain 354
The Factors of Production 367
Circular Flow Model of a Market Economy 378
Supply and Demand for Strawberries 380
Payments for Resources .383
The Importance of Corporations 385
Methods that Employers and Unions
Use in Disputes 391
Membership in American Labor Unions 393
Types of Income 403
Median Credit Card Debt 405
Personal Consumption, 2003 411
Common Savings Plans 413
Types of Insurance 415
Career Outlook, 2000–2010 418
Gross Domestic Product, 1992-2002 444
The Federal Budget for 2002 445
Tax Deductions from Your Paycheck 446
Annual Budget Surpluses and Deficits 448
The Parts of the Money Supply, 2003 463

Insured Financial Institutions in the
United States, 2003 466
The Story of a Check 472
Government's Role in the Circular Flow of
Economic Activity 484
Calculating GDP 487
Gross Domestic Product .488
Characteristics of a Good Tax 492
Regressive Tax Summary .494
Use of Budget Policy to Stabilize the Economy 499
National Debt 1993-2003 501
Types and Causes of Crime 539
Types of Serious Crimes in 2002 543
Criminal Law: From Arrest to Conviction 546
Prisoners Under State Jurisdiction, 2002 549
Civil Cases in U.S. District Courts, 1988-2002 572
Alternatives to a Civil Trial 576
Top Civil Cases Awards in 2002 580
American Political Parties .598
Party Identification in the United States,
1952-2000 602
Voting Methods 618
Political Action Committee Contributions 625
Propaganda Techniques .626
The Electoral College 636
United States Defense Spending 1980-2002 647
Conflict and Resolution .662
Comparison of Selected Nations 674
Types of Conflict 680

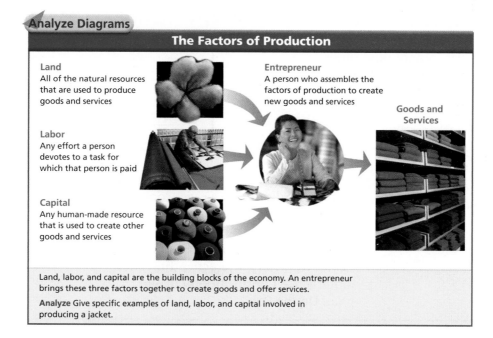

Analyze Diagrams

The Factors of Production

Land
All of the natural resources that are used to produce goods and services

Labor
Any effort a person devotes to a task for which that person is paid

Capital
Any human-made resource that is used to create other goods and services

Entrepreneur
A person who assembles the factors of production to create new goods and services

Goods and Services

Land, labor, and capital are the building blocks of the economy. An entrepreneur brings these three factors together to create goods and offer services.

Analyze Give specific examples of land, labor, and capital involved in producing a jacket.

Learning With Technology

In *Civics: Government and Economics in Action* you will learn about the United States government and economy —and how **you** can participate as an active citizen. Technology will help you put what you learn to work in your community, your state, and your nation.

Civics: Government and Economics in Action Video Program

The *Civics: Government and Economics in Action Video Program* created with our partner, the Close Up Foundation, explores government and economics in real life. Each video segment consists of three sections: an **Overview** of a government or economics issue, an **Up Close** section that focuses on a topic in depth, and an **Economic Impact** activity. Look for references in every unit.

Watch the **Civics: Government and Economics in Action** videos to learn about immigrants' own stories.

Video: Overview ▶Video: Up Close

Go Online
PHSchool.com

For: Writing Activity
Visit: PHSchool.com
Webcode: mpd-6181

Go Online at PHSchool.com

Use the Web Code in each Go Online Box to access exciting information or activities at PHSchool.com.
How to Use the Web Code:
1. Go to PHSchool.com
2. Enter the Web Code
3. Click Go!

Interactive Textbook

The *Civics: Government and Economics in Action* Interactive Textbook brings your textbook to life. Learn about government and economics using interactive charts, graphs, and other activities. Define and understand vocabulary words at the click of a mouse.

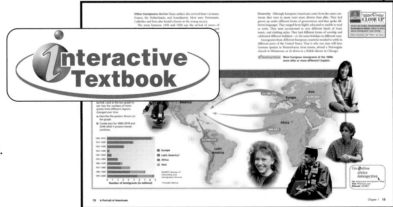

Go Online
civics
interactive

Civics Interactive

Your *Civics: Government and Economics in Action* textbook contains special Web links to make civics come alive. Look for the Civics Interactive box on these activities:
- Local Citizenship Activities
- Civics Interactive Charts, Graphs, Diagrams, and Maps
- Links to History Interactive Timelines
- Interactive Constitution Activities
- You Decide Poll

Target Reading Skills

The Target Reading Skills will help you understand the social studies reading you do. Each chapter focuses on one of these reading skills. If you develop a bank of reading strategies, or skills, you may draw on the particular strategies that will help you understand the text you are reading.

Reading Process

Previewing can help you understand and remember what you read. This skill involves practicing these previewing skills: setting a purpose for reading, predicting what the text will be about, and asking questions before you read.

▶ **Chapters 2, 16, and 23**

Clarifying Meaning

If you do not understand something you are reading right away, you can use several skills to clarify the meaning of the word or idea. This skill involves practicing these strategies for clarifying meaning: rereading, reading ahead, paraphrasing, and summarizing.

▶ **Chapters 1, 9, 15, and 22**

Main Idea

Since you cannot remember every detail of what you read, it is important to identify the main ideas. The main idea of a section or paragraph is the most important point and the one you want to remember. This skill involves practicing these skills: identifying both stated and implied main ideas and identifying supporting details.

▶ **Chapters 3, 11, and 24**

Cause and Effect

Recognizing cause and effect will help you understand relationships among the situations and events you are reading about. This skill involves practicing these cause-and-effect skills: identifying cause and effect, recognizing multiple causes, and understanding effects.

▶ **Chapters 4, 14, and 21**

Context

Using the context of an unfamiliar word can help you understand its meaning. Context includes the words, phrases, and sentences surrounding a word. This skill involves practicing using these context clues: definitions, contrast, and your own general knowledge.

▶ **Chapters 5, 10, and 17**

Sequence

A sequence is the order in which events occur. Sequencing skills will help you understand and remember the events. This skill involves practicing these sequencing skills: understanding sequence and recognizing words that signal sequence.

▶ **Chapters 6, 13, and 20**

Word Analysis

When you come across unfamiliar words, word analysis can help you figure out their meanings. This skill involves practicing these word analysis skills: analyzing word parts and recognizing word origins.

▶ **Chapters 7 and 18**

Comparison and Contrast

You can use comparison and contrast to sort out and analyze information you are reading. Comparing means examining the similarities between things. Contrasting is looking at differences. This skill involves practicing these skills: comparing and contrasting, identifying contrasts, and making comparisons.

▶ **Chapters 8, 12, 19, and 25**

Reading Informational Texts

Reading a magazine, an Internet page, or a textbook is not the same as reading a novel. The purpose of reading nonfiction texts is to acquire new information. On page M18 you'll read about some **Target Reading Skills** that you'll have a chance to practice as you read this textbook. Here we'll focus on a few skills that will help you read nonfiction with a more critical eye.

Analyze the Author's Purpose

Different types of materials are written with different purposes in mind. For example, a textbook is written to teach students information about a subject. The purpose of a technical manual is to teach someone how to use something, such as a computer. A newspaper editorial might be written to persuade the reader to accept a particular point of view. A writer's purpose influences how the material is presented. Sometimes an author states his or her purpose directly. More often, the purpose is only suggested, and you must use clues to identify the author's purpose.

Distinguish Between Facts and Opinions

It's important when reading informational texts to read actively and to distinguish between fact and opinion. A fact can be proven or disproven. An opinion cannot—it is someone's personal viewpoint or evaluation.

For example, the editorial pages in a newspaper offer opinions on topics that are currently in the news. You need to read newspaper editorials with an eye for bias and faulty logic. For example, the newspaper editorial at the right shows factual statements in blue and opinion statements in red. The underlined words are examples of highly charged words. They reveal bias on the part of the writer.

More than 5,000 people voted last week in favor of building a new shopping center, but the opposition won out. The margin of victory is irrelevant. Those radical voters who opposed the center are obviously self-serving elitists who do not care about anyone but themselves.

This month's unemployment figure for our area is 10 percent, which represents an increase of about 5 percent over the figure for this time last year. These figures mean that unemployment is worsening. But the people who voted against the mall probably do not care about creating new jobs.

Identify Evidence

Before you accept an author's conclusion, you need to make sure that the author has based the conclusion on enough evidence and on the right kind of evidence. An author may present a series of facts to support a claim, but the facts may not tell the whole story. For example, what evidence does the author of the newspaper editorial on the previous page provide to support his claim that the new shopping center would create more jobs? Is it possible that the shopping center might have put many small local businesses out of business, thus increasing unemployment rather than decreasing it?

Evaluate Credibility

Whenever you read informational texts, you need to assess the credibility of the author. This is especially true of sites you may visit on the Internet. All Internet sources are not equally reliable. Here are some questions to ask yourself when evaluating the credibility of a Web site.

❑ Is the Web site created by a respected organization, a discussion group, or an individual?

❑ Does the Web site creator include his or her name as well as credentials and the sources he or she used to write the material?

❑ Is the information on the site balanced or biased?

❑ Can you verify the information using two other sources?

❑ Is there a date telling when the Web site was created or last updated?

Writing for Social Studies

Writing is one of the most powerful communication tools you will ever use. You will use it to share your thoughts and ideas with others. Research shows that writing about what you read actually helps you learn new information and ideas. A systematic approach to writing—including prewriting, drafting, revising, and proofing—can help you write better, whether you're writing an essay or a research report.

Narrative Essays

Writing that tells a story about a personal experience

1 Select and Narrow Your Topic

A narrative is a story. In social studies, it might be a narrative essay about how an event affected you or your family.

2 Gather Details

Brainstorm a list of details you'd like to include in your narrative.

3 Write a First Draft

Start by writing a simple opening sentence that conveys the main idea of your essay. Continue by writing a colorful story that has interesting details. Write a conclusion that sums up the significance of the event or situation described in your essay.

4 Revise and Proof

Check to make sure you have not begun too many sentences with the word *I*. Replace general words with more colorful ones.

Main idea

Details

Significance of narrative

In my last year of college, I volunteered for an organization called Amigos De Las Americas (Friends of the Americas). I was sent to a remote village in Brazil and worked with villagers to improve the community's water supply and sanitation systems. The experience made me realize I wanted to work in the field of public health. When I went to Brazil, I never imagined what an incredible sense of purpose it would add to my life.

Persuasive Essays

Writing that supports an opinion or position

1 Select and Narrow Your Topic

Choose a topic that provokes an argument and has at least two sides. Choose a side. Decide which argument will appeal most to your audience and persuade them to understand your point of view.

2 Gather Evidence

Create a chart that states your position at the top and then lists the pros and cons for your position below, in two columns. Predict and address the strongest arguments against your stand.

3 Write a First Draft

Write a strong thesis statement that clearly states your position. Continue by presenting the strongest arguments in favor of your position and acknowledging and refuting opposing arguments.

4 Revise and Proof

Check to make sure you have made a logical argument and that you have not oversimplified the argument.

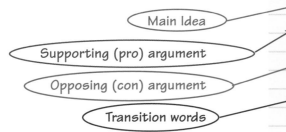

Main Idea

Supporting (pro) argument

Opposing (con) argument

Transition words

It is vital to vote in elections. When people vote, they tell public officials how to run the government. Not every proposal is carried out; however, politicians do their best to listen to what the majority of people want. Therefore, every vote is important.

Expository Essays

Writing that explains a process, compares and contrasts, explains causes and effects, or explores solutions to a problem

1 Identify and Narrow Your Topic

Expository writing is writing that explains something in detail. It might explain the similarities and differences between two or more subjects (compare and contrast). It might explain how one event causes another (cause and effect). Or it might explain a problem and describe a solution.

2 Gather Evidence

Create a graphic organizer that identifies details to include in your essay.

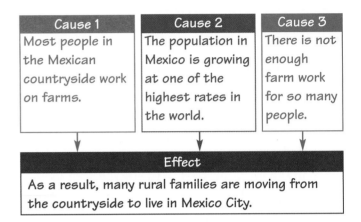

Cause 1	Cause 2	Cause 3
Most people in the Mexican countryside work on farms.	The population in Mexico is growing at one of the highest rates in the world.	There is not enough farm work for so many people.

Effect

As a result, many rural families are moving from the countryside to live in Mexico City.

3 Write Your First Draft

Write a topic sentence and then organize the essay around your similarities and differences, causes and effects, or problem and solutions. Be sure to include convincing details, facts, and examples.

4 Revise and Proof

Research Papers

Writing that presents research about a topic

1 Narrow Your Topic

Choose a topic you're interested in and make sure that it is not too broad. For example, instead of writing a report on Panama, write about the creation of the Panama Canal.

2 Acquire Information

Locate several sources of information about the topic from the library or the Internet. For each resource, create a source index card like the one at the right. Then take notes using an index card for each detail or subtopic. On the card, note which source the information was taken from. Use quotation marks when you copy the exact words from a source.

Source #1
McCullough, David. *The Path Between the Seas: The Creation of the Panama Canal, 1870-1914.* N.Y., Simon and Schuster, 1977.

3 Make an Outline

Use an outline to decide how to organize your report. Sort your index cards into the same order.

Outline
I. Introduction
II. Why the canal was built
III. How the canal was built
    A. Physical challenges
    B. Medical challenges
IV. Conclusion

> **Introduction**
> **Building the Panama Canal**
> Ever since Christopher Columbus first explored
> the Isthmus of Panama, the Spanish had been
> looking for a water route through it. They wanted
> to be able to sail west from Spain to Asia without
> sailing around South America. However, it was not
> until 1914 that the dream became a reality.

> **Conclusion**
> It took eight years and more than 70,000
> workers to build the Panama Canal. It
> remains one of the greatest engineering
> feats of modern times.

❶ Write a First Draft

Write an introduction, a body, and a conclusion. Leave plenty of space between lines so you can go back and add details that you may have left out.

❷ Revise and Proof

Be sure to include transition words between sentences and paragraphs. Here are some examples:

To show a contrast—*however, although, despite.*

To point out a reason—*since, because, if.*

To signal a conclusion—*therefore, consequently, so, then.*

Evaluating Your Writing

Use this table to help you evaluate your writing.

	Excellent	Good	Acceptable	Unacceptable
Purpose	Achieves purpose— to inform, persuade, or provide historical interpretation— very well	Informs, persuades, or provides historical interpretation reasonably well	Reader cannot easily tell if the purpose is to inform, persuade, or provide historical interpretation	Purpose is not clear
Organization	Develops ideas in a very clear and logical way	Presents ideas in a reasonably well-organized way	Reader has difficulty following the organization	Lacks organization
Elaboration	Explains all ideas with facts and details	Explains most ideas with facts and details	Includes some supporting facts and details	Lacks supporting details
Use of Language	Uses excellent vocabulary and sentence structure with no errors in spelling, grammar, or punctuation	Uses good vocabulary and sentence structure with very few errors in spelling, grammar, or punctuation	Includes some errors in grammar, punctuation, and spelling	Includes many errors in grammar, punctuation, and spelling

UNIT
1

Foundations of Citizenship

What's Ahead in Unit 1

In Unit 1 you will be taking a look at the ideas and beliefs that Americans share. You will begin to learn what it means to be an American citizen and what rights and responsibilities citizens share.

CHAPTER 1
A Portrait of Americans

CHAPTER 2
American Society and Its Values

CHAPTER 3
The Meaning of Citizenship

Why Study Civics?

What does it mean to be an American? What do we believe about our country and government? How do we know what to expect from our government? How do we know what is expected of us? These are all questions that can be addressed by the study of civics.

Watch the **Civics: Government and Economics** videos for an overview of U.S. Immigration

▶**Video**: Overview   Video: Up Close

Standards for Civics and Government

National

The following National Standards are covered in this unit.

II. What are the foundations of the American political system?

B. What are the distinctive characteristics of American society?

C. What is American political culture?

D. What values and principles are basic to American constitutional democracy?

State

Go Online
PHSchool.com

For: Your state's Civics standards
Visit: PHSchool.com
Webcode: mpe1001

1

A Portrait of Americans

What's Ahead in Chapter 1

In this chapter you will read about the many different kinds of people who are Americans and about some of the important ideas and values that bind us together as a nation and as a people.

SECTION 1
Who Americans Are

SECTION 2
America: A Cultural Mosaic

SECTION 3
The Values That Unite Us

TARGET READING SKILL

Clarifying Meaning In this chapter you will focus on clarifying meaning to help you better understand what you read. Clarifying meaning includes reading ahead, rereading, and para-phrasing.

These American students ▶ come from a variety of backgrounds.

The following National Standards are covered in this chapter.

II. What are the foundations of the American political system?

B. What are the distinctive characteristics of American society?

C. What is American political culture?

D. What values and principles are basic to American constitutional democracy?

Active Citizen — Civics in the Real World

Meet four American citizens, each with a unique and interesting story. Follow their stories throughout the chapter.

Miguel Espinoza I am nineteen and attend California State University. Before I was born, my parents left Mexico and came to the United States. My mother and father are citizens of Mexico and permanent U.S. residents. I am a U.S. citizen.

Thomas Pham I am twenty eight years old. I was born in Vietnam, and I came to the United States with my family in 1986. In 1991 we all became American citizens. Today I have my own software distribution business in Denver, Colorado.

Emily Shultz I am eighty-one years old. I grew up on a farm in Kansas. My father, who came to this country from Scotland, and my mother, who was born in Germany, homesteaded a farm near Dodge City, Kansas. I live in the small town of Sublette.

Jean Reardon I am forty-nine. I grew up in the South, and I participated in the civil rights marches in Selma, Alabama, in 1965. Today I live in Tucker, Georgia, a suburb of Atlanta, and I work as a computer analyst.

Citizen's Journal Write a paragraph about a friend, a family member, or yourself like the ones written by Miguel, Thomas, Emily, and Jean. Include age, birthplace, family background, and anything else that tells a unique story.

Who Americans Are

Reading Preview

Objectives
In this section you will
- Discuss the variety of places where Americans live.
- Find out how the American work force is changing.
- Learn why the average age of Americans is increasing.
- Explore how our varied backgrounds contribute to what it means to be a United States citizen.

Taking Notes
Make a diagram like the one below. As you read the section, complete the diagram with information about who Americans are.

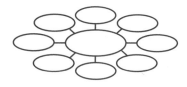

Key Terms
demography
Sunbelt
service job
baby boom
diversity

Main Idea
American society is made up of people from diverse backgrounds. Recent trends include changes in where Americans live, in the work force, and in the average age of the population.

Target Reading Skill
Read Ahead Rereading can help you understand words and ideas in the text. If you do not understand a word or idea, it might help you to read ahead, because a word or idea might be made clear later on.

How would you answer the question "Who are Americans?" As you can see from reading about Miguel, Thomas, Emily, and Jean, not all Americans are alike. The study of the size, growth, and distribution of human populations is called **demography.** Gathering demographic information can help to make a portrait of the American people.

Where Americans Live

Americans live in almost every kind of terrain the world has to offer. We live on high mountains and broad prairies. From Alaska to Texas and Hawaii to Maine, the United States is a vast and varied land.

Variety of Homes When Miguel Espinoza goes home, he climbs the stairs to his family's apartment in San Francisco, California, a city of 746,000 people. Jean lives in a condominium in Tucker, Georgia, a suburb with a population of about 26,000. Emily's home is in Sublette, Kansas, a farming town of 1,400 people.

New England village (left) and New Mexican adobe (right).▶

New Construction
Population growth in some states in the West and South has resulted in a need for new housing and office space. **Predict** *What might be the economic consequences of this growth?*

Americans on the Move Early in our history, most people lived on farms or in small towns along the eastern seacoast. As more people came to North America, our population spread westward.

Gradually, people began to concentrate in urban areas where jobs were available in factories and offices. Today, four out of five Americans (about 217 million) live in urban areas.

Americans have not only moved from farms to cities. They also have moved from the North and the East toward the South and the West, settling in the **Sunbelt**—warm weather states such as Georgia, Florida, Texas, and Arizona.

✓ Reading Check   **Why might Americans have moved to urban areas and, more recently, to the Sunbelt?**

The Work Force

Americans have always worked hard. The first settlers from Europe supported themselves by scratching farms out of the wilderness in Virginia and Massachusetts. Since then, we have cultivated land on both coasts and in the fertile plains and valleys across the continent. We have built houses, stores, factories, and office buildings. We have manufactured a vast array of products and sold them at home and in countries around the world.

American Workers Our work force is made up of about 60 million women and 70 million men working in nearly 30,000 different occupations. Many people in your age group join the work force by taking part-time and summer jobs.

Civics and Economics

The Bureau of Labor Statistics What jobs are likely to be available when you enter the job market? One good place to find out is the Bureau of Labor Statistics (BLS). The BLS is the principle fact-finding agency for the federal government in the field of economics and statistics. Thinking of becoming a computer software engineer, desktop publisher, or medical assistant? Those are among the fastest growing occupations. Thinking advertising or film making? Be ready for stiff competition for jobs and long hours.

Analyzing Economics
1. What does the continuing growth of jobs in computer-related fields suggest about the American economy?
2. Go to the Bureau of Statistics homepage (www.bls.gov). Choose a link and write a brief oral report on what you find there.

Target Reading Skill

Read Ahead Read the first paragraph under the heading Ages of Americans. Then keep reading to see why the percentages of people in different age groups have varied.

More Service Jobs A hundred years ago, most Americans worked in farming and manufacturing. However, modern farm machinery and the increasing use of technology in our factories have brought about a change.

By the year 2006, nearly 75 percent of American workers are expected to hold **service jobs,** or jobs in which a person makes a living by providing a service for other people. Your doctor, your teacher, your dentist, and the person who fixes your family's car are all engaged in service jobs.

✓ Reading Check **How has the American work force changed over the last hundred years?**

Ages of Americans

To answer the question, "Who are Americans?" you will need some information about how old we are. At different times in our history, the percentage of people in different age groups has varied.

In 1850, more than half of Americans were children. About 44 percent were in the 20–59 age range, while a very small percentage were of retirement age. By the beginning of the twenty-first century, these numbers had changed significantly. (See Skills for Life on page 26 for a look at how the United States population is projected to change from 2000 to 2025.)

More Older Americans Today there are more older Americans than ever before. One reason is that improvements in medical care have increased our life expectancy. More and more Americans are living past age sixty. On average, a person in your age group today can expect to live to be about 76 years old.

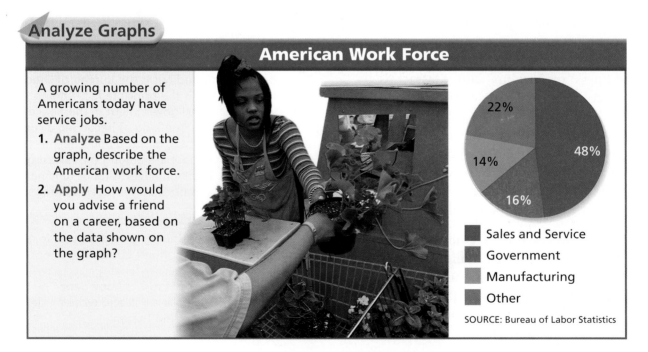

Analyze Graphs

A growing number of Americans today have service jobs.

1. **Analyze** Based on the graph, describe the American work force.
2. **Apply** How would you advise a friend on a career, based on the data shown on the graph?

American Work Force

22%
48%
14%
16%

■ Sales and Service
■ Government
■ Manufacturing
■ Other

SOURCE: Bureau of Labor Statistics

Active Citizen
Students Make a Difference

To Joey Peña, a junior at St. Joseph Academy in Brownsville, Texas, knowledge of current events is key to serving his community. Joey is a member of the National Hispanic Institute, an organization that provides young Latinos with a forum to discuss issues relevant to their communities.

One program established by the National Hispanic Institute is the Lorenzo de Zavala Youth Legislative Session. It is a mock youth government that introduces students to public policy issues that affect Latinos.

Service Learning

How can you educate people in your community about the issues relevant to them?

▲ Students can help make a difference by educating each other about topics that affect them.

Baby Boomers Another reason is the "**baby boom,**" or the dramatic rise in the number of births that occurred between 1946 and 1964. During these years following World War II, many American couples had three or more children. Today, the large number of people born during the baby boom has swelled the ranks of Americans in the 40-to-60 age group. Your grandparents and even your parents are likely to be baby boomers.

In addition, although there are more adults of child-bearing age than ever before, they are having fewer children than did people of their parents' generation. This is one reason why the percentage of younger people in our population has declined.

Population experts predict that, by the year 2050, more than one in four Americans will be age 65 or older. This surge in the population of older Americans will strain Social Security benefits and medical services. At the same time, there will be fewer people in the work force to support our aging population. The aging of our population will have other major effects on our society.

✓ Reading Check **What is meant by the "baby boom generation" and what is its effect on American society?**

Americans' Varied Backgrounds

Americans are a people who are known for their **diversity** or differences. Our diversity is reflected in our different jobs, home towns, ages—and especially in our backgrounds. Our backgrounds differ because we are from many different cultures and belong to different races and ethnic groups.

Miguel Espinoza's family speaks both Spanish and English and has strong ties to Mexican culture. They return to Mexico once a year to visit relatives. The Espinozas are members of a large group of Hispanic Americans, also called Latinos.

Thomas and his family have been Americans for about fifteen years. The Phams were born in Vietnam and grew up speaking Vietnamese. The Phams now think of themselves as Americans whose background is Vietnamese.

Jean's family has lived in America for almost 300 years. She considers herself to be an American of African background.

Emily's father was born in Scotland and her mother, in Germany. Emily is not unusual. Many Americans have ancestors from more than one country.

As you explore what it means to be a citizen of the United States, it will be useful to look more closely at the diversity of our backgrounds and learn how that diversity contributes to who we are as a people.

√ Reading Check **Predict some of the challenges of a diverse society.**

SECTION **1** **Assessment**

Key Terms

Use each of the key terms in a sentence that explains its meaning: demography, Sunbelt, service job, baby boom, diversity

Target Reading Skill

1. **Read Ahead** What word or idea were you better able to understand by reading ahead?

Comprehension and Critical Thinking

2. **a. Describe** What are two population shifts in the United States?
   b. Infer Why are Americans moving to the South and West?

3. **a. Recall** How is the American work force changing?
   b. Check Consistency Are jobs in your community consistent with trends you read about in this section?

4. **a. Recall** Why is the average age of Americans shifting?
   b. Predict What might be the economic effects for a society in which the average age is very young or very old?

5. **a. Explain** List and explain examples of diversity in American society.
   b. Determine Relevance Why is understanding diversity an important part of understanding citizenship?

Writing Activity

You have been asked to address a group of foreign dignitaries on the topic "Who Americans Are." Using the information from this section and your own observations, write a short speech that gives a snapshot of life in the United States today.

Go Online
PHSchool.com

For: Speech Writing
Visit: PHSchool.com
Web Code: mpd-1011

How to Volunteer

Americans are known for their strong tradition of community involvement. You too can become involved by contributing your time and talents to make a difference in your school and community.

Below, Carlos Lopez describes his experience looking for a volunteer job. As you read, think about the steps he went through to become a volunteer for a program that teaches inline skating to inner city children.

Carlos Lopez comes from a family of volunteers. His mother, a teacher, volunteers her time after school to help recent immigrants learn English. His father helps out once a month in a local soup kitchen.

Carlos too wanted to help his community, so he looked into possibilities for community service. He talked to friends in the Service Learning Club at school. He also looked online to learn more about national organizations such as Habitat for Humanity and Meals on Wheels. He looked at volunteer opportunities listed in his local newspaper. Soon Carlos had a list of ten possibilities to consider.

Carlos then had to decide how much time he could spend volunteering. Between homework, chores, and sports, Carlos figured he could volunteer about three hours a week, as long as his volunteer job was close by.

Carlos also considered his strengths and interests in choosing where to volunteer. He liked teaching younger children and he wanted to be outdoors.

Carlos saw a notice at school asking for volunteers to teach inline skating to inner city children, using donated skates and gear. He talked to classmates who volunteered for the program and visited it the next week.

Today the children are learning a new skill and getting fresh air and exercise. Carlos is feeling the satisfaction of helping others who would not otherwise have this opportunity.

Learn the Skill

To find a volunteer job, follow these steps:

❶ **Research your options.** Find out about possible volunteer jobs in your community.

❷ **Determine your strengths, interests, and availability.**

Practice the Skill

❶ Make a list of at least five volunteer opportunities you have heard or read about.

❷ List your own strengths, interests, and availability.

❸ Decide what volunteer opportunities on your list would be best for you.

Apply the Skill

Find out about volunteer opportunities in your community. Research one and report your findings to the class.

Go **Online**
**civics
interactive**

For: Local Citizenship
Visit: PHSchool.com
Web Code: mpp-1011

America: A Cultural Mosaic

Reading Preview

Objectives

In this section you will

- Explain what is meant by the American identity.
- Discuss the contributions of European, Hispanic, African, Asian, and Native Americans to American society.
- Describe the U.S. population today.

Taking Notes

Make a diagram like the one below. As you read the section, complete the diagram with information about different groups of Americans.

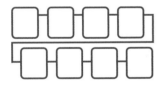

Key Terms

immigrants   exclusion laws
discrimination   census
racism

Main Idea

Americans are part of a mosaic in which each piece is an essential part of American society.

Target Reading Skill

Rereading is a strategy that can help you understand unfamiliar words and ideas. If a certain passage is not clear when you read it the first time, reread it to look for connections between words and sentences.

"America was built by a nation of strangers. From a hundred different places they have poured forth joining and blending in one mighty and irresistible tide. The land flourished because it was fed from so many sources—because it was nourished by so many cultures and traditions and people."

—President Lyndon B. Johnson, 1965

The American Identity

America has been called a nation of **immigrants**, people who move from one country to make their homes in another. Immigrants brought to America the customs and traditions of their homelands as well as their dreams for a better life. Because we are a nation of immigrants, we are a very diverse people.

Passports and new ▶
European arrivals

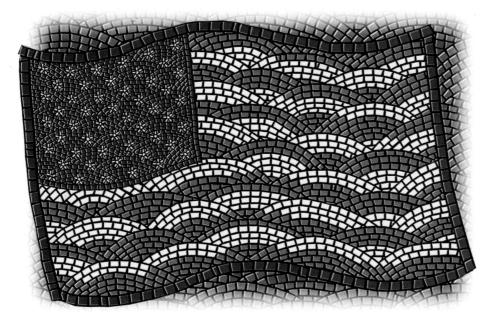

American Mosaic
Like mosaic tiles, the diverse groups in the United States form a whole nation.
Draw Inferences *How does immigration contribute to the American mosaic?*

A Melting Pot? The United States has sometimes been referred to as a "melting pot." This term reflects the idea that people from all over the world came here and melted into American society, giving up the heritage of their native lands.

However, many immigrants have continued to speak their native language in their homes and with friends, and to follow their native customs. You can see evidence of these diverse cultures in the wide variety of international foods we can buy.

Such examples of our cultural differences make clear that Americans have not melted together to form one identity. Instead of giving up our separate cultures, we have retained parts of them and, in the process, have enriched American culture as a whole.

The American Mosaic A mosaic (moh ZAY ik) is made of small tiles of different sizes, shapes, and colors. When they are all fitted together, these many tiles create a whole picture. Like mosaic tiles, all the groups in the United States fit together to form a whole nation. Thus, when we ask "Who are Americans?" we may answer that they are part—not of a melting pot—but of a mosaic in which each different tile is an essential part of the picture.

√ Reading Check **Why is it inaccurate to say that America is a melting pot?**

Target Reading Skill
Reread Read back over the sections titled A Melting Pot? and The American Mosaic to be sure you understand why American culture is best compared to a mosaic.

European Americans

Among the first immigrants to the land that became the United States were Europeans seeking religious freedom, political freedom, and opportunities to have their own farms and businesses. In the 1600s and 1700s they came mostly from England, Ireland, and Scotland. They brought their language—English—and their traditions of government, which would deeply influence the future nation.

Other Europeans Arrive Many settlers also arrived from Germany, France, the Netherlands, and Scandinavia. Most were Protestants. Catholics and Jews also found a haven in the young society.

The years between 1830 and 1920 saw the arrival of waves of Central and Eastern Europeans, including Germans, Slavs, and Russians. Denied political and economic freedom at home, these immigrants, many of them Jews, sought new opportunities in the United States. Meanwhile, Irish, Italians, Greeks, and others suffering from crop failures and lack of adequate farmlands also immigrated in large numbers.

The waves of immigrants from Europe have dwindled today. Nevertheless, European Americans still make up the largest segment of our population.

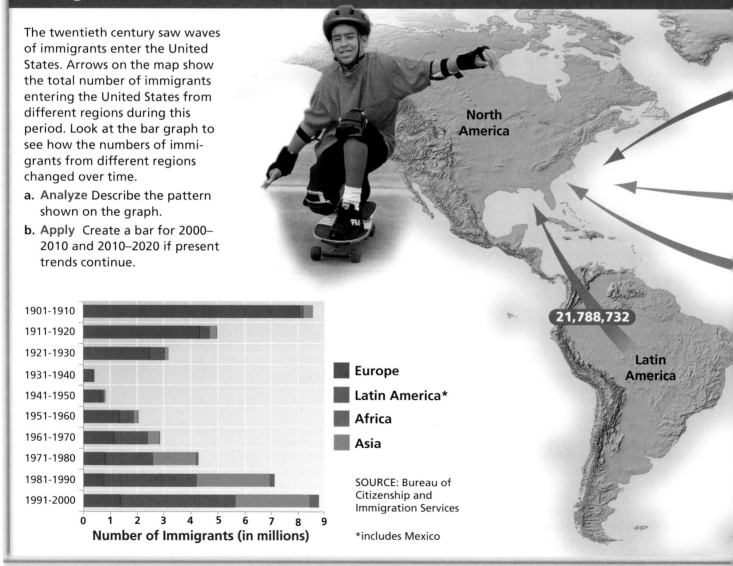

Analyze Maps and Graphs

Immigration to the United States, 1900–2000

The twentieth century saw waves of immigrants enter the United States. Arrows on the map show the total number of immigrants entering the United States from different regions during this period. Look at the bar graph to see how the numbers of immigrants from different regions changed over time.

a. **Analyze** Describe the pattern shown on the graph.

b. **Apply** Create a bar for 2000–2010 and 2010–2020 if present trends continue.

North America

21,788,732

Latin America

Europe
Latin America*
Africa
Asia

1901-1910
1911-1920
1921-1930
1931-1940
1941-1950
1951-1960
1961-1970
1971-1980
1981-1990
1991-2000

0 1 2 3 4 5 6 7 8 9
Number of Immigrants (in millions)

SOURCE: Bureau of Citizenship and Immigration Services

*includes Mexico

Diversity Although European Americans came from the same continent, they were in many ways more diverse than alike. They had grown up under different forms of government, and they spoke different languages. They ranged from highly educated to unable to read or write. They were accustomed to very different kinds of food, music, and clothing styles. They had different forms of worship and celebrated different holidays—or the same holidays in different ways.

Immigrants from different European countries tended to settle in different parts of the United States. That is why you may still hear German spoken in Pennsylvania farm towns, attend a Norwegian church in Minnesota, or sit down to a Polish dinner in Chicago.

✔ **Reading Check** **Were European immigrants of the 1800s more alike or more different? Explain.**

Watch the **Civics: Government and Economics in Action** videos to learn about immigrants' own stories.

Video: Overview ▶ Video: Up Close

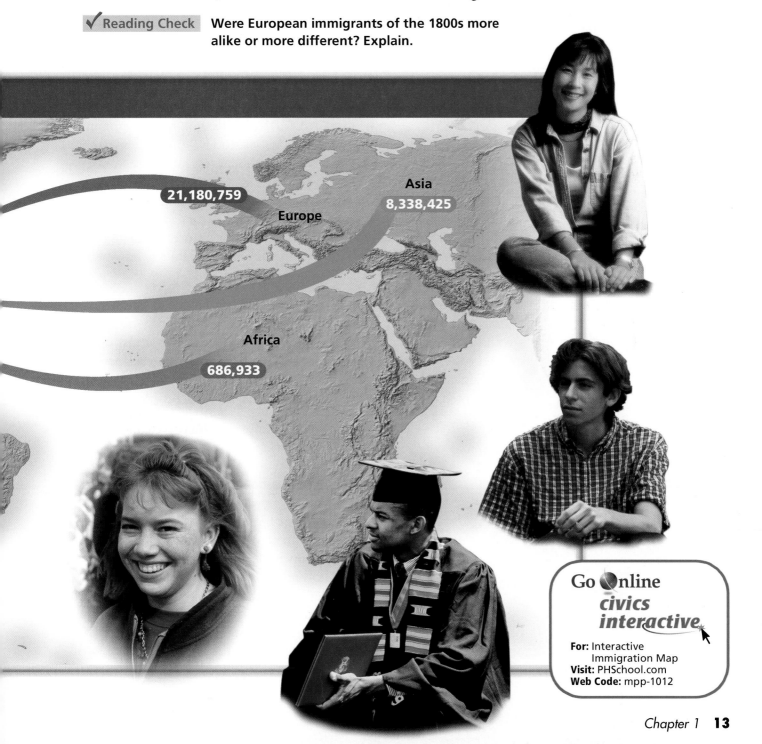

Europe 21,180,759

Asia 8,338,425

Africa 686,933

Go Online
*civics
interactive*

For: Interactive Immigration Map
Visit: PHSchool.com
Web Code: mpp-1012

Hispanic Americans

Hispanic Americans, or Latinos, share a common culture and language from Spanish-speaking countries. Hispanic Americans can be of any race.

Hispanics have a long history in the United States. As the nation expanded in the 1800s, it added areas that had been settled by Spaniards and later by people from Mexico, then a Spanish colony. The inhabitants of these regions—including the present-day states of Florida, Louisiana, Texas, Arizona, New Mexico, and California—became American citizens. Today, Latino immigrants come from Mexico, Central and South America, and the Caribbean.

Latino Culture It's not uncommon in American cities today to hear Spanish spoken. In fact, Spanish-speakers form the largest language minority in the United States.

Latino foods, music, and architecture have greatly influenced U. S. culture. Perhaps you have noticed foods such as tortillas, tomatillos, and bins of dried chiles in your local grocery store. In areas like southern California with large Latino populations, retailers are opening entire grocery stores catering to Hispanic tastes.

Challenges As for all immigrants, finding a place for themselves in this country has been easier for some Hispanics than for others. Those with professional training have often made the quickest adjustment. Others do not speak English or lack the skills needed for a well-paying job. Education is key for assuring that Hispanic Americans are well represented in professions such as medicine, law, and business.

Latinos and African Americans make up the two largest U.S. minorities.
▼

✓ Reading Check **What are some examples of Hispanic culture in the United States today?**

African Americans

Unlike immigrants who came to America by choice, African Americans did not come here voluntarily. Their ancestors were brought to this country as slaves, beginning in early colonial times. Although slavery was ended legally in 1865, it has taken a long time to change the way African Americans are treated. African Americans have suffered from **discrimination**, the unfair treatment of a group of people compared with another group.

Struggle for Equality For many years, in various communities and states, African Americans were barred from voting, from attending schools with white students, and from living in neighborhoods with whites. Many restaurants, hotels, and theaters had signs warning "For Whites Only." Even public buses had seats reserved for whites, with black riders having to sit or stand in the back.

Discrimination is the result of **racism**, the belief that members of ones' own race are superior to those of other races. Courageous African Americans have struggled against racism and sought to obtain equality. From the 1960s to the present, inspired by the example of leaders like the Reverend Dr. Martin Luther King, Jr., African Americans have called attention to the unequal treatment of blacks. As a result, opportunities in education, jobs, and housing have expanded.

African Americans Today Equal treatment for all is a goal that has not yet been completely achieved. Many African Americans live in poverty due to lack of opportunities. Nevertheless, the number of African Americans with at least a high school diploma increased from 63 percent in 1990 to 72 percent in 2000, up from 51 percent in 1980. Percentages of African Americans with college and advanced degrees have also steadily increased, as have home ownership and the number of African-American-owned businesses.

✔ Reading Check **How have African Americans worked toward achieving equality in American society?**

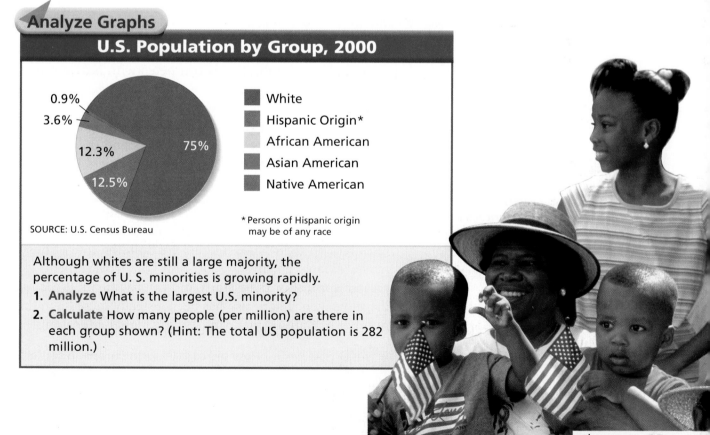

Analyze Graphs

U.S. Population by Group, 2000

0.9%
3.6%
12.3%
12.5%
75%

- White
- Hispanic Origin*
- African American
- Asian American
- Native American

SOURCE: U.S. Census Bureau

* Persons of Hispanic origin may be of any race

Although whites are still a large majority, the percentage of U. S. minorities is growing rapidly.

1. **Analyze** What is the largest U.S. minority?
2. **Calculate** How many people (per million) are there in each group shown? (Hint: The total US population is 282 million.)

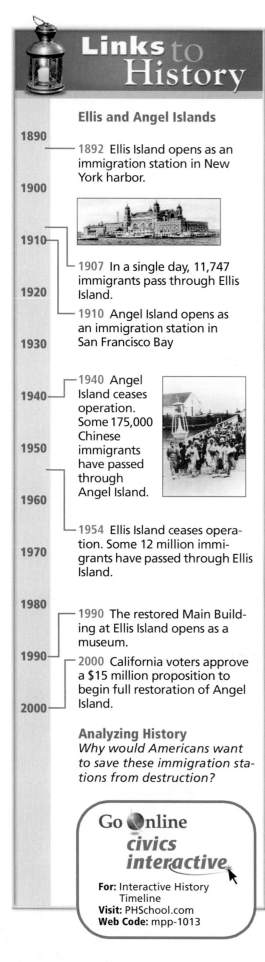

Links to History

Ellis and Angel Islands

1890

1900

1910

1920

1930

1940

1950

1960

1970

1980

1990

2000

1892 Ellis Island opens as an immigration station in New York harbor.

1907 In a single day, 11,747 immigrants pass through Ellis Island.

1910 Angel Island opens as an immigration station in San Francisco Bay

1940 Angel Island ceases operation. Some 175,000 Chinese immigrants have passed through Angel Island.

1954 Ellis Island ceases operation. Some 12 million immigrants have passed through Ellis Island.

1990 The restored Main Building at Ellis Island opens as a museum.

2000 California voters approve a $15 million proposition to begin full restoration of Angel Island.

Analyzing History
Why would Americans want to save these immigration stations from destruction?

Go Online
civics
interactive

For: Interactive History Timeline
Visit: PHSchool.com
Web Code: mpp-1013

Asian Americans

Among the first Asians to come to America were young men from villages in southeastern China. They had heard of the discovery of gold in California in 1849 and came to North America to make money to send home to their families. Many set up small businesses to supply the miners' needs. Later arrivals found work building the railroads of the West and on farms and in fisheries. As Japanese workers began to arrive, they also prospered in farming and business.

The success of these immigrants bred resentment among other groups, who accused the Asians of taking away jobs. As a result, laws were passed in 1882 and 1907. These **exclusion laws** prohibited any further immigration from China and Japan.

The last of these laws were repealed in 1952. After 1972, immigrants from Southeast Asia began arriving, driven from their homes by wars and revolutions. Today there are over ten million Asian Americans living in the United States.

✔ Reading Check **What was the result of the repeal of the Asian exclusion laws?**

Native Americans

Native American groups had been living in North America thousands of years before Columbus arrived. Some relied on farming, while others hunted, fished, and gathered wild plants for food and clothing. A few groups built large cities, and others lived in villages or moved from place to place.

European Settlement As European settlers began to arrive in large numbers, they competed with Native Americans for land. Although Native Americans fought for their lands in many bloody battles, they were gradually pushed west, often onto the poorest lands for farming and hunting. By the late 1800s, wars with settlers and the effects of the unfamiliar diseases brought by the settlers had taken their toll. Many thousands of Indians had died.

Living in Modern America To meet the challenges facing them today, some groups are developing mineral resources on their lands. Others are building tourist businesses. Many groups are pressing the government for greater control of their lands and for payments for lands illegally taken. There also has been a steady increase in the number of Native Americans seeking higher education.

✔ Reading Check **How did contact with European settlers affect Native Americans by the 1800s?**

Our Population Today

A **census** is a population survey that is taken every ten years. The 2000 census shows that the population of the United States is becoming more diverse. In 1990, about 20% of the population was nonwhite. In 2000, that number increased to 25%. The number of Hispanic Americans grew quickly, from about 9% to more than 12% of the population. And for the first time, the number of Hispanic Americans was larger than that of African Americans.

The United States is diverse because our ancestors come from the many Native American cultures and from all over the world—Europe, Latin America, Africa, and Asia, as well as Australia and Oceania. Despite this wide diversity, all have the same goals: to build better lives for themselves and their families and to share in "the land of opportunity."

All these individuals and groups fit together to form a whole nation. Each of these groups adds to the richness of our society.

American Faces
Americans come from a wide variety of backgrounds.
Draw Inferences *In what ways are Americans diverse?*

✓ Reading Check **How did the United States population change between 1990 and 2000? What might be the social effects of these changes?**

SECTION 2 Assessment

Key Terms

Use each of the key terms in a sentence that explains its meaning: immigrants, discrimination, racism, exclusion laws, census

Target Reading Skill

1. **Reread** What word or idea in this section were you able to clarify by rereading?

Comprehension and Critical Thinking

2. **a. Describe** How is American culture like a mosaic?
   b. Determine Relevance Does your community reflect the American mosaic? Explain.

3. **a. Recall** What are two important facts about each group described in this section?
   b. Distinguish False from Accurate Images Stereotypes are overly simplified images of certain groups. Choose a stereotype and explain why it is inaccurate.

4. **a. Explain** What did the 2000 census reveal about diversity?
   b. Predict Name some effects of increasing diversity.
   c. Identify Alternatives What might be the disadvantages of a society that is not diverse?

Writing Activity

Write a journal entry from the point of view of someone belonging to one of the groups described in this section. Discuss the challenges you and the members of your group face and how you might meet these challenges.

Go Online
PHSchool.com

For: Journal Entry
Visit: PHSchool.com
Web Code: mpd-1012

The Values That Unite Us

Reading Preview

Objectives
In this section you will
- Learn why equal respect is part of the American Dream.
- Describe the basic values that unite us as a nation.
- Understand how Americans can help achieve our ideals.

Taking Notes
Make a diagram like the one below. As you read the section, complete the diagram with the definition of the basic American values.

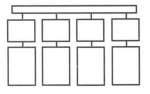

Key Terms
beliefs   freedom
values   justice
equality

Main Idea
Americans value the ideal of equal respect, but work still needs to be done to ensure that the rights to equality, freedom, and justice for all Americans are protected.

Target Reading Skill
Paraphrasing can help you understand what you read. When you paraphrase, you restate what you have read in your own words.

Each American is part of the cultural mosaic that makes up American society. As you have learned, we are a diverse people. Despite our differences, we have survived as a nation for more than two hundred years. What unites us as one people, one nation?

Equal Respect: The American Dream

Americans are held together by certain shared beliefs and values. **Beliefs** are certain ideas that we trust are true. Values are our standards of behavior. Values help us decide how we should act and how we should live our lives.

The beliefs and values on which our nation was founded have attracted many immigrants who have come to the United States. Peter Ky remembers when his father first spoke of leaving Vietnam:

> "My father was discouraged by how hard life was for us in Vietnam. We had so little freedom and so few opportunities to improve our lives. My father said that in America, people were treated with respect and dignity. We would have a chance to make a good life for ourselves there."

Mr. Pham's dream of a better life in America is based on a basic American belief: that everyone, regardless of age, sex, race, wealth, opinions, or education, has worth and importance.

✓ Reading Check   **What is the role of beliefs and values in American society?**

Basic American Values

We believe that all people—unique tiles in our cultural mosaic—deserve the same chance to realize their full potential and to contribute their talents and ideas to society. In other words, every person has the right to be treated with equal respect.

The American belief that all people deserve equal respect is supported by three basic values: equality, freedom, and justice. To see what these values mean, consider the experiences of Jean Reardon. Jean, an African American woman, often relied on these three values to support her efforts to gain equal respect as a computer analyst, which is traditionally a white, male occupation.

Equality Equal respect is based on the belief that everyone can contribute to society. To make this contribution, everyone must have the same rights and opportunities in life. The condition of everyone having the same rights and opportunities is called **equality**.

Jean learned that even though equality is one of our basic values, equal opportunity is not always available for every citizen in America. She recalls:

> "Job hunting was tough at first. I thought I'd never get that first interview. Then, when I walked into the room, the interview committee—all white men—looked at me and then at each other as if to say, "We knew she was a woman, but black, too?" I didn't get the job, and I have a strong feeling that my being a black woman had something to do with it."

Jean's experience is not uncommon. Even though discrimination because of race or sex is against the law, it still affects the lives of many people.

Becoming Citizens
These immigrants have just become U.S. citizens.
Demonstrate Reasoned Judgment *Why might this be a time of deep emotion for the new citizens?*

The basic American values are expressed in the Bill of Rights. The Bill of Rights consists of the first 10 amendments to the United States Constitution. It lists the fundamental rights held by the people.

1. What basic values are shown in the cartoon?
2. What kinds of freedom are protected by the Bill of Rights?
3. Why does the cartoonist use the Bill of Rights as a crown?

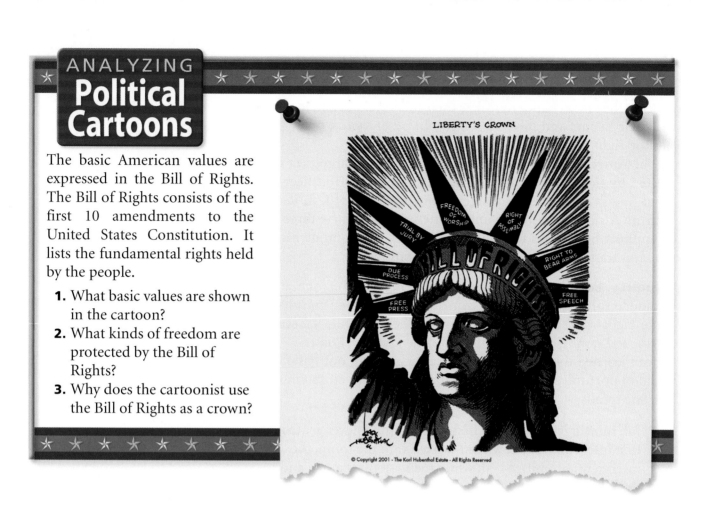

LIBERTY'S CROWN

FREEDOM OF WORSHIP · RIGHT OF ASSEMBLY · TRIAL BY JURY · BILL OF RIGHTS · DUE PROCESS · RIGHT TO BEAR ARMS · FREE PRESS · FREE SPEECH

© Copyright 2001 - The Karl Hubenthal Estate - All Rights Reserved

Target Reading Skill

Paraphrase the section under the heading *Equal Opportunity* on this page. Your paraphrase should explain in your own words what equal opportunity is and what it is not.

Equal Opportunity In this chapter, you have learned just how varied the backgrounds, lifestyles, and occupations of Americans can be. Everyone has different skills and abilities. You may be a natural at math, for example, while your best friend's greatest talent is on the soccer field. Your cousin might have great talent as a trumpet player, while you have to struggle to play a note.

Our opportunities in life may be limited by our abilities. Your friend may be less likely to get a job as a math teacher than you are. You might be less likely to play in an orchestra than your cousin.

Our opportunities may also be limited by our energy and interests. Although your friend could have a career as a soccer player, he or she might not like training so hard and traveling so much. Your cousin might to want to put in the hours of practice necessary to play the trumpet in an orchestra.

However, our race, sex, religion, background, and opinions should not be used to deny us an equal chance to succeed in life. Jean, confident of her ability and training, knew she had the right to an equal opportunity. Says Jean:

"I didn't give up. I had interviews at many companies. Then I finally landed a job with a company that judges me by the quality of my work, not by the color of my skin or by my sex. It feels good to work where I'm treated as an equal."

Freedom When you try to define freedom, you may explain that it means having the ability to say what you want, go where you want, choose the friends you want. **Freedom is the ability to make choices.** Jean knows that freedom also means being able to choose where you want to work and with whom you want to work. She says:

> "Thinking back on that first interview, I know I wouldn't have accepted the job even if it had been offered to me. I just didn't feel comfortable with the men on that committee. It was good to know that I was free to look for a job that I felt better about."

If you believe in equal respect, you give the same freedoms to others that you expect for yourself. However, you must not be so free in your actions that you end up interfering or limiting someone else's freedom.

For example, you are free to listen to music you like. However, if you walk down the street playing your favorite CD at full volume, you may interfere with the right of other people to stroll quietly or listen to their own music. Can you think of another situation in which your freedom is limited because of respect for others' freedom?

Law and the Real World

Equality in the Work Place

Your right to equal opportunity in the work place is protected by several laws. These laws include:

- the Civil Rights Act of 1964, which prohibits job discrimination based on race, color, religion, sex, or national origin;
- the Equal Pay Act of 1963, which requires that employers pay men and women equally when they perform equal work in the same establishment;
- the Americans with Disabilities Act of 1990, which prohibit job discrimination against people with disabilities.

Applying the Law

1. **Analyzing Information** Which of these laws would apply to you if you were seeking a job now?
2. **Draw Conclusions** Why do we need so many laws to protect a single right?

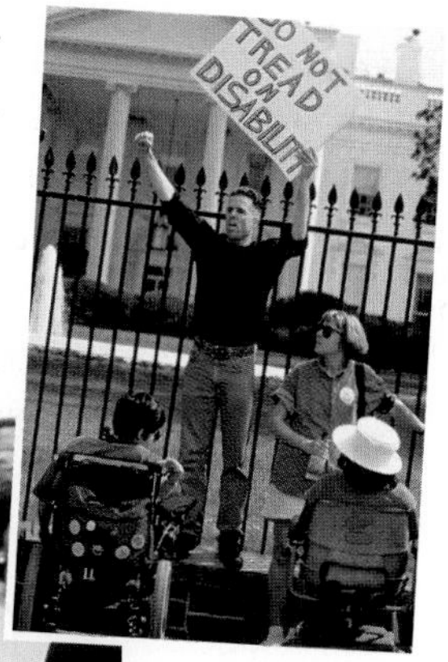

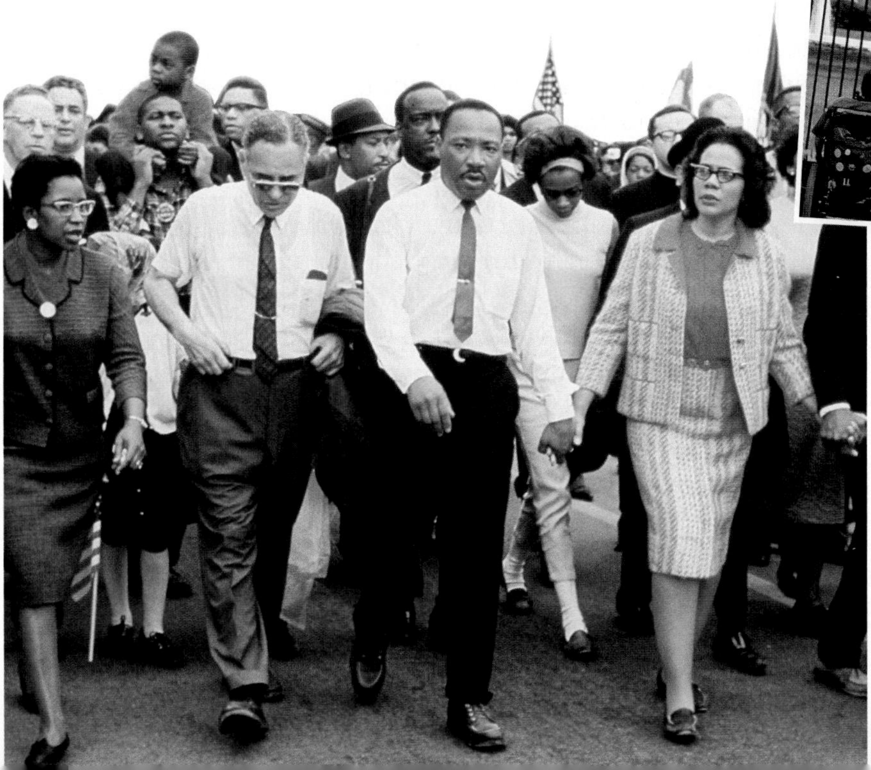

Respect and Justice
Led by Dr. Martin Luther King, Jr., the civil rights movement of the 1960s led to greater justice for minorities (left). Disabled Americans lobby for equality (above).
Draw Inferences *What do both groups pictured here have in common?*

Justice Equal respect also means that everyone deserves to be treated fairly. The third basic value, **justice** can also be thought of as fairness. For example, you should not be paid more or get better grades or a better job because of your race, gender, or connections to powerful people.

Justice, however, does not require that people always be treated the same. In the work place, for example, people with greater skills and experience are rewarded with more pay or responsibility than those with fewer skills or less experience.

When Jean was hired, she became the newest employee in the company. She made less money than employees who were more experienced. As Jean continued to work, she gained experience and showed her ability to do a good job. Her pay was raised to match that of people with equal experience and performance.

✓ **Reading Check** **Describe and give examples of the three basic American values.**

Citizens and the American Ideal

American society is held together by our shared belief in equality, freedom, and justice. These beliefs and values form an ideal of the kind of nation we want the United States to be. We judge our society by how well we live up to this ideal.

An Imperfect Society We do not always achieve our ideal. Thomas Pham found that his first few years in the United States were sometimes difficult. In Vietnam he had been told that everyone in America enjoyed freedom and equality. He found out that this statement did not always represent the truth.

Thomas recalls something that happened when he was nine years old and had been in his new homeland for only one year.

"I was out in the street playing with some kids. Two boys began choosing teams for kickball. The other kids begged to be picked. My English wasn't so good, so I kept quiet. Finally, I was the only one left to be picked—and I was the only Asian in the bunch. The two boys stared at me. "You take him," one said, pointing at me. "Forget it," the other said, "I don't want him." He looked at me. "What's the matter?" he jeered, "Don't you speak English?" Then he pulled at the corners of his eyes, to make them slanted, and laughed. I ran home crying. That was my first experience with racism. I'll never forget it. Never."

Equality in the Classroom Classrooms in the 1950s (bottom) were very different from the classrooms of today (top). **Compare and Contrast** *What differences do you see between the 1950s classrooms and today's classroom?*

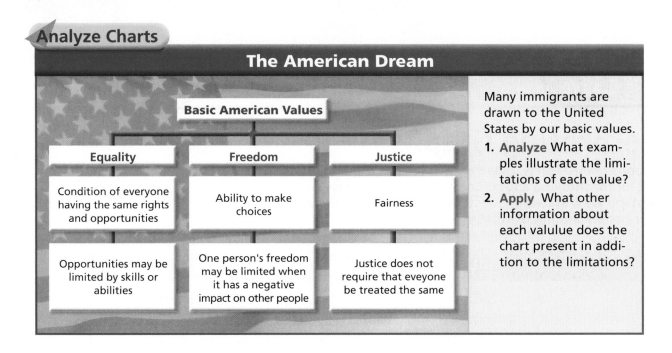

The American Dream

Basic American Values

Equality	Freedom	Justice
Condition of everyone having the same rights and opportunities	Ability to make choices	Fairness
Opportunities may be limited by skills or abilities	One person's freedom may be limited when it has a negative impact on other people	Justice does not require that eveyone be treated the same

Many immigrants are drawn to the United States by our basic values.

1. **Analyze** What examples illustrate the limitations of each value?

2. **Apply** What other information about each valulue does the chart present in addition to the limitations?

The American Ideal and the Future Our nation is held together by the fundamental belief in equal respect for all. Yet Thomas Pham's story illustrates that not everyone lives according to this ideal.

We do not always respect newcomers and those who are different than us. We sometimes distrust people who look different from ourselves or have beliefs unlike our own. The difference between the ideal of equal respect and its reality shows us the work that still needs to be done to ensure that the rights of all Americans to equality, freedom, and justice are protected.

✓ Reading Check **How does Thomas's story illustrate the work that still needs to be done to ensure equal respect for all?**

SECTION 3 Assessment

Key Terms

Use each of the key terms in a sentence that explains its meaning: beliefs, values, equality, freedom, justice

Target Reading Skill

1. **Paraphrase** Paraphrase the section under the heading Freedom on page 23.

Comprehension and Critical Thinking

2. **a. Explain** What is meant by equal respect?

b. Identify Central Issues Why are immigrants sometimes willing to risk their lives to come to the U.S.?

3. **a. Describe** Give an example of each American value.

b. Determine Relevance How do Jean's experiences reflect American values?

4. **a. Recall** What is the American ideal?

b. Draw Conclusions Describe how we sometimes live up to our ideal and sometimes fall short.

Writing Activity

Write an essay describing how you have met (or how you would meet) a challenge stemming from inequality or injustice. Be sure to use examples to illustrate your points.

TIPS
- Be sure that your essay has a beginning, a middle, and an end.
- Use specific, concrete details to help explain your point.

Interpreting Graphs

Bar graphs present facts, called data, in picture form. Bar graphs are useful for showing a lot of information in an easy-to-understand way. Knowing how to read bar graphs will give you a greater understanding of what you read.

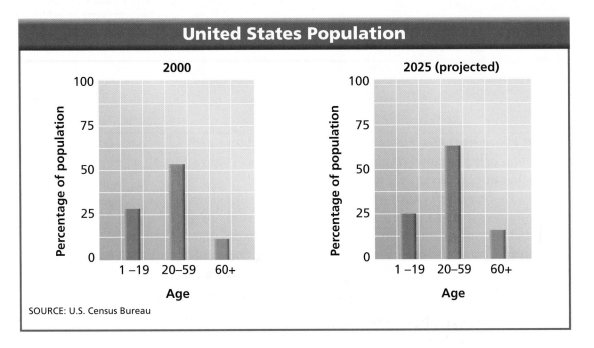

United States Population

2000

2025 (projected)

SOURCE: U.S. Census Bureau

Learn the Skill

Follow these steps to learn how to make sense of a bar graph:

1 **Subject** Read the title of the graph. The title will tell you the subject of the graph and what information is being presented.

2 **Type** Identify the type of graph. Bar graphs compare amounts of different items.

3 **Labels** Read the labels on the graph. For bar graphs, the labels will help you find out what information is provided across the bottom of the graph (the horizontal axis) and along the side of the graph (the vertical axis).

4 **Amounts** For bar graphs, match the top of each bar with the value of the vertical axis to find out how much each bar represents.

Practice the Skill

Look at the graphs above and answer these questions:

1 What is the subject of each of the graphs?

2 Of what type are the graphs?

3 **a.** What are the labels on the graphs?
   b. What do the labels tell you about the information presented on the graphs?

4 **a.** What is the value of each of the bars on the left hand graph?
   b. What is the value of each of the bars on the right hand graph?

Apply the Skill

Suppose you are writing a report on the number of immigrants from Latin America to the United States over the past three decades. How could a bar graph help you organize your information?

Review and Assessment

Chapter Summary

Section 1
Who Americans Are
(pages 4–8)

- Americans are known for diversity, or differences.

- Americans live in varied regions, work at different jobs, and come from different backgrounds.

- Recent trends include population growth in the South and West, more Americans working in service jobs, and an aging population as the baby boom generation grows older.

Section 2
America: A Cultural Mosaic
(pages 10–17)

- European, Hispanic, African, Asian, and Native Americans have all made important contributions to American society.

- European Americans make up the largest segment of the population.

- Hispanic Americans are the fastest growing segment of the population.

- African Americans have achieved greater equality in American society through a long civil rights struggle and changing American attitudes.

- Although exclusion laws prevented many Asians from immigrating to the United States in the past, today there are millions of Asian Americans coming from diverse cultural backgrounds.

- Many Native Americans work to balance their cultural traditions with the culture of modern American society.

- Many immigrants to the United States have faced discrimination and racism.

- Despite these obstacles, the many groups in the United States fit together to form a single, united nation.

Section 3
The Values That Unite Us
(pages 18–23)

- Americans share a belief that all people deserve equal respect.

- The American dream of equal respect for all Americans is based on the values of equality, freedom, and justice.

- These American values continue to attract immigrants, although our society sometimes does not reflect these ideals.

Copy the chart below and use it to help you summarize the chapter.

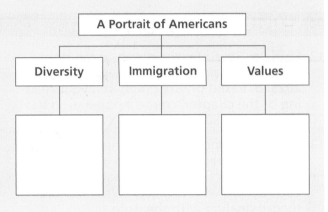

```
          A Portrait of Americans

   Diversity    Immigration    Values

   [        ]   [          ]   [      ]
```

Go Online
PHSchool.com

For: Self-Test
Visit: PHSchool.com
Web Code: mpa-1013

Reviewing Key Terms

Fill in the blank with one of the key terms from the list below.

values   immigrants
racism   diversity
service jobs   exclusion laws
census   discrimination

1. A series of _____ prevented Asians from settling in the United States between the 1880s and the 1950s.

2. Basic American _____ include equality, freedom, and justice.

3. If an employer decides not to hire a job applicant because she is a woman, the employer is guilty of _____.

4. Many _____ come to the United States each year from other nations around the world.

5. Nearly 75 percent of American workers are expected to hold _____ by 2006.

6. The _____ of American society is reflected in the many different backgrounds of its people.

7. The belief that one's own race is superior to others is called _____.

8. The most recent _____ documented the rapid growth of the Hispanic American population.

Comprehension and Critical Thinking

9. a. **Describe** What are three ways that the U.S. population has changed?
   b. **Draw Conclusions** What are the economic effects of these changes?
   c. **Draw Inferences** In what other ways is American society diverse?

10. a. **Explain** How are the five main groups of immigrants similar? How are they different?
    b. **Demonstrate Reasoned Judgment** What are the advantages and disadvantages of a diverse population?
    c. **Synthesize Information** Describe what is meant by "the American Identity."

11. a. **Recall** What are the shared beliefs and values that unite Americans?
    b. **Express Problems Clearly** Using examples, explain why justice does not always require that all people be treated the same.
    c. **Analyze Information** What can Americans do to better live up to the American ideal?

Activities

12. **Skills a.** Based on the graph to the right, describe the projected U.S. population in 2025. **b.** Based on the graph and your reading of the chapter, create a population bar graph for 2050.

13. **Writing** Suppose you are running for school president and have to give a speech on the subject "Why it is important to treat each person with respect." Write a short speech dealing with the issue.

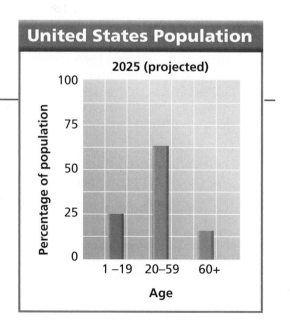

United States Population

2025 (projected)

Percentage of population

Age: 1–19, 20–59, 60+

14. **Active Citizen** How can students make a difference for new immigrants to the United States? Write an action plan explaining your idea and the steps needed to carry it out.

15. **Math Practice** Turn to the bar graph on page 12. Calculate the percentage of immigrants from each region (Europe, Latin America, Asia, and Africa) for 1901–1910 and 1991–2000. What conclusions can you draw from your calculations?

16. **Civics and Economics** You are the President's Chief Economic Advisor. Write a memo predicting the likely economic effects of an aging population on American society.

17. **Analyzing Visuals** Explain how the photograph above reflects diversity and American values.

Standardized Test Prep

Test-Taking Tips

Some questions on standardized tests ask you to analyze a reading selection. Study the passage below. Then follow the tips to answer the sample question.

TIP The first sentence gives clues about what follows. You know to look for three reasons.

Between 1866 and 1915, immigrants came to the United States for three reasons. First, the promise of freedom and hopes for a better life attracted poor and oppressed people. Then, once settled, the newcomers encouraged family and friends to come to the United States. Jobs were another reason for immigrants to leave home. American factories needed workers, and factory owners sent agents to Europe and Asia to hire workers at low wages.

Pick the letter that best completes the statement.

1. Which reason below is NOT a reason why immigrants came to the United States?

   TIP Notice the word "NOT" in the question.

   A family and friends already settled in the United States
   B the discovery of oil
   C factory jobs
   D freedom and a better life

   The correct answer is **B**. Note that the question asks you to choose the reason that is NOT stated in the passage.

2. How did the United States benefit from immigrants?
   A Immigrants provided labor.
   B Newcomers encouraged family and friends to emigrate.
   C Immigrants hoped for a better life.
   D People were oppressed at home.

American Society and Its Values

What's Ahead in Chapter 2

In this chapter you will read about why people belong to groups, and how groups influence what we believe and how we act.

SECTION 1
Groups and Institutions

SECTION 2
Society's Training Grounds

SECTION 3
The Economy

SECTION 4
Government:
Meeting Society's Needs

TARGET READING SKILL

Reading Process In this chapter, you will focus on the reading process to help you better understand the texts you read. The reading process includes setting a purpose for reading, making predictions, asking questions, and using prior knowledge.

Celebrating graduation ▶

National Standards for Civics and Government   **State**

The following National Standards for Civics and Government are addressed in this chapter:

I. What are civic life, politics, and government?

A. What is civic life? What is politics? What is government? Why are government and politics necessary? What purposes should government serve?

II. What are the foundations of the American political system?

B. What are the distinctive characteristics of American society?

Go Online
PHSchool.com

For: Your state's standards
Visit: PHSchool.com
Webcode: mpe-1020

Active Citizen ▶ Civics in the Real World

When Doris Hollingsworth was in high school, she faced an important decision about her future.

"I had always been an average student, and doing well in school did not really matter to me. Some of my friends thought we should all quit school and get jobs at the same place so we could hang out and have fun. But my parents were urging me to finish high school.

In my junior year, everything changed. Mrs. Hansen, my math teacher, said she saw a lot of potential in me. She offered to help me after school. I agreed, but I did not think I would do any better. I was wrong. By the end of the semester, I was getting A's in math and my other grades were improving too. I don't know where I would be today if Mrs. Hansen had not pushed me to see that doing well in school could make a big difference in my life."

When Doris was in high school, she was getting advice from several different groups to which she belonged—her family, her friends, and her teachers at school. Like Doris, everyone belongs to groups that influence the way we think and feel.

Citizen's Journal   Choose one group of people that influences your behavior—your friends, family, teachers or any other group. Write a paragraph explaining how this groups influences you. What advice do they give you? Do you always follow it? Why or why not?

Groups and Institutions

Objectives

In this section you will

- Learn why people form groups.
- Describe the five major social institutions.

Taking Notes

Make a diagram like the one below. As you read the section, fill in the diagram to compare informal groups with social institutions.

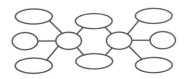

Key Terms

socialization   social institutions
rules

Main Idea

People form groups to satisfy many of their needs. Groups have rules that their members must follow in order to get along with each other. Needs that cannot be met by groups are fulfilled by social institutions.

Target Reading Skill

Set a Purpose Setting a purpose for reading can help you better understand what you read. To set a purpose for reading, look at the headings and visuals to see what the text is about. Then, use this information to give yourself a focus for reading.

Everybody has needs. For example, people have physical needs for such things as food and shelter. They have emotional needs such as the desire for love and companionship. They have spiritual needs for answers to questions about the meaning of life and death.

People form groups to satisfy many of their needs. Of course, simply being born makes you a member of some groups, such as your family. You are required to join other groups, such as a school, and you choose some groups, such as clubs and circles of friends. In any case, groups meet particular needs in people's lives. By looking at a group of friends it may be easier to understand how belonging to groups affects our lives.

Participating in a Group

Miguel Espinoza's best friends are Alex and Carol. The three of them spend a lot of time together. As a group, their goal is to provide each other with companionship and a sense of belonging.

◄ Friends make up a group that meets important needs in our lives.

Becoming a Group Member The process of learning how to participate in a group is called **socialization**. Socialization also means learning to accept the values of a group and learning the rules for behavior within it. Values are standards that guide our behavior. **Rules** are specific expectations about what our behavior should be. Rules are based on values.

Melissa, a girl at Miguel's school, went through the process of socialization when she joined Miguel's group. Soon after joining the group, Melissa ran into trouble with her new friends. She agreed to join them for a beach trip one afternoon at two o'clock. But she did not take the meeting time seriously and showed up hours late. Her new friends were worried about her, and they were angry that their afternoon was ruined.

Following the Group's Rules Melissa had run into one of the group's important values: being considerate. One of the rules based on this value is that everyone should show up for activities on time. Melissa had broken this rule, which brought her into conflict with the group.

Melissa was upset that she had angered her friends. Her need for friendship led her to accept the group's values and to agree to change her behavior. By socializing new members, groups can continue to meet their members' needs.

✓ Reading Check **What needs do people meet by joining a group?**

Target Reading Skill
Set a Purpose Preview the headings and visuals on this page. What do you expect to read about?

Learning the Rules
A group of friends shares common values and rules of behavior. A new member will need to learn these rules. **Identify Cause and Effect** *What are the benefits of following a group's rules?*

Five Social Institutions

Social institutions provide the framework for our lives. They meet our most basic physical, emotional, spiritual, and economic needs. Their values shape our own personal values, and their rules determine how we behave much of the time.

1. **Analyze** Briefly describe the needs that are met by each of the five social institutions.

2. **Apply** How might our society be different if these institutions did not exist?

Economy
The institution of the economy helps meet individuals' wants and needs by providing a system for producing and distributing goods and services.

Family
The family is society's most basic institution. It meets the physical needs of individuals by providing food, clothing, and shelter. It also provides a sense of belonging and support to meet emotional needs. This institution teaches the basic values of society as well as rules of behavior.

Education
The institution of education meets important needs by helping individuals fit into our society. This institution provides individuals with the skills and knowledge to succeed later in life. It also teaches them how to live and work together.

Religion
Religion fosters a sense of community and belonging. It also teaches the basic values of society. Most importantly, this institution meets important emotional needs by giving people comfort in difficult times and providing answers to important spiritual questions.

Government
Government is one of the most important social institutions. Government meets a society's need for law and order, security, and public services, such as schools and transportation. This institution also helps to maintain the other institutions in our society.

Social Institutions

Groups are important, but they do not satisfy all of our needs. For example, they do not provide food or shelter. They do not make laws. Groups are unable to perform these functions by themselves.

These functions are taken care of by **social institutions**, systems of values and rules that determine how our society is organized. Five major social institutions in all societies are the family, religion, education, the economy, and government.

Every society needs these institutions in one form or another. Social institutions not only satisfy needs and teach values, they also provide a framework within which groups and organizations can exist.

The institution of the family, for example, provides the framework for how individual families are set up and how they work in our society. Parents do not just make up the ideas that they will raise their children and that they will have the power to make rules for their children's behavior. These ideas about how to raise their children come from the institution of the family.

✔ Reading Check   **How do social institutions meet people's needs?**

Civics and Economics

The Cost of Raising Children   Each year, the United States Department of Agriculture (USDA) releases a report detailing the average amount of money that two-parent families in the United States will spend to raise a child from birth to age 17. In 1995, it cost the average middle-income family $145,320 to raise a child. In 2002, it cost $173,880 to raise a child, which represents an increase of about 19 percent from 1995.

Analyzing Economics
1. How much more money did it cost to raise a child in 2002 than it did in 1995?
2. What kinds of expenses related to raising a child do you think families have? Explain.
3. Assuming that costs keep rising at the same rate, how much will it cost to raise a child in 2009?

SECTION 1 Assessment

Key Terms

Use each of the key terms in a sentence that explains its meaning: rules, socialization, social institutions

Target Reading Skill

1. **Set a Purpose** What purpose did you set for reading this section? How did previewing the headings and visuals help you to set this purpose?

Comprehension and Critical Thinking

2. **a. Describe** Why do people join groups?

b. Make Generalizations What are values? What is the relationship between values and rules? Why do groups have rules?

3. **a. Recall** List the five major social institutions found in all societies.
b. Draw Conclusions Why do we need other social institutions in addition to the family? What needs do these institutions meet that are not met by the institution of the family?

Writing Activity

Think of several groups to which you belong. Write a journal entry in which you discuss what needs of yours are met by each of these groups.

TIP Brainstorm a list of the different groups to which you belong. For each group, think about why you belong to it. Determine the needs you have that are fulfilled by this group.

Society's Training Grounds

Reading Preview

Objectives

In this section you will

- Identify the ways that families meet people's needs.
- Explain the role of religion.
- Describe the importance of education.

Taking Notes

Make a diagram like the one below. As you read the section, fill in the diagram with information about the institutions of family, religion, and education.

Key Terms

family   blended families

Main Idea

Family, religion, and education are important social institutions that help shape the behavior and values of our society.

Target Reading Skills

Predict Making predictions while you read can help you to set a purpose for reading. Preview the section by first looking at the headings, the visuals, and anything else that stands out to help you make a prediction. As you read, connect what you read to your prediction. If what you learn does not support your prediction, revise your prediction.

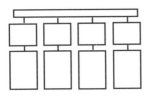

A growing number of families are headed by a single parent. ▶

The institutions of the family, religion, and education play very important parts in shaping the behavior and the values of the members of society. As you read this section, think about how these institutions affect you and the people you know.

The Family

The **family** is the most basic social institution in any society. From birth, you depend on your family to provide you with food, clothing, and shelter. Your family gives you a sense of security and belonging. Your family also teaches you many of the values you need to participate in society and contribute to it.

The American family has changed over the past century. Families are now smaller. The cost of raising and educating children continues to rise. More women now work outside the home. Therefore, many couples decide to have fewer children, or none.

The structure of some families includes a father, mother, and children. Some families are headed by a single parent because of divorce, death, or personal choice. Some families are **blended families**, or families made up of adults and their children from previous marriages. Children whose parents are not able to care for them may become part of other families through adoption or foster care.

Rules of Daily Life The family is where you learn many of the rules that govern daily life. These rules may include keeping your room clean, finishing your homework, and not playing your radio too loudly. Such rules reflect the values that parents think children ought to live by: being responsible, clean, and respectful of others.

Every teen has experienced punishments, such as being grounded, for breaking such rules. Of course, there are rewards for following the rules, too, such as praise from your parents.

How the Family Benefits Society The rules of conduct you learn at home do not disappear when you step out the door. Society has created similar rules called laws. For example, your parents have taught you to put trash in the garbage can rather than let it pile up on the floor. Society has a rule against littering as well.

This simple example illustrates the point that rules established within the family often reflect the values held by society as a whole. In a real sense, the family benefits society by serving as a kind of training ground for adults-to-be.

✓ Reading Check   **How does the family serve as a training ground for young people?**

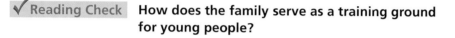

Families with Children Under 18

11%
89%
1970

20%
80%
1980

24%
76%
1990

28%
72%
2000

■ One-parent families
■ Two-parent families

SOURCE: U.S. Bureau of the Census

The percentage of one-parent families rose from 1970 to 2000.

1. **Analyze** What percentage of families with children under 18 had two parents in 1980?
2. **Calculate** In which decade did the number of single-parent families increase the most?

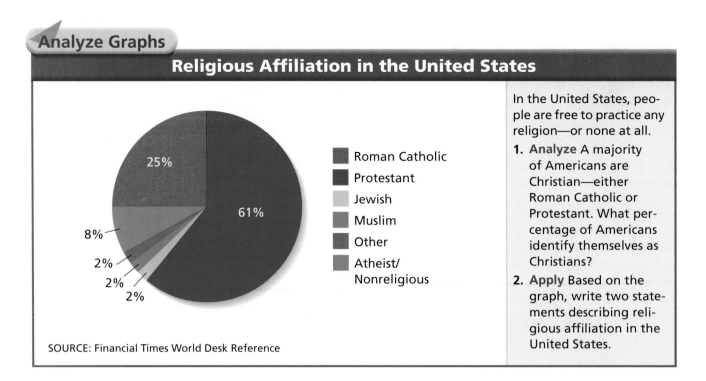

Religious Affiliation in the United States

- Roman Catholic
- Protestant
- Jewish
- Muslim
- Other
- Atheist/ Nonreligious

25%

61%

8%

2%

2%

2%

SOURCE: Financial Times World Desk Reference

In the United States, people are free to practice any religion—or none at all.

1. **Analyze** A majority of Americans are Christian—either Roman Catholic or Protestant. What percentage of Americans identify themselves as Christians?

2. **Apply** Based on the graph, write two statements describing religious affiliation in the United States.

Religion

Not everyone in America belongs to a religious group. However, the institution of religion plays an important part in our society. Religion meets important individual needs, such as the need for comfort in times of sorrow and the need to find answers to spiritual questions about the meaning of life and death.

Like the family, religious groups can also give people a sense of belonging. Religious groups give their members a feeling of being part of a community of people who have similar goals and similar ways of looking at life. Religions provide people with moral standards that they can use to decide how to live their lives.

A Sense of Community Emily Shultz cannot imagine life without her church. It helps to draw the members together, giving them a sense of belonging to a community that can support them in times of trouble. Her church is a place where members can meet to observe their faith together.

Rules to Live By Every religion has a moral code that sets expectations for people's behavior and helps them judge right from wrong. A religious group can exert a powerful influence on its members to live according to its rules. Each religion has punishments for those who stray from its moral path. One form of punishment is to withdraw the emotional and spiritual support the group provides. An individual can also be threatened with punishment after death.

People who follow the rules of their religion are rewarded by the acceptance and approval of the group. Most religions promise faithful members some kind of reward after death. Obeying religious rules and embracing the values they reflect also give people confidence that they are living moral and good lives.

Target Reading Skill

Predict Did you correctly predict what the text on this page would be about? Do you need to revise your prediction?

How Religion Affects Society Many of the rules that guide people's behavior in our society are written into laws. However, members of religious communities who help each other in times of crisis are not required by law to do so. They act out of the belief that charity—helping others who are less fortunate—is good.

Charity, sympathy, and loyalty to friends and family are values that cannot be written into laws. However, when people live their lives according to such values, the whole society benefits. By teaching values, and by passing them on from generation to generation, the institution of religion makes an important contribution to American society.

Conflicting Religious Values The diverse people who make up American society belong to many religious groups. In fact, more than 1,200 different religious groups can be found in the United States today.

Not all of these religious groups share the same values and rules. If one religious group tries to impose its values on the rest of society, serious conflicts can arise. In the United States today, disagreements about such issues as the teaching of evolution are often based on the values of different religious groups.

As we debate such issues, we face the challenge of balancing two of our most important rights: freedom of speech and freedom of religion. One test of whether or not we as Americans are living up to our ideal of equal respect is whether members of religious groups (and people who adhere to no religion at all) can act according to their own beliefs and values while still respecting the right of others to believe differently.

✔ Reading Check **How does the institution of religion make an important contribution to American society?**

Charity
Whether providing meals or homes for those less fortunate, members of religious communities make important contributions to our society.
Draw Conclusions *What are some other contributions that members of religious communities make to society?*

Education

Think back to your first days in elementary school. There were dozens of new rules to learn. Many of the rules and skills were new to you. However, as you moved into the larger world outside your family and your neighborhood, your needs began to change. The institution of education exists to meet those needs.

Preparing for the Future
Education provides students with the skills and knowledge they will need as working adults.
Draw Inferences *Why is college or additional training after high-school so important these days?*

Why People Need Education Whatever your dreams might be, you have hopes for a career that uses your skills and talents, provides you with a comfortable life, and gives you a sense of self worth. To achieve this goal, you will need an education. Education is increasingly important in our society. Because we live in a time of rapid technological change, more and more of the available jobs require a great deal of knowledge or special skills. The institution of education has another important effect on you. School is one of the first places where you meet people from different backgrounds and with different values. In school you begin to recognize the importance of respecting others.

Meeting Society's Needs The institution of education also serves our society. Society needs to train its citizens to do the work that keeps society functioning. We need trained workers to run businesses and all the other services of our society. In addition, our society needs to prepare its citizens to live together as a nation. The children who enter our schools are as diverse as American society itself. The values and customs they bring from home often differ from those of their classmates.

Analyze Charts

Occupations and Education

Occupation	Earnings (yearly)	Educational Requirements
Bank Teller	$9.21 (hourly)	At least a high school diploma, though a college degree is becoming increasingly important
Newspaper Reporter	$26,900.00	Bachelor's degree in Journalism
Computer Specialist	$36,460.00	Associate's or bachelor's degree in computer science
High School Teacher	$39,845.00	All states require general education teachers to have a bachelor's degree and teacher training certificate
Anesthesiologist	$210,000.00	4 years of undergraduate school, 4 years of medical school, and 3 to 8 years of internship and residency

SOURCE: U.S. Department of Labor, Bureau of Labor Statistics

The chart above lists the earnings and educational requirements for different occupations.
1. **Analyze** What are the educational requirements for a teacher?
2. **Apply** What relationship do you see between the amount of money earned in each occupation and the educational requirements for the occupation?

Teaching Young Citizens Society has entrusted the schools with the task of teaching the rules and values by which Americans are expected to live. Schools teach us to think critically, form opinions, make judgments, and solve problems.

Our schools also offer us knowledge of our history, culture, and government. Our schools transmit society's ideal of equal respect and the values of freedom, equality, and justice that support it. Through the institution of education, American society assures that this country will continue to be a free, democratic nation.

Education's Rewards The rewards of your education can go far beyond grades and paychecks. By the time you finish high school, you may have spent the better part of 13 years in school. When you leave school, you will probably have some good memories. Perhaps you will also leave school with a better sense of who you are and how you can contribute to American society.

Citizen Profiles

Michele Foreman (1946–) is a social studies teacher at Middlebury Union High School in Middlebury, Vermont. In 2001, she was voted National Teacher of the Year. Foreman earned the honor through her excellence in teaching and devotion to her students. Foreman saw that the Middle East was playing a vital role in world affairs. She learned Arabic and now teaches it in a popular before-school class. Asked about her philosophy of education, Foreman said, "A good teacher needs not only a good understanding of what he or she teaches, but also a sense of excitement in learning."

Citizenship
What impact would studying Arabic have on understanding the role that the Middle East plays in the world?

✓ Reading Check **Why is the opportunity to meet people from different backgrounds an important part of education?**

SECTION 2 Assessment

Key Terms

Use each of the key terms in a sentence that explains its meaning:
family, blended families

Target Reading Skill

1. Predict What prediction did you make about this section before you began reading? How did your prediction help guide your reading?

Comprehension and Critical Thinking

2. a. Recall How has the family changed over the past century?

b. Analyze Information How does the family form the foundation of society?

3. a. Describe What social benefits are provided by the institution of religion?

b. Identify Cause and Effect What causes conflict between people of different religions?

4. a. Explain Why do people need an education? What needs of society are met by the institution of education?

b. Predict What have you learned from your education so far that will help you later in adult life?

Writing Activity

You are writing a letter to a pen pal in another country who is interested in the United States. In your letter, explain the importance of family, religion, and education as social institutions and how they influence American life.

TIP Make a brief outline. Under each topic (family, religion, and education), identify two or three points that explain how each influences American life.

Debating the Issues

CLOSE UP FOUNDATION

The debates in this feature are based on *Current Issues*, published by the Close Up Foundation. Go to **PHSchool.com**, Web Code mph-1025, to read the latest issue of *Current Issues* online.

The United States guarantees every child a free public school education through the 12th grade. Unfortunately, many public schools are overcrowded and understaffed. Many school buildings are in disrepair. Some schools do not have enough books or desks to go around. One alternative is private school, but many families can't afford the fees. Recently, school voucher programs in some communities have provided some families with money to apply toward private school tuition. However, there is no nationwide school voucher program.

Should the Federal Government Give Parents Vouchers for Private School Tuition?

YES	NO
• No student should be denied opportunities because his or her parents cannot pay school fees. Vouchers would eliminate the unfairness of a system in which students from wealthy families can get a better education than children from poor families.	• As more students leave public schools because of vouchers, these schools will become even more cash-strapped. Since vouchers do not pay the full cost of a private education, only the poorest students will be left behind in even more impoverished public schools.
• As public schools lose more and more students to private schools, they will also lose funding. They will be forced to improve or close down. This will make sure that only good schools survive	• The United States Constitution forbids the government to support religious organizations. However, school vouchers can be used to pay tuition at a religious school. All taxpayers, not just the parents of school-age children, pay for these vouchers. This forces Americans to support religious organizations.

What Is Your Opinion?

1. **Support a Point of View** Do you think the government should spend money for tuition at religious schools? Explain.

2. **Identify Cause and Effect** How might the threat of losing funding result in improvements in public schools?

3. **Writing to Persuade** Your state is about to vote on a school voucher program. Write a newspaper editorial urging readers to vote for or against the program. State your position clearly and give your reasons.

Go Online
civics interactive

For: You Decide Poll
Visit: PHSchool.com
Webcode: mpp-1022

The Economy

Reading Preview

Objectives
In this section you will
- Explain characteristics of the American economy.
- Identify American economic freedoms.
- Describe your role in the American economy.

Key Terms
economy   price
consumer   money
market

Main Idea
The American economy is an exchange of goods and services that is supported by economic freedoms.

Target Reading Skills
Preview and Ask Questions
Asking questions as you read can help you better understand the text. Preview the headings and visuals to see what the section is about. Then, ask some questions that might be answered by what you will read.

Taking Notes
Make a diagram like the one below. As you read the section, fill in the diagram with information about the American economy.

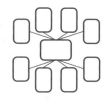

Suppose that one day you are baking brownie bars and you get an idea: why not make a huge batch of these bars and trade them for things that you need? Surely no one could resist the taste of your new creation, which you call the BarWonder.

At Jane's farm, you exchange a dozen eggs for one BarWonder. Then you are off to the tailor to trade him 30 BarWonders for a pair of pants. You have provided yourself with food and clothing, which are physical products called goods.

Your next stop is Danny's Handyman Shop. You ask Danny to fix your television and repair your flat bicycle tire. Danny agrees to perform these services—work you will pay to have done—in exchange for two dozen BarWonders.

The American Economy

Every society has an **economy**—a system for producing and distributing goods and services to fulfill people's wants. It also has a set of rules and expectations for its members.

Exchanging Services
In an economy, goods and services are exchanged.
Analyze Information *Explain how this image illustrates the concept of an economic exchange.*

Characteristics of Our Economy In our economy, each of us is a **consumer**, a person who uses, or consumes, goods and services to satisfy his or her wants. Most people are also workers. They provide the skills and the labor necessary to produce goods or to provide services.

People exchange goods or services in a **market**. In some markets, such as stores, people meet face-to-face to exchange what they have for what they want. In other markets, such as stock exchanges, buyers and sellers never meet, but make transactions using complicated accounting systems.

The amount you must pay for a good or service in a market is its **price**. You used the barter system when you exchanged your Bar-Wonders for eggs, blue jeans, flour, and repair services. Although bartering is one way to pay for what you want, people in modern socities usually use money. **Money** is anything, from beads to coins to checks, which is generally accepted as payment for a good or a service.

Analyze Diagrams

American Economic Freedom

Freedom is a basic value that is at the core of the American economy. Our economy has five important economic freedoms.

a. Which of these freedoms apply both to sellers and buyers?

b. Should any of these freedoms be limited? Why or why not?

Employed Persons by Age, 2002

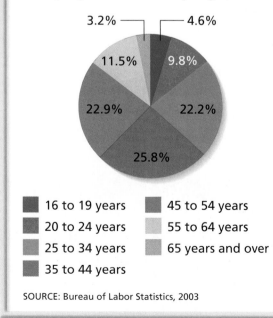

3.2%   4.6%
11.5%   9.8%
22.9%   22.2%
25.8%

- ■ 16 to 19 years   ■ 45 to 54 years
- ■ 20 to 24 years   ■ 55 to 64 years
- ■ 25 to 34 years   ■ 65 years and over
- ■ 35 to 44 years

SOURCE: Bureau of Labor Statistics, 2003

Freedom to Buy and Sell

You have the right to buy and sell goods and services. Having a wide variety of goods and services available helps keep the economy strong.

Freedom to Compete

You may compete against other sellers. Competition promotes innovation and improvements in products and services.

American Economic Freedoms Built into our economy are rules protecting five important freedoms.

- You have the freedom to buy or sell goods or services to anyone you wish. You are also free to charge whatever price you think you can get for them.

- You have the freedom to compete against others who are selling goods or services.

- You have the freedom to earn a profit. Profits encourage people to produce goods and services.

- You have the right of ownership of your goods until you sell them. The right to buy and sell your own property is a basic rule of the American economic system.

- You are free to pursue any career you wish. Your success depends on whether there are jobs available and on whether you have the proper training and skills.

Freedom to Own Property

You have the right of ownership of your own property until you choose to sell it. You may buy, sell, and use your property as you wish.

Freedom to Choose an Occupation

You have the freedom to pursue any career you wish. Your success depends on the availability of jobs and your preparation for your career.

Freedom to Make a Profit

You have the freedom to earn a profit, if you can sell a product or service for more than it costs you to produce. Earning profits encourages businesses to produce more goods and provide more services.

Go Online
civics
interactive

For: American Economic Freedoms
Visit: PHSchool.com
Webcode: mpp-1023

Fairness In addition to protecting freedom, the rules of our economic system are based on the idea of fairness. If you make an agreement to do a job, sell a product, or pay a worker, you may not break it. Furthermore, you may not make a product that does not work the way that you claim it does.

✓ Reading Check **What is the purpose of an economy?**

America's Economy and You

Target Reading Skill
Preview and Ask Questions
Ask (and answer) a question about this paragraph.

As you have read, our economic system gives people the freedom to make their own choices. We are free, for example, to buy and sell goods and services. We also are free to pursue the careers we wish. Yet not everyone has the job he or she wants, and most people cannot buy all the goods and services they would like to have. There are also many people in our country who are very poor. They often cannot buy the goods and services they need. On the whole, however, our economic system succeeds. The goods and services we desire are produced, distributed, and sold. We have the freedom to try to achieve our dreams—to have the lifestyles of our own choosing. In these ways, we benefit from the institution of the economy in the United States.

✓ Reading Check **How do people benefit from the American economy?**

SECTION 3 Assessment

Key Terms

Use each of the key terms in a sentence that explains its meaning: economy, consumer, market, price, money

Target Reading Skill

1. **Preview and Ask Questions** What questions did you ask yourself that helped you learn something from this section?

Comprehension and Critical Thinking

2. **a. Describe** How does bartering work?

   b. Explain Why are markets an important part of an economy?

3. **a. Recall** What is the freedom to compete?

   b. Check Consistency How does the price of a good or service influence your decisions as a consumer?

4. **a. Describe** List at least one way the American economy does not work for people.

   b. Make Generalizations How does the American economy work for most people?

Writing Activity

Write a report about how the freedoms of the American economy help Americans gain a better life.

TIP Examine each economic freedom and write at least one reason it helps Americans achieve their dreams.

Government: Meeting Society's Needs

Reading Preview

Objectives

In this section you will

- Learn why government is needed.
- Explain how three different forms of government work.
- Describe the roles of law in government.

Key Terms

monarchy   patriotism
dictatorship political socialization
democracy

Main Idea

There are different forms of government. Each tries to establish order. Where they differ is the amount of freedom each provides.

Target Reading Skills

Use Prior Knowledge Using prior knowledge refers to building on what you already know to help you better understand new information. Spark your memory by looking at the headings and the visuals of your reading assignment. What do you already know about what you see?

Taking Notes

Make a diagram like the one below. As you read the section, fill in the diagram with information about the different functions of government.

Suddenly, in the middle of the night, soldiers rush into your best friend's home and arrest his parents. He never sees them again. A president and other officials appoint themselves to permanent office. All elections are cancelled indefinitely. Religion is outlawed. Churches, temples, and mosques are locked and barred. Do you think these scenes could take place in the United States?

These scenes are an everyday reality for people in many countries. Individuals live in constant fear because their rights are not protected. For them, their government is the enemy.

Life in the United States is different. Our government was formed to protect our rights and to ensure that events such as the ones described above do not occur.

The Role of Government

Without government, life would be chaos. There would be no order to the way roads were built or towns and cities planned. People would disagree about ways to settle arguments and deal with crime. We would have no proper way to defend our nation from attack.

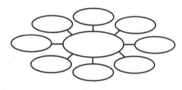

By preventing crime and protecting ▶ community safety, police officers help government maintain law and order in our society.

Target Reading Skill
Use Prior Knowledge What do you already know about what the government does that will help you understand its various responsibilities?

Keeping the Peace Government makes and enforces laws that protect rights and ensure that people's lives can proceed in a peaceful, orderly way. Through courts, our government can also settle disputes and punish law breakers.

Protecting the Country Government provides for our defense against outside attack by maintaining armed forces and weapons. Our government makes treaties with other countries in which both sides agree to keep the peace or to help each other in case of attack.

Providing Necessary Services Government provides services we need but cannot depend on private businesses to provide. Such services include building and maintaining roads, sewers, and schools.

Maintaining Other Institutions Government can help to maintain the other institutions in society. For example, in the United States, government protects our freedom of religion, provides schools, and offers hundreds of services to families, from health care to aid in the event of a natural disaster.

✓ Reading Check **What is the role of the courts in our government?**

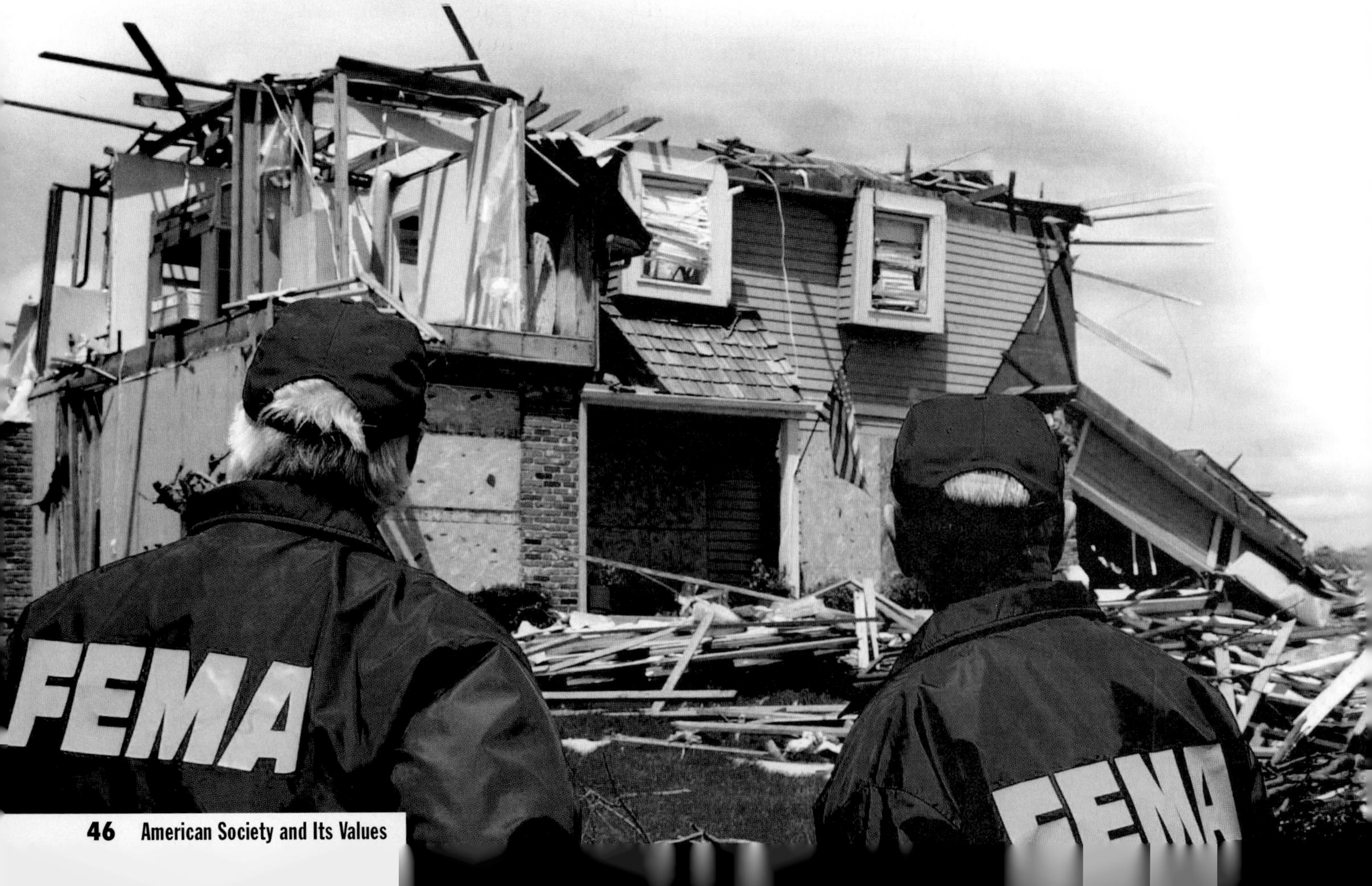

Disaster Relief
The Federal Emergency Management Agency (FEMA) is a government agency that helps people before and after disasters.
Draw Conclusions *Why does the government provide assistance to Americans after serious disasters?*

In 2003, many states faced serious budget crises due to a poor national economy and a decrease in aid from the federal government. As a result, funding for education in many states was cut severely.

1. What is the main idea of the cartoon?

2. How does the cartoonist use humor to make his point?

High Sch ol Dipl ma

THIS CERTIFI S TH T
(FILL IN YOUR NAME)
HAS RECEIV D A COMPL TE EDUC TION
DESP TE ALL THE BUDG T CUTS

Forms of Government

There are many forms of government. In the world today, monarchy, dictatorship, and democracy are three of the most common forms of government.

Monarchy A **monarchy** is a form of government in which all or most of the power is in the hands of one individual, the monarch. The monarch's authority is hereditary; it stays in the family, usually being passed down to a son or daughter. King, queen, and emperor are some of the titles that have been given to monarchs.

Monarchies were once the most common type of government in the world. Today, however, real monarchies—in which the monarch holds all the power—are rare. An example of such a modern-day monarchy is the kingdom of Saudi Arabia.

Dictatorship A **dictatorship** is a government controlled by one person, called a dictator. A dictator is different from a monarch because a dictator usually takes power by force, rather than by inheriting it. Historically, dictators have usually come to power when an existing government is weak or has lost public support.

Dictators are frequently military leaders. They rely heavily on the support of the armed forces and the police to maintain their power. Laws or legislatures do not limit their actions. Military dictatorships of the twentieth century include Germany under Adolf Hitler and Iraq under Saddam Hussein.

Democracy A third form of government is a **democracy**, a system in which the power is shared by all the people. Democracy means "government by the people." By voting and by choosing representatives, the people decide how their government will meet their needs and protect their rights and freedoms.

The United States was the first modern democracy. Since our nation was founded, countries all over the world have adopted democratic forms of government. Most countries that were once monarchies have become democracies. Many of these countries, such as Great Britain and Japan, still have monarchs with ceremonial duties, but real power is held by democratically elected representatives. Countries with this form of democratic government are often called constitutional monarchies.

✓ Reading Check **What is the main difference between a monarchy and a dictatorship?**

Laws: The Rules of Government

Laws are the formal rules that govern our behavior in society. The most basic and important laws of our nation are written down in a document called the Constitution. The Constitution tells what the government can and cannot do, and lists the rights guaranteed to states and to citizens. In the United States, governments at the town, county, state, and national levels can make laws, as long as these laws are not in conflict with the Constitution.

Following and Breaking Laws Laws influence nearly everything we do, from driving a car to getting a fishing license. By following our laws, we ensure that rights are protected and order maintained in society.

Breaking laws can lead to very specific punishments. The seriousness of the punishment depends on the seriousness of the crime. For example, if you were to break the speed limit or litter, you would probably have to pay a fine. If you were to rob a bank, you could spend years in jail.

Changing the Laws In a democracy, the citizens have a right to express their opinions and work with others to try to make laws they think are needed. They can also try to change laws they think are unfair or harmful to society.

Our government responds to our demands, but only when it hears them. People's opinions do make a difference when they are made known to lawmakers and other government officials.

✓ Reading Check **How do citizens help make the laws in a democracy?**

▲ British Prime Minister Tony Blair meets with Queen Elizabeth II (above). The Queen's duties are mostly ceremonial. For example, each year, the British monarch officially opens the session of Parliament (top).

Political Socialization

On September 11, 2001, terrorists attacked the United States. This attack resulted in nationwide displays of patriotism. **Patriotism** is the demonstration of love and devotion to one's country. Following September 11th, people displayed the American flag. Schools called for students to say the Pledge of Allegiance to the flag. How do people in a society learn about patriotism?

An individual learns correct and incorrect political behavior in our culture. We learn how to behave politically and patriotically. We learn from our parents, our teachers, our church, the media, and many others. The process of learning how to behave politically is called **political socialization**. Through political socialization, we learn why it is important to defend freedom of speech and to dissent responsibly. We understand why it is important to say the Pledge of Allegiance and to respect the will of the people through the majority vote.

✓ **Reading Check** How do people in a society learn about patriotism?

Law and the Real World

The USA Patriot Act

After the terrorist attack on the World Trade Center, President Bush signed the USA Patriot Act on October 25, 2001. The law begins with a description of its purpose: "to deter and punish terrorist acts in the United States and around the world."

Legislators believed that United States law enforcement and intelligence agencies could not track down terrorists because they did not have enough access to information.

The law raised immediate concern among some Americans. It expanded the power of law enforcement to use phone wiretaps, searches of computer e-mail, Internet use, and other tools. Several states passed resolutions against the act because they believed that it violated free speech rights.

Applying the Law

1. **Summarize** What is the USA Patriot Act?
2. **Draw Conclusions** Why did some people disagree with this law?

SECTION 4 Assessment

Key Terms

Use each of the key terms in a sentence that explains its meaning: monarchy, dictatorship, democracy, patriotism, political socialization

Target Reading Skill

1. **Use Prior Knowledge** How did what you learned in this section relate to what you already knew?

Comprehension and Critical Thinking

2. **a. Recall** What are the roles of government?

b. Predict What kinds of problems would result if government did not provide public services?

3. **a. Recall** How do most dictators come to power?

b. Contrast How is a democracy different from a dictatorship?

4. **a. Describe** What is the role of the constitution in a democracy?

b. Summarize How can people help make or change the laws?

Writing Activity

Find out about a current issue that is being considered in Congress. Write a letter to your Congressional representative to express your opinions about the issue.

Go Online
PHSchool.com
For: Writing Activity
Visit: PHSchool.com
Webcode: mpd-1024

Identifying Points of View

An editorial is a kind of newspaper article that expresses an opinion. When you read an editorial, look for clues that tell about the writer's point of view. Then think about whether or not you agree with the writer's point of view.

The following excerpt is from an editorial that discusses music file-sharing on the Internet. Record companies are beginning to sue people who download music files for breaking copyright laws.

Suing a 12-year-old girl for illegal file sharing is hardly a way to generate good press. . . . Music companies are right to aggressively pursue people, even minors, who steal their products, but that alone will not solve their problems. They need to change how they do business, and fast, if they want to survive in the 21st century. . . .

Some downloaders have reacted angrily to the lawsuits, claiming that they did not know swapping music files was illegal, or that it is justified by high CD prices. But stealing is stealing, online or in a store, and this theft has real victims. It robs artists of their livelihoods and . . . makes it harder for new acts to break in. The only way for the industry to defend itself is to litigate hard, and publicly, against the copyright infringers. But it also needs to adapt to the times.

Learn the Skill

Follow these steps to identify points of view:

1 Identify the source. Knowing the background of the writer or the publication can help you figure out the point of view.

2 Note the frame of reference. Time, place, and circumstances can influence a person's opinion.

3 Find main ideas. Look for the writer's main point. This will help you identify his or her point of view on the subject

4 Look for emotionally charged words. The way information is presented often shows the writer's point of view.

5 Identify the point of view. Where does the writer or speaker "stand" in regards to the main idea?

Practice the Skill

Read the editorial and answer these questions:

1 What are the two sides of the issue discussed in the editorial?

2 What is the main point of the editorial?

3 List at least three words or phrases that indicate the writer's point of view.

4 Identify the writer's point of view. What evidence does the author use to support his or her point of view?

Apply the Skill

Use the Internet to find a recent political speech. Read the speech and use the steps above to identify the speaker's point of view.

Review and Assessment

Chapter Summary

Section 1
Groups and Institutions
(pages 30–33)

- People form groups to satisfy many of their needs.
- Socialization is the process of learning how to be a member of a group.
- Rules are specific expectations about what our behavior should be.
- The five social institutions that help organize society are the family, religion, education, the economy, and government.

Section 2
Society's Training Grounds
(pages 34–39)

- The structure of the American family has changed over the past century to include single-parent and blended families.
- The family is the first place people learn the rules of daily life.
- Religion teaches values and provides people with a sense of community.
- With so many religions in the United States, our different religious values and beliefs sometimes come into conflict.
- Education provides training for future employment and also brings children into contact with others of different backgrounds.

Section 3
The Economy
(pages 41–44)

- In an economy, consumers exchange goods and services in a market where everything has a price.
- Barter and money are two ways people use to pay one another for their goods and services.

- The American economy has the following five freedoms: to buy and sell, to compete, to make a profit, to own property, and to choose one's occupation.
- The American economy gives people the freedom to achieve their dreams, although it does not guarantee that everyone will be equally successful at doing so.

Section 4
Government: Meeting Society's Needs
(pages 45–49)

- The role of government is to provide for law and order, security, public services, and to maintain other institutions such as schools.
- The most common forms of government in the world today are monarchy, dictatorship, and democracy.
- Laws are the formal rules that govern behavior in society.
- Patriotism is the expression of love for one's country.
- Political socialization is the process by which people learn to be citizens of the political world.

Copy the chart below and use it to help you summarize the chapter.

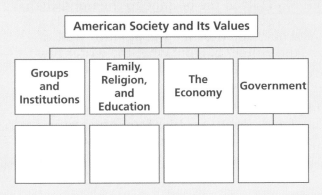

Review and Assessment Continued

Go Online
PHSchool.com

For: Self-Test
Visit: PHSchool.com
Webcode: mp9-1026

Reviewing Key Terms

Fill in the blank with one of the key terms from the list below.

price	market
socialization	rules
economy	social institutions
monarchy	democracy

1. A government ruled by a king is a _____.

2. Specific expectations about behavior are called _____.

3. Religion, education and government are examples of _____.

4. The amount you pay for a good or service is its _____.

5. The system of government in which power is shared by all the people is called _____.

6. The system for producing and distributing goods is called the _____.

7. The process of learning how to participate in a group is called _____.

8. A place where goods and services are exchanged is called a _____.

Comprehension and Critical Thinking

9. a. **Describe** Why do people join groups?
   b. **Contrast** What is the difference between values and rules?
   c. **Evaluate Information** How do a group's rules contribute to socialization?

10. a. **Explain** How do the family, religion, and education shape the values of American society?
    b. **Analyze** What happens when people of different religious views try to impose those views on others?
    c. **Draw Inferences** How do freedom of religion and freedom of speech come into conflict in American society?

11. a. **Recall** What are the five freedoms of the American economy?
    b. **Draw Conclusions** How does competition benefit consumers?
    c. **Identify Cause and Effect** How would the absence of competition hurt consumers?

12. a. **Recall** List four roles of government.
    b. **Compare** How are monarchy and dictatorship similar?
    c. **Draw Inferences** Why is the military an important part of most dictatorships?

Activities

13. **Skills** Read the passage to the right, then answer the questions that follow. a. How would you describe the point of view of the writer? b. From what the writer has written, infer who does not benefit from competition.

14. **Writing** Write a short essay comparing democracy to another form of government and explaining which form of government is best.

> Some people think it is better to limit competition. I don't. Competition benefits both consumers and producers. Consumers benefit because competition forces producers to make the highest quality product for the lowest price. Producers benefit because there is opportunity for someone with a new or better idea.

15. **Active Citizen** Think about a recent shopping experience. Make a list of the number of stores you visited and the questions you asked yourself about the goods you looked at. Be sure to include the reasons you used to make or not make the purchase.

16. **Math Practice** At a bake sale you sell 85 brownies at $0.50 a piece and 68 muffins at $0.75 a piece. Your costs for ingredients is 12 cents per brownie and 22 cents per muffin. How much money did you make from the bake sale, and what is your profit?

17. **Civics and Economics** Write a brief essay about why two functions provided by government—roads and education—are vital to the health of the American economy.

18. **Analyze Visuals** Explain how the photo above illustrates American values.

Standardized Test Prep

Some questions on standardized test ask you to analyze a reading selection. Study the passage below. Then follow the tips to answer questions that follow.

TIP The first sentence tells you what will have happened by the end of the paragraph. Read the paragraph with that end in mind.

> There is a pattern to the beginnings of dictatorships. In many countries an elected government adopts policies that threaten the country's military or its wealthiest, most powerful citizens. The military ousts the government and takes power to "restore law and order." The law and order it restores is a law and order that is favored by the wealthy few. From a group of generals who organize the takeover, one leader takes power and rules, creating laws and policies that protect the interests of the wealthy at the expense of the interests and freedom of the majority of the people.

1. What causes the military to oust a democratically elected government?
   A It is angry it lost the election.
   B The government adopts polices that threaten the military or the country's wealthy and powerful.
   C The majority of people don't like the government.
   D Most people prefer to live in dictatorships.

   The correct answer is **B**. The answer is directly stated in the second sentence of the passage.

2. What happens to the majority of people in a dictatorship?
   A They lose their freedom.
   B They get to serve in the army.
   C Their interests are represented instead of the interests of the wealthy.
   D All of the above.

The Meaning of Citizenship

What's Ahead in Chapter 3

In this chapter you will read about how a person becomes a citizen of the United States. You will also learn about the rights, duties, and responsibilities associated with citizenship.

SECTION 1
What it Means to be a Citizen

SECTION 2
Rights, Duties, and Responsibilities

SECTION 3
Citizenship and Our Other Roles

TARGET READING SKILL

Identify Main Ideas In this chapter you will focus on identifying the main idea of a paragraph or section. This skill will help you better understand what you read. This skill includes identifying supporting details and identifying main ideas that are implied, or stated indirectly.

A naturalization ceremony ▶

National Standards for Civics and Government

State

The following National
Standards for Civics and
Government are covered
in this chapter:

V. What are the roles of

the citizen in American
democracy?

A. What is citizenship?

B. What are the rights of citizens?

C. What are the responsibilities of citizens?

D. How can citizens take part
in civic life?

Go Online
PHSchool.com

For: Your state's
standards
Visit: PHSchool.com
Web Code: mpe-1031

Active Citizen ▶ Civics in the Real World

The Pledge of Allegiance first appeared in 1892 in a magazine
called *The Youth's Companion.* The original Pledge was
attributed to Francis Bellamy. Bellamy was chairman of a
committee of state superintendents in the National Education Association. As chairman, he organized a program for
public schools to celebrate the quadricentennial of Columbus
Day in 1892. The program included a flag raising ceremony
and a flag salute—the Pledge of Allegiance. The original
Pledge stated: "I pledge allegiance to my Flag and the Republic for which it stands; one Nation indivisible with liberty
and justice for all."

The Pledge has been changed a few times since then. In 1924
"my Flag" was changed to "the Flag of the United States of
America" by the National Flag Conference. Congress officially recognized the Pledge in 1942 by including it in the
Flag Code. The last change to the Pledge occurred on Flag
Day, June 14, 1954. President Dwight D. Eisenhower
approved adding the words "under God."

*I pledge allegiance to the Flag of the United States of Amer-
ica, and to the Republic for which it stands, one nation
under God, indivisible, with liberty and justice for all.*

Citizen's Journal Write a paragraph explaining your understanding of what citizenship means. After you have studied the
chapter, reread your paragraph. Write a new paragraph explaining how your understanding has grown.

What it Means to be a Citizen

Reading Preview

Objectives
In this section you will
- Discuss who a citizen is and how a person becomes an American citizen.
- Discuss what the office of citizen is and what important powers citizens possess.

Taking Notes
Make a diagram like the one shown. As you read this section, complete the diagram to outline the meanings of citizenship.

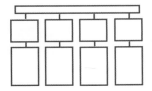

Key Terms
citizen   alien
naturalized   representatives

Main Idea
Americans become citizens in a variety of ways. Each citizen holds an office—the office of citizen—that comes with important rights and duties.

Target Reading Skill
Identify Main Ideas Identifying main ideas helps you grasp the most important issues as you read. If you are unsure of the main ideas of a section as you read, look for the ideas in a passage that are key to your understanding.

An immigrant who wishes to become an American citizen must be able to read, write, and speak English.
▼

Emily Shultz lives in Sublette, Kansas. She is a citizen of her town, state, and nation. A **citizen** is a person with certain rights and duties under a government. As a citizen, therefore, Emily has certain rights and duties. She has the right to express an opinion and the right to protection under the law. She has the duty to obey the law and to pay taxes. Each of us is a citizen of the town, state, and nation in which we live, and each of us has certain rights and duties.

Who Is a Citizen?

Our Constitution says that a citizen of the United States is a person who by birth or choice owes allegiance to this nation. You are legally an American citizen if any of these statements is true.

- You were born in the United States or in one of its territories. (This is true even if your parents were not citizens, unless they were living in the United States as representatives of a foreign government.)

- At least one of your parents was a United States citizen when you were born. As long as one of your parents is a citizen, it does not matter where you were born.

- You have been **naturalized**, which means you have gone through the process of becoming a citizen.

- You were less than eighteen years old when your parents were naturalized.

The Naturalization Process

Step 1
APPLICATION

The applicant submits an application to the Immigration and Naturalization Service (INS).

Step 2
EXAMINATION

The applicant must prove the following qualifications for citizenship:
- Age 18 or older
- Legal residence in the country for at least 5 years; in state for at least 3 months
- Good moral character (for example, not having been convicted of certain crimes)
- Loyalty to the principles of the U.S. Constitution
- Ability to read, write, and speak English
- Knowledge of the history and form of government of the United States

Step 3
FINAL HEARING

The applicant appears before a citizenship court.
- INS responds to the application.
- A judge asks the applicant to take an oath of loyalty to the United States.
- The applicant receives a certificate of citizenship.

People who wish to become citizens must meet certain requirements and take a test.

1. **Analyze** In what subjects must applicants demonstrate ability and knowledge?

2. **Apply** Why do you think it's important for an applicant to know the history and form of government of the U.S.?

Naturalization When Thomas Pham's family came to this country from Vietnam, they were considered aliens. An **alien** is a citizen of one country who lives in another country. As aliens, the Phams had many of the same rights and duties as American citizens. However, they could not vote or hold government office.

To become citizens, Thomas' parents went through the process of naturalization. (See the chart above). They learned English, studied American history, and learned the values, laws, rights, and duties of citizens. Since Thomas was under eighteen, he automatically became a citizen, too.

Naturalized Citizens Naturalized citizens have all the rights and duties of citizens by birth except the right to be President or Vice President. Once you are a citizen, you will always be a citizen except in a few special cases. For example, a person can decide to give up citizenship or become a citizen of another country. Citizenship may be taken away from a person who is convicted of trying to overthrow the United States government by force.

> **Target Reading Skill**
> **Identify Main Ideas** Read the paragraph under the heading *Naturalized Citizens*. Look for the central idea of the paragraph. You may want to write down key words or phrases that help you identify the main idea.

✓ Reading Check **How do the rights and duties of naturalized citizens differ from those of citizens by birth?**

The Office of Citizen

Each citizen holds a very important position of authority. Abraham Lincoln observed that ours is a government "of the people, by the people, [and] for the people." He meant that our government can operate—make laws, build roads, collect taxes, make agreements with other countries—only if we citizens want it to. When we say that the power of our government is based on "the consent of the governed," we mean that citizens have the power to decide what our government will and will not do.

Voting in elections is one of the most important jobs we have as citizens of the United States. ▶

However, it would be impossible for each citizen to represent himself or herself in government. As citizens, we elect **representatives,** people who are chosen to speak and act for their fellow citizens in government. We elect members of Congress as well as the President, city council members, mayors, governors, and many of our judges. They have the power to make decisions and to pass laws.

However, our representatives hold office only as long as we want them to. We delegate—or lend—our power to them. The real power belongs to us. If citizens are unhappy with the way in which someone represents them in government, for example, they can vote the person out of office. In this way, each of us holds an office—the "office of citizen." In our society, that is the most important office there is. As citizens we hold it for life.

✓ Reading Check **How do American citizens invest their representatives with political power?**

SECTION 1 Assessment

Key Terms

Use each of the key terms in a sentence that explains its meaning: citizen, naturalized, alien, representatives

Target Reading Skill

1. **Identify Main Ideas** Reread the first paragraph on this page. What is the main idea of this paragraph?

Comprehension and Critical Thinking

2. **a. Recall** What are the four ways in which a person may be defined as an American citizen?
   b. Draw Inferences Why do you think legal aliens must go through the process of naturalization in order to become citizens?

3. **a. Describe** What are some of the jobs held by our elected representatives?
   b. Predict What do you think might happen to our political system if our representatives were not elected by citizens?

Writing Activity

A friend of yours in another country hopes to move to America and become a naturalized citizen. She is unsure of how the naturalization process works. Using the information from this section, write her a letter in which you describe the process that she will need to go through.

Go Online
PHSchool.com

For: Journal Activity
Visit: PHSchool.com
Web Code: mpd-1031

Rights, Duties, and Responsibilities

Reading Preview

Objectives
In this section you will
- Explore some of the many rights guaranteed to American citizens.
- Learn about the many duties and obligations citizens share.
- Find out about some of the responsibilities citizens honor to keep our country strong and united.

Key Terms
rule of law
jury of peers
witnesses
common good
candidate

Main Idea
Citizenship is not just a connection to your country of origin or naturalization. All citizens must uphold the rights, duties, and responsibilities of citizenship.

Target Reading Skill
Identify Supporting Details Supporting details reinforce the main idea. When you identify the supporting details, it helps you understand the main idea better.

Taking Notes
Make a diagram like the one shown. As you read this section, complete the diagram with information about the rights, duties, and responsibilities of citizens.

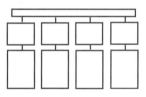

Having a driver's license gives you certain rights. These include the right to drive on public roads and highways, and to park where the law allows. As a driver you also have duties. Your duties, which are required by law, include observing traffic signals and signs and obeying the speed limit. In addition to your duties, you have responsibilities. You are expected to drive in a way that will not endanger others and that will protect the safety of other drivers, cyclists, and pedestrians. Holding the "office of citizen" is like being a licensed driver—in both situations you have important rights, duties, and responsibilities.

Rights of Citizens

Here are some rights of American citizens.
- the right to vote and to hold elected office
- the right to say what you think in speech or in writing
- the right to practice your own religion
- the right to have a fair trial

These rights, and our other rights as citizens, are based on the fundamental beliefs and values we Americans share: equal respect, freedom, equality, and justice. Our rights are guaranteed to us by our Constitution and protected by our laws and our courts.

✓ **Reading Check** **How do the rights held by American citizens suggest the importance of "equal rights for all"?**

Your passport identifies you as a citizen of the United States.
▼

The Supreme Court

Go Online
civics
interactive

For: Interactive Constitution with Supreme Court Cases
Visit: PHSchool.com
Web Code: mpp-1032

Korematsu v. *United States* (1944)

Why It Matters The main question of this case is whether the government has the right to limit the civil rights of certain Americans during national emergencies. As the United States deals with the threat of terrorism, this question arises again today.

Background During World War II, the United States government forced thousands of Japanese and Japanese Americans to move to internment camps. The government feared that people of Japanese ancestry might help Japan attack the West Coast.

Toyosaburo Korematsu [KOR-eh-MAHT-soo], a native-born American citizen, refused to leave his home and go to the camps. He was arrested, charged with failure to report for relocation, and was convicted in federal district court. After losing in the Court of Appeals, he appealed to the United States Supreme Court.

The Decision The Court upheld the government's action. It noted that national emer-gencies, such as war, may sometimes justify limiting the civil rights of a single racial group. The Court noted, however, that it is not justified to restrict civil rights because of racial ill will.

Understanding the Law

1. Why did the government feel justified in sending people of Japanese ancestry to internment camps?
2. Why is this case relevant as the United States struggles with the threat of terrorism?

Duties of Citizens

Just as a licensed driver has certain duties that go with the right to drive, citizens have duties, too. These duties include:

- obeying the laws.
- defending the nation.
- serving on a jury or as a witness in court.
- paying taxes.
- attending school.

By performing each of these duties, we, as citizens, support our government's efforts to meet our needs as a society.

Obeying the Law Your family and your classroom have rules that keep them running in an orderly way. A society's formal rules are called laws. Some laws are to keep us from hurting each other. They range from laws requiring drivers to stop at stop signs to laws against murder and armed robbery. Other laws establish the rules for making agreements and for settling disagreements. We also must obey laws that protect citizens' rights.

The Rule of Law In a democracy, no individual—even the President—is above the law. This concept of a government of laws, rather than of men and women, is called the **rule of law**. Officials must base their decisions on the law, not on personal opinion. If an official breaks the law, he or she must be treated like any other citizen. Our laws are also public, and citizens know the basic law of the land. This is an important protection against government tyranny.

Defending the Nation Helping our country defend itself is another duty of citizens. The United States maintains armed services even in peacetime. In this way, the nation can defend itself in case of attack and can help other countries protect themselves.

When you are eighteen years old or older, you may volunteer to serve in the army, navy, air force, or marines. In addition, young men must register for military service when they reach age eighteen. Registering does not mean that they will have to serve in the armed forces, but it does mean that they can be called to serve when there is a national emergency. A man whose moral beliefs prohibit him from fighting may ask to be considered a conscientious objector. If his request is approved, he will be assigned to some other kind of public service, such as working in a hospital.

Armed Forces
A member of the armed forces passes out fliers to citizens interested in recruitment opportunities.
Draw Conclusions *Why is it important for citizens to serve in the armed forces?*

Serving on a Jury One basic right of citizens is the right to a fair trial. In our legal system no person may be found guilty of a crime unless that guilt can be proved "beyond a reasonable doubt." We believe that the best way to determine a person's guilt or innocence is to conduct a trial, with citizens participating in the process.

Experts, such as lawyers, police officers, and psychologists, may play an important part in a criminal trial. However, experts do not make the final decision as to innocence or guilt. A judge does not make the final decision, either, unless the accused person gives such permission. Instead, our Constitution guarantees that anyone accused of a crime may have the case decided by a **jury of peers**—a group of ordinary citizens who hear the case and decide whether the accused person is innocent or guilty.

Analyze Diagrams

Citizenship and You

As American citizens, we place great importance on our rights and freedoms. However, our government must depend on its citizens to support its institutions and help keep the country running smoothly and safely. Therefore, citizens have duties they must uphold.

a. Why is attending school and important duty of citizenship?

b. If citizens were not expected to carry out these duties, how would this affect the ability of our government to fulfill our needs? For example, what would our society be like if citizens were not required to obey the law?

Defending the Nation

Our country requires armed forces to protect itself and help other countries in need of military aid. It is expected that citizens will help defend the nation by joining the armed forces.

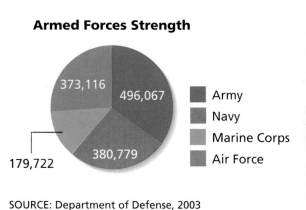

Armed Forces Strength

373,116
496,067
179,722
380,779

- Army
- Navy
- Marine Corps
- Air Force

SOURCE: Department of Defense, 2003

Obeying the Law

Laws protect people and ensure that people treat each other in fair and peaceful ways. A driver's ed class, for example, teaches you important motor vehicle laws. If drivers did not know the laws and obey them, our streets and highways would be very dangerous places.

Serving as a Witness During the trial, the lawyers may call witnesses to prove their case. **Witnesses** are people who have seen events related to the crime or who have special information that may help determine the guilt or innocence of the person on trial. Criminal trials use witnesses and juries. However, criminal trials are not the only ones that use witnesses and juries. People may also ask a court to decide cases in which they think their rights have been violated or they have been treated unfairly. If two people cannot settle a dispute, for example, they can go to court. They can call witnesses to help them by testifying on their behalf.

As you can see, juries and witnesses play an important part in assuring that a trial is fair. Because Americans have a right to a fair trial, it is the duty of all adult citizens to serve as jurors and act as witnesses when they are called to do so.

Go Online
civics
interactive

For: Citizenship and You Interactive
Visit: PHSchool.com
Web Code: mpp-1033

Duties of Citizens

Serving on a Jury or as a Witness

A person's right to a fair trial when convicted of a crime can only be assured when citizens participate in the process. Therefore, it is our duty to serve as a juror on a trial or as a witness on a trial when asked.

Attending School

Our society depends on our schools to teach citizens the knowledge and skills they need when they become adults. Education helps to ensure the survival of a society of responsible and active citizens.

Paying Taxes

Without taxes, our local, state, and federal governments would not be able to pay for the services that make our lives better. When we pay sales tax on the meals we eat, we are doing our duty as American citizens.

The Soup Shack
25 Main Street

REG   MC#01 12:13 PM 067081

1   Sweet Corn Chowder $3.99
1   Ham Sandwich $4.49
2   Medium Lemonade $3.00

SUBTOTAL $11.48

TAX $0.91

TOTAL $12.39

****
THANK YOU, PLEASE COME AGAIN

Target Reading Skill

Identify Supporting Details Read the section entitled "Attending School." Consider the many supporting details. These supporting details should help focus your attention on the main idea of the paragraph.

Paying Taxes Are you a taxpayer? A few students earn enough money at part-time jobs or through savings accounts or investments that they pay income tax to the government. Many students pay sales tax on items they buy, such as clothes and CDs.

As an adult, you will pay other taxes as well. Through taxes, our local, state, and national governments raise money to pay for the services that citizens ask them to provide.

Attending School Every time you go to school you are performing one of your duties as a citizen. Society depends on schools to make sure that young people are prepared for the future.

Another important task of the schools is to give students the knowledge, skills, and experiences they need to carry out the duties and responsibilities of the "office of citizen." Each of us must be educated about our history, government, and the workings of our society.

✓ Reading Check **Why are public officials governed by the same rules and laws as ordinary citizens?**

Active Citizen

Students Make a Difference

For Cadet Lieutenant Colonel Khandi Johnson, serving her community is about "uplifting pride." As Army JROTC Battalion Commander at Marlboro County High School in Bennettsville, South Carolina, Khandi trains new battalion members in drill and ceremony. She also serves as the JROTC spokesperson for Freedom's Answer, a non-profit organization that registers voters.

Khandi also sets aside time as a volunteer. She has given her time and energy to many groups such as the March of Dimes and Relay for Tots.

Service Learning

How can you make a difference to people in need in your community?

▲ Students can help make a difference by volunteering their time.

Although citizens are not required by law to vote, it is one of our most important responsibilities of American citizens.

1. Describe what is happening in this cartoon.

2. How do the man's and the woman's attitudes toward citizenship differ?

3. How does this cartoon illustrate the importance of our civic responsibility to vote?

Responsibilities of Citizens

As citizens we have responsibilities as well. Unlike duties, responsibilities are fulfilled by choice—they are voluntary. However, even though we are not required by law to fulfill our responsibilities, doing so is just as important a part of being a citizen as performing our duties.

Working Toward the Common Good The basic responsibility of citizens is to contribute to the **common good,** or the well being of all members of society. Contributing to the common good means acting in ways that protect the rights and freedoms of other Americans and that make our communities good places to live.

The responsibilities of citizenship include the many ways we participate in our political process. For example, as citizens we vote for government representatives. Some of us agree to hold office ourselves. We also work to influence government decisions.

Voting The right to vote is one of the basic rights of American citizens and one of our most important responsibilities. We vote for representatives at all levels of government, from President of the United States to members of the local school board.

In addition, in our states and our local communities citizens are often asked to vote on issues. We may be asked to make decisions about such public issues as building schools.

General Colin Powell spoke the following words at the 1997 President's Summit for America's Future.

"Above all, we pledge to reach out to the most vulnerable members of the American family, our children. As you've heard, up to 15 million young Americans today are at risk....Fifteen million young lives are at risk, may not make it unless we care enough to do something about it. . . .

"We know what they need. They need an adult caring person in their life, a safe place to learn and grow, a healthy start, marketable skills and an opportunity to serve so that early in their lives they learn the virtue of service so that they can reach out then and touch another young American in need."

Analyze Primary Sources
How does Colin Powell connect the "virtue of service" to the needs of young Americans?

To make good decisions and vote wisely, citizens have the responsibility to inform themselves. You can get information by reading, asking questions, and discussing the candidates and issues with other people. It is always important, when preparing to vote, to try to separate facts from opinions, and to try to base your decisions on reasons instead of personal likes and dislikes.

Holding Government Office The people who agree to hold government office are fulfilling another important responsibility of citizenship. They have accepted the responsibility of learning about the issues and trying to make decisions that are in the best interests of the people they represent.

Citizens who hold office include our elected city council members, mayors, governors, and state and national representatives and senators. They also include appointed officials, such as members of local water boards and planning commissions, as well as advisors to the President.

Holding office
Christopher Portman is sworn in as the mayor of Mercer, Pennsylvania in 2002. Portman, who was 19 when elected, was the town's first teen-age mayor. ▼

Participating in Election Campaigns One important way to fulfill the responsibilities of citizenship is to help a **candidate**, or person running for office, in his or her election campaign. Listen to Emily Shultz talking about the people who helped her father win public office:

"When my father ran for election to the Kansas state House of Representatives, our neighbors really helped out. They wrote letters, made phone calls, and knocked on doors, telling people about my father and what a good representative he would be for our area.

When my father gave speeches, his campaign workers were there, handing out information. And on election day they went around, reminding people to vote and driving them to their voting place. Thanks to them he was elected."

There are a number of ways that students might help a candidate. They include carrying a campaign sign at a rally, stuffing envelopes with information to send to voters, and making phone calls to encourage people to vote for your candidate.

Influencing Government Another way you can fulfill the "office of citizen" is to influence government to take action in a cause you believe in. Citizens of any age can influence the government by expressing their opinions in letters to elected representatives and to newspapers, and by speaking at city council and school board meetings. You can also join or create an organization that influences government. Here is Thomas Pham's experience:

> "One year some friends and I noticed that the trashcans in the school lunchroom were overflowing with cans and bottles that kids had thrown away. We went to the school board and asked them to provide special bins for cans and bottles. Now people can't remember a time when there wasn't recycling at the school."

Serving the Community Not all of the responsibilities of citizenship are directly connected with government. Each of us is responsible for doing whatever we can to make our communities better places to live in. When you listen with respect to the opinion of a person who disagrees with you, when you make a new student feel welcome in your school, or pick up a candy wrapper someone else dropped on the sidewalk, you are acting as a responsible citizen. You are fulfilling the "office of citizen" by contributing to the common good.

✓ Reading Check **Why is it important to study and understand the issues that get decided in elections?**

Cleaning Up
Bette Midler, a singer and actress, is the founder of the New York Restoration Project, an organization that restores and maintains public parks in New York City.

SECTION 2 Assessment

Key Terms
Use each of the key terms in a sentence that explains its meaning: rule of law, jury of peers, witnesses, common good, candidate

Target Reading Skill
1. **Identify Supporting Details** What supporting details in this section gave you a better understanding of the main idea?

Comprehension and Critical Thinking
2. **a. Describe** What are some of the rights that all American citizens share?

   b. Make Generalizations Which values or beliefs are apparent in the rights guaranteed to American citizens?

3. **a. Explain** In what way are citizens obligated to defend the nation?

   b. Contrast How do witnesses differ from jurors?

4. **a. Recall** What responsibilities do citizens share in promoting the common good?

   b. Identify Alternatives What are some of the ways in which citizens can support a candidate running for office?

Writing Activity
You are the mayor of a small town. Your town needs improved upkeep of local streets and parks. Address your constituents in a speech. Propose a program that would improve the overall quality of life.

> **TIPS**
> - Make sure your speech identifies any problems that need to be improved in the community.
> - Make clear to your listeners that their involvement is essential.

How to Interview for a Job

A job interview gives you a chance to tell employers your strengths and show them that you can communicate well.

Interviews can be intimidating. If you know what to expect, you'll be less nervous. Making a good impression at an interview can help you get the job.

Below is an example of a student's job interview at a bookstore. Observe how he shows he would be right for the job.

Employer: What made you decide to apply for this job?

Student: I am familiar with bookstores because I like to read. I usually stop by this store every week or so after school.

Employer: That's good to hear. Have you ever worked in a bookstore?

Student: No, but my dad's office had a huge book sale last summer, and I worked at it for a few weeks. We had to sort books by category, help people find books they were looking for.

Employer: That sounds like a good introduction to book selling. Would you like to work more with books in the future?

Student: I'm not sure yet, but I think I would like to work in a library.

Employer: Wonderful. We are looking for someone to unload shipments of books, record them, and put them out on the shelves. Does that sound interesting to you?

Student: Yes, very interesting.

Learn the Skill

To have a successful interview, follow these steps:

❶ **Dress nicely.** Do not look sloppy.

❷ **Make a good impression.**

❸ **Answer questions honestly.** You may be asked about your skills, experiences, goals, and reasons for wanting the job.

❹ **Ask questions.** Show that you are interested in the job.

Practice the Skill

❶ Think of a job that you would like to do.

❷ In the interview above, replace the bookstore with your job.

❸ Write down answers to each of the employer's questions.

Apply the Skill

❶ Find a partner in class. One of you will interview the other for a job as a lifeguard.

❷ Switch roles so that the person who asked the questions is now being interviewed for a job at a restaurant.

Go **O**nline
civics
inter*active*

For: Local Citizenship
Visit: PHSchool.com
Web Code: mpp-1034

Citizenship and Our Other Roles in Society

Reading Preview

Objectives

In this section you will

- Learn about playing social roles.
- Discuss how social roles involve expected behaviors.
- Consider the different levels of participation involved in social roles.
- Explore how to play the role of citizen.

Key Terms

social roles

Main Idea

Social roles are part of our everyday lives. We play many different social roles. Each one requires a certain kind of behavior. Each also requires a certain level of participation over the course of our lives.

Target Reading Skill

Identify Implied Main Ideas Sometimes the main idea of a section is not directly addressed. Sometimes it is implied or hinted at. By identifying implied main ideas, you can better understand the central idea of a passage.

Taking Notes

Copy this web graphic organizer. As you read this section, fill in the web organizer to illustrate how one person plays different social roles at the same time.

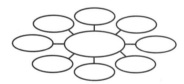

Here is a typical day for Jean Reardon: She begins by reading a newspaper article about a new public library. Then she helps her daughter prepare for a test. At work she has a conference with her boss and goes for lunch with two college friends. On the way home from work, she picks up some groceries. After dinner, she watches some TV with her husband before going to bed.

In the course of her day, Jean acted as a citizen, family member, member of a social group, worker, friend, and consumer. She also acted as her own person—herself—in making choices.

Playing Social Roles

When you think of the word *role*, you may think of an actor playing a role in a film or play. However, we all play **social roles**, which are roles that people play in real life.

Everyday Roles When Jean helped her daughter with her homework, she was playing the mother role. Having dinner and watching television with her husband were part of her wife role. The roles of mother and wife are both part of Jean's family member roles.

Social Roles As a carpool member, Jean was playing social group roles. The social groups of which we are members can range in size from small to large. Two people painting a poster for the school dance make up a social group. Other examples of social groups are all students or all workers.

This man plays a social group role as a construction worker.

▼

The Seven Social Roles

Every citizen plays different social roles in society.

1. **Analyze** Do you think the social roles a person plays changes over his or her lifetime? Why or why not?

2. **Apply** To which social groups do you belong?

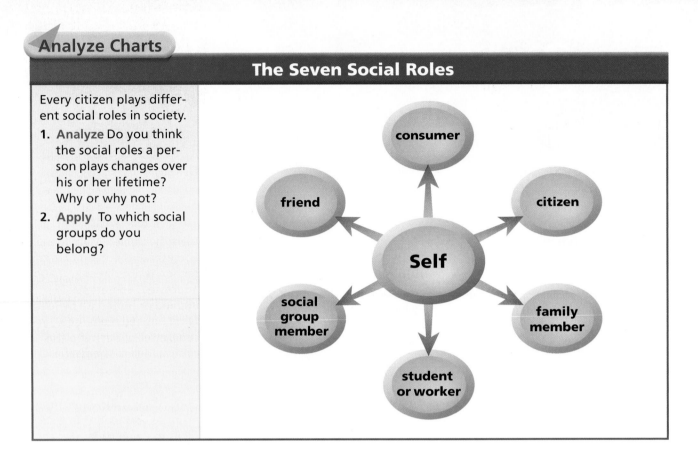

Citizen Roles When she was reading the newspaper, Jean was playing the citizen role by informing herself on a government issue. She was playing the mother role when she helped her daughter prepare for a test. Watching TV with her husband was part of her wife role. The roles of wife and mother are both part of Jean's family member roles. Jean played a worker role when meeting with her boss, a friend role at lunch with friends, and a consumer role when she shopped for groceries. Finally, as she played all her roles, Jean was also playing the self role. She was guided by a sense of who she is as a person.

Our Many Social Roles Like Jean, you play many different social roles in the course of a day and in the course of your life. Some roles you play because you were born into them. Some roles you play because you are required to play them. Some roles you choose as a family member for yourself.

You were born into your family, where you may play several roles: son or daughter, sister or brother, grandchild, or cousin. At this point in your life, you are required to be a student, which is another social role. Later, you may be required to pay taxes and serve as a juror, which are citizen roles. Roles you choose now may include being a friend, being a member of a club, and being a consumer.

✓ Reading Check **What are some of the other social roles Jean Reardon might experience in any given day?**

Roles as Expected Behaviors

In each of your roles you behave differently. What causes you to act the way you do when you are playing a certain role? Partly, your behavior is determined by a set of expectations that people have of how someone in that role should act.

A cheerleader, for example, is expected to wear school colors and to jump, dance, and lead the crowd in school cheers. A member of the marching band is expected to wear a uniform and to know the music. If you want to be a member of a group, you will make an effort to learn the expected behaviors for that group.

The way you play a role also depends on how you want to play it and on the kind of person you are. People who know you begin to expect certain behaviors from you when you play your roles. A brother may always grumble when it is his turn to do the dishes. On the other hand, he may be the kind of brother who volunteers to do the dishes for his sister when he sees that she has too much homework.

Changing Roles Sometimes a person plays the same role in different ways, depending on the situation. In Chapter 2 you read about Miguel Espinoza and his friends. For Miguel, playing the role of friend to Carol, Alex, and Melissa includes being sympathetic, sharing biology notes, and going to the beach. Miguel plays the friend role differently with his friend Jerry. Jerry and Miguel both like to read science fiction novels, and when they get together, it is often to swap books and talk about their favorite authors. So, even when we play the same role in different situations, we do not always play it the same way.

Roles can also change over time. Emily Shultz has been a daughter and a wife. However, since the death of her parents and her divorce, she no longer plays those roles.

The way Emily plays her role as a mother has changed, too. Once she fed and bathed her babies. Later she helped make them Halloween costumes, attended their track meets and school plays, and made sure they had finished their homework. Today her children are adults with children of their own, living in other states. She now writes them letters, sends them presents on their birthdays, and gets together with them for family reunions. Her role as mother has changed over time.

The Roles We Play
These boys are playing a certain role as members of their high school soccer team. They are expected to show up to practice and perform their best. **Make Generalizations** *What are some of the expected behaviors of a particular social group to which you belong?*

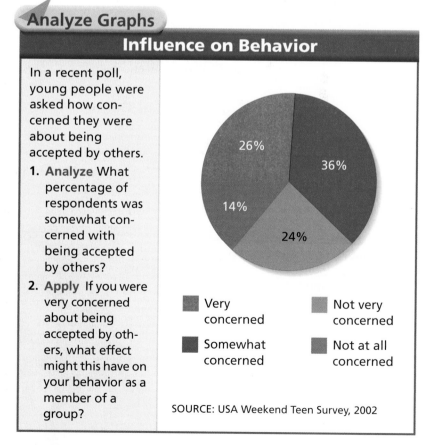

Analyze Graphs

Influence on Behavior

In a recent poll, young people were asked how concerned they were about being accepted by others.
1. **Analyze** What percentage of respondents was somewhat concerned with being accepted by others?
2. **Apply** If you were very concerned about being accepted by others, what effect might this have on your behavior as a member of a group?

26%

36%

14%

24%

■ Very concerned

■ Somewhat concerned

■ Not very concerned

■ Not at all concerned

SOURCE: USA Weekend Teen Survey, 2002

Overlapping Roles As you think about your many roles, you will realize that sometimes you are playing more than one at the same time. When Miguel gets together with friends to study for a biology test, he is playing two roles, friend and student. When he volunteers his time as a tutor, he is playing a citizen role, serving the common good by helping others.

Conflicting Roles You may also find that the demands of your roles conflict with each other. For example, suppose you want to go to an amusement park with friends, but you have already agreed to take a babysitting job that day. In this case, your social group role is in conflict with your worker role, forcing you to make a difficult decision.

Often, being aware of the values that guide your behavior can be helpful making a decision. Suppose you do not need a new pair of sneakers, but everyone you know is buying the latest style. Think about the values expressed in these statements:

- It is not good to spend money on items I do not really need.
- Being accepted by the social group that wears the latest fashions is important to me.

What decision would you make in this situation? How would your values affect your decision?

✓ Reading Check   **What are some changing or conflicting social roles that you have experienced?**

Conflicting Roles
When the demands of your social roles conflict, making choices is not easy.
Identify Cause and Effect *What would you choose to do in this situation? Explain your answer.*

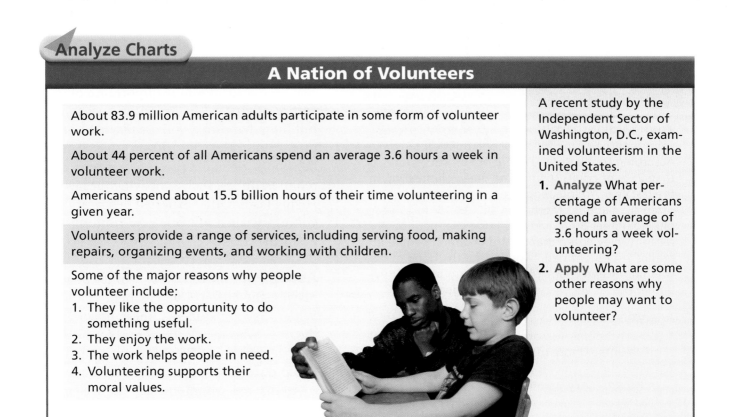

A Nation of Volunteers

About 83.9 million American adults participate in some form of volunteer work.

About 44 percent of all Americans spend an average 3.6 hours a week in volunteer work.

Americans spend about 15.5 billion hours of their time volunteering in a given year.

Volunteers provide a range of services, including serving food, making repairs, organizing events, and working with children.

Some of the major reasons why people volunteer include:
1. They like the opportunity to do something useful.
2. They enjoy the work.
3. The work helps people in need.
4. Volunteering supports their moral values.

A recent study by the Independent Sector of Washington, D.C., examined volunteerism in the United States.

1. **Analyze** What percentage of Americans spend an average of 3.6 hours a week volunteering?

2. **Apply** What are some other reasons why people may want to volunteer?

Level of Participation

As you play your social roles, you will have to make choices about how actively you want to participate in a given role at any time. These choices, too, are based on your values and your sense of what is most important to you.

Suppose you think that there are not enough social activities at your school. What will you do? You can choose to do nothing. Alternatively, you can get a group of students to help you plan a dance, hire a band, and decorate the gym. You could also decide to not take a leadership role in planning the dance, but instead offer to help with a certain task. The course of action you choose depends on how much time and energy you are willing to devote and how important it is to you to have a dance.

You have a choice about your level of participation. However, you must realize that you will have to take the consequences of participating or deciding not to participate. In the case of the school dance, if you do nothing, you will have no activity, or perhaps someone else will plan an activity you do not enjoy. If you choose to take an active role, you are likely to have the kind of school activity you enjoy. Most people find that when they participate fully in a role, they feel satisfaction and get a better sense of who they are.

✓ Reading Check   **What are some of the consequences of participating passively rather than actively in a social role?**

Young Volunteers How many young Americans volunteer their time for social and political causes? According to the Bureau of Labor Statistics, more than 25% of adults spent some time volunteering in the last year. Young people tend to volunteer more often than adults. More than 40% of 15- to 25-year-olds volunteer during a typical one-year period. A recent survey noted that a third of young people in grades 7–12 identified "working for the good of my community and country" and "helping others or volunteering" as very important future goals.

Analyzing Economics

1. What economic reasons might allow young people to volunteer more often than adults?
2. Take a survey among your classmates. Find out how much time they spend volunteering.

Target Reading Skill

Identify Implied Main Ideas Read this passage. Identify the implied main idea of the paragraph. Pay attention to some of the other ideas expressed in the passage.

The Citizen Role

You have read about the importance of the "office of citizen" in American society. In fulfilling that office, you are playing a very important role: the citizen role. Some behaviors people expect of citizens are required duties, such as obeying the law or paying taxes. Other expected behaviors are voluntary, such as voting or running for political office.

Active Participants For some people playing the citizen role has high priority. When they are students, these people are the ones who take leadership roles in student government. They plan school activities and work to solve school problems.

Adults for whom the citizen role has high priority may run for government office. They may volunteer to serve on committees that study government problems or plan for parks and recreation. They may devote much of their time to helping with political campaigns or working for organizations that try to influence government decisions.

Other people spend less time playing the citizen role. Some are satisfied simply to keep informed, to vote, or perhaps to give money to support candidates and issues.

As with your other roles, you cannot always participate in citizenship activities as actively as you might want to. Miguel would like to be more active in student government. However, he knows that at this stage in his life, he needs to spend most of his time studying and preparing for the future.

Contributing to the Common Good Being a responsible citizen is not limited to participating in political activities. Earlier in this chapter you learned that the overall responsibility of every citizen is to contribute to the common good. Many people are making such a contribution to the common good when they play roles that they may not think of as citizen roles.

For example, Emily Shultz helps at the church thrift shop. The money the shop raises goes to buy medicine and food for elderly people in the community. In this way, Emily is contributing to the common good while playing a role in a social group in her church.

When Emily was secretary to the superintendent of schools, she was playing a worker role. The work she did supported the town's efforts to educate its children. Therefore, Emily was contributing to the common good in her role as worker.

Civic Responsibilities
These senior citizens are attending a town hall meeting to discuss issues important to their lives.
Synthesize Information *What do you think might happen in your community if no one chose to perform the voluntary activities of the citizen role?*

Setting Priorities for Citizenship How much time and energy will you devote to fulfilling your responsibilities as a citizen? This decision is one that you will make again and again in your life. Each time, that decision will be influenced by the other roles you are playing and how important they are to you. It will also be influenced by your age, your values, and your particular talents and interests.

Playing the citizen role in a political way may not always be a high priority for you. However, as a citizen you share the responsibility of all Americans to protect the basic values that unite us as a people and as a society. Therefore, if you choose never to play the citizen role, you are giving up your right to have a voice in your government and to make a difference in your community.

✓ **Reading Check** What influences how much time you devote to your duties as a citizen?

SECTION 3 Assessment

Key Terms
Use the key term in a sentence that explains its meaning:
social roles

Target Reading Skill
1. **Identify Implied Main Idea** What ideas were easier to understand when you identified the implied main idea?

Comprehension and Critical Thinking
2. **a. Recall** What are some of the social roles you play?
   b. Predict What are some of the social roles you envision for yourself in the future?

3. **a. Explain** How might your behavior change when you want to become a member of a new group?
   b. Check Consistency Why might a person assume different roles in a single day?
4. **a. Recall** What kinds of choices do people make as they play their social roles?
   b. Identify Cause and Effect Suppose a student chooses not to vote in an election for student president. Why might that student feel unsatisfied about the outcome?
5. **a. Describe** Give two examples of how people behave when playing the citizen role.

   b. Compare How does your commitment to citizenship compare to your commitments to other endeavors?

Writing Activity
Write an entry in your journal in which you consider the many social roles you experience in a single day.

TIPS
- Consider listing your different social roles in chronological order to give structure to your account.
- Use concrete descriptions to explain your different roles.

Transferring Information

Information can be presented in many forms. Sometimes it is useful to organize information to make it easier to read and evaluate. One way to do this is to put data into a table or pie chart.

The following paragraph discusses recent immigration into the United States. Read the paragraph. Then look below at the pie graph to see how that data was presented in a new way.

Immigration in the early twenty-first century has continued at a pace on par with recent decades. Thirty-two percent of all immigrants emigrated from Asian countries and Australia. About half as many (17%) Europeans immigrated to the United States. Nine percent of immigrants came from the Caribbean. Emigration continued from both Central America (6%) and South America (7%). Only 6% of immigrants in 2002 came from Africa.

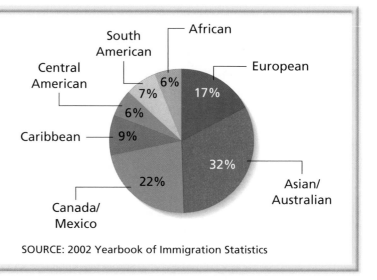

SOURCE: 2002 Yearbook of Immigration Statistics

Learn the Skill

Follow these steps to transfer information from one form to another:

1 **Identify the raw data.** Identify facts and statistics as you read. Think about how you can best organize the data so it is easy to see and use.

2 **List the data.** Make a list of facts and organize them. Organize percentages from greatest to least, for example.

3 **Transfer the data.** To make a pie chart, divide a circle into parts that add up to 100. Color a portion of the circle to represent each percentage you want to include. Label the chart.

4 **Draw conclusions based on the data.** What can be learned by looking at the data in this form?

Practice the Skill

Study the pie chart above and answer these questions:

1 In 2002, what percentage of immigrants to the United States was from Europe? From Asia/Australia?

2 List the data in the paragraph in order of percentage from greatest to least.

3 Where did the largest group of immigrants come from in 2002?

4 How does the pie graph help make data easier to understand?

Apply the Skill

Look through Unit 1 and find population data for two different years. Draw a pie chart for each year. Then compare them to see how the population has changed.

Review and Assessment

Chapter Summary

Section 1
What It Means to Be a Citizen
(pages 56–58)

- Americans become citizens in a variety of ways.

- Aliens from other countries must get naturalized in order to become American citizens.

- American citizens are able to elect representatives who serve them in office in local, state, and national government.

Section 2
Rights, Duties, and Responsibilities
(pages 59–67)

- American citizens have important rights granted to them by the Constitution that guarantee them freedom, equality, and justice.

- In addition to their basic rights, citizens have a duty to obey all laws.

- The rule of law governs all citizens, and all laws are public.

- Citizens have a duty to defend their nation.

- Basic rights of citizens include the right to a fair trial decided by a jury of peers, and to be presumed innocent before proven guilty.

- As part of their civic duty, citizens may serve as jurors or witnesses in trials.

- Citizens bear a responsibility to work toward the common good to benefit all members of society.

- Citizens also have the opportunity to participate in election campaigns and lend their support to a candidate for office.

Section 3
Citizenship and Our Other Roles in Society
(pages 69–75)

- Citizens play different social roles in their everyday interactions with family, friends, coworkers, neighbors, and fellow citizens.

- Each social role has expected behaviors associated with it, and as these roles change over time, the behaviors change with them.

- Sometimes social roles overlap or conflict with each other.

- Social roles demand different levels of participation, depending on the interest of the individual.

- The citizen role is an important social role in which all citizens take part whenever they vote, volunteer, serve their community, or help candidates get elected.

Copy the chart below and use it to help you summarize the chapter:

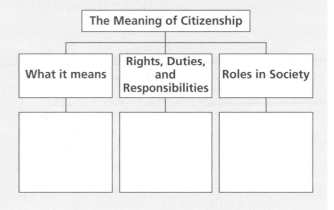

Review and Assessment Continued

Go Online PHSchool.com

For: Self-Test
Visit: PHSchool.com
Web Code: mpa-1033

Reviewing Key Terms

Fill in each blank with one of the key terms from the list below.

social roles	representatives
citizen	aliens
candidate	naturalized
witnesses	common good

1. Throughout the course of her day, Nigella contributed to the _____. She volunteered at a nursing home and helped her elderly neighbors register to vote.

2. The defendants benefited from the numerous _____ who testified about their honesty and generosity.

3. Because she was a _____ citizen, Marisa was unable to run for Vice-President.

4. Stanley made an excellent _____ for office. He has a vast amount of experience and many supporters in his home district.

5. Some of the elected _____ supported a plan to help ease traffic problems in the region.

6. Each year, thousands of _____ went through the process of becoming naturalized citizens.

7. Some of the many _____ that Miles played over the course of his day included those of son, husband, father, boss, and neighbor.

8. Because she took being a _____ seriously, Mrs. Jensen always abided by the laws, upheld her civic duties, and fulfilled her social obligations.

Comprehension and Critical Thinking

9. a. **Describe** Why might a citizen choose to give up his or her citizenship?
   b. **Make Predictions** Why do you think citizens would not be likely to give up their citizenship lightly?
   c. **Summarize** What are some advantages of American citizenship?

10. a. **Recall** What are some of the basic duties of American citizens?
    b. **Categorize** How do witnesses and jurors participate in some of the duties of American citizenship?

   c. **Synthesize Information** Why is working toward the common good one responsibility of American citizens?

11. a. **Explain** How can citizens play more than one social role at a time?
    b. **Draw Conclusions** Why do social roles tend to change over time?
    c. **Identify Main Ideas** Why is the "office of citizen" an important social role?

Activities

12. **Skills a.** Immigrants from which region became naturalized citizens most quickly in 2001? **b.** Based on the table, create a bar graph that compares the time it took immigrants to become citizens in 2000 and 2002.

13. **Writing** You have been asked to write an article for a newsletter for new citizens. Explain why contributing to the common good is an important responsibility of citizenship.

Median Years of Residence by Year of Naturalization and Region of Birth			
Region of Birth	2002	2001	2000
Africa	7	10	8
Asia	8	8	8
Europe	7	7	8
North America	11	11	11
Oceania	9	10	11
South America	8	9	10

Source: U.S. Citizenship and Immigration Services, 2003

14. **Active Citizen** How can students make a difference in their community? Brainstorm some of the ways in which you can contribute to your local community.

15. **Math Practice** Review the Civics and Economics information on page 74. Using the statistics in this section, estimate the number of young volunteers aged 15–25 in America. Determine what portion of that population consists of people aged 15 to 25. Then calculate the number of volunteers using the percentages given.

16. **Civics and Economics** Write a letter to the President. Detail the effects of steady immigration on the national economy.

17. **Analyzing Visuals** Explain how the photograph above reflects the role of the citizens in influencing government.

Standardized Test Prep

Test-Taking Tips

Some questions on standardized tests ask you to analyze information in a chart. Study the chart from the U.S. Department of Housing and Urban Development (HUD) below. Then follow the tips to answer the sample question.

TIP When you consider a chart, look at the title of the chart to understand what is being illustrated

Households by Region and Citizenship of Householder

Region	Native Citizen Households	Naturalized Citizen Households	Noncitizen Households
Northeast	17,651,029	1,440,401	1,297,526
Midwest	23,676,358	577,185	556,927
South	35,113,525	1,397,335	1,591,955
West	18,709,217	2,192,469	2,203,025
Total	**95,150,129**	**5,607,390**	**5,649,432**

Pick the letter that best completes this statement

1. All of the regions have more noncitizen households than naturalized citizen households EXCEPT:

   TIP Notice the word "EXCEPT" in the question.

   A Northeast and Midwest

   B Midwest and South

   C South and Northeast

   D West and South

   The correct answer is **A**. Note that the questions asks you to choose the exception to the rule.

2. In which region of the United States would you expect to find the most registered voters?

   A Northeast

   B Midwest

   C South

   D West

UNIT 2

Creating a Lasting Government

What's Ahead in Unit 2

Unit 2 will explore the origins of our government. You will see how colonists' beliefs about citizenship and government led to the creation of the Constitution that has guided our nation for more than 200 years.

CHAPTER 4
America's Political Heritage

CHAPTER 5
Creating the Constitution

CHAPTER 6
The Bill of Rights

CHAPTER 7
Our Enduring Constitution

Why Study Civics?

Why did the Americans fight for freedom from England in the Revolutionary War? What kind of government did they wish to establish? What is the Constitution of the United States? What is the Bill of Rights? How is the Constitution active in our lives today? These are all questions that can be addressed by the study of civics.

Watch the **Civics: Government and Economics** videos for an overview of creating the Constitution.

▶ **Video:** Overview   Video: Up Close

Standards for Civics and Government

National

The following National Standards are covered in this unit.

II. What are the foundations of the American political system?

B. What are the distinctive characteristics of American society?

C. What is American political culture?

D. What values and principles are basic to American constitutional democracy?

State

Go Online
PHSchool.com

For: Your state's Civics standards
Visit: PHSchool.com
Webcode: mpe2001

4

America's Political Heritage

What's Ahead in Chapter 4

In this chapter you will explore the origins of the American belief in government by the consent of the people—a rare form of government in the history of the world.

SECTION 1
The Colonial Experience

SECTION 2
Roots of American Government

SECTION 3
Moving Toward Nationhood

TARGET READING SKILL

Cause and Effect Recognizing the relationships between causes and effects can help you better understand what you read. Cause and effect includes recognizing multiple causes, identifying causes and effects, and understanding effects.

This illustration was ▶ created by Currier & Ives to celebrate the 100th anniversary of the Revolutionary War.

National | Standards for Civics and Government | State

The following National Standards for Civics and Government are covered in this chapter:

I. What are civic life, politics, and government?

A. What is civic life? What is politics? What is government? Why are government and politics necessary? What purposes should government serve?

II. What are the foundations of the American political system?

A. What is the American idea of constitutional government?

Go Online
PHSchool.com

For: Your state's standards
Visit: PHSchool.com
Web Code: mpe-2040

Active Citizen — Civics in the Real World

The date was November 11, 1620. A lone ship, the *Mayflower*, lay anchored off the rugged Massachusetts coast. Aboard the vessel were 102 passengers. Many of them were English Puritans seeking religious freedom. Other passengers had made the stormy two-month voyage from England in search of wealth and better lives.

Although they had come to America for different reasons, the travelers knew that they would all have to work together to survive the approaching winter. They would have to establish order and make laws. The men gathered in the ship's cabin and emerged with the Mayflower Compact—a signed agreement to make and obey "just and equal" laws for the "general good of the colony."

In the 1600s, most people in the world had to obey laws made without their consent. The Mayflower Compact was a bold step toward self-government. The rights and responsibilities of citizens continued to expand as the colonies grew, leading to the founding of the United States of America—a nation governed by its citizens.

Citizen's Journal Suppose you were aboard the *Mayflower* in 1620. What is one law you would want the Mayflower Compact to establish for the colony? Write a paragraph explaining your choice.

The Colonial Experience

Reading Preview

Objectives

In this section you will

- Learn how the colonists acquired a voice in their government.
- Understand the meaning of citizenship in the colonies.
- Explore some roots of individual freedom in America.
- Describe the colonists' signs of discontent with English rule.

Taking Notes

Make a diagram like the one below. As you read this section, fill in the diagram to show the rights associated with self-government.

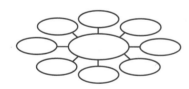

Key Terms

heritage   charter
legislature   tyranny

Main Idea

During the colonial period, Americans established traditions of freedom and self-government.

Target Reading Skill

Recognize Multiple Causes
A cause may be an event that makes something else happen or a situation that leads to a new situation. As you study history, it is helpful to identify the many causes that contribute to one effect.

Many American traditions took root during the colonial period. The values and experiences of the settlers in the thirteen English colonies make up an important part of our **heritage**, the traditions passed down to us from generation to generation.

A Voice in Government

From the beginning, the colonists were used to having a voice in their government. It was one of their rights as citizens of England. In each colony, citizens could elect representatives to the **legislature**, a group of people chosen to make the laws. They had a degree of self-government that was rare in the world at that time.

Representative government in America began in the year 1619. In that year, the colonists of Virginia elected representatives called burgesses. Other colonial legislatures followed as more colonies were founded. But the colonists did not have complete control over their government. They were still subject to England.

Royal Authority The English monarch established each colony through a **charter**, a document giving permission to create a government. Any colony that challenged England's authority might be stripped of its charter. It would then become a royal colony under the control of the monarch, who appointed a royal governor.

In theory, England had final authority over the colonies. However, throughout the 1600s and early 1700s, England was busy fighting wars and had little time to pay attention to colonial laws. Thus the colonists largely governed themselves.

Preserving Rights Used to having a voice in government, colonial citizens resisted any efforts to ignore their rights or to weaken their legislatures. Typically those efforts were made by colonial governors. The governors were usually appointed to their posts rather than elected. Moreover, they usually represented England's interests rather than those of the colonists.

From time to time, the legislatures became involved in power struggles with colonial governors. For instance, the Virginia House of Burgesses declared that the governor could not tax citizens without the legislature's consent.

✔ Reading Check **Why did the American colonists have such an unusual degree of self-government?**

Target Reading Skill
Recognize Multiple Causes
Reread the first paragraph on this page. Notice that the last sentence tells you that colonists already enjoyed a degree of self-rule. As you continue reading this section, look for other reasons why colonists wanted full independence.

Patrick Henry (left), a leading figure in the fight for self-government, gives a speech to the Virginia House of Burgesses. ▼

Citizenship in the Colonies

Being an English citizen in the 1600s and 1700s differed in some important ways from being an American citizen today. First of all, only white men who owned a certain amount of land were allowed to vote or hold office. The Africans brought to the colonies as slaves were not only denied the vote, but they were legally considered property rather than people.

It is important to recognize that relatively few people in the colonies were allowed to vote. But during the 1600s and early 1700s, citizens in most nations and colonies did not have any rights. The English colonies in America were one of the few places in the world where citizens participated in their government.

Analyze Maps

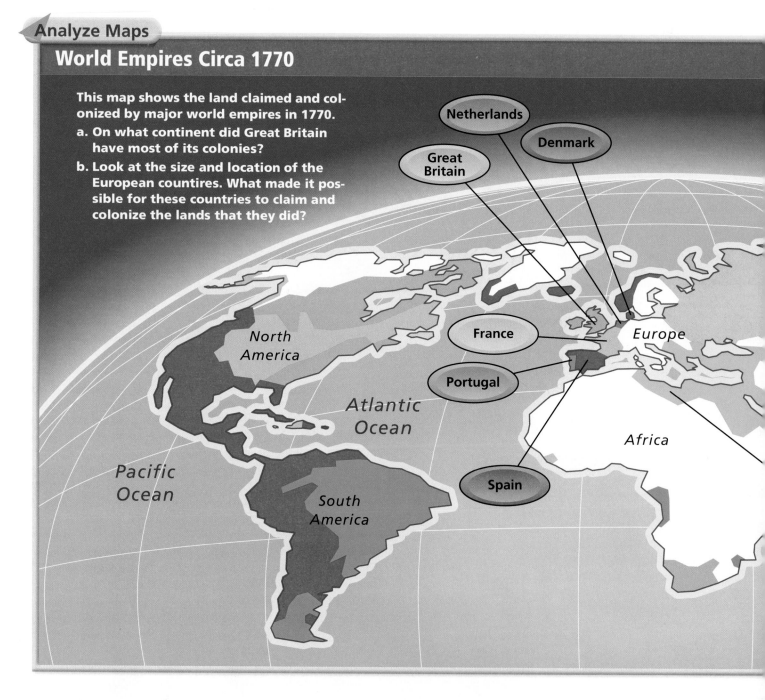

World Empires Circa 1770

This map shows the land claimed and colonized by major world empires in 1770.

a. On what continent did Great Britain have most of its colonies?

b. Look at the size and location of the European countires. What made it possible for these countries to claim and colonize the lands that they did?

Netherlands

Denmark

Great Britain

France

Europe

Portugal

North America

Atlantic Ocean

Africa

Pacific Ocean

Spain

South America

Colonial citizens, like citizens today, had a responsibility to work for the common good. They helped their communities in various ways, such as serving on juries and becoming members of the local militia, or volunteer army.

Citizens also served their communities by supporting education. For instance, the Puritans in New England set up a public school system to make sure that people could read and understand the Bible. In the middle and southern colonies, where there were few public schools, parents usually sent their children to private schools or taught them at home.

✓ **Reading Check** **What did it mean to be a citizen in the American colonies?**

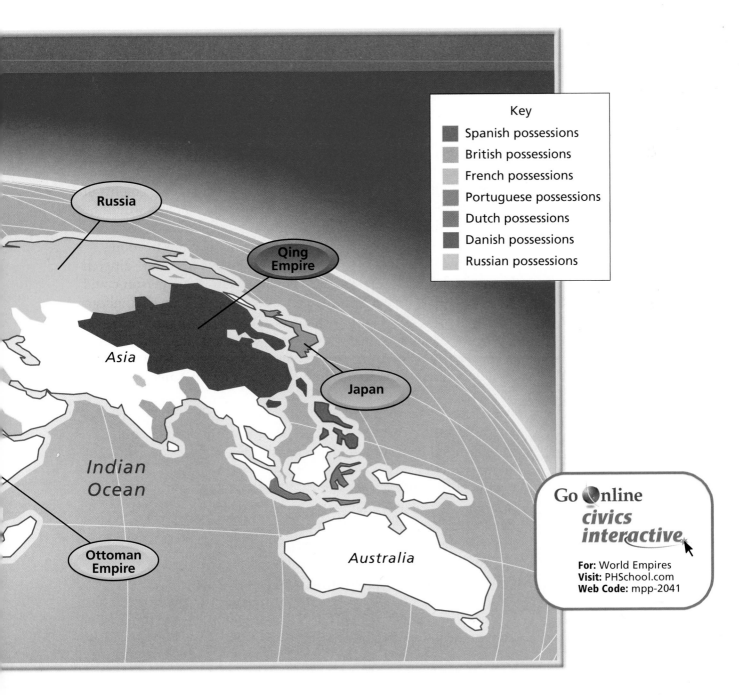

Key

- Spanish possessions
- British possessions
- French possessions
- Portuguese possessions
- Dutch possessions
- Danish possessions
- Russian possessions

Russia

Qing Empire

Japan

Asia

Indian Ocean

Ottoman Empire

Australia

Go Online
civics interactive

For: World Empires
Visit: PHSchool.com
Web Code: mpp-2041

Some Roots of Freedom

Individual freedoms, such as freedom of religion or freedom of speech, were unknown for most of human history. They became part of our heritage mainly through the efforts of the colonists.

Greater Religious Freedom The colonists lived at a time when religion was closely tied to government in most parts of the world. All English citizens, for instance, had to pay taxes to support the official Church of England. Many colonists, including the Pilgrims on the *Mayflower* and the Puritans who founded the Massachusetts Bay Colony, had left England because they were persecuted for disagreeing with the Church of England.

Although the Puritans had fled persecution in England, they in turn denied religious freedom to those who disagreed with them. They forced a minister named Roger Williams to leave their colony after he criticized church leaders. In 1636, Williams founded the colony of Rhode Island, whose charter promised that no colonist would be punished "for any differences in opinions in matters of religion." Before long, other colonies were also allowing religious freedom.

Actually, the colonists' definition of "religious freedom" differed from our definition today. They usually meant that a person could belong to any Christian church, such as the Presbyterian or Anglican churches. They did not mean freedom for members of non-Christian religions. Nevertheless, considering the world in which they lived, the colonists were taking an important step—one that would eventually lead to freedom of religion for all Americans.

A Call for Freedom of the Press When colonial newspapers appeared in the early 1700s, they became an important source of information. However, under English law, a publisher was not allowed to criticize the government.

One of the earliest arguments for freedom of the press was made in 1735. On trial was John Peter Zenger, the publisher of a New York newspaper. Zenger had printed articles accusing the New York governor of abusing his power by accepting bribes and interfering with elections. Furious, the governor accused Zenger of trying to stir up rebellion against the government, and he had Zenger jailed.

Zenger's lawyer, Andrew Hamilton, argued that Zenger was innocent if what he had written was true. Hamilton declared that freedom of the press was a basic right.

The Outcome The jury found Zenger not guilty. Zenger was released from jail and went back to publishing his newspaper.

The Zenger case did not change English law or guarantee freedom of the press. However, it did inspire other colonists to fight for freedom of the press and to criticize abuses of power.

✔ Reading Check **Why were freedom of religion and freedom of the press important to the colonists?**

Signs of Discontent

By the mid-1700s, England had tightened its control over the colonies. Many colonists were angry with royal governors who used power without regard for citizens' rights.

As people complained about royal governors, the word *tyranny* was increasingly used throughout the colonies. **Tyranny** meant the abuse of power. A growing number of colonists began to wonder whether England might eventually try to strip them of their rights and silence their voice in government.

▲ Alexander Hamilton's defense of John Peter Zenger helped establish freedom of the press in the United States.

✔ Reading Check **Why do you think England tightened its control over the colonies?**

SECTION 1 Assessment

Key Terms

Use each of the key terms in a sentence that explains its meaning: heritage, legislature, charter, tyranny

Target Reading Skill

1. **Recognize Multiple Causes** List three different causes that contributed to the colonists' discontent with England.

Comprehension and Critical Thinking

2. **a. Recall** Why were the American colonies largely left to govern themselves?
   b. Predict What effect might this experience of self-government have on the colonists

when England tried to exercise more control over them?

3. **a. Describe** What were the basic responsibilities of a colonial citizen?
   b. Draw Inferences What do these responsibilities suggest about citizens' attitudes toward their communities?

4. **a. Explain** Why did the jury find John Peter Zenger innocent of the charges made against him?
   b. Determine Relevance Why did the colonists believe in freedom of the press?

5. **a. Describe** Why did the royal governors' activities anger the colonists?

b. Identify Cause and Effect How were the colonists likely to respond to the governors' actions?

Writing Activity

Write an essay describing why freedom of the press is as important in our society today as it was in the 1700s. Use current events to help you illustrate your point.

Go Online
PHSchool.com
For: Writing Activity
Visit: PHSchool.com
Web Code: mpd-2041

Analyzing Political Cartoons

One of our rights as citizens is the freedom to express our political views, even when we disagree with government policies. Political cartoons use humor and exaggeration to comment on issues, and often to criticize the government. The political cartoon below was drawn by Benjamin Franklin; it appeared in his newspaper in 1754.

Learn the Skill

Follow these steps to to analyze a political cartoon:

❶ **Identify the symbols.** A political cartoon often uses symbols to convey its message. Symbols are drawings of people, animals, or objects that stand for something else. What do the symbols in the cartoon represent?

❷ **Study the words and images.** Political cartoons use few words, so the words that are used are important to understand. Labels help identify symbols and captions help explain a cartoon's meaning.

❸ **Analyze the meaning.** What is the point of view of the cartoonist?

❹ **Interpret the cartoon.** Draw conclusions about the cartoon. What is the cartoonist saying about the issue?

Practice the Skill

Read the passage above and answer the following questions:

❶ What does the snake represent?

❷ **(a)** What do the labels on each piece of the snake's body mean? **(b)** What does the caption mean?

❸ **(a)** How did Franklin feel about the political issue of independence from Great Britain? **(b)** How can you tell?

Apply the Skill

Find a political cartoon in a newspaper and analyze it. Describe how the cartoonist uses symbols and words to convey his or her opinion about the issue.

SECTION 2 · Roots of American Government

Reading Preview

Objectives
In this section you will
- Discuss how the colonists looked to ancient Greece and Rome for models of government.
- Examine how the English tradition influenced American government.
- Understand how relying on reason helped shape the American government.

Key Terms
direct democracy
republic
natural rights
separation of powers

Main Idea
American colonists began to think about what they wanted from their government. They looked to models from ancient Greece and Rome, English history, and European philosophers.

Target Reading Skill
Identify Causes and Effects A cause makes something happen. An effect is what happens. By identifying causes and effects, you can better understand relationships among situations or events.

Taking Notes
Make a diagram like the one below. As you read this section, complete the diagram with information comparing a monarchy to a representative system of government.

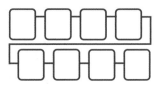

The American colonists had the benefit of other people's experiences and ideas about government. John Adams, one of our nation's founders, once urged his fellow colonists to look to the past for inspiration:

> "Let us study the law of nature; search into the spirit of the British constitution; . . . [think about] the great examples of Greece and Rome; set before us the conduct of our own British ancestors."

Looking to Ancient Greece and Rome

What did John Adams mean by "the great examples of Greece and Rome"? The Athenians created the world's first **direct democracy**, a form of government in which laws are made directly by the citizens. The citizens of Athens met regularly to discuss ways to make life better for their community. Centuries later some American colonists practiced direct democracy by holding town meetings to vote on local issues.

In 509 B.C., the Romans founded a republic, a government in which representatives were elected to make laws. Colonial legislatures resembled the Roman form of government.

✓ Reading Check **What did the colonial government have in common with the government of ancient Athens?**

Coin minted by the Roman government.
▼

The Signing of the Magna Carta
King John is surrounded by nobles who force him to sign the Magna Carta.
Analyzing *Why was limiting the monarch's power a necessary first step to a representative government?*

Target Reading Skill
Identify Causes and Effects
Look for the causes of the Magna Carta and the effects of this charter.

The English Tradition

The people in the English colonies saw the democracy of Athens and the **republic** (a government in which representatives were elected to make laws) of Rome as noble examples of governments designed to prevent tyranny. Unfortunately, those governments eventually gave way to government by force.

After the end of the Roman republic, government by the people disappeared for hundreds of years. Then, in the year A.D. 1215, a dramatic conflict took place in England. It was a conflict that changed the course of English history and laid the groundwork for the type of government we have today.

The Magna Carta For centuries, monarchs had ruled with complete authority over the English people. The people were not citizens. Instead, they were subjects—they were subject to the monarch's command. Some monarchs used their powers wisely and justly. But others were tyrants who stirred resentment among many of their subjects.

By the early 1200s, English nobles had become strong enough to challenge royal power. In 1215 they forced King John to sign the Magna Carta, or Great Charter. This document listed rights that even the English monarch would not have the power to take away. Among these rights were the right to a fair trial.

The rights in the Magna Carta applied only to nobles. But the Magna Carta was an important step in gaining basic rights for all English people. For the first time the monarch's power had been limited. Eventually, the rights it listed were given to all English citizens—including the colonists.

The English Bill of Rights Once the monarch's power had been limited, a representative government soon followed. By the late 1200s, a legislature called Parliament was well established in England. Over the centuries, Parliament gradually became more powerful than the monarch.

In 1689, Parliament passed the English Bill of Rights, which further limited the power of the monarch. For example, the king or queen would no longer be able to limit free speech in Parliament or to collect taxes without Parliament's approval.

The English Bill of Rights listed the rights of all English citizens, not just nobles. It proclaimed that everyone, even government leaders, must obey the law. It declared that all people have the right to a trial by jury and the right to make a formal petition, or request, to the government.

By stating the rights of English citizens, the Magna Carta and the English Bill of Rights provided protections against tyranny. The colonists in America treasured these protections of their rights.

✓ Reading Check **What does English history suggest about how the English people felt about government?**

Analyze Charts

Influences on American Government

Source	Concepts
Ancient Athenians	Citizens make laws as part of a direct democracy.
Ancient Romans	Representatives make laws in a republican form of government.
Magna Carta	The power of the highest leader (in this case, a monarch) is limited.
English Bill of Rights	Everyone must obey the law, even government leaders. Citizens have the right to a trial by jury. Citizens have the right to make a formal petition to the government.
John Locke	Governments exist for the people, not people for the government. The purpose of government is to protect the natural rights of life, liberty, and property.
Baron de Montesquieu	Government should be divided into three branches: legislative, executive, and judicial.

There have been many influences on American government. One was the English bill of Rights, passed during the reign of King William III and Queen Mary II.

1. Analyze Which of John Locke's ideas had an influence on American government?

2. Apply Why do you think so many of the influences on American government were British?

The writings of John Locke had so much influence that he has sometimes been called "the intellectual ruler of the eighteenth century."

▼

Relying on Reason In the 1600s and early 1700s, many European philosophers wrote that people have the power of reason, the ability to think clearly. People could use reason to recognize their **natural rights**, rights they are born with and that no government can take away. Two philosophers who inspired the colonists were the English writer John Locke and the French writer Montesquieu (mon tes KYOO).

John Locke argued that representative government is the only reasonable kind. He wrote that government exists to serve the people, rather than the other way around. He said the purpose of government is to protect natural rights—the rights to life, liberty, and property. Any government that abuses its power should not be obeyed.

Colonial leaders knew that power could lead to tyranny. Therefore, they were drawn to Montesquieu's proposal for **separation of powers**, dividing government power among legislative, executive, and judicial branches. The legislature would only make the laws; the executive, such as a governor, would only enforce the laws; the judges would only interpret the meaning of the laws. Such a system would guard against tyranny because no government official or branch of government could gain too much power.

✓ Reading Check **Would Montesquieu and Locke have agreed with one another's ideas? Why or why not?**

SECTION 2 **Assessment**

Key Terms

Use each of the key terms in a sentence that explains its meaning: direct democracy, republic, natural rights, separation of powers

Target Reading Skill

1. **Identify Cause and Effect** Reread the text on page 93. Identify one cause of the English Bill of Rights and one effect of the document.

Comprehension and Critical Thinking

2. **a. Describe** Describe the government of ancient Athens.

b. Compare What was the most important thing the Athenian and Roman governments had in common?

3. **a. Recall** List the important freedoms set forth in the English Bill of Rights.
b. Contrast What was the major difference between the English Bill of Rights and the Magna Carta?

4. **a. Explain** Explain Montesquieu's proposed design for a government.
b. Determine Relevance How did Montesquieu's system reflect John Locke's ideas about government?

Writing Activity

Write a short biography about either Montesquieu or Locke. Focus on the details of your chosen writer's career, his major works and ideas, and his influence on other thinkers. Use reliable sources from the library or the Internet.

TIP Make an outline before you begin writing. Organize your information under major headings. This will help you to include only the most important main ideas and supporting details.

Moving Toward Nationhood

Reading Preview

Objectives

In this section you will

- Explain the clash of views that brought the colonists into open conflict with England.
- Summarize the Declaration of Independence.
- Describe how the Americans organized a new government.
- Understand the challenges that a struggling American government would have to face.

Key Terms

compact   ratification

Main Idea

After becoming dissatisfied with English rule, the colonies declared themselves an independent nation. After winning the American Revolution, they turned to the task of strengthening and improving their new government.

Target Reading Skill

Understand Effects An effect is the result of an event or action. As you read this section, take note of the effects of England's attempts to tighten control over the colonies.

Taking Notes

Make a diagram like the one below. As you read this section, complete the diagram with information about the events that led to American independence.

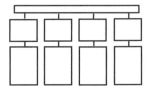

If the colonists had inherited their tradition of representative government from England, why did they become dissatisfied with English rule? Why did relations between the colonies and England eventually explode into war and lead to American independence? Let's find out by looking at how tensions developed over the issue of representation in government.

A Clash of Views

The English colonists had different views on important issues than the English government did. These differences would soon bring the colonists into conflict with England.

Government and Trade England believed that Parliament represented all English citizens—including the colonists. The colonists believed that they were only represented by their own legislatures. The colonists could not vote for members of Parliament, and no colonists were members themselves. Unlike the colonial legislatures, Parliament had little understanding of the colonists' needs.

The colonists and the English government also had opposing views on colonial trade. Parliament permitted the colonies to trade only with England. The colonists wanted the freedom to sell their products to any country.

Despite these differences, many colonists were still loyal English citizens. In fact, they helped England defeat France in the French and Indian War in 1763.

TEA THROWN INTO BOSTON HARBOR DEC. 16 1773.

◀ The colonists became angry when England added a tax to tea. Colonists in Boston, Massachusetts, responded by dumping British tea into Boston Harbor.

One of the major causes of the American Revolution was the colonists' anger over being taxed by England without representation in the British government. In this cartoon, a group of colonists protest the Stamp Act of 1764, which was a new tax for the colonists.

1. What does the sign that the man is carrying say? Restate its meaning in your own words.

2. What kind of effect do you think this cartoon had on the colonists? Explain your answer.

"No Taxation Without Representation" Facing huge war debts, Parliament decided to squeeze money out of the colonies through taxes. The colonists protested that they should not be taxed unless their own representatives approved such taxes. The colonists believed that taxation without representation was taking people's property without their consent. Soon the cry of "no taxation without representation" was heard throughout the colonies.

To make people pay the taxes, Parliament gave the governors greater power. Colonists accused of breaking tax laws were thrown in jail. Parliament ignored all protest, claiming that it had the power to make laws for the colonies "in all cases whatsoever."

Steps Toward Independence Some colonists organized Committees of Correspondence to pass news from colony to colony about how England was violating colonists' rights. Eventually many colonial legislatures saw the need for a united response to Parliament's threats. They called for a congress, or formal meeting, of representatives from all the colonies.

In 1774, delegates from 12 colonies met in Philadelphia for the First Continental Congress. The delegates hoped to convince the English government to respect colonists' rights. To pressure Parliament, they pledged to cut off all trade with England. They agreed to meet the following year if the situation did not improve.

Target Reading Skill

Understand Effects As you read Steps Toward Independence, think about the actions the colonists took in response to England's attempt to assert its powers. Read on to understand the further effects of England's actions.

A Year Later Far from improving, the situation got worse. By the time the Second Continental Congress met in 1775, colonists in Massachusetts were already fighting English soldiers. Delegate Patrick Henry argued for independence, stating that the war had already begun and that there was no turning back.

Many colonists feared independence, however. Even if they fought and won, they thought, what future would they face without the security of being part of a strong nation like England?

The writings of Thomas Paine changed many people's minds. In 1776, Paine published his pamphlet titled *Common Sense*, in which he presented his argument:

> "To be always running three or four thousand miles with a tale or a petition, waiting four or five months for an answer, which when obtained requires five or six more [months] to explain it in, will in a few years be looked upon as folly and childishness— There was a time when it was proper, and there is a proper time for it to cease. . . . England [belongs] to Europe, America to itself."

✔ Reading Check   **Why do you think Thomas Paine titled his pamphlet *Common Sense*?**

The Declaration of Independence

Popular support for separation from England increased. The delegates to the Second Continental Congress finally voted for independence. They appointed a committee to write a declaration of independence. Among the committee members were Thomas Jefferson, Benjamin Franklin, and John Adams. Jefferson was asked to do the actual writing.

The ringing phrases of the Declaration of Independence capture many of the colonists' beliefs about natural rights:

> "We hold these truths to be self-evident, that all men are created equal, that they are endowed by their Creator with certain unalienable Rights, that among these are Life, Liberty, and the pursuit of Happiness."

As did John Locke, Jefferson described these rights as "unalienable"—meaning that no government has the power to take them away. Further reflecting Locke's views, Jefferson described the purpose of government:

> ". . .to secure these rights, Governments are instituted [established] among Men, deriving their just powers from the consent of the governed."

▲ Thomas Paine was a respected political theorist and essayist. *Common Sense* was widely read and did much to sway hearts and minds toward the patriot cause.

In other words, the people give power to their government as long as it protects their rights. If a government abuses its powers, the people may change it or do away with it:

> "... whenever any Form of Government becomes destructive of these ends, it is the Right of the People to alter or to abolish it, and to institute new Government."

Jefferson then listed the ways in which England had ignored the colonists' rights as English citizens—proof that England was trying to rule the colonies with "absolute Tyranny."

The Declaration concludes with the signers pledging to support it with "our Lives, our Fortunes, and our sacred Honor." Adopted in Philadelphia on July 4, 1776, the Declaration of Independence proclaimed that "these United Colonies are, and of Right ought to be Free and Independent States." *The full text of the Declaration of Independence can be found on pages 106–109.*

✓ Reading Check **What was the purpose of the Declaration of Independence?**

Thomas Jefferson was chosen to draft the Declaration of Independence. He is shown here (wearing a red vest), presenting the document to the Second Continental Congress.
▼

Organizing a New Government

Now that the colonies had become "free and independent states," each had to organize its own government. Because the colonies had been established by charters, people were used to the idea of having a written plan of government. People also remembered that the *Mayflower* passengers had made a **compact**, a written agreement to make and obey laws for the welfare of the group.

State Constitutions Each state created a constitution, or plan of government. By creating written constitutions, the states were clearly spelling out the limits on government power. Some state constitutions also included a list of citizens' rights, such as trial by jury and freedom of religion.

To help guard against tyranny, each state constitution limited the number of years a governor could hold office. As a further protection against abuse of power, each state used Montesquieu's idea of separating government into legislative, executive, and judicial branches. Of the three branches, the legislature was given the most power because it most directly represented the interests of citizens.

The Articles of Confederation Although the states were united in opposing England, they were still 13 separate governments. During the war against England, the delegates to the Second Continental Congress debated how to form a national government.

The delegates faced a difficult task. Conflicts with the English king and Parliament had made the colonists fearful of giving power to a central government. Also, the states disagreed on how many representatives each should have in the government. Large states like Virginia wanted the number of representatives to be based on population. Small states like Rhode Island feared that large states would then have too much power. They argued that each state should have the same number of votes.

The Continental Congress drew up a plan for a loose confederation, or alliance of independent states, in 1777. This compact, known as the Articles of Confederation, called for a national legislature in which each state would have one vote. There would be no executive or judicial branches of government. The state legislatures feared that these branches might try to take power away from them.

The national legislature, known as Congress, was given power to declare war, make treaties with foreign countries, and work out trade agreements between states. However, it was not given the power to tax or to enforce any laws it made. Therefore, most of the power would remain with the states.

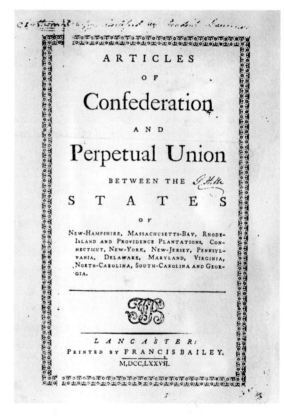

Toward a Central Government
The Articles of Confederation established a national legislature, or Congress, which was given certain powers. It took four years to ratify.
Drawing Inferences *Why do you think the compact took so long to ratify?*

John Dickinson (1732–1808) of Pennsylvania stirred up colonial opposition to English taxes in his *Letters from a Farmer in Pennsylvania* (1767–1786). The *Letters* paved the way for Thomas Paine's *Common Sense*. Unlike Paine, Dickinson hoped to come to an agreement with England. He was the only man in Congress who refused to sign the Declaration of Independence. He was opposed to independence. However, Dickinson headed the committee that drafted the Articles of Confederation. He also served in the Continental army and later published essays urging public support for the Constitution.

Citizenship

Why do you think Dickinson served and supported the new nation when he did not believe the colonies should have become independent?

Before the Articles of Confederation could go into effect, they needed the **ratification,** or approval, of all 13 states. At first it seemed the states would reject the plan because many state legislatures still did not trust a central government. Even while fighting the Revolutionary War, it took four years for the states to agree on a plan of government. Finally, the states realized that they had to cooperate or lose the war. The Articles were ratified in 1781.

✔ Reading Check **Why were the states reluctant to give any power to a central government?**

A Limping Government

You know the story of how the patriots under General George Washington won our independence in the Revolutionary War. However, after winning the war the new government had to face another challenge. A struggling economy made life difficult for Americans and their new government.

Problems with Debt and Trade Congress and the states had borrowed a large amount of money to buy war supplies to fight for independence. Now they could not pay off these huge debts because they did not have enough gold and silver to back up their printed money. Many Americans and foreigners lost confidence in the value of American money.

Another problem was that the new Congress had no power to regulate trade with England. Americans were buying most of their manufactured goods from England because prices were low. American merchants could not sell their goods as cheaply as the English. Congress could not help because it did not have the power to raise the prices of English goods by taxing them. England no longer allowed Americans to trade with English colonies in the British West Indies. This had been one of the most important markets for American crops and manufactured goods.

Shays' Rebellion Many farmers slid into debt, largely because they could not sell their crops to the Caribbean colonies. Farmers in Massachusetts faced an added problem. To pay its war debts, the state legislature had sharply raised taxes on land. Many farmers who were unable to pay the taxes faced loss of their farms. Local courts threatened to sell the farms and use the money to pay the taxes.

In 1786, hundreds of angry Massachusetts farmers, led by a former war hero named Daniel Shays, stormed into courthouses to disrupt court business. Congress did not have the power to force other states to help put down the uprising. Massachusetts had to use its own state militia to crush the rebellion.

Newspapers quickly spread word of the violent clash, which shocked people throughout the states. Many Americans called for a stronger national government, one that would keep law and order and solve the economic problems that had led to Shays' Rebellion. George Washington thought that the Articles of Confederation had weakened Congress, leaving it unable to keep order, raise money through taxes, or deal effectively with European nations.

Most Americans agreed that the 13 proud and independent states would have to face the challenge of establishing a stronger government. Their future was at stake.

▲ Daniel Shays' army of farmers gather on the courthouse steps during Shays' Rebellion in 1786.

✓ Reading Check **What was the importance of Shays' Rebellion?**

SECTION 3 Assessment

Key Terms

Use each of the key terms in a sentence that explains its meaning: compact, ratification

Target Reading Skill

1. **Understanding Effects** Reread the text on this page. List one effect of Shays' Rebellion.

Comprehension and Critical Thinking

2. **a. Explain** How did the conflict between England and the colonies develop?
   b. Draw Conclusions Why did Parliament refuse to listen to the colonists' protests?

3. **a. Recall** What was the purpose of the Declaration of Independence?
   b. Identify Main Ideas What are the most important ideas in the Declaration of Independence?

4. **a. Recall** List the powers reserved for the central government in the Articles of Confederation.
   b. Analyze Information Why do you think the colonists wanted state governments to have more power than the central government?

5. **a. Describe** What challenges did the new national government face at the end of the American Revolution?
   b. Predict How might Congress meet these challenges?

Writing Activity

You are a delegate to Congress from one of the 13 states. You believe that the central government must be made stronger. Give a speech in which you urge the other delegates to give Congress greater powers.

TIP Include specific reasons to support your argument. Remember that political speeches often use emotional language to persuade listeners to vote a certain way.

Debating the Issues

CLOSE UP FOUNDATION

The debates in this feature are based on *Current Issues*, published by the Close Up Foundation. Go to **PHSchool.com**, Web Code mph-2044 to read the latest issue of *Current Issues* online.

The United States has a history of helping nations around the world. After World War II, the Marshall Plan sent millions of dollars in aid to western European nations to help them rebuild. Japan and the United States were enemies during the war, but American aid helped Japan become an economic superpower. In 2003, the United States ousted the Iraqi dictator Saddam Hussein. Afterward, the United States attempted to help Iraq launch a new government, rebuild its cities, and feed its people.

Should the United States Lead Nation-Building Efforts Around the World?

YES	NO
• The United States is an extremely wealthy nation and the world's only remaining superpower. It has both the financial and human resources to help nations rebuild.	• The United States should not try to be an international police force. Instead, the United Nations should help nations solve their problems.
• Any conquering nation has a responsibility to help its defeated enemies. It is only right that the United States should try to help repair the damage it causes.	• The United States should turn its attention to troubles at home. Problems such as poverty and hunger have not yet been solved within our own country. It would be best if each nation took care of itself to the best of its ability.
• By helping nations rebuild, the United States gains valuable allies. With growing anti-American sentiment in some parts of the world, the United States needs to establish and encourage friendly relations with all nations.	• Many countries do not welcome what they regard as American interference. Terrorist attacks against American targets show that there is much anti-American feeling in the world today.

What Is Your Opinion?

1. **Determine Relevance** What factors should the U.S. government take into account when deciding to send military or financial aid to another nation? Explain.

2. **Support a Point of View** Do you believe that the United Nations, not the United States, should lead global nation-building efforts? Why?

3. **Writing to Persuade** Suppose that you are the president of the United States. You believe you should send aid to help a war-torn African nation rebuild its government and infrastructure. Write a short, informal speech you will make at a Cabinet meeting to persuade your Cabinet to support your position.

Go Online
civics interactive

For: You Decide Poll
Visit: PHSchool.com
Web Code: mph-2043

Review and Assessment

Chapter Summary

Section 1
The Colonial Experience
(pages 84–89)

- The values and experiences of the settlers in the 13 English colonies, such as religious freedom and freedom of the press, are an important part of America's heritage.

- England established each colony by granting it a charter, which could be taken away if a colony challenged England's authority.

- In the colonies, white men who owned property were citizens, able to participate in government by electing representatives to the legislature.

- When the royal governors began showing signs of tyranny, the colonists began to worry that they would lose their freedoms.

Section 2
Roots of American Government
(pages 91–94)

- As they began thinking about self-government, the colonists looked to the direct democracy of ancient Athens and the republic of ancient Rome.

- The colonists believed Locke's idea that government should exist to protect people's natural rights.

- Montesquieu's system of separation of powers within the government influenced the Americans.

Section 3
Moving Toward Nationhood
(pages 95–101)

- The First and Second Continental Congresses pressured Parliament to respect colonists' rights and eventually declared independence.

- The Declaration of Independence emphasized the importance of basic rights and declared the colonists' separation from England.

- The Articles of Confederation was a compact that established a national Congress but left the individual states with most of the powers of government.

- After a long period of ratification, the Articles of Confederation were adopted, but they proved to be seriously flawed.

Copy the chart below and use it to help you summarize the chapter:

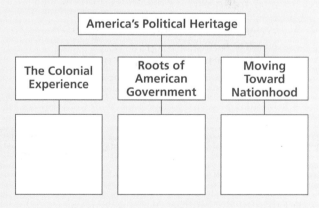

Go Online
PHSchool.com
For: Self-Test
Visit: PHSchool.com
Web Code: mpa-2043

Reviewing Key Terms

Write the term that makes each sentence correct on a separate piece of paper.

1. A (direct democracy, legislature) made the laws in each colony.

2. The English monarch granted each colony a (charter, compact).

3. (Natural rights, Separation of powers) ensured that no branch of the government would become too strong.

4. The states hesitated to agree to the Articles of Confederation because they feared the (direct democracy, tyranny) of a central government.

5. The Declaration of Independence stressed the importance of an individual's (compact, natural rights).

6. The (charter, republic) of ancient Rome provided one model of government for the Americans.

7. In a (direct democracy, republic), the people make the laws themselves.

8. The success of the Mayflower (Charter, Compact) reminded the Americans that they needed an agreement to make laws for the welfare of the entire nation.

Comprehension and Critical Thinking

9. a. **Describe** Did colonial citizens in America enjoy greater or fewer rights than citizens of other countries at the time?
   b. **Analyze Information** Why did citizens believe in a number of individual freedoms, such as freedom of religion and freedom of the press?
   c. **Determine Relevance** What is the connection between good citizenship and freedom?

10. a. **Recall** Why did King John sign the Magna Carta?
    b. **Draw Conclusions** Why did English citizens eventualy become dissatisfied with the Magna Carta?

   c. **Identify Cause and Effect** How did the signing of the Magna Carta lead to the passage of the English Bill of Rights?

11. a. **Describe** What did the Declaration of Independence say about natural rights?
    b. **Analyze Primary Sources** Why did Jefferson state that men were entitled to "life, liberty, and the pursuit of happiness?"
    c. **Identify Bias** How could Congress agree to sign a document stating that "all men are created equal" and not immediately outlaw the enslavement of Africans?

Activities

12. **Skills** On March 5, 1770, citizens of Boston clashed with English soldiers. Paul Revere published this image of the event (at right). a. How does this image portray the English army? b. What did the artist want people to think about the clash between England and the colonies?

13. **Writing** You are a newspaper publisher in Philadelphia in 1776. Write an editorial dated July 5, 1776, in which you support or oppose the Declaration of Independence.

14. **Active Citizen** Read the first section of a newspaper. Find a government policy with which you disagree. With a small group of classmates, form a plan to protest this policy.

15. **Math Practice** By 1790, the United States was made up of 16 states. Find out the population of each of the states in 1790. Decide which state should have the most votes in national government, based on its population, and which state should have the least votes.

16. **Civics and Economics** You are a member of Congress who supports changes to the Articles of Confederation. Write a speech describing the economic issues facing the states, such as debt, taxes, and trade, that Congress should pass laws to solve.

The Thirteen Original Colonies

17. **Analyze Visuals** Study the map above of the 13 colonies. Explain why the Congress chose to meet in Philadelphia.

Standardized Test Prep

Test-Taking Tips

Sometimes a standardized test will ask you to analyze a primary source. Below is an excerpt from a letter John Adams wrote to his wife Abigail on July 3, 1776. Read the excerpt and answer the questions.

TIP When there is an unfamiliar word in a primary source, examine the entire sentence or passage to figure out the meaning.

"Yesterday the greatest Question was decided, which ever was debated in America, and a greater perhaps, never was or will be decided among Men. A Resolution was passed without one dissenting Colony 'that these united Colonies are, and of right ought to be free and independent States. . . . ' You will see in a few days a Declaration setting forth the Causes, which have impelled Us to this mighty Revolution, and the Reasons which will justify it, in the Sight of God and Man."

Choose the letter that best completes the statement.

1. Adams uses the word *dissenting* to explain that no colony_____ the resolution.
   A suggested
   B wrote
   C agreed with
   D disagreed with

   TIP Go back to the excerpt and reread the sentence in which the word *dissenting* appears.

   The correct answer is **D**. Since Adams states that the resolution was passed, it must be because none of the colonies disagreed with it.

2. Adams says that the purpose of the Declaration of Independence was to
   A make the colonies come together.
   B show that no colony dissented from the resolution.
   C explain why the colonies decided to break away from England.
   D prove that England's king was a tyrant.

The Declaration of Independence

The Declaration of Independence has four parts: the Preamble, the Declaration of Natural Rights, the List of Grievances, and the Resolution of Independence. The Preamble states why the Declaration was written. The document will explain to the world the reasons why the colonists feel **impelled**, or forced, to separate from Great Britain.

The Declaration of Natural Rights lists the basic rights to which all people are entitled. These rights are **unalienable**; they cannot be taken away. The purpose of government is to protect these natural rights. When a government does not protect the rights of the people, the people must change the government or create a new one. The colonists feel that the King's repeated **usurpations**, or unjust uses of power, are a form of **despotism**, or tyranny, that denied them their basic rights.

★ In Congress, July 4, 1776

The Unanimous Declaration of the Thirteen United States of America

When in the Course of human events, it becomes necessary for one people to dissolve the political bands which have connected them with another and to assume among the powers of the earth, the separate and equal station to which the Laws of Nature and of Nature's God entitle them, a decent respect to the opinions of mankind requires that they should declare the causes which impel them to the separation.

We hold these truths to be self-evident, that all men are created equal, that they are endowed by their Creator with certain unalienable Rights, that among these are Life, Liberty and the pursuit of Happiness. That to secure these rights, Governments are instituted among Men, deriving their just powers from the consent of the governed. That whenever any Form of Government becomes destructive of these ends, it is the Right of the People to alter or to abolish it, and to institute new Government, laying its foundation on such principles and organizing its powers in such form, as to them shall seem most likely to effect their Safety and Happiness. Prudence, indeed, will dictate that Governments long established should not be changed for light and transient causes; and accordingly all experience hath shown that mankind are more disposed to suffer, while evils are sufferable than to right themselves by abolishing the forms to which they are accustomed. But when a long train of abuses and usurpations, pursuing invariably the same Object evinces a design to reduce them under absolute Despotism, it is their right, it is their duty, to throw off such Government, and to provide new Guards for their future security. Such has been the patient sufferance of these Colonies; and such is now the necessity which constrains them to alter their former Systems of Government. The history of the present King of Great Britain is a history of repeated injuries and usurpations, all having in direct object the establishment of an absolute Tyranny over these States. To prove this, let Facts be submitted to a candid world.

> The List of Grievances details the colonists' complaints against the British government, and King George III in particular. The colonists have no say in determining the laws that govern them and they feel King George's actions show little or no concern for the well being of the people.

He has refuted his Assent to Laws, the most wholesome and necessary for the public good.

He has forbidden his Governors to pass Laws of immediate and pressing importance, unless suspended in their operation till his Assent should be obtained; and when so suspended, he has utterly neglected to attend to them.

He has refused to pass other Laws for the accommodation of large districts of people, unless those people would relinquish the right of Representation in the Legislature, a right inestimable to them and formidable to tyrants only.

> The colonists refuse to **relinquish**, or give up, the right to representation, which they feel is **inestimable**, or priceless.

He has called together legislative bodies at places unusual, uncomfortable, and distant from the depository of their Public Records, for the sole purpose of fatiguing them into compliance with his measures.

He has dissolved Representative Houses repeatedly, for opposing with manly firmness his invasions on the rights of the people.

He has refused for a long time, after such dissolutions, to cause others to be elected, whereby the Legislative Powers, incapable of Annihilation, have returned to the People at large for their exercise; the State remaining in the mean time exposed to all the dangers of invasion from without, and convulsions within.

> The king has refused to allow new legislators to be elected. As a result, the colonies have not been able to protect themselves against foreign enemies and **convulsions**, or riots, within the colonies.

He has endeavoured to prevent the population of these States; for that purpose obstructing the Laws for Naturalization of Foreigners; refusing to pass others to encourage their migrations hither, and raising the conditions of new Appropriations of Lands.

> The king has tried to stop foreigners from coming to the colonies by refusing to pass naturalization laws. Laws for naturalization of foreigners are laws that set up the process for foreigners to become legal citizens.

He has obstructed the Administration of Justice by refusing his Assent to Laws for establishing Judiciary Powers.

He has made Judges dependent on his Will alone for the tenure of their offices, and the amount and payment of their salaries.

> The king alone has decided a judge's **tenure**, or term. This grievance later would result in Article 3, Section 1 of the Constitution, which states that federal judges hold office for life.

He has erected a multitude of New Offices, and sent hither swarms of Officers to harass our people and eat out their substance.

He has kept among us, in times of peace, Standing Armies without the Consent of our legislatures.

He has affected to render the Military independent of and superior to the Civil Power.

He has combined with others to subject us to a jurisdiction foreign to our constitution, and unacknowledged by our laws; giving his Assent to their Acts of pretended Legislation:

For quartering large bodies of armed troops among us:

> Forced by the king, the colonists have been **quartering**, or lodging, troops in their homes. This grievance found its way into the Constitution in the Third Amendment.

For protecting them, by a mock Trial from punishment for any Murders which they should commit on the Inhabitants of these States:

For cutting off our Trade with all parts of the world:

For imposing Taxes on us without our Consent:

For depriving us in many cases, of the benefit of Trial by Jury:

For transporting us beyond Seas to be tried for pretended offences:

For abolishing the free System of English Laws in a neighbouring Province, establishing therein an Arbitrary government, and enlarging its Boundaries so as to render it at once an example and fit instrument for introducing the same absolute rule into these Colonies

> The king has taken away the rights of the people in a nearby province (Canada). The colonists feared he could do the same to the colonies if he so wished.

For taking away our Charters, abolishing our most valuable Laws and altering fundamentally the Forms of our Governments:

For suspending our own Legislatures, and declaring themselves invested with power to legislate for us in all cases whatsoever.

He has abdicated Government here, by declaring us out of his Protection and waging War against us.

He has plundered our seas, ravaged our Coasts, burnt our towns, and destroyed the lives of our people.

He is at this time transporting large Armies of foreign Mercenaries to complete the works of death, desolation, and tyranny, already begun with circumstances of Cruelty and perfidy scarcely paralleled in the most barbarous ages, and totally unworthy the Head of a civilized nation.

> The king has hired foreign **mercenaries**, or soldiers, to bring death and destruction to the colonists. The head of a civilized country should never act with the cruelty and **perfidy**, or dishonesty, that the king has.

He has constrained our fellow Citizens taken Captive on the high Seas to bear Arms against their Country, to become the executioners of their friends and Brethren, or to fall themselves by their Hands.

He has excited domestic insurrections amongst us, and has endeavoured to bring on the inhabitants of our frontiers, the merciless Indian Savages whose known rule of warfare, is an undistinguished destruction of all ages, sexes and conditions.

> The colonists have tried repeatedly to petition the king to **redress,** or correct, these wrongs. Each time, they have been ignored by the king or punished by new laws. Because of the way he treats his subjects, the king is not fit to rule a free people.

In every stage of these Oppressions We have Petitioned for Redress in the most humble terms: Our repeated Petitions have been answered only by repeated injury. A Prince, whose character is thus marked by every act which may define a Tyrant, is unfit to be the ruler of a free People.

Nor have We been wanting in attentions to our British brethren. We have warned them from time to time of attempts by their legislature to extend an unwarrantable jurisdiction over us. We have reminded them of the circumstances of our emigration and settlement here. We have appealed to their native justice and magnanimity, and we have conjured them by the ties of our common kindred. to disavow these usurpations, which would inevitably interrupt our connections and correspondence. They too have been deaf to the voice of justice and of consanguinity. We must, therefore, acquiesce in the necessity, which denounces our Separation, and hold them, as we hold the rest of mankind, Enemies in War, in Peace Friends.

We, therefore, the Representatives of the United States of America, in General Congress, Assembled, appealing to the Supreme Judge of the world for the rectitude of our intentions, do, in the Name, and by Authority of the good People of these Colonies, solemnly publish and declare, That these United Colonies are, and of Right ought to be Free and Independent States, that they are Absolved from all Allegiance to the British Crown, and that all political connection between them and the State of Great Britain, is and ought to be totally dissolved; and that as Free and Independent States, they have full Power to levy War, conclude Peace contract Alliances, establish Commerce, and to do all other Acts and Things which Independent States may of right do. And for the support of this Declaration, with a firm reliance on the protection of Divine Providence, we mutually pledge to each other our Lives, our Fortunes and our sacred Honor.

> The colonists have appealed to the British people. They have asked their fellow British subjects to support them. However, like the king, the British people have ignored the colonists' requests.

> The Resolution of Independence boldly asserts that the colonies are now "free and independent states." The colonists have proven the **rectitude**, or justness, of their cause. The Declaration concludes by stating these new states have the power to wage war, establish alliances, and trade with other countries.

John Hancock, *President from Massachusetts*

Georgia
Button Gwinnett
Lyman Hall
George Walton

North Carolina
William Hooper
Joseph Hewes
John Penn

South Carolina
Edward Rutledge
Thomas Heyward, Jr.
Thomas Lynch, Jr.
Arthur Middleton

Maryland
Samuel Chase
William Paca
Thomas Stone
Charles Carroll
of Carrollton

Virginia
George Wythe
Richard Henry Lee
Thomas Jefferson
Benjamin Harrison
Thomas Nelson, Jr.
Francis Lightfoot Lee
Carter Braxton

Pennsylvania
Robert Morris
Benjamin Rush
Benjamin Franklin
John Morton
George Clymer
James Smith
George Taylor
James Wilson
George Ross

Delaware
Caesar Rodney
George Read
Thomas McKean

New York
William Floyd
Philip Livingston
Francis Lewis
Lewis Morris

New Jersey
Richard Stockton
John Witherspoon
Francis Hopkinson
John Hart
Abraham Clark

New Hampshire
Josiah Bartlett
William Whipple
Matthew Thornton

Massachusetts
Samuel Adams
John Adams
Robert Treat Paine
Elbridge Gerry

Rhode Island
Stephen Hopkins
William Ellery

Connecticut
Samuel Huntington
William Williams
Oliver Wolcott
Roger Sherman

Creating the Constitution

What's Ahead in Chapter 5

In this chapter you will read about how the United States Constitution was written, the debate about its ratification, and how the Constitution set up the democratic government that has lasted more than 200 years.

SECTION 1
The Constitutional Convention

SECTION 2
The Struggle for Ratification

SECTION 3
The Supreme Law of the Land

TARGET READING SKILL

Context In this chapter you will focus on using context to help you better understand what you read. Context includes using context clues to figure out or clarify the meaning of a word. It also includes interpreting nonliteral meanings in texts.

The National Constitution ▶ Center opened on July 4, 2003, in Philadelphia.

The following National Standards are covered in this chapter:

II. What are the foundations of the American political system?

A. What is the American idea of constitutional government?

III. How does the government embody the purposes, values, and principles of American democracy?

A. How are the government's power and responsibility distributed, shared, and limited by the United States Constitution?

Go Online
PHSchool.com

For: Your state's standards
Visit: PHSchool.com
Web Code: mpe-2051

Active Citizen — Civics in the Real World

It is May 1787, and the United States is facing a serious crisis. The government is unable to deal with the challenges of leading a large country. It is overwhelmed by a failing economy and war debt. Riots and talk of rebellion are spreading through many of the thirteen states.

In response to this crisis, many of the nation's most respected citizens have traveled to Philadelphia to serve as delegates to the Constitutional Convention. George Washington is here, as is James Madison and Benjamin Franklin. Most of the delegates agree that a stronger national government is needed, but there is little agreement about what form this government should take. The delegates are preparing for long days of hard work and heated debates.

In late May the convention begins. The country's future is at stake. It needs a new government. But can the delegates agree on and fashion a government that will work, solve the problems the day, and yet be flexible enough to grow and endure in the future?

Citizen's Journal   **How can people who have different ideas arrive at an agreement they can all support? If you were a delegate to the Constitutional Convention, what approach would you use to both win support for your views and also arrive at solutions with people who don't agree with you?**

The Constitutional Convention

Reading Preview

Objectives

In this section you will

- Discuss the debate among delegates over the kind of national government that was needed.
- Describe steps the delegates took in getting organized for the Constitutional Convention.
- Explain James Madison's plan for the national government.
- Understand the compromises made as the national government was created.
- Describe the powers granted to the executive and judicial branches.
- Recall what took place at the signing of the Constitution.

Taking Notes

Make a diagram like the one below. As you read this section, complete the diagram to show the sequence of events that took place at the Constitutional Convention.

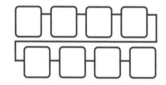

Key Terms

bicameral
Great Compromise
Three-Fifths Compromise

Main Idea

The delegates to the Constitutional Convention debated different arrangements of sharing power. After much debate, they created the United States Constitution.

Target Reading Skill

Use Context Clues You can sometimes figure out the meaning of an unfamiliar word by looking at clues in the context, or the surrounding words and sentences. As you read this section, use context clues to help you understand the meaning of words you do not know.

As you saw in Chapter 4, Shays' Rebellion raised doubts about the young government under the Articles of Confederation. With no power to tax or to enforce laws, Congress seemed unable to deal with the country's debts or to settle disputes between the states. Therefore, in 1787 Congress approved a convention "for the sole and express purpose of revising the Articles of Confederation."

Agreement and Disagreement

Even before the convention began, most delegates agreed that a national government was needed, not just an alliance of states. Also, they recognized the need to guard against abuse of power. Many delegates agreed with Montesquieu's principle of separation of powers among three branches of government: legislative, executive, and judicial. They also agreed that the government's power must be limited by dividing power between the states and the national government.

On other important questions, the delegates were sharply divided. How many representatives should each state have in the national government? How much power should the government be given? As the delegates packed their bags and left for Philadelphia, they braced themselves for a long convention.

✓ **Reading Check** On what issues did most delegates to the convention agree?

Getting Organized

The Constitutional Convention took place at the Pennsylvania State House, where the Declaration of Independence had been signed in July 1776. Summer in Philadelphia meant heat, humidity, and flies. Thomas Jefferson is said to have joked that the Declaration was signed quickly because flies were biting the signers. Actually, the Declaration had been signed only after long debate, and the convention of 1787 promised more of the same.

Washington Is Selected On Friday, May 25 1787, the convention began with the unanimous selection of George Washington as the presiding officer. The delegates realized, however, that it would take more than Washington's popularity to keep the convention on course. Without clear rules, the meeting could end in confusion, and the young country might fall apart.

Setting the Rules Several of the rules the convention adopted were aimed at keeping the discussions secret. It was feared that if their debates were reported in the newspapers, delegates would not feel free to change their minds. They might also fail to consider the good of all the states rather than just the interests of people back home. They thus decided that no one should remove notes from the meeting room. They also agreed that conversations about the proceedings should take place only inside the State House. Doors and windows were to be kept shut.

▼ Convention delegates meet in the Pennsylvania State House. George Washington (standing to the right) presides over the delegates.

James Madison (1751–1836) was born in Virginia. In 1786, he and Alexander Hamilton took the lead in calling for a Constitutional Convention. Madison was the author of the Virginia Plan and of much of the Constitution itself. After the convention Madison, Hamilton, and John Jay wrote articles collected in *The Federalist* supporting ratification of the Constitution. Serving in the first Congress, Madison was a leader in adopting the Bill of Rights. He was elected the fourth President of the U.S. in 1808 and served two terms, including during the War of 1812.

Citizenship

What role did Madison play at the Constitutional Convention?

Other Rules The delegates established other rules for voting procedures and behavior during meetings. Each state had one vote, regardless of its number of delegates. The debate rules allowed for each person's opinion to be heard. No one was to whisper, pass notes, or read while another delegate was speaking.

The delegates met six days a week from 10:00 a.m. until 4:00 p.m., without stopping for a meal. They also met with each other before and after the formal sessions. Although some of the 55 delegates left Philadelphia for brief times, an average of 40 were present on any given day.

✔ Reading Check **What decision did the delegates make about secrecy at the convention?**

Madison's Plan

As one of their first acts, the delegates voted not to revise the Articles of Confederation. Most of them believed that government under the Articles was so weak that a new plan was needed. Few delegates, though, had specific ideas about how to organize the new government.

One person who did have some definite ideas was Virginia's James Madison. Madison proposed a strong national government with legislative, executive, and judicial branches. The legislative branch would have two parts: a House of Representatives and a Senate. The people would elect members of the House directly. Members of the House would choose the senators. The number of seats in the House and the Senate would be based on each state's population.

Madison's proposal, known as the Virginia Plan, dominated discussion for the entire convention. Madison was calling for a strong national government to replace the alliance of independent states. Many of the delegates feared that under Madison's plan the national government would be too strong, snatching away important powers of the state legislatures. Many delegates from the smaller states, such as Delaware, Maryland, and New Jersey found Madison's plan to be too radical.

✔ Reading Check **How did Madison want the legislative branch to work under the Virginia Plan?**

Sharing Power

Many delegates feared that a strong national government might abuse its powers, treating the states in much the same way England had treated the colonies. Throughout much of the long, hot summer, delegates argued over how power would be shared between the national government and the states. Eventually, the delegates decided which powers would be given to the national government, which would be kept by the states, and which would be shared by both.

One issue was whether each state would have the power to either protect or abolish the slave trade. Several northern states wanted the national government to regulate all trade and to outlaw slavery. The southern states opposed this idea because their plantations depended upon slave labor. Eventually the delegates compromised because they saw the urgent need to form a new government. They agreed that the national government could regulate trade in general. It could not, however, interfere with the slave trade until 1808. Some delegates hoped that slavery would be abolished once a national government was created.

 Reading Check **What compromise was reached over slavery?**

Target Reading Skill
Use Context Clues Reread the sentence beginning "One issue was. . ." If you do not know what *abolish* means, consider words that act as context clues in the sentence: *Abolish* is the opposite of *protect*, so it means "to do away with."

Reaching Compromise

Reaching agreement on the powers of the national government was only part of the struggle. The delegates also had to decide how that government would be organized. Since the core of a representative government is the legislature, the delegates focused mainly on issues relating to representation in Congress.

The Virginia and New Jersey Plans The major question was how many representatives each state would have in the legislature. In Madison's Virginia Plan each state's population would determine the number of its representatives. The small states, however, objected that the large states would always outvote them. They supported a plan proposed by William Paterson of New Jersey. Known as the New Jersey Plan, it called for a one-house legislature in which each state would have an equal number of votes.

As supporters of each plan argued back and forth, tempers flared in the June heat. The convention seemed to be going nowhere.

The Great Compromise
Delegates finally compromised by combining aspects of both plans.
Analyze *What aspects of each plan ended up in the compromise?*

Virginia Plan
Two-house legislature; representation based on each state's population

Compromise
Two-house legislature; House of Representatives elected on basis of state population; two Senators for each state, regardless of population

New Jersey Plan
One-house legislature; representation equal for all states

From the Articles of Confederation to the Constitution

As this chart shows, the Constitution created a much stronger national government than had existed under the Articles of Confederation.

1. **Analyze** What are two powers that the national government gained under the Constitution?
2. **Apply** What are two powers that state governments lost under the Constitution?

Government under the Articles of Confederation 1781	Government under the Articles of Confederation 1789
A loose alliance of independent states	A national government representing all citizens
A one-house legislature	A two-house legislature
No executive or judicial branches	Executive and judicial branches established
Only states can tax	Congress also given the power to tax
States may coin money	Only the national government may coin money
No regulation of trade between states	National government regulates trade between states
Most power held by states	Power shared by national and state governments

▲
These colonial coins were made in the Massachusetts colony. Under the Articles of Confederation of 1789, however, only the national government could coin money.

The Great Compromise Realizing that they were making no progress, the delegates considered a plan proposed by Roger Sherman of Connecticut. Like the Virginia Plan, it called for a **bicameral**, or two-house, legislature. The House of Representatives would be elected on the basis of state population. In the Senate each state would have two senators, regardless of its population. This plan gave the large states more power in the House of Representatives, but each state had equal power in the Senate.

Although no one was completely satisfied with Sherman's plan, the delegates finally approved it by the narrow margin of one vote. The plan became known as the **Great Compromise** because each side gave up part of what it wanted in order to benefit all. If both sides had been unwilling to give and take, the convention probably would have failed.

Ensuring Fairness Although they had argued over the number of representatives, most delegates agreed that a two-house legislature was a good idea. It would help ensure that fair laws were passed because each law would have to be approved by both houses.

Jefferson was out of the country serving as ambassador to France at the time. He is later said to have asked Washington why the delegates had established a Senate in addition to a House of Representatives. Washington is said to have replied by asking, "Why do you pour your coffee into a saucer?"

"To cool it," Jefferson answered.

Washington replied, "Even so, we pour legislation into the senatorial saucer to cool it."

The Three-Fifths Compromise The Great Compromise kept the convention alive. It did not, however, settle the question of how to count state populations when determining representation in the House. Although slaves were treated as property, the southern states wanted to count each slave as a person when figuring state populations. The northern states objected that this would give the southern states more members in the House.

Once again the delegates compromised. This compromise, known as the **Three-Fifths Compromise**, counted each slave as three fifths of a person when a state's population was calculated.

✓ Reading Check   **What was the purpose of the Three-Fifths Compromise?**

Executive and Judicial Branches

Under the Articles of Confederation there had been no executive branch to enforce the laws and no judicial branch to interpret the laws. The delegates felt these branches were needed to provide for separation of powers.

The delegates decided that one President, rather than a committee of leaders, should be given executive power. They broadly defined the powers and duties of the President. In establishing the judicial branch, they created a Supreme Court that would have authority to interpret laws. It would be able to settle conflicts between states.

A Government by the People? The delegates generally agreed on the functions of each branch of government. They argued, however, about who should elect the President and the Congress. Should all the citizens vote in a direct election or just the members of the state legislatures?

Some delegates argued for direct election because it would take into account the opinions of a wide variety of people. Others, however, distrusted the people's judgment. Roger Sherman stated that average citizens "will never be sufficiently informed."

Voting and Elections As part of the Great Compromise, the delegates decided that all eligible citizens—that is, white men with property—would elect members of the House. State legislatures would select senators. A group of electors known as the Electoral College would select the President. Each state legislature could determine how that state's electors would be chosen.

✓ Reading Check   **What arguments were used against direct election of the President?**

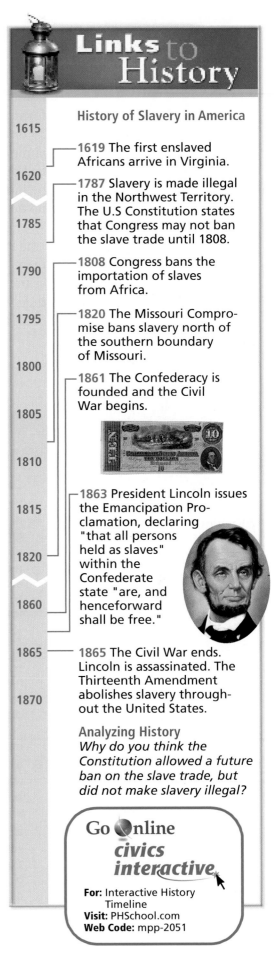

Links to History

History of Slavery in America

1615

1619 The first enslaved Africans arrive in Virginia.

1620

1787 Slavery is made illegal in the Northwest Territory. The U.S Constitution states that Congress may not ban the slave trade until 1808.

1785

1808 Congress bans the importation of slaves from Africa.

1790

1820 The Missouri Compromise bans slavery north of the southern boundary of Missouri.

1795

1800

1861 The Confederacy is founded and the Civil War begins.

1805

1810

1863 President Lincoln issues the Emancipation Proclamation, declaring "that all persons held as slaves" within the Confederate state "are, and henceforward shall be free."

1815

1820

1860

1865 The Civil War ends. Lincoln is assassinated. The Thirteenth Amendment abolishes slavery throughout the United States.

1865

1870

Analyzing History
Why do you think the Constitution allowed a future ban on the slave trade, but did not make slavery illegal?

Go Online
civics interactive

For: Interactive History Timeline
Visit: PHSchool.com
Web Code: mpp-2051

The Signing

Through the hot Philadelphia summer, the delegates took up resolution after resolution. Finally, in early September, a committee was named to arrange the articles and put the Constitution into its final form. In mid-September the convention finally drew to a close, with 39 delegates signing the Constitution on September 17, 1787. Benjamin Franklin was impressed that the debate and the compromises had produced such a strong plan. On the final day of the convention, he stated, "Thus I consent, Sir, to this Constitution because I expect no better, and because I am not sure that it is not the best."

The delegates to the Constitutional Convention are often called "the Framers" because they framed, or shaped, our form of government. Over the years changes have been made in the Constitution, as the Framers expected there would be. However, if they could see their work today, they would still recognize the basic plan of government they created over 200 years ago.

▲
Washington's chair at the Constitutional Convention

✓ Reading Check **How is our government today similar to the one outlined by the Framers of the Constitution?**

SECTION 1 Assessment

Key Terms

Use each of the key terms in a sentence that explains its meaning: bicameral, Great Compromise, Three-Fifths Compromise

Target Reading Skill

1. **Use Context Clues** Find the word *alliance* on page 114. Use context clues to find out its meaning. What clues helped you?

Comprehension and Critical Thinking

2. **a. Describe** What issues divided delegates before the convention?
b. Draw Inferences Why do you think delegates agreed about the separation of powers?

3. **a. Recall** Who was elected to be the presiding officer of the Constitutional Convention?
b. Predict What do you think would have happened if the

Convention did not adopt secrecy rules?

4. **a. Describe** Under the Virginia Plan, how were the number of seats each state would receive in the House and Senate determined?
b. Analyze Information Why were some states unhappy with the Virginia Plan?

5. **a. Explain** Why did many delegates fear the power of the national government?
b. Draw Conclusions How did the delegates limit the power of the national government?

6. **a. Describe** What was the New Jersey Plan?
b. Contrast How did Virginia and New Jersey Plans differ?

7. **a. Recall** Who was eligible to vote at the time of the convention?
b. Check Consistency How did the Electoral College show what the Framers thought

about the idea of people electing the President?

8. **a. Recall** When was the Constitution signed?
b. Recognize Points of View Why do you think Benjamin Franklin said about the Constitution "I am not sure that it is not the best"?

Writing Activity

You are a delegate to the Constitutional Convention. Write a journal entry about one of the issues dealt with at the Convention. Take a position on the issue, explain the opposing view, and describe the compromise that resulted.

TIP First identify a specific issue covered in this section. Then outline the opposing viewpoints and the compromise that resulted.

How to Analyze Public Documents

Public documents are valuable sources of information about history and government. Reading these documents helps us to understand what life was like and how people felt in a particular historical period.

Below is letter written by Benjamin Franklin. In 1785, a Massachusetts town that had been named in his honor asked him to donate a bell for the town's meeting house. The letter is his reply to the town's request.

My nephew. Mr. Williams, will have honor of delivering you this line [letter]. It is to request from you a list of a few good books to the value of about twenty-five pounds, such as are most proper to inculcate [teach] principles of sound religion and just government. A new town in the State of Massachusetts having done me the honor of naming itself after me, and proposing to build a steeple to their meeting house if I would give them a bell, I have advised sparing themselves the expense of a steeple at present, and that they would accept books instead of a bell, sense being preferable to sound. These are therefore intended as the commencement [beginning] of a little parochial [local] library for the use of a society of intelligent, respectable farmers such as our country people generally consist of. With the highest esteem and respect, I am ever, my dear friend, yours most affectionately,

B Franklin,

Learn the Skill

To analyze public documents, follow these steps:

❶ Identify the author or authors and the date of the document.

❷ Read the document carefully. Underline important parts. Look up unfamiliar words.

❸ Think about the author's point of view. Do some research to learn more about the historical issue(s) in the document.

Practice the Skill

❶ Read Franklin's letter. Restate the letter in your own words.

❷ What is Franklin's point of view about the town's request? What does he mean when he says that "sense" is preferable to "sound"?

Apply the Skill

❶ At the library, find and read two historical documents.

❷ Fill out a chart with the following columns: the date, author, purpose, and other historical information about each document.

❸ Present your findings to the class.

Go Online
civics interactive

For: Local Citizenship
Visit: PHSchool.com
Web Code: mpp-2052

The Struggle for Ratification

Reading Preview

Objectives
In this section you will
- Identify the views of the Federalists.
- Discuss the views of the Anti-Federalists.
- Explore the role of *The Federalist* in the debate over the Constitution.
- Learn the outcome of the struggle over ratification.

Key Terms
ratified   Anti-Federalists
Federalists

Main Idea
The campaign to ratify the Constitution pitted the Federalists, who favored a strong national government, against the Anti-Federalists, who feared the power of a national government.

Target Reading Skill
Interpret Nonliteral Meanings Nonliteral language uses images or comparisons to vividly communicate an idea. As your read, identify any images or comparisons that help to make a point in the text.

Taking Notes
Make a diagram like the one below. As you read the section, complete the diagram with arguments made by the Federalists and the Anti-Federalists.

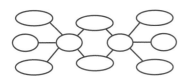

Federalists
Supported a strong national government to:
- *protect the states*
- *maintain order*
- *regulate trade*
- *guarantee rights of citizens*

Anti-Federalists
Supported a weak national government and strong state governments to:
- *allow politicians to be closer to their constituents*
- *protect people's liberties*
- *limit abuses of power by federal governments*

To go into effect, the Constitution had to be **ratified**, or approved, by at least nine state conventions. Only those states that ratified the new Constitution would be part of the new nation.

While all discussions had been secret during the Constitutional Convention, the issues were now out in the open. When the Constitution was published in newspapers, a storm of debate arose. People argued in churches, meetinghouses, roadside inns, and town squares. Some strongly supported the plan while others loudly opposed it.

The Federalists

The supporters of the Constitution were known as **Federalists** because they supported a strong federal, or national, government. The Federalists argued that individual states might not be able to protect themselves against foreign nations. A strong national government, they declared, would provide protection, maintain order, regulate trade, and guarantee the rights of citizens. It would also ensure that the nation's debts were paid and that American money had a stable value at home and abroad.

✔ Reading Check   **What position did Federalists take on the Constitution?**

◄
The Federalists and Anti-Federalists strongly disagreed about the power of the national government.

This 1788 cartoon was drawn during the battle over ratification. It took the approval of nine states to approve the Constitution. The writing in all capital letters is Latin and means "The Great Times Will Move Forward."

1. What do the pillars symbolize?
2. How does the Latin inscription relate to the subject of the cartoon?
3. What does the saying next to the hand mean?

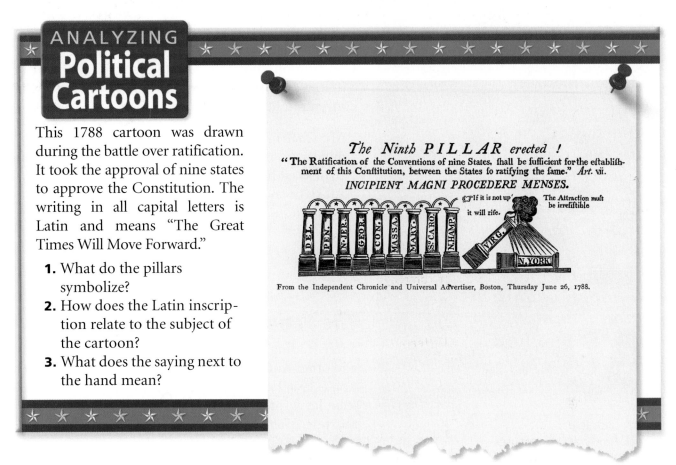

The Ninth PILLAR erected !
" The Ratification of the Conventions of nine States, fhall be fufficient for the eftablifhment of this Conftitution, between the States fo ratifying the fame." *Art.* vii.
INCIPIENT MAGNI PROCEDERE MENSES.

From the Independent Chronicle and Universal Advertiser, Boston, Thursday June 26, 1788.

The Anti-Federalists

The opponents of the Constitution were called **Anti-Federalists.** They feared that a strong central government would endanger the people's liberties. According to them, a central government that met so far away from local communities could not truly be called a government by consent of the people. The Anti-Federalists believed that representatives should meet in a location close to the people whose interests they sought to protect.

Laws "Necessary and Proper" One statement in the Constitution especially worried those who feared a strong national government. This was the statement giving Congress power to make laws "necessary and proper" to carry out its stated powers. Anti-Federalists argued that this wording left the door open to an abuse of power because term "necessary and proper" was open to interpretation. A strong national government, they said, could interpret "necessary and proper" as allowing laws that swallowed up state governments.

The Bill of Rights Issue The Anti-Federalists were also troubled by what was left out of the Constitution: a bill of rights. They feared that a strong national government might not respect citizens' rights. The Federalists responded that a bill of rights listing the rights of citizens was unnecessary because the Constitution already limited the government's powers.

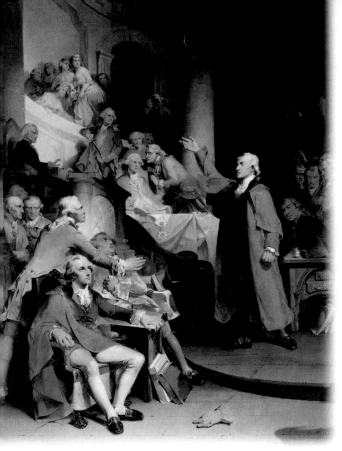

▲ Patrick Henry addresses a session of the Virginia House of Burgesses.

Revolutionary War hero Patrick Henry provided a strong Anti-Federalist voice in this debate. Calling the Constitution "horridly defective," he led the fight in Virginia against ratification. At the Virginia ratifying convention he warned:

"Mr. Chairman, the necessity for a bill of rights appears to me to be greater in this government than ever it was in any government before... All rights not expressly reserved to the people are relinquished [given up] to rulers."

✓ Reading Check **Why did Anti-Federalists favor a bill of rights?**

The Federalist Papers

Some leading Federalists responded to Patrick Henry and other Anti-Federalists in a series of pro-Constitution essays. James Madison, Alexander Hamilton, and John Jay wrote the essays, which were collected under the title *The Federalist*. The essays were written in 1787 and 1788. They were published in several newspapers in New York State. In all, there were 85 essays outlining the need for a new government and the form that this new government should take.

Alexander Hamilton argued that the Articles of Confederation were insufficient and a better form of government was needed. In one of his essays, he attempted to convince readers of the need for the Constitution:

"In the course of the preceding papers, I have endeavored, my fellow-citizens, to place before you, in a clear and convincing light, the importance of Union to your political safety and happiness. I have unfolded to you a complication of dangers to which you would be exposed, should you permit that sacred knot which binds the people of America together be severed or dissolved."

Target Reading Skill

Interpret Nonliteral Meanings Reread the sentence beginning "The Federalist also emphasized..." Notice the phrase "a weak, immature nation." Does the author mean that America was childish? If not, what do you think the nonliteral meaning of *immature* is?

Madison argued that the Constitution would protect the liberty of every citizen. With a national government representing all the people, no group would be able to ignore the rights of everyone else. Instead, to reach some of its goals, each group would have to compromise with other groups.

The Federalist also emphasized the problems America faced as a weak, immature nation on a large continent. If the states did not unite under a strong national government, the forces of Spain, England, and France might overpower them.

✓ Reading Check **What was the purpose of *The Federalist*?**

Ratification

The Federalists' effective campaign and the support of Washington and Franklin persuaded many Americans to support the new Constitution. Many more were won over after the Federalists agreed to propose a bill of rights if the Constitution was ratified. In several cases the Constitution was approved by only a few votes. Finally, in June 1788, the new government was officially born when New Hampshire became the ninth state to ratify the Constitution.

The government would not last long, however, without the support of the remaining four states, which included more then 40 percent of the nation's people. After bitter debate, Virginia ratified the document by only ten votes (89–79). New York approved by the slim margin of three votes (30–27). By the spring of 1790, all 13 states had ratified the new Constitution. The loose union of independent states had become the United States of America.

Ratifying the Constitution

State	Date of Ratification
Delaware	December 7, 1787
Pennsylvania	December 12, 1787
New Jersey	December 18, 1787
Georgia	January 2, 1788
Connecticut	January 9, 1788
Massachusetts	February 6, 1788
Maryland	April 28, 1788
South Carolina	May 23, 1788
New Hampshire	June 21, 1788
Virginia	June 25, 1788
New York	July 26, 1788
North Carolina	November 21, 1788*
Rhode Island	May 29, 1790

*Second vote; ratification was originally defeated on August 4, 1788, by a vote of 184-84

✓ **Reading Check** Why was it important that all 13 states ratify the Constitution?

SECTION 2 Assessment

Key Terms

Use each of the key terms in a sentence that explains its meaning: ratified, Federalists, Anti-Federalists

Target Reading Skill

1. **Interpret Nonliteral Meanings** Find the statement "A strong national government..." on page 121. In your own words, explain the meaning of this sentence.

Comprehension and Critical Thinking

2. **a. Explain** What reasons did the Federalists give for their position on ratification?
   b. Check Consistency How consistent were the Federalists' views with the original purpose of the convention?

3. **a. Recall** Why did Anti-Federalists oppose ratification of the Constitution?
   b. Support a Point of View Whose position on the Bill of Rights do you think was correct, the Federalists or the Anti-Federalists? Why?

4. **a. Describe** What was *The Federalist*?
   b. Evaluate Information How effective was Madison in responding to the concerns about liberty expressed by Patrick Henry and others?

5. **a. Recall** What decision by the Federalists helped the cause of ratification?
   b. Make Predictions What do you think would have happened if some states had not approved ratification?

Writing Activity

You are a citizen living in 1788. Write a letter to the editor of a newspaper that states your position on ratification and tries to win support for your point of view.

TIP

- Be sure to provide specific reasons that support your position.
- Think about the opposing position when stating your reasons.

The Supreme Law of the Land

Reading Preview

Objectives

In this section you will

- Learn the goals of our government stated in the Preamble to the Constitution.
- Explore the Articles of the Constitution.
- Analyze the principles of limited government.

Taking Notes

Make a diagram like the one below. As you read this section, complete the diagram with the main ideas and supporting details that describe the structure of the U.S. government.

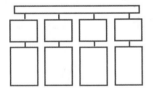

Key Terms

amendments
federalism
concurrent powers

reserved powers
checks and balances
impeach

Main Idea

The Constitution establishes a federal government, protects the rights of citizens, and provides general rules that government must follow.

Target Reading Skill

Use Context Clues You can sometimes clarify the meaning of a word by using context clues. Context clues are the surrounding words, phrase, and sentences. As you read this section, use context clues to help you clarify the meanings of unknown words.

The Constitution establishes our form of government, a republic. As you recall from Chapter 4, a republic is a government in which citizens elect their representatives. As the "supreme law of the land," the Constitution protects the rights of citizens by providing general rules that the national government and the state governments must follow.

The Goals of Our Government

The Constitution begins by stating the goals of our government. In the Preamble, or introduction, the Framers listed six goals:

To Form a More Perfect Union Framers were seeking a better government than the one under the Articles of Confederation. Their main concern was to unite the 13 separate states under an effective national government.

Establish Justice We have a legal system that seeks fair ways to settle disputes between individuals, between individuals and the government, between states, and between the national and state governments.

Insure Domestic Tranquility Our government tries to establish a peaceful society in which people are protected from the unlawful acts of others.

Provide for the Common Defense Our government seeks to protect citizens from attacks by other countries.

Promote the General Welfare Our government tries to create conditions that will benefit all Americans.

Secure the Blessings of Liberty to Ourselves and Our Posterity Our government seeks to give people the freedom to choose where they work, where they live, what they believe, and who shall represent them in government. However, our liberty as Americans does not leave us free to do whatever we want. Our actions should not interfere with the rights of others. The government protects the liberty of all citizens. It also protects future Americans—our posterity, or descendants.

✓ Reading Check **Which goal of government pledges to protect our basic freedoms?**

The Articles

Following the Preamble, the Framers laid out the plan for our government. This plan is organized into seven parts called articles. The articles are divided into subsections called clauses. Some of the key ideas in the articles are described below.

Article 1: The Legislative Branch Article 1 describes the organization and powers of the national legislature, called the Congress of the United States. Congress is divided into two houses: the House of Representatives and the Senate.

The most important power of Congress is to make laws. A proposed law, called a bill, must gain a majority vote in both houses of Congress before it goes to the President for approval. If the President signs the bill, it becomes law. The President may veto, or reject, the bill. However, Congress has the final word. A vetoed bill can still become a law if Congress votes on it again, with two thirds of the members of each house approving it.

At the Capitol
Senators John McCain of Arizona (left) and Russell Feingold of Wisconsin (right) walk down the steps of the Senate. **Analyze** *Which article of the Constitution describes the role of Senators?*

Target Reading Skill

Use Context Clues Sometimes the context will restate the meaning of a word. Reread the first sentence on this page. In this sentence, the context shows that the word *delegated* means *assigned*.

The powers assigned to Congress are known as delegated powers. Most of these delegated powers—such as the power to coin money, to declare war, and to regulate trade—are specifically listed in Article 1, Section 8. However, not all of Congress's powers are listed. Congress may also make laws that are "necessary and proper" for carrying out the powers that are listed.

By using the words "necessary and proper," the Framers wanted to give the government flexibility to carry out its work and change with the times. For this reason the "necessary and proper clause" is sometimes called "the elastic clause." This flexible wording troubled the Anti-Federalists and continues to bother Americans who worry that Congress might abuse its powers. It is important to note, however, that Article 1 also limits the government's power by stating which actions Congress may not take.

Article 2: The Executive Branch The powers of the legislative branch are shared by hundreds of members of Congress. The Framers gave the power of the executive branch, however, to one person—the President. By establishing the office of President, they created something very new in the world: a leader who has some of the strengths of a monarch, but whose authority is based on the consent of the people. In order to continue in office after their four-year term, both the President and the Vice-President have to be re-elected.

The painful memory of the colonies' experience with King George of England was still fresh in the Framers' minds. To avoid having another monarch, they made it clear that the President's job is to execute, or carry out, the laws—not to make them. They also put limits on the power of the President. For example, the President is the head of the armed forces, but only Congress can declare war. The President may make treaties, but they are only binding if approved by the Senate. The President may also nominate judges, but the Senate has the right to reject the President's nominees. The President can appoint ambassadors to foreign countries. However, the Senate must approve these appointments as well.

The Constitution is far less specific on the office of President than it is on the national legislature. There had never been a President before. Most delegates to the Constitutional Convention believed that George Washington would be elected as the first President and that he could best create the office, setting an example for later Presidents.

Presidential Power
The Framers limited the power of the President. They determined that the responsibility of the executive branch is to execute laws, not make them. Here President George W. Bush authorizes a bill. **Demonstrate Reasoned Judgement** *Why would the Framers want to limit the President's power?*

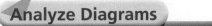

Sharing the Power

Powers of the National Government

Maintain army and navy

Declare war

Coin money

Regulate trade between states and with foreign nations

Make all laws necessary for carrying out delegated powers

Shared Powers

Enforce laws

Establish courts

Borrow money

Protect the safety of the people

Build roads

Collect taxes

Powers of the State Governments

Conduct elections

Establish schools

Regulate businesses within a state

Establish local governments

Regulate marriages

Assume other powers not given to the national government or denied to the states

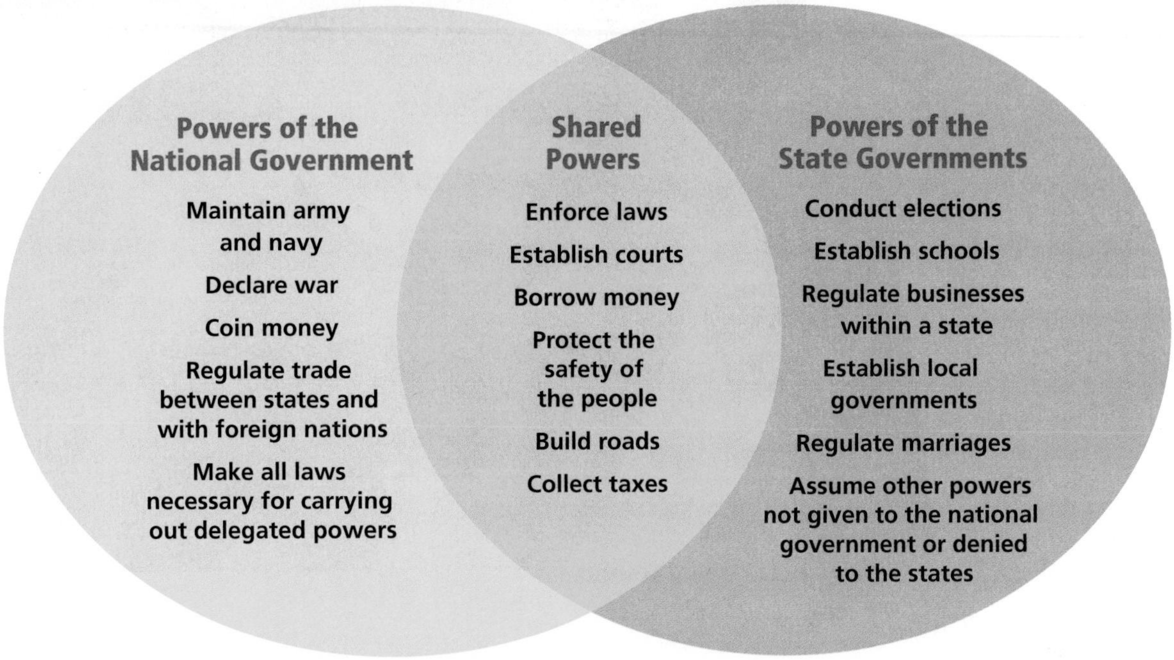

Under the Constitution, some powers are shared by the national and state governments.

1. **Analyze** Which government is responsible for regulating trade with foreign nations?

2. **Apply** If certain powers are not given to the national government or denied to state governments, to which government do they belong?

Article 3: The Judicial Branch Although each state had its own courts, the Framers wanted a national court system to settle disputes between states. The Framers agreed that neither Congress nor the President should control the national courts. Thus the President nominates judges, but the Senate must approve the nominations. Once appointed, judges may serve for life as long as they demonstrate "good behavior."

One of the most important contributions of the Framers was the creation of the Supreme Court. This court has the final say in all cases involving the Constitution. Important cases on which lower courts disagree can be appealed to the Supreme Court for a final decision, thus ensuring that legal issues affecting the nation will not be left unsettled.

Article 4: The States To ensure that the rights of the states are respected, each state must honor the laws of other states. A New York marriage license, for instance, is valid in any other state. Requiring states to respect each other's laws helps preserve each state's rights and reduces the possibility of conflict between states.

Constitutional Amendments
Franklin Delano Roosevelt successfully ran for a third term in 1940 and a fourth term in 1944. Many people became very concerned with limiting a President's terms in office. As a result, the 22nd Amendment was passed in 1951, limiting a President to two terms.
Draw Inferences *Why do you think people wanted to limit the amount of time a President could serve?*

Article 5: Amending the Constitution The Framers knew that future Americans might want to change the Constitution. Therefore, they included in the Constitution instructions for making **amendments**, or changes. To ensure that each change reflects the will of the people, three fourths of the states must approve an amendment.

Article 6: The Supremacy of the Constitution Since both state and national governments may pass laws, the Framers wanted to avoid any uncertainty about which laws take priority. Therefore, Article 6 requires officials in state and national government to take an oath to support the Constitution as "the supreme law of the land." No state law may violate the Constitution. Also, if a state law conflicts with a federal—or national—law, the federal law takes priority.

Article 7: Ratification The last article of the Constitution establishes the procedure for ratification, or approval, of the Constitution.

Amendments to the Constitution When you read the Constitution, you will see that a series of amendments follow the seven articles. The first ten amendments, ratified in 1791, are called the Bill of Rights and were added in response to the concerns of the Anti-Federalists. Since the approval of the Bill of Rights, only seventeen other amendments have been added. Clearly, the Constitution has stood the test of time.

✔ Reading Check **Summarize the duties of the legislative, the executive, and the judicial branches of government.**

Limited Government

The Constitution creates a government with powers limited by consent of the people. It is based on the idea of popular sovereignty—letting the people rule. Three main principles limit the government's power: federalism, separation of powers, and checks and balances.

Federalism The Constitution establishes a principle of **federalism**, the division of power between the states and the federal, or national, government. Under federalism, some powers belong only to the national government, some powers belong only to the states, and some are shared by both. The diagram on page 127 shows how the powers are divided and shared.

The delegated powers are those that belong to Congress. A number of these powers, such as the power to coin money or declare war, are denied to the states.

The **concurrent powers** are powers shared by the federal and state governments. For instance, the states as well as the federal government can collect taxes, establish courts, and borrow money.

The **reserved powers** are powers that the Constitution neither gives to Congress nor denies to the states. For example, two of the powers reserved to the states are the authority to establish schools and to form police organizations.

By dividing power between the federal and state governments, the system of federalism gives the federal government the authority it needs while helping to protect each state's rights. This system also allows the federal government to deal with issues affecting all citizens, while each state government can better serve the particular needs of its people.

Civics and Economics

The Census The U.S. Census Bureau does more than just count the population every ten years. It analyzes and processes the data it gathers. This data is important for many social institutions and businesses. School officials use the information to predict how many children will be entering their schools. Social service agencies use the data to determine what services people will need. Government and private businesses can make predictions about such things as energy and transportation needs. Marketers learn where their customers are located.

Analyzing Economics
Why do you think the government, rather than private business, has the responsibility for counting the population every ten years?

Highway projects, such as this overpass in Louisiana, are one example of powers shared by state and national governments.
▼

Checks and Balances

Under the system of checks and balances, each branch of govern-ment limits the power of the other two branches.

1. Which branch of government has the power to declare laws unconstitutional?
2. In what ways does the executive branch limit the power of the legislative branch?

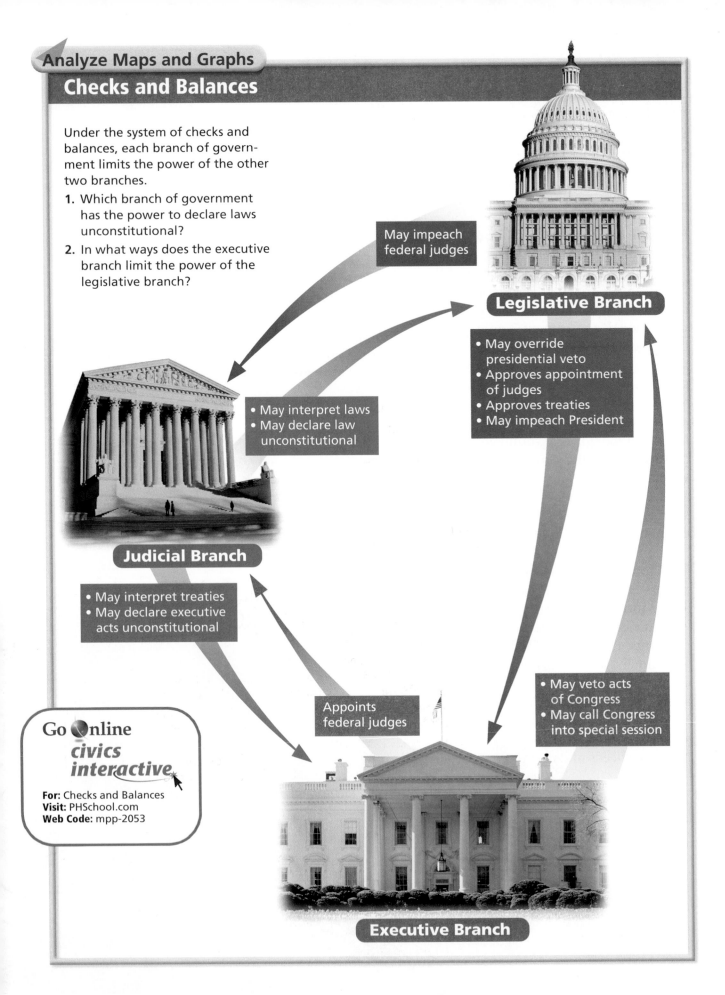

May impeach federal judges

Legislative Branch

- May override presidential veto
- Approves appointment of judges
- Approves treaties
- May impeach President

- May interpret laws
- May declare law unconstitutional

Judicial Branch

- May interpret treaties
- May declare executive acts unconstitutional

Appoints federal judges

- May veto acts of Congress
- May call Congress into special session

Executive Branch

Go Online
civics
interactive

For: Checks and Balances
Visit: PHSchool.com
Web Code: mpp-2053

Separation of Powers Under our Constitution, power is not only divided between the state and federal governments; it is also divided within the federal government. From the previous chapter, you will remember that the concept of separation of powers in the work of John Locke and Montesquieu was a major influence on the Framers. The Framers wanted to prevent the abuse of power which led the colonies to fight for independence from Great Britain. Dividing power among the executive, legislative, and judicial branches helps prevent any one branch from abusing its power.

Checks and Balances The Constitution protects against abuse of power in the federal government through checks and balances. The system of **checks and balances** gives each branch of government ways to limit the powers of the other two. This system is illustrated on the opposite page.

For instance, the President can check the actions of Congress by vetoing bills that are not in the best interest of the nation. Meanwhile, the judicial branch checks the power of the other two branches by determining whether laws passed by Congress or actions taken by the President are constitutional. The House can **impeach**, or accuse, the President or other high officials of serious wrongdoing. If found guilty in a trial in the Senate, the official will be removed from office. By checking and balancing each other, the three branches of government ensure that they work together for the welfare of citizens.

✔ Reading Check   **Why are checks and balances important to the American system of government?**

SECTION 3 Assessment

Key Terms

Use each of the key terms in a sentence that explains its meaning: amendments, federalism, concurrent powers, reserved powers, checks and balances, impeach

Target Reading Skill

1. **Use Context Clues** Find the word *posterity* on page 125. Use the context to find out what *posterity* means.

Comprehension and Critical Thinking

2. **a. Recall** What are the six goals of government stated in the Preamble to the Constitution?

   b. Compare Compare the goals "insure domestic tranquility" and "provide for the common defense." In what way are these goals similar?

3. **a. Explain** What is the "elastic clause"?

   b. Draw Conclusions Given that a national court system was created in the Constitution, why was the creation of the Supreme Court so important?

4. **a. Describe** What three principles limit the power of the government?

   b. Synthesize Information How do these principles work together to restrict the government's power?

Writing Activity

You are an editorial writer on a newspaper in 1788. Write an editorial about one part of the Constitution in which you analyze its strengths and weaknesses. Include a prediction about what kind of government you think will result.

Go Online
PHSchool.com
For: Writing Activity
Visit: PHSchool.com
Web Code: mpa-2053

Analyzing Primary Sources

To gain an accurate understanding of important events, it is helpful to analyze the words of people who were present when the events took place. Primary sources are accounts of past events by people who observed or were directly involved in the events being described. They may include letters, journal entries, speeches, and even photographs.

The excerpt below is part of a speech given by Benjamin Franklin during the Constitutional Convention of 1787. In his speech, the 81-year-old Franklin urged his fellow delegates to forget the bitter quarrels and debates of the previous months and to sign the Constitution that had finally been finished.

> Mr. President
>
> I agree to this Constitution with all its faults, if they are such, because I think a general Government necessary for us. . . . I doubt too whether any other Convention we can obtain may be able to make a better Constitution. For when you assemble a number of men to have the advantage of their joint wisdom, you inevitably assemble with these men, all their prejudices, their passions, their errors of opinion, their local interests, and their selfish views. From such an Assembly can a perfect production be expected? It therefore astonishes me, Sir, to find this system approaching as near to perfection as it does . . . . Thus I consent, Sir, to this Constitution because I expect no better, and because I am not sure, that it is not the best. . . .
>
> On the whole, Sir, I cannot help expressing a wish that every member of this Convention who may still have objections to it, would with me, on this occasion doubt a little of his own infallibility—and to make manifest our unanimity, put his name to this instrument.

Learn the Skill

To analyze a primary source:

1 **Identify the writer.** Knowing who wrote a document helps you evaluate the information presented and the point of view.

2 **Identify the context.** When was the document produced? What purpose did it serve? Under what circumstances was it written?

3 **Identify the main idea.** What is the main idea of the document?

4 **Look for words that indicate the point of view.** Find the words that express emotion. They can tell you how the writer feels about the subject matter.

5 **Analyze.** What conclusions can you draw about the writer and the information given?

Practice the Skill

Read the primary source above and answer these questions:

1 What does the speech tell you about Benjamin Franklin and his view of the Constitution?

2 Why did Franklin urge his fellow delegates to join him in signing the Constitution?

3 What does Franklin's speech tell you about the Constitutional Convention of 1787?

Apply the Skill

Use the steps presented in Learn the Skill to analyze another primary source about the Constitution, such as an excerpt from The Federalist Papers or the transcripts of the Congressional debates of 1787.

Chapter Summary

Section 1
The Constitutional Convention
(pages 112–118)

- Delegates to the Constitutional Convention disagreed about how much power the national government should have.

- The Virginia Plan called for representation in Congress to be based on the states' populations. The New Jersey Plan called for equal representation from each state.

- Delegates were concerned that the new national government would have too much power. They divided powers between the federal government and the states. They split the federal government into three branches.

- The Great Compromise created a bicameral legislature that based representation in the House of Representatives on population. It also gave each state equal representation in the Senate.

- The Three-Fifths Compromise counted a slave as three fifths of a person when calculating a state's population.

- The Framers of the Constitution signed the document on September 17, 1787.

Section 2
The Struggle for Ratification
(pages 120–123)

- The Federalists favored the Constitution. The Anti-Federalists opposed it.

- The supporters of ratification put forth their views in The Federalist.

- The Federalists' promise to add a bill of rights helped persuade people to support the Constitution. The Constitution was ratified by all 13 states by 1790.

Section 3
The Supreme Law of the Land
(pages 124–131)

- The Constitution states the structure of our government. It also explains how amendments can be added to the Constitution.

- Three main principles in the Constitution limit the government's power: federalism, separation of powers, and checks and balances. An example of checks and balances is the power of Congress to impeach the President.

- Under federalism, concurrent powers are shared by the federal and state governments. Reserved powers are neither given to Congress nor denied to the states.

Copy the chart below and use it to help you summarize the chapter:

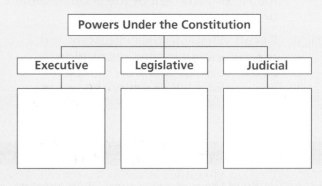

Review and Assessment Continued

Go Online
PHSchool.com
For: Self-Test
Visit: PHSchool.com
Web Code: mpa-2054

Reviewing Key Terms

Fill in each blank with one of the key terms from the list below.

checks and balances   concurrent powers
amendments   reserved powers
bicameral   federalism
Anti-Federalists   ratified
Federalists

1. The _____ favored ratification of the Constitution.

2. Changes made to the Constitution are called _____.

3. The Constitution created a _____ legislature.

4. Powers shared by the federal government and the states are _____.

5. The ability of one branch of government to limit the power of the other two branches is called _____.

6. The _____ argued against ratification of the Constitution.

7. To be approved, the Constitution needed to be _____ by at least nine states.

8. The division of power between the national government and the states is called _____.

9. _____ are powers the Constitution does not give to the federal government and does not deny to the states.

Comprehension and Critical Thinking

10. a. **Explain** Explain the Virginia Plan and the New Jersey Plan.
    b. **Synthesize Information** What did each side win in the Great Compromise?
    c. **Demonstrate Reasoned Judgment** Did the Great Compromise reflect the idea of government by the people? Why or why not?

11. a. **Recall** What was the "necessary and proper" clause in the Constitution?
    b. **Draw Conclusions** How did the absence of a bill of rights add to Anti-Federalists' fears about the Constitution?

    c. **Evaluate Information** Were the Anti-Federalists correct in their concern about the "necessary and proper" clause? Explain.

12. a. **Describe** Describe at least two goals of government stated in the Preamble to the Constitution.
    b. **Analyze Primary Sources** What are the guarantees and limits of liberty in the last goal of the Preamble?
    c. **Support a Point of View** How successful is the Constitution at meeting the goals set forth in the Preamble? Explain.

Activities

13. **Skills** Read the passage at right, then answer these questions. **a.** What is the main idea of Jefferson's letter to Madison? **b.** What reason does Jefferson give for including a bill of rights in the Constitution?

14. **Writing** The Great Compromise was a key event at the Constitutional Convention. Write a short essay on the importance of compromise in making a democracy like that of the United States' work.

" The general voice from north to south... calls for a bill of rights. It seems pretty generally understood that this should go to juries, habeas corpus, standing armies, printing, religion and monopolies. I conceive there may be difficulty in finding general modifications of these suited to the habits of all the States. But if such cannot be found, then it is better to establish [them] . . . in all cases . . . than not to do it in any. The few cases wherein these things may do evil cannot be weighed against the multitude wherein the want of them will do evil. "

—Thomas Jefferson to James Madison, 1788

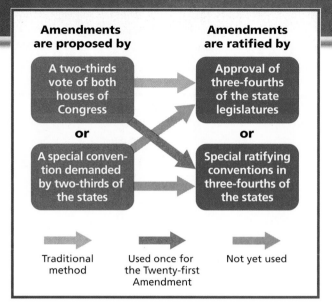

Amendments are proposed by | Amendments are ratified by

A two-thirds vote of both houses of Congress → Approval of three-fourths of the state legislatures

or | or

A special convention demanded by two-thirds of the states → Special ratifying conventions in three-fourths of the states

Traditional method — Used once for the Twenty-first Amendment — Not yet used

15. **Active Citizen** Choose a problem that is of public concern for your community or for the nation. Work with a classmate to outline different views of the issue. Then work together to write a plan that represents a compromise between the differing views.

16. **Math Practice** In 1790, Virginia had a population of about 700,000, and slightly more than 340,000 people lived in New York. Approximately how many times larger was Virginia's population than New York's?

17. **Civics and Economics** Find an article in a newspaper that deals with an action taken on economic activity by the government. Identify the branch of government taking the action. Which article in the Constitution describes the powers of that branch?

18. **Analyzing Visuals** The diagram above shows the different ways that the Constitution may be amended. By which method was the Twenty-first Amendment proposed and ratified?

Standardized Test Prep

Test-Taking Tips

Some questions on standardized tests ask you to analyze information in a table. Study the table. Then follow the tips to answer the sample question.

TIP When analyzing a table, be sure to read the headings for each column carefully.

Delegates to the Constitutional Convention		
State	Number Who Attended	Number Who Signed Constitution
New Hampshire	2	2
Massachusetts	4	2
Rhode Island	0	0
Connecticut	3	2
New York	3	1
New Jersey	5	4
Pennsylvania	8	8
Delaware	5	5
Maryland	5	3
Virginia	7	3
North Carolina	5	3
South Carolina	4	4
Georgia	4	2

1. How many delegates from Virginia and Pennsylvania signed the Constitution?
   A 7
   B 10
   C 11
   D 15

   The correct answer is **C**. Note that the question asks you to find the number of delegates in Virginia and Pennsylvania that *signed* the Constitution.

2. How many delegates attended the convention from Maryland, Virginia, North Carolina, South Carolina, and Georgia?
   A 25
   B 22
   C 19
   D 15

The Constitution of the United States

A Note on the Text of the Constitution

The complete text of the Constitution, including amendments, appears on the pages that follow. Spelling, capitalization, and punctuation have been modernized, and headings have been added. Portions of the Constitution altered by later amendments or that no longer apply are printed in blue. Commentary appears in the right column of each page.

> **The Preamble** The Preamble describes the purpose of the government set up by the Constitution. Americans expect their government to defend justice and liberty, and provide peace and safety from foreign enemies.

Preamble

We the people of the United States, in order to form a more perfect union, establish justice, insure domestic tranquillity, provide for the common defense, promote the general welfare, and secure the blessings of liberty to ourselves and our posterity, do ordain and establish this Constitution for the United States of America.

Article I ★ Legislative Branch

Section 1. Legislative Powers; The Congress

> **Section 1** The Constitution gives Congress the power to make laws. Congress is divided into the Senate and the House of Representatives.

All legislative powers herein granted shall be vested in a Congress of the United States, which shall consist of a Senate and House of Representatives.

Section 2. House of Representatives

1. Election of Members The House of Representatives shall be composed of members chosen every second year by the people of the several states, and the electors in each state shall have the qualifications requisite for electors of the most numerous branch of the state legislature.

2. Qualifications No person shall be a representative who shall not have attained to the age of twenty-five years, and been seven years a citizen of the United States, and who shall not, when elected, be an inhabitant of that state in which he shall be chosen.

3. Apportionment Representatives and direct taxes shall be apportioned among the several states which may be included within this Union, according to their respective numbers, which shall be determined by adding to the whole number of free persons, including those bound to service for a term of years and excluding Indians not taxed, three fifths of all other persons. The actual enumeration shall be made within three years after the first meeting of the Congress of the United States, and within every subsequent term of ten years, in such manner as they shall by law direct. The number of representatives shall not exceed one for every thirty thousand, but each state shall have at least one representative; and until such enumeration shall be made, the state of New Hampshire shall be entitled to choose three, Massachusetts eight, Rhode Island and Providence Plantations one, Connecticut five, New York six, New Jersey four, Pennsylvania eight, Delaware one, Maryland six, Virginia ten, North Carolina five, South Carolina five, and Georgia three.

4. Filling Vacancies When vacancies happen in the representation from any state, the executive authority thereof shall issue writs of election to fill such vacancies.

5. Officers; Impeachment The House of Representatives shall choose their Speaker and other officers; and shall have the sole power of impeachment.

Section 3. Senate

1. Composition; Term The Senate of the United States shall be composed of two senators from each state chosen by the legislature thereof, for six years, and each senator shall have one vote.

2. Classification; Filling Vacancies Immediately after they shall be assembled in consequence of the first election, they shall be divided as equally as may be into three classes. The seats of the senators of the first class shall be vacated at the expiration of the second year, of the second class at the expiration of the fourth year, and of the third class at the expiration of the sixth year, so that one third may be chosen every second year; and if vacancies happen by resignation, or otherwise, during the recess of the legislature of any State, the executive thereof may make temporary appointments until the next meeting of the legislature, which shall then fill such vacancies.

Clause 1 *Electors* refers to voters. Members of the House of Representatives are elected every two years. Any citizen allowed to vote for members of the larger house of the state legislature can also vote for members of the House.

Clause 3 The number of representatives each state elects is based on its population. An *enumeration*, or census, must be taken every 10 years to determine population. Today, the number of representatives in the House is fixed at 435. Clause 3 contains the Three-Fifths Compromise worked out at the Constitutional Convention. *Persons bound to service* meant indentured servants. *All other persons* meant slaves. All free people in a state were counted. However, only three fifths of the slaves were included in the population count. This three-fifths clause became meaningless when slaves were freed by the Thirteenth Amendment.

Clause 4 *Executive authority* means the governor of a state. If a member of the House leaves office before his or her term ends, the governor must call a special election to fill the seat.

Clause 5 The House elects a Speaker. Also, only the House has the power to *impeach*, or accuse, a federal official of wrongdoing.

Clause 2 Every two years, one third of the senators run for reelection. The Seventeenth Amendment changed the way of filling *vacancies*, or empty seats. Today, the governor of a state must choose a senator to fill a vacancy that occurs between elections.

Clause 5 *Pro tempore* means temporary. The Senate chooses one of its members to serve as president pro tempore when the Vice President is absent.

Clause 6 The Senate acts as a jury if the House impeaches a federal official. The Chief Justice of the Supreme Court presides if the President is on trial. Two thirds of all senators present must vote for conviction, or finding the accused guilty. No President has ever been convicted. The House impeached President Andrew Johnson in 1868, but the Senate acquitted him of the charges. In 1998–99, President Bill Clinton became the second President to be impeached and acquitted.

Clause 1 Each state legislature can decide when and how congressional elections take place, but Congress can overrule these decisions. In 1842, Congress required each state to set up congressional districts with one representative elected from each district. In 1872, Congress decided that congressional elections must be held in every state on the same date in even-numbered years.

Clause 1 Each house decides whether a member has the qualifications for office set by the Constitution. A *quorum* is the smallest number of members who must be present for business to be conducted. Each house can set its own rules about absent members.

Portions of the Constitution altered by later amendments or that no longer apply are printed in blue.

3. Qualifications No person shall be a senator who shall not have attained to the age of thirty years, and been nine years a citizen of the United States, and who shall not, when elected, be an inhabitant of that state for which he shall be chosen.

4. President of the Senate The Vice President of the United States shall be president of the Senate, but shall have no vote, unless they be equally divided.

5. Other Officers The Senate shall choose their other officers, and also a president pro tempore, in the absence of the Vice President, or when he shall exercise the office of the President of the United States.

6. Impeachment Trials The Senate shall have the sole power to try all impeachments. When sitting for that purpose, they shall be on oath or affirmation. When the President of the United States is tried, the Chief Justice shall preside; and no person shall be convicted without the concurrence of two thirds of the members present.

7. Penalty on Conviction Judgment in cases of impeachment shall not extend further than to removal from office, and disqualification to hold and enjoy any office of honor, trust or profit under the United States: but the party convicted shall nevertheless be liable and subject to indictment, trial, judgment, and punishment, according to law.

Section 4. Elections and Meetings

1. Election of Congress The times, places, and manner of holding elections for senators and representatives, shall be prescribed in each state by the legislature thereof; but the Congress may at any time by law make or alter such regulations, except as to the places of choosing senators.

2. Sessions The Congress shall assemble at least once in every year, and such meeting shall be on the first Monday in December, unless they shall by law appoint a different day.

Section 5. Legislative Proceedings

1. Organization Each house shall be the judge of the elections, returns, and qualifications of its own members, and a majority of each shall constitute a quorum to do business; but a smaller number may adjourn from day to day, and may be authorized to compel the attendance of absent members, in such manner, and under such penalties, as each house may provide.

2. Rules Each house may determine the rules of its proceedings, punish its members for disorderly behavior, and with the concurrence of two thirds, expel a member.

3. Record Each house shall keep a journal of its proceedings, and from time to time publish the same, excepting such parts as may in their judgment require secrecy; and the yeas and nays of the members of either house on any question shall, at the desire of one fifth of those present, be entered on the journal.

4. Adjournment Neither house, during the session of Congress, shall, without the consent of the other, adjourn for more than three days, nor to any other place than that in which the two houses shall be sitting.

Section 6. Compensation, Immunities, and Disabilities of Members

1. Salaries; Immunities The senators and representatives shall receive a compensation for their services, to be ascertained by law, and paid out of the Treasury of the United States. They shall in all cases, except treason, felony, and breach of the peace, be privileged from arrest during their attendance at the session of their respective houses, and in going to and returning from the same; and for any speech or debate in either house, they shall not be questioned in any other place.

2. Restrictions on Other Employment No senator or representative shall, during the time for which he was elected, be appointed to any civil office under the authority of the United States, which shall have been created, or the emoluments whereof shall have been increased during such time; and no person holding any office under the United States shall be a member of either house during his continuance in office.

Section 7. Revenue Bills, President's Veto

1. Revenue Bills All bills for raising revenue shall originate in the House of Representatives; but the Senate may propose or concur with amendments as on other bills.

2. How a Bill Becomes Law; the Veto Every bill which shall have passed the House of Representatives and the Senate shall, before it become a law, be presented to the President of the United States; if he approve, he shall sign it, but if not, he shall return it, with his objections, to that house in which it shall have originated, who shall enter the objections at large on their journal, and proceed to reconsider it. If after such reconsideration two thirds of that house shall agree to pass the bill, it shall be sent, together with the objections, to the other house, by which it shall likewise be reconsidered, and if approved by two thirds of that house, it shall become a law. But in all such cases the votes of both houses shall be determined by yeas and nays, and the names of the persons voting for and against the bill shall be entered on the journal of each house respectively. If any bill shall not be returned by the President within ten days (Sundays excepted) after it shall have been presented to him, the same shall be a law, in like manner as if he had signed it, unless the Congress by their adjournment prevent its return, in which case it shall not be a law.

3. Resolutions Passed by Congress Every order, resolution, or vote to which the concurrence of the Senate and House of Representatives may be necessary (except on a question of adjournment) shall be presented to the President of the United States; and before the same shall take effect, shall be approved by him, or being disapproved by him, shall be repassed by two thirds of the Senate and House of Representatives, according to the rules and limitations prescribed in the case of a bill.

Clause 4 Neither house can *adjourn*, or stop meeting, for more than three days unless the other house approves. Both houses must meet in the same city.

Clause 1 Congress decides the salary for its members. While Congress is in session, a member is free from arrest in civil cases and cannot be sued for anything he or she says on the floor of Congress. This allows for freedom of debate. However, a member can be arrested for a criminal offense.

Clause 2 *Emolument* means salary. A member of Congress cannot hold another federal office during his or her term. A former member of Congress cannot hold an office created while he or she was in Congress. An official in another branch of government cannot serve at the same time in Congress.

Clause 1 *Revenue* is money raised by the government through taxes. Tax bills must be introduced in the House. The Senate, however, can make changes in tax bills.

Clause 2 A *bill*, or proposed law, that is passed by a majority of the House and Senate is sent to the President. If the President signs the bill, it becomes law.

A bill can also become law without the President's signature. The President can refuse to act on a bill. If Congress is in session at the time, the bill becomes law 10 days after the President receives it.

The President can veto, or reject, a bill by sending it back to the house where it was introduced. Or if the President refuses to act on a bill and Congress adjourns within 10 days, then the bill dies. This way of killing a bill without taking action is called the *pocket veto*.

Congress can override the President's veto if each house of Congress passes the bill again by a two-thirds vote.

Congress's power is expressed directly in the Constitution. Article I, Section 8 lists most of the expressed powers of Congress. Numbered from 1 to 18, these powers are also known as enumerated powers.

Clause 1 *Duties* are tariffs. *Imposts* are taxes in general. *Excises* are taxes on the production or sale of certain goods.

Clause 4 *Naturalization* is the process whereby a foreigner becomes a citizen. *Bankruptcy* is the condition in which a person or business cannot pay its debts. Congress has the power to pass laws on these two issues. The laws must be the same in all parts of the country.

Clause 6 *Counterfeiting* is the making of imitation money. *Securities* are bonds. Congress can make laws to punish counterfeiters.

Clause 11 Only Congress can declare war. Declarations of war are granted at the request of the President. *Letters of marque and reprisal* were documents issued by a government allowing merchant ships to arm themselves and attack ships of an enemy nation. They are no longer issued.

Clauses 15, 16 The *militia* is a body of citizen soldiers. Congress can call up the militia to put down rebellions or fight foreign invaders. Each state has its own militia, today called the National Guard. Normally, the militia is under the command of a state's governor. However, it can be placed under the command of the President.

Portions of the Constitution altered by later amendments or that no longer apply are printed in blue.

Section 8. Powers of Congress

The Congress shall have power

1. To lay and collect taxes, duties, imposts, and excises, to pay the debts and provide for the common defense and general welfare of the United States; but all duties, imposts and excises shall be uniform throughout the United States;

2. To borrow money on the credit of the United States;

3. To regulate commerce with foreign nations, and among the several states, and with the Indian tribes;

4. To establish an uniform rule of naturalization, and uniform laws on the subject of bankruptcies throughout the United States;

5. To coin money, regulate the value thereof, and of foreign coin, and fix the standard of weights and measures;

6. To provide for the punishment of counterfeiting the securities and current coin of the United States;

7. To establish post offices and post roads;

8. To promote the progress of science and useful arts by securing for limited times to authors and inventors the exclusive right to their respective writings and discoveries;

9. To constitute tribunals inferior to the Supreme Court;

10. To define and punish piracies and felonies committed on the high seas and offenses against the law of nations;

11. To declare war, grant letters of marque and reprisal, and make rules concerning captures on land and water;

12. To raise and support armies, but no appropriation of money to that use shall be for a longer term than two years;

13. To provide and maintain a navy;

14. To make rules for the government and regulation of the land and naval forces;

15. To provide for calling forth the militia to execute the laws of the Union, suppress insurrections, and repel invasions;

16. To provide for organizing, arming, and disciplining the militia, and for governing such part of them as may be employed in the service of the United States, reserving to the states, respectively, the appointment of the officers, and the authority of training the militia according to the discipline prescribed by Congress;

17. To exercise exclusive legislation in all cases whatsoever, over such district (not exceeding ten miles square) as may, by cession of particular states, and the acceptance of Congress, become the seat of the government of the United States, and to exercise like authority over all places purchased by the consent of the legislature of the state in which the same shall be, for the erection of forts, magazines, arsenals, dock-yards, and other needful buildings; —and

18. To make all laws which shall be necessary and proper for carrying into execution the foregoing powers, and all other powers vested by this Constitution in the government of the United States, or in any department or officer thereof.

Section 9. Powers Denied to Congress

1. The Slave Trade The migration or importation of such persons as any of the states now existing shall think proper to admit, shall not be prohibited by the Congress prior to the year one thousand eight hundred and eight, but a tax or duty may be imposed on such importation, not exceeding ten dollars for each person.

2. Writ of Habeas Corpus The privilege of the writ of habeas corpus shall not be suspended, unless when in cases of rebellion or invasion the public safety may require it.

3. Bills of Attainder; Ex Post Facto Laws No bill of attainder or ex post facto law shall be passed.

4. Apportionment of Direct Taxes No capitation, or other direct, tax shall be laid, unless in proportion to the census or enumeration herein before directed to be taken.

5. Taxes on Exports No tax or duty shall be laid on articles exported from any state.

6. Special Preference for Trade No preference shall be given by any regulation of commerce or revenue to the ports of one state over those of another; nor shall vessels bound to, or from, one state, be obliged to enter, clear, or pay duties in another.

7. Spending No money shall be drawn from the Treasury, but in consequence of appropriations made by law; and a regular statement and account of the receipts and expenditures of all public money shall be published from time to time.

8. Titles of Nobility No title of nobility shall be granted by the United States; and no person holding any office of profit or trust under them, shall, without the consent of the Congress, accept of any present, emolument, office, or title, of any kind whatever, from any king, prince or foreign state.

Section 10. Powers Denied to the States

1. Unconditional Prohibitions No state shall enter into any treaty, alliance, or confederation; grant letters of marque and reprisal; coin money; emit bills of credit; make any thing but gold and silver coin a tender in payment of debts; pass any bill of attainder, ex post facto law, or law impairing the obligation of contracts, or grant any title of nobility.

2. Powers Conditionally Denied No state shall, without the consent of the Congress, lay any imposts or duties on imports or exports, except what may be absolutely necessary for executing its inspection laws; and the net produce of all duties and imposts, laid by any state on imports or exports, shall be for the use of the Treasury of the United States; and all such laws shall be subject to the revision and control of the Congress.

Clause 18 Clause 18 gives Congress the power to make laws as needed to carry out the first 17 clauses. It is sometimes called the elastic clause because it lets Congress stretch the meaning of its power.

Clause 1 *Such persons* means slaves. In 1808, as soon as Congress was permitted to abolish the slave trade, it did so.

Clause 2 A *writ of habeas corpus* is a court order requiring government officials to bring a prisoner to court and explain why he or she is being held. A writ of habeas corpus protects people from unlawful imprisonment. The government cannot suspend this right except in times of rebellion or invasion.

Clause 3 A *bill of attainder* is a law declaring that a person is guilty of a particular crime. An *ex post facto* law punishes an act which was not illegal when it was committed. Congress cannot pass a bill of attainder or ex post facto laws.

Clause 7 The federal government cannot spend money unless Congress *appropriates* it, or passes a law allowing it. The government must publish a statement showing how it spends public funds.

Clause 1 The writers of the Constitution did not want the states to act like separate nations, so they prohibited states from making treaties or coining money. Some powers denied to the federal government are also denied to the states.

Clauses 2, 3 Powers listed here are forbidden to the states, but Congress can pass laws that give these powers to the states.
Clause 2 forbids states from taxing imports and exports without the consent of Congress. States may charge inspection fees on goods entering the states. Any profits go the United States Treasury.

Clauses 2, 3 Some writers of the Constitution were afraid to allow the people to elect the President directly. Therefore, the Constitutional Convention set up the electoral college. Clause 2 directs each state to choose electors, or delegates to the electoral college, to vote for President. A state's electoral vote is equal to the combined number of senators and representatives. Each state may decide how to choose its electors. Members of Congress and federal officeholders may not serve as electors. This much of the original electoral college system is still in effect.

Clause 3 Clause 3 called upon each elector to vote for two candidates. The candidate who received a majority of the electoral votes would become President. The runner-up would become Vice President. If no candidate won a majority, the House would choose the President. The Senate would choose the Vice President.

The election of 1800 showed a problem with the original electoral college system. Thomas Jefferson was the Republican candidate for President, and Aaron Burr was the Republican candidate for Vice President. In the electoral college, the vote ended in a tie. The election was finally decided in the House, where Jefferson was chosen President. The Twelfth Amendment changed the electoral college system so that this could not happen again.

Portions of the Constitution altered by later amendments or that no longer apply are printed in blue.

3. Other Denied Powers No state shall, without the consent of Congress, lay any duty of tonnage, keep troops, or ships of war in time of peace, enter into any agreement or compact with another state, or with a foreign power, or engage in war, unless actually invaded, or in such imminent danger as will not admit of delay.

Article II ★ Executive Branch

Section 1. President and Vice President

1. Chief Executive; Term The executive power shall be vested in a President of the United States of America. He shall hold his office during the term of four years, and, together with the Vice President, chosen for the same term, be elected as follows:

2. Electoral College Each state shall appoint, in such manner as the legislature thereof may direct, a number of electors, equal to the whole number of senators and representatives to which the state may be entitled in the Congress: but no senator or representative, or person holding an office of trust or profit under the United States, shall be appointed an elector.

3. Former Electoral Method The electors shall meet in their respective states, and vote by ballot for two persons, of whom one at least shall not be an inhabitant of the same state with themselves. And they shall make a list of all the persons voted for, and of the number of votes for each; which list they shall sign and certify, and transmit sealed to the seat of the government of the United States, directed to the president of the Senate. The president of the Senate shall, in the presence of the Senate and House of Representatives, open all the certificates, and the votes shall then be counted. The person having the greatest number of votes shall be the President, if such number be a majority of the whole number of Electors appointed; and if there be more than one who have such majority, and have an equal number of votes, then the House of Representatives shall immediately choose by ballot one of them for President; and if no person have a majority, then from the five highest on the list the said House shall in like manner choose the President. But in choosing the President, the votes shall be taken by states, the representation from each state having one vote; a quorum for this purpose shall consist of a member or members from two thirds of the states, and a majority of all the states shall be necessary to a choice. In every case, after the choice of the President, the person having the greatest number of votes of the electors shall be the Vice President. But if there should remain two or more who have equal votes, the Senate shall choose from them by ballot the Vice President.

4. Time of Elections The Congress may determine the time of choosing the electors, and the day on which they shall give their votes; which day shall be the same throughout the United States.

5. Qualifications for President No person except a natural-born citizen, or a citizen of the United States at the time of the adoption of this Constitution, shall be eligible to the office of President; neither shall any person be eligible to that office who shall not have attained to the age of thirty-five years, and been fourteen years a resident within the United States.

6. Presidential Succession In case of the removal of the President from office, or of his death, resignation, or inability to discharge the powers and duties of the said office, the same shall devolve on the Vice President, and the Congress may by law provide for the case of removal, death, resignation or inability, both of the President and Vice President, declaring what officer shall then act as President, and such officer shall act accordingly, until the disability be removed, or a President shall be elected.

7. Salary The President shall, at stated times, receive for his services, a compensation, which shall neither be increased nor diminished during the period for which he shall have been elected, and he shall not receive within that period any other emolument from the United States, or any of them.

8. Oath of Office Before he enter on the execution of his office, he shall take the following oath or affirmation:—"I do solemnly swear (or affirm) that I will faithfully execute the office of the President of the United States, and will to the best of my ability, preserve, protect, and defend the Constitution of the United States."

Section 2. Powers of the President

1. Military Powers The President shall be commander in chief of the army and navy of the United States, and of the militia of the several states, when called into the actual service of the United States; he may require the opinion, in writing, of the principal officer in each of the executive departments, upon any subject relating to the duties of their respective offices, and he shall have power to grant reprieves and pardons for offenses against the United States, except in cases of impeachment.

2. Treaties; Appointments He shall have power, by and with the advice and consent of the Senate, to make treaties, provided two thirds of the senators present concur; and he shall nominate, and by and with the advice and consent of the Senate, shall appoint ambassadors, other public ministers and consuls, judges of the Supreme Court, and all other officers of the United States, whose appointments are not herein otherwise provided for, and which shall be established by law: but the Congress may by law vest the appointment of such inferior officers, as they think proper, in the President alone, in the courts of law, or in the heads of departments.

3. Temporary Appointments The President shall have power to fill up all vacancies that may happen during the recess of the Senate, by granting commissions which shall expire at the end of their next session.

Clause 6 The powers of the President pass to the Vice President if the President leaves office or cannot discharge his or her duties. The Twenty-fifth Amendment replaced this clause.

Clause 7 The President is paid a salary. It cannot be raised or lowered during his or her term of office. The President is not allowed to hold any other federal or state position while in office.

Clause 1 The President is the head of the armed forces and the state militias when they are called into national service. So the military is under *civilian*, or nonmilitary, control. The President can get advice from the heads of executive departments. In most cases, the President has the power to grant a *reprieve*, or pardon. A reprieve suspends punishment ordered by law. A *pardon* prevents prosecution for a crime or overrides the judgment of a court.

Clause 2 The President has the power to make treaties with other nations. Under the system of checks and balances, all treaties must be approved by two thirds of the Senate.

The President has the power to appoint ambassadors to foreign countries and to appoint other high officials. The Senate must confirm, or approve, these appointments.

Section 3. Duties of the President

He shall from time to time give to the Congress information of the state of the Union, and recommend to their consideration such measures as he shall judge necessary and expedient; he may, on extraordinary occasions, convene both houses, or either of them, and in case of disagreement between them, with respect to the time of adjournment, he may adjourn them to such time as he shall think proper; he shall receive ambassadors and other public ministers; he shall take care that the laws be faithfully executed, and shall commission all the officers of the United States.

Section 4. Impeachment

The President, Vice President and all civil officers of the United States, shall be removed from office on impeachment for, and conviction of, treason, bribery, or other high crimes and misdemeanors.

> **Section 4**
> *Civil officers* include federal judges and members of the Cabinet. *High crimes* are major crimes. *Misdemeanors* are lesser crimes. The President, Vice President, and others can be forced out of office if impeached and found guilty of certain crimes.

Article III ★ Judicial Branch

Section 1. Courts, Terms of Office

The judicial power of the United States shall be vested in one Supreme Court, and in such inferior courts as the Congress may from time to time ordain and establish. The judges, both of the Supreme and inferior courts, shall hold their offices during good behavior, and shall, at stated times, receive for their services, a compensation, which shall not be diminished during their continuance in office.

Section 2. Jurisdiction

1. Scope of Judicial Power The judicial power shall extend to all cases, in law and equity, arising under this Constitution, the laws of the United States, and treaties made, or which shall be made, under their authority;—to all cases affecting ambassadors, other public ministers and consuls;—to all cases of admiralty and maritime jurisdiction;—to controversies to which the United States shall be a party;—to controversies between two or more states; between a state and citizens of another state; —between citizens of different states;—between citizens of the same state claiming lands under grants of different states, and between a state, or the citizens thereof, and foreign states, citizens, or subjects.

2. Supreme Court In all cases affecting ambassadors, other public ministers and consuls, and those in which a state shall be a party, the Supreme Court shall have original jurisdiction. In all the other cases before mentioned, the Supreme Court shall have appellate jurisdiction, both as to law and fact, with such exceptions, and under such regulations as the Congress shall make.

> **Clause 1** *Jurisdiction* refers to the right of a court to hear a case. Federal courts have jurisdiction over cases that involve the Constitution, federal laws, treaties, foreign ambassadors and diplomats, naval and maritime laws, disagreements between states or between citizens from different states, and disputes between a state or citizen and a foreign state or citizen.

> **Clause 2** *Original jurisdiction* means the power of a court to hear a case where it first arises. The Supreme Court has original jurisdiction over only a few cases, such as those involving foreign diplomats. More often, the Supreme Court acts as an appellate court. An *appellate* court does not decide guilt. It decides whether the lower court trial was properly conducted and reviews the lower court's decision.

> Portions of the Constitution altered by later amendments or that no longer apply are printed in blue.

3. Trial by Jury The trial of all crimes, except in cases of impeachment, shall be by jury; and such trial shall be held in the state where the said crimes shall have been committed; but when not committed within any state, the trial shall be at such place or places as the Congress may by law have directed.

Section 3. Treason

1. Definition Treason against the United States shall consist only in levying war against them, or in adhering to their enemies, giving them aid and comfort. No person shall be convicted of treason unless on the testimony of two witnesses to the same overt act, or on confession in open court.

2. Punishment The Congress shall have power to declare the punishment of treason, but no attainder of treason shall work corruption of blood or forfeiture except during the life of the person attained.

Article IV ★ Relations Among the States

Section 1. Full Faith and Credit

Full faith and credit shall be given in each state to the public acts, records, and judicial proceedings of every other state. And the Congress may by general laws prescribe the manner in which such acts, records, and proceedings shall be proved, and the effect thereof.

> Each state must recognize the official acts and records of any other state. For example, each state must recognize marriage certificates issued by another state. Congress can pass laws to ensure this.

Section 2. Privileges and Immunities of Citizens

1. Privileges The citizens of each state shall be entitled to all privileges and immunities of citizens in the several states.

2. Extradition A person charged in any state with treason, felony, or other crime, who shall flee from justice, and be found in another state, shall on demand of the executive authority of the state from which he fled, be delivered up, to be removed to the state having jurisdiction of the crime.

> **Clause 2** *Extradition* means the act of returning a suspected criminal or escaped prisoner to a state where he or she is wanted. State governors must return a suspect to another state. However, the Supreme Court has ruled that a governor cannot be forced to do so if he or she feels that justice will not be done.

3. Fugitive Slaves No person held to service or labor in one state, under the laws thereof, escaping into another, shall in consequence of any law or regulation therein, be discharged from such service or labor, but shall be delivered up on claim of the party to whom such service or labor may be due.

> **Clause 3** *Persons held to service or labor* refers to slaves or indentured servants. This clause required states to return runaway slaves to their owners. The Thirteenth Amendment replaces this clause.

Section 3. New States and Territories

1. New States New states may be admitted by the Congress into this Union; but no new states shall be formed or erected within the jurisdiction of any other state; nor any state be formed by the junction of two or more states, or parts of states, without the consent of the legislatures of the states concerned as well as of the Congress.

> **Clause 1** Congress has the power to admit new states to the Union. Existing states cannot be split up or joined together to form new states unless both Congress and the state legislatures approve. New states are equal to all other states.

2. Federal Lands The Congress shall have power to dispose of and make all needful rules and regulations respecting the territory or other property belonging to the United States; and nothing in this Constitution shall be so construed as to prejudice any claims of the United States, or of any particular state.

Section 4. Protection Afforded to States by the Nation

The United States shall guarantee to every state in this Union a republican form of government, and shall protect each of them against invasion; and on application of the legislature, or of the executive (when the legislature cannot be convened) against domestic violence.

Article V ★ Provisions for Amendment

The Congress, whenever two thirds of both houses shall deem it necessary, shall propose amendments to this Constitution, or, on the application of the legislatures of two thirds of the several states, shall call a convention for proposing amendments, which, in either case, shall be valid to all intents and purposes, as part of this Constitution, when ratified by the legislatures of three fourths of the several states, or by conventions in three fourths thereof, as the one or the other mode of ratification may be proposed by the Congress; provided that no amendment which may be made prior to the year one thousand eight hundred and eight shall in any manner affect the first and fourth clauses in the ninth section of the first Article; and that no state, without its consent, shall be deprived of its equal suffrage in the Senate.

Article VI ★ National Debts, Supremacy of National Law, Oath

Section 1. Validity of Debts

All debts contracted and engagements entered into, before the adoption of this Constitution, shall be as valid against the United States under this Constitution, as under the Confederation.

Section 2. Supremacy of National Law

This Constitution, and the laws of the United States which shall be made in pursuance thereof, and all treaties made, or which shall be made, under the authority of the United States, shall be the supreme law of the land; and the judges in every state shall be bound thereby, anything in the constitution or laws of any state to the contrary notwithstanding.

Section 4 In a *republic*, voters choose representatives to govern them. The federal government must protect the states from foreign invasion and from domestic, or internal, disorder if asked to do so by a state.

The Constitution can be *amended*, or changed, if necessary. An amendment can be proposed by (1) a two-thirds vote of both houses of Congress or (2) a national convention called by Congress at the request of two thirds of the state legislatures. (This second method has never been used.) An amendment must be *ratified*, or approved, by (1) three fourths of the state legislatures or (2) special conventions in three fourths of the states. Congress decides which method will be used.

Congress has proposed each of the 27 amendments to the Constitution by a vote of two-thirds in both houses. The only amendment ratified by constitutional conventions of the states was the Twenty-first Amendment. State legislatures have ratified all other amendments.

Section 2 The "supremacy clause" in this section establishes the Constitution, federal laws, and treaties that the Senate has ratified as the *supreme*, or highest, law of the land. Thus, they outweigh state laws. A state judge must overturn a state law that conflicts with the Constitution or with a federal law.

Portions of the Constitution altered by later amendments or that no longer apply are printed in blue.

Section 3. Oaths of Office

The senators and representatives before mentioned, and the members of the several state legislatures, and all executive and judicial officers, both of the United States and of the several states, shall be bound by oath or affirmation, to support this Constitution; but no religious test shall ever be required as a qualification to any office or public trust under the United States.

Article VII ★ Ratification of Constitution

The ratification of the conventions of nine states shall be sufficient for the establishment of this Constitution between the states so ratifying the same.

Article VII During 1787 and 1788, states held special conventions. By October 1788, the required nine states had ratified the United States Constitution.

Done in convention by the unanimous consent of the states present the seventeenth day of September, in the year of our Lord one thousand seven hundred and eighty-seven, and of the independence of the United States of America the twelfth. In Witness whereof, we have hereunto subscribed our names.

Attest: William Jackson, SECRETARY
George Washington, PRESIDENT and deputy from Virginia

New Hampshire
   John Langdon
   Nicholas Gilman

Massachusetts
   Nathaniel Gorham
   Rufus King

Connecticut
   William Samuel Johnson
   Roger Sherman

New York
   Alexander Hamilton

New Jersey
   William Livingston
   David Brearley
   William Paterson
   Jonathan Dayton

Pennsylvania
   Benjamin Franklin
   Thomas Mifflin
   Robert Morris
   George Clymer
   Thomas Fitzsimons
   Jared Ingersoll
   James Wilson
   Gouverneur Morris

Delaware
   George Read
   Gunning Bedford, Jr.
   John Dickinson
   Richard Bassett
   Jacob Broom

Maryland
   James McHenry
   Dan of St. Thomas Jennifer
   Daniel Carroll

Virginia
   John Blair
   James Madison, Jr.

North Carolina
   William Blount
   Richard Dobbs Spaight
   Hugh Williamson

South Carolina
   John Rutledge
   Charles Cotesworth Pinckney
   Charles Pinckney
   Pierce Butler

Georgia
   William Few
   Abraham Baldwin

The Amendments The *Amendments* are changes made to the Constitution, which has been amended 27 times since it was originally ratified in 1788. The first 10 amendments are referred to as the Bill of Rights. These amendments give rights to the people and states, thus putting limits on the power of government.

First Amendment The First Amendment protects five basic rights: freedom of religion, speech, the press, assembly, and petition. Congress cannot set up an established, or official, church or religion for the nation, nor can it forbid the practice of religion. During the colonial period, most colonies had established churches. However, the authors of the First Amendment wanted to keep government and religion separate.

Congress may not *abridge*, or limit, the freedom to speak and write freely. The government may not censor, or review, books and newspapers before they are printed. This amendment also protects the right to assemble, or hold public meetings. *Petition* means ask. *Redress* means to correct. *Grievances* are wrongs. The people have the right to ask the government for wrongs to be corrected.

Portions of the Constitution altered by later amendments or that no longer apply are printed in blue.

Amendments

First Amendment ★

(1791) Freedom of Religion, Speech, Press, Assembly, and Petition

Congress shall make no law respecting an establishment of religion, or prohibiting the free exercise thereof; or abridging the freedom of speech, or of the press; or the right of the people peaceably to assemble, and to petition the government for a redress of grievances.

Second Amendment ★

(1791) Bearing Arms

A well-regulated militia being necessary to the security of a free state, the right of the people to keep and bear arms shall not be infringed.

Third Amendment ★

(1791) Quartering of Troops

No soldier shall, in time of peace, be quartered in any house, without the consent of the owner; nor in time of war, but in a manner to be prescribed by law.

Fourth Amendment ★

(1791) Searches and Seizures

The right of the people to be secure in their persons, houses, papers, and effects, against unreasonable searches and seizures, shall not be violated, and no warrants shall issue, but upon probable cause, supported by oath or affirmation, and particularly describing the place to be searched, and the persons or things to be seized.

Fifth Amendment ★

(1791) Criminal Proceedings; Due Process; Eminent Domain

No person shall be held to answer for a capital, or otherwise infamous, crime, unless on a presentment or indictment of a grand jury, except in cases arising in the land or naval forces, or in the militia, when in actual service in time of war or public danger; nor shall any person be subject for the same offense to be twice put in jeopardy of life and limb; nor shall be compelled, in any criminal case, to be a witness against himself; nor be deprived of life, liberty, or property, without due process of law; nor shall private property be taken for public use, without just compensation.

Sixth Amendment ★

(1791) Criminal Proceedings

In all criminal prosecutions, the accused shall enjoy the right to a speedy and public trial, by an impartial jury of the state and district wherein the crime shall have been committed, which district shall have been previously ascertained by law, and to be informed of the nature and cause of the accusation; to be confronted with the witnesses against him; to have compulsory process for obtaining witnesses in his favor, and to have the assistance of counsel for his defense.

Seventh Amendment ★

(1791) Civil Trials

In suits at common law, where the value in controversy shall exceed twenty dollars, the right of trial by jury shall be preserved, and no fact tried by a jury shall be otherwise re-examined in any court of the United States, than according to the rules of the common law.

Eighth Amendment ★

(1791) Punishment for Crimes

Excessive bail shall not be required, nor excessive fines imposed, nor cruel and unusual punishments inflicted.

Fifth Amendment This amendment protects the rights of the accused. *Capital crimes* are those that can be punished with death. *Infamous crimes* are those that can be punished with prison or loss of rights. The federal government must obtain an *indictment*, or formal accusation, from a grand jury to prosecute anyone for such crimes. A *grand jury* is a panel of between 12 and 23 citizens who decide if the government has enough evidence to justify a trial. This procedure prevents the government from prosecuting people with little or no evidence of guilt.

Double jeopardy is forbidden by this amendment. This means that a person cannot be tried twice for the same crime. However, if a court sets aside a conviction because of a legal error, the accused can be tried again. A person on trial cannot be forced to *testify*, or give evidence, against himself or herself. A person accused of a crime is entitled to *due process of law*, or a fair hearing or trial.

Finally, the government cannot seize private property for public use without paying the owner a fair price for it.

Sixth Amendment In criminal cases, the jury must be *impartial*, or not favor either side. The accused is guaranteed the right to a trial by jury. The trial must be speedy. If the government purposely postpones the trial so that it becomes hard for the person to get a fair hearing, the charge may be dismissed. The accused must be told the charges and be allowed to question all witnesses. Witnesses who can help the accused can be ordered to appear in court. The accused must be allowed a lawyer.

Seventh Amendment *Common law* refers to rules of law established by judges in past cases. This amendment guarantees the right to a jury trial in lawsuits where the sum of money at stake is more than $20. An appeals court can set aside a verdict only if legal errors made the trial unfair.

Ninth Amendment ★

(1791) Unenumerated Rights

The enumeration in the Constitution, of certain rights, shall not be construed to deny or disparage others retained by the people.

Tenth Amendment ★

(1791) Powers Reserved to the States

The powers not delegated to the United States by the Constitution, nor prohibited by it to the states, are reserved to the states respectively, or to the people.

Eleventh Amendment ★

(1798) Suits Against States

The judicial power of the United States shall not be construed to extend to any suit in law or equity, commenced or prosecuted against one of the United States by citizens of another state, or by citizens or subjects of any foreign state.

Twelfth Amendment ★

(1804) Election of President and Vice President

The electors shall meet in their respective states, and vote by ballot for President and Vice President, one of whom, at least, shall not be an inhabitant of the same state with themselves; they shall name in their ballots the person voted for as President, and in distinct ballots the person voted for as Vice President, and they shall make distinct lists of all persons voted for as President, and of all persons voted for as Vice President, and of the number of votes for each, which lists they shall sign and certify, and transmit sealed to the seat of the government of the United States, directed to the president of the Senate; the president of the Senate shall, in the presence of the Senate and the House of Representatives, open all the certificates and the votes shall then be counted;—the person having the greatest number of votes for President shall be the President, if such number be a majority of the whole number of electors appointed; and if no person have such a majority, then from the persons having the highest numbers not exceeding three on the list of those voted for as President, the House of Representatives shall choose immediately, by ballot, the President.

Ninth Amendment The rights of the people are not limited to those listed in the Bill of Rights. In the Ninth Amendment, the government is prevented from claiming these are the only rights people have.

Tenth Amendment Powers not given to the federal government belong to the states. Powers reserved to the states are not listed in the Constitution.

Eleventh Amendment A private citizen from one state cannot sue the government of another state in federal court. However, a citizen can sue a state government in a state court.

Twelfth Amendment This amendment changed the way the electoral college voted as outlined in Article II, Clause 3.

This amendment provides that each elector choose one candidate for President and one candidate for Vice President. If no candidate for President receives a majority of electoral votes, the House of Representatives chooses the President. If no candidate for Vice President receives a majority, the Senate elects the Vice President. The Vice President must be a person who is eligible to be President.
This system is still in use today. However, it is possible for a candidate to win the popular vote and lose in the electoral college. This happened in 1888 and in 2000.

Portions of the Constitution altered by later amendments or that no longer apply are printed in blue.

But in choosing the President, the votes shall be taken by states, the representation from each state having one vote; a quorum for this purpose shall consist of a member or members from two thirds of the states, and a majority of all states shall be necessary to a choice. [should this be blue] And if the House of Representatives shall not choose a President whenever the right of choice shall devolve upon them, before the fourth day of March next following, then the Vice President, shall act as President, as in the case of death or other constitutional disability of the President.–The person having the greatest number of votes as Vice President, shall be the Vice President, if such a number be a majority of the whole number of electors appointed, and if no person have a majority, then from the two highest numbers on the list, the Senate shall choose the Vice President; a quorum for the purpose shall consist of two thirds of the whole number of senators, and a majority of the whole number shall be necessary to a choice. But no person constitutionally ineligible to the office of President shall be eligible to that of Vice President of the United States.

Thirteenth Amendment ★

(1865) Slavery and Involuntary Servitude

Section 1. Outlawing Slavery Neither slavery nor involuntary servitude, expect as a punishment for crime whereof the party shall have been duly convicted, shall exist within the United States, or any place subject to their jurisdiction.

Section 2. Enforcement Congress shall have power to enforce this article by appropriate legislation.

Thirteenth Amendment The Emancipation Proclamation (1863) freed slaves only in areas controlled by the Confederacy. This amendment freed all slaves. It also forbids *involuntary servitude*, or labor done against one's will. However, it does not prevent prison wardens from making prisoners work. Congress can pass laws to carry out this amendment.

Fourteenth Amendment ★

(1868) Rights of Citizens

Section 1. Citizenship All persons born or naturalized in the United States, and subject to the jurisdiction thereof, are citizens of the United States and of the state wherein they reside. No state shall make or enforce any law which shall abridge the privileges or immunities of citizens of the United States; nor shall any state deprive any person of life, liberty, or property, without due process of law; nor deny to any person within its jurisdiction the equal protection of the laws.

Section 2. Apportionment of Representatives Representatives shall be apportioned among the several states according to their respective numbers, counting the whole number of persons in each states, excluding Indians not taxed. But when the right to vote at any election for the choice of electors for President and Vice President of the United States, representatives in Congress, the executive and judicial officers of a state, or the

Fourteenth Amendment, Section 1 This amendment defines citizenship for the first time in the Constitution. It was intended to protect the rights of the freed slaves by guaranteeing all citizens "equal protection under the law."

Fourteenth Amendment, Section 2 This section replaced the three-fifths clause. It provides that representation in the House of Representatives is decided on the basis of the number of people in the state. It also provides that states which deny the vote to male citizens over age 21 will be punished by losing part of their representation in the House. This provision has never been enforced.

members of the legislature thereof, is denied to any of the male inhabitants of such state, being twenty-one years of age, and citizens of the United States, or in any way abridged, except for participation in rebellion, or other crime, the basis of representation therein shall be reduced in the proportion which the number of such male citizens shall bear to the whole number of male citizens twenty-one years of age in such state.

Section 3. Former Confederate Officials No person shall be a senator or representative in Congress, or elector of President and Vice President, or hold any office, civil or military, under the United States, or under any state, who having previously taken an oath, as a member of Congress, or as an officer of the United States, or as a member of any state legislature, or as an executive or judicial officer of any state, to support the Constitution of the United States, shall have engaged in insurrection or rebellion against the same, or given aid or comfort to the enemies thereof. But Congress may, by a voted of two thirds of each house, remove such disability.

Section 4. Public Debt The validity of the public debt of the United States, authorized by law, including debts incurred for payment of pensions and bounties for services in suppressing insurrection or rebellion, shall not be questioned. But neither the United States nor any state shall assume or pay any debt or obligation incurred in aid of insurrection or rebellion against the United States, or any claim for the loss of emancipation of any slave; but all such debts, obligations and claims shall be held illegal and void.

Section 5. Enforcement The Congress shall have power to enforce, by appropriate legislation, the provisions of this article.

Fifteenth Amendment ★

(1870) Right to Vote–Race, Color, Servitude

Section 1. Extending the Right to Vote The Right of citizens of the United States to vote shall not be denied or abridged by the United States or by any state on account of race, color, or previous condition of servitude.

Section 2. Enforcement The Congress shall have power to enforce this article by appropriate legislation.

Sixteenth Amendment ★

(1913) Income Tax

The Congress shall have power to lay and collect taxes on incomes, from whatever source derived, without apportionment among the several states, and without regard to any census or enumeration.

Fifteenth Amendment, Section 1
Previous condition of servitude refers to slavery. This amendment gave African Americans, both former slaves and free African Americans, the right to vote. In the late 1800s, southern states used grandfather clauses, literacy tests, and poll taxes to keep African Americans from voting.

Fifteenth Amendment, Section 2
Congress can pass laws to carry out this amendment. The Twenty-fourth Amendment barred the use of poll taxes in national elections. The Voting Rights Act of 1965 gave federal officials the power to register voters where there was voting discrimination.

Sixteenth Amendment Congress has the power to collect taxes on people's income. An income tax can be collected without regard to a state's population. This amendment changed Article 1, Section 9, Clause 4.

Portions of the Constitution altered by later amendments or that no longer apply are printed in blue.

Seventeenth Amendment ★

(1913) Popular Election of Senators

Section 1. Method of Election The Senate of the United States shall be composed of two senators from each state, elected by the people thereof, for six years; and each senator shall have one vote. The electors in each state shall have the qualifications requisite for electors of the most numerous branch of the state legislatures.

Section 2. Vacancies When vacancies happen in the representation of any state in the Senate, the executive authority of such state shall issue writs of election to fill such vacancies: provided, that the legislature of any state may empower the executive thereof to make temporary appointments until the people fill the vacancies by election as the legislature may direct.

Section 3. Those Elected Under Previous Procedure This amendment shall not be so construed as to affect the election or term of any senator chosen before it becomes valid as part of the Constitution.

> **Seventeenth Amendment, Section 1** This amendment replaced Article 1, Section 2, Clause 1. Before it was adopted, state legislatures chose senators. This amendment provides that senators are directly elected by the people of each state.

Eighteenth Amendment ★

(1919) Prohibition of Intoxication Liquors

Section 1. Ban on Alcohol After one year from the ratification of this article, the manufacture, sale, or transportation of intoxicating liquors within, the importation thereof into, or the exportation thereof from the United States and all territory subject to the jurisdiction thereof for beverage purposes is hereby prohibited.

Section 2. Enforcement The Congress and the several states shall have concurrent power to enforce this article by appropriate legislation.

Section 3. Method of Ratification This article shall be inoperative unless it shall have been ratified as an amendment to the Constitution by the legislatures of the several states, as provided in the Constitution, within seven years from the date of the submission hereof to the states by Congress.

> **Eighteenth Amendment** This amendment, known as Prohibition, banned the making, selling, or transporting of alcoholic beverages in the United States. Later, the Twenty-first Amendment *repealed*, or canceled, this amendment.

Nineteenth Amendment ★

(1920) Women's Suffrage

Section 1. The Right to Vote The right of citizens of the United States to vote shall not be denied or abridged by the United States or by any state on account of sex.

Section 2. Enforcement Congress shall have power to enforce this article by appropriate legislation.

> **Nineteenth Amendment** Neither the federal government nor state governments can deny the right to vote on account of sex. Thus, women won *suffrage*, or the right to vote. Before 1920, some states had allowed women to vote in state elections.

Section 1. The date for the inauguration of the president was changed to January 20th, and the date for Congress to begin its term changed to January 3rd. Prior to this amendment, the beginning of term date was set in March. The outgoing officials with little or no influence on matters were not effective in office. Being so inactive, they were called "lame ducks."

Section 3. If the President-elect dies before taking office, the Vice President becomes President. If no President has been chosen by January 20 or if the elected candidate fails to qualify for office, the Vice President-elect acts as President, but only until a qualified President is chosen.

Finally, Congress has the power to choose a person to act as President of neither the President-elect nor the Vice President-elect is qualified to take office.

Twentieth Amendment ★

(1933) Commencement of Terms; Sessions of Congress; Death or Disqualification of President-Elect

Section 1. Beginning of Terms The terms of the President and Vice President shall end at noon on the 20th day of January, and the terms of senators and representatives at noon on the 3rd day of January, of the years in which such terms would have ended if this article had not been ratified; and the terms of their successors shall then begin.

Section 2. Congressional Sessions The Congress shall assemble at least once in every year, and such meeting shall begin at noon on the 3rd day of January, unless they shall by law appoint a different day.

Section 3. Presidential Succession If, at the time fixed for the beginning of the term of the President, the President-elect shall have died, the Vice President-elect shall become President. If a President shall not have been chosen before the time fixed for the beginning of his term, or if the President-elect shall have failed to qualify, the Vice President-elect shall act as President until a President shall have qualified; and the Congress may by law provide for the case wherein neither a President-elect nor a Vice President-elect shall have qualified, declaring who shall then act as President, or the manner in which one who is to act shall be selected, and such person shall act accordingly until a President or Vice President shall have qualified.

Section 4. Elections Decided by Congress The Congress may by law provide for the case of the death of any persons from whom the House of Representatives may choose a President whenever the right of choice shall have devolved upon them, and for the case of the death of any of the persons from whom the Senate may choose a Vice President whenever the right of choice shall have devolved upon them.

Section 5. Date of Implementation Sections 1 and 2 shall take effect on the 15th day of October following the ratification of this article.

Section 6. Ratification Period This article shall be inoperative unless it shall have been ratified as an amendment to the Constitution by the legislatures of three fourths of the several states within seven years from the date of its submission.

Twenty-first Amendment, Section 1 The Eighteenth Amendment is repealed, making it legal to make and sell alcoholic beverages. Prohibition ended December 5, 1933.

Portions of the Constitution altered by later amendments or that no longer apply are printed in blue.

Twenty-first Amendment ★

(1933) Repeal of Prohibition

Section 1. Repeal The eighteenth article of amendment to the Constitution of the United States is hereby repealed.

Section 2. State Laws The transportation or importation into any state, territory, or possession of the United States for delivery or use therein of intoxicating liquors, in violation of the laws thereof, is hereby prohibited.

Section 3. Ratification Period This article shall be inoperative unless it shall have been ratified as an amendment to the Constitution by conventions in the several states, as provided in the Constitution, within seven years from the date of the submission hereof to the states by the Congress

Twenty-second Amendment ★

(1951) Presidential Tenure

Section 1. Two-Term Limit No person shall be elected to the office of the President more than twice, and no person who has held the office of President, or acted as President, for more than two years of a term to which some other person was elected President shall be elected to the office of President more than once. But this article shall not apply to any person holding the office of President when this article was proposed by the Congress, and shall not prevent any person who may be holding the office of President, or acting as President, during the term within which this article becomes operative from holding the office of President or acting as President during the remainder of such term.

Section 2. Ratification Period This article shall be inoperative unless it shall have been ratified as an amendment to the Constitution by the legislatures of three fourths of the several states within seven years from the date of its submission to the state by the Congress.

> **Twenty-second Amendment, Section 1**
> This amendment provides that no President may serve more that two terms. A President who has already served more than half of someone else's term can only serve one more full term. Before Franklin Roosevelt became President, no President served more than two terms in office. Roosevelt broke with this custom and was elected to four terms. The amendment, however, did not apply to Harry Truman, who became President after Franklin Roosevelt's death in 1945.

Twenty-third Amendment ★

(1961) Presidential Electors for the District of Columbia

Section 1. Determining the Number of Electors The district constituting the seat of government of the United States shall appoint in such manner as the Congress may direct:

A number of electors of President and Vice President equal to the whole number of senators and representatives in Congress to which the district would be entitled if it were a state, but in no event more than the least populous state; they shall be in addition to those appointed by the states, but they shall be considered, for the purposes of the election of President and Vice President, to be electors appointed by a state; and they shall meet in the district and perform such duties as provided by the twelfth article of amendment.

Section 2. Enforcement The Congress shall have power to enforce this article by appropriate legislation.

> **Twenty-third Amendment, Section 1**
> This amendment gives the residents of Washington, D.C., the right to vote in presidential elections. Until this amendment was adopted, people living in Washington, D.C., could not vote for President because the Constitution had made no provision for choosing electors from the nation's capital. Washington, D.C., has three electoral votes.

Twenty-fourth Amendment ★

(1964) Right to Vote in Federal Elections–Tax Payment

Section 1. Poll Tax Banned The right of citizens of the United States to vote in any primary or other election for President or Vice President, for electors for President or Vice President, or for senator or representative in Congress, shall not be denied or abridged by the United States or any state by reason of failure to pay any poll tax or other tax.

Section 2. Enforcement The Congress shall have the power to enforce this article by appropriate legislation.

> **Twenty-fourth Amendment, Section 1**
> A *poll tax* is a tax on voters. This amendment bans poll taxes in national elections. Some states used poll taxes to keep African Americans from voting. In 1966, the Supreme Court struck down poll taxes in state elections, also.

(1967) Presidential Succession, Vice Presidential Vacancy, Presidential Inability

Twenty-fifth Amendment, Section 1
If the President dies or resigns, the Vice President becomes President. This section clarifies Article 2, Section 1, Clause 6.

Twenty-fifth Amendment, Section 3
If the President declares in writing that he or she is unable to perform the duties of office, the Vice President serves as acting President until the President recovers.

Twenty-fifth Amendment, Section 4
Two Presidents, Woodrow Wilson and Dwight Eisenhower, have fallen gravely ill while in office. The Constitution contained no provision for this kind of emergency. Section 3 provided that the President can inform Congress he or she is too sick to perform the duties of office. However, if the President is unconscious or refuses to admit to a disabling illness, Section 4 provides that the Vice President and Cabinet may declare the President disabled. The Vice President becomes the acting President until the President can return to the duties of office. In case of a disagreement between the President and the Vice President and Cabinet over the President's ability to perform the duties of office, Congress must decide the issue. A two-thirds vote of both houses is needed to find the President is disabled or unable to fulfill the duties of office.

Section 1. President's Death or Resignation In case of the removal of the President from office or of his death or resignation, the Vice President shall become President.

Section 2. Vacancies in Vice Presidency Whenever there is a vacancy in the office of the Vice President, the President shall nominate a Vice President who shall take office upon confirmation by a majority vote of both houses of Congress.

Section 3. Disability of the President Whenever the President transmits to the President pro tempore of the Senate and the Speaker of the House of Representatives his written declaration that he is unable to discharge the powers and duties of his office, and until he transmits to them a written declaration to the contrary, such powers and duties shall be discharged by the Vice President as acting President.

Section 4. Vice President as Acting President Whenever the Vice President and a majority of either the principal officers of the executive departments or of such other body as Congress may by law provide, transmit to the President pro tempore of the Senate and the Speaker of the House of Representatives their written declaration that the President is unable to discharge the powers and duties of his office, the Vice President shall immediately assume the powers and duties of the office as Acting President.

Thereafter, when the President transmits to the President pro tempore of the Senate and the Speaker of the House of Representatives his written declaration that no inability exists, he shall resume the powers and duties of his office unless the Vice President and a majority of either the principal officers of the executive department or of such other body as Congress may by law provide, transmit within four days to the President pro tempore of the Senate and the Speaker of the House of Representatives their written declaration that the President is unable to discharge the powers and duties of his office. Thereupon Congress shall decide the issue, assembling within forty-eight hours for that purpose if not in session. If the Congress, within twenty-one days after receipt of the latter written declaration, or, if Congress is not in session, within twenty-one days after Congress is required to assemble, determines by two-thirds vote of both Houses that the President is unable to discharge the powers and duties of his office, the Vice President shall continue to discharge the same as Acting President; otherwise, the President shall resume the powers and duties of his office.

Twenty-sixth Amendment ★

(1971) Right to Vote–Age

Section 1. Lowering the Voting Age The right of citizens of the United States, who are eighteen years of age or older, to vote shall not be denied or abridged by the United States or by any state on account of age.

Section 2. Enforcement The Congress shall have the power to enforce this article by appropriate legislation.

Twenty-sixth Amendment, Section 1
In 1970, Congress passed a law allowing 18-year-olds to vote. However, the Supreme Court decided that Congress could not set a minimum age for state elections.

Twenty-seventh Amendment ★

(1992) Congressional Pay

No law, varying the compensation for the services of the senators and representatives, shall take effect until an election of representatives shall have intervened.

Twenty-seventh Amendment
If members of Congress vote themselves a pay increase, it cannot go into effect until after the next congressional election. This amendment was proposed in 1789. In 1992, Michigan became the thirty-eighth state to ratify it.

The Bill of Rights

What's Ahead in Chapter 6

Why is the Bill of Rights so important and how did it become part of the Constitution? This chapter will answer these questions and help you understand the value of your rights as an American citizen.

SECTION 1
Adding the Bill of Rights

SECTION 2
Protections in the Bill of Rights

SECTION 3
Interpreting the Bill of Rights

TARGET
READING SKILL

Sequence In this chapter you will focus on sequence to help you better understand what you read. Sequence includes understanding a sequence, or order, of events and recognizing words that signal sequence.

Protesters at the ▶
Supreme Court

National | **Standards for Civics and Government** | **State**

The following National Standards for Civics and Government are covered in this chapter:

II. What are the foundations of the American political system?

D. What values and principles are basic to American constitutional democracy?

V. What are the roles of the citizen in American democracy?

B. What are the rights of citizens?

Go Online
PHSchool.com

For: Your state's standards
Visit: PHSchool.com
Web Code: mpe-2061

Active Citizen — Civics in the Real World

In Civics class, Mr. Walker asked his students to make a detailed list of everything they had seen and done since they woke up that morning. The students raised their eyebrows but began to write.

"Now," said Mr. Walker, "What were some things on your lists?" Marie said she had watched the morning news while eating breakfast. Jason reported that he had gotten up early to deliver newspapers. Tamara laughed when she said it had taken her a long time to decide what clothes to wear.

"These things are just common, everyday activities," said Mr. Walker. "Yet each one is, in a way, an example of our rights as citizens." The students stopped to consider this. It was true— their daily routines would be completely different without the freedoms they took for granted.

"As American citizens, we have many important rights, and without them, our lives might be very different," Mr. Walker concluded. "These rights are guaranteed in the first ten amendments to the Constitution. Together they make up the Bill of Rights."

Citizen's Journal What important rights do you live by every day? Write a paragraph describing how your daily activities reflect your rights as an American citizen.

The Constitutional Convention

Objectives

In this section you will

- Understand the amendment process.
- Learn about the debate in Congress over the Bill of Rights and its ratification.

Taking Notes

Make a diagram like the one below. As you read the section, complete the diagram with information about the sequence of events from the ratification of the Constitution to the adoption of the Bill of Rights.

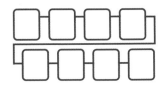

Key Terms

Bill of Rights
amendment
  process

convention

Main Idea

After some debate, the Bill of Rights was added to the Constitution to protect Americans' individual rights and freedoms.

Target Reading Skill

Understand Sequence A sequence is the order in which a series of events occurs. Noting the sequence of important events can help you understand and remember the events. As you read this section, write the sequence of events in your Taking Notes graphic organizer.

W hy did the **Bill of Rights**, a list of citizens' rights, become part of the Constitution? Quite simply, the framers thought that it was unnecessary. They believed that the Constitution already guarded against tyranny by limiting the government's power.

The Anti-Federalists disagreed and put up a stiff fight against ratification. James Madison and other Federalists promised that a bill of rights could be added in the form of amendments. If they had not done so, the Constitution might not have been ratified.

After the ratification, Madison was determined to fulfill his promise to the Anti-Federalists. Adding a bill of rights would be an important step toward gaining their support for the new government.

The stage was set for the first changes in the Constitution. This was the first test of the **amendment process**, or the way in which changes are added to the Constitution.

The Amendment Process

The Constitution requires that any amendment must be approved at both the national and state levels. First an amendment is approved at the national level—usually by Congress—and proposed to the states. Then the states either ratify it or reject it.

There are two ways to propose an amendment to the states. Congress may propose an amendment if it has been approved by a two-thirds vote in both the Senate and the House of Representatives. Congress proposed the 27 amendments that are part of our Constitution today.

A **national convention**, or assembly, may propose amendments. The convention must be called for by two thirds of the state legislatures. This method, however, has not yet been used.

There are two ways for the states to ratify an amendment. The usual route is approval by three fourths of the nation's state legislatures. The other method is approval by special conventions in three fourths of the states. Congress chooses which method will be used.

✔ Reading Check   **Why is having a formal amendment process important?**

The Debate in Congress

In the case of the Bill of Rights, the amendment process began in Congress. James Madison spoke to fellow members of the House in June 1789. He declared that many Americans believed that the Constitution did not adequately protect their rights. Madison argued that Congress needed to propose a bill of rights. This would earn the people's trust and lay a solid foundation for the new republic.

The newly-elected Congress, however, was impatient to begin passing laws. Madison urged Congress to prepare a bill of rights. By doing so, he declared, Congress would "make the Constitution better in the opinion of those who are opposed to it without weakening its frame... in the judgment of those who are attached to it."

Analyze Graphs

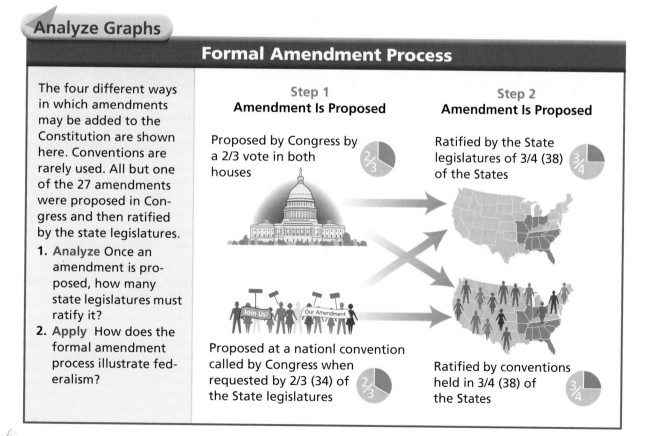

Formal Amendment Process

The four different ways in which amendments may be added to the Constitution are shown here. Conventions are rarely used. All but one of the 27 amendments were proposed in Congress and then ratified by the state legislatures.

1. **Analyze** Once an amendment is proposed, how many state legislatures must ratify it?
2. **Apply** How does the formal amendment process illustrate federalism?

Step 1
Amendment Is Proposed

Proposed by Congress by a 2/3 vote in both houses

Proposed at a nationl convention called by Congress when requested by 2/3 (34) of the State legislatures

Step 2
Amendment Is Proposed

Ratified by the State legislatures of 3/4 (38) of the States

Ratified by conventions held in 3/4 (38) of the States

George Mason wrote Virginia's Declaration of Rights, which became a model for the Bill of Rights.

Target Reading Skill

Understand Sequence What important events led up to the ratification of the Bill of Rights on December 15, 1791?

Preparing the Bill of Rights Two months later, members of Congress began preparing the Bill of Rights. After some debate, they produced a list that drew on many earlier statements of individual rights. These statements included the Magna Carta, the English Bill of Rights, colonial charters, and state constitutions.

The next issue was where in the Constitution to place the Bill of Rights. Madison wanted the rights within the articles of the Constitution to link them to limits already placed on the government.

A majority of members of Congress voted to attach the list of rights to the end of the document. Some Congress members wanted the Bill of Rights at the end because they did not want to give them the same importance as the original Constitution.

The Proposal and the Ratification A committee of Congressmen wrote final versions of 12 amendments, including ten that protected citizens' rights. Congress approved the amendments and proposed them to the states in September of 1789.

The amendments were welcomed by people who distrusted the new government. Only two proposals failed: to enlarge the House and to limit when Congress might raise its salaries. By December 15, 1791, the states had ratified ten amendments protecting citizens' rights. The Bill of Rights had become part of the Constitution.

✓ Reading Check **Why was there a debate over where to place the Bill of Rights in the Constitution?**

SECTION 1 Assessment

Key Terms

Use each of the key terms in a sentence that explains its meaning: Bill of Rights, amendment process, convention

Target Reading Skill

1. **Understand Sequence** Place the following events in the correct order:
   - Congress proposed a final version of the Bill of Rights to the states.
   - James Madison spoke to the House of Representatives about the importance of a bill of rights.
   - The ten amendments known as the Bill of Rights were rat-ified by the states and became a part of the Constitution.
   - Congress began preparing a bill of rights.

Comprehension and Critical Thinking

2. **a. Recall** List each of the ways an amendment can be proposed and ratified.
   b. Determine Relevance How does the amendment process reflect the idea of democracy?

3. **a. Explain** Why did James Madison propose a bill of rights?

   b. Describe Which proposal method was used to add the Bill of Rights to the Constitution?

Writing Activity

It is 1788. Your state legislature is debating whether it will ratify the new Constitution without a bill of rights. Write a letter to your representative to convince him of the importance of a bill of rights. Give at least three reasons to support your argument.

TIP Give your letter a strong, persuasive introduction and conclusion, and state your points clearly.

Protections in the Bill of Rights

Reading Preview

Objectives

In this section you will

- Understand how the First Amendment protects individual freedoms.
- Find out how the Bill of Rights protects people against abuse of power by the government.
- Learn how the Bill of Rights protects people accused of crimes.
- Discuss the protections of other rights outlined in the Ninth and Tenth Amendments.

Key Terms

separation of church and state
eminent domain
due process of law
double jeopardy

Main Idea

The Bill of Rights was added to the Constitution to guarantee the basic rights of citizens. These rights include protections of individual freedoms, protections against the government's abuse of power, and protections of the accused.

Target Reading Skill

Understand Sequence Recall that the order in which a series of events occurs is called sequence. As you read this section, consider the order of the ten amendments that make up the Bill of Rights.

Taking Notes

Make a diagram like the one below. As you read the section, complete the diagram with information about the rights protected in the Bill of Rights.

The first ten amendments to the Constitution were added to protect citizens' rights against actions by the national government. The Bill of Rights did not change any principles in the Constitution. Instead, these ten amendments spell out basic rights that are protected under our form of government. These rights fall into three main categories: (1) individual freedoms, (2) protections against government abuse of power, and (3) rights of citizens accused of crimes.

Protections of Individual Freedoms

What if you could be arrested for criticizing a government official? What if the government could decide which books or magazines may be published and which movies or television shows you may watch? What if daily newspapers could publish no articles critical of the government? What if a person could be jailed because of religious beliefs?

You may be asking, "What is the point of supposing things that could never happen?" The answer is that they do happen. Millions of people in the world today are denied the rights that we Americans often take for granted. These rights include a number of freedoms protected by the First Amendment.

At one time or another, these books were banned from libraries.
▼

Freedom of Religion The First Amendment provides for freedom of religion. Every American is free to follow the religion of his or her choice, or not to practice any religion at all. Also, the First Amendment establishes **separation of church and state**, the situation in which the government may not favor any religion or establish an official religion.

Freedom of Speech Freedom of speech is another right protected by the First Amendment. As an American you have the right to speak and write freely.

Does freedom of speech mean that you may say anything, whenever and wherever you please? No. You are not free to slander, or tell lies that damage another person's reputation.

Freedom of the Press Freedom of the press guarantees that people may criticize the government without fearing arrest. In many countries today, the government controls newspapers and radio or television stations. In the United States, the First Amendment helps guarantee that citizens can get information and hear different opinions.

Analyze Diagrams and Charts

The Bill of Rights

The Bill of Rights, comprised of the first ten amendments to the Constitution, spell out the basic rights protected by our government. The First Amendment protects a number of very important rights and freedoms.

1. Why are the rights and freedoms protected by the First Amendment necessary for a democracy to function properly?
2. In your own words, summarize the overall goal of the Bill of Rights.

Freedom of the Press

Freedom of Speech

1st Amendment: Guarantees freedom of religion, of speech, and of the press; the right to assemble peacefully; and the right to petition the government.

2nd Amendment: Protects the right to possess firearms.

3rd Amendment: Declares that the government may not require people to house soldiers during peacetime.

4th Amendment: Protects people from unreasonable searches and seisures.

5th Amendment: Guarantees that no one may be deprived of life, liberty, or property without due process of law.

Freedom of the press has its limits. For instance, a newspaper is not free to libel, or print lies about, a person. Also, both freedom of speech and freedom of the press may be limited when what is said or written endangers the lives of citizens, as when a person falsely shouts "Fire" in a theater and causes a panic.

Freedom of Assembly Under the First Amendment, citizens also have the right to assemble, or meet together. For instance, a group may hold a demonstration to protest a new law as long as their demonstration is peaceful and does not violate the rights of other citizens.

Freedom of Petition Any citizen or group of citizens has the right to ask a government representative to change a law, to make a new law, or to solve problems that arise in other ways. A citizen may make such a request by writing a letter, by sending an email, by telephoning, or by sending a petition—a request signed by many citizens—to a representative in Congress.

✔ Reading Check **What are some ways that you exercise the basic freedoms of the First Amendment every day?**

Go Online
civics
interactive

For: Interactive Place Holder
Visit: PHSchool.com
Web Code: mpp-2061

The Right to Assemble Peacefully

The Right to Petition Government

6th Amendment: Guarantees the right to a trial by jury in criminal cases.

7th Amendment: Guaranteees the right to a trial by jury in most civil cases.

8th Amendment: Prohibits excessive bail, fines, and punishments.

9th Amendment: Declares that rights not mentioned in the Constitution belong to the people.

10th Amendment: Declares that powers not given to the national government belong to the states or to the people.

Following the attacks of September 11, 2001, the government increased its policing powers to combat terrorism.

1. Why is the man in the foreground wearing a ribbon labeled "Bill of Rights"?

2. What is the cartoonist's point of view about the government's war on terrorism and citizen's rights? Do you agree or disagree? Why?

Protections Against Abuse of Power

The Second, Third, Fourth, and Fifth amendments all help protect citizens from abuse of power by police and judges, or by any other government officials. These amendments stem from the colonists' experience under the rule of England.

Gun Ownership The Second Amendment deals with the rights of citizens to own guns. The Amendment states:

"A well-regulated militia being necessary to the security of a free state, the right of the people to keep and bear arms shall not be infringed."

When this amendment was written, the American Revolution was fresh in the minds of citizens. Americans remembered that militias, or groups of citizens armed to defend themselves, had played an important role in achieving victory over the powerful British.

Throughout our nation's history, citizens have debated the exact meaning of the Second Amendment. Do Americans have a constitutional right to own guns for personal use? Should the government have the right to restrict the sale and use of guns? These questions are still being debated today.

The Housing of Soldiers During the colonial period, England had allowed English soldiers to use colonists' homes as living quarters against the colonists' wishes. The Third Amendment states that the government must obtain the owner's consent first. During wartime a citizen may have to provide soldiers with lodging, but only if Congress passes laws requiring it.

Unreasonable Searches and Seizures "Open up! This is the police. We have a warrant to search your house!" You have probably seen TV shows and movies in which police officers say this when entering the home of a suspect. Under the Fourth Amendment, officers cannot search a citizen or a citizen's home without a valid reason. Usually they must obtain a search warrant—written permission from a judge—to search citizens, their homes, or their belongings. To obtain a warrant, the police must convince a judge that they are likely to find evidence of a crime.

▲ A police officer conducts a search in a public school.

During the years leading to the American Revolution, as tensions between England and the colonies increased, Parliament allowed officers to make unlimited searches and seizures. Homes and businesses could be searched without warning or reason. Through the Fourth Amendment, Americans were guarding against any such abuse of power by the new government.

Protecting Property Rights May the government take away your property to build a freeway, subway, or other public project? Yes, it may. The government has the power of **eminent domain (EM eh nehnt do MAYN), the power to take private property for public use.** Recognized public use includes schools, parks, highways, fire and police stations, and public buildings. However, the Fifth Amendment protects citizens from an abuse of this power by requiring the government to pay owners a fair price for their property.

✓ Reading Check How do the amendments that protect against abuse of power suggest Americans' right to privacy?

Civics and Economics

Department of the Interior The government exercises its power of eminent domain when land will be used to benefit the public. For example, the land may be used to build highways, railroads, or reservoirs. Only a small fraction of land controlled by the government has been seized from private landowners through eminent domain. In parts of the United States, particularly in the west, the federal government has owned vast areas of land for more than a century. The Department of the Interior manages all of these federal lands, which amount to about one fifth of all land in the United States.

Analyzing Economics
Read more about the Department of the Interior through library or online research. How are funds generated by the federal government's use of public land?

Protections of the Accused

When arresting a person suspected of a crime, a police officer makes a statement like the following.

> "You have the right to remain silent. Anything you say can and will be used against you in a court of law. You are entitled to have an attorney present when you are questioned. If you cannot afford an attorney, one will be provided for you at public expense."

The Miranda Warning
A law enforcement officer holds up a Miranda Card. Law enforcement officers are required to read out the rights stated on the Miranda Card to all suspects taken into custody. **Predict** *How might the Miranda rights, such as "the right to remain silent," interfere with law enforcement?*

This statement is part of the Miranda warning, which is named after a man who was arrested without being informed of his rights. As a result of a Supreme Court decision in 1966, police officers must state the Miranda warning to anyone they arrest.

The rights of the accused are spelled out in the Fifth, Sixth, Seventh, and Eighth amendments. These amendments reflect English legal tradition dating back to the Magna Carta. This document stated that no person could be deprived of life, liberty, or property except by "the law of the land." The Constitution continues English tradition by stating that citizens are entitled to **due process of law**, a process by which the government must treat accused persons fairly according to rules established by law. People accused of crimes have rights under the Constitution.

The Fifth Amendment The Miranda warning mentions the right to remain silent because the Fifth Amendment says that nobody may be forced to "be a witness against himself." This is why accused persons sometimes say, "I take the Fifth" or "I refuse to answer on the grounds that it may incriminate me [make me appear guilty]." In some countries, police use torture or other methods to pressure citizens into confessing to crimes. Under the Fifth Amendment, any confessions must be freely given, not forced.

The Fifth Amendment also states that persons suspected of committing serious crimes such as murder must be indicted(in DYE ted), or accused, by a grand jury. A grand jury determines whether there is enough evidence to put the person on trial. Citizens are also protected from **double jeopardy (JEP ur dee)**, being placed on trial twice for the same crime. Thus, a person who has been found "not guilty" of a crime in a federal court cannot be put on trial again for the same offense.

Right to Trial by Jury A key element of due process of law is trial by jury. The Sixth Amendment guarantees a citizen's right to a speedy, public, and fair trial in any case involving a crime. A person may not be tried in secret or kept in jail for a long time awaiting trial. An accused person has the right to the advice of a lawyer. The Supreme Court has ruled that a defendant who cannot afford to pay a lawyer has the right to consult a lawyer paid by the government. An accused person also has the right to know what the accusations are and the right to ask questions of any witnesses during the trial. The accused has the right to see his or her accuser in court under ordinary circumstances.

The Seventh Amendment permits jury trials in cases where there are conflicts over property or money—as long as the value in dispute is over twenty dollars. The Sixth and Seventh amendments reflect the belief that trial by jury is important if people are to have trust and confidence in the law. The work of the courts is open to public view and public participation. When people serve as jurors, they help to make sure that their fellow citizens are treated fairly.

Law and the Real World

The Death Penalty, the U.S. Constitution, and DNA

A U.S. District Court judge in New York ruled in 2002 that the death penalty is unconstitutional because there is a risk that innocent people may be executed. In some cases, people sentenced to death several years ago have challenged their sentence using new DNA evidence. DNA tests have shown that occasionally, the wrong person was convicted of a crime. New DNA evidence is now being used to throw out convictions from past trials in which DNA tests were not available.

People who favor the death penalty believe that it is a constitutional form of punishment because the convict is sentenced by a jury. They argue that that it promotes justice, deters crime, and saves lives.

Applying the Law

1. What are the arguments for and against the death penalty?
2. Does the use of DNA tests support or weaken the arguments against the death penalty? Explain.

Bail, Fines, and Punishments The Eighth Amendment protects accused persons from unfair treatment both before and after a trial. Instead of having to stay in jail until the trial, an accused person may be allowed to deposit with the court a certain amount of money—called bail. This money is a pledge that the person will appear at the trial.

The Eighth Amendment forbids the amount of bail from being unfairly high. When the person appears at the trial, the bail is returned. This system protects the accused person from long-term imprisonment before being convicted of a crime. The Eighth Amendment also protects people from "cruel and unusual punishments." Whipping, branding, and other physical punishments were common in England and America during the 1700s. The debate continues today over whether the death penalty should be considered "cruel and unusual punishment."

Bail bonds are short-term loans that help people post bail.

✓ **Reading Check** Why is it important that all people be allowed the due process of law?

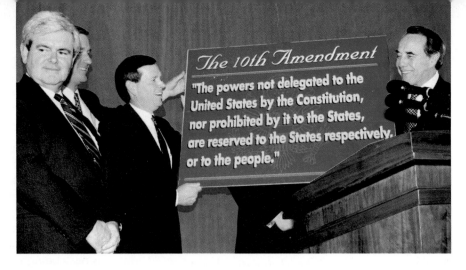

Power to the People
Republican Congressional leaders and a state governor display a placard stating the Tenth Amendment at a press conference.
Draw Conclusions *What point might these politicians be trying to make by calling attention to the Tenth Amendment?*

Target Reading Skill

Understand Sequence As you read the section Protections of Other Rights, consider the amendments that came before the Ninth and Tenth Amendments. How did those amendments influence the Ninth and Tenth Amendments?

Protections of Other Rights

One of the objections to adding a bill of rights had been that all rights could not possibly be included. James Madison, however, provided a solution to this problem. Madison suggested an amendment stating that citizens' rights are not limited to the ones listed in the Constitution. This proposal became the Ninth Amendment.

The Tenth Amendment settles a question arising from Article 1 of the Constitution. Article 1 describes which powers Congress has and does not have, and which powers are denied to the states. Who has the powers not mentioned? The Tenth Amendment declares that those powers belong to the state governments or to the people.

✓ **Reading Check** **How might the Ninth and Tenth Amendments have helped form a lasting Constitution?**

SECTION 2 **Assessment**

Key Terms

Use each of the key terms in a sentence that explains its meaning: separation of church and state, eminent domain, due process of law, double jeopardy

Target Reading Skill

1. **Understand Sequence** Place the events in the correct order:
   - An amendment says that citizen's rights are not limited to those in the Bill of Rights.
   - An amendment protects individual liberties.
   - An amendment addresses powers not mentioned in Article 1.
   - Amendments protect those accused of crimes.

Comprehension and Critical Thinking

2. **a. Recall** How does the First Amendment guarantee freedom of expression?
   b. Identify Cause and Effect How have First Amendment freedoms affected your school or neighborhood?

3. **a. Explain** How does the Bill of Rights limit government?
   b. Support a Point of View Are those restrictions on the government effective today?

4. **a. Recall** How does the Bill of Rights guarantee rights beyond those listed in the Constitution?
   b. Predict What problems might have arisen without the Tenth Amendment?

Writing Activity

Choose an amendment that you feel is important. Write a speech in which you argue why your chosen amendment is essential to the democratic system of government.

Go Online PHSchool.com

For: Journal Activity
Visit: PHSchool.com
Web Code: mpd-2062

Identifying Causes and Effects

When studying historical events, it is important to recognize the previous events that caused them. It is also necessary to understand the effects of an event. Understanding the chain of causes and effects gives you insight into why things happened the way they did.

The chart below shows some of the causes that led to the meeting of a constitutional convention and some effects of the meeting.

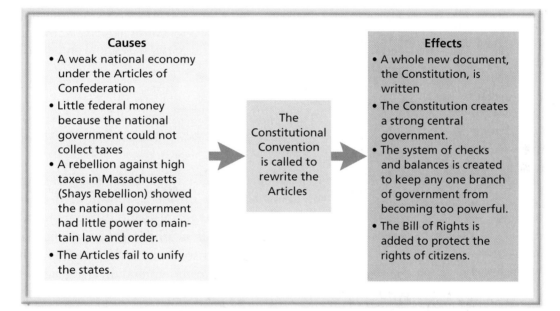

Causes	The Constitutional Convention is called to rewrite the Articles	Effects
• A weak national economy under the Articles of Confederation • Little federal money because the national government could not collect taxes • A rebellion against high taxes in Massachusetts (Shays Rebellion) showed the national government had little power to maintain law and order. • The Articles fail to unify the states.		• A whole new document, the Constitution, is written • The Constitution creates a strong central government. • The system of checks and balances is created to keep any one branch of government from becoming too powerful. • The Bill of Rights is added to protect the rights of citizens.

Learn the Skill

Follow these steps to identify causes and effects:

❶ **Identify the historical event.** Think about the time it occurred, who was involved, and other circumstances.

❷ **Identify the causes.** Consider decisions, problems, or other actions that led up to the event.

❸ **Identify the effects.** These are the results of the event. What happened because of the event?

❹ **Analyze the connection between causes and effects.** Think about how the causes led to the event and how the effects resulted from the event.

Practice the Skill

Look at the chart above and answer these questions:

❶ What event is the subject of the cause-and-effect chart?

❷ Identify two causes of the event.

❸ Identify two effects of the event.

❹ How did the U.S. Constitution address the problems that led up to the Constitutional Convention?

Apply the Skill

Think of an event you have observed. Draw up a cause-and-effect chart listing causes of the event and effects that resulted from the event.

Interpreting the Bill of Rights

Reading Preview

Objectives

In this section you will

- Determine the role of the courts in interpreting citizens' rights.
- Examine the definition of freedom of speech and students' rights in the *Tinker* case.
- Describe how the courts protected freedom of expression for extreme groups in the *Skokie* case.
- Understand that protecting the rights of citizens is a continuing challenge for all.

Taking Notes

Make a diagram like the one below. As you read the section, complete the diagram with information about the causes and effects of decisions made in the cases discussed in this section.

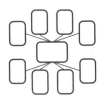

Key Terms

freedom of the press

freedom of speech

case studies

Main Idea

Many different situations call into question the meaning of our rights under the Constitution. It is the role of the courts to interpret the Bill of Rights and to apply them to each case.

Target Reading Skill

Recognize Words That Signal Sequence Signal words point out relationships among ideas or events. As you read, help keep the order of events clear by looking for words like *first, at that time, in [date]* that signal sequence.

What happens when people disagree about the meaning of our rights under the Constitution? Consider **freedom of the press**, the right to publish newspapers, magazines, and other materials without governmental restriction. Is a school principal violating students' rights when he or she censors an article that was written for the school newspaper? Is the government endangering rights when it passes libel laws that forbid people to print damaging and false statements about others?

Consider **freedom of speech**, the right to express one's opinions publicly. Does a person have the right to make a speech that causes listeners to riot, causing injury to others and damaging public and private property? Does a speaker have the right to call for violence against another person? Does a person have the right to tell damaging lies about a public figure on the radio or television?

The rights of citizens are often difficult to interpret. The framers of the Bill of Rights could not have predicted the many ways the ten amendments could be tested in just a single day. The first ten amendments to the Constitution are broad descriptions of rights. They were not intended to explain how those rights apply to every situation. And sometimes certain rights have to be weighed against other rights. For example, suppose a person wants to make a speech that may cause a violent reaction. The right of that person's free speech must be weighed against the importance of providing for the safety of other citizens.

The Role of the Courts

The people who tackle the difficult job of interpreting the meaning of citizens' rights are the judges in our nation's courts. As legal experts, they decide whether people's rights are being violated by the actions of other citizens. They also decide whether rights have been violated by any laws.

Usually cases involving citizens' rights are first brought before local judges. If necessary, the decisions of these judges may be examined by higher courts, such as state courts. A few cases that start out in local courts eventually reach the United States Supreme Court. These cases often have far-reaching consequences for the nation.

You will now be reading about two challenging court cases that reached the Supreme Court. Both cases involve First Amendment rights. The decisions of the Court are presented as **case studies**, which are descriptions of situations or conflicts, the issues involved, and the decisions made.

Case studies can help you see principles of the Constitution being put into action. You can see how an ideal, such as freedom of speech, applies to a real situation. As you read each case study, picture yourself as one of the nine justices of the Supreme Court. Think about how you would decide the case.

✓ **Reading Check** Describe a conflict involving citizens' rights in which neither party is clearly right or wrong.

Freedom of the Press
Students work on their school newspaper.
Analyze *Do school administrators have a say over what student editors publish in the school newspaper?*

▲
Mary Beth and John Tinker display the black armbands that the Supreme Court ruled were a form of speech protected by the First Amendment. The case has had important implications for the right of students to protest.

Students and Free Speech

Mary Beth Tinker and Christopher Eckhardt were students in Des Moines, Iowa, in 1965. A community group decided to protest American involvement in the Vietnam War. All the protestors would wear black armbands. Thirteen-year-old Mary Beth and 16-year-old Christopher came to school one day wearing the black armbands. The next day Mary Beth's 15-year-old brother John also wore a black armband to school. The students felt it was their right to protest the war in school. Their small protest would have important implications for freedom of speech and eventually cause the Supreme Court to wrestle with two questions. What is meant by "speech" in freedom of speech? What rights do students have under the Constitution?

The Case When Des Moines school officials first learned of the students' plan to protest, they forbade the wearing of armbands. When the students wore armbands anyway, they were suspended. The Tinkers' parents argued that the school board was denying the students' right to freedom of speech. They declared that the students had not disrupted classes or interfered with other students' rights. School officials defended the armband rule, stating that it preserved discipline. They argued that schools were not places for political demonstrations.

The Court's Decision The case first came before a local court, which ruled that the armband rule was necessary to avoid disruption of classes. A higher court also affirmed the school district's decision. However, the Tinkers did not give up. The students had one last hope: the Supreme Court.

The Supreme Court heard the case and ruled in favor of the students. It held that armbands were a form of "speech" because they were symbols representing ideas. The justices also said that the protest was protected by the First Amendment because it had not interfered with other students' right to an education.

Most importantly, the Court emphasized that students do have a basic right to free speech. The Court declared:

"It can hardly be argued that students or teachers shed their constitutional rights to freedom of speech or expression at the schoolhouse gate... Students in school as well as out of school are "persons" under our Constitution."

Think about the Court's ruling. Why is it important for students to have freedom of speech? How should that freedom be limited? What responsibilities go along with it?

✓ Reading Check   **What are some other symbols that are protected by the First Amendment?**

Target Reading Skill
Recognize Words That Signal Sequence As you read about the Skokie case, look for words that signal the sequence of events. Which words show the order of events in the "Background" paragraph?

The Skokie Case: Freedom for Nazis?

When may freedom of expression be limited? What other rights must be considered? What if a person or group expresses ideas that most people find shocking or despicable? All of these questions were involved in the Skokie case, one of the most controversial in our nation's history.

Background In the 1930s, members of dictator Adolf Hitler's Nazi (NOT zee) Party attacked the homes of Jews throughout Germany. Between 1938 and 1945, the Nazis forced millions of Jews and other people into camps to be starved, tortured, and killed.

Conflict in Skokie The year was 1977. The place was Skokie, Illinois. The town's residents included 40,000 Jews. Many of these people had survived the horror of Nazi camps, but many of their relatives had not. In May a small group of uniformed men applied for a permit to march through Skokie. These men were members of the American Nazi Party. Each wore a large black swastika—the symbol of the Nazi Party.

These plans shocked and enraged Skokie officials, who wanted to prevent the march. They informed the American Nazi group that it would have to obtain $350,000 of insurance before a permit to march would be issued. Town officials hoped that the cost of this insurance would discourage the Nazis from marching in Skokie.

Frank Collin led the American Nazi group that fought to march on Skokie, Illinois. ▼

The following excerpt is from a letter to the editor written in 1978 by a citizen concerned about the planned Nazi march in Skokie, Illinois.

"Our founding fathers provided that what is meant by any part of the Constitution or its amendments should be decided by the courts—not by you, me, or any other individual—not even the President of the United States, not by police, army, navy, air force, or marines, not by state or national legislature or village board. If and when the Nazis march in Skokie, will the people of the village choose to be governed by emotion or by law?"

James S. Ayars
Urbana, Ill.

Analyze Primary Sources

Which side of the Skokie case does this citizen support? How can you tell?

Then when the Nazis planned a rally to protest the insurance requirement, the county court stated that the group could not hold a demonstration. The court forbade anyone to march in a Nazi uniform, display the swastika, or distribute material promoting hatred.

The Court Battle Begins A long and painful court battle began. From the Illinois courts to the United States Supreme Court, judges faced a challenging question: does the First Amendment protect even Nazis and their message of hatred?

The case stirred nationwide interest. Many people argued that the First Amendment does not protect people who want to destroy freedom and spread violence. As one citizen stated, "Freedom of expression has no meaning when it defends those who would end this right for others." Another said, "In Germany they also started with a bunch of crazies... Anybody who advocates killing should not be allowed to rally."

Those who argued that Nazis do have a right to freedom of expression included members of the American Civil Liberties Union (ACLU). The ACLU is an organization devoted to defending citizens' rights under the First Amendment. ACLU lawyers asked a basic question: if the government may deny freedom of expression to one group, what will prevent it from denying that right to any other group? A Jewish member of the ACLU summed up this argument by saying, "The First Amendment has to be for everyone—or it will be for no one."

Clearly, the Skokie case presented a major challenge for the courts. There were powerful arguments and strong feelings on both sides.

Appealing the Case The American Nazi group was unwilling to accept the county court order. They took their case to the Illinois Supreme Court.

In response, the Illinois Supreme Court refused to overrule the county court order or to rule on the fairness of the Skokie laws. Therefore, the Nazis asked the United States Supreme Court to hear their case.

On June 14, 1977, the Supreme Court ordered Illinois to hold a hearing on their ruling against the Nazis. The Court did not discuss either the county court order or the Skokie laws. But its decision led the Illinois and U.S. District courts to examine those laws closely in light of the First Amendment.

Protecting First Amendment Rights For almost a year, the Illinois and U.S. District courts struggled with the issue of limits on the American Nazis' right to freedom of expression. The courts finally decided that the Skokie law requiring insurance violated the First Amendment. The courts stated that the insurance was too costly for most groups. It limited their freedoms of speech and assembly. Also, the law had not been applied equally. The town officials required the Nazis to pay for insurance, but other groups were allowed to hold rallies without insurance.

The courts also concluded that the Nazis had a right to distribute material expressing hatred. The First Amendment protects the expression of all ideas—even beliefs that threaten the basic principles of our nation.

The court rulings drew upon old Supreme Court precedents protecting the right to free speech, no matter how cruel or unpopular. As Justice Oliver Wendell Holmes once said, our Constitution protects "the principle of free thought—not free thought for those who agree with us but freedom for the thought that we hate."

Active Citizen

Students Make a Difference

Clem Woods, a senior at Phillips Academy in Andover, Maryland, is the editor-in-chief of The Phillipian, the Phillips Academy student-run weekly newspaper. He understands that the decisions he makes can influence public discussion.

Clem's role as a journalist has fueled his enthusiasm for government. Since his freshman year, Clem has participated in Model United Nations, a program that simulates the United Nations system. He has been a delegate from Canada and has been a justice, presiding over cases on the International Criminal Court.

▲ Students can help make a difference by keeping their peers informed about important issues.

Service Learning

How does being an informed citizen benefit your community?

Symbols as Speech The courts discussed whether the Nazi uniform and swastika symbol were protected by the First Amendment. Earlier court decisions, particularly the Tinker case, had established that symbols were a form of speech. The issue was whether the hated swastika symbol would cause a violent reaction, threatening public safety. Were the Nazis guilty of trying to start a fight?

The courts heard strong testimony from Jews in Skokie about the meaning of the swastika to them. One concentration camp survivor angrily declared, "I do not know if I could control myself if I saw the swastika in a parade." Skokie attorneys argued that, for Jews, seeing the swastika was just like being physically attacked.

The Illinois Supreme Court deeply sympathized with the Skokie residents but decided that the swastika could not be banned. Otherwise, the mere possibility of violence could keep anyone from exercising the right to freedom of expression. The court reluctantly concluded that the Nazis could wear their symbol. The United States Supreme Court agreed.

In the summer of 1978 the Nazis finally held two rallies, but not in Skokie. Both rallies were in Chicago, and the Nazis faced thousands of people demonstrating against them. A heavy guard of Chicago police officers was assigned to prevent any violence.

A Marketplace of Ideas The Skokie case showed that the First Amendment protects both popular and unpopular beliefs. The First Amendment makes possible what Justice Holmes called "a marketplace of ideas," in which all views may be expressed. Holmes believed that people should be allowed to hear many different ideas. According to Justice Holmes, the test of a good idea is "the power of the thought to get itself accepted in the competition of the market."

✓ Reading Check   **How did the Skokie case prove the need for courts to interpret citizens' rights?**

Exchange of Ideas
A man reads a newspaper editorial (above). People meet to discuss issues and ideas (right).
Draw Inferences *How do these two photographs illustrate what Justice Holmes termed "a marketplace of ideas"?*

The Continuing Challenge

Protecting the rights of citizens is not just the responsibility of judges and laws. It is a continuing challenge that we all share. Another famous American judge, Learned Hand, made this point in the following way:

> "I often wonder whether we do not rest our hopes too much upon constitutions, upon laws, and upon courts. These are false hopes... Liberty lies in the hearts of men and women; when it dies there, no constitution, no law, no court can even do much to help it. While it lies there it needs no constitution, no law, no court to save it."

As Judge Learned Hand emphasized, the rights of American citizens are not protected just because they have been written down in our nation's Constitution. We as citizens of the United States—even while still students—play a key role in protecting our rights. By respecting each other's rights, we help guarantee that the Bill of Rights survives.

✓ **Reading Check** **What are some ways that you can help protect and uphold the rights of others around you?**

▲ Learned Hand (1872–1961) served on the federal court system's Second Circuit Court of Appeals from 1924 to 1951. He was a committed defender of free speech and one of the finest legal minds of his day.

SECTION 3 Assessment

Key Terms

Use each of the key terms in a sentence that explains its meaning: freedom of the press, freedom of speech, case studies

Target Reading Skill

1. **Recognize Words That Signal Sequence** Review the paragraphs after the heading *Conflict in Skokie*. Identify the words that signal the sequence of events in Skokie that led up to the court battle.

Comprehension and Critical Thinking

2. **a. Describe** What is the relationship between the courts and the Bill of Rights?
b. Identify Cause and Effect How do the courts determine the limits of the First Amendment's guarantee of freedom of expression?

3. **a. Explain** Why did the Supreme Court find in favor of the students in the Tinker case?
b. Predict If the students in the Tinker case had posted anti-war signs in classrooms, might the outcome of the case have been different? Why or why not?

4. **a. Recall** On what grounds did the Illinois Supreme Court decide to allow the Nazi rally?
b. Determine Relevance How does a "marketplace of ideas" reflect the American ideal of democracy?

5. **a. Explain** Why does Judge Hand call constitutions, laws, and courts "false hopes"?
b. Draw Conclusions How do you, your classmates, and your family demonstrate Hand's belief that "liberty lies in the hearts of men and women"?

Writing Activity

Select one of the case studies from this chapter and write an essay discussing the arguments of the two opposing side in the case. Compare and contrast their interpretations of citizens' rights.

TIP Before you write, brainstorm a list of similarities and differences between the two parties' interpretations of the Bill of Rights. Use this as a guide to writing a strong essay that moves clearly and logically from one point to the next.

Debating the Issues

CLOSE UP FOUNDATION

The debates in this feature are based on *Current Issues*, published by the Close Up Foundation. Go to **PHSchool.com**, Web Code mph-2063, to read the latest issue of *Current Issues* online.

The Charitable Choice provision of the 1996 Welfare Reform Act allows religious organizations to compete for federal funds. These funds may only be used for social programs such as drug treatment or feeding the homeless. The money may not be used to pay for religious services or activities. This policy was expanded in 2000. The money for these funds comes from taxpayers.

Should the Federal Government Fund Faith-Based Providers of Social Services?

YES	NO
• Many religious groups have a long-standing record of excellence in community and social service. The government is right to encourage these faith-based organizations to expand social programs and give direct help to those in need.	• The United States Constitution forbids the government to support any religious organization. No such organization can separate its religious agenda from the social services it provides.
• The Constitution does not forbid the government from giving funds to religious organizations. Under Charitable Choice, federal funds are equally available to all denominations.	• Taxpayers should not be forced to donate money to religious organizations whose teachings they do not support. The Charitable Choice program gives some of their tax money to religious organizations whether the taxpayers like it or not.
• Faith-based organizations are friendly and approachable. People in need can ask for and receive direct help simply by walking in the door. Government social programs often involve detailed application forms and long waiting lists.	• Religious organizations tend to hire only those workers who share their faith. The government should not use taxpayers' money to fund social programs with discriminatory hiring practices such as this.

What is Your Opinion?

1. **Analyze Primary Sources** Read the First Amendment to the Constitution. Does it prohibit the government from funding social programs run by religious organizations? Explain.

2. **Make Decisions** The law states that religious organizations may discriminate according to faith when hiring workers for federally funded programs. Do you agree with this law? Why or why not?

3. **Writing to Persuade** You are a candidate for a Senate seat. Write a speech you will give at a rally, outlining your position on federally funded faith-based programs. Make specific arguments that will rally support for your position.

Go Online
civics
interactive
For: You Decide Poll
Visit: PHSchool.com
Web Code: mpp-2063

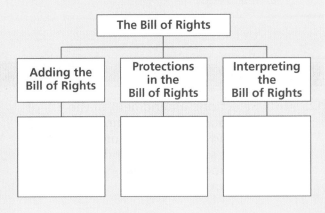

Chapter Summary

Section 1
Adding the Bill of Rights
(pages 160–162)

- The Bill of Rights was added to the Constitution to protect the individual rights of citizens.

- In the amendment process, Constitutional amendments are proposed by Congress or by a national convention and must be ratified by state legislatures or state conventions.

- The promise of the addition of a bill of rights to the Constitution helped earn people's trust in the new federal government.

- In 1791, the states ratified the first ten amendments to the Constitution that make up the Bill of Rights.

Section 2
Protections in the Bill of Rights
(pages 163–170)

- The First Amendment to the Constitution protects individual freedoms such as the freedoms of religion, speech, the press, assembly, and petition.

- The First Amendment also calls for the separation of church and state, which states that the government may not favor any religion or establish an official religion.

- The Bill of Rights protects citizens from abuse of power by the government by limiting its ability to interfere with their property.

- The government has the power of eminent domain, but it must compensate owners for their property.

- Under the Bill of Rights, people accused of crimes have the right to due process of law, including a fair trial by jury, and are protected from double jeopardy.

- The Ninth and Tenth Amendments state that citizens' rights are not limited to the ones in the Constitution and reserves all powers not specifically addressed in the Constitution to the states or to the people.

Section 3
Interpreting the Bill of Rights
(pages 172–179)

- The courts interpret the meaning of rights such as freedom of the press and freedom of speech, and apply these interpretations in different situations.

- Case studies of important court decisions show how the principles of the Constitution are put into action.

- In the *Tinker* case, the Supreme Court decided that symbols such as armbands are forms of free speech and that students have the right to free speech.

- The First Amendment protects the expression of unpopular ideas, as long as the ideas do not directly endanger other citizens.

- Citizens play a key role in protecting individual rights by their actions and behaviors towards one another.

Copy the chart below and use it to help you summarize the chapter.

```
          The Bill of Rights
   ┌───────────┬───────────────┬────────────┐
 Adding the   Protections      Interpreting
 Bill of Rights   in the           the
              Bill of Rights   Bill of Rights
   ┌──────┐   ┌──────┐         ┌──────┐
   │      │   │      │         │      │
   └──────┘   └──────┘         └──────┘
```

Review and Assessment Continued

Reviewing Key Terms

Fill in each blank with one of the key terms from the list below.

eminent   Bill of Rights
domain   separation of church and
due process of   state
    law   freedom of the press
freedom of   double jeopardy
speech   amendment process

1. The Bill of Rights guarantees _____ so that newspapers, magazines, and other materials may be published without government limits.

2. Although the government has the power of _____, it must pay citizens for any property it takes away.

3. Every citizen accused of a crime is entitled to _____.

4. The Constitution establishes the _____ in order to prevent the government from setting a national religion.

5. The first ten amendments to the Constitution make up the _____.

6. The _____ allows citizens to express their political views freely through writing, speaking, or the use of symbols.

7. The Constitution may be changed through the _____.

8. The Bill of Rights upholds the rights of accused persons by protecting them from _____.

Comprehension and Critical Thinking

9. a. **Recall** What are the two steps of the amendment process?
   b. **Analyze Information** How does the amendment process balance power between the national government and the states?
   c. **Summarize** Why did the promise of a bill of rights encourage states to ratify the Constitution?

10. a. **Describe** In what ways does the Bill of Rights protect the rights of citizens?
    b. **Synthesize Information** How does the separation of church and state guarantee freedom?

    c. **Determine Relevance** How does the Bill of Rights reflect the American idea of democracy?

11. a. **Explain** How has the Supreme Court defined "freedom of speech"?
    b. **Synthesize Information** How does Justice Holmes' belief in a "marketplace of ideas" relate to the practice of free speech?
    c. **Draw Conclusions** Why is it necessary for courts to interpret our legal rights under the Constitution?

Activities

12. **Skills** Select one amendment in the Bill of Rights. Conduct research online or in a library to find out more about it. Then, identify at least one cause and two effects of the addition of that amendment to the Constitution.

13. **Writing** Observe how people around you live by the rights guaranteed in the Bill of Rights. In what ways do they respect the rights of others? For one week, keep a journal in which you list your observations.

14. **Active Citizen** The Bill of Rights guarantees your freedom to express your political views. Look through a newspaper and select a political issue that is important to you. Then, write a letter to the editor in which you explain your opinion of the issue.

15. **Math Practice** The amendment process has been used 27 times between 1791 and 1992. On average, how often have amendments been added between 1791 and 1992?

16. **Civics and Economics** Journalists work by exercising the rights of free speech and freedom of the press. Do some Internet research to find out about careers in journalism. Summarize your findings in a brief report.

17. **Analyzing Visuals** In what ways does the Bill of Rights protect these protesters?

Standardized Test Prep

Test-Taking Tips

Some questions on standardized tests ask you to analyze primary sources. Study the quote below. Then follow the tips to answer the sample question.

> First Amendment freedoms are most in danger when the government seeks to control thought... The right to think is the beginning of freedom, and speech must be protected from the government because speech is the beginning of thought.
>
> —Supreme Court Justice Anthony M. Kennedy

TIP Always keep in mind who the speaker or author is.

Choose the letter of the statement that best answers each question.

1. How does Justice Kennedy feel about free speech?

   TIP Words like *should* or *must* are clues that point to the speaker's opinion.

   A Free speech should only be limited by the government.

   B It is more important to protect freedom of thought than free speech.

   C Free speech must be protected because it allows freedom of thought.

   D Courts must limit freedom of thought.

   The correct answer is **C**. Note that the question asks you to determine Justice Kennedy's opinion about free speech.

2. Why might freedoms be in danger when the government controls thought?

   A People would not be allowed to express their thoughts.

   B Citizens would forget their First Amendment freedoms.

   C The government would put the lives of citizens in danger.

   D The courts would favor freedom of thought over free speech.

CHAPTER 7

Our Enduring Constitution

What's Ahead in Chapter 7

In this chapter, you will learn how the Constitution of the United States continues to respond to the changing needs of society. You will read about the amendments to the Constitution that brought equality to a greater number of Americans. You will learn about the role of the Supreme Court in applying constitutional principles.

SECTION 1
Changing the Law of the Land

SECTION 2
A Flexible Framework

TARGET READING SKILL

Word Analysis In this chapter you will focus on analyzing words in order to better understand them. Analyzing words includes breaking words down into parts, such as prefixes and roots, and recognizing word origins.

Over 200,000 people ▶ attended Martin Luther King's March on Washington for civil rights in 1963

National | **Standards for Civics and Government** | **State**

The following National Standards for Civics and Government are addressed in this chapter:

I. What are Civic Life, Politics, and Government?
C. What are the nature and purposes of constitutions?

II. What are the foundations of the American political system?
C. What is American political culture?

Go Online
PHSchool.com
For: Your state's standards
Visit: www.PHSchool.com
Web Code: mpe-2071

Active Citizen   Civics in the Real World

One Monday morning Mrs. Taylor made a surprise announcement to her Civics class: they were going to elect a student committee to recommend rules for the class. At first the students responded enthusiastically, but then Mrs. Taylor stunned them by saying: "In order to vote for committee members, you must be a boy and you must be white."

Immediately students began to protest. Why were the girls not allowed to vote? Why could the African American, Hispanic American, and Asian American students not vote?

After listening to the objections, Mrs. Taylor replied, "Actually, I agree with you. It is unfair. But I wanted to make a point about our nation. For much of our history, most states allowed only white males to vote. Fortunately, this is not longer the case because the Constitution has been changed."

Our Constitution has survived for over two centuries because it responds to the needs of a growing and changing society. Despite changes in attitudes and conditions over the years, Americans have not had to create a whole new Constitution.

Citizen's Journal   Our Constitution is described as a flexible document. Write a paragraph explaining why you think this flexibility has been important to our nation. Then, after studying the chapter, reread your paragraph. Write a new paragraph, explaining how your understanding has grown.

Changing the Law of the Land

Reading Preview

Objectives

In this section you will

- Learn how slavery was abolished.
- Find out more about how African Americans gained the right to vote.
- Explore how women gained the right to vote.
- Discuss how youth gained the right to vote.
- Learn how the Constitution adapts to the needs of society.

Taking Notes

Make a flow map organizer like the one below. As you read the section, complete the diagram to record the amendments discussed.

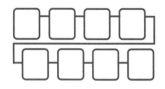

The Statue of Freedom atop the Capitol building in Washington, D.C.

Key Terms

poll tax   suffrage

Main Idea

Citizenship and voting rights have undergone dramatic changes in our country's history. The amendment process enables our Constitution to adapt to a constantly changing society.

Target Reading Skill

Analyze Word Parts Breaking down difficult words into parts may enable you to recognize a word meaning and pronunciation. You may find roots, prefixes, or suffixes. A root is the base of a word that has meaning by itself. A prefix goes in front of the root and changes the meaning.

Since the Bill of Rights became part of the Constitution, 17 other amendments have been added. Most of these amendments reflect efforts to change the Constitution to meet changing needs and attitudes. For example, over time there has been a great change in the attitude of Americans about who has the right to vote.

Originally, the Constitution let the states decide who was qualified to be a citizen. Most states granted citizenship only to white men who owned property. Today, however, anyone born or naturalized in the United States is a citizen. Any citizen who is at least 18 years old may vote.

As you know, the Constitution begins with the words "We the people of the United States." Why is the meaning of "we the people" so much broader today than it was in 1787? In the following pages you will step back into history to trace the changes in citizenship and voting rights that have taken place in this country over the years. You will see how the amendment process helps the Constitution adjust to changing times.

Abolishing Slavery

Many people were denied citizenship in the early years of our nation. Among them were enslaved African Americans. The United States was founded on freedom. Why did it permit slavery? Why was slavery eventually abolished by an amendment to the Constitution? Finding the answers requires looking at the history of slavery in our nation.

Amendments 11–27

Amendment	Year Ratified	Subject
11th	1795	Lawsuits against states
12th	1804	Separate voting for President and Vice President
13th	1865	Abolition of slavery
14th	1868	Citizenship and civil rights
15th	1870	Voting rights for African American men
16th	1913	Income tax
17th	1913	Direct election of senators
18th	1919	Prohibition of alcoholic beverages
19th	1920	Voting rights for women
20th	1933	Term of President, Vice President, and Congress
21th	1933	Repeal of Eighteenth Amendment
22th	1951	President limited to two terms
23th	1961	Electoral votes for the District of Colombia
24th	1964	Abolition of poll taxes
25th	1967	Presidential disability and succession
26th	1971	Voting age lowered to eighteen
27th	1992	Congressional Pay

After the first ten amendments in the Bill of Rights, our Constitution has been amended only 17 more times.

1. **Analyze** Which amendment lowered the voting age to 18? When was it passed?
2. **Apply** Which amendments broadened voting rights?

Slavery and the Framers The Constitutional Convention probably would have failed without a compromise on slavery. Southerners believed that their farming economy would collapse without slave labor. However, by that time many northern states had banned slavery within their borders, and wanted slavery to be made illegal nationwide. The framers needed both the northern and southern states to ratify the Constitution. Therefore, the framers avoided deciding whether to abolish slavery. Nowhere in the Constitution is the word *slavery* even mentioned. Instead, the framers used phrases such as *all other persons* and *such people* to refer to slaves without using the words *slave* or *slavery*.

To avoid angering the southern states, the framers even tried to make slavery seem acceptable. They agreed that slaves could be counted as part of a state's population and that runaway slaves had to be returned to their owners. However, neither the northern nor southern states were completely satisfied by the compromises. Many Americans wondered whether a nation so divided over slavery could survive.

Tension Between North and South As new states joined the nation during the early 1800s, the North and the South competed for power in Congress. The more populous northern states controlled a majority in the House. However, the North argued that including enslaved people in population counts gave southern states more representatives than they deserved. The South, in turn, feared that the North might use its political power to abolish slavery everywhere.

Congress tried to avoid a serious conflict by passing the Missouri Compromise in 1820. This law divided new lands into "slave" territories and "free" territories. Nevertheless, Americans increasingly saw slavery as an "all or nothing" issue. On one side were those who defended the right to own slaves anywhere. On the other side were those who wanted slavery to be banned everywhere.

Further efforts at compromise seemed hopeless. Therefore, Congress later tried the principle of majority rule, allowing settlers in each territory to vote on whether to allow slavery there. However, this only sparked conflict among settlers. Tension within the nation continued to build.

A Controversial Court Decision A tense nation awaited a Supreme Court decision on a case in 1857. Many people hoped this case would finally settle the slavery issue.

A slave named Dred Scott had traveled with his slaveholder to Illinois and the Wisconsin territory where slavery was illegal. After they returned to Missouri, Scott argued that his residence in a free territory had made him a free person. Now the Court had to decide whether or not Scott was free according to the Constitution.

The Court ruled that, according to the Constitution, slaves were property. The Court also ruled that Congress could not prevent slaveholders from taking slaves anywhere they wished. The Constitution was interpreted as allowing slavery. Despite the decision, Americans who opposed slavery did not give up hope that things would change.

The Thirteenth Amendment Change finally came after the Civil War, which took the lives of more than 600,000 Americans. The North's victory in the war paved the way for the Thirteenth Amendment, which abolished slavery in 1865.

A Case for Freedom
In 1857, the front page of *Frank Leslie's Illustrated Newspaper* featured an article about the Dred Scott case. **Draw Conclusions** *Do you think* Frank Leslie's Illustrated Newspaper *was a newspaper from the North or the South? Why?*

✓ Reading Check **Why was the outcome of the Dred Scott case considered a victory for defenders of slavery?**

Slave States and Free States, 1854

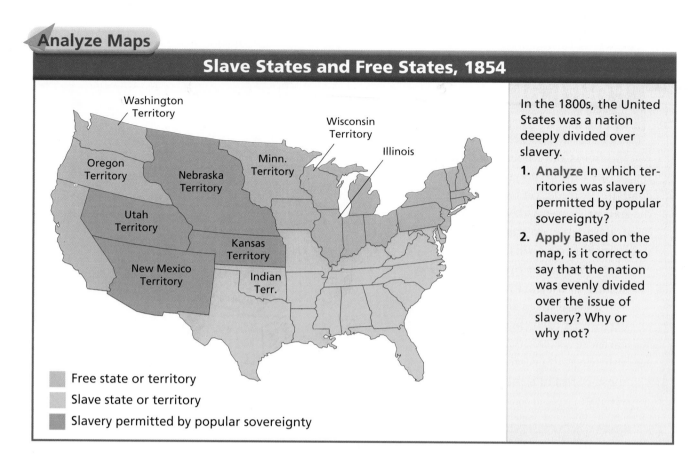

Washington
Territory

Oregon
Territory

Nebraska
Territory

Utah
Territory

New Mexico
Territory

Kansas
Territory

Minn.
Territory

Wisconsin
Territory

Illinois

Indian
Terr.

Free state or territory
Slave state or territory
Slavery permitted by popular sovereignty

In the 1800s, the United States was a nation deeply divided over slavery.

1. **Analyze** In which territories was slavery permitted by popular sovereignty?

2. **Apply** Based on the map, is it correct to say that the nation was evenly divided over the issue of slavery? Why or why not?

African Americans and the Right to Vote

The Constitution now banned slavery. But the struggle for citizenship and voting rights for African Americans had only begun. Even those who had been free long before the Civil War knew that freedom did not mean equality. For one thing, the states still had the power to decide who could be a citizen. Most states—both northern and southern—continued to deny citizenship to African Americans.

The Fourteenth Amendment This amendment, adopted in 1868, ensured citizenship for African Americans. It takes the power to grant citizenship away from the states. The amendment states that "All persons born or naturalized in the United States . . . are citizens of the United States and of the state wherein they reside." It also declares that no state may "deprive any person of life, liberty, or property without due process of law" or "deny to any person . . . the equal protection of the laws."

Why were these statements added when there was already a Bill of Rights? Actually, the first ten amendments say only that Congress must respect citizens' rights. The Fourteenth Amendment specifically requires the states to do so. Therefore, it has often been called the "second Bill of Rights."

The Fourteenth Amendment did not automatically ensure equal treatment. The Supreme Court had ruled that state governments could not treat African Americans unfairly. This did not prevent private citizens, such as employers, from discriminating against them.

The First Vote
This drawing by A.R. Waud shows African American men voting in the first state election during reconstruction in the South.
Draw Conclusions *Why do you think there are no African American women voting?*

Amendments have been made to the Constitution to reflect the changing attitudes on issues facing the nation. Some issues that were once acceptable or tolerated are now considered unconstitutional.

1. Describe the action in the setting of the cartoon.
2. What issues does the cartoonist include in the cartoon?
3. Why does the cartoonist put these issues in a museum setting?

CLOSE★UP®
FOUNDATION

Watch the **Civics: Government and Economics in Action** videos to learn about liberty and equality.

Video: Overview   ▶Video: Up Close

Target Reading Skill

Analyze Word Parts Breaking apart a word into its parts can help you understand its meaning. For example, if *in-* means "not," what is the meaning of *injustice?*

The Fifteenth Amendment In some states being a citizen did not guarantee **suffrage,** or the right to vote. To keep states from denying voting rights to African Americans, the Fifteenth Amendment, added in 1870, declares that states may not deny the vote to any person on the basis of "race, color, or previous condition of servitude."

The Twenty-Fourth Amendment Despite the Fifteenth Amendment, some states found a number of ways to prevent African Americans from voting. Some states required citizens to pay a **poll tax,** or fee for voting. Many were unable to vote because they were too poor to pay the tax.

The passage of the Twenty-fourth Amendment in 1964 finally made poll taxes illegal. This amendment was an important step toward protecting the rights of African Americans and undoing the injustice done against them.

Changes in the Constitution do not guarantee that attitudes and conditions in society will change completely and immediately. It took more than 100 years for the nation to make real progress toward ending discrimination against African Americans and other racial groups.

✔ Reading Check   **Why is the Fourteenth Amendment to the Constitution sometimes called the "second Bill of Rights"?**

Women and the Right to Vote

African Americans were not the only group left out of "we the people" in 1787. Women, too, faced a long struggle for full citizenship rights. Unlike slavery, women's rights did not even seem to be an issue in the minds of the framers. Traditional ideas about the role of women help to explain why most states denied them voting rights for many years.

Traditional Ideas About Women Long before the founding of our country, most people believed that women belonged in the home caring for the family. They believed women were unable to handle many of the jobs that men performed. Large numbers of women took factory jobs during the 1800s. But still, laws treated them differently from men. Some laws allowed women to do only specific—usually low-paid—jobs.

People who held the traditional view disapproved of women voting or holding political office. They argued that politically active women would leave their family responsibilities behind. This would upset the stability of family life. They also thought that women were less intelligent than men. They believed that women were less able to make political decisions.

Primary Sources

Susan B. Anthony was a well known American suffragist. In 1872, she was arrested for voting in a presidential election. She delivered a speech in 1873 that reflected on women's right to vote.

"[The Constitution states] we, the people; not we, the white male citizens; nor yet we, the male citizens; but we, the whole people, who formed the Union. And we formed it, not to give the blessings of liberty, but to secure them; not to the half of ourselves and the half of our posterity, but to the whole people—women as well as men. And it is a downright mockery to talk to women of their enjoyment of the blessings of liberty while they are denied the use of the only means of securing them provided by this democratic-republican government—the ballot."

Analyze Primary Sources How does Susan B. Anthony's interpretation of the opening words of the preamble to the Constitution support her argument?

Challenging the Traditional View By the late 1800s, people's views toward women began to change. More women took jobs. Many women also became active in social and political issues.

Soon, some women began to insist on the right to vote. A declaration from the Seneca Falls women's rights convention in 1848 stated, "We hold these truths to be self evident: that all men and women are created equal." Nevertheless, by 1900 only a handful of states had granted suffrage to women.

During the late 1800s and early 1900s, supporters of women's suffrage gained the public's attention. These supporters were known as suffragists. They marched, gave speeches, wrote to government officials and newspapers, and even went on hunger strikes. A proposed amendment giving suffrage to women was introduced—but failed to pass—in almost every session of Congress for 40 years, from 1878 to 1918.

Women suffragists attempted to capture the public's attention for their cause.

The Nineteenth Amendment By 1916, an overwhelming majority of suffrage organizations were united behind the goal of a constitutional amendment. In 1917, New York gave women the right to vote. A year later, President Woodrow Wilson, who previously opposed suffrage, changed his position to support an amendment. The tide began to turn and the suffragists' determination paid off. A breakthrough came in January 1918 at an emotional session of the House of Representatives. The visitors' galleries were packed as the House prepared to vote. Several congressmen voted despite illness. One was even brought in on a stretcher. Another left his gravely ill wife, at her request, to cast his vote. This time the House approved the amendment. The Senate approved it the following year. The Nineteenth Amendment was ratified by the states in 1920. Women were now truly part of "we the people."

✔ Reading Check **How did women show that they deserved the right to vote?**

Analyze Maps and Graphs

Voting in the United States

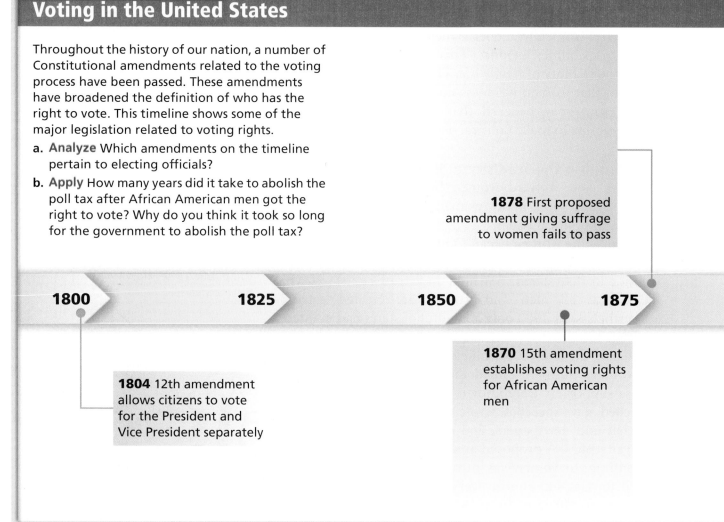

Throughout the history of our nation, a number of Constitutional amendments related to the voting process have been passed. These amendments have broadened the definition of who has the right to vote. This timeline shows some of the major legislation related to voting rights.

a. **Analyze** Which amendments on the timeline pertain to electing officials?

b. **Apply** How many years did it take to abolish the poll tax after African American men got the right to vote? Why do you think it took so long for the government to abolish the poll tax?

1878 First proposed amendment giving suffrage to women fails to pass

1800   1825   1850   1875

1804 12th amendment allows citizens to vote for the President and Vice President separately

1870 15th amendment establishes voting rights for African American men

Youth and the Right to Vote

The most recent voting rights amendment lowered the voting age to 18. Until the middle of the twentieth century, the voting age was 21. However, millions of young people served in World War II, the Korean War, and the Vietnam War. Many Americans came to believe that citizens old enough to fight and to die for their country should not be denied the right to vote. Public support grew for lowering the voting age.

The Twenty-Sixth Amendment Congress passed a law in 1970 giving 18-year-olds the right to vote in national, state, and local elections. However, the Supreme Court later ruled that Congress could set the voting age only for national—not state or local—elections. After the Court decision, it seemed that the only way to guarantee 18-year-olds the right to vote in all elections was by changing the Constitution. Congress overwhelmingly approved the new amendment in March 1971.

✓ Reading Check **What explains public support for lowering the voting age from 21 to 18?**

Go Online
civics
interactive

For: Interactive Time Line
Visit: www.PHSchool.com
Web Code: mpp-2071

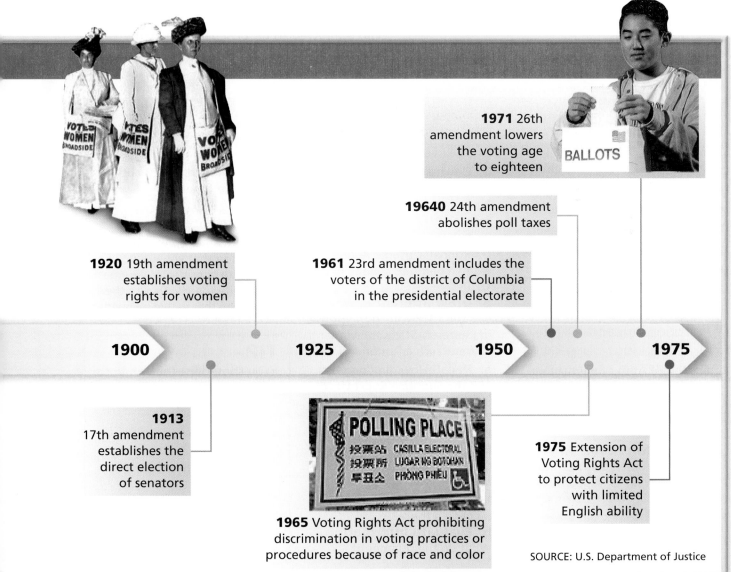

1971 26th amendment lowers the voting age to eighteen

19640 24th amendment abolishes poll taxes

1920 19th amendment establishes voting rights for women

1961 23rd amendment includes the voters of the district of Columbia in the presidential electorate

1900   1925   1950   1975

1913 17th amendment establishes the direct election of senators

POLLING PLACE

1975 Extension of Voting Rights Act to protect citizens with limited English ability

1965 Voting Rights Act prohibiting discrimination in voting practices or procedures because of race and color

SOURCE: U.S. Department of Justice

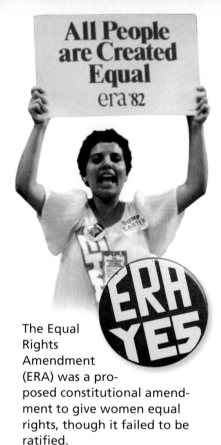

The Equal Rights Amendment (ERA) was a proposed constitutional amendment to give women equal rights, though it failed to be ratified.

The Voice of the People

The voting rights amendments show that the Constitution can be changed in response to new attitudes and conditions in society. The Thirteenth, Fourteenth, and Fifteenth amendments came about largely as a result of the Civil War. However, all the other changes in the Constitution were made through peaceful efforts of citizens.

The most recent amendment to the Constitution was the Twenty-seventh Amendment, ratified in 1992. This amendment states that if members of Congress vote to increase their salaries, the change cannot go into effect until after the next election. This way, members of Congress are accountable to the voters for their actions.

Amendments are frequently suggested and debated by citizens. You might be tempted to ask, "Is our Constitution truly a good plan of government?" A quick look back at history will provide the answer. If the framers had written a poor plan, we would have had hundreds, maybe thousands, of amendments by now. Perhaps we would even have a whole new constitution. Instead, we have had only 27 amendments. The voice of the people has been heard.

✓ **Reading Check** **Who is allowed to propose changes to the Constitution?**

SECTION 1 Assessment

Key Terms

Use each of the key terms in a sentence that explains its meaning: poll tax, suffrage

Target Reading Skill

1. Apply your knowledge of the suffix -ist. What does *suffragist* mean?

Comprehension and Critical Thinking

2. **a. Recall** At the time the Constitution was written in 1787, what bodies had the authority to decide who was qualified to be a citizen?
   b. Draw Inferences Why were the framers reluctant to abolish slavery in the Constitution?

3. **a. Describe** How did the Fourteenth Amendment ensure citizenship for African Americans?

   b. Contrast How did the Twenty-fourth Amendment differ from the Fifteenth and Fourteenth Amendments?

4. **a. Explain** Why did people's traditional attitudes about women begin to change in the 1800s?
   b. Draw Inferences Why was the 1918 vote in the House of Representatives for women's suffrage such an emotional one?

5. **a. Recall** How did Congress and the Supreme Court view lowering the voting age from 21 to 18?
   b. Identify Cause and Effect What spurred the growth in public sentiment for a lowered voting age?

6. **a. Recall** How many amendments are there?
   b. Evaluate Information What do the number of

amendments suggest about our government?

Writing Activity: Petition

Propose an amendment to the Constitution that you would like Congress to consider. In your petition, specify the changes to the Constitution that would be needed.

TIP
- You should list the demands of your petition at the beginning of your proposed amendment.
- Your proposed amendment must use formal language, and be concise, clear, and logical.
- You may want to consult some amendments to the Constitution to get a sense of amendment language.

Analyzing Photographs

Photographs can be valuable primary source documents. They help us understand the circumstances surrounding an event, and how people felt. Examining them carefully gives us clues about the event that is captured. Keep in mind, too, that photographers, like writers, may sometimes betray their own point of view in their work.

The women's suffrage movement gained momentum during the 1910s as more and more women joined the fight for their rights. Pickets and parades became common events. The photograph below shows a women's suffrage parade in New York City on May 6, 1912.

Learn the Skill

Follow these steps to analyze a photograph:

❶ **Identify the subject.** What does the photograph show?

❷ **Look for details.** Examine the photograph closely. Identify people, objects, and any other things that give clues about the circumstances of the event shown in the photograph. Try to identify where and when it was taken?

❸ **Analyze the photographer's intent.** Why do you think the photographer took this picture? Was the picture posed, or was it taken as it happened?

❹ **Draw conclusions.** What can you learn from this photograph? What factual information does it convey? How does it further your understanding of history?

Practice the Skill

Look at the photograph above and answer these questions:

❶ To what does the phrase on the banner "DEMAND EQUAL REPRESENTATION FOR EQUAL TAXATION" allude?

❷ What does the children's presence at the parade suggest?

❸ What did you learn from this photograph?

Apply the Skill

Analyze another photograph in this chapter. Identify the subject and details and describe what you learned from the photo.

SECTION **2**

A Flexible Framework

Reading Preview

Objectives

In this section you will

- Discuss the role of the Supreme Court.
- Explore how equality and segregation were at odds in our nation's history.
- Consider equality and affirmative action in our nation's history.
- Take a look at women and equality.
- Understand how the Constitution provides a framework for the future.

Taking Notes

Make a diagram like the one below. As you read the section, use the diagram to record one of the Supreme Court decisions described that provided citizens with equal protection under the law.

Key Terms

equal protection
segregation

affirmative
action

Main Idea

Amendments to the Constitution have enlarged the rights of African Americans and women with respect to equality. The Supreme Court applies the principles of the Constitution to the cases or issues that it hears.

Target Reading Skill

Recognize Word Origins A word's origin is where the word comes from. Knowing the origin of root words can help you determine the meanings of unfamiliar words.

Amendments enable the Constitution to change with the times. Now you will take a closer look at why very few changes have been needed. The framers realized that specific instructions for running a government in 1787 might not work years later. By providing general principles, they gave later generations freedom to fill in the details. In this way, the Constitution does not have to be changed constantly.

The Role of the Supreme Court

If the Constitution does not spell out in detail how to follow the principles, who makes sure that they are being followed correctly? This is where the courts, especially the Supreme Court, enter the picture. The Supreme Court has the final say over whether constitutional government officials and other citizens have correctly followed principles. By deciding whether a certain action violates the Constitution, the Court makes that action either legal or illegal.

Overturning a Decision However, a Court decision is not necessarily permanent. It may be overturned by an amendment that changes, removes, or adds a constitutional principle. For example, the Dred Scott decision was overturned when the Thirteenth Amendment abolished slavery.

A decision may also be overturned by a later Court decision. New evidence or new ideas may lead the Court to change an earlier interpretation of a constitutional principle.

Interpreting a Principle How has the Supreme Court applied broad constitutional principles to a changing society? One way to answer this question is to see how the Court's interpretation of one principle changed over the course of several important cases. A good example is the Fourteenth Amendment principle that each state must provide citizens with "equal protection of the laws."

Equal protection means that people must be treated fairly, but it does not mean that everyone must be treated in exactly the same way. For instance, a bank does not have to lend money to every customer, but it must be fair in deciding who will receive loans. It may base its decision on a customer's ability to repay the money. It may not base its decision on a customer's race or gender.

Denying a loan to a person because of race or gender is, of course, an example of discrimination. Human history has been scarred by many forms of discrimination. The following cases focus on two forms that have been particularly common: racial discrimination and discrimination against women. As you read, think about the Supreme Court's important role in applying the general principles of our Constitution to these situations.

✔ Reading Check   **How can Supreme Court decisions be overturned?**

Equality and Segregation

The principle of equal protection was originally intended to prevent states from denying rights to African Americans. Over the years the Court has interpreted the meaning of equal protection in many situations that might involve racial discrimination.

***Plessy* v. *Ferguson* (1896)** The Fourteenth Amendment had given African Americans citizenship. However, many states passed laws requiring **segregation,** or separation, of blacks and whites in public places such as hotels, schools, restaurants, and trains. Did segregation violate the principle of equal protection?

Segregation in America
An African American woman is directed away from a 'whites only' room at a Dallas bus station in 1961.
Draw Conclusions *Why do you think states passed segregation laws?*

Target Reading Skill

Recognize Word Origins
Reread the sentence "Plessy argued that the Louisiana law . . .". The word *segregate* comes from the Latin root *greg-* meaning "herd." Based on your knowledge of the meaning of the word, what do you think the prefix *se-* means?

Ending Segregation
U.S. troops escorted nine African American students into Central High School in Little Rock, Arkansas, in 1957.
Draw Conclusions *Why did troops have to escort these students to school?*

The Court faced this question in 1896, when it heard a Louisiana case involving Homer Plessy. Plessy was an African American man who had refused to leave a "whites only" railroad car. Plessy argued that the Louisiana law requiring segregation violated his right to equal protection. In a famous decision, *Plessy* v. *Ferguson*, the Court ruled that the Louisiana law did not violate the Fourteenth Amendment as long as the cars for blacks and for whites were of equal quality. For more than 50 years after the decision, this "separate but equal" standard was accepted as a justification for laws that segregated blacks from whites.

Opposition to Segregation Not everyone agreed that "separate but equal" facilities truly guaranteed equal protection of the laws. Many schools and other facilities for African Americans were not as good as those for whites. Furthermore, even when the facilities were equal in quality, the fact of being separated by law made many African Americans feel that they were treated as inferior to whites. Could it really be said, then, that they were being treated equally?

By the early 1950s, many Americans were questioning the fairness of segregation. Among them was Thurgood Marshall, a lawyer for the National Association for the Advancement of Colored People (NAACP). He and other NAACP lawyers brought before the Court several cases involving facilities that were segregated but equal in quality. They knew that such cases would force the Court to decide whether "separate but equal" facilities truly represented "equal protection."

At the center of one of these cases was a schoolgirl from Topeka, Kansas. Linda Brown was about to play a role in overturning a Supreme Court ruling that had permitted segregation for more than half a century.

***Brown* v. *Board of Education of Topeka* (1954)** Linda Brown, an African American girl, lived only 7 blocks from a school for white children. By law, however, she was required to attend a school for African American children 21 blocks away. Linda's parents thought she should be able to attend the neighborhood school. Therefore they took the school board to court, with the help of the NAACP.

In arguing the case before the Supreme Court, Thurgood Marshall presented evidence that separate schools had a harmful effect on both black and white children. Black children were made to feel inferior to whites, he argued, while white children learned to feel superior to African American children. Therefore, Marshall concluded, "separate but equal" schools could never be equal.

All of the justices on the Supreme Court were convinced by Marshall's reasoning. The Court agreed that segregation of African Americans creates "a feeling of inferiority as to their status in the community that may affect their hearts and minds in a way unlikely ever to be undone." Separate educational facilities, the Court ruled, were "inherently [by their very nature], unequal" and therefore violated the principle of equal protection.

The Court determined that the "separate but equal" standard established in *Plessy* v. *Ferguson* had no place in public education. Thus, the decision in *Brown* v. *Board of Education of Topeka* overturned the decision in *Plessy v. Ferguson* and made all segregation laws unconstitutional. Thus, it is a significant example of how Supreme Court rulings can keep the Constitution flexible.

✓ Reading Check **What impact did the Supreme Court decision in *Brown* v. *Board of Education of Topeka* have on segregation?**

Equality and Affirmative Action

The Court's ruling gave a powerful constitutional weapon to Americans who were fighting racial discrimination. Spurred on by the Brown case and by increasing public pressure during the 1960s, Congress passed a series of laws—known as civil rights laws—to guard against racial discrimination. However, these laws could not undo the effects of years of discrimination against African Americans, Hispanic Americans, Asian Americans, and Native Americans, particularly in the workplace.

Starting in the late 1960s, as a result of the civil rights movement, the government worked to correct the effects of unfair hiring practices. It required companies to take **affirmative action,** steps to counteract the effects of past racial discrimination and discrimination against women. Colleges and universities that seemed to favor white males when hiring staff and admitting students were required to take similar steps.

Some people have argued that affirmative action does not result in equal treatment. They say that affirmative action leads to discrimination against white male applicants. Faced with the question of whether affirmative action programs really do lead to fair treatment of applicants, the Court took another close look at the meaning of "equal protection."

Traditional views of women's roles and rights have changed as more women, like this astronaut, take on jobs previously held by men.

The Supreme Court

Go Online
civics
interactive

For: Interactive Constitution
with Supreme Court Cases
Visit: PHSchool.com
Web Code: mpp-2072

The Supreme Court *Grutter* v. *Bollinger* (2003)

Why It Matters Colleges and universities consider many factors when admitting students. Many consider applicants' race and ethnicity, among other factors. This policy is known as affirmative action. Affirmative action developed as a way to increase diversity and to reduce educational disadvantages facing minority students.

Background Barbara Grutter, a white student, was denied admission to the University of Michigan Law School in 1996. Grutter discovered that minority students with lower test scores than her own had been admitted. Grutter sued the university and its president, Lee Bollinger. Grutter claimed that she was discriminated against based on her race. The university argued that affirmative action was necessary.

Barbara Grutter won her case in the U.S. District Court. The decision was later overturned on appeal. Grutter then appealed her case to the U.S. Supreme Court.

The Decision The Court ruled in favor of the University of Michigan. The Court said that no illegal discrimination had occurred. In the majority opinion, Justice Sandra Day O'Connor wrote that the policy of affirmative action was still needed. She held that it would ensure a diverse student body and would help undo past wrongs.

Understanding the Law

1. What is affirmative action?
2. How does *Grutter* v. *Bollinger* affect college admissions?

***Regents of the University of California v. Bakke* (1978)**
One school with an affirmative action program was the medical school of the University of California at Davis. The school reserved places in each entering class for African American, Hispanic American, Asian American, and Native American students. In 1973 and again in 1974 a white applicant, Allan Bakke, was rejected for admission. Some members of other racial and ethnic groups were admitted with lower grade-point averages, test scores, and interview ratings. Bakke took the university to court, arguing that he was a victim of reverse discrimination.

Bakke posed a challenge for the Supreme Court. Unlike the Brown case, the justices were sharply divided. Some thought the admissions program was a reasonable way to overcome effects of discrimination. The majority, however, agreed with Bakke.

The Court ruled that under the equal protection principle it was unconstitutional for an admissions program to discriminate against whites only because of their race. However, the Court stated that race could be one of the factors considered if the school wished to create a more diverse student body while treating white applicants fairly.

Affirmative action was challenged further in 1996 when California voters approved Proposition 209. This law prohibited state universities and employers from considering race or ethnicity when accepting students or hiring employees. The Supreme Court refused to review the case in 1997 when opponents tried to overturn the law. In 2003, however, the Court's decision in *Grutter* v. *Bollinger* held that considering race or ethnicity is a legal and necessary tool in college admissions.

✓ Reading Check **What was affirmative action originally designed to counteract?**

Women and Equality

The Court has also applied the equal protection principle to other issues, such as whether companies may treat male employees differently from female employees. May a company hire only males for certain jobs? May they have different rules for women and men? As more women entered the workplace over the years, traditional views on women's roles and rights changed. The following case illustrates how the Court has addressed such questions.

Changes in the Workplace Asian American working mothers demonstrate for child care services.
Draw Inferences *Why is child care and important issue for working mothers?*

WORKING MOTHERS NEED QUALITY DAY CARE

為工作母親爭取良好托兒服

Students Make a Difference

Christopher Elmore, Senior Class President at Fairview High School in Boulder, Colorado, believes it is important for students to have a voice on issues concerning school policy. For three years, he has served as Chair of the Student Accountability Advisory Committee (SAAC), a student committee that represents student issues to the professional staff and school board of the Boulder Valley School District. "I enjoy having the opportunity to represent the students of the district and to effect positive change."

Service Learning

How can you effect policy change in your local school district?

▲ Students can help make a difference by learning more about issues concerning school policy.

Phillips v. Martin Marietta Corporation (1971) Ida Phillips applied for a position with the Martin Marietta Corporation in Florida. Part of the corporation's screening process was to find out whether female applicants had young children. In the corporation's view, young children take up a lot of women's time and energy. The corporation felt that this would interfere with work performance. Women such as Ida Phillips, who had two pre-schoolers, were denied jobs for that reason.

When Ida Phillips was rejected for the job, she decided to take the corporation to court. She argued that she had not been treated equally. She charged the company with discriminating against women because male applicants were not questioned about their children. Men were hired whether they had young children at home or not.

The Court ruled in favor of Ida Phillips, declaring that the company could not have "one hiring policy for women and another for men."

✓ Reading Check **How was the equal protection clause applied by the Supreme Court in the Phillips case?**

A Framework for the Future

The cases you have just examined all show how the Supreme Court applies general principles of the Constitution to new situations or issues. A hundred years ago, most Americans could not have foreseen that racial discrimination against a white man would ever become an issue, as happened in the Bakke case. However, the equal protection principle can be applied just as well to racial discrimination of any type.

Similarly, equality in the workplace did not become a major issue until relatively recently. As more women have taken jobs outside the home, however, they have called attention to cases of unequal treatment. In response, the Supreme Court has applied the old principle of equal protection to this new situation.

The general principles of our living Constitution have guided our nation for over two centuries and can be expected to do so in the future. Judging from past history, amendments may be required from time to time, but the Constitution's sturdy framework of principles will most likely remain intact.

✓ **Reading Check** **What does the Bakke case demonstrate about the principle of equal protection?**

SECTION 2 Assessment

Key Terms

Use each of the key terms in a sentence that explains its meaning: equal protection, segregation, affirmative action

Target Reading Skill

1. **Word Origins** If *super-* means "above," what do you think the word *supervise* means?

Comprehension and Critical Thinking

2. **a. Recall** Who has final authority concerning constitutional principles?
   b. Draw Inferences Why does it make sense that a Supreme Court decision is not permanently binding?

3. **a. Explain** What racial concept did the *Plessy* v. *Ferguson* decision bring into being?

   b. Identify Main Ideas What did segregation opponents hope to achieve with *Brown* v. *Board of Education of Topeka?*

4. **a. Describe** What did many of the civil rights laws of the 1960s hope to achieve?
   b. Draw Inferences Where might racial and gender discrimination commonly occur?

5. **a. Explain** How did the Supreme Court use the equal protection principle to address discrimination in the workplace?
   b. Compare In what ways are gender and racial discrimination similar?

6. **a. Recall** What do all of the cases in this chapter have in common?

   b. Draw Inferences Why did gender discrimination in the workplace become a major issue only relatively recently?

Writing Activity: Biography

Use the Internet to research an important figure in the civil rights movement. Write a brief biographical essay of the person you chose.

Go Online
PHSchool.com
For: Writing Activity
Visit: PHSchool.com
Web Code: mpd-2072

Debating the Issues

CLOSE UP FOUNDATION

The debates in this feature are based on *Current Issues*, published by the Close Up Foundation. Go to **PHSchool.com**, Web Code mph-1025, to read the latest issue of *Current Issues* online.

The United States is largely an English-speaking nation. Our founding documents were written in English. Our government conducts its business in English. However, there is no law that requires this. The United States is also a nation of immigrants from all over the world. Our citizens and immigrants speak a wide variety of languages.

RESTRICTED AREA DO NOT ENTER BETRETEN VERBOTEN SE PROHIBE EL PASO 立入禁止

Should the Government Make English the Nation's Official Language?

YES

- Every nation should have an official language in which it can conduct business, both within and outside of its borders. In the United States, it should be English because that is the language most Americans speak.

- If English were the official language, immigrants would have a greater incentive to learn to speak English quickly. This in turn would widen their opportunities for higher education and careers.

- The establishment of an official language does not mean that other languages may not be spoken. The United States is a nation of immigrants whose people will continue to speak a variety of languages.

NO

- The United States is a nation of immigrants. The English language should not be considered better than other languages that make up our nation.

- At the turn of the last century, more than 10 percent of the U.S. population was foreign-born. Printing government forms in English only would make life very difficult for these thousands of immigrants.

- With the exception of Native Americans, every citizen of the United States is either an immigrant or the descendant of immigrants. Making English the official language would insult the languages and cultures of the millions of immigrants who have helped to build this nation since its founding.

What Is Your Opinion?

1. **Identify Cause** Why has English become the dominant language of the United States? Use your knowledge of history to answer.

2. **Identify Alternatives** More than 14 million Spanish-speaking immigrants live in the United States. Should the United States have two official languages—English and Spanish? Why or why not?

3. **Writing to Persuade** Suppose that Congress is about to vote on a bill that would make English the nation's official language. Write a letter urging your congressman to vote for or against the bill. Explain your reasons in detail.

Go Online
civics
interactive

For: You Decide Poll
Visit: PHSchool.com
Web Code: mph-2072

Review and Assessment

Chapter Summary

Section 1
Changing the Law of the Land
(pages 176–184)

- Amendments to the Constitution reflect the changing needs and attitudes of the American people.

- Slavery was abolished by the Thirteenth Amendment in 1865.

- The Fourteenth and Fifteenth Amendments (1868 and 1870) guaranteed African Americans the rights of citizenship, including the right to vote. Nevertheless, many states imposed requirements such as poll taxes, which were outlawed by the Twenty-Fourth Amendment in 1964.

- Women were not granted suffrage, or the right to vote, until the Nineteenth Amendment was ratified in 1920.

- The Twenty-Sixth Amendment, ratified in 1971, gave people aged 18 and older the right to vote.

Section 2
A Flexible Framework
(pages 186–193)

- The Supreme Court determines whether actions or legislation have violated the Constitution. Its decisions must be obeyed by the President and Congress.

- The Fourteenth Amendment's principle of equal protection was intended to prevent discrimination based on race. The Supreme Court upheld the idea that segregation of African American citizens was acceptable, as long as the separate accommodations were of equal quality. However, the Court ended the official approval of the "separate but equal" principle in the 1950s. Legalized segregation was abolished.

- Women were denied the right to vote for many years. Many women had difficulty getting certain jobs and were not as well paid for their work as men.

- Affirmative action policies were intended to create opportunities for many Americans who experienced discrimination based on race, ethnicity, and gender.

- The Constitution can be amended to adapt to great changes in American society. The difficulty of the amendment process ensures that there are no frivolous changes made to the Constitution.

Copy the chart below and use it to help you summarize the chapter:

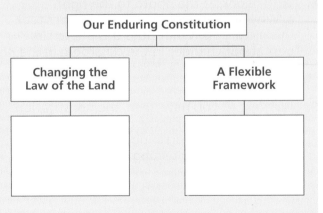

Our Enduring Constitution

Changing the Law of the Land

A Flexible Framework

Go Online
PHSchool.com

For: Self-Test
Visit: PHSchool.com
Web Code: mpa-2072

Reviewing Key Terms

Fill in each blank with one of the key terms from the list below.

poll tax   affirmative action
suffrage   equal protection
segregation

1. Amendments that proposed giving _____ to women were introduced in almost every session of Congress in the 40 years from 1878 to 1918.

2. Legalized _____ required separate public places for African Americans and white Americans.

3. Some states imposed a _____ to prevent nonwhites from voting.

4. The principle of _____ is guaranteed in the Fourteenth Amendment.

5. The policy of _____ was designed, in part, to correct the effects of unfair hiring practices.

Comprehension and Critical Thinking

6. a. **Recall** Why did the framers of the Constitution decide not to abolish slavery?
   b. **Summarize** What was the Supreme Court's ruling in the Dred Scott case?
   c. **Draw Conclusions** How did the Fourteenth Amendment guarantee citizenship to African Americans?

7. a. **Explain** What powers does the Supreme Court have with respect to the Constitution?

   b. **Predict** What do you think would happen if the Constitution were a list of very specific rules for the government to follow?
   c. **Synthesize Information** How do the cases of *Plessy* v. *Ferguson* and *Brown* v. *Board of Education of Topeka* illustrate the flexibility of the Constitution?

Activities

8. **Skills** Look at the photo to the right.
   a. Why do you think the photographer took this picture? b. What does this photo suggest about changes in the classroom in the years after *Brown* v. *Board of Education of Topeka*?

9. **Writing** As you have seen, the Constitution alone cannot guarantee citizens' rights. Write an essay describing the role citizens should play in protecting each other's rights.

10. **Active Citizen** Create a bill of rights for your class. First, working in small groups, come up with two or three amendments that would help protect the rights of both teachers and students. As a class, debate each proposed amendment. Finally, vote on each amendment.

11. **Math Practice** Turn to the chart on page 187. What is the average number of years between amendments to the Constitution in the years displayed?

12. **Civics and Economics** Most single-parent families in the United States are headed by women. How might employment discrimination based on gender affect the incomes of these families?

13. **Analyzing Visuals** What does the photograph above suggest about citizens' abilities to change the Constitution??

Standardized Test Prep

Test-Taking Tips

Some questions on standardized tests ask you to analyze a reading selection. Study the passage below which was written by President Johnson in 1965. Then follow the tips to answer the sample question.

TIP The first sentence gives clues and explains the purpose of what follows.

The bill that I am presenting to you will be known as a civil rights bill . . .

Because all Americans just must have the right to vote. . .

All Americans must have the privileges of citizenship regardless of race. . .

But I would like to caution you and remind you that to exercise these privileges takes much more than just legal right. It requires a trained mind and a healthy body. It requires a decent home, and the chance to find a job, and the opportunity to escape from the clutches of poverty.

Pick the letter that best completes this statement.

1. According to the speaker, all of the following are things that Americans deserve EXCEPT

   TIP Notice the word "EXCEPT" in the question.

   A trained minds and healthy bodies

   B exercise

   C privileges of citizenship

   D the right to vote

   The correct answer is **B**. Note that the questions asks you to choose the exception to the rule.

2. Which of the following best describes the tone of the passage?

   A frustrated

   B positive

   C determined

   D tentative

   The correct answer is **C**. President Johnson is presenting a bill that he hopes will change the situation in America and give more rights to its citizens.

The Federal Government

What's Ahead in Unit 3

Unit 3 will examine the three branches of the federal government. You will see how each branch works, and how each checks and balances the power of the other two. You will also analyze the vital role you play in helping all three branches of our government work as an effective team.

CHAPTER 8
The Legislative Branch

CHAPTER 9
The Executive Branch

CHAPTER 10
The Judicial Branch

Why Study Civics?

Why did the framers of the Constitution establish the legislative, executive, and judicial branches of federal government? How is the power to govern divided among three branches of federal government? How does this division of power serve to balance the federal government and protect the welfare of citizens? These are all questions that can be addressed by the study of civics.

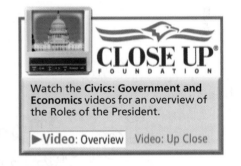

Watch the **Civics: Government and Economics** videos for an overview of the Roles of the President.

▶**Video:** Overview   Video: Up Close

Standards for Civics and Government

National

The following National Standards are covered in this unit.

II. What are the foundations of the American political system?

B. What are the distinctive characteristics of American society?

C. What is American political culture?

D. What values and principles are basic to American constitutional democracy?

State

For: Your state's Civics standards
Visit: PHSchool.com
Webcode: mpe3001

The Legislative Branch

What's Ahead in Chapter 8

In this chapter you will learn about the lawmaking powers given to Congress by the Constitution. You will find out how Congress is organized and follow a bill as it makes its way through Congress.

SECTION 1
The Members of Congress

SECTION 2
The Powers of Congress

SECTION 3
How Congress is Organized

SECTION 4
Following a Bill in Congress

TARGET READING SKILL

Comparison and Contrast In this chapter you will focus on comparing and contrasting. Comparing and contrasting includes recognizing and using signal words, making comparisons, identifying contrasts, and identifying similarities and differences.

Joint session of Congress ▶

The following National Standards for Civics and Government are covered in this chapter:

III. How does the government established by the Constitution embody the purposes, values, and principles of American democracy?

A. How are power and responsibility distributed, shared, and limited in the government established by the United States Constitution?

D. What is the place of law in the American constitutional system?

Active Citizen — Civics in the Real World

Teenager Diana Perez earned the minimum wage working in a small grocery store. She enjoyed earning her own spending money.

Anne Petrini worked with Diana at the grocery store. Anne used her salary to support her two children. Diana could not imagine how Anne could feed two children and pay her bills on this salary. Anne agreed that it wasn't easy.

One day in the break room, Diana picked up the newspaper. The front page described a bill that would raise the minimum wage. The Senate would soon begin debate on the bill. Anne read the story over Diana's shoulder.

"We should write to our senators," said Diana.

"They'll never pay any attention to us," Anne objected.

"Are you sure that raising the minimum wage is a good idea?" asked Christine, looking up from her lunch. "The boss says that she can't afford to pay us more. If Congress raises the minimum wage, some of us may lose our jobs."

The three women decided to find out more about the issue. Could Congress pass laws about how much a worker should be paid? Would a senator or representative pay any attention to letters from citizens? How do members of Congress make up their minds about laws when people have strong feelings for or against them?

Citizen's Journal Do you think the minimum wage should be raised? After you read this chapter, write a letter to your senators. Tell them whether you would like to see a minimum-wage increase. Include your reasons.

The Members of Congress

Reading Preview

Objectives

In this section you will

- List the responsibilities of lawmaking.
- Describe the day of a member of Congress at work.
- Explore the jobs of representatives and senators.
- Identify the requirements, salaries, and benefits of being a representative or senator.

Taking Notes

Make a double word web like the one below. As you read this section, use it to compare and contrast the Senate and the House of Representatives.

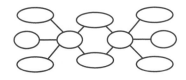

Key Terms

constituents
bill
interest
  groups

lobbyists
census
congressional
  district

Main Idea

The legislative branch of the United States government is called the Congress. Laws are made by 100 senators and 435 representatives.

Target Reading Skill

Identify Signal Words Certain words and phrases in a text can indicate that the writer is going to compare or contrast two concepts, people, or things.

Congress is the legislative, or lawmaking, branch of the national government. It is made up of two houses, the Senate and the House of Representatives.

The most important job of Congress is to make laws. Laws do not simply state what you can and cannot do. A law can establish a national policy, a plan of action designed to achieve a certain goal. Laws spell out how the government raises and spends its money.

The Responsibilities of Lawmaking

Members of Congress have responsibilities to different groups of people. Lawmaking involves balancing many responsibilities and handling conflicting pressures.

Local versus National Needs Each member of Congress represents a group of citizens much smaller than the nation. One of a member's major responsibilities is to his or her **constituents (kun STICH oo ents)**, the people he or she represents. Constituents expect senators and representatives to be their voice in Congress.

A member of Congress also has a responsibility to the whole nation. The laws Congress makes can affect all Americans. Sometimes, the needs of a member's constituents are in conflict with the needs of Americans in general. For example, a representative from a wheat-growing region may confront a law that helps wheat farmers but would anger consumers by raising the price of bread.

Political Parties A member of Congress also has a responsibility to his or her political party. A party is an organization of people who share certain ideas about what government should do. Most members of Congress today belong to either the Republican party or the Democratic party. Each party works to elect its candidates to Congress. In return, the party expects its members to support the party's position on issues before Congress.

This responsibility may present a member of Congress with a difficult choice. The senator who received Diana Perez's letter about the **bill**, or proposed law, to increase the minimum wage was pressured from two sides. As a Republican, he felt he should follow his party's position and oppose the bill. However, most of the letters he had received from constituents supported of the bill.

Interest Groups Members of Congress who want to run for re-election try to gain support for campaigns. They often get help from **interest groups**, groups of people who work together for similar interests or goals. Interest groups can supply both votes and money. Examples of well-known interest groups are the American Medical Association and the American Farm Bureau Foundation.

Interest groups work to convince senators and representatives to support bills that help their members and to oppose bills that hurt them. This is done by hiring **lobbyists**, people who represent interest groups. For example, hotel owners formed one interest group to oppose the minimum wage bill. They argued it would increase their costs by forcing them to pay workers more. Their lobbyists tried to convince members of Congress to oppose the bill.

Often, a member of Congress supports the goals of a particular interest group. In return, that group encourages its members to vote for him or her in the next election.

Influencing Legislation Representatives of interest groups testify before Congress on legislation.
Identify Cause and Effect *How might such groups' efforts affect laws made by Congress?*

Multiple Responsibilities Representatives Loretta (left) and Linda (right) Sanchez of California are sworn in by House Speaker Dennis Hastert of Illinois.
Make Predictions *Why might a representative vote against legislation that would benefit his or her home district?*

Factors in Decision Making A member of Congress votes on hundreds of bills every year. He or she must weigh conflicting information and arguments presented by constituents, fellow party members, and lobbyists. A member must also search his or her own conscience and values. Predicting what the result of a bill will be in the long run can be difficult, but the member must consider that, too.

Servants of the People A member of Congress plays a second important role as servant of the people. In this role, a member gives information and help to constituents who have special problems. The owner of a business, for example, may want to know the latest government rules that apply to her business. Many members of Congress place a great deal of emphasis on this role because it helps a member's constituents directly—and makes them more likely to vote for him or her for re-election.

✓ Reading Check **Explain what is meant by the phrase *servant of the people*.**

Members of Congress at Work

Members of Congress spend a great deal of time learning about the wide range of issues on which they must vote. For example, members need to know about issues ranging from use of the American military and trade with the Middle East to air pollution and child care.

Members of Congress try to be present on the floor of the House or Senate chamber as much as possible. There, they listen to and give speeches, and vote on bills.

Every day, members of Congress go to meetings. Every day, dozens of people compete for their time—a fellow member with questions about a bill, a lobbyist with arguments against one, a constituent visiting the Capitol. Between meetings, members prepare bills, study reports, and read many letters from constituents.

A Representative's Duties
House Minority Leader Nancy Pelosi of California is shown speaking with Puerto Rican leaders about the budget; addressing the media; and breaking ground on a new federal building.
Demonstrate Reasoned Judgment *How do these activities reflect Pelosi's primary responsibility as a maker of laws?*

Members of Congress rely heavily on their personal staffs. Administrative assistants run a member's offices in his or her home state and in Washington, D.C. Legislative assistants study bills. Caseworkers handle requests from constituents.

✔ Reading Check **What does a senator or representative do on a typical day in Washington?**

Representatives and Senators

The number of members of Congress is determined in two different ways. Each state has two senators. The number of House members is determined by the state's population.

Representatives The Constitution requires a **census**, an official count of the population made every ten years. The census is used to find out how many representatives each state should have. Congress gives each state a fair proportion of the 435 seats in the House of Representatives. For example, the 2000 census determined that California, with the biggest population, should have 53 representatives. Vermont, with a very small population, has only one representative. States can gain or lose representatives after each census. Each state must have at least one representative.

The area that a member of the House represents is called a **congressional district**. Each state is divided into as many congressional districts as it has representatives in the House. By law, all congressional districts must have about the same number of people. Today, districts contain an average of 647,000 people.

The process of drawing district boundaries is controlled by state governments. The process can lead to controversy.

Target Reading Skill
Identify Signal Words Look at the phrase *about the same* in the fourth paragraph on this page. This phrase highlights a comparison—a mention of similar numbers of people in each congressional district. Read on to look for other words and phrases that signal comparison or contrast.

Representations in Congress

Florida and Mississippi each elect two senators, despite a huge difference in their populations.

1. **Analyze** Which state will have more influence in the House of Representatives, Mississippi or Florida?

2. **Apply** How does the distribution of Senate seats among the states illustrate the principle of federalism?

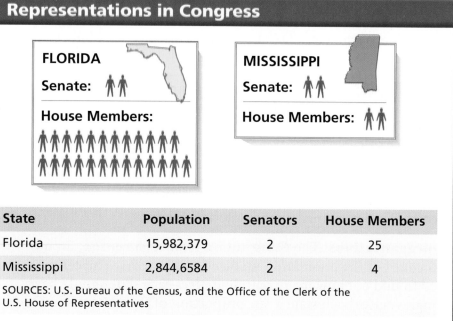

State	Population	Senators	House Members
Florida	15,982,379	2	25
Mississippi	2,844,6584	2	4

SOURCES: U.S. Bureau of the Census, and the Office of the Clerk of the U.S. House of Representatives

Representatives serve for two years. All 435 representatives end their terms of office on every other January 3rd. They must run for re-election or retire. There is no limit to the number of times a representative can be re-elected. If they wish to stay in office for more than two years, representatives must constantly work to earn the approval of the people in their districts. A typical representative spends more than one fourth of his or her time working for constituents—writing letters, receiving visitors, and doing casework.

Senators

In the Senate, each state is represented by two senators. Thus, a senator focuses on the interests of the whole state, not just one district. For example, a representative from central Illinois is likely to be very interested in farm policies. A senator from Illinois, in contrast, is concerned not only with farming, but also with other parts of the state's economy, including manufacturing, banking, and shipping.

Senators are elected for six-year terms. One third of the senators are elected every two years. Unlike the terms of representatives, the terms of senators overlap. Therefore, there are always a number of experienced senators in the Senate.

The framers of the Constitution hoped that longer, overlapping terms would make senators less sensitive to the shifting moods of the people than representatives. As a stable body, the Senate was expected to prevent quick, unwise changes in the law.

✓ Reading Check   **Why did the authors of the Constitution want senators' terms to overlap?**

Requirements, Salary, and Benefits

Senators and representatives must live in the states in which they are elected. Representatives must be at least 25 years old, and senators must be at least 30 years old. A representative must have been a citizen of the United States for at least seven years, but a senator must have been a citizen for at least nine years.

A member of Congress received an annual salary of $154,700 in 2003; majority and minority leaders earned $171,900, and the Speaker of the House received $198,600. A member can have two offices, one in Washington, D.C., and one in his or her congressional district or state. A member receives allowances for running both offices and paying staff salaries, as well as money to travel home to meet with constituents. Members also have free use of the postal service to send mail, such as newsletters, to constituents.

Civics and Economics

The Fair Labor Standards Act Congress first established a federal minimum wage in 1938 during the Great Depression. At the time, unemployment was high and workers competing for jobs had driven down wages.

The Fair Labor Standards Act guaranteed certain workers 25 cents an hour. Congress has raised the minimum wage many times since then. It has also expanded coverage to almost all hourly workers. The minimum wage in 2003 was $5.15 an hour for the first 40 hours worked in a week, and $7.72 for every hour after that. Although the minimum wage has increased several times, an hour's wage buys less than it did 30 years ago because of inflation.

Analyze Economics

The minimum wage has increased over time. What does that suggest about the American economy?

✔ **Reading Check** What are the minimum job requirements for senators and representatives?

SECTION 1 Assessment

Key Terms

Use each of the key terms in a sentence that explains its meaning: constituents, bill, interest groups, lobbyists, census, congressional district

Target Reading Skill

1. **Identify Signal Words** List one word or phrase in the text that signals a comparison and one that signals a contrast. Explain what or who is being compared or contrasted.

Comprehension and Critical Thinking

2. **a. Define** What is the primary responsibility of a member of Congress?

   b. Solve Problems How can a member of Congress balance responsibilities that conflict?

3. **a. Describe** What are congressional staff members' duties?

   b. Draw Inferences Why do members of Congress need large staffs?

4. **a. Describe** How long is a senator's term, and what fraction of the senate is up for re-election at one time?

   b. Draw Conclusions Why do senators serve longer terms than representatives?

5. **a. Recall** List the financial benefits members of Congress receive in addition to salaries.

   b. Identify Effect What advantages do ordinary citizens gain from these benefits?

Writing Activity

A friend in another country wants to know how Congress works. Write a letter listing and describing the powers of Congress.

> **TIP** Since this is a friendly letter, keep your language informal and your sentences clear and easy to read. Remember to include details to help your friend understand.

The Powers of Congress

Objectives

In this section you will
- List and describe the powers given to Congress.
- Identify limits on the powers of Congress

Taking Notes

Make a tree map like the one below. As you read this section, use it to outline the delegated powers of Congress.

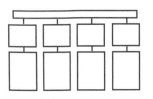

Key Terms

budget   bill of attainder
impeach

Main Idea

The Constitution grants Congress specific and general powers to make laws. The Constitution also specifies limits to those powers.

Target Reading Skill

Make Comparisons Comparing two or more concepts or laws can help you see their similarities. Phrases or words such as *similar to, about the same as,* and *like* may indicate comparisons.

C ongress has the power to try to solve some of the problems of the nation. Other problems are left to local and state governments.

Which problems Congress can try to solve is determined in part by the powers given to it by the Constitution. These powers are broad, but they have their limits.

Powers Given to Congress

In deciding which powers to give to Congress, the framers of the Constitution had the goals of the Preamble in mind. These goals are "to form a more perfect union, establish justice, insure domestic tranquility, provide for the common defense, promote the general welfare, and secure the blessings of liberty." Each power reflects one or more of these goals.

Promoting the General Welfare The term *general welfare* refers to the needs of all the people of a nation. Congress promotes the general welfare by making laws that help people live better.

Many of these laws are based on the power of Congress to regulate commerce, or business, with foreign nations and between states. For example, a law sets up an agency that controls air traffic in the nation and writes and enforces rules for air safety.

Congress can limit commerce in order to promote the general welfare. For example, Congress passed a law in 1808 forbidding traders to bring African slaves into the United States. Today, there is a law requiring companies to pay workers at least minimum wage or they cannot ship their goods to other states.

Congress also has the power to collect taxes and to borrow money. Without money the government could not function. Any bill that has to do with raising money must begin in the House of Representatives. After a money bill has been introduced in the House, the Senate may then act on it by proposing amendments.

In addition, Congress has the power to decide how the money it collects will be spent. Congress determines how much money will go to education, space programs, law enforcement, and so on.

Congress has the "power of the purse" because it has final approval of the government's **budget,** or plan for raising and spending money. Congress can act as a check on the executive branch, because without money, the President can do very little.

Providing for Defense Congress has the power to establish and maintain an army and a navy. Congress also has the sole power to declare war. The last time Congress used this power was during World War II, when the United States declared war on Japan in 1941.

In the 1960s presidents sent troops into battle in the Vietnam War even though Congress did not declare war. In 1973, Congress passed the War Powers Resolution, commonly known as the War Powers Act. That law limits the President's power to send troops into combat without approval by Congress. In the years since, however, Presidents and Congress have continued to debate the question of when congressional approval is needed. This debate intensified when the United States went to war with Iraq in 2003. War was never declared, although Congress had passed a resolution authorizing President George W. Bush to invade Iraq under certain circumstances. Debate continues, however, over the question of when such an authorization would not be enough.

Commander in Chief
The prospect of military action in Iraq in 2003 provoked much debate.
Summarize *What is the source of disagreement between the President and Congress over Presidential use of military force?*

Powers of Congress

The Constitution grants Congress a wide range of powers.

1. **Analyze** Name two nonlegislative powers granted to Congress.
2. **Apply** Which has greater powers, the House or the Senate? Explain.

Legislative Powers
- Collect taxes
- Borrow money
- Regulate trade with foreign nations and among the states
- Make laws about naturalization
- Coin money and set a standard of wieghts and measures
- Establish post offices and highways
- Issue patents and copyrights
- Declare war
- Create, maintain, and make rules for armed forces
- Make laws for the District of Columbia

Nonlegislative Powers
- Elect a President (House) and a Vice President (Senate) if no candidate gets a majority in the electoral college
- Confirm appointments and treaties made by the President (Senate)
- Proposes amendments to the Constitution
- Call conventions to propose amendments if demanded by states
- Admit new states to the Union
- Bring impeachment charges (House)
- Try impeachment cases (Senate)

Target Reading Skill

Make Comparisons The important powers of Congress are listed on pages 219 and 220. Think about what all these powers have in common.

Establishing Justice Congress may create federal courts below the Supreme Court. The appointment of judges to these courts and to the Supreme Court must be approved by the Senate.

Another power of Congress is the power to **impeach**, or accuse an official, such as the President or a federal judge, of serious wrongdoing. Only the House can impeach. The Senate, however, has the power to put the impeached official on trial. If found guilty, the official is removed from office. Only two Presidents have been impeached—Andrew Johnson in 1868 and Bill Clinton in 1998. In both cases, the Senate voted not to convict the President.

Unlisted Powers A clause in the Constitution allows Congress to make all laws that are "necessary and proper" for carrying out the listed powers. In order to coin money, Congress set up a mint to design coins and bills, buy metal and paper, hire workers, and distribute the money to banks. None of these powers are listed in the Constitution. The "elastic clause" helps the government carry out its work and change with the times.

Nonlegislative Powers The Constitution grants Congress several important nonlegislative powers. Congress also has the power to conduct investigations. It can gather information to help it make laws. It can also find out how the executive branch is enforcing laws.

✓ Reading Check **List the major powers the Constitution grants the Congress.**

Limits on the Powers of Congress

There are both general and specific limits to the powers of Congress. The general limits come from the system of checks and balances you read about in Chapter 5. The executive branch is able to veto proposed laws, and the judicial branch can declare laws unconstitutional.

The specific limits are listed in Article 1, Section 9 of the Constitution. The most important of these limits protect the rights of citizens.

In some countries, a person can be held in jail without having been charged with a crime and given a trial. In the United States, if you are held in jail without a charge, a lawyer or friend can get a writ of habeas corpus (HAY bee uhs KOR pus). This paper orders the police to bring you into court. The court then decides if the police have enough evidence to keep you in jail. If not, you must be released. The Constitution says that Congress cannot take away a citizen's right to a writ of habeas corpus except in times of invasion or civil war.

The Constitution also prevents Congress from passing bills of attainder. A **bill of attainder** is a law that convicts a person of a crime without a trial. In addition, Congress cannot pass ex post facto laws. Such a law makes a particular act a crime and then punishes people who committed the act before the law was passed. For example, you cannot be punished for something you do in April if a law against the act was not established until May.

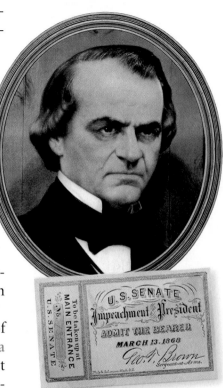

▲ Andrew Johnson, President from 1865–1869, was one of only two Presidents ever to be impeached. He was found not guilty of his charges by one vote.

✓ Reading Check **Why does the Constitution place specific limits on Congressional powers?**

SECTION 2 Assessment

Key Terms

Use each of the key terms in a sentence that explains its meaning: budget, impeach, bill of attainder

Target Reading Skill

1. **Make Comparisons** What is the common characteristic of all major powers of Congress?

Comprehension and Critical Thinking

2. **a. Recall** What is Congress' role in declaring war?

b. Analyzing Primary Sources How does this role reflect the words of the Constitution quoted on page 218?

3. **a. Identify** What allows Congress to take actions not specified in the Constitution?

b. Draw Conclusions Why did the authors of the Constitution permit this?

4. **a. Explain** How does the Constitution limit Congressional power?

b. Compare What do these specific limits have in common?

Writing Activity

Read the sections of the Constitution (pages 136–157) that describe the powers of Congress. Write a report explaining what these powers are.

TIP Make an outline before you begin writing. List each power granted to Congress, then note the major aspects of that power. This will help you organize your report.

Debating the Issues

CLOSE UP FOUNDATION

The debates in this feature are based on *Current Issues*, published by the Close Up Foundation. Go to **PHSchool.com**, Web Code mph-3082, to read the latest issue of *Current Issues* online.

The worldwide computer network known as the Internet was created in 1969. Today, hundreds of millions of people go online to send e-mail, do research, pay bills, and shop. Online transactions require you to enter information such as telephone and account numbers. Software today allows companies to track individuals' information. Many Americans are worried about privacy.

Should the Government Regulate the Internet to Protect Users' Privacy?

YES

- Companies on the Internet are concerned primarily with making money. User privacy is a secondary concern at best. Government regulations would ensure that online businesses handle user information responsibly.

- Today, Internet sites are not required to tell researchers and shoppers how their personal information will be used. Individuals have a right to know this for their own protection. Government regulations would force online businesses to disclose what they do with the information they collect.

NO

- Online businesses want to keep their customers coming back. It is in every Internet company's interest to make sure online users' privacy is protected. Government regulations are unnecessary when a business will regulate itself.

- Today, computer software can scramble credit card numbers, which protects users from having their information stolen and misused. Software is updated and improved much more rapidly than regulations could be rewritten to keep pace with it.

What Is Your Opinion?

1. **Draw Conclusions** What dangers do you see in having your personal information available on an unregulated Internet?

2. **Compare** Passing the new Clean Air Act in 1990, Congress further regulated air pollution produced by cars. Go online to find out how this has affected the auto industry and car buyers. How does this compare to what might happen if the Internet were regulated? Explain.

3. **Writing to Persuade** You run a successful Internet-based book and CD store. New regulations you might have to comply with are truth in advertising, no marketing to children under 13, and ensuring the privacy of your customers. Write a memo to your staff explaining why you have decided either to fight or support this regulation. Include specific reasons that will convince your staff to agree with your point of view.

Go Online
civics interactive

For: You Decide Poll
Visit: PHSchool.com
Web Code: mpp-3082

How Congress Is Organized

Reading Preview

Objectives

In this section you will

- Identify the leaders of both houses of Congress.
- Describe the work of congressional committees.
- Describe the President's role in legislation.

Key Terms

Speaker of the House
president pro tempore

floor leaders
pocket veto

Main Idea

Both houses of Congress choose leaders and assign members to committees. The committees work on bills before they are voted on. The President can sign or veto a bill.

Target Reading Skill

Identify Contrasts When you contrast two positions or organizations, you observe their differing characteristics. Phrases or words such as unlike, in contrast to, and than may indicate contrasts.

Taking Notes

Make a diagram like the one below. As you read this section, use it to outline the structure and leaders of each house of Congress.

The terms, or meeting periods, of Congress have been numbered in order since the first Congress met in 1789. The 108th Congress began in 2003. Each two-year term of Congress is divided into two sessions, one for each year. Each house stays in session from January 3 until its members vote to end the session. Sessions often last until October.

The Constitution does not tell Congress how to make laws. Over time, Congress developed procedures to consider bills. One important way was to divide the work of preparing bills among committees, or small working groups. Another way was to choose leaders to oversee the process of committee work.

First-time members of the House of Representatives line up at the start of the 108th Congress in 2002.

▼

The Growth of Congress

	1st Congress	108th Congress
Members of the House	65	435
Members of the Senate	26	100
Standing Committees	0	35
Budget	$374,000	$3.3 billion
Salary	$6.00/day	$154,700/year

SOURCES: Clerk of the U.S. House of Representatives, U.S. Senate

The size and budget of Congress have increased greatly since it was established. Frederick Muhlenberg (above) was a representative from Pennsylvania in the first Congress. Sheila Jackson-Lee (left) was a representative from Texas in the 108th.

1. **Analyze** How many more representatives are there now than in the first Congress? How many more senators?
2. **Apply** Why do you think Congress and its budget have grown so much?

Leadership in Congress

The Constitution states that the House of Representatives must choose a presiding officer called the **Speaker of the House**. Second, it says that the Vice President of the United States is to serve as the presiding officer, or president, of the Senate. Of the two positions, the Speaker of the House is by far the more important and more powerful. Finally, the Constitution directs the Senate to choose an officer called the **president pro tempore (pro TEMP puh ree)**, who will preside over the Senate when the Vice President is absent. This officer is also called president pro tem, for short.

Today the Democratic and Republican parties make the decisions about leadership in Congress. In both the House and the Senate, the party with more members is called the majority party. The one with fewer members is called the minority party.

Before a new Congress begins, members of each party hold meetings to select congressional leaders. The majority party in the House chooses the Speaker of the House. Likewise, the majority party in the Senate chooses the president pro tem.

Speaker of the House The Speaker is the most powerful member of the House. The Speaker presides over sessions, deciding the order of business and who may speak. The Speaker also appoints members of committees and refers bills to committees. These powers give the Speaker great influence over which bills pass or fail in the House.

President of the Senate As presiding officer of the Senate, the Vice President is in charge of sessions. However, he cannot take part in debates and can vote only in case of a tie. Because the Vice President often is busy with executive duties, the president pro tem usually acts as the Senate's presiding officer.

Floor Leaders The chief officers of the majority and minority parties in each house are the **floor leaders**. Next to the Speaker of the House, they are the most important officers in Congress. They are responsible for guiding bills through Congress. Floor leaders work closely with committee leaders and party members to persuade them to accept compromises or trade-offs in order to win votes on bills.

Assistant floor leaders, called whips, aid floor leaders in each house. Whips try to persuade members to support the party's position on key issues and to be present when it is time to vote. On important issues, when close votes are expected, much depends on the skill of a party's floor leader and whip.

✓ Reading Check   **Who are the leaders of the Senate?**

Working in Committees

More than 10,000 bills are introduced in a term of Congress. It would be impossible for a member to study each bill and decide how to vote. Therefore, both the Senate and the House have set up a system of committees. Much of the most important work of lawmaking is done in the committees.

Introducing Bills Citizens, interest groups, and the executive branch can draw up bills. However, only a member of Congress can introduce bills. A representative introduces a bill in the House by dropping it in a special box called a *hopper*. A senator introduces a bill by reading it aloud from the Senate floor. All bills introduced during a term are marked HR in the House and S in the Senate. They are given numbers in the order in which they are introduced. For example, when the minimum wage bill was introduced in the Senate in 1998, it was marked S.1805.

Standing Committees In the House and Senate, a bill is sent to a standing committee for action. There are 16 permanent standing committees in the Senate and 19 in the House. Each committee deals with a certain area, such as education or banking.

Committees control the fate of bills. First, a standing committee carefully studies a bill. Next, it holds hearings, or public meetings, at which numerous speakers are often heard. The committee may propose changes in the bill. Finally, the committee decides whether to recommend that the entire House or Senate vote on the bill. If the committee does not recommend it, the bill dies.

Target Reading Skill
Identify Contrasts This page describes one type of Congressional committee. As you continue reading, note the differences between standing committees and other Congressional committees.

The Hopper
Members of the House introduce bills for consideration by placing them into this wooden box, called a hopper.
Contrast *Who can write up proposed bills? Who can introduce bills?*

This cartoon shows a legislator speaking in Congress and proposing a 'solution' to a problem.

1. What solution is the legislator proposing?

2. What point is the cartoonist trying to make about Congress?

3. The problem the legislators are trying to solve is never identified. How is this significant?

"The only solution I can see is to hold a series of long and costly hearings in order to put off finding a solution."

Every committee has Democratic and Republican members. The chairperson of every committee belongs to the majority party. These leaders have great power over bills because they decide which bills their committees will study. They also decide when and if the committees will meet and whether or not hearings will be held.

Select and Joint Committees Sometimes the House or Senate will form a select committee to deal with a problem not covered by any standing committee. For example, in 2003 the House of Representatives set up a select committee on homeland security to address terrorist threats to the United States. A joint committee is made up of members of both the House and the Senate. Joint committees are usually select committees, formed to conduct investigations.

Conference Committees Before a bill can go to the President to be signed, it must be passed by both houses. Sometimes a bill passes one house but is changed in the other. If the two houses cannot agree, a temporary joint committee, called a conference committee, is formed. This committee, made up of both senators and representatives, tries to settle the differences. The conference committee's version of the bill must then be passed by both houses in order for it to move on.

✔ Reading Check **What is the difference between a select committee and a standing committee?**

How a Bill Becomes a Law

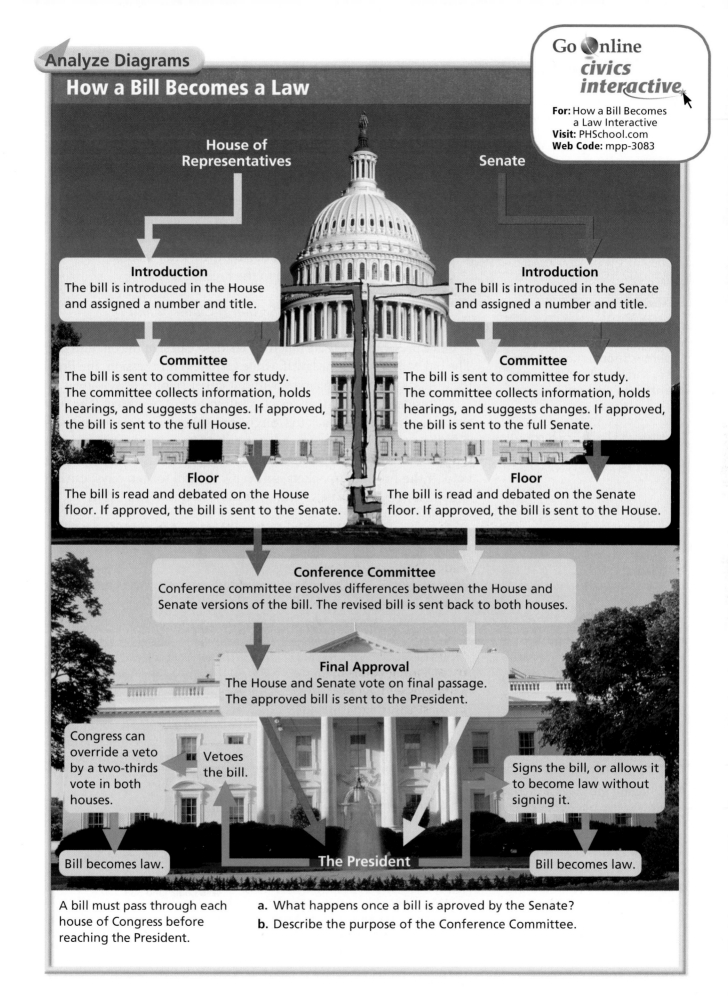

Go Online
civics interactive

For: How a Bill Becomes a Law Interactive
Visit: PHSchool.com
Web Code: mpp-3083

House of Representatives

Senate

Introduction
The bill is introduced in the House and assigned a number and title.

Introduction
The bill is introduced in the Senate and assigned a number and title.

Committee
The bill is sent to committee for study. The committee collects information, holds hearings, and suggests changes. If approved, the bill is sent to the full House.

Committee
The bill is sent to committee for study. The committee collects information, holds hearings, and suggests changes. If approved, the bill is sent to the full Senate.

Floor
The bill is read and debated on the House floor. If approved, the bill is sent to the Senate.

Floor
The bill is read and debated on the Senate floor. If approved, the bill is sent to the House.

Conference Committee
Conference committee resolves differences between the House and Senate versions of the bill. The revised bill is sent back to both houses.

Final Approval
The House and Senate vote on final passage. The approved bill is sent to the President.

Congress can override a veto by a two-thirds vote in both houses.

Vetoes the bill.

Signs the bill, or allows it to become law without signing it.

Bill becomes law.

The President

Bill becomes law.

A bill must pass through each house of Congress before reaching the President.

a. What happens once a bill is aproved by the Senate?
b. Describe the purpose of the Conference Committee.

The President's Role

After the same bill has been passed by a majority vote in both houses of Congress, it is sent to the President. As the Constitution states,

Tax Veto
In 1985, President Reagan and Governor Thomas Kean of New Jersey showed the President's intention to veto tax increases.

"Every Bill which shall have passed the House of Representatives and the Senate, . . . [and] Every Order, Resolution, or vote to which the Concurrence of the Senate and House of Representatives may be necessary (except on a question of Adjournment) shall be presented to the President . . ."

—*Article I, Section 7, Clauses 2 and 1*

Once presented with the bill, the President can sign the bill into law. The bill will also become law if, while Congress is in session, the President holds the bill for ten days without either signing or vetoing it.

A President may veto, or reject, a bill in one of two ways. The first way is to send the bill back to Congress unsigned. Congress can override the veto by passing the bill again by a two-thirds vote of both houses. The second way a President can veto a bill is called a **pocket veto**. If the President pockets, or keeps, the bill for ten days, during which Congress ends its session, the bill will not become law.

✓ Reading Check **Why might a President want to exercise a pocket veto?**

SECTION 3 Assessment

Key Terms

Use each of the key terms in a sentence that explains its meaning: Speaker of the House, president pro tempore, floor leaders, pocket veto

Target Reading Skill

1. What are the major differences among the categories of Congressional committees?

Comprehension and Critical Thinking

2. **a. Describe** What are the duties of the various Congressional leaders?

   b. Contrast Which leadership position do you think is the most important? Why?

3. **a. Explain** What steps does a House or Senate standing committee take when it is given a bill to consider?

   b. Determine Relevance Why does Congress send bills to committees instead of having all members consider each bill?

4. **a. Recall** What is the President's role in passing legislation?

   b. Identify Alternatives Why does the President need more than one method of passing or vetoing legislation?

Writing Activity

Go online to either **www.senate.gov** or **www.house.gov** and research a committee of your choice. Write a report about some aspect of the committee's history, structure, membership, or recent legislation.

Go Online PHSchool.com
For: Report on Congress
Visit: PHSchool.com
Web Code: mpd-3083

Following a Bill in Congress

Reading Preview

Objectives

In this section you will

- Describe the process of stopping a bill from being passed.
- Discuss how compromise bills are agreed to and become law.

Key Terms

filibuster   cloture

Main Idea

Either party can use rules of order and procedure on the House or Senate floor to prevent a bill from being passed. Members of Congress try to compromise on controversial legislation so that they can agree to pass bills. Some bills don't survive committee study.

Target Reading Skill

Compare and Contrast When you compare two things, you note similarities. When you contrast them, you note differences.

Taking Notes

Make a tree map like the one below. As you read this section, use it to outline information about the minimum-wage legislation.

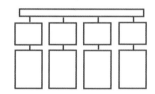

Suppose you have been hired to work as a summer intern for one of your state's senators. The senator wants to introduce a bill to raise the minimum wage, but she asks you to research some background information.

As you begin researching, you quickly learn that the minimum wage is a controversial issue. Since the Fair Labor Standards Act set the first minimum wage at 25 cents per hour in 1938, Americans have been debating whether increasing the minimum wage helps or hurts our economy. Some people argue that minimum wage increases help low-income workers support themselves and their families. Others disagree, insisting that increases in the minimum wage hurt workers. Businesses may not able to afford the wage increase, these opponents argue, and they may have to lay off workers. So what has happened in the past when minimum wage bills have been introduced in Congress?

Minimum Wage
Workers stringing tennis rackets are paid minimum wage. **Identify Cause and Effect** *What are the possible effects of an increase in the minimum wage on these workers? How might it affect their employer?*

Students Make a Difference

Sarah Keister, a senior at Vernon Hills High School in Vernon Hills, Illinois, is a legislative intern for her state representative. While working as an intern, Sarah has attended meetings addressing local issues in her legislative district and participated in information fairs.

Through her participation in the democratic process, Sarah has gained an understanding of how government works. "I became interested in politics because I like to be aware of the current issues surfacing in my community."

Service Learning

How can you make a difference on issues important to your legislative district?

Stopping a Bill

Since 1938 the minimum wage has been part of American working life. During Harry Truman's Fair Deal, Congress raised the minimum wage from 40 cents to 75 cents an hour. Six years later, it rose to $1.00 an hour. Another six years took it to $1.25.

Senator Edward Kennedy, a Democrat from Massachusetts, introduced the Minimum Wage Restoration Act, numbered S.837, in March 1987. The bill was assigned to the Labor and Human Resources Committee.

The Democrats were the majority party in the Senate at this time, so the chairperson on every committee was a Democrat. Senator Kennedy was chairman of the Labor and Human Resources Committee. From this powerful position he moved the minimum wage legislation forward by scheduling hearings on the bill. At the hearings, committee members listened to testimony from supporters and opponents of S.837.

The Labor and Human Resources Committee sent S.837 to the full Senate in July 1988. It recommended that the bill be approved. This is called reporting the bill.

The Senate began its debate on S.837. Senator Orrin Hatch, a Republican from Utah, felt the bill would be bad for the American economy. To try to block passage of the bill, Senator Hatch and some fellow Republicans started a **filibuster**, which is the use of long speeches to prevent a vote on a bill. In an attempt to wear down the opposition, well-known filibusters have lasted as long as 15 and even 24 hours. Filibusters cannot happen in the House, where time limits are set for debates.

The Democrats tried to stop the filibuster on September 22 by calling for **cloture** (KLO chur), or agreement to end the debate on a bill. Cloture requires a three-fifths vote. At the final count only 53 senators voted in favor of cloture. The next day, the Democrats tried again but failed. Without an end to the filibuster, the Senate could not vote on the bill. Even though they were the minority party in the Senate, the Republicans had stopped the bill.

Filibuster
Senator Orrin Hatch of Utah started a filibuster against the passage of S.837 that prevented its passage.

✓ **Reading Check** **How did the Republicans prevent the minimum-wage bill from coming to a vote?**

Analyze Graphs

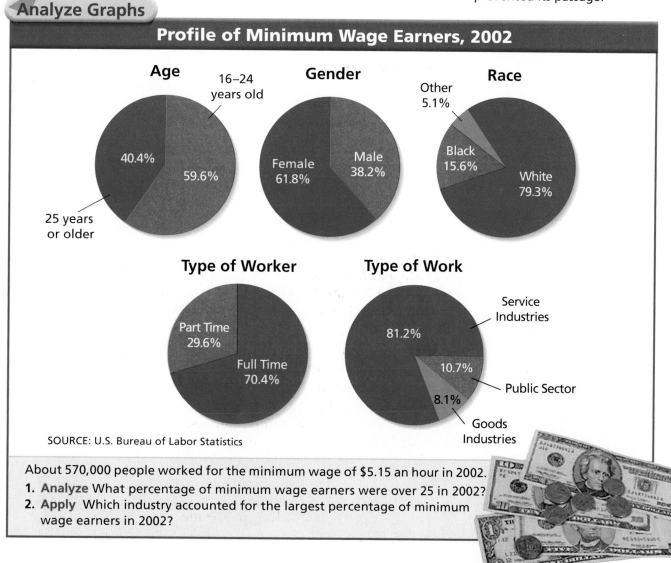

Profile of Minimum Wage Earners, 2002

Age
16–24 years old
40.4%
59.6%
25 years or older

Gender
Female 61.8%
Male 38.2%

Race
Other 5.1%
Black 15.6%
White 79.3%

Type of Worker
Part Time 29.6%
Full Time 70.4%

Type of Work
Service Industries 81.2%
Public Sector 10.7%
Goods Industries 8.1%

SOURCE: U.S. Bureau of Labor Statistics

About 570,000 people worked for the minimum wage of $5.15 an hour in 2002.
1. **Analyze** What percentage of minimum wage earners were over 25 in 2002?
2. **Apply** Which industry accounted for the largest percentage of minimum wage earners in 2002?

Compromise Bills

In the next Congress, Senator Kennedy introduced S.4, a new minimum wage bill. This time, several changes were made in the bill. Some Republicans liked it better, and the Senate passed it.

Meanwhile, the House also passed a minimum wage bill, numbered HR.2. Because the two bills were not exactly alike, a conference committee formed to write a compromise bill. This bill was passed by both houses of Congress and sent to the President. President George Bush believed a minimum wage increase would hurt the economy. He vetoed the bill.

After failing to override the veto, Congress worked out a compromise bill that satisfied the President, who signed it into law in November. This law increased the minimum wage to $4.25 per hour in 1991.

The minimum wage remained at $4.25 until 1996. At this time, the Republicans were the majority party in both the House and the Senate. Representative Bill Archer, a Republican from Texas, introduced HR.3448, the Small Business Job Protection Act of 1996. One of this bill's provisions was a two-stage increase in the minimum wage—to $4.75 per hour in 1996, and to $5.15 in 1997.

The bill HR.3448 was sent to the Committee on Ways and Means, which approved the bill. The bill was then passed by the full House. Several weeks later, the Senate passed a similar bill. A conference committee worked out a compromise bill that was then passed by both houses of Congress. President Clinton signed the bill in August, making it law.

✓ Reading Check **Why was a conference committee formed for bill S.4?**

A Bill Becomes Law
President Bill Clinton signs HR.3448 in 1996, raising the federal minimum wage. Summarize *What happens when the House and the Senate approve bills that are similar in goal but not identical?*

Strengthening America's Families
A New Minimum Wage

A Bill Dies in Committee

Senator Edward Kennedy introduced S.1805, the Fair Minimum Wage Act, in 1998. When introducing this bill in the Senate chamber, Kennedy explained its purpose to his colleagues:

"The federal minimum wage is now $5.15 an hour. Our bill will raise it by $1.00 over the next two years—a 50 cent increase on January 1, 1999, and another 50 cent increase on January 1, 2000, so that the minimum wage will reach the level of $6.15 at the turn of the century."

James Jeffords
Senator James Jeffords of Vermont chaired the Labor and Human Resources Committee that failed to support S.1805.

The bill S.1805 was sent to the Labor and Human Resources Committee, chaired by Republican Senator Jim Jeffords of Vermont. It failed to gain the support of a majority of committee members. Without that support, the bill "died" when the 105th Congress ended.

By following these minimum wage bills through Congress, you have learned a lot about lawmaking. Clearly, a bill must overcome many hurdles before becoming a law. Realize that passing a bill is difficult for a reason. The framers wanted Congress to take its time. They wanted every bill to be studied and debated carefully. Any bill that makes it through this process has an excellent chance of being a good law.

✓ **Reading Check** **Why did Senator Kennedy want to raise the minimum wage?**

SECTION 4 Assessment

Key Terms
Use each of the key terms in a sentence that explains its meaning:
filibuster, cloture

Target Reading Skill
1. **Compare and Contrast** What are the major similarities and differences in the stories of the minimum-wage bills?

Comprehension and Critical Thinking
2. **a. Recall** How did the Democrats respond to the Republican filibuster of S.387?

   b. Analyze Information Why did the Republicans want to prevent the vote?

3. **a. Describe** How did Congress respond to President Bush's veto of the compromise minimum-wage bill?

   b. Draw Inferences Why did Congress take this action?

4. **a. Explain** What happened to bill S.1805?

   b. Check Consistency Why did Congress react differently to the different minimum-wage bills?

Writing Activity
Go online or to the library to find out more about one of your state's senators. Write a one-page biography that describes his or her career in the Senate and discusses legislation in which he or she played a central role.

> **TIP** It will be difficult to cover your Senator's entire career in one page. Choose the highlights that you find most significant.

Sequencing

When studying past events, it is important to consider the sequence, or order, in which the events take place. Once you know the correct sequence, you can begin to see how events relate to one another.

The following paragraph and table deal with a series of laws passed from the late 1880s through the 1910s.

From 1887 to 1914, Congress passed legislation to put a stop to business abuses. The first important law was the Interstate Commerce Act in 1887. It set up a commission to regulate railroads. Next was the Sherman Anti-Trust Act in 1890. In 1903, the Elkin Act outlawed railroad abuses by big companies. It was followed in 1906 by several laws, including the Meat Inspection Act. After Woodrow Wilson's election to the presidency in 1912, Congress passed several additional laws, among them the Federal Reserve Act and the Clayton Anti-Trust Act.

Examples of Reform Laws		
Year	Law	Content
1887	Interstate Commerce Act	Regulated railroads
1890	Sherman Anti-Trust Act	Outlawed trusts
1903	Elkins Act	Outlawed railroad abuses for big shippers
1906	Pure Food and Drug Act	Created standards for food and drugs
1913	Federal Reserve Act	Established the Federal Reserve Bank
1914	Clayton Anti-Trust Act	Strengthened Sherman Anti-Trust Act

Learn the Skill

Follow these steps to sequence information:

❶ **Identify the order in which events happened.** Place the events in chronological order. Start with the event that has the earliest date.

❷ **Identify time-order words.** To establish sequence, look for words such as *first, next, later, now, then, before,* and *after.*

❸ **Figure out time intervals.** Calculate the time between events.

❹ **Make connections.** How are the events related?

Practice the Skill

Look at the information above and answer these questions.

❶ What year was the Interstate Commerce Act passed?

❷ What event happened the year before the Federal Reserve Act?

❸ The Meat Inspection Act and the Federal Reserve Act were passed how many years apart?

Apply the Skill

Look around your neighborhood. Do some library research to find out the sequence of events that led to the construction of a building or monument, or to the beginning of a town fair or event.

Review and Assessment

Chapter Summary

Section 1
The Members of Congress
(pages 212–217)

- Members of the two houses of Congress make laws. As they consider each bill, they must balance the needs of their constituents and their political parties with the needs of the nation. Members of interest groups employ lobbyists to try to influence the decisions of members of Congress.

- Each member of the House of Representatives is elected to represent a congressional district in his or her home state. A state's number of representatives depends on its population.

Section 2
The Powers of Congress
(pages 218–221)

- Congress has the power to make laws, oversee the budget, and impeach government officials. Congress possesses other unspecified powers it may need to carry out the specific ones.

- The Constitution denies Congress the power to jail anyone without charging him or her with a crime.

Section 3
How Congress Is Organized
(pages 223–228)

- The ruling party in each house of Congress chooses that body's leaders. The Senate is led by a president pro tempore who presides when the Vice-President is absent. The House is led by the *Speaker of the House.* Each house also has a number of floor leaders.

- Most of the work of making laws is done in standing (permanent) committees, select (temporary special) committees,

and joint and conference committees (with members from both houses).

- The President of the United States can make a bill into law (by signing it or by waiting for ten days) or veto it (by refusing to sign it or by a pocket veto). Congress can override a presidential veto with a two-thirds vote of both houses.

Section 4
Following a Bill In Congress
(pages 229–233)

- If a bill is up for a vote in the Senate, Senators in opposition to the bill can stop the vote with an endless series of speeches called a filibuster. To override the filibuster, the Senate must successfully vote for cloture.

- If both houses pass similar but different versions of legislation, a conference committee can draft a compromise bill. If the President vetoes this bill, Congress can amend it and send it back for presidential approval.

- If committee members cannot agree on a bill, they do not send it to the floor for a vote, and the bill dies.

Copy the chart below and use it to help you summarize the chapter:

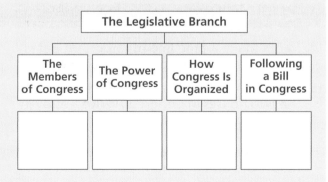

Reviewing Key Terms

Circle the term that makes each sentence correct.

1. (Floor leaders, Lobbyists) pressure members of Congress to listen to the needs of interest groups.

2. The Constitution calls for a (bill of attainder, census) of the population once every ten years.

3. The (president pro tempore, Speaker of the House) is appointed to take the place of the Vice-President in the Senate.

4. Each (congressional district, interest group) sends one representative to the House.

5. Senators can (filibuster, impeach) when they want to prevent a vote on a bill.

6. The term (cloture, pocket veto) means holding a bill for ten days during which a session of Congress ends.

7. (Floor leaders, Interest groups) often donate money to political parties in hopes of influencing legislation.

8. (Census, Cloture) is an agreement to end a debate on a bill.

9. A piece of legislation on which Congress will vote is called a (bill, budget).

Comprehension and Critical Thinking

10. a. **Recall** Identify the groups to which members of Congress are responsible.
    b. **Contrast** What is the difference between lobbyists and interest groups?
    c. **Identify Effects** What effect do you think lobbyists and interest groups have on the passage or failure of legislation?

11. a. **Describe** What are some of the ways in which Congress can check the power of the executive branch?
    b. **Evaluate Information** How effective are these checks on the President's power?
    c. **Predict** How might Congress react if a President took actions with which it disagreed?

12. a. **Explain** What are the duties of the Speaker of the House?
    b. **Analyze Information** How can the majority party use its leadership positions to maintain power in Congress?
    c. **Identify Alternatives** How could an equal balance of power between the two parties in Congress be achieved?

13. a. **Recall** What did Senator Kennedy do after minimum-wage bill S.837 failed?
    b. **Draw Inferences** Why did the Senator take this action?
    c. **Identify Effects** What are the consequences of repeated attempts to pass certain legislation, such as a minimum-wage bill?

Activities

14. **Skills** Make a time line of important dates in minimum-wage legislation since 1987.

15. **Writing** You have read a great deal about the two houses of Congress. Write a essay in which you compare and contrast the membership, structure, and functions of the House and the Senate. You may wish to read more about Congress before you begin your essay.

16. **Active Citizen** Go to **www.house.gov** to read about your representative in the House. Find a piece of legislation that you want to see passed. Write a letter urging your representative to support this legislation. Explain why you support it.

17. **Math Practice** Find out what the minimum wage is today and multiply it by 40 hours to get an average weekly wages. How much would you earn in a year if you worked 40 hours per week at the minimum wage?

18. **Civics and Economics** You have been asked to testify before a Senate committee studying a minimum-wage bill. A senator asks what you think the minimum wage should be and if and when it should be raised. Write your answer and your reasons for feeling this way.

19. **Target Reading Skills** Make a table that compares and contrasts the jobs of senators and representatives.

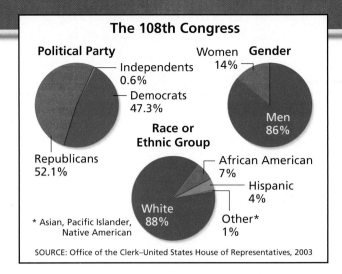

The 108th Congress

Political Party
Independents 0.6%
Democrats 47.3%
Republicans 52.1%

Gender
Women 14%
Men 86%

Race or Ethnic Group
White 88%
African American 7%
Hispanic 4%
Other* 1%
* Asian, Pacific Islander, Native American

SOURCE: Office of the Clerk–United States House of Representatives, 2003

20. **Analyzing Visuals** These three circle graphs describe the membership of the 108th Congress. Write a paragraph explaining whether you think Congress fairly represents the general population.

Standardized Test Prep

Test-Taking Tips

Sometimes a standardized test will ask you to analyze a primary source. Below is an excerpt from a speech made by Senator Edward Kennedy in the spring of 2002. Read the speech and answer the questions that follow.

TIP When the answer to a question is not given directly in the passage, read it carefully to help you make the correct inference.

> I propose increasing the federal minimum wage to $6.65 an hour. This modest increase would add $3,000 to the income of full-time, year-round workers. That's enough money for a low-income family of three to afford over 15 months of groceries, over 7 months of utilities, or two years' tuition for a community college degree. . . . It will enable hard-working Americans to afford a decent home and a better quality of life. No one who works for a living should have to live in poverty.

Choose the letter of the best answer.

1. Kennedy suggests that the minimum wage
   A was far above the poverty level.
   B was just above the poverty level.
   C was about equal to the poverty level.
   D had no relationship to the poverty level.

   TIP Reread the sentence in which Kennedy uses the word *poverty.*

   The correct answer is **C**. The final sentence of the passage suggests minimum-wage earners live in poverty; if the wage is raised, they won't live in poverty any longer.

2. How much did Kennedy suggest a family of three spends on groceries every month?
   A $200
   B $3,000
   C $15
   D $150

The Executive Branch

What's Ahead in Chapter 9

In this chapter you will read about the responsibilities of the President. You will also learn about the responsibilities of the executive branch of the government that the President heads.

SECTION 1
The Roles of the President

SECTION 2
The Organization of the Executive Branch

SECTION 3
Presidents and Power

TARGET
READING SKILL

In this chapter you will focus on clarifying meaning to help you better understand what you read. Clarifying meaning includes reading ahead, rereading, and paraphrasing.

The White House ▶

National | **Standards for Civics and Government** | **State**

The following National Standards for Civics and Government are covered in this chapter:

III. How does the government established by the Constitution embody American democracy?

A. How are power and responsibility distributed, shared, and limited in the government?

B. What does the national government do?

Go Online
PHSchool.com

For: Your state's standards
Visit: PHSchool.com
Web Code: mpe-3091

Active Citizen ▶ Civics in the Real World

Have you ever wondered what it would be like to be President of the United States? Here is what several Presidents have said about the job.

Though I occupy a very high position, I am the hardest working man in the country.

—James K. Polk (1845–1849)

I have thoroughly enjoyed being President. But I believe I can also say that I am thoroughly alive to the tremendous responsibilities of the position.

—Theodore Roosevelt (1901–1909)

Being a President is like riding a tiger. A man has to keep on riding or be swallowed.

—Harry S Truman (1945–1953)

No easy problems ever come to the President of the United States. If they are easy to solve, somebody else has solved them.

—Dwight D. Eisenhower (1953–1961)

There is no experience you can get that can possibly prepare you adequately for the presidency.

—John F. Kennedy (1961–1963)

Citizen's Journal When discussing their time in the White House, Presidents have often described the presidency as an extremely difficult job. Why do you think the presidency is such a demanding position? Write a paragraph explaining your opinion on this question.

The Roles of the President

SECTION 1

Reading Preview

Objectives

In this section you will
- Learn why the framers created the office of President with limits.
- Describe the various roles of the President.
- Identify which of the President's roles have been created by tradition.

Taking Notes

Make a diagram like the one below. As you read the section, complete the diagram with information about the different roles of the President of the United States.

▲ Presidents are often associated with events that took place during their terms. Abraham Lincoln was President during the Civil War.

Key Terms

executive branch
foreign policy
ambassadors
executive agreements
domestic policy

Main Idea

The President of the United States is a very powerful person who plays many roles in the government. However, the President's power is deliberately limited by the Constitution.

Target Reading Skill

Reading Ahead Reading ahead can help explain something you have just read. If an idea or word is not clear, keep reading, because something in the next paragraph or two may help clarify the meaning of what you were unsure about.

As our highest elected official, the President of the United States represents all Americans, not just citizens of one state or congressional district. It is the President who usually meets with leaders of other nations, and whose daily activities are closely followed by the television networks, newspapers, and news magazines. Just about everyone knows who the President is.

How many Americans, though, have a clear picture of what the President does? The President is the head of the **executive branch**, the branch of government responsible for executing, or carrying out, the law. However, carrying out laws is only part of the President's job. The most important duty is to set goals for the nation and to develop policies, which are methods for reaching those goals.

This heavy responsibility goes with an office that many think is the most powerful in the world. The office of President also has limits, though, which are set by the Constitution. To understand the powers and responsibilities of the presidency, as well as its limits, you need to look first at how the office was created.

Creating the Office of President

In creating the presidency, the Framers did not want a leader with unlimited powers. The memory of the tyranny of the British king was fresh in the minds of many Americans. To calm the people's fears, the Framers gave very few specific powers to the President. They also included ways to prevent abuse of power.

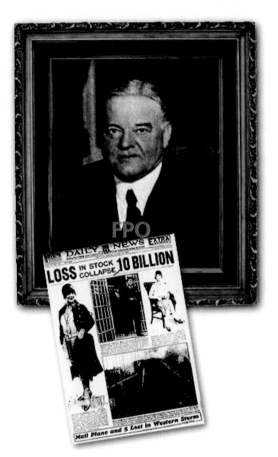

Term of Office One limit on the President's power is the term of office. The President is elected for a term of four years and must run for re-election in order to serve a second term. No President may hold office for more than two terms.

Limited Power Another protection is the separation of powers among the three branches of government. The President cannot make laws, only carry out the ones made by Congress. The Supreme Court has the power to decide if a law is constitutional.

The system of checks and balances also limits the President's power. Congress must approve many presidential decisions. In cases of serious wrongdoing, Congress may remove the President from office. Furthermore, the Supreme Court can decide whether actions taken by the President are allowed by the Constitution.

Qualifications and Salary To be President, a person must be at least 35 years old and a natural-born citizen of the United States. He or she must have lived in the United States for at least 14 years. The President's yearly salary is set by Congress.

✓ Reading Check   **How many years is one term of office for the President?**

▲
Herbert Hoover (top left) was President when the country fell into the Great Depression. Jimmy Carter (top right, standing in the middle) helped to bring peace between Israel and Egypt. Woodrow Wilson (above) took the United States into World War I.

A Leader with Many Roles

The framers knew that the nation needed a leader who could both carry out laws and represent the nation in meeting leaders of other countries. The office of President was new in a world of nations led by monarchs. Therefore, the Framers did not describe exactly how the President should fulfill the duties of this new office. Expecting that George Washington would be elected as the nation's first leader, they trusted that he would become a model of what a President should be. As Washington himself noted:

> "I walk on untrodden ground. There is scarcely any part of my conduct which may not hereafter be drawn into precedent [made an example of]."

Through the examples of Washington and the Presidents who followed him, the roles of the President have become more clearly defined over the years.

Analyze Diagrams

Roles of the President

As leader of the executive branch, the President has many important roles. The images on this page and the next illustrate some of the many functions of the office of the President.

a. Why do you think the role of chief diplomat is an important one for the President?

b. Which of the President's roles do you think is the most difficult? Why?

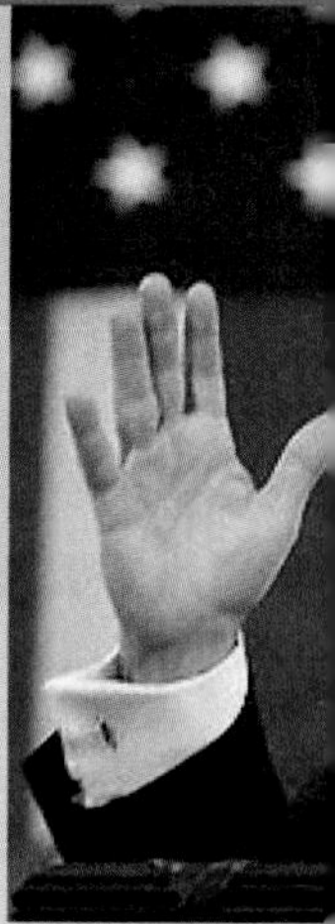

Legislative Leader
One of the President's duties as legislative leader is to give an annual State of the Union address to all Americans. Here President George W. Bush delivers his address before of cials from all three branches of government.

Chief Diplomat
Acting as chief diplomat, President Richard Nixon made a historic trip to the People's Republic of China in 1972. Nixon's visit to China was hailed as a diplomatic triumph during the Cold War.

Commander in Chief
In this photo, Franklin Delano Roosevelt (center) meets with Richard Byrd (left), an admiral in the U.S. Navy.

Chief Executive The President serves as chief executive, or head of the executive branch. The Constitution states that the President must "take care that the laws be faithfully executed." To execute laws means to make sure that they are carried out. Although Congress makes the laws, it is up to executive branch officials to decide just how to carry out laws and other policies.

As leader of the executive branch, the President usually makes only the broadest decisions, leaving the details to other officials. One way in which the President gives orders is through executive orders, which are rules and regulations that governments must follow. The power to make executive orders, however, is limited. The President's orders may not violate the Constitution or laws passed by Congress.

As chief executive, the President also has the power to appoint about 4,000 executive branch officials. As a check on that power, Congress must confirm, or approve, many top appointments.

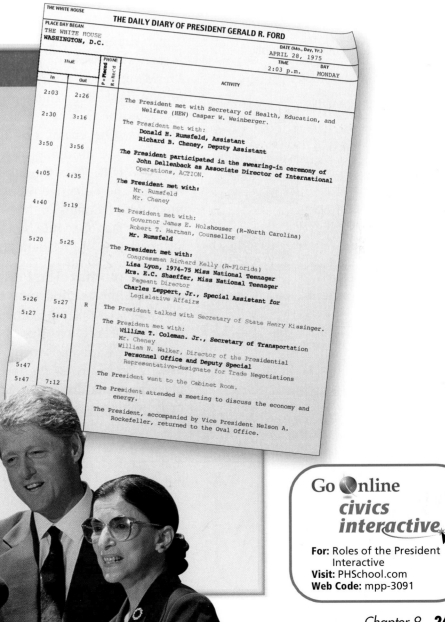

Judicial Powers
The President chooses justices for the Supreme Court and other federal courts. In 1993, President Bill Clinton appointed Ruth Bader Ginsburg as Justice to the Supreme Court. As leader of the executive branch, the President has many important roles.

Go Online
civics
interactive

For: Roles of the President Interactive
Visit: PHSchool.com
Web Code: mpp-3091

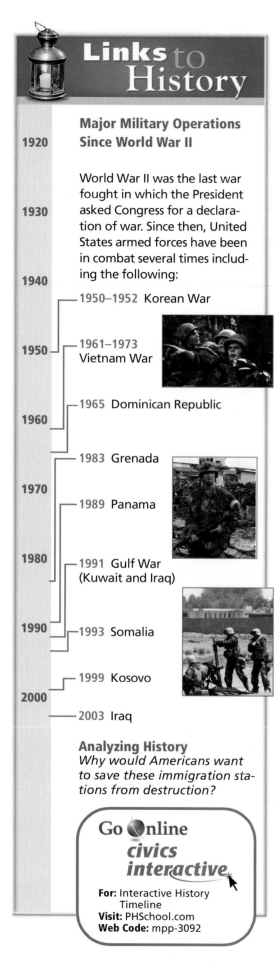

Major Military Operations Since World War II

World War II was the last war fought in which the President asked Congress for a declaration of war. Since then, United States armed forces have been in combat several times including the following:

1920
1930
1940

1950–1952 Korean War

1950

1961–1973 Vietnam War

1965 Dominican Republic

1960

1983 Grenada

1970

1989 Panama

1980

1991 Gulf War (Kuwait and Iraq)

1990

1993 Somalia

1999 Kosovo

2000

2003 Iraq

Analyzing History
Why would Americans want to save these immigration stations from destruction?

Go Online
civics interactive

For: Interactive History Timeline
Visit: PHSchool.com
Web Code: mpp-3092

Commander in Chief The Constitution says that "the President shall be commander in chief of the army and navy of the United States." This statement points to the President's important role as leader of the armed forces. This role was given to the President because the framers of the Constitution wanted to maintain civilian authority over the military.

While the President is expected to set military goals and approve military tactics, military leaders and specialists often discourage the commander in chief from getting involved in daily operations. Yet when the nation is at war, the President makes the most important decisions.

To protect American interests, the President may send troops to a foreign country even if Congress has not declared war. However, the War Powers Resolution, passed after the Vietnam War, says that such troops may not remain for more than 60 days without the approval of Congress.

The President's role as head of the armed forces has grown dramatically since the days of George Washington. It carries an awesome power that can weigh heavily on the President. Besides affecting American soldiers who are sent to fight on foreign soil, the President's decisions can also alter the lives of other nations and change the course of history. One example of the sober nature of this responsibility is the dropping of the atomic bomb on Japan in World War II. Even though there was much consultation between the executive branch, the armed forces, and the members of Congress, the plan to end the war with Japan with this action could not have proceeded without the authorization of President Harry S. Truman.

Chief Diplomat The President is also our chief diplomat, the most important representative of the United States in relations with other nations. The President leads in making **foreign policy**, the set of plans for guiding our nation's relationships with other countries. Although they usually seek advice on foreign policy, Presidents must make the final decisions. As President Truman put it, "I make foreign policy."

Foreign policy is clearly the President's "territory," but Congress may set limits. For instance, the President may make treaties, or formal agreements with other countries, but the Senate may reject any treaty.

The Senate must also approve the President's appointments of ambassadors. **Ambassadors** are the official representatives to foreign governments.

Shaping Our Laws
President George W. Bush is shown promoting his No Child Left Behind Act, which his administration hoped would improve education in American schools.
Draw Inferences *Why do you think the Constitution prevents Congress from acting along in making laws?*

Target Reading Skill
Read Ahead Read the first paragraph under the heading *Legislative Leader.* Then keep reading to find out about the President's power to influence lawmaking.

The President does have freedom, though, to make **executive agreements**, agreements with other countries that do not need Senate approval. Executive agreements may have a wide range of purposes. They may set goals for trade or make promises to give aid to other countries.

Legislative Leader Congress makes our nation's laws. The President, however, has a good deal of power to influence what those laws will be and how they are enforced. The Constitution states that the President may recommend to Congress "such measures as he shall judge necessary and expedient." This means that Congress is expected to consider the President's ideas rather than act alone in making laws.

Early each year, the President gives a speech to both houses of Congress. In this State of the Union Address, the President sets forth ideas about what America's foreign policy should be. The President also talks about problems at home, such as taxes and health care. By describing these problems and giving ideas for solving them, the President helps to set **domestic policy**, a set of plans for dealing with national problems.

How does a President get Congress to turn foreign and domestic policy into laws? One way is by getting members of Congress to write bills. Another is by calling and meeting with members of Congress, urging them to support the President's program. Speeches to interest groups and to the public also help gain support for bills the President wants passed.

A powerful tool for influencing Congress to take action is the veto. The threat of a veto is often enough to get Congress to change a bill to make it more to the President's liking. Congress has overridden about 4 percent of the more than 2,500 vetoes in our nation's history.

Franklin Delano Roosevelt, known as FDR, was the President who brought the United States out of the Great Depression. He did so by pressuring Congress to enact a sweeping series of programs known as the New Deal.

1. What does the snail represent? Why do you think the cartoonist chose to use a snail?
2. What point does the cartoon make about the President's power as legislative leader?

Another way in which the President acts as legislative leader is in making the budget. To put policy ideas into action costs money. Every year the President consults committees and advisors, then prepares a budget, a plan for how to raise and spend money to carry out the President's programs.

Congress does not pass all the laws the President asks for, and it almost always makes changes in the President's budget. However, Congress cannot ignore the President's power as legislative leader.

Finally, the President has the power to call special sessions of Congress if Congress is not meeting. Today, however, Congress meets for almost the whole year, and the power is not much used.

Judicial Powers As part of the system of checks and balances, the President chooses Supreme Court justices and other federal judges. Of course, the President's power is balanced by the Senate, which must confirm these appointments.

The President may limit the power of the judicial branch by putting off or reducing the punishment of someone convicted of a crime in federal courts. The President may even do away with the punishment by granting a pardon, or release from punishment.

✓ Reading Check   **How does the President influence the making of laws?**

Roles Created by Tradition

Over the years, the President has taken on two other roles: party leader and chief of state. Neither role is mentioned explicitly in the Constitution, yet both are natural results of the President's position and power.

The President is a member of a political party, typically either the Democratic party or the Republican party. As our highest elected official, the President is seen as the leader of that party. The President's power and prestige can be used to support party goals or candidates. Frequently, during election years, the President will give speeches and attend fundraisers throughout the country to help support members of the party who are running for important offices.

As chief of state, the President speaks for the whole nation, expressing the values and goals of the American people. The President carries out many ceremonial duties, such as greeting visiting leaders and giving medals to citizens. In this role, the President is very much like a monarch, who traditionally carries out ceremonial duties. As chief of state, the President stands for a national unity that overshadows differences between the political parties. The President also stands as a symbol of the United States of America.

✔ **Reading Check** **What two other roles has the President taken on over the years that are not mentioned in the Constitution?**

▲ In 2000, Marian Wright Edelman, President of the Children's Defense Fund, was awarded the Presidential Medal of Honor.

SECTION 1 Assessment

Key Terms
Use each of the key terms in a sentence that explains its meaning: executive branch, foreign policy, ambassadors, executive agreements, domestic policy

Target Reading Skill
1. **Read Ahead** Turn back to page 245. How did reading ahead help you better understand how the President sets domestic policy?

Comprehension and Critical Thinking
2. **a. Recall** For how many terms may a President hold office?

   b. Demonstrate Reasoned Judgment Why do you think Congress, rather than the Constitution, sets the President's salary?

3. **a. Describe** What is the military role of the President?

   b. Draw Inferences How do the actions of Presidents help define the office of President?

4. **a. Describe** What does the President do as head of a political party?

   b. Check Consistency How do the President's two roles as party leader and chief of state conflict?

Writing Activity
Write a letter to James Madison, the "Father of the Constitution." Tell Madison how the office of the President has evolved since his lifetime. In your letter, explain the different responsibilities and powers of the presidency today.

TIP Write an outline using the heads of each sub-section in Section 1. Find a detail or two you can use to illustrate the main idea of each paragraph.

How to Conduct a Survey

The United States is a representative democracy. This means that public officials act on behalf of the citizens who elected them. To do this effectively, they must know how citizens feel about different issues.

Surveys are a good way of determining public opinion. A survey is a list of questions. Many people answer these questions. The results of a survey give a good idea of how people generally feel about different issues.

Forced-Choice Questions

A forced-choice question makes the person give a definite answer. For example, the person may have to choose either "yes" or "no."

Example: The minimum voting age should be raised to 21.

____ yes ____ no

Scaled Questions

Scaled questions ask a person to gauge how strongly they feel about an issue.

Example: Circle your reaction to the following statement: The Constitution continues to meet the needs of America today.

Strongly Disagree   Agree   Strongly Agree

Ranked Questions

A ranked question gives a list of items. The person must put them in order of importance to him or her.

Example: Rank the following in order of importance. Use a 1 for the freedom you think is most important and a 3 for the freedom of least importance.

____ freedom of the press

____ freedom of speech

____ freedom of assembly

Learn the Skill

To conduct a survey, follow these steps:

❶ **Choose an issue.** Think of an issue that is of importance to many people.

❷ **Write the survey questions.** Include each type of question. Try to make your questions fair and unbiased.

❸ **Ask people to fill out the survey.** Ask at least ten people.

❹ **Compile the results.** How many people answered each question the same way?

Practice the Skill

❶ Write two examples of each type of question.

❷ Have a partner read your questions to make sure they are clear and worded fairly.

Apply the Skill

❶ Choose an issue and write six survey questions about it.

❷ Ask 20 people to complete your survey.

❸ Compile the results and report them to the class.

Go Online
civics interactive

For: Local Citizenship
Visit: PHSchool.com
Web Code: mpp-3093

The Organization of the Executive Branch

Reading Preview

Objectives

In this section you will

- Learn about the Executive Office of the President.
- Identify the executive departments.
- Identify the independent agencies.
- Understand the civil service system.

Key Terms

bureaucracy   cabinet
administration

Main Idea

The executive branch of the government includes the President, the White House staff, the Vice President, the executive departments, and the independent agencies.

Target Reading Skill

Paraphrase Paraphrasing is the skill of putting something you have read in your own words. It can help you confirm your understanding of what you have just read.

Taking Notes

Make a diagram like the one below. As you read the section, complete the diagram with information about the way the executive branch is organized.

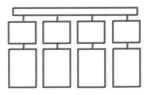

As our nation has grown, the President's duties have grown, too. Each year hundreds of laws must be carried out. Decisions must be made on a wide range of foreign and domestic policy issues. To fulfill their many duties, Presidents have needed more and more help. The executive branch has grown from a few hundred officials in George Washington's time to about 3 million employees today. It is now the largest branch of government.

As it has grown, the executive branch has become a huge bureaucracy. A **bureaucracy** (**byoo RAH kruh see**) is an organization of government departments, agencies, and offices. Most people who work in the bureaucracy are not chosen to work just for one President. They are hired as permanent employees.

To help direct the bureaucracy, the President appoints an **administration**, a team of executive branch officials. The nearly 2,000 members of the administration lead the three main parts of the executive branch: (1) the Executive Office of the President, (2) the executive departments, and (3) the independent agencies.

The Executive Office of the President

The Executive Office of the President (EOP) is largely made up of people the President chooses to help make foreign and domestic policy. Unlike the other parts of the executive branch, the main job of the Executive Office is not to carry out laws directly, but to advise the President on important matters.

▲
The Federal Bureau of Investigations (FBI), part of the Department of Justice, is one of the many executive departments in our government.

▲
Gerald Ford served as Vice President under Richard Nixon. When Nixon resigned in 1974, Ford then became President.

The White House Staff At the center of an administration is the White House staff. It includes the President's most trusted advisors and assistants. They give the President advice and information about national security, the economy, and other subjects. The White House staff also helps guide the bureaucracy toward meeting the President's goals.

Some Presidents prefer to have several staff people report directly to them on issues relating to the executive departments. Other Presidents have depended on one powerful chief of staff to whom other staff members report.

The staff includes a chief of staff, key advisors, press secretaries, legal experts, speechwriters, office workers, and researchers. All members of the White House staff are appointed or hired by the President and without need for Senate approval.

The Vice President The Constitution gives the Vice President no duties aside from presiding over the Senate. It is the President who decides what the Vice President will do. Some Presidents ask the Vice President to play an active role. This role might include heading special commissions, making trips to other countries, and working with Congress. Historically, however, the Vice President has been almost invisible. Fearing this fate, some leaders have refused to run for Vice President. Daniel Webster, for instance, said in 1848 that "I do not propose to be buried until I am dead."

If the President dies, though, the Vice President may become President. This transition has taken place eight times in our nation's history. The Vice President may also be asked to serve as "acting President" if the President falls seriously ill.

Analyze Charts

Vice Presidents Who Succeeded the President

Vice President	Year of Succession	Reason
John Tyler	1841	Death of William Henry Harrison
Millard Fillmore	1849	Death of William Zachary Taylor
Andrew Johnson	1965	Assassination of Abraham Lincoln
Chester A. Arthur	1881	Assassination of James A. Garfield
Theodore Roosevelt	1901	Assassination of William McKinley
Calvin Coolidge	1923	Death of Warren G. Harding
Harry S. Truman	1945	Death of Franklin D. Roosevelt
Lyndon B. Johnson	1963	Assassination of John F. Kennedy
Gerald R. Ford	1974	Resignation of Richard Nixon

Source: Encyclopedia Britannica Almanac, 2003

The Vice President succeeds the President if the President dies or leaves office by resignation or impeachment.

1. **Analyze** How many Vice Presidents have become President due to the assassination of the elected President?
2. **Apply** Which Vice President succeeded Warren G. Harding?

Special Advisory Groups The Executive Office of the President also includes several special groups that help the President make decisions on domestic and foreign policy. Two important groups are the Office of Management and Budget (OMB) and the National Security Council (NSC).

The OMB decides how much the President's policy goals will cost. The President may change the goals in light of the price tags provided by the OMB. Then the OMB prepares the budget that is sent to Congress.

The National Security Council plays a major role in helping the President make foreign policy. The NSC includes top military officers and advisors from other government agencies and departments concerned with foreign affairs and national defense.

✔ Reading Check **What three groups make up the Executive Office of the President?**

Civics and Economics

The Office of Management and Budget

The Office of Management and Budget was created in 1970. It has several responsibilities. Its primary duty is to prepare the President's annual budget for Congress.

The OMB also helps the President to manage the executive branch by promoting good management practices throughout the executive branch and reviewing the regulatory acts of federal agencies.

Analyzing Economics

1. What is the primary responsibility of the Office of Management and Budget?
2. Go online and find the OMB's web page. Find out more about the OMB's history and responsibilities. Write a brief report on what you find there.

The Executive Departments

Over the years, the number of executive departments has grown. Today they number 15 and form the largest part of the executive branch. They do much of the work connected with carrying out the nation's laws and running government programs.

Each executive department helps fulfill one or more of the President's duties. The Department of State, for example, handles relations with other countries and helps put the President's foreign policy decisions into action. The Department of Defense helps the President fulfill the duty of commander in chief by running the armed forces.

Presidential Advisors President George W. Bush meets with the National Security Council, one of the advisory groups in the Executive Office of the President. **Demonstrate Reasoned Judgment** *Why is it important for the President to have groups of advisors such as the NSC?*

Executive Departments

 Department of State (1789)

Carries out foreign policy.
Supervises ambassadors and other U.S. diplomats.
Represents the U.S. at the United Nations.

 Department of State (1789)

Collects federal taxes through the Internal Revenue Service (IRS).
Prints money and postage stamps; makes coins.

 Department of Defense (1789, reorganized in 1947)

Maintains the Army, Navy, Marine Corps, and Air Force.
Does research on military weapons.
Builds and maintains military bases.

Department of Interior (1849)

Manages national parks and other federal lands.
Protects fish, wildlife, and other natural resources.

 Department of Agriculture (1862)

Provides assistance to farmers.
Inspects food processing plants.
Runs the food stamp and school lunch programs.
Works to control animal and plant diseases (in conjunction with DHS).

Department of Justice (1870)

Investigates and prosecutes violations of federal laws.
Operates federal prisons. Runs the Federal Bureau of Investigation (FBI).
Represents the federal government in lawsuits.

Department of Commerce (1903)

Provides assistance to American businesses.
Conducts the national census.
Issues patents and trademarks for inventions.
Maintains official weights and measures.

Department of Labor (1903)

Enforces laws on minimum wage, job discrimination, and working conditions.
Helps run job training and unemployment programs.
Provides statistics on changes in prices and levels of employment.

 Department of Health & Human Resources (1953)

Directs Medicare Program.
Runs the Food and Drug Administration (FDA).
Runs the Public Health Service.
Runs the Family Support Administration.

 Department of Education (1953)

Provides assistance to elementary, high school, and college education programs.
Conducts research and provides statistics on education.
Promotes equal access to educational opportunities.

 Department of Housing & Urban Development (1965)

Helps provide housing for low-income citizens.
Assists state and local governments in financing community development and housing projects.

 Department of Transportation (1966)

Helps state and local governments maintain highways.
Enforces transportation safety standards.

 Department of Energy (1977)

Conducts research on sources of energy.
Promotes the conservation of fuel and electricity, and directs programs to deal with possible shortages.

 Department of Veteran's Affairs (1989)

Gives medical, educational, and financial help to people who have served in the armed forces.

 Department of Homeland Security (2003)

Runs the Federal Emergency Management Agency (FEMA).
Runs Transportation Security Administration (TSA).
Protects the President and Vice President through the Secret Service.
Operates the United States Coast Guard and the U.S. Customs Service.

Much of the work of running government is done by the executive departments.

1. **Analyze** Which executive department is in charge of managing our public parks?
2. **Apply** Do you think any of the responsibilities of these departments overlap? Which ones do you think might overlap? Why?

Source: U.S. Office of Personnel Management

The Department of Homeland Security President George W. Bush created the Department of Homeland Security in response to the terrorist attacks of September 11, 2001. The duty of the Department of Homeland Security is to safeguard our country from terrorism. In this role, the Department coordinates the anti-terrorist activities of many federal agencies, including the Coast Guard, the Immigration and Naturalization Service, and the Federal Emergency Management Agency.

The Cabinet The President appoints the head of each executive department. As a check on presidential power, the Senate must approve each appointment. The head of the Department of Justice is called the Attorney General. The other department heads are called secretaries, such as the Secretary of State and the Secretary of the Treasury. The department secretaries and the Attorney General form the core of the **Cabinet**, an important group of policy advisors to the President.

√ Reading Check   **What is the role of the executive departments in the President's Cabinet?**

Target Reading Skill
Paraphrase Paraphrase the section under the sub-heading *The Cabinet.* Your paraphrase should include information about who makes up the President's Cabinet and how they are appointed.

The Independent Agencies

The executive departments do not carry out all the duties of today's executive branch. Many tasks, from making rules about the environment to providing farm loans, are carried out by approximately 60 independent agencies. There are three types of agencies: executive agencies, regulatory commissions, and government corporations.

Executive Agencies Executive agencies are under the direct control of the President, who can choose or remove their directors. Among the most important agencies are the National Aeronautics and Space Administration (NASA) and the Environmental Protection Agency (EPA).

Regulatory Commissions Congress has formed 12 regulatory commissions. Each one makes and carries out rules for a certain business or economic activity. The Federal Communications Commission (FCC), for instance, makes rules for radio and television stations. The Consumer Product Safety Commission (CPSC) sets safety standards for products you might find around the house. The regulatory commissions also settle disputes between businesses they regulate.

The regulatory commissions are meant to be fairly free from political influences. The President chooses members of the boards that run the commissions. Each member has a long term so that no single President can choose all of a board's members.

NASA is one of the agencies under the President's control. Founded in 1958, it oversees the American space program.
▼

Civil Servants
The Federal Deposit Insurance Corporation (FDIC) is a government corporation that helps support the banking system. Its directors are appointed by the President. All other staff members are part of the Civil Service system.
Demonstrate Reasoned Judgment *Why is it important that all agency staff members should not be appointed by the President?*

Government Corporations Government corporations are like private businesses in that they try to make a profit. However, most of them provide public services that may be too risky or expensive for a private business to undertake. The United States Postal Service is one example of a government corporation.

✓ Reading Check **What are the three types of independent agencies?**

The Civil Service System

As you might imagine, the executive branch includes a wide variety of employees, from budget experts at the OMB to rocket engineers at NASA. The President chooses less than 1 percent of the workers in the executive branch. How do all the others get their jobs?

For many years, government jobs were likely to go to friends and supporters of the President. Loyalty to the President was more important than knowing how to do the job.

In 1883, however, Congress set up the civil service system. Under this system most government workers, called civil servants, are hired on the basis of merit. There are tests for most kinds of jobs, and workers are hired from among those with the highest scores. The civil service system provides for a group of trained workers who stay on the job from administration to administration.

✓ Reading Check **On what basis are most federal government workers hired today?**

SECTION 2 **Assessment**

Key Terms

Use each of the key terms in a sentence that explains its meaning: bureaucracy, administration, cabinet

Target Reading Skill

1. **Paraphrase** Paraphrase the information about civil service on this page.

Comprehension and Critical Thinking

2. **a. Explain** What is the Vice President's most important role?
   b. Draw Conclusions Why doesn't the President need Senate approval to appoint members of the White House staff?

3. **a. Recall** What is the role of the Department of State?
   b. Identify Cause and Effect How did the terrorist attacks of September 11, 2001 lead to the formation of the Department of Homeland Security?

4. **a. Recall** What type of independent agency is the Environmental Protection Agency?
   b. Draw Inferences Why were the regulatory commissions set up to be largely free from political influence?

5. **a. Recall** About how many workers in the Executive branch are covered by the Civil Service System?

   b. Analyze Information How does the Civil Service System improve the quality of government?

Writing Activity

Choose one executive department. Visit its Web site and explore one important issue that this department deals with. Write a newspaper article describing the department's work on this issue.

Go Online
PHSchool.com
For: Newspaper Article
Visit: PHSchool.com
Web Code: mpd-3092

Presidents and Power

Reading Preview

Objectives

In this section you will

- Understand the limits of the President's freedom to take action.
- Discuss how government leaders seek a balance between strong Presidential leadership and the needs of democracy.
- Learn how past Presidents have used the power of the office.

Key Terms

treaties   executive privilege

Main Idea

The power of the President has expanded since George Washington's time. The President's power is still balanced by the other two branches of the government.

Target Reading Skill

Reread Rereading a certain passage that is not clear when you first read it can help you better understand what you read.

Taking Notes

Make a diagram like the one below. As you read the section, complete the diagram with information about the advantages and disadvantages of limiting a President's power.

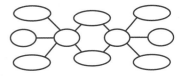

As our first President, George Washington was the leader of a small nation of about four million people. Today, the President's actions affect our nation of about 281 million people. They also affect nations and peoples around the world.

In setting up the office of President, the Framers could not have known how much the power and duties of the office would grow. Today, many people fear that too much power is in the hands of one leader. How much power should a President have? How free should a President be from checks and balances by the legislative and judicial branches of government?

President George W. Bush meeting with the President of Indonesia. The President sets much of the country's international policy.

▼

Freedom to Take Action

In fact, the President has a good deal of freedom to take action to meet goals. For example, the President and presidential advisors do not need permission from Congress to hold talks with representatives of other countries. Many talks result in executive agreements, agreements with other countries, which do not need Senate approval. Other talks lead to **treaties**, or formal agreements between nations. Even though the Senate has the power to reject any treaty, once the President has committed the United States to a treaty, it is hard for the Senate to say no.

A protection for the President's independence is **executive privilege,** the right to keep some information secret from Congress and the courts. Sometimes, for instance, the nation's safety depends on keeping certain information secret.

✓ Reading Check **What are two examples of a President's freedom to take action?**

Seeking a Balance

Why should the President be able to act independently of the other branches of government? One reason is that the President can act quickly when necessary, such as in a crisis.

Suppose, however, that a President often made important decisions without asking Congress or thinking about the constitutionality of the decision. Clearly, the need for strong leadership must be balanced against the need to protect against abuse of power.

✓ Reading Check **Why should the President be able to act without the approval of Congress when necessary?**

Active Citizen
Students Make a Difference

Cadet First Lieutenant Laquanda Leaven is a member of the JROTC and junior at Marlboro County High School in Bennettsville, South Carolina. She has gained recognition in her community for her academic achievements and volunteer activities.

Because of her achievements, Laquanda was selected to be a chemical engineer intern for a program run by the National Aeronautics and Space Administration (NASA). Among the many scientific interests pursued there, Laquanda studied different life forms found on Mars.

Service Learning

How can you use your education to benefit your community?

▲ Students can help make a difference by making good use of their education.

Presidential Power

The following examples show how three Presidents have used their powers at certain times. As you read, think about the effects of each President's action. Was the President right to take that action?

Jefferson and the Louisiana Purchase President Thomas Jefferson had a great opportunity in 1803. Napoleon, the ruler of France, had offered to sell the huge Louisiana Territory for $15 million. By buying Louisiana, Jefferson could double the size of the United States.

Although Jefferson thought that the purchase would be good for the young nation, he was troubled because the Constitution did not say that the President or Congress could buy territory. Jefferson thought that a constitutional amendment might solve the problem, but time was short. Napoleon was showing signs of changing his mind.

Knowing that he had to act quickly, Jefferson turned to his advisors, especially James Madison, who was then Secretary of State. Madison believed that the President's power to make treaties gave Jefferson the right to buy Louisiana. After carefully thinking about Madison's advice, Jefferson accepted Napoleon's offer. The Senate ratified the treaty, and Congress agreed to pay France for the territory.

Truman and the Steel Mills In 1952, during the Korean War, President Harry Truman faced a problem. The steelworkers said they would not work unless certain demands were met. The steel-mill owners would not agree to their demands.

President Truman knew that steel was needed to make weapons for the soldiers in Korea. He gave an executive order placing the Secretary of Commerce in control of the mills for the time being. The steel companies said that the President had no right to take control of private property. Truman said that he was acting as commander in chief to protect American troops.

The case came before the Supreme Court. The Court ruled that the President had no power to take private property, even in a national emergency. His duty, the Court said, was to carry out laws passed by Congress, not to use executive orders to make his own laws.

▲ French and American representatives signed the official purchase of the Louisiana Territory on April 30, 1803, in Paris.

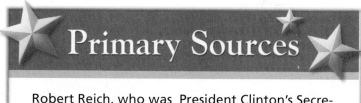

Primary Sources

Robert Reich, who was President Clinton's Secretary of Labor, noted the unique challenges facing the President.

"Unlike Britain and other democratic monarchies, we ask our country's leader to do two jobs simultaneously, to act both as head of government and as the symbol of the nation. It's a hard act. Governing involves tough compromises and gritty reality. Symbolism requires nobility and grandeur."

Analyzing History
In what ways is the President like a king in a democratic monarchy?

Target Reading Skill

Rereading Reread these paragraphs. Be sure you understand how Nixon used executive privilege and why the Supreme Court ordered him to turn over the tapes.

Watergate
The Watergate scandal demonstrated that Presidential power is not unlimited and that the President is not above the law. **Draw Inferences** *Why do you think President Nixon chose to resign rather than be impeached?*

Nixon and Watergate On August 9, 1974, President Richard Nixon left office as a result of the Watergate scandal. Nixon and members of his staff were accused of covering up White House involvement in a 1972 break-in at the Democratic National Committee Headquarters in the Watergate office building in Washington, D.C. The goal of the break-in was to help get Nixon re-elected by finding out about the Democrats' campaign plans.

After the burglars were caught in the act, newspaper reporters discovered that members of the White House staff had helped plan the burglary and later tried to cover up the crime. Later, FBI agents discovered that the Watergate break-in was part of a larger campaign of political spying on behalf of the effort to get President Nixon elected for a second term.

A special Senate committee and, later, the House Judiciary Committee began an investigation of the President. Investigators found that the President had taped all of his White House conversations. When they asked to examine the tapes, however, Nixon refused to release them, claiming executive privilege. In July 1974, the Supreme Court ordered Nixon to turn over the tapes, saying that executive privilege was not an unlimited power, particularly if used to hide possible criminal actions. Based on the tapes and other facts, the House Judiciary Committee recommended that Nixon be impeached, or put on trial. Nixon resigned before the full House could vote. In his resignation speech, Nixon explained why he felt he had to resign:

"From the discussions I have had with Congressional and other leaders, I have concluded that because of the Watergate matter I might not have the support of the Congress that I would consider necessary to back the very difficult decisions and carry out the duties of this office in the way the interests of the Nation would require."

◀ President Jimmy Carter meets with his top advisors.

Sharing the Power The stories you have just read show that the President does not govern alone. Instead, power is shared among the three branches of government—the "three horse team" as President Franklin D. Roosevelt described them. The system of checks and balances helps to make sure that the government acts in the best interests of the people. In this way the "three horse team" works together for the good of the nation.

✓ Reading Check **Of the three examples given, which is an example of an opportunity and which is an example of a crisis?**

SECTION 3 Assessment

Key Terms

Use each of the key terms in a sentence that explains its meaning:
treaties, executive privilege

Target Reading Skill

1. **Reread** Reread the passage on page 244 entitled "The President as Chief Diplomat." What information provided later in the chapter helps you to understand this passage better?

Comprehension and Critical Thinking

2. **a. Recall** How are executive agreements an example of presidential freedom of action?

b. Contrast How do executive agreements and executive privilege contrast with the system of checks and balances?

3. **a. Describe** What problem led President Truman to take control of the steel mills?

b. Demonstrate Reasoned Judgment Was Truman's action a threat to the Constitution?

4. **a. Explain** What is the "three-horse team" that Roosevelt described?

b. Evaluate Information Did the Framers of the Constitution do a good job in designing the federal government? Explain.

Writing Activity

Write a newspaper editorial in which you describe the problems Jefferson faced in completing the Louisiana Purchase. Conclude by explaining whether you think Jefferson made the correct decision or not.

TIPS
- Organize your essay into two parts: a presentation of the facts and then an evaluation of Jefferson's action.
- Make an outline of Jefferson's options and the consequences of each choice.

Drawing Inferences

Writers will sometimes imply meanings rather than stating them directly. When this happens, you need to *infer* the writer's meaning by using what you already know to interpret the writer's meaning.

Read this passage about President John F. Kennedy and the Cuban Missile Crisis. Then, answer the questions that follow.

> On October 14, 1962, the Pentagon provided the White House with photographs proving that the Soviets were building nuclear military installations in Cuba. Because a previous attack on Cuba had been an embarrassing failure for the United States, President Kennedy took his time deciding on his response to this threat. After discussion with his cabinet, the President ordered a naval blockade of the Gulf of Mexico.
>
> On October 26, Soviet Premier Nikita Khrushchev offered to withdraw all the missiles from Cuba in exchange for an American pledge not to invade the island nation. The President and his cabinet agreed to respond positively to this offer. On the following day, however, they were halted by a second letter from Moscow, which now asked for the removal of American missile bases in Turkey.
>
> Attorney General Robert Kennedy, the President's brother and his most trusted adviser, suggested that the United States respond as planned to the first letter and ignore the existence of the second. Khrushchev accepted the United States pledge not to invade Cuba, and by November the missiles had been sent back to the Soviet Union and the naval blockade lifted.

Learn the Skill

Follow these steps to draw inferences:

❶ **Identify main ideas.** What is the main idea of the passage?

❷ **Look for facts and opinions.** What information is directly stated by the author?

❸ **Identify unstated ideas.** What ideas or information are implied but not directly stated in the passage?

❹ **Identify the point of view.** Based on the inferences you made, how do you think the writer feels about the topic?

Practice the Skill

Read the passage above and answer the following questions:

❶ What is the main idea of this passage about the Cuban Missile Crisis?

❷ (a) Find two stated facts. (b) Find two stated opinions.

❸ What are some advantages and disadvantages of each solution?

❹ What is the best solution? Why?

Apply the Skill

Read a magazine article about a recent action taken by the President of the United States. What does the writer of the article imply about the President's action?

Review and Assessment

Chapter Summary

Section 1
The Roles of the President
(pages 240–247)

- The President heads the executive branch of the government.

- The Constitution spells out requirements, responsibilities, and powers of the presidency.

- The President serves as chief executive, commander in chief, chief diplomat, and legislative leader. The President also appoints judges and other officials, leads a political party, and serves as chief of state.

- As part of foreign policy, the President negotiates treaties, appoints ambassadors, and makes executive agreements.

- As legislative leader, the President sets domestic policy.

Section 2
The Executive Branch
(pages 249–254)

- The executive branch is a large bureaucracy of government departments and agencies.

- The President's administration heads an executive branch made up of three parts: the Executive Office of the President, which advises the President, and the executive departments and the independent agencies, which enforce laws and provide services.

- The President appoints the heads of the executive departments. With other executive officials, they make up the Cabinet.

- The Civil Service System fills the positions not appointed directly by the President, These executive department employees are hired on the basis of merit.

Section 3
Presidents and Power
(pages 255–259)

- The President can use executive agreements and executive privilege to act without consulting with other branches of the government. Some executive agreements lead to treaties that need approval by the Senate.

- The President must seek a balance between the need for immediate action and the constitutional need to consult with Congress.

- Presidents may, rightly or wrongly, try to use executive powers during times of great opportunity or crisis. Presidents Jefferson, Truman, and Nixon are examples of presidents who tried to use their powers, rightly or wrongly, during great opportunities or crises.

- Government works best when power is shared among the three branches of government.

Copy the chart below and use it to help you summarize the chapter.

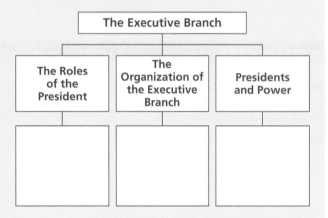

Go Online
PHSchool.com

For: Self-Test
Visit: PHSchool.com
Web Code: mpa-3093

Reviewing Key Terms

Fill in each blank with one of the key terms from the list below.

bureaucracy   ambassadors
domestic policy   executive agreements
executive branch   Cabinet
treaties   foreign policy

1. Agreements with other countries that do not need Senate approval are called _____.

2. The branch of government charged with executing the laws is the _____.

3. The official representatives of foreign governments are called _____.

4. An organization of government departments, agencies, and offices is called a _____.

5. The heads of the executive departments are members of the President's _____.

6. The set of plans that guides our nation's relationships with other countries is called _____.

7. Formal agreements with other countries are called _____.

8. The President's plan for dealing such national issues as health care and taxes is called _____.

Comprehension and Critical Thinking

9. **a. Describe** What three roles does the President have in the government?
   b. Make Generalizations How is the President's power limited by the other branches of government?
   c. Draw Inferences Besides the veto, how can the President influence Congress?

10. **a. Recall** What are the duties of the Department of State?
    b. Contrast How do the duties of the Department of Defense differ from those of the Department of State?

    c. Predict How might the interests of the Department of State and the Department of Defense conflict?

11. **a. Recall** What countries and leaders were involved in the Louisiana Purchase?
    b. Analyze Information What constitutional issues were involved in the Louisiana Purchase?
    c. Synthesize Information How was the outcome of the Louisiana Purchase an example of the expanding power of the President?

Activities

12. **Skills** Read the text to the right. **a.** Why did Richardson and Ruckelshaus resign? **b.** Why did Bork fire Cox?

13. **Writing** Choose an issue facing the country right now. Write a short essay that explains the President's powers to deal with the issue, the forces of the Executive Branch that would deal with the issue, and the limits on presidential power in place.

A significant point of the Watergate Crisis was an event the press called the "Saturday Night Massacre." The Department of Justice had appointed a special prosecutor, Archibald Cox, to investigate the case. Cox asked the White House to turn over tapes made by the President. Nixon refused and ordered Attorney General Elliot Richardson to fire Cox. Richardson instead resigned, as did his deputy. The third most important official left at the Justice Department, Solicitor General Robert Bork, then fired Cox.

14. **Active Citizen** How could you let the President know your opinion on than issue of national importance?

15. **Math Practice** The United States paid France $15 million for the Louisiana Purchase, an area of 828,000 square miles. Which of the following is closest to the price of the Louisiana Purchase per square mile?

    a. $12   **b.** $18   **c.** $24

16. **Civics and Economics** If the President decided to increase funding for the teaching of math in the schools, which departments and branches of government would be involved in carrying out this decision?

17. **Analyzing Visuals** The map shows the area of the Louisiana Purchase. Identify all present-day states that made up the Louisiana Purchase.

Standardized Test Prep

Test-Taking Tips

Most Presidents have retired from public life when they have left the presidency. There have been a few notable exceptions to this rule. President John Quincy Adams, who served from 1825 to 1829, was elected to Congress after leaving the White House. He served for many years as an early opponent of slavery. President William Howard Taft, who served from 1909 to 1913, was later appointed Chief Justice of the Supreme Court. President Jimmy Carter (1977–1981) has been active in international affairs as head of the Carter Center. In addition to their public service, all three former Presidents have something else in common. All were defeated in their quest for a second term of office.

TIP Sometimes, the main idea is inferred rather than stated. Remember also that important details can be at the end of the paragraph.

Pick the letter that best answers the question.

1. What shared fact makes the three Presidents unusual?
   A They all served in Congress after leaving the Presidency.
   B They all served on the Supreme Court.
   C They have had careers in public life after serving single terms in office.
   D They all served two terms as President.

   The correct answer is **C**. Note the main idea is inferred rather than directly stated.

2. Which statement below do you think is a correct assessment of the three Presidents?
   A They needed to continue working because they needed the money.
   B Having served two terms as President, they still had a desire to serve.
   C Having been defeated for reelection, they still had a desire to serve.
   D They were not qualified for any other line of work.

10

The Judicial Branch

What's Ahead in Chapter 10

In this chapter you will read about the judicial branch of the federal government. Led by the Supreme Court, the judicial branch helps protect the rights of American citizens by judging federal laws and interpreting the Constitution.

SECTION 1
The Role of the Federal Courts

SECTION 2
The Organization of the Federal Courts

SECTION 3
The Supreme Court

TARGET READING SKILL

Context In this chapter you will focus on using context to help you better understand what you read. Context includes using context clues to figure out a word's meaning and interpreting nonliteral meanings in text.

The United States ▶ Supreme Court

National Standards for Civics and Government

State

The following National Standards for Civics and Government are covered in this chapter:

III. How does the government established by the Constitution embody the purposes, values, and principles of American democracy?

A. How are power and responsibility distributed, shared, and limited in the government?

B. What does the national government do?

E. What is the place of law in the American constitutional system?

Go Online
PHSchool.com

For: Your state's standards
Visit: PHSchool.com
Web Code: mpa-3101

Active Citizen

Civics in the Real World

You are visiting the Supreme Court building in Washington, D.C. As you sit facing a long bench with nine dark leather chairs behind it, a clerk suddenly pounds a gavel and declares:

The Honorable, the Chief Justice and the Associate Justices of the Supreme Court of the United States!

Everyone in the courtroom stands as the nine justices in black robes enter and take their seats behind the bench. You sit down quietly along with the rest of the audience.

A lawyer steps forward and begins arguing the first case of the day. Her client has been found guilty of first-degree murder by a state court and sentenced to death. When he committed the crime, however, he was under the age of eighteen. The lawyer argues that a law allowing the death penalty for a person who has not yet reached adulthood is cruel and unusual punishment and therefore unconstitutional.

Next, the lawyer for the state presents his argument, justifying the state's law. The justices ask the lawyers many questions. Then they leave the courtroom to discuss their ruling privately. You wonder how the justices will decide this important case.

Citizen's Journal Suppose you are a Supreme Court justice. In one paragraph, describe the beliefs and principles that would guide your decisions. Keep your answer in mind as you read this chapter.

The Role of the Federal Courts

Reading Preview

Objectives

In this section you will

- Understand the need for laws and courts in our society.
- Learn what courts do.
- Discuss and compare the roles of state courts and federal courts.

Taking Notes

Make a diagram like the one below. As you read this section, complete the diagram with information about the role of the federal courts.

Key Terms

plaintiff   original jurisdiction
defendant   appeal
prosecution   appellate
precedent   jurisdiction

Main Idea

Our legal system provides a framework for resolving conflicts and protecting the rights of citizens. Federal and state courts hear criminal and civil cases. The Supreme Court hears a handful of those cases on appeal.

Target Reading Skill

Use Context Clues Context clues can help you understand words and ideas in the text. When you come across an unfamiliar word in this section, try to figure out its meaning by looking for clues in the surrounding words and sentences.

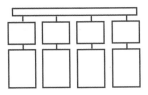

There are so many laws in our country that law books could fill entire libraries.

The judicial branch of the federal government is made up of the Supreme Court and more than 100 other federal courts. The most important members of the judicial branch are judges. They work quietly, away from the hubbub of politics that surrounds the President and members of Congress. However, the judges of the judicial branch have a very important role in our government.

Laws and Courts

In our society, disputes involving laws are resolved in the legal system. To understand the need for a legal system, consider the following example. A legislative body makes a law prohibiting one person from purposely damaging another's property. If a junior high student is then accused of throwing a baseball through someone else's window, several issues may have to be decided. Was the ball thrown on purpose? Has the law been broken? Is the accused person innocent or guilty? How shall the person who threw the baseball repay the person whose window was broken? These questions may be decided by the people involved in the incident, but if the matter is serious enough, it may have to be decided within the legal system.

✓ **Reading Check** What is the purpose of a legal system?

What Courts Do

Legal conflicts in our country are resolved by courts of law. All courts perform the same basic function: to apply the law to an actual situation. Courts interpret the law and then determine how to apply the law to the given situation.

Courts in our legal system resolve two kinds of legal conflicts: criminal and civil cases. In a criminal case, a court determines whether a person accused of breaking a law is innocent or guilty. If the person is found guilty, the court also decides what the punishment will be.

In a civil case, a court settles a disagreement. The disagreement can arise over such issues as who broke a contract. Other conflicts may concern divorce, or violations of constitutional rights. The federal courts hear both civil and criminal cases. Both kinds of cases can find their way to the Supreme Court.

The Parties in the Conflict Every court case involves two opposing sides, or parties. Who these parties are depends on whether the case is civil or criminal.

The typical civil case is brought to court by a party called the **plaintiff**, an individual or a group of people who bring a complaint against another party. The party who answers a complaint and defends against it is called the defendant. The defendant may be an individual, a group, or a government body.

Suppose that Mabel Edwards brought the Techno Corporation to court, claiming that the company had denied her a job because of her race. She would be the plaintiff in this civil case, and the company would be the defendant. The case would be called *Edwards* v. *The Techno Corporation*. When referencing a civil case, the name of the plaintiff is listed first. The name of the defendant is listed last. If Ted Burke were suing Mercy Hospital because the hospital had failed to diagnose his illness, the case would be called *Burke* v. *Mercy Hospital*.

In contrast, a criminal case is always brought to court by the **prosecution**, a government body that brings a criminal charge against a defendant who is accused of breaking one of its laws. The prosecution is referred to as "The People" and is represented by a government lawyer known as a prosecutor.

What if Arlo Ashley was accused of robbing a convenience store in Lima, Ohio? The state of Ohio would bring him to court on charges of theft. The criminal case would be called *The People of the State of Ohio* v. *Ashley*. When referencing a criminal case, the prosecution is listed first. The defendant is listed last.

Settling Disagreements
Civil courts settle disagreements, such as who is responsible for an auto accident.
Analyze Information *Do you think a case involving an auto accident might also end up in criminal court? Why or why not?*

Violent Video Games and Free Speech

A federal judge can review laws passed by local governments when constitutional issues are at stake. In a case in St. Louis County, Missouri, a federal judge ruled that the county could keep people under the age of 17 from buying, renting, or playing violent video games without a parent's consent. The county law reflects society's view that violence is harmful to children and can result in violent behavior. The Interactive Digital Software Association argued that video games have First Amendment protection, just like movies and books. However, the judge ruled that video games are not a form of speech protected by the First Amendment.

Applying the Law

1. **Analyzing Information** What constitutional issue was at stake in the case described above?
2. **Support a Point of View** Do you think people under the age of 17 should be able to play, rent, and buy violent video games? Why or why not?

The Members of the Court In a court the job of a judge is to apply the law to the conflict between the plaintiff or prosecution and the defendant. This means determining which side's argument is most in keeping with the law. The judge directs the proceedings but must remain neutral and not take sides in the conflict.

Many legal cases also involve a jury, which decides the facts of a case—such as what happened and who did it. A trial by jury is one of the rights guaranteed by the Constitution to a person accused of a crime.

Interpreting the Law In the process of hearing a case, a court may have to decide what the law in question means. For example, does a law banning "motor vehicles" in a park also ban radio-controlled model cars? A court may also have to decide if the law is allowed by the Constitution. This process of interpretation is an important job of the courts.

Although the legal system deals with individual cases, a court's decision in a case can have very broad effects. This is because a court's decision can establish a **precedent**, a guideline for how all similar cases should be decided in the future. A precedent makes the meaning of a law or the Constitution clearer. It also determines how the law should be applied, both inside and outside the legal system. For example, the Court's decision in Brown v. Board of Education established a precedent that made any law segregating blacks and whites unconstitutional.

Trial By Jury
These jurors are deciding the outcome of a court case.
Draw Conclusions *Why do you think the framers of the Constitution made trial by jury a right of each citizen?*

✓ Reading Check **Who are the parties in civil and criminal trials?**

State Courts and Federal Courts

Our legal system is made up of two separate but interconnected court systems—those of the states and those of the federal government. Decisions that establish the broadest precedents are made in the highest federal courts. However, most legal cases begin in a lower court, often at the level of state government. To understand the federal court system, it helps to know about the state court system.

Each state has courts at different levels of government and courts for different purposes, such as traffic courts and juvenile courts. Municipal courts operate on the city level and hear cases involving small sums of money or misdemeanors like traffic violations. All of these courts are considered part of the state court system. Most of the laws that govern our everyday actions are state and local laws. Therefore, most legal disputes and violations of the law are decided in state courts.

Jurisdiction The court to which a legal case first goes has **original jurisdiction**, the authority to hear a case first. A court with original jurisdiction determines the facts in a case. Often this occurs during a trial conducted with a jury. In certain cases a judge hears the case alone. Because they hold trials to resolve cases, courts with original jurisdiction are also called trial courts.

What happens if the court of original jurisdiction makes a decision that the plaintiff or defendant in the case believes is unjust? Then he or she has the right to **appeal**, to ask a higher court to review the decision and determine if justice was done. In each state, there are appeals courts set up just for the purpose of hearing cases appealed from lower state courts. These courts have **appellate jurisdiction**, the authority to hear an appeal.

Analyze Graphs

The Federal Court System

The federal courts have jurisdiction over a wide range of cases.

1. **Analyze** What kinds of federal law cases are heard by federal courts?
2. **Apply** Why would a case involving an American ship at sea be heard by a federal court?

Cases Heard by Federal Courts
Cases that raise constitutional questions
Cases involving federal laws, such as treason and tax evasion
Cases in which the federal government is the defendant
Disagreements between people from different states when more than $75,000 is in dispute
Cases involving treaties signed by the United States
Cases involving American ships at sea
Cases involving ambassadors and other foreign representatives

Target Reading Skill

Use Context Clues Sometimes a sentence will restate the meaning of an unfamiliar word. Look for a statement that provides a definition for the word *affirm*. What does *affirm* mean?

An appeals court does not hold a trial, nor does it determine the facts in a case. It reviews the legal issues involved. Then it determines if the law was applied fairly and if due process of law was followed.

An appeals court may decide to affirm, or let stand, the lower court's decision. However, if it decides that the trial was unfair, it may reverse the lower court's decision. When that happens, the appeals court may order another trial. The new trial is held in the court of original jurisdiction. When a plaintiff is declared innocent, however, the prosecution may not appeal. The Constitution prohibits double jeopardy—being tried again for the same crime.

The appeals process may go beyond the first appeals court. In most states, the final court of appeals is the state supreme court. Although state court systems differ, most have three levels: trial courts, appeals courts, and a court of final appeals.

Cases Heard by Federal Courts Federal courts hear two kinds of cases. First, they hear cases involving federal laws and issues beyond the authority of individual states. In these cases, the federal courts have original jurisdiction. Second, they hear cases appealed from state supreme courts. These cases must involve a federal law or a constitutional issue. They are heard only by the Supreme Court. This gives the Supreme Court and the federal judicial branch the leadership role in our legal system.

√ **Reading Check** How does a case go from a trial court to the Supreme Court?

SECTION 1 Assessment

Key Terms

Use each of the key terms in a sentence that explains its meaning: plaintiff, defendant, prosecution, precedent, original jurisdiction, appeal, appellate jurisdiction

Target Reading Skill

1. **Use Context Clues** Find the word *reverse* on page 269. Use context clues to find out its meaning. What do you think it means? What clues helped you arrive at a meaning?

Comprehension and Critical Thinking

2. **a. Explain** What is the purpose of our legal system?
   b. Make Predictions What might happen if we didn't have an organized legal system?

3. **a. Recall** What two kinds of cases are heard by the federal courts?
   b. Draw Inferences Why might the establishment of a new precedent have broad effects?

4. **a. Describe** What are the levels of a typical state court system?

   b. Sequence How might a case work its way from a state court to the Supreme Court?

Writing Activity

Suppose you are a journalist working for your hometown newspaper. Write an article about a fictional civil trial, describing the conflict and giving details about the parties involved.

Go Online
PHSchool.com

For: Article
Visit: PHSchool.com
Web Code: mpd-3101

The Organization of the Federal Courts

Reading Preview

Objectives

In this section you will

- Learn what district courts do.
- Discuss the role of the courts of appeals.
- Consider the purpose of the Supreme Court.
- Examine what federal court judges do.

Key Terms

courts of appeals circuit courts

Main Idea

The structure of our federal court system has changed since the Judiciary Act was passed in 1789. Today, the system is made up of district courts, courts of appeals, the Supreme Court, and a few specialized courts.

Target Reading Skill

Interpret Nonliteral Meanings
Sometimes words mean something other than exactly what they say. In other words, they have nonliteral meanings. As your read, identify nonliteral language, such as images or comparisons, that helps express an idea in the text.

Taking Notes

Make a diagram like the one below. As you read the section, complete the diagram with information about the organization of the federal court system.

The Constitution created the framework for the federal court system in Article III. However, the Constitution did not spell out how the inferior, or lower, courts would be set up. One of the first acts passed by the First Congress in 1789 was the Judiciary Act. It created the district courts and courts of appeals. Many of the details of the Judiciary Act have since been changed. However, the federal court system it created is much the same more than 200 years later.

The District Courts

The workhorses of the federal court system are the 94 district courts scattered across the United States. These courts handle some 300,000 cases a year, about 80 percent of the federal caseload. Each state has at least one district court. Some larger states, such as New York, have as many as four. The number of judges in one district court ranges from 1 to 28, depending on the size of the district and its workload. As courts of original jurisdiction, the district courts are the first to hear cases such as those involving kidnapping or a city's failure to obey federal air pollution standards.

Like a state trial court, witnesses are called. A jury normally decides the facts in the case. One judge directs the proceedings and applies the law.

✔ Reading Check **Which courts do the bulk of the work in the federal court system?**

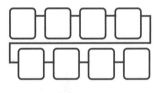
The Scales of Justice
▼

Louis Brandeis (1856–1941) was an outspoken advocate for poor people and workers during his 22 years as a Supreme Court justice. President Woodrow Wilson nominated Brandeis to the Supreme Court in 1916. Brandeis became the first Jewish Supreme Court justice in the nation's history. He worked tirelessly for social and economic reform. In his decisions, he often dissented from the majority vote to stand up for what he believed was morally and legally correct. Brandeis supported unions and small business, and he argued for a balance of power between owners and employees.

Citizenship

What contributions did Louis Brandeis make during his service on the Supreme Court?

The Courts of Appeals

At the next highest level of the federal court system are the 12 United States courts of appeals. The **courts of appeals** handle appeals from the federal district courts. Each court of appeals takes cases from a group of district courts within a particular geographic area. This area is called a circuit. In fact, the courts of appeals are often called **circuit courts.** A thirteenth court of appeals has appellate jurisdiction over cases appealed from certain special federal courts and agencies of the executive branch. It is called the Court of Appeals for the Federal Circuit. Look at the map on the next page to see how the nation is divided into 12 regions.

A court of appeals has no jury, calls no witnesses, and does not examine any evidence. Instead, lawyers for the defendant and the plaintiff or prosecution make arguments in front of a panel of three judges. The judges decide either to affirm the lower court's decision or to reverse it. Like state appeals courts, the courts of appeals are not concerned with guilt or innocence. They are only concerned with whether the original trial was fair and whether the law was interpreted correctly.

✓ Reading Check   **How does a court of appeals arrive at a verdict?**

The Supreme Court Justices in a recent portrait: (standing, left to right) Ruth Bader Ginsburg, David Souter, Clarence Thomas, Stephen Breyer; (sitting, left to right) Antonin Scalia, John Paul Stevens, Chief Justice William Rehnquist, Sandra Day O'Connor, Anthony Kennedy. ▼

Federal Court Circuits

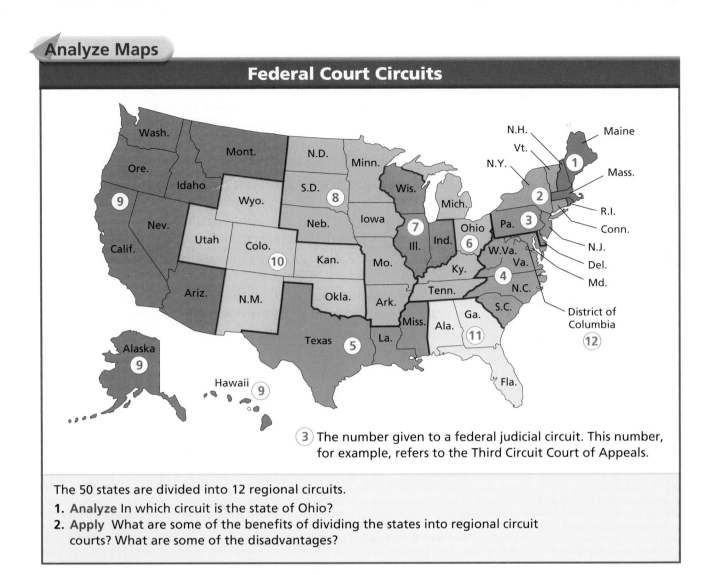

③ The number given to a federal judicial circuit. This number, for example, refers to the Third Circuit Court of Appeals.

The 50 states are divided into 12 regional circuits.

1. **Analyze** In which circuit is the state of Ohio?
2. **Apply** What are some of the benefits of dividing the states into regional circuit courts? What are some of the disadvantages?

The Supreme Court

The Supreme Court is the highest court in the federal court system. The major purpose of the Supreme Court is to serve as the final court of appeals for both the state and federal court systems.

The Supreme Court, however, does have original jurisdiction over a few special kinds of cases. These include cases involving representatives of foreign governments and disputes between state governments. The role of the Supreme Court in the legal system and in the federal government is so important that it will be discussed in detail in the next section.

There are also many additional federal courts. These special courts include the Court of Claims, the Court of Customs and Patent Appeals, and the Tax Court. Each of these courts was established by Congress for a special purpose. Appeals from some of these courts are sent directly to the Supreme Court. Others must first pass through a court of appeals or a higher special court.

✓ **Reading Check** **In what kinds of cases does the Supreme Court have original jurisdiction?**

Federal Court Judges

Just as members of Congress do the work of the legislative branch, federal judges do the work of the judicial branch. A judge's role in government, however, is very different from that of a legislator.

A legislator is open to the influence of citizens, interest groups, other legislators, and the President. A judge, in contrast, must be impartial. A judge must not favor one party or the other. A legislator seeks to solve broad problems by making laws, whereas a judge can only settle individual cases. By applying the law to specific cases, however, judges help define and clarify the work of legislators.

In part because judges' jobs are different from those of legislators, judges are selected in a different way. All federal judges are appointed by the President and confirmed by the Senate. They serve life terms and can be removed from office only by the impeachment process.

Federal judges shoulder great responsibility. They must balance the rights of individuals with the interests of the nation as a whole. Often they are forced to make decisions that seem fair to one side but unfair to the other.

Of all federal judges, the nine Supreme Court justices have the most responsibility. From time to time the entire nation waits in anticipation for them to make a decision. Although they are only deciding a specific case, perhaps involving just one or two people, their decision may have very important consequences for the nation.

✓ Reading Check **How do federal judges differ from legislators?**

Target Reading Skill

Interpret Nonliteral Meanings Sometimes nonliteral language can communicate an idea more vividly than literal language. Restate the following sentence from this paragraph in your own words: "From time to time the entire nation waits in anticipation for them to make a decision."

SECTION 2 Assessment

Key Terms

Use each of the key terms in a sentence that explains its meaning: courts of appeals, circuit courts

Target Reading Skill

1. **Interpret Nonliteral Meanings** Reread the first paragraph of this section. Explain in your own words what it means.

Comprehension and Critical Thinking

2. **a. Recall** When were the district courts and courts of appeals created?
   b. Draw Inferences Why were two kinds of courts created by our nation's founders?

3. **a. Explain** What kind of jurisdiction does a federal court of appeals have?
   b. Compare How are state appeals courts similar to federal courts of appeals?

4. **a. Describe** What is the main purpose of the Supreme Court?
   b. Draw Conclusions Why do you think the Supreme Court has original jurisdiction in special kinds of cases?

5. **a. Explain** What are two differences between a federal judge and a member of Congress?
   b. Analyze Information Why are federal judges appointed instead of elected?

Writing Activity

Research a current or former Supreme Court justice. Then write a short biography describing that justice's background and impact on the Court.

TIPS

- Consider writing your biography in chronological order.
- Remember to include important details about the person you are profiling, including any major cases that he or she ruled on.

Skills for Life ✓

Evaluating the Validity of Internet Sources

There are millions of information-packed Web sites on the Internet. Before you use information from a Web site, however, it is very important that you check the validity of the site.

Government, educational, nonprofit, and news Web sites are usually good sources of accurate information. Look especially for Web sites whose addresses end in .gov (government), .org (organization), and .edu (education).

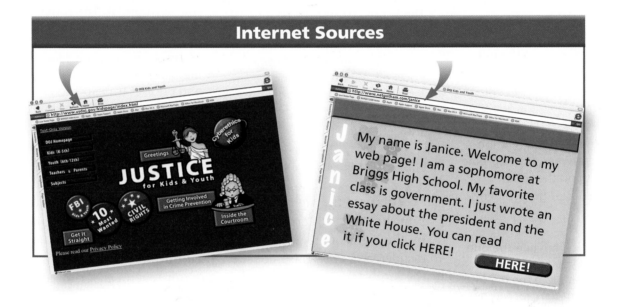

Internet Sources

JUSTICE for Kids & Youth

My name is Janice. Welcome to my web page! I am a sophomore at Briggs High School. My favorite class is government. I just wrote an essay about the president and the White House. You can read it if you click HERE!

HERE!

Learn the Skill

Follow these steps to evaluate Internet sources:

❶ **Evaluate the source.** Is the Web site sponsored by an established organization? Web suffixes can tell you something about who is behind the site. Government, organization, and education Web sites usually have the most reliable information.

❷ **Determine the Web site's purpose.** What information does the Web site provide? Is it trying to promote a specific point of view or to sell something?

❸ **Examine the information.** Does the site include visuals? Does it include primary source materials?

❹ **Compare the information to what you already know.** Does the information on the site agree with information found in reliable print sources?

Practice the Skill

Look at the two Web sites above and answer these questions:

❶ Who is responsible for each Web site?

❷ What is the purpose of each Web site?

❸ What kind of information does each Web site provide?

❹ Which Web site would you use to gather information for a report? Why?

Apply the Skill

Type a key word about a topic of interest into an Internet search engine. Choose two or three sites the search engine presents and use the steps you learned to determine if the information on each site is reliable.

The Supreme Court

Reading Preview

Objectives

In this section you will

- Analyze the importance of judicial review.
- Learn about the Supreme Court justices and the work they do.
- Explore some of the influences on judicial decision making.
- Describe how the Supreme Court is a changing court.
- Understand the relationship between the Supreme Court and the other branches of government.

Taking Notes

Make a diagram like the one below. As you read this section, complete the diagram with information about how a case reaches the Supreme Court.

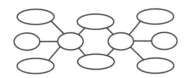

Key Terms

judicial review   judicial activism
opinion   judicial restraint

Main Idea

The Supreme Court is the highest court in the United States. It has the final say about what the Constitution means. The Supreme Court establishes the longest-lasting precedents in our legal system.

Target Reading Skill

Use Context Clues Sometimes the meaning of a word or phrase makes sense only in its context—the words, phrases, or sentences that surround it. The context may restate the word, give an example, or make a comparison. As you read this section, consider the meanings of surrounding words and phrases to help you understand words you do not know.

W hat are the rights of people accused of crimes? What kinds of punishments are "cruel and unusual"? What activities are protected by the right of free speech? When the Supreme Court is asked to decide cases that raise constitutional questions, Americans can see the importance of the Court's role in our federal government.

Lower state and federal courts make rulings in cases that involve constitutional issues. However, their rulings are not necessarily final. Only the Supreme Court has the final say about what the Constitution means and what laws it will allow. A Supreme Court decision establishes the broadest and longest-lasting kind of precedent in our legal system.

Judicial Review

One of the most important powers of the Supreme Court is **judicial review,** the power to overturn any law that the Court decides is in conflict with the Constitution. Judicial review gives the judicial branch the final say over whether any law is valid. Judicial review is not spelled out in the Constitution. The Supreme Court asserted this power for itself early in its history.

A court can interpret law only as it relates to the specific case it is hearing. The Supreme Court could not simply declare one day that it had the power of judicial review. It had to do so in relation to a particular case.

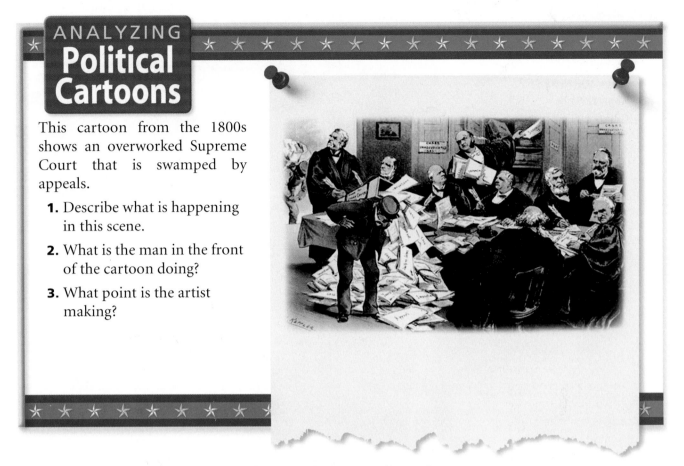

This cartoon from the 1800s shows an overworked Supreme Court that is swamped by appeals.

1. Describe what is happening in this scene.
2. What is the man in the front of the cartoon doing?
3. What point is the artist making?

Marbury v. Madison William Marbury sued James Madison, then serving as Secretary of State, in 1803. Marbury was suing because he did not get a government job promised to him by then-President John Adams. Marbury brought his case directly to the Supreme Court. The Judiciary Act of 1789 gave the Court original jurisdiction in such matters. The Court focused its attention on the law that had allowed Marbury to bring his case before the Court in the first place.

The Judiciary Act had given the Supreme Court original jurisdiction in cases involving government officials. However, the Constitution only gave the Court appellate jurisdiction in such cases. Therefore, the Court decided, the part of the Judiciary Act that gave the Court original jurisdiction in Marbury's case was unconstitutional.

Chief Justice John Marshall wrote the Court's opinion. The Supreme Court had a sworn duty to uphold the Constitution. Therefore, Marshall argued, it also had a responsibility to declare unconstitutional any law that violated the Constitution.

Marbury v. *Madison* established a precedent that gave the Court one of its most important powers. Judicial review was later extended to cover acts of the executive branch and the states. Since 1803, more than 1,000 state and local laws and more than 100 federal laws have been overturned as a result of the Supreme Court's judicial review.

▲
John Marshall was appointed Chief Justice by President John Adams in 1801. He helped shape the Supreme Court we know today.

✓ Reading Check **Why is judicial review an important power of the Supreme Court?**

A Tireless Worker for Civil Rights
Thurgood Marshall (1908–1993) was the first African American Supreme Court Justice. He was appointed to the Court by President Lyndon Johnson in 1967.

The Justices

If the justices of the Supreme Court are to use the power of judicial review in a way that defends the Constitution, they must have the highest moral standards. They must also have a thorough knowledge of the law, the Constitution, and American history.

The Constitution lists no qualifications for the position of Supreme Court justice. However, the way justices are selected helps ensure that they will be qualified for the job. The President chooses a justice from among the most respected judges, lawyers, and legal scholars in the country. Then the Senate must approve the President's appointment.

The Supreme Court is made up of the Chief Justice of the United States, whose office is established by the Constitution, and eight associate justices. There have been 108 justices who have served on the Court. All but four have been white men. Two of the exceptions are Thurgood Marshall and Clarence Thomas, African American men appointed in 1967 and 1991. The other two are Sandra Day O'Connor and Ruth Bader Ginsburg, white women appointed in 1981 and 1994. The Chief Justice earns $198,600 a year, and Associate Justices $190,100. 213,400   223,500

Sonya Sotom 2009
Elena Kaygen 2010

The Work of the Supreme Court

The decisions of the nine justices of the Supreme Court can affect the lives of millions of people for years or even decades after they make their decisions. How do the justices make sure their decisions are carefully reasoned and fair?

Selecting Cases Each year, the Court chooses which cases to hear. By law, it must hear certain kinds of appeals from federal and state courts that involve the federal government or federal laws. It must also hear the cases over which it has original jurisdiction, such as cases involving representatives of foreign governments and disputes between state governments.

The remainder of the cases the Court hears each year are chosen from among the more than 8,000 requests for appeal it receives from lower courts. In most cases, petitions for review are denied, usually for one of two reasons. This is usually either because most of the justices agree with the decision of the lower court or believe that the case involves no significant point of law. Altogether, the Court hears arguments and writes full opinions on only about 100 cases a year. The cases the Court chooses are generally those that raise the most important constitutional issues.

Hearing Arguments When a case is put on the Court's calendar, each side in the case submits briefs, or written arguments. The justices study the briefs and other records of the case. Then attorneys for each side present oral arguments before the Court. Each attorney has only half an hour to present the arguments. The justices usually ask many questions of the attorneys to challenge and clarify their arguments.

Making a Decision After hearing oral arguments, the Court meets to discuss that case and vote on it. Only the justices are allowed to attend. The Chief Justice leads the discussion of each case, summarizing it and offering an opinion. Then each justice has an opportunity to comment. Finally, the Chief Justice calls for a vote. A simple majority decides the case, although justices may change their votes during the opinion-writing.

Civics and Economics

The Economics of the Court Supreme Court decisions may affect financial resources and federal funding for organizations. For example, in recent years the Supreme Court ruled that Congress can require public libraries to equip their computers with filters that block objectionable materials.

The 6-3 ruling reinstated a previous law that told libraries to install the filters or give up funding from the federal government. According to the majority opinion, "To the extent that libraries wish to offer unfiltered access, they are free to do so without federal assistance."

Analyzing Economics
1. What does the Supreme Court's influence on the nation's economy suggest about the Court's power?
2. Go to the Landmark Supreme Court Cases section on page 719. Find a case in which the Supreme Court's decision made an economic impact. Explain how the Supreme Court decision affected the economy.

Our Justices
Sandra Day O'Connor has served as Justice since 1981. She was the first woman to serve on the Supreme Court.
Support a Point of View *Do you think the makeup of the Supreme Court should reflect the diversity American society? Why or why not?*

Writing Opinions Most Supreme Court decisions are accompanied by an **opinion,** a written statement explaining the reasons for the decision. A Supreme Court opinion shows exactly how the law must be applied, or how the Constitution must be interpreted in a specific situation.

The Court's opinion, called the majority opinion, is written by one of the justices in the majority—the winning side of the vote. A draft of the opinion is circulated among the justices. It is often modified to keep the support of the other justices in the majority.

A justice who agrees with the majority opinion but has different reasons for supporting it may write a concurring opinion. A justice who does not agree with the majority's decision may write a dissenting opinion.

After all opinions have been written and finalized, the justices announce their final decision. Then copies of the opinions are distributed to news reporters. You can also read the justices' opinions on the Internet.

✓ Reading Check **What determines the outcome of a case heard by the Supreme Court?**

Analyze Diagrams and Tables

Appealing a Case to the Supreme Court

Appealing a case to the Supreme Court involves many steps. This diagram shows the typical path a case can take.

a. According to the diagram, what must happen first before a case is appealed to the Supreme Court?

b. Appealing a case can take a great deal of time and money. Why then is the process made up of so many steps?

Federal District Court

Step 1
Case is filed and ruled upon in a federal district court.

Step 2
Case is appealed to a federal court of appeals.

Cases Before the Supreme Court, 1997 to 2001			
Year	Number of Cases Before the Court	Number of Cases Disposed of	Number of Cases Heard by the Court
1997	7,692	6,759	96
1998	8,083	7,045	90
1999	8,445	7,369	83
2000	8,965	7,762	82
2001	9,176	8,072	88
Source: Administrative Office of the U.S. Courts			

Influences on Judicial Decision Making

What factors can influence how the justices vote when they decide a case? Like any judge, a justice is most concerned with the law and how it has been applied up to that point. The justices firmly believe that laws and the Constitution reflect the will of the people. Therefore, it is their responsibility to make sure they apply the law appropriately when making decisions.

The justices, therefore, carefully review the laws involved in each case. They must consider all related precedents that have been established by any court. Precedent is always a factor in a justice's decision. A basic principle of the American legal system is to respect past judicial decisions. In this way, our country develops a consistent body of law.

The justices also try to determine the intentions of lawmakers at the time they made a particular law when making decisions on cases that come before the Court. For a constitutional question, for example, the justices may read historical documents such as *The Federalist Papers* or even letters and journals to try to determine the intent of the framers.

Go Online
civics
interactive

For: Interactive Diagram
Visit: PHSchool.com
Web Code: mpp-3103

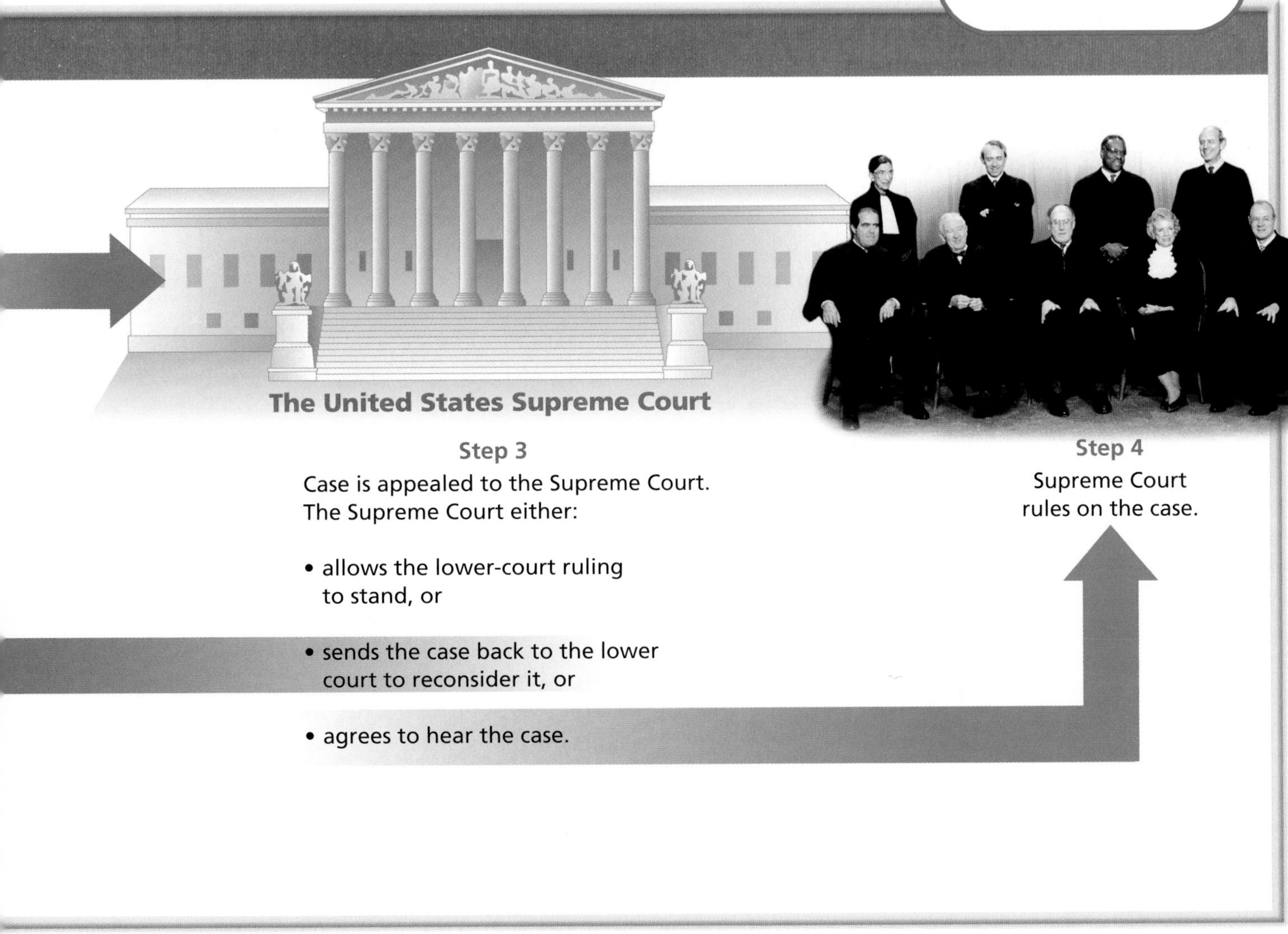

The United States Supreme Court

Step 3
Case is appealed to the Supreme Court. The Supreme Court either:

- allows the lower-court ruling to stand, or

- sends the case back to the lower court to reconsider it, or

- agrees to hear the case.

Step 4
Supreme Court rules on the case.

Go Online
civics
interactive

For: Interactive Constitution with Supreme Court Cases
Visit: PHSchool.com
Web Code: mpp-3104

The Supreme Court

United States v. *Nixon* (1974)

Why it Matters This decision made clear that the President is not above the law.

Background President Richard Nixon ran for reelection against Democrat Senator George McGovern in 1972. Five months before the election, an alert security guard found burglars in the Democratic Party headquarters in Washington's Watergate apartment complex. Reporters following the story connected the burglars to high-ranking officials in the White House. Nixon denied any connection to the break-in. However, an independent investigation revealed the existence of audio tapes of the President discussing the break-in with its organizers.

Nixon refused to turn the tapes over to Congress. The District Court ruled against Nixon. The President appealed and the case quickly reached the Supreme Court.

The Decision The Supreme Court decided unanimously in July 1974 that Nixon must hand over the tapes. They revealed that he

had participated in the cover-up of the burglary. Within a few days, Congress began impeachment proceedings and rather than face impeachment, Nixon resigned from office.

Understanding the Law

1. What was Nixon's legal justification for not handing over the audio tapes?
2. What reasons did the Supreme Court give for ruling against Nixon?

Supreme Court justices try to be impartial and to respect precedent. However, it can be difficult for them to put aside their personal views completely. The justices, after all, are only human.

Presidents usually try to appoint to the Court people who agree with their political views. Presidents know that the personal views of Supreme Court justices can affect their decisions. A President hopes that if the appointee becomes a justice, he or she will favor the President's position on important issues. Because Supreme Court justices serve for life, presidential appointments to the Court can influence the Court's decisions for many years.

✓ Reading Check **Why do Supreme Court justices try to determine the intentions of lawmakers at the time they made a law?**

A Changing Court

Throughout its history, the Supreme Court has gone through important changes in how it views its role in government and how it interprets the Constitution. These changes have been the result of shifts in public opinion and in the justices' own personal beliefs.

Since the 1950s, the Court has had three different "personalities," reflecting the views of the Chief Justice at the time. From 1953 to 1969, the Supreme Court was called the "Warren Court" after Chief Justice Earl Warren. The Warren Court was known for its defense of the rights of people accused of crimes.

One of the Warren Court's noted decisions was in the case of *Miranda* v. *Arizona*. In this case, the Court ruled that when a person is arrested, police must inform him or her of the constitutional rights to remain silent and to have the advice of a lawyer. The decisions of the Warren Court are examples of what is called **judicial activism,** an effort by judges to take an active role in policy making by overturning laws relatively often.

From 1969 to 1986, Warren Burger was Chief Justice. The decisions of the "Burger Court" differed from those of the Warren Court in that they were often characterized by **judicial restraint,** an effort by judges to avoid overturning laws and to leave policymaking up to the other two branches of government. The Burger Court, however, made one of the most controversial decisions of the twentieth century in the case of *Roe* v. *Wade.* In this case the Supreme Court said that no state could make a law that forbids a woman to have an abortion.

The Court today is often called the "Rehnquist Court," after Chief Justice William Rehnquist. The Rehnquist Court has made a number of important decisions limiting the federal government's authority over the states.

✔ Reading Check **What was the Warren Court known for?**

Supreme Court Confirmations for Each President

George Washington	10	Abraham Lincoln	5	Calvin Coolidge	1
John Adams	3	Andrew Johnson	0	Herbert Hoover	2
Thomas Jefferson	3	Ulysses S. Grant	5	Franklin D. Roosevelt	8
James Madison	2	Rutherford B. Hayes	2	Harry S. Truman	4
James Monroe	1	James A. Garfield	1	Dwight D. Eisenhower	5
John Quincy Adams	1	Chester A. Arthur	3	John F. Kennedy	2
Andrew Jackson	7	Grover Cleveland	2	Lyndon B. Johnson	2
Martin Van Buren	2	Benjamin Harrison	4	Richard M. Nixon	4
William H. Harrison	0	Grover Cleveland	2	Gerald R. Ford	1
John Tyler	1	William McKinley	1	Jimmy Carter	0
James Polk	2	Theodore Roosevelt	3	Ronald Reagan	3
Zachary Taylor	0	William H. Taft	5	George H.W. Bush	2
Millard Filmore	1	Woodrow Wilson	3	William J. Clinton	2
Franklin Pierce	0	Warren G. Harding	4	George W. Bush	0
James Buchanan	1				

Source: www.senate.gov

This table shows the number of justices confirmed to the Supreme Court for each President.

1. **Analyze** Which Presidents had the most justices confirmed? Which had the least?
2. **Apply** Why is the number of justices a Persident has confirmed significant?

▲ Salmon P. Chase was appointed Chief Justice of the Supreme Court by President Lincoln in 1864.

The Court and Other Branches of Government

Judicial review gives the Supreme Court an important check on the power of the legislative and the executive branches. Some people argue that judges should not have what amounts to veto power over laws passed by legislators. But nearly everyone agrees that the overall system of checks and balances prevents even the most active Court from abusing its power.

The President's Power One of the checks on the Supreme Court is the President's power to appoint justices. This power can be exercised only when a justice dies or retires, creating an opening on the Court. President Carter was not able to appoint a single Supreme Court justice. President Reagan, in contrast, appointed three justices—Sandra Day O'Connor, Antonin Scalia, and Anthony Kennedy. President George H. W. Bush appointed David Souter and Clarence Thomas. President Clinton appointed Ruth Bader Ginsburg and Stephen Breyer. A President who is able to have justices confirmed who share his views can exercise great power long after his term has ended.

The Power of Congress The Senate can check the power of the President and the Supreme Court by refusing to confirm presidential appointments to the Supreme Court. In this way, the Senate can weed out appointees who it believes are unsuited for the job.

Occasionally, a Supreme Court appointee becomes the focus of a political battle between the other two branches of government. Such a battle occurred in 1987 when President Reagan appointed Robert Bork. After four months of hearings, the Senate refused to confirm Bork. In 1991 Clarence Thomas, appointed by President George H. W. Bush, also faced intense questioning by the Senate Judiciary Committee. Thomas, however, was confirmed in a close vote.

Congress can also check the power of the Court through a constitutional amendment. If ratified by the states, an amendment proposed by Congress can nullify, or cancel out, a Supreme Court decision. When the Fourteenth Amendment was ratified in 1868, for example, it nullified the Supreme Court's decision in the Dred Scott case.

Citizen Participation Citizens have several avenues through which they can influence policies. If the Supreme Court makes a decision that goes against the wishes of the majority, citizens can always turn to Congress and the amendment process. They can elect a President who promises to appoint justices whose ideas they like. If citizens wish to make such changes happen, however, they must participate in government.

Target Reading Skill
Use Context Clues Find the word *nullify* on this page. Use context to determine its meaning.

✓ Reading Check   **What power does the President have over the Supreme Court?**

SECTION 3 Assessment

Key Terms

Use each of the key terms in a sentence that explains its meaning: judicial review, opinion, judicial activism, judicial restraint

Target Reading Skill

1. **Use Context Clues** Look for the word *briefs* on page 279. What do you think it means? What clues helped you arrive at a meaning?

Comprehension and Critical Thinking

2. **a. Describe** How did *Marbury v. Madison* give the Court the power of judicial review?

   b. Determine Relevance Why was this an important case in our nation's history?

3. **a. Recall** What are the qualifications for the position of Supreme Court justice?

   b. Contrast How does a dissenting opinion differ from a concurring opinion?

4. **a. Describe** What factors unrelated to the law can influence how justices vote?

   b. Analyze Information Why might the Supreme Court's view of its role in government change over time?

5. **a. Explain** What two checks does Congress have on the Supreme Court?

   b. Predict How might citizens influence the Supreme Court?

Writing Activity

Write a speech announcing the President's nominee for a vacant seat on the Supreme Court. The speech should describe why your candidate is qualified for the job.

TIPS
- Mention specific experience and credentials that the nominee has.
- Try to address any questions or issues that opponents to your candidate may have.

Debating the Issues

CLOSE UP
FOUNDATION

The debates in this feature are based on *Current Issues*, published by the Close Up Foundation. Go to **PHSchool.com**, Web Code mph-1025, to read the latest issue of *Current Issues* online.

Supreme Court justices may remain on the Court until they die or choose to retire. The longest-serving justice on the Supreme Court was William O. Douglas (right). He was appointed to the Court in 1939 by President Franklin Delano Roosevelt. When he retired in 1975, Douglas had served as a justice for 37 years.

Should the Government Set Term Limits for Supreme Court Justices?

YES

- Presidents often appoint justices who agree with their political and social views. If one President appoints several justices, the court might favor a particular agenda for many years. Term limits would allow more Presidents to appoint justices, making the Court more balanced.

- If a sitting justice and a President held opposing views, the justice might put off retirement simply to prevent the president from appointing a new justice. Term limits would prevent justices from remaining on the Court for political reasons like this.

- There is no retirement age for justices. Term limits would make them step down before they become too physically or mentally frail for the job.

NO

- The Supreme Court needs to be free of any outside influence. Since justices serve for life, they are always free to rule according to the merits of the case before them, without pressure or fear.

- The Constitution states that justices may serve "during good behavior." They can already be removed from office for crimes or misdeeds. There is no need to establish term limits to ensure a lack of corruption.

- The Supreme Court plays a crucial role in establishing our nation's laws. The more time justices serve on the Court, the more knowledge and experience they bring to their decisions. Term limits might force outstanding justices to step down when they could do valuable work for many years to come.

What Is Your Opinion?

1. **Identify Effect** What are the most important effects of allowing justices to serve for life?

2. **Demonstrate Reasoned Judgment** Do you think there should be a mandatory retirement age for justices? Why, or why not?

3. **Writing to Persuade** Suppose that you are a senator proposing a term-limits amendment. Decide how long a term should be, whether justices should be able to serve more than one term, and whether they should be reconfirmed each time. Write the speech you will give on the Senate floor. Include specific arguments to persuade listeners to vote for your amendment.

Go Online
civics interactive

For: You Decide Poll
Visit: PHSchool.com
Web Code: mpp-3105

10 Review and Assessment

Chapter Summary

Section 1
The Role of the Federal Courts
(pages 266–270)

- The judicial branch of the federal government consists of the Supreme Court and more than 100 other federal courts.

- Laws and courts allow parties to settle disputes in civil and criminal cases.

- Criminal cases are always brought to court by the prosecution.

- A court's decision can establish a new precedent.

- If a court of original jurisdiction makes a decision that the plaintiff or defendant considers unjust, he or she has the right to appeal to a new court that has appellate jurisdiction.

Section 2
The Organization of the Federal Courts
(pages 271–274)

- The 94 district courts scattered across the United States hear the most federal cases.

- Twelve federal courts of appeals handle appeals from the federal district courts. The courts of appeal are often called circuit courts.

- The Supreme Court is the highest court in the federal court system.

- Special federal courts exist to handle specific issues.

- Federal Court judges are impartial and removed from political influence.

Section 3
The Supreme Court
(pages 276–285)

- The Supreme Court has the power of judicial review, which allows it to overturn any laws that are unconstitutional.

- The Supreme Court chooses a limited number of cases to hear each year. The Court accompanies each decision with a written opinion.

- Supreme Court justices review laws and consider precedents when making their decisions.

- The Warren Court (1953–1969) was known for its judicial activism. The Burger Court (1969-1986) was known for its judicial restraint.

- The President has the power to appoint Supreme Court justices.

- The Senate checks the power of the President and the Supreme Court. The Senate may refuse to confirm presidential appointments and may introduce amendments to the Constitution.

- The Supreme Court checks the power of the legislative and executive branches with its power of judicial review.

Copy the chart below and use it to help you summarize the chapter:

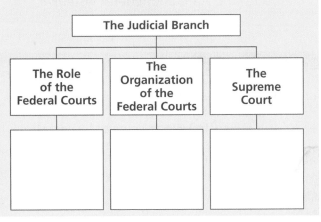

Review and Assessment Continued

Reviewing Key Terms

Choose the best term to complete each of the following sentences.

1. The Supreme Court established its power of _____ by declaring a law unconstitutional in *Marbury* v. *Madison.* (judicial restraint, judicial review)

2. The _____ rested its criminal case after making closing arguments about the defendant's wrongdoing. (prosecution, plaintiff)

3. One justice wrote the majority _____ that pronounced the law unconstitutional. (precedent, opinion)

4. The Supreme Court under Chief Justice Warren Burger was characterized by its _____. (judicial restraint, judicial review)

5. Because of the overwhelming amount of evidence against her, the _____ was found guilty of assault. (plaintiff, defendant)

6. After he was found guilty of murder, the defendant brought his case to a court with _____. (original jurisdiction, appellate jurisdiction)

7. Judges often look to a(n) _____ to help them come to a decision in a case. (appeal, precedent)

8. As the victim of the pickpocket on trial, the _____ hoped that she would learn what happened to her grandmother's antique watch. (defendant, plaintiff)

Comprehension and Critical Thinking

9. a. **Describe** What are the three levels of most state court systems?
   b. **Summarize** How might an appeals court respond to a lower court's decision?
   c. **Evaluate Information** How does the Supreme Court connect the state and federal court systems?

10. a. **Recall** What is the job of a court of appeals?
    b. **Make Generalizations** Why does it make sense for the Supreme Court to serve as the final court of appeals for both the state and federal systems?

   c. **Synthesize Information** Why do you think federal judges are appointed for life?

11. a. **Explain** How does the selection of Supreme Court justices show the balance of power between the executive and legislative branches?
    b. **Identify Alternatives** What advantages would there be to electing Supreme Court justices?
    c. **Draw Conclusions** Why do you think the selection process of justices can sometimes lead to an impasse?

Activities

12. **Skills** Visit the following Web page: http://www.uscourts.gov **a.** What is the purpose of this Web site? What kinds of information can you access from the page? **b.** What organization is behind the Web site? Do you think the information on this site is valid? Why or why not?

13. **Writing** You are a Senator considering a presidential nominee for Supreme Court justice. Write a list of ten hard-hitting questions that you would ask the nominee. These questions should be related to political issues.

14. **Active Citizen** Working with a partner, research a law that was declared unconstitutional by the Supreme Court. Prepare an oral presentation for your classmates. Describe the law and why the Court declared it unconstitutional.

15. **Math Practice** Review the annual salaries for the Chief Justice and Associate Justices of the Supreme Court on page 278. What is the total cost for their salaries each year?

16. **Civics and Economics** Federal District Court judges earn about $150,000 each year. Suppose the judges are arguing that they deserve more pay for the amount of work they do. Would you agree or disagree? Explain.

17. **Analyzing Visuals** Explain how the photograph above reflects the importance of the legal system in settling disputes.

Standardized Test Prep

Test-Taking Tips

Some questions on standardized tests require that you analyze a reading selection using your own knowledge. Study the passage below. Then follow the tips to answer the sample question.

TIP Note that the passage discusses the organization of the federal court system when it was created in 1789.

The Judiciary Act of 1789 divided the court into 13 judicial districts, which were, in turn, organized into three circuits: the Eastern, Middle, and Southern. The Supreme Court, the country's highest judicial tribunal [court], was to sit in the Nation's Capital, and was initially composed of a Chief Justice and five Associate Justices. For the first 101 years of the Supreme Court's life . . . the Justices were also required to "ride circuit," and hold circuit court twice a year in each judicial district.

Source: *Supreme Court of the United States*

Pick the letter that best completes the statement.

1. The following statements are true of the early Court and today's Court EXCEPT:

    TIP Notice the word "EXCEPT" in the question.

    A The Supreme Court is the country's highest court.

    B The Supreme Court is located in the nation's capital.

    C The Supreme Court is composed of a Chief Justice and five associate justices.

    D The Supreme Court has authority over all other courts in the nation.

    The correct answer is **C**. Note that the question asks you to choose the statement that does NOT apply to both the early and present-day Supreme Court.

2. What did the Judiciary Act of 1789 do?

    A It divided the country into three districts.

    B It created a Northern circuit.

    C It created a Supreme Court with a Chief Justice and eight associate justices.

    D It divided the country into 13 districts, which were organized into three circuits.

UNIT 4

State and Local Government

What's Ahead in Unit 4

In Unit 4 you will learn how state and local governments are organized and what powers they have. You will also see that they offer you many opportunities to participate directly in the process of government.

CHAPTER 11
State Government

CHAPTER 12
Local Government

Active Citizen

Why Study Civics?

What do state governments provide their citizens? What do local governments provide their citizens? How do the three levels of government—federal, state, and local—share the costs and responsibilities for the many programs and services they provide for their citizens? These are all questions that can be addressed by the study of civics.

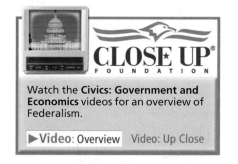

CLOSE UP FOUNDATION

Watch the **Civics: Government and Economics** videos for an overview of Federalism.

▶ **Video**: Overview   Video: Up Close

Standards for Civics and Government

National

The following National Standards are covered in this unit.

II. What are the foundations of the American political system?

B. What are the distinctive characteristics of American society?

C. What is American political culture?

D. What values and principles are basic to American constitutional democracy?

State

Go Online
PHSchool.com

For: Your state's Civics standards
Visit: PHSchool.com
Webcode: mpe4001

State Government

What's Ahead in Chapter 11

In this chapter you will read about how state governments work. You will also learn how they relate to the federal government in the system known as federalism.

SECTION 1
Federalism: One Nation and Fifty States

SECTION 2
State Legislatures

SECTION 3
The State Executive Branch

SECTION 4
State Courts

TARGET READING SKILL

Main Idea In this chapter you will focus on identifying the main idea of what you read. Identifying the main idea includes the skills of identifying supporting details and identifying a main idea that is implied, rather than directly stated.

Utah's state capitol ▶ building in Salt Lake City

The following National Standards for Civics and Government are covered in this chapter:

III. How does the government established by the

Constitution embody the purposes, values, and principles of American democracy?

A. How are power and responsibility distributed, shared,

and limited in the government established by the United States Constitution?

C. How are state and local governments organized and what do they do?

Active Citizen — Civics in the Real World

Suppose you live in a densely populated state. Each year, thousands of acres of your state's farmland and forests are replaced with development and suburban sprawl. Environmental groups, farmers, local politicians, and students, determined to preserve a significant amount of the state's remaining natural areas, join together in an effort to convince your state government to protect the land.

With so much public pressure, the state government responds. The state legislature agrees to place an ambitious conservation plan on the ballot. In the next election, voters are given the chance to approve the plan, which would use state money to buy and preserve acres of undeveloped land across the state. Voters respond by approving the plan.

Your state governor is proud of the people in the state: "Pat yourselves on the back and say, this is the importance of getting involved in your government."

Citizen's Journal Think about the effort made by these people to preserve their state's undeveloped land. Write a paragraph describing an action that you believe should be taken in your own state. Explain how you think this action would improve life in your state.

Federalism: One Nation and Fifty States

Reading Preview

Objectives

In this section you will

- Understand that public policy is a major concern of all levels of government.
- Understand how federalism involves state powers and shared powers.
- Explore the concept of federalism in action.

Taking Notes

Make a diagram like the one below. As you read the section, complete the diagram with information about the relationship between the national and state governments under the federalist system.

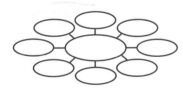

Key Terms

public policy unitary system
federalism

Main Idea

Under federalism, some powers are reserved for the states, some are shared by the states and federal government, and some are reserved for the federal government.

Target Reading Skill

Identify Main Ideas It is difficult to remember everything you read. One solution is to focus on the main idea of each paragraph. In most of what you read, the main idea will be directly stated, often in the first sentence of the paragraph.

If your public school had problems, would you write to the President? Probably not, because most of the laws and policies that affect public schools are made by state and local governments, not by the government in Washington, D.C. In fact, our state governments carry out much of the work of meeting citizens' needs. These governments have primary responsibility for public education, transportation, health and safety.

Public Policy

Consider the following problems:

- You have homework due tomorrow and your favorite TV show is on tonight.
- Drivers ages 16 to 21 have a much higher accident rate than do other groups of drivers.

The first situation is a private problem, since you are the person who must decide whether to do your homework or watch TV. The second situation affects many people. Therefore, it is a public problem.

Public Policy Issues If people do not agree on the solution to a public problem, issues arise. An issue is a point of conflict or a matter of debate. When people ask government to help solve a public problem, the issues that arise become public issues. Government response to public issues is known as **public policy**. Although all levels of government set public policy, the policies set by state and local government often affect your life most directly.

Public Policy Choices In making public policy, government officials must make choices and trade-offs. You, too, must make choices when deciding which solution to support.

Solving public problems requires the effort of the people we elect to public office. Keep in mind that solving public problems also requires that individual citizens take responsibility for their actions. The key to finding and carrying out solutions to the public problems that face us lies in government, community, and individuals working together.

✔ Reading Check How does public policy relate to public problems?

Federalism

Some delegates at the Constitutional Convention argued that only a strong national government could handle the problems facing the country. Other delegates wanted the states to keep most of the power. In trying to bring together these points of view, the Framers settled on the system of federalism. **Federalism** is the system that divides some powers between the national and state governments while allowing them to share other powers. The Constitution lists the powers of the national government. They include the power to declare war and make treaties with other countries.

Powers of the States The Constitution does not specifically list the powers of the states. Instead, the Tenth Amendment gives to the states all powers not given to the national government or denied to the states. Powers that the states alone hold include the power to set up local governments, conduct elections, set up public school systems, and oversee businesses. The states also make laws such as traffic laws that protect health and safety.

Shared Powers The national government and state governments also share many powers. They both collect taxes, borrow money, set up courts, enforce laws, and punish lawbreakers.

Unitary Government Our system of federalism is unusual. A more common system is the **unitary system**, in which practically all political power lies with a central government. A large and diverse country like the U.S. would be difficult to serve with a unitary government, however.

✔ Reading Check How does the Tenth Amendment give powers to the states?

Federalism in Action
Federalism allows national and state governments to divide and share their power. State and local governments create laws and oversee programs and services to meet the needs of their particular state, such as transportation, with assistance from the national government. **Draw Inferences** *What are the benefits of having state and national governments share responsibility for services, such as transportation?*

Linda Chavez is the president of the Center for Equal Opportunity in Washington, D.C. In this excerpt, she maintains that more power to the states helps keep power closer to the citizens of this country.

" Whenever the federal government gives money to the states or to local governments or agencies, certain obligations or rules follow. . . . But many . . . functions that the federal government performs, and taxes citizens to pay for, would be better decided on and funded at the local or state level, where people can keep track of what is being done and how much it costs."

Analyze Primary Sources

Why does Chavez feel that the states should be responsible for certain functions performed by the federal government?

Federalism in Action

Some people think of federalism as being like a layer cake. In this view, "layers" of government—national and state—are seen as separate, with different powers. In action, however, federalism is more like a marble cake, with the powers mixed and overlapping.

The way the powers of national government and state governments mix and overlap is not set. Some people press to keep the national government out of what they see as the states' business. Others think that the national government's power over the states should increase.

Power to the States Those in favor of states' rights feel that state governments can serve their people better than the national government can. State governments, they argue, should be allowed to fit laws and programs to the particular needs of their states.

Analyze Maps

State Constitutions

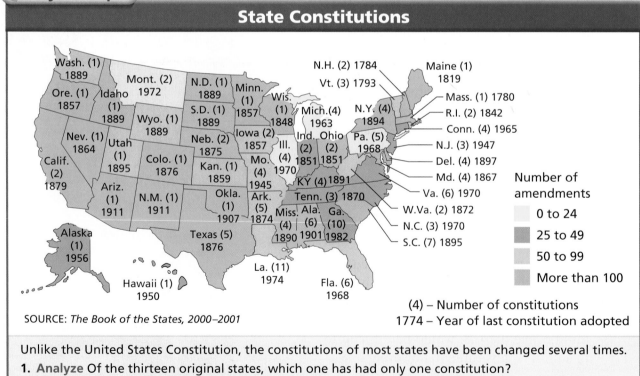

SOURCE: *The Book of the States, 2000–2001*

Number of amendments

0 to 24
25 to 49
50 to 99
More than 100

(4) – Number of constitutions
1774 – Year of last constitution adopted

Unlike the United States Constitution, the constitutions of most states have been changed several times.

1. **Analyze** Of the thirteen original states, which one has had only one constitution?
2. **Apply** Which state has added more than 100 amendments and has had the most constitutions?

Power to the National Government

Those who favor a strong national government point out that the opportunities in different states are not always equal. For example, some states might spend more money per student on education than other states. Thus, critics of states' rights argue, the national government needs to play a stronger role to ensure equal opportunity in all the states.

Some problems are too big for individual states to solve. Following the terrorist attacks on September 11, 2001, Congress took over the job of overseeing airport security. It believed that the task of airport security was too important and too large for any state or private company to manage. Doing so represented a huge increase in the role of the federal government.

Whether providing security for airports or building a dam, some tasks cost more than a state can afford. The state needs the help of the federal government. Sometimes, too, a problem involves several states. For example, if a state's factories are causing pollution in another state, the federal government may have to step in.

▲ Following the terrorist attacks on September 11, 2001, the national government took over the job of overseeing airport security.

Target Reading Skill

Identify Main Ideas What is the main idea of this paragraph?

✓ Reading Check **Why do some people argue for less federal power over state decisions?**

SECTION 1 Assessment

Key Terms

Use each of the key terms in a sentence that explains its meaning:
public policy, federalism, unitary system

Target Reading Skill

1. **Identify the Main Idea**
   State the main idea for each of the three major parts of Section 1.

Comprehension and Critical Thinking

2. **a. Recall** What are some powers shared by the national government and the states?

   b. Demonstrate Reasoned Judgment Why do you suppose the Framers gave the power to declare war, to make treaties, and to coin money *only* to the national government?

3. **a. Explain** Why might some people want the national government to have a strong role over the states?

   b. Recognize Points of View If someone believed that the best government was local government, would you describe them as a supporter of strong national government or of states' rights?

Writing Activity

Identify a local issue that you are concerned about. Then write a brief report that explains which levels of government are involved in the problem. Propose possible solutions to the problem.

> **TIP** Make an outline that identifies the main idea of each paragraph. Supply one or two supporting details for each main idea.

State Legislatures

Reading Preview

Objectives
In this section you will
- Learn who state legislators are.
- Discuss the organization of state legislatures.
- Find out how states make laws.
- Learn about financing state governments.

Taking Notes
Make a diagram like the one below. As you read the section, complete the diagram with information about state legislatures.

Key Terms
apportioned
initiative
referendum
recall
impeach

revenue
sales tax
excise tax
income tax
bonds

Main Idea
State legislatures are organized much like Congress. States have procedures for making laws and creating taxes to pay for state services.

Target Reading Skill
Identify Implied Main Ideas
Sometimes the main idea of a paragraph will be implied rather than directly stated. The details in a paragraph or section will add up to a main idea, but you will have to state this main idea for yourself.

Because your state legislators usually get less news coverage than members of Congress do, you might be less aware of the activities of lawmakers in your state. However, state legislators make most of the laws that affect your day-to-day life.

Who Are State Legislators?

In the early years of our nation's history, the states were mostly rural, with small populations. The demands on state governments were not great. Legislators would leave their jobs as farmers, lawyers, or business people for a few weeks each year to go to legislative sessions. Over time, however, rapid growth of industries and cities led to new responsibilities for state government. As legislatures met more often and for longer sessions, citizen legislators found it difficult to balance their government duties with the demands of their jobs.

Today, many state legislators are full-time lawmakers. The typical legislator has studied political science, law, or public administration and has spent time in government service before running for office. Often state legislators plan on a life-long career in politics.

✓ Reading Check **Why are more state legislators full-time lawmakers today than in early years of the United States?**

Kentucky state senators review legislative materials during a General Assembly Senate session.

Organization of State Legislatures

All states except Nebraska have a **bicameral**, or two-house, legislature with an upper house called a senate. The lower house is usually known as the house of representatives, although in some states the lower house is called the assembly or general assembly.

Sessions State governments, like the national government, divide legislative terms into sessions. Most states hold annual sessions, while a few meet every other year. Most states limit these sessions from anything from 20 days to 6 months. However, the governor may call special sessions.

Representation Seats in state legislatures are **apportioned**, or divided among districts, on the basis of equal representation. Legislators represent districts with about the same population.

Sets used to be apportioned on a geographical basis, like the United States Senate. One legislator might have represented a rural district with a few hundred people, while another represented all the people in a large city.

In *Reynolds* v. *Sims* (1964), the Supreme Court ruled that the apportionment of both houses of state legislatures must be based on population. Today, most states reapportion seats in their legislatures every ten years, based on the results of the United States census.

▲
Nebraska has a unicameral, or one house, state legislature.

✓ Reading Check **What issue was decided in the Supreme Court Case *Reynolds* v. *Sims*?**

ANALYZING Political Cartoons

Today, districts are redrawn after every census so that each district has roughly the same population. However, in some cases, boundaries of the districts are redrawn to influence the outcome of elections. This results in very oddly-shaped districts.

1. How does the cartoonist show changes in the districts' shapes and sizes?

2. Why does the cartoonist use puzzle pieces for the districts?

Making Laws

The major job of a state legislature is to make laws. By and large, the process is the same as in Congress. Bills are introduced, discussed in committees, and debated on the floor. Both houses must agree on the final bill, which the governor must then approve. A major difference between lawmaking in Congress and in state legislatures, however, is that in some states citizens have a greater voice in the laws that are made.

Initiative   One method of giving lawmaking power to citizens is called the **initiative**, the process by which citizens can propose laws. In this process, citizens gather signatures on a petition. When enough people have signed the petition (usually 5 to 10 percent of the registered voters), the proposed law is put to a vote in a statewide election. If a majority of the voters approve the proposal, it becomes state law.

Referendum   Another way that citizens can participate in lawmaking is the **referendum**, the process by which a law is referred to the voters to approve or reject. Almost every state requires a referendum on constitutional amendments proposed by the legislature.

Both the initiative and referendum are ways that citizens can take lawmaking into their own hands. If enough people believe that a certain law is needed, or that a bad law should be removed, they can use an initiative or referendum.

Recall   Citizens in some states also have the power of **recall**, a process for removing elected officials from office. A recall effort is usually begun by citizens who believe that an official is not doing a good job or is dishonest. Citizens begin a recall by gathering voters' signatures on a petition. If, in the recall election that follows, a majority of voters agree with the recall, the official must leave office.

Citizen Power
A citizen holds a sign urging voters to reject Proposition 209 on the election ballot (above, left). In California, citizens gather signatures on a petition to recall Governor Gray Davis (right).
Draw Inferences *Why should citizens want to be more involved in lawmaking?*

Students Make a Difference

Emily Meade, a junior at Canton High School in Canton, Illinois believes that school funding initiatives deserve more attention from the people most affected by them: the students. "When I heard that our school district was in financial trouble and that extracurriculars might be cut, I became alarmed."

Emily is a member of Students First Illinois, a non-partisan, statewide, grassroots coalition fighting for equal, high-quality public education for every student. She has spoken at rallies and visited the Illinois State Capital to speak and work with legislators.

▲ Students can help make a difference by becoming more involved in issues related to their schools

Service Learning

How can you contribute to education reform in your community?

The California Recall More than 25 states authorize the recall as an option. However, it has been used infrequently. The most recent recall election occurred in California in 2003. Voters felt that Governor Gray Davis was not doing a good job, especially because the state was facing a serious economic crisis. Voters, faced with a ballot of over 100 candidates, voted to recall Governor Davis and they elected the Austrian actor Arnold Schwarzenegger. Davis was only the second governor to be recalled in the history of our country.

Checking the Other Branches State legislatures have the power to oversee, or to check, the activities of the executive and the judicial branches. In many states, the legislature must approve officials and judges who are appointed by the governor. State legislatures also must approve the governor's budget. In this process, the legislature examines how well executive agencies are doing their jobs. State legislators also review how federal funds are spent in their state. Legislatures in most states have the power to **impeach**, or bring charges against, executive and judicial officers and to determine their guilt or innocence. By and large, the impeachment process in the states is much the same as the process followed in Congress.

> **Target Reading Skill**
> **Identify the Implied Main Idea** Reread this paragraph carefully, paying attention to the details. What is the implied main idea of this paragraph?

✓ Reading Check **How do state legislatures check the executive branch?**

Financing State Government

State governments need money to meet the needs of citizens for important services. Where does the money come from?

Taxes   States raise more than 50 percent of their **revenue**, or income, from taxes. Most of state tax revenue comes from two sources: sales taxes and income taxes.

Most states have two kinds of **sales taxes**, or charges made on purchases of goods and services. The general sales tax places a charge on almost all goods sold in a state. This charge usually is a percentage of the price of a product. A second kind of sales tax is the **excise tax**, a charge on certain goods, such as alcoholic beverages, gasoline, and tobacco. Most states also have an **income tax**, a tax on what individuals and businesses earn. The income tax is a percentage of the money a person or business makes.

Bonds and Lotteries   Sometimes states borrow money by selling **bonds**, certificates that people buy from the government. The government agrees to pay back the cost of the bond, plus interest, after a set period of time. States often use this method of raising revenue for such projects as building a school or convention center.

Some states also raise money through lotteries. About 60 percent of the money from lottery ticket sales goes toward prizes. The remaining 40 percent goes to the state, often to help pay for educational programs.

✔ Reading Check   **What are the different ways that a state can raise money?**

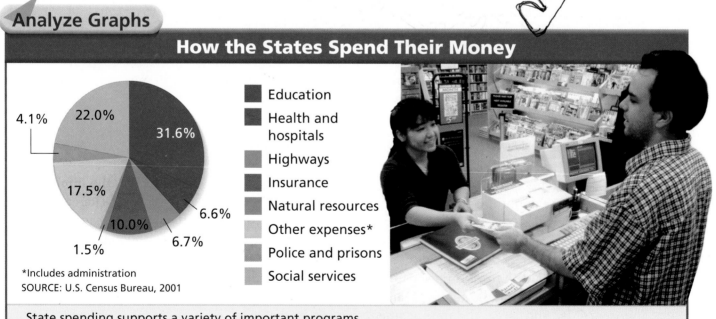

Analyze Graphs

How the States Spend Their Money

4.1%   22.0%   31.6%

17.5%

10.0%   6.6%

1.5%   6.7%

- Education
- Health and hospitals
- Highways
- Insurance
- Natural resources
- Other expenses*
- Police and prisons
- Social services

*Includes administration
SOURCE: U.S. Census Bureau, 2001

State spending supports a variety of important programs.
1. **Analyze** Which two services make up more than 50% of the money that states spend?
2. **Calculate** Which service gets the largest portion of the money?

States can use block grants for programs of their choosing, such as immunization services.

Federal Funds Over time, state and local governments have increasingly turned to Congress for money. Federal money comes to the states in several forms. Two of the most widely used forms are categorical grants and block grants.

Categorical grants are given for specific purposes, such as a job training program or highway construction. These grants come with "strings attached"—certain conditions that must be met before the state may use the funds. Block grants are given for more general purposes. The state can decide for which programs to use the block grant funds.

SECTION 2 Assessment

Key Terms

Use each of the key terms in a sentence that explains its meaning: apportioned, initiative referendum, recall, impeach, revenue, sales taxes, excise tax, income tax, bonds

Target Reading Skill

1. **Identify Implied Main Ideas** State the main ideas of the four parts of Section 2.

Comprehension and Critical Thinking

2. **a. Recall** In the early years of the United States, how long were states' legislative sessions?
   b. Draw Inferences What plans do you think many state

legislators have for their careers?

3. **a. Describe** How many houses do most state legislatures have? What are they called?
   b. Synthesize Information How does the Federal government assist the states in apportioning legislative seats?

4. **a. Describe** What is the major job of state legislatures?
   b. Contrast What is the difference between an initiative and a referendum?

5. **a. Recall** What are the two leading sources of state tax revenue?
   b. Contrast What is the difference between sales tax and income tax?

Writing Activity

Find a local issue that is important to you. It could be about schools, the environment, roads, taxes, traffic, or some other issue. Write a letter to your state legislator in which you express your concerns and make recommendations as to what should be done.

TIP Organize your essay using an outline, setting up paragraphs to identify the issue, express why it is important to you, and then express your opinion.

How to Write a Letter to the Editor

The Constitution of the United States guarantees all citizens the right to express their views on political issues. One way to do this is to write a letter to the editor of your local newspaper. If your letter is printed, other citizens will be able to read your opinion.

Below is a letter to the editor from a concerned citizen. Read the letter and think about the citizen's opinion. Has he expressed it clearly? Has he given good reasons for feeling the way he does? Does the letter influence you?

Editor:

Thank you for the articles in your paper identifying the importance of recycling. It is the responsibility of every citizen to care for our environment, and recycling is a simple and effective way of caring. Before our family began recycling, we were not aware of how much newspaper, glass, aluminum, paper, and plastic we used. We have been amazed at the amounts we accumulate each week.

The new city program offering curbside pick-up service makes recycling easy and convenient. We urge everyone to participate in the new program. To learn more, contact the city manager's office.

Sincerely,
Matt Reilly

Learn the Skill

To write an effective letter to the editor, follow these steps:

❶ **Briefly summarize the issue.** Begin your letter with an interesting statement to get the reader's attention.

❷ **State your opinion.** Give two reasons why you feel the way you do. Support your reasons with evidence or examples.

❸ **Reaffirm your point of view.** You may also share your suggestions for overcoming the problem or working out the issue.

Practice the Skill

❶ Brainstorm a list of three issues. For each one, write one statement which expresses your opinion. Write at least two reasons or examples to support your opinion.

❷ Take turns sharing your ideas with a classmate. You should be able to understand each other's views on the issues each of you has chosen.

Apply the Skill

❶ Select one of your three issues and write a letter to the editor.

❷ Send your letter to the editor of your local newspaper.

Go **O**nline
civics interactive

For: Local Citizenship
Visit: PHSchool.com
Web Code: mpp-4113

The State Executive Branch

Reading Preview

Objectives
In this section you will
- Discuss the roles of the governor.
- Learn about other state executive officials.
- Learn about state executive agencies.

Key Terms
item veto
lieutenant governor

Main Idea
The governor's powers and duties are similar to the president's domestic powers.

Target Reading Skill
Identify Supporting Details
The main idea of a paragraph is supported by details that give more information about it. The details can explain the main idea or provide examples or reasons in support of it.

Taking Notes
Make a diagram like the one below. As you read the section, complete the diagram with information about the various roles of a state governor.

A governor and a group of executive officials lead the executive branch of state government. These officials help run the many agencies that enforce the laws and carry out the state's programs. Early state constitutions greatly limited the power of the governor. Over the years, however, many state constitutions have been changed in order to give the governor more power to take on the growing responsibilities of state government.

The Roles of the Governor

If the state and federal executive branches are similar, would it be correct to describe the governor as the "president of the state"? Presidents and governors do play similar roles. However, there are differences between the two offices, as well.

Chief Executive The governor's role of chief executive is similar to that of the President. He or she oversees the executive branch and makes sure laws are enforced. The governor is commander-in-chief of the state militia, or National Guard, and can call on it in the event of a riot or disaster.

As chief executive, the governor has the power to appoint hundreds of officials to carry out the state's day-to-day work. However, as you will see, limits on governors' powers of appointment can greatly affect their ability to achieve their goals.

A governor's seal.

Perhaps the greatest source of executive power is the governor's budget-making role. Of course, the legislature must approve the governor's budget, and no state money may be spent without the legislature's approval. However, because the governor usually writes the budget, he or she still has a good deal of control over how much money various agencies get.

Legislative Leader Like the President, the governor has legislative powers. The governor may propose legislation in the form of a bill, a budget, or a speech to the state legislature. The governor can also influence lawmaking by talks with legislators or by whipping up public support. In these ways, the governor makes clear what programs he or she wants lawmakers to set up and provide funds for.

Target Reading Skill

Identify Supporting Details
Find two details that support the main idea of the paragraph entitled "Legislative Leader."

Analyze Diagrams

The Duties and Powers of the Governor

The governor's role of chief executive is similar to that of the President.

a. What are two ways the governor can influence the State legislature?

b. How is the governor similar to the President as commander-in-chief?

Proposes new laws and influences lawmaking: approves or vetoes bills

Appoints certain state officials

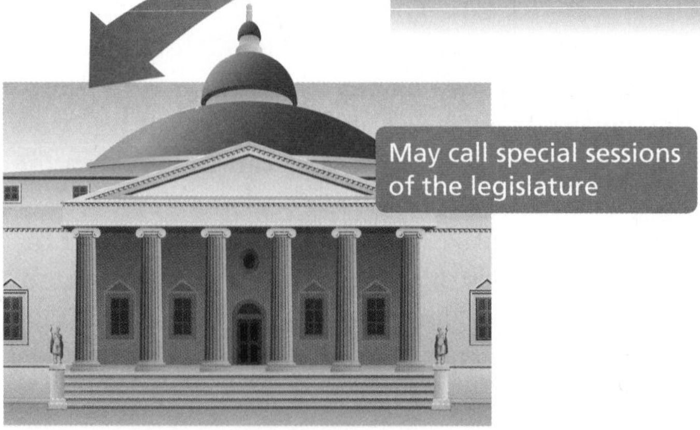

May call special sessions of the legislature

GOVERNOR

Another legislative power of the governor is the veto. In 43 states governors have the **item veto**, the power to reject particular parts, or items, of a bill. A state legislature may override the governor's veto. However, even the threat of a veto gives the governor a good deal of power over the legislature because it usually takes more than 50 percent of the legislature to override it.

Judicial Role Like the President, a governor has certain judicial powers. For example, some state governors appoint certain state judges. The governor can also reduce or overturn the sentences of people convicted of crimes.

✓ Reading Check **What is the governor's greatest source of executive power?**

Go Online
civics
interactive

For: The Duties and Powers of the Governor
Visit: PHSchool.com
Web Code: mpp-4113

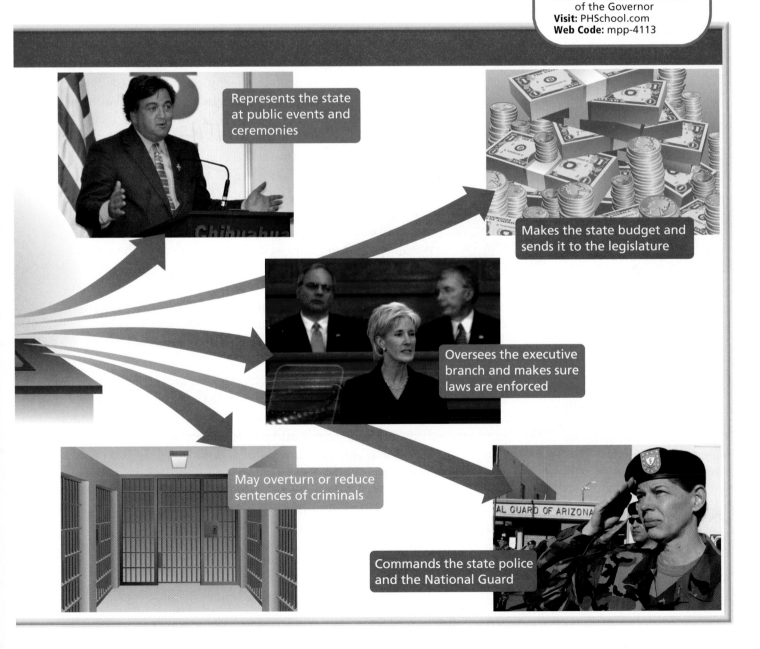

Represents the state at public events and ceremonies

Makes the state budget and sends it to the legislature

Oversees the executive branch and makes sure laws are enforced

May overturn or reduce sentences of criminals

Commands the state police and the National Guard

The Department of Health
A state's department of health is responsible for making sure businesses, such as restaurants, follow health codes. Following the blackout of 2003, for example, New York State health inspectors made sure that supermarkets did not violate state health codes by selling spoiled foods.

State Executive Agencies

Just like the federal government, much of the work of running a state government is done by executive agencies. Each agency helps by carrying out the day-to-day work of the executive branch. Departments of health, revenue, and natural resources are examples of executive agencies.

To better understand what executive agencies do, take a look at one of the largest in every state—the agency in charge of education. This agency's major responsibility is to make sure that national and state education laws are carried out. One such law sets the number of school days in a year. Laws also set the subjects you have to study and how many classes you must pass to graduate.

The state education agency works with local school districts to make sure that they meet these requirements. It also sets standards for teachers. The education agency makes sure that funds are spent as the law requires.

Another important state agency in each state oversees transportation. This agency works to provide and maintain transportation systems, from highways to railroads. A state transportation agency ensures the safe mobility of people and goods within the state. It also balances the need for transportation systems with the preservation of the state's environment and communities.

As you have seen, keeping our states running takes many people, whether they be elected, appointed, or hired. In fact, our states employ millions of people.

✓ Reading Check   **What executive agency is usually one of the largest in state government?**

Other Executive Officials

A team of executive officials assists the governor. The **lieutenant governor** is the state official second in rank to the governor. The lieutenant governor performs a role similar to that of the Vice President. The secretary of state has charge of official records and documents and supervises elections. The secretary of state is usually second in the line of succession behind the governor and lieutenant governor. The attorney general serves as the state's chief legal officer. The treasurer or comptroller is the chief financial officer of the state.

Some people have compared state executive officials to the President's Cabinet. However, Presidents can select their own Cabinet members, while the voters elect many state executive officers. Therefore, the governor may have to work with executive officials who do not share the same goals and may belong to a different political party.

✓ Reading Check **What is the job of the attorney general?**

Civics and Economics

State Budgets   Forty-nine states have laws requiring the state budget be balanced. (Vermont is the sole exception.) A balanced budget means that the money the state intends to spend must be the same as it expects to earn.

For state budget makers, there is a lot of guesswork in arriving at those numbers. Revenues are mostly in the form of taxes. Tax revenues depend on how much people and businesses earn and how much other taxes like sales taxes and excise taxes bring in.

Expenses are easier to project. Even then, budget makers have to account unexpected events. For example, severe weather or a bad economy may lead to an increase in payments for public assistance and unemployment.

Analyzing Economics
Why does balancing a state budget involve guesswork?

SECTION 3 Assessment

Key Terms

Use each of the key terms in a sentence that explains its meaning: item veto, lieutenant governor

Target Reading Skill

1. **Identify Supporting Details** State the details on pages 306–307 that support the idea that a state's governor has legislative powers similar to the President's.

Comprehension and Critical Thinking

2. **a. Describe** How does the governor control how much money each state agency gets to spend?

   b. Compare How are the governor's powers similar to some powers of the President?

3. **a. Recall** What state official performs a role similar to that of the Vice President?

   b. Contrast How do state executive officers differ from members of the President's Cabinet?

4. **a. Recall** Departments of health, revenue and natural resources are examples of what type of state government?

   b. Draw Inferences Why does it take so many people to staff state executive agencies?

Writing Activity

Use the Internet to identify a state executive agency in your state's government. Find out about the work it does. Write a report in which you explain the responsibilities and major activities of the agency.

Go Online PHSchool.com

For: Writing Activity
Visit: PHSchool.com
Web Code: mpd-4113

SECTION 4 State Courts

Reading Preview

Objectives
In this section you will
- Learn what state courts do.
- Learn about judges in state courts.
- Discuss a case study in federalism and the courts.

Taking Notes
Make a tree map graphic organizer like the one below. As you read the section, fill it in with a description of a state court system. Use the red headings in the section as main topics.

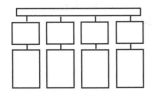

Key Terms
Missouri Plan   judicial action commissions

Main Idea
State courts handle cases of state law. They also act as a check on the other two branches of state government.

Target Reading Skill
Identify Supporting Details Chapters, sections, subsections, and paragraphs all feature a main idea supported by details. These details explain the idea and make it more meaningful to the reader.

We are all subject to two levels of law: state law and federal law. Just as federal courts interpret the United States Constitution and apply federal laws, state court systems interpret state constitutions and laws. State courts handle cases that are close to people's everyday lives, such as divorces, wills, drunk driving, robberies, and murders. The organization of courts, and even their names, varies from state to state. The way judges are selected and the terms they serve vary, too. As you read about the state courts, keep in mind that this is a general description. As a citizen, you will want to know more about the special features of the court system in your own state.

Most state judicial systems have three levels. On the first level, the state's trial courts hear both civil cases and criminal cases. On the second level, state appeals courts review cases appealed from the trial courts. Cases that go beyond the first appeals court are heard in the state's supreme court, the highest court in the state system.

What State Courts Do

Like the federal judiciary, state courts act as a check on the two other branches of state government. For example, state courts may decide that a law passed by the state legislature violates the state constitution. Like the federal judiciary, state courts have the duty of protecting the rights and freedoms guaranteed to each citizen by a state's constitution.

Perhaps the best-known tasks of the state courts involve hearing civil and criminal cases. State courts hear more than ten million cases each year. (See Unit 6 for more on courts.)

✓ Reading Check **What are the three levels of a state court system?**

Judges in State Courts

Judges are the foundation of the state court system. State court judges perform many of the same duties as federal judges. However, the way judges are selected and the lengths of their terms vary, depending on the state and on the level of court.

Selection of Judges There are several advantages of having judges run for election. First, an elected judge is responsible to the public, whose lives and property may be directly affected by the judge's decisions. Second, election checks the power of a governor, who might want to appoint friends and supporters even if they are not well qualified to be judges.

Opponents of electing judges, however, say that a judge must make decisions based on the law and the facts of the case, not on what might please the voters during an election campaign. People who hold this view believe that judges should be chosen on merit, or ability, alone, and should not have to face election.

Some states have adopted a method of choosing judges known as the **Missouri Plan**. Under this plan, the governor appoints a judge from a list prepared by a commission of judges, lawyers, and ordinary citizens. Then, in the next election, voters cast a "yes" or "no" vote on whether they want the judge to stay in office for a twelve-year term. Many people feel that it combines the best qualities of appointment and election.

Target Reading Skill
Identify Supporting Details
List the supporting details in the final paragraph of *Selection of Judges*.

The State Court System
State courts, such as this one in Virginia, hear civil and criminal cases, review appeal cases, and rule on the constitutionality of state laws.
Draw Inferences *Why do states need their own court systems?*

The Supreme Court

Go Online
civics
interactive

For: Interactive Constitution
with Supreme Court Cases
Visit: PHSchool.com
Web Code: mpp-4114

Reno v. *Condon* (2000)

Why It Matters This case determined that the federal government has the right to decide what can be done with the information contained on people's driver's licenses.

Background Rebecca Schaeffer, a popular young TV actress, was killed by an obsessed fan in 1989. The murder investigation revealed that the killer had gotten Schaeffer's address from her driver's license. Many states routinely sold information on licenses to direct marketing companies and other businesses. In response, Congress passed the Driver's Privacy Protection Act. This law prohibited states from selling the information to private companies.

South Carolina's Attorney General, Charlie Condon, sued to have the law declared unconstitutional. (The suit was called *Reno* v. *Condon* because Janet Reno was the Attorney General of the United States at the time

of the lawsuit.) Condon did not disagree with the terms of the act. But he believed that since the states issued driver's licenses, regulating driver's licenses was a state matter, not a federal one. Condon won his case in both the District Court and the Court of Appeals.

The Decision The Supreme Court reversed the lower courts' decision unanimously. The lower courts had agreed with South Carolina's charges that the law asserted federal power into the states' business. The Supreme Court redefined the issue. It stated that the information on driver's licenses was an "item of commerce." As such, the information's use could be regulated by the federal government.

Understanding the Law

1. Why did Charlie Condon object to the Driver's Privacy Protection Act?
2. What grounds did the Supreme Court use to reverse the lower court decisions?

Terms of Service The length of time judges spend in office depends on the state and on the level of the court. Most terms run from 4 to 15 years. In Rhode Island, judges have life appointments, while in some states judges serve until age 70.

Most judges may be removed by the voters at the end of their terms. State constitutions in most states also allow for judges to be impeached, and four states allow for the recall of judges. These powers, however, have rarely been used.

Most states have **judicial action commissions**, official governmental bodies that handle situations in which judges might not be doing their job well. Such a commission looks into complaints against the judge, holds hearings, reports on the judge's guilt or innocence, and decides penalties.

✓ Reading Check   **What is the Missouri Plan for selecting judges?**

Case Study: Federalism and the Courts

Some state constitutions offer greater rights and freedoms than the federal Constitution. When an individual rights case comes up in one of these states, which applies—the federal Constitution or the state constitution?

Two U.S. Supreme Court cases, one in Oregon and one in California, help answer this question. In each case, the owners of a shopping mall took to court members of citizens' groups who had passed out leaflets and gathered signatures at the mall. The owners claimed that it was their right to ban such activity on their property. The citizens' groups stated that they were exercising their right to freedom of speech.

In its review of the Oregon case, the Supreme Court found that the owners of the mall had a right to use their property as they wanted. In the California case, however, the Court found for the citizens' groups, pointing out that California's constitution offers greater protection of free speech than does the federal Constitution. Thus, the federal Constitution was applied in the Oregon case, while in California the state constitution was applied.

The line between federal power and state power is not always an easy one to draw. These two cases demonstrate the important role the judicial branch plays in deciding questions of federalism.

✓ Reading Check **How would you define the line between federal power and state power?**

SECTION 4 Assessment

Key Terms

Use each of the key terms in a sentence that explains its meaning: Missouri Plan, judicial action commissions

Target Reading Skill

1. **Identify Supporting Details** State the details on this page that support the idea that the "line between federal power and state power is not always an easy one to draw."

Comprehension and Critical Thinking

2. **a. Recall** What level of state courts hear all civil and criminal cases?

   b. Compare How are state courts similar to federal courts?

3. **a. Describe** What is the advantage of the Missouri Plan for selection judges?

   b. Draw Inferences In the Missouri Plan, why is the make-up of the panel that submits a list of possible judges to the governor so important?

4. **a. Recall** What was the issue in the two constitutional cases in Oregon and California?

   b. Synthesize Information How is the U.S. Supreme Court reviews of the two cases an example of federalism in action?

Writing Activity

Use research materials to find out how judges are selected in your state. Write a report that explains the selection process and the length of terms of offices for different judges.

TIP Take notes on the details of becoming a judge in your state. Arrange them in outline form under the following headings: Selection Process, Term of Office.

Comparing Maps Over Time

Maps can show historical or political change. The two maps below show the United States in 1860 and today.

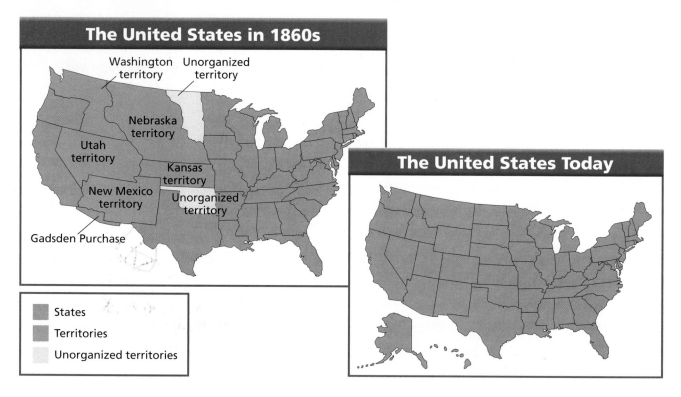

The United States in 1860s

Washington territory
Unorganized territory
Nebraska territory
Utah territory
Kansas territory
New Mexico territory
Unorganized territory
Gadsden Purchase

The United States Today

States
Territories
Unorganized territories

Learn the Skill

Follow these steps to compare maps over time:

1 Check the subject and area shown on each map. Understand what the titles and labels indicate.

2 Study the map key. Figure out which symbols or colors are used to present specific information.

3 Compare maps. Use the data to make comparisons. Note changes over time.

4 Interpret the maps. Think over what you already know about this period. Draw conclusions or make predictions.

Practice the Skill

Look at the maps above and answer these questions:

1 What area is shown on each map? How are they alike? How are they different?

2 What do the map keys symbolize?

3 Identify ten states on Map B that were not states in 1860.

4 Was the direction of settlement from east to west or west to east?

Apply the Skill

Choose a city that interests you. Then look in a historical atlas or online for maps of that area from two different time periods. How did the area change? Why do you think it changed? Do some more research to find out.

Review and Assessment

Chapter Summary

Section 1
Federalism: One Nation and Fifty States
(pages 294–297)

- A major concern of the government is setting public policy, making decisions that address public concerns.

- Unlike the unitary system, in which most power is held by the central government, federalism is the system that divides some powers between the national and state governments.

Section 2
State Legislatures
(pages 298–303)

- State legislators tend to be full-time lawmakers, serving districts apportioned by population.

- Citizens have a greater voice in state legislation through the use of initiative, referendum, and recall.

- Among state legislatures' checks on other branches of state government is the power to impeach.

- State governments get their revenue from such sources as sales taxes, excise taxes, income taxes, and bonds.

Section 3
The State Executive Branch
(pages 305–309)

- The governor's role as chief executive of the state is similar to that of the President.

- Many governors have the legislative power of the item veto, a power the President lacks.

- States have other executive officials, such as the lieutenant governor, many of whom are elected rather than appointed by the governor.

- State executive agencies carry out the day-to-day work of the executive branch.

Section 4 State Courts
(pages 310–313)

- State trial courts hear civil and criminal cases, and usually have three levels: trial courts, appeals courts, and the state supreme court.

- Some states elect judges, others appoint judges, and some use the Missouri Plan, which combines both appointment and election. Judicial action commissions handle situations in which judges are not doing their job well.

Copy the chart below and use it to help you summarize the chapter:

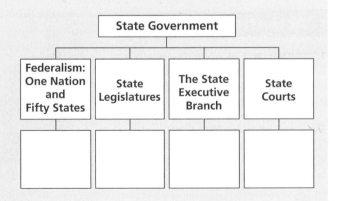

Go Online
PHSchool.com

For: Self–Test
Visit: PHSchool.com
Web Code: mpa-4114

Reviewing Key Terms

Fill in each blank with one of the key terms from the list below.

excise tax	public policy
initiative	income tax
federalism	bonds
item veto	apportioned
recall	

1. Seats in state legislatures are _____ on the basis of equal representation.

2. The system that divides some powers between the national and state governments while allowing them to share other powers is called _____.

3. The process for removing an elected official from office is called the _____.

4. Certificates that people buy from the government are called _____.

5. Government response to the concerns of the public is called _____.

6. A tax on such goods as tobacco or alcohol is called an _____.

7. The power to reject particular parts of a bill is called the _____.

8. A tax on the money people or businesses earn is called _____.

9. The process in which citizens can propose laws is called the _____.

Comprehension and Critical Thinking

10. a. **Recall** What powers do the states hold alone?
    b. **Make Generalizations** What advantages do state governments have in meeting people's needs?

11. a. **Explain** How are block grants different from categorical grants?
    b. **Draw Conclusions** Why do you think federal officials might prefer giving categorical grants to the states?

12. a. **Recall** What is one power that most governors have that the President does not have?

    b. **Make Generalizations** How might the governor's ability to lead be affected by state executive officers who come from a different political party?

13. a. **Describe** What are two advantages to electing judges?
    b. **Draw Inferences** How might the Missouri Plan restrict qualified people from becoming judges?

Activities

14. **Skills a.** On Map A, in what country is Santa Fe located?
    b. On Map B in what state is Santa Fe located?

15. **Writing** Write a short report that gives an example of federalism in action in your community.

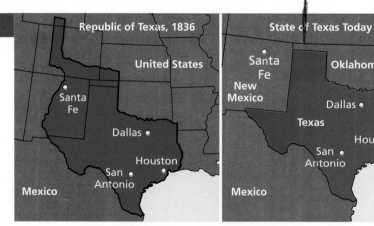

Republic of Texas, 1836

State of Texas Today

North Dakota Employment, 2002

Manufacturing	23,700
Information	7,900
Professional & Business Services	24,100
Financial Activities	17,850
Utilities	3,400
Mining & Construction	18,250
Wholesale & Retail Trade	58,650
Transportation & Warehousing	9,650
Educational Services	3,100
Health Care & Social Assistance	43,550
Leisure and Hospitality	29,900
Other Services	89,450
TOTAL Nonfarm Employment	**329,500**

16. **Active Citizen** Research how one of your state legislators has voted on a key issue before the state legislature. Write him or her a letter expressing your support or disapproval for his or her position.

17. **Math Practice** A state has 4,500,000 people. There are 150 seats in the State Assembly. How many people should each assemblyperson represent if the seats are equally apportioned?

18. **Civics and Economics** Every state has a department of labor or employment that monitors jobs in the state and provides training and other services for workers. Find out what services the Department of Labor in your state provides and which might be useful to you when you are looking for a job.

19. **Analyzing Visuals** What is the largest sector of the North Dakota economy? How many people work in manufacturing?

Standardized Test Prep

The Taft Family of Ohio

TIP The main idea is sometimes in the first sentence of the paragraph.

The Taft family has been prominent in politics for nearly a century. William Howard Taft (1857–1930) was elected President of the United States in 1908. He served one term and was defeated for reelection. But in 1921 he became the only ex-president to serve on the U.S. Supreme Court. Taft was named Chief Justice and served to his death in 1930.

President Taft's son, Robert Alphonso Taft (1889–1953) served in the U.S. Senate for many years. Taft was known as "Mr. Republican" and in several elections was a leading candidate for his party's nomination for the presidency.

Senator Taft's grandson, Robert A. Taft II (1942–), was elected governor of Ohio in 1998.

1. What is the main idea of the selection?
   A William Howard Taft (1857–1930) was elected President of the United States in 1908.
   B The Taft family has been prominent in politics for nearly a century.

   The correct answer is **B**. Note that the main idea is the first sentence of the paragraph.

2. What detail best supports the statement that the Taft family has been prominent in politics?
   A Senator Taft's grandson, Robert A. Taft II (1942–) was elected governor of Ohio in 1998.
   B Taft was named Chief Justice and served until his death in 1930.
   C Taft was known as "Mr. Republican."
   D William Howard Taft served one term as President and was defeated for reelection.

Local Government

What's Ahead in Chapter 12

In this chapter you will take a look at different kinds of local governments. You will find out what they do. You will also learn how they work with each other and with state and federal governments.

SECTION 1
Types of Local Government

SECTION 2
Local Government Services and Revenues

SECTION 3
Conflict and Cooperation Between Governments

TARGET READING SKILL

Comparison and Contrast In this chapter you will focus on comparing and contrasting to help you better understand what you read. Comparing and contrasting includes making comparisons, identifying contrasts, and using signal words.

Ossining, New York ▶

National Standards for Civics and Government   State

The following National Standards for Civics and Government are covered in this chapter:

III. How does the government established by the

Constitution embody the purposes, values, and principles of American democracy?

C. How are state and local governments organized and what do they do?

V. What are the roles of the citizen in American democracy?

C. What are the responsibilities of citizens?

E. How can citizens take part in civic life?

Go Online
PHSchool.com

For: Your state's standards
Visit: PHSchool.com
Web Code: mpe-4121

Active Citizen   Civics in the Real World

"No one has the right to force you to breathe smoke," says a resident of Denver, Colorado. The city government agrees. It has passed laws that ban cigarette smoking in many public places.

Although hundreds of local governments across the nation have passed anti-smoking laws, there are many people who are opposed to such legislation. As a citizen in North Carolina says, "We don't need to make a bunch of rules as to what people do with their private lives."

As these examples show, communities can be torn between respecting a person's right to smoke and promoting public health. Whatever their beliefs are on this issue, however, most people agree that laws about smoking should be set by local governments. Governments at this level have the best idea of what their citizens want. In fact, local governments were first formed to meet people's everyday needs—from fighting fires to collecting garbage.

Citizen's Journal What do you think about the debate over anti-smoking laws? Do people have the right to smoke in public? Or is protecting non-smokers from secondhand cigarette smoke more important than an individual's right to smoke? Write a paragraph explaining your opinion on how local governments should deal with this issue.

Types of Local Government

Reading Preview

Objectives

In this section you will

- Describe counties and townships.
- Explain how New England towns are run.
- Learn about special districts.
- Describe the different types of city government.

Taking Notes

Make a diagram like the one below. As you read this section, complete the diagram with information about types of local government.

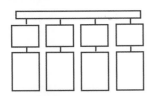

▲ Many states are divided into counties.

Key Terms

board
ordinances

municipality
charters

Main Idea

There are many varieties of local governments. Certain governmental structures are ideal for small towns. Large city governments are organized in a different fashion.

Target Reading Skill

Compare and Contrast When you compare two or more things, you notice how they are alike. When you contrast them, you look for differences. As you read this section, think about the similarities and differences among various types of local government.

The Constitution gives powers to the federal and state governments, but not to local governments—counties, cities, and towns. Local governments are created by the states and have only those powers that state governments give them. The powers that state governments give to local governments help meet the many needs of communities throughout the nation.

Many people you see every day work for local governments—teachers, librarians, bus drivers, police officers, and others. Your daily life runs on the services of local governments, such as garbage collection, road repair, and water supply. Local government is the level that is closest to you. It has the greatest effect on your everyday life.

Counties and Townships

Our oldest unit of local government is the county. Rooted in England, the county form of government came to North America with the English colonists. Settlers divided colonies into counties to carry out laws in rural areas. Because farmers lived far apart, county business was done at a place most people could reach within a day's wagon journey. This distance to the "county seat" set the boundaries of many counties.

Today, most counties help state governments keep law and order and collect taxes. Counties may also offer many other services, from libraries to health care.

County Officials Most counties are governed by county boards. A **board** is a group of people who manage the business of an organization. Most county boards, which are also called commissions, have three to five elected members, called commissioners or supervisors. Board members set up county programs and pass **ordinances**, which are local laws. The county board shares its power with other boards, which run hospitals, libraries, and other special programs.

Perhaps the best-known elected county official is the sheriff. The office of sheriff has its roots in England, just like the county form of government itself. The sheriff, with the help of deputies, runs the county jail and makes sure people obey the law. Sheriffs often work in rural areas not covered by city or state police. Other county officials may include the assessor, who figures property values; the treasurer, who sends the property tax bill; and the county clerk, who keeps official records such as marriage certificates.

Townships In the Middle Atlantic states and in the Midwest, counties are often divided into townships. At first, townships were needed to help carry out duties such as setting up schools and repairing roads in rural areas far from the county seat. Over the years, though, cities have grown larger and transportation has improved, so most of these duties have been taken over by county and city governments. In many urban areas, townships just elect representatives to serve on the county board.

Deputy Sheriff
The sheriff's office plays an important role in maintaining law and order. Here a deputy dusts evidence for fingerprints.

✔ Reading Check   **What is the difference between a county and a township?**

Local Elections
County officials for Broward County, Florida, meet to discuss upcoming elections.

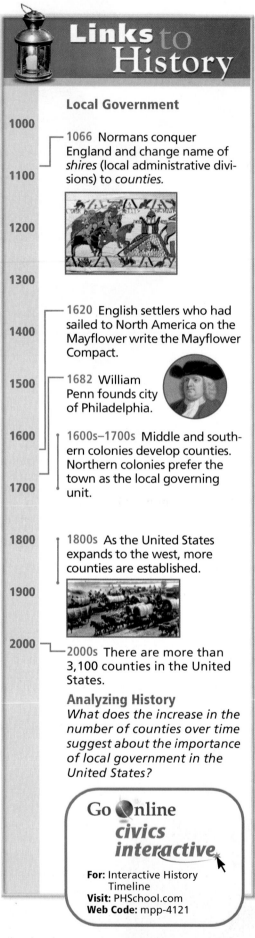

1000

1066 Normans conquer England and change name of *shires* (local administrative divisions) to *counties*.

1100

1200

1300

1400

1620 English settlers who had sailed to North America on the Mayflower write the Mayflower Compact.

1500

1682 William Penn founds city of Philadelphia.

1600

1600s–1700s Middle and southern colonies develop counties. Northern colonies prefer the town as the local governing unit.

1700

1800

1800s As the United States expands to the west, more counties are established.

1900

2000

2000s There are more than 3,100 counties in the United States.

Analyzing History
What does the increase in the number of counties over time suggest about the importance of local government in the United States?

Go Online
civics
interactive

For: Interactive History Timeline
Visit: PHSchool.com
Web Code: mpp-4121

New England Towns

In New England, another form of rural government grew up—the town. When people from other countries came to the New England colonies, they were given land. Groups of settlers started a town by building villages with homes, a church, and a school. They also planted crops in the nearby farmlands. The town was made up of both the village and the farmlands.

Citizens took an active part in local government in the early New England towns. The voters met once a year at town meetings to pass laws, set taxes, and decide how the money should be spent. This kind of town meeting still takes place today in some small New England towns. It is the closest thing we have to direct democracy.

At the yearly town meeting in a New England town, citizens elect a board of three to five members. The board carries on town business during the year. Other officials, such as the school board members, the town clerk, the assessor, and the treasurer, are chosen by the town board or elected by the voters. As you can see, towns in New England have most of the duties that counties have in other regions.

Like townships, New England towns have changed over the years. Because some towns have become large, it is not easy for all the citizens to gather together to decide things. Therefore, in many large towns the voters choose representatives to attend town meetings. Some towns have hired managers to take care of the town's business.

✔ **Reading Check** **What makes a town meeting the closest thing we have to direct democracy?**

Special Districts

Sometimes it does not make sense for a community to handle certain matters alone. For example, it would not make sense for each community in a dry region to build its own water supply system. It would be too much work and cost too much money. In such a case, all the communities in the region ask the state to make a special water district to supply water to the whole region.

A special district is a unit of government that generally provides a single service. It can serve one community or cover parts or all of several communities. Special districts serve many needs. In cities, they provide subways and parks. Rural special districts protect people from fires or control insects. Most such districts are run by a board. One special district that you know about is your school district.

✔ **Reading Check** **What can a special district do that an individual community cannot?**

Cities

A government that serves people who live in an urban area is called a **municipality**. Most municipalities, especially those that serve large populations, are called cities. Some municipalities that serve small populations are called towns or villages.

As the population of the United States has grown, so also have the sizes of our cities. Today a mid-sized American city has between 25,000 and 250,000 citizens. Several cities have millions of people. Governments of large cities must meet many different needs, including pollution control and drug abuse programs.

The boundaries and powers of a municipality—which can be a city, town, or village—are set by the state. Some communities write **charters**, or plans of government, that must be approved by the state. In other communities, the plan of government is set by state laws. No matter how they are formed, the governments of most municipalities follow one of three plans: mayor-council, council-manager, or commission.

Cities and Towns
Running a large city poses very different challenges to local leaders than does meeting the needs of a small town.
Contrast *What are some needs of large city that you would not expect to find in a small town?*

The Mayor-Council Plan The mayor-council plan also comes from England. The mayor, like the English prime minister or the American President, is the executive. The council, like the English Parliament or the American Congress, is the legislative branch. About 35 percent of the cities in the United States use the mayor-council plan. Under this plan, the duties and powers of city officials depend on whether the city uses a weak-mayor plan or a strong-mayor plan.

Under the weak-mayor plan, the mayor does not have special executive powers. In fact, most of the power rests with the council. The council is elected by the people and acts as both a legislative and executive body. The council can choose the mayor from among its members. The council also chooses other officials, makes ordinances, and decides how money should be spent.

The weak-mayor plan dates back to the colonies. The early settlers in the colonies did not trust the English government. When they formed their own city governments, they did not want to give too much power to one person.

Mayor-Council Plans

Mayors have different powers under different types of local government.
1. **Analyze** Under the strong-mayor plan, how are the department heads chosen?
2. **Apply** How does the role of voters differ in each plan?

In the early 1900s, New York City was under the control of a political machine known as Tammany Hall. In this cartoon, artist Thomas Nast explores the corruption of local government.

1. Describe what is happening in the cartoon. Do the voters look happy or angry?
2. What important point about election corruption does the cartoon make? What do you think Nast hoped to do by publishing this cartoon?

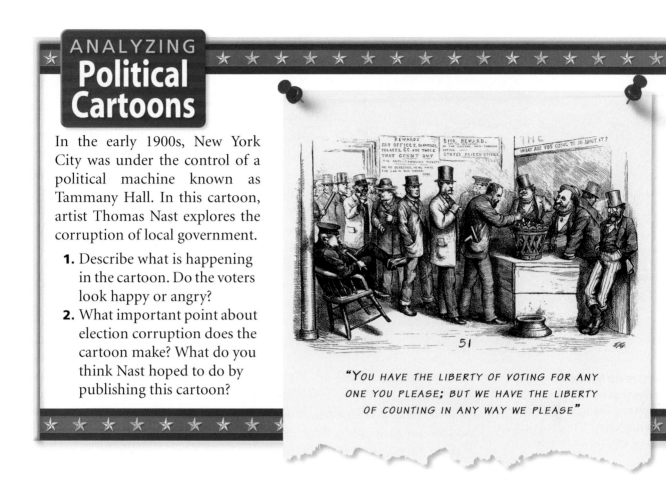

"YOU HAVE THE LIBERTY OF VOTING FOR ANY ONE YOU PLEASE; BUT WE HAVE THE LIBERTY OF COUNTING IN ANY WAY WE PLEASE"

During the first century of our nation's history, most cities used the weak-mayor plan. As cities grew in size, however, stronger leadership was needed in city hall. By the late 1800s, most large cities had switched to a strong-mayor plan. In this plan, the relationship between the mayor and the council is more like that between the President and Congress. The council makes ordinances, but the mayor is elected by the voters and is in charge of the budget, makes policies, and chooses city officials.

The Council-Manager Plan By the early 1900s, many cities were in the grasp of political groups called "machines." City officials did favors for the machine, such as giving jobs to politicians and friends. In return, the machine helped the officials get elected again. This arrangement often led to corruption. Officials looked after their own interests instead of looking after the public interest.

To create honest government, some people came up with the council-manager plan. The goal of this plan is to run government like a business. In the council-manager plan, the council is chosen through an election in which candidates have no political ties. The council makes ordinances and hires a city manager to handle day-to-day city business. It is the manager, not the mayor, who prepares the budget and is in charge of people who work for the city. Because the manager is not elected, he or she is supposed to be free from political pressures.

Target Reading Skill
Compare and Contrast As you read about the council-manager plan, compare and contrast it to the mayor-council plan. How are they similar? How are they different?

The Great Storm
The destruction of the city of Galveston, Texas, in 1900 led to the creation of the commission form of city government.

The Commission Plan Another reform of city government took place in Galveston, Texas, in 1900. The city had been destroyed by a hurricane. The weak-mayor government that Galveston had at that time could not manage the rebuilding. Local citizens convinced the state to approve a new form of government called a commission plan. Under this plan, voters choose several commissioners who make ordinances together. In addition, each commissioner directs one of the city's departments.

The commission plan worked so well in rebuilding Galveston that hundreds of other cities decided to try it. However, the plan does not provide for a single leader to control the budget and make the departments work together. In the past few years Galveston and most other cities that tried the plan have decided not to use it any more.

No matter what the strengths and the weaknesses are of a plan of local government, its success or failure lies in the hands of its citizens. Today, most cities seek advice from groups made up of people who live there. Citizens *can be* heard in city hall.

✓ Reading Check **What are the strengths and weaknesses of the commission plan?**

SECTION 1 Assessment

Key Terms

Use each of the key terms in a sentence that explains its meaning: board, ordinances, municipality, charters

Target Reading Skill

1. Compare and Contrast What are the most important similarities and differences among the various types of local government?

Comprehension and Critical Thinking

2. a. Recall What are the duties of county board members?
b. Support a Point of View Which county officials are the

most important? Why?

3. a. Describe How is the government of a New England town run?
b. Link Past and Present Why do you think New England towns continue to use this method of governing?

4. a. Explain What is the purpose of a special district?
b. Make Decisions Give an example of a situation that would best be dealt with by a special district.

5. a. Describe Describe the two types of mayor-council plans.
b. Contrast In which of these two plans do the citizens play a more active role? Explain.

Writing Activity

Do some research online or at the library to find out how your own local government is structured. Write a report that identifies the type of government, explains how it works, and lists and describes its most important officials.

TIP Make an outline before you start writing. Identify major topics and subtopics of your research. This will help you write a well-organized report.

Local Government Services and Revenue

Reading Preview

Objectives
In this section you will
- Examine how local governments provide education, health, and public safety services.
- Discuss how local governments provide utilities.
- Understand how local governments control land use.
- Learn how local governments collect revenue to pay for services.

Key Terms
utilities   intergovernmental
zoning   revenue
property tax   grant

Main Idea
Local governments provide a wide variety of important everyday services. Several sources of revenue help pay for these services.

Target Reading Skill
Use Signal Words Signal words point out relationships among ideas or events. For example, words that have opposite meanings often signal a contrast. As you read this section, take note of signal words that indicate comparison or contrast.

Taking Notes
Make a diagram like the one below. As you read this section, complete the left side of the diagram with information about local government services. Complete the right side with information about local government revenues.

In one town, a concerned mother wants the city council to ban skateboarding in public places. She feels it is dangerous to pedestrians. A skateboarder disagrees. Instead, he wants the town to build a skatepark for skateboarders.

We ask local governments to help us in many ways. They provide **utilities**, or services needed by the public, such as water, gas, and electricity. They build parks, schools, and roads. They plan for community growth.

Every time officials decide to handle a problem in a certain way, they are making policy. If the council bans skateboarding, it is making a public safety policy. Another policy might be to build a skate park.

Policy decisions often depend on money. Because no government has all the money it needs, officials must decide which services to offer. The council might decide that it does not have enough money to build a skate park, but it will allow skateboarders to use an empty parking lot. Perhaps the park could be built if skateboarders were charged money to use it.

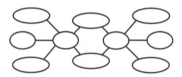

◄ Local leaders decide if skateboarding is allowed in parks.

Education, Health, and Public Safety

Local governments provide many services that meet many citizens' human needs. Those services include education, health and welfare services, and public safety.

High School Exit Exams

A student's education is affected by local, state, and federal levels of government. Many states have passed laws requiring students to pass an exit exam in order to receive a high school diploma.

★ The purpose of statewide exit exams is to hold students accountable for meeting state standards for reading, writing, mathematics, and other subjects.

★ In Florida, more than 12,000 students were not allowed to graduate in 2003. Many were students just learning the English language.

★ In Nevada, one out of twelve high school seniors did not pass the exit exam. Ninety-eight percent of those that failed could not pass the math portion.

Applying the Law

1. **Analyzing Information** Why have state legislatures passed laws requiring high school exit exams?
2. **Solve Problems** How might local governments respond to high failure rates?

Target Reading Skill

Use Signal Words Identify the signal word in the paragraph that begins "Most programs...." Does it indicate a comparison or a contrast? How?

Education The service that local governments spend the most money on is education. Local governments—counties, cities, and school districts—provide all public education from elementary through high school. Some also are in charge of two-year colleges. Local school boards build schools and hire teachers and staff to run them. Many local boards have a strong say in what courses will be taught.

The federal and state governments are also important in public education. State officials set standards for school employees and buildings. State governments have a strong say in how schools are run because they pay about one third or more of schooling costs. The federal government helps to pay for buildings, school lunch programs, and programs for children with special needs.

Local and state governments often do not agree about which of them should have greater control over state education money. State officials make sure state standards are met. They also make sure that children in all school districts have equal opportunities. On the other hand, local control can be good for schools because local citizens know what the students need.

Health and Welfare Millions of Americans are poor, too ill to work, or unable to find jobs or homes. Many people help the needy, but it is a very big job. Local governments play a part by offering health and child care to families that need extra assistance. Other local programs train people for new careers and provide low-cost places to live.

Most programs giving public assistance, or welfare, are paid for by federal, state, and local governments together. However, local officials carry out the programs. The city of Atlanta, Georgia, for example, was recently recognized for its success in using federal funds to improve low-cost public housing in several Atlanta neighborhoods.

Communities also look after public health. In many cases, local officials carry out state health laws. Local health officials inspect restaurants, markets, hotels, and water to be sure that state and federal standards are met. Many communities also make sure that federal and state laws to control pollution are obeyed.

Public Safety If you had an emergency, what would you do? You might call the police or fire department, or dial 911. If you were witnessing a crime, the Police Department would send a police office to stop the crime and speak with you about what happened. Other members of the department would follow up on the crime to recover lost property and bring the criminal to justice. If you called 911 to report a fire, the Fire Department would dispatch a fire truck to put out the fire, help people affected by the fire, and protect nearby buildings. In the case of a medical emergency, a local dispatcher might send an ambulance to help. The ambulance would bring the sick or injured person to a local hospital or medical center where doctors would treat the patient regardless of ability to pay.

Police officers and firefighters also look after the public safety in non-emergencies. The police help citizens stop crime by teaching them how to keep people from breaking into their homes. The fire department checks for fire hazards, such as faulty wiring, and teaches safety rules to children.

Local governments also hire people to make sure that safety rules, called codes, are followed. A fire code may say that all buildings must have smoke alarms. Building codes make sure that new buildings are built safely.

Firefighters
Your local fire department is an important service provided by your local government.

✓ Reading Check   **What role does a local government play in community health?**

Students Make a Difference

Ryan Melville has always had a deep interest in politics and history. At Peabody Veterans Memorial High School, Ryan is Senior Class President, an active member of student council, and participates in Northeastern University's Model Arab League.

Ryan also participates in the Yankee Division Veteran's Association history project. One year, he toured World War II historical sites in Europe with the group and recorded their stories. He then presented lectures on the group's history to local community groups.

Service Learning

How can you make a difference for local veterans' groups in your community?

▲ Students can help make a difference by learning from their elders.

Steam rises from a nuclear reactor in Stedman, Missouri.
▼

Utilities

You may not even notice some local government services. However, you would certainly notice if you no longer had them. These government services include the utilities. Utilities is a term that describes such services as water, gas, electricity, sewage treatment plants, and garbage collection.

In many cases, water and sewage treatment plants are owned and run by local governments. Communities often arrange for private companies to supply gas and electricity and to pick up garbage. The state makes rules to make sure the companies deliver good services at fair rates.

Utilities are best provided at the local level, where they can be planned to fit a community's needs. For example, in Emmonak, Alaska, the ground freezes in winter. Sewer pipes are not put underground because they would freeze, too. Instead, sewer pipes made of materials that will not freeze are laid above ground—a method that fits the Arctic climate. If utilities were provided at the state or federal level, these governments would not be well equipped to meet the different needs of local communities.

Land Use

In many communities, homes and businesses are in separate areas. This is the result of **zoning**, local rules that divide a community into areas and tell how the land in each area can be used. For example, zoning may keep a factory from being built next to your home. Zoning is a tool used by local governments to plan and control the growth of their communities.

Things to Consider The people who plan communities think about where roads, parks, factories, and homes should be built. They must also think about how a new factory will affect the lives of people in the community. They must think about who will be using a park and whether it will need a playground or picnic tables. Will a new road bring too much traffic into downtown? Are there enough low-cost houses and apartments for families with low incomes? Planners must also look at how development affects the environment. Will the new factory have anti-pollution controls?

The Planning Process Planning is made up of many steps. A local government appoints a planning commission to set goals and get information about the community, such as its growth rate and types of businesses. Most commissions are made up of interested citizens, such as builders, environmentalists, and business leaders.

Commission members work with a staff that looks at requests from builders and reads reports about what building will do to the environment. The staff tells the commission what they think should be done about each request. The commission decides what to do. Then it presents the matter to the city council or county board, which makes the final decision.

Downtown Los Angeles
Los Angeles, which is one of the most densely populated cities in the United States, has grown in size over the years. One purpose of land-use planning is to prevent uncontrolled growth in towns and cities. **Predict** *What might happen to our towns and cities without land-use planning?*

▲
The city of Reno (left) gets its water from the Truckee River.

Some of the most heated battles in planning are over how fast communities should grow. New businesses mean more jobs and more tax money. However, new businesses may bring in more people, who will need water, schools, and parks. New businesses may also bring more traffic and pollution.

The city of Reno, Nevada grew rapidly during the 1980s and 1990s. This growth brought thousands of new jobs and lots of tax money to Reno. Local officials pointed out, however, that quick growth meant the city would also need more water. Reno gets its water from the Truckee River. The city could make land-use plans, but it could not make more water flow from the river. Planners must think about the resources they have as well as the short-term and long-term needs of citizens.

✔ Reading Check **List some important questions that may be asked when determining land use.**

Revenue: Paying for Services

To provide services to citizens, local governments need money. Like state governments, local governments depend on several sources of revenue.

Taxes About 25 percent of local government revenue comes from **property tax, a tax on land and buildings.** The county assessor decides how much the property is worth. He or she charges the property owner a fixed percentage of that value. Many people feel property tax is fair because the more property that citizens own, the more services they use, such as water and fire protection.

Some communities bring in money through other taxes, such as a local sales tax. About 3,300 local governments in more than a dozen states put an income tax on the salaries of people who work there. The idea is to collect money from people who use city services during the work day but live somewhere else.

Service Charges and Profits Cities often charge money for certain services, such as inspecting buildings to see that they meet safety codes. Communities also get money from bridge tolls, park entrance fees, and parking meters.

Some local governments make money by running businesses. For instance, the city of Naperville, Illinois, runs a parking garage. It brings in money while providing parking spaces for people who work and shop in the city. Government-owned utilities, such as electric companies, also bring in money and give low-cost service to local citizens and businesses.

Borrowing When revenue from taxes, fees, and city-owned businesses is not enough to cover their costs, local governments can borrow money. For short-term needs, they may borrow from banks. To pay for big projects, such as school buildings, communities borrow money by selling bonds.

Sharing Revenue **Intergovernmental revenue** money given by one level of government to another, is another source of funding for local government. Federal and state governments often give money to local communities. This money is called a **grant**. Grants are a way to make sure that services of national or state importance are provided at the local level.

Some grants are for special uses, such as summer job programs for youth, or large building projects. Others are block grants for general uses such as education. Block grants allow local officials to decide how best to use the money.

Analyze Charts

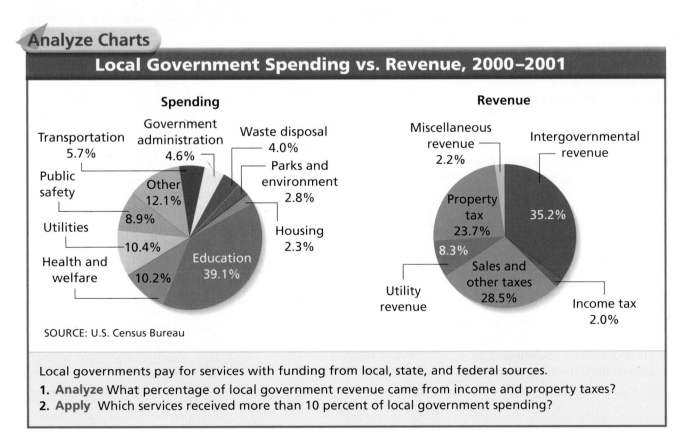

Local Government Spending vs. Revenue, 2000–2001

Spending

- Transportation 5.7%
- Government administration 4.6%
- Waste disposal 4.0%
- Parks and environment 2.8%
- Public safety
- Other 12.1%
- Housing 2.3%
- Utilities 8.9%
- Health and welfare 10.4%
- Education 39.1%
- 10.2%

Revenue

- Miscellaneous revenue 2.2%
- Intergovernmental revenue 35.2%
- Property tax 23.7%
- Utility revenue 8.3%
- Sales and other taxes 28.5%
- Income tax 2.0%

SOURCE: U.S. Census Bureau

Local governments pay for services with funding from local, state, and federal sources.

1. **Analyze** What percentage of local government revenue came from income and property taxes?
2. **Apply** Which services received more than 10 percent of local government spending?

▲ Former Mayor Willie Brown, Jr. of San Francisco

Limits on Revenue Most communities face problems in paying for services. The demand for services is generally greater than the amount of money available to the community to pay for them. Sources of money may "run dry." Another problem is that the power to tax is controlled by the state. The state spells out what kinds of taxes may be collected and how the money may be used.

Large cities can have a particularly difficult time balancing the money in the city treasury with the need for services. Former San Francisco mayor Willie Brown, Jr. discussed this challenge when presenting his year 2003 budget to the people of San Francisco.

"Confronted with the harsh realities of a struggling national economy, a catastrophic state budget crisis and severely diminished local tax revenues, my administration set out to craft a balanced spending plan that protects the people of San Francisco and lays out the groundwork for economic recovery."

✔ Reading Check **Why do cities tax people who live elsewhere?**

SECTION 2 Assessment

Key Terms

Use each of the key terms in a sentence that explains its meaning: utilities, zoning, property tax, intergovernmental revenue, grant

Target Reading Skill

1. **Make Comparisons** What do local government services have in common? Explain.

Comprehension and Critical Thinking

2. **a. Recall** Identify the important human services that local governments provide to individuals in their communities.
   b. Identify Cause Why is local government, rather than state or federal government, in charge of running these services?

3. **a. Describe** What role do local governments play in providing utilities?
   b. Identify Effect How would things change in your community if the state or federal government controlled or provided utilities?

4. **a. Explain** Why are local zoning laws necessary?
   b. Make Generalizations When do you think a government should agree to waive or change zoning laws?

5. **a. Recall** What are a local government's sources of revenue?
   b. Explain Do you think the relationship between local taxes and services is reasonable? Why or why not?

Writing Activity

You are the head of the zoning board in a large city. The major-league baseball team is ready to build a new 50,000-seat stadium. The team is asking the board to waive the zoning laws so that it can build on a large plot of land near a quiet residential neighborhood. Write a letter to the team owner explaining why your board will or will not allow the stadium to go up on that site.

TIP Before you begin writing, think about the impact a stadium would have on a neighborhood. Consider such factors as parking, noise, and local opinion.

Debating the Issues

CLOSE UP FOUNDATION

The debates in this feature are based on *Current Issues*, published by the Close Up Foundation. Go to **PHSchool.com**, Web Code mph-4122, to read the latest issue of *Current Issues* online.

More than 65 million immigrants have moved to the United States since 1820. As the population grew, Congress began to limit immigration. In spite of these limits, people are still moving to the United States—some illegally. Some stay here after their visas or work permits expire. Others come secretly, without these documents. Illegal immigrants come for many of the same reasons that legal immigrants do—economic opportunity and freedom. Illegal immigrants often have little difficulty finding jobs because they are generally willing to work for very low pay. Since 1996, illegal immigrants have been entitled to no benefits except emergency medical care, immunization programs, and disaster relief.

Should the Government Provide Social Services to Illegal Immigrants?

YES

- It is cruel and unfair to deny basic health and welfare services to people in need, even if they are citizens.
- Immigrants will continue to come to the United States no matter what the laws are. Denying them social services will not keep them away. It will only prevent them from getting health care or an education. In the long run, this will harm the United States.

NO

- Illegal immigrants are not citizens. They should not be allowed to take advantage of the privileges of citizenship when they do not pay taxes or vote. It is not fair to make citizens pay for social services for non-citizens.
- If the government denied social services to illegal immigrants, it would discourage them from entering the country illegally.

What Is Your Opinion?

1. **Link Past and Present** With the exception of Native Americans, every U.S. citizen is either an immigrant or the descendant of immigrant. Given this history, should the United States deny social services to illegal immigrants? Explain.

2. **Make Predictions** Assume that Congress is about to grant full social services to all immigrants. Predict the consequences. Give reasons for your predictions.

3. **Writing to Persuade** Suppose you run a health clinic. You and your staff must decide whether to accept illegal immigrants as patients. Write a memorandum giving your opinion, including reasons that will convince the staff that your position is the correct one.

Go Online
civics interactive

For: You Decide Poll
Visit: PHSchool.com
Web Code: mpp-4122

Conflict and Cooperation Between Governments

Reading Preview

Objectives

In this section you will

■ Describe relations between local governments and between local and state governments.

■ Examine relations between local, state, and federal governments.

Taking Notes

Make diagram like the one below. As you read this section, complete the diagram with information about how local governments conflict and cooperate with other levels of government.

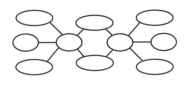

Key Terms

councils of governments
home rule

Main Idea

Local governments work with other local governments, their state government, and the federal government to get things done. These working relationships involve both cooperation and conflict.

Target Reading Skill

Make Comparisons Comparing two or more things helps you remember what they have in common and how they relate to one another. As you read this section, compare the responsibilities of our local, state, and federal governments.

U.S. Conference of Mayors
Newly elected president James A. Garner (left) shakes hands with outgoing president Thomas M. Menino (right).

Look in your phone book and see how many levels of government are listed that serve you. Like most citizens, you probably live under at least four layers of government.

Almost every town, city, and township lies inside a county or parish. All these local governments must answer to their state governments. Of course, the nation as a whole is guided by the federal government. As the layers overlap, governments cooperate and come into conflict.

Relations Between Local Governments

A county official in the Detroit area became alarmed in 1954 that the region's services were not keeping up with its growth. As the Detroit area grew, development crossed city and county lines. He met with officials of neighboring counties to figure out how to meet area-wide needs. Soon other regions were holding meetings, too. Groups that work together to meet regional needs became known as **councils of governments**.

Other groups, such as the United States Conference of Mayors, are also ways of linking local governments. Officials from these groups talk about matters that affect them all, and they work together to look for solutions. Since cooperation would seem to help everyone, what causes conflicts between local governments?

Conflict One big cause of conflicts between local governments is economics. Communities often compete to attract new businesses, which pay new property taxes. Communities also compete to get federal money.

Another cause of conflicts is the effect of one community's policies on neighboring communities. One city may zone an area for new factories. However, when the pollution from that factory zone blows into a neighboring city, the stage is set for conflict.

Cooperation Problems can also lead to cooperation. Sometimes communities work together to provide services that would cost too much for each to provide for itself. Townships have teamed up to answer emergency calls. Each township's fire department offers something different, such as clothing that protects people from fire or training for emergencies.

Small communities may also turn to counties for help. A county can build a jail or hospital to serve several small towns.

Library Funding
Some local governments have worked together to build libraries for communities that do not have the money to build one on their own.

✓ Reading Check **How do citizens benefit when local governments work together?**

Local and State Governments

Many states have a strong voice in deciding how local governments will be set up. Other states have granted cities and some counties **home rule**, the right to write their own charter.

Conflict The question of what is a local matter and what is also a state matter can lead to conflict. For example, California wanted to build a sewage plant for the city of Arcata. The state had received federal money for the plant. However, Arcata would have had to pay millions of dollars, as well.

Arcata came up with a plan for a cheaper sewage system, but the state said no. City officials spent two years meeting with state officials. Finally, Arcata won the right to build the system it wanted instead of the system preferred by the state of California. When local and state laws come into conflict, however, state law is almost always enforced.

Civics and Economics

LOVE Park Skateboarders everywhere traveled to Philadelphia to skate in its famous LOVE Park. With its granite and marble ledges and steep inclines, LOVE Park helped draw the X Games to Philadelphia two years in a row. This brought the city millions of dollars in revenue from athletes and spectators.

LOVE Park is also a popular spot for tourists who come to see Robert Indiana's well-known sculpture of the word "LOVE." In 2002, the park was renovated to make it more pleasant for visitors. The mayor banned skating from the park. The X Games did not return to Philadelphia the following year.

Analyzing Economics
How do you think banning skateboarding from LOVE Park affected the economy of Philadelphia?

Cooperation Many state governments work directly with local governments to solve local problems. The city of Evanston turned to the Illinois Environmental Protection Agency for help in building a park over what had been a garbage dump. The job was hard because rotten garbage is not a stable surface and makes a gas that can blow up if trapped. Together, city and state officials worked out plans to cover the garbage with a layer of clay and to build a vent for the gas to escape.

States often work with local governments to carry out state programs. When a state highway commission plans a road that will cut through a city, it consults with the city council. Both levels of government work together to make sure state and local needs are met. States also help local programs run smoothly. State officials help local officials in finance, law enforcement, health, and education. Also, states license local government workers, such as public school teachers and doctors at public hospitals.

✓ Reading Check **Why do you think state governments usually win conflicts with local governments?**

Analyze Diagrams

Relations Among Governments: The No Child Left Behind Act

This diagram shows how the three levels of government—federal, state, and local—work together to ensure that each child receives a good education.

The No Child Left Behind Act became law in 2002. The law requires that public schools in every state meet national education standards. Under the law, federal funding for public schools is tied to school performance in each state.

a. What are the responsibilities of each state government?

b. What are the responsibilities of the federal government after each state submits its test results?

1 Federal government establishes national education standards.

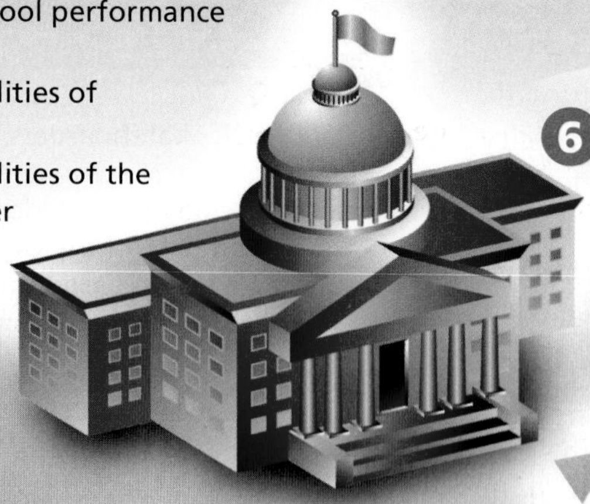

6 Federal government reviews test results. Federal funds given to state are dependent on school performance.

Federal

5 State compiles test results from all public schools and reports results to federal government.

Local, State, and Federal Governments

Money is the key to the relations of local governments to state and federal governments. The federal government gives grants and loans to local governments for housing, public assistance, and other uses. The idea is to use federal money at the local level to meet national goals. For example, the federal government gives grants to states for job-training programs. Then the states decide how to divide up the money among local governments that run the programs. The federal government also gives aid directly to local governments.

Federal, state, and local governments also work together to improve education. For example, President George W. Bush signed the No Child Left Behind Act into law in 2002. Under this law, states must show that their public schools make yearly progress by testing students in reading and math. The amount of federal funding a state can receive for education depends on how well the students perform in that state's schools. Local state, and federal governments must cooperate to make sure children receive proper education.

Target Reading Skill

Make Comparisons Reread the two paragraphs on this page. Compare the examples that show how federal money is used at the local level to meet national goals.

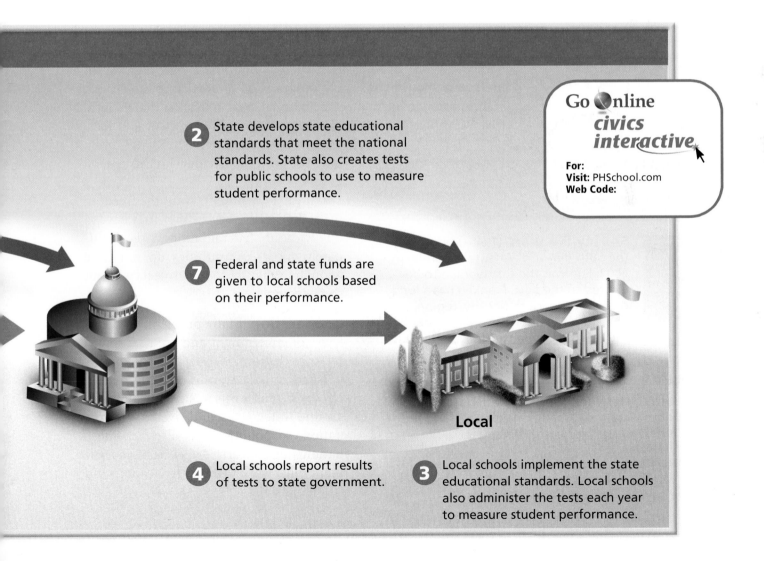

Go Online
civics interactive

For:
Visit: PHSchool.com
Web Code:

2 State develops state educational standards that meet the national standards. State also creates tests for public schools to use to measure student performance.

7 Federal and state funds are given to local schools based on their performance.

Local

4 Local schools report results of tests to state government.

3 Local schools implement the state educational standards. Local schools also administer the tests each year to measure student performance.

Big Dig
The Massachusetts Central Artery project (known as "Big Dig"), is the largest public works project in American history. Funding for this highway project came from federal, state, and local sources.
Make Generalizations *Why would the federal government be interested in improving the highway system of a particular state?*

Conflict Sometimes local officials disagree with federal and state officials over how to spend grant money. Most federal money for local governments can be used only in certain ways. Funding can be marked for very specific uses, such as building a new highway or funding a medical research program at a particular university. Grants given to help meet a national goal may not match local needs. Conflicts can also arise between state government and local leaders over funding. The states often have the power to decide who gets federal grants.

If local governments want the freedom to set their own policies, they may have to do without federal money. Unfortunately, most communities do not have enough money to do big projects without some federal help.

Cooperation Many problems affect all levels of government and are best solved by cooperation. If one factory dumps poisonous wastes, it is a local matter. However, poisonous wastes have polluted ground water, lakes, and rivers across the nation, so pollution has also become a nationwide concern. All levels of government must work together to clean up and stop pollution.

Citizen Profiles

Shirley Franklin (1945–) became the 58th mayor of Atlanta, Georgia, in 2002. She was the first woman to be elected to the post. Franklin has a long career of service to her city, region, and state. While she was a member of the Atlanta Committee for the Olympic Games and Vice-Chairman of the Georgia Regional Transportation Authority, she formed strong ties with regional and state leaders. She has used these close working relationships to help Atlanta secure state and federal funding for major city projects.

Citizenship
Why would Franklin's ties to regional and state leaders be helpful to her as mayor of Atlanta?

Local, state, and federal governments also cooperate in providing services, such as law enforcement. The Federal Bureau of Investigation (FBI) trains local police in the latest ways of fighting crime. Local police turn to the FBI for records of suspected criminals. Local, state, and federal officers work together to solve crimes like bank robbery and kidnapping.

The federal-state-local partnership is a good way to deal with nationwide issues. It also brings local problems to national attention because local officials can tell state and federal officials what their citizens want. Even though there are conflicts, they can lead to creative solutions.

Individuals at all levels of state government can work together to advance their common interests. It is not unusual for a member of Congress to work with a state legislator who represents the same constituents to find federal funding for a local need. In the same way, a mayor can call a state legislator for help with a local problem. In a serious case, mayors can contact Congressional representatives for help. If you want to take part in finding solutions, local government is a good place to start.

✔ Reading Check **How might citizens in one community benefit from a faraway community's relationship with the federal government?**

SECTION 3 Assessment

Key Terms

Use each of the key terms in a sentence that explains its meaning: councils of governments, home rule

Target Reading Skill

1. **Use Signal Words** List one word or phrase from this section that signals a comparison and one that signals a contrast. Explain what or who is being compared or contrasted.

Comprehension and Critical Thinking

2. **a. Describe** What economic reasons cause conflict and competition between local governments?

    b. Solve Problems How might two local governments resolve such a conflict?

3. **a. Recall** What kinds of problems do state governments help local ones out with?

    b. Draw Inferences Why are state governments willing to help local ones?

4. **a. Explain** Why does the federal government give grants and loans to local communities?

    b. Identify Alternatives What can local governments do if they want to use federal money for a special project?

Writing Activity

Go online to your state's web site. Look for information about the relationship between the state government and the smaller local governments. Write an essay describing the ways in which your state and local governments are working together.

Go Online
PHSchool.com

For: Essay
Visit: PHSchool.com
Web Code: mpd-4123

Distinguishing Facts and Opinions

When reading any text, it is important to be able to distinguish between facts and opinions. A fact can be proven right or wrong. "Chicago is the largest city in the United States" is a statement of fact because it can be proven wrong. An opinion cannot be proven. "I like Chicago better than New York" is an opinion because it tells how someone feels about something.

Excerpt from a Letter in a Local Newspaper

The school budget is set at $6.2 million. That is a 10% increase over last year's budget of $5.58 million. Five percent of that 10% figure is a result of rising health care costs. We have no direct control over that number. But 3% of the increase is going towards such items as buying new buses and renovating the music room, and I think these choices are wrong. We can save money by simply repairing the buses that need repairs. And the music room is fine the way it is. Spending $51,000 on the music room is just crazy. We also need to look for other items to cut from the budget. I think that people should look for ways to save money in these hard times instead of looking for ways to get something new.

Learn the Skill

Follow these steps to distinguish fact from opinion:

① **Identify statements of fact.** Find the statements that can be proven. These may include numbers, dates, or events that have happened.

② **Identify statements of opinion.** Find statements that cannot be proven. One clue is sentences that begin "I think," "I believe," or "I feel." Also look for emotion-packed words that tell how the writer feels.

③ **Note how opinions and facts are related.** Are the opinions supported by facts?

④ **Identify points of view.** What is the writer's point of view about the topic?

Practice the Skill

Read the excerpt above and answer the following questions:

① (a) Identify one statement of fact.
(b) Explain how the fact could be proven.

② (a) Identify one statement of opinion.
(b) Find an emotion-packed word.

③ Is each opinion presented supported by facts?

④ How would you summarize the writer's point of view on the issue?

Apply the Skill

Find an editorial or a letter to the editor in a newspaper about a topic you are interested in. Underline the statements of fact and circle the statements of opinion. Then write a brief statement that accurately shows the writer's point of view.

CHAPTER 12

Review and Assessment

Chapter Summary

Section 1
Types of Local Government
(pages 320–326)

- County governments may include smaller township governments within their borders.
- A county is usually governed by a **board** that sets up programs and passes **ordinances.**
- The town is a form of rural government that began in New England.
- A special district is a unit of government that provides a single service for one or several communities.
- A **municipality** may have a **charter,** or plan of government, that is approved by the state.
- City governments may use a strong or weak mayor-council plan, a council-manager plan, or a commission plan.

Section 2
Local Government Services and Revenue
(pages 327–334)

- Local governments provide services related to education, health, and public safety.
- Local governments own or supervise **utilities** within the community.
- **Zoning** helps local governments plan and control land use in their communities.
- In exchange for the services the local government provides, citizens pay a variety of taxes and fees, including a **property tax.**
- To fund certain services or special programs, local governments can borrow money or receive **intergovernmental revenue** in the form of a state or federal grant.

Section 3
Conflict and Cooperation Between Governments
(pages 336–341)

- Local governments often work together as **councils of governments** on projects or concerns that one government could not afford or manage on its own.
- Local governments sometimes come into conflict over economic and other issues.
- Local governments can turn to state governments for help with major public-engineering projects.
- Some state governments grant cities and counties **home rule,** the right to write their own charter.
- Federal governments will help local governments financially with problems that affect the nation.

Copy the chart below and use it to help you summarize the chapter:

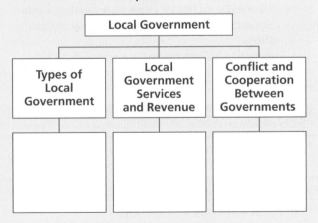

Review and Assessment Continued

Reviewing Key Terms

Fill in each blank with one of the key terms from the list below.

board
charters
home rule
utilities
zoning

municipality
intergovernmental revenue
grant
ordinances
property tax

1. A large city is also known as a _____.

2. _____ allows local governments to decide on the proper mix of businesses and residences in their communities.

3. _____ include electricity, water, and gas.

4. Local governments use the _____ that you pay on your land and buildings to provide essential services.

5. If your community needs money for a special project, it can apply for a _____ from the federal government.

6. When a city is granted _____, it can write its own charter.

7. A county is usually governed by a _____ of elected members.

8. _____ are local laws.

Comprehension and Critical Thinking

9. **a. Describe** Describe the various types of city governments.
   b. Compare and Contrast What are the advantages of each of the two types of mayor-council plans?
   c. Demonstrate Reasoned Judgment Which city-government plan do you think is best? Why?

10. **a. Explain** What are the purposes of zoning laws?
    b. Identify Effects How can zoning laws accomplish their purposes? Give examples.
    c. Predict What might happen in a community if there were no zoning laws?

11. **a. Recall** Why do local governments sometimes work together?
    b. Identify Alternatives What happens when local governments can't agree on an issue?
    c. Make Generalizations Why do local governments need to cooperate with each other in the end?

Activities

12. **Skills** Read the paragraph to the right and answer the following questions. **a.** Identify a statement of fact and explain why it is a fact. **b.** Identify a statement of opinion and explain why it is an opinion.

13. **Writing** Find a local-government issue on which you have a strong opinion. Write a letter to the head of your local government, urging him or her to support your position on this issue.

Chicago and the state of Illinois had almost finished an underground walkway between the city hall and the state government building in 1989. City workers had tunneled from one direction and state workers from the other. As the two teams approached one another in the center, the workers realized that one team had built its half of the walkway nine inches higher than and eight inches to one side of the other half. Obviously, not enough planning had gone into the project.

14. **Active Citizen** Find out about volunteer opportunities within your local government, such as cleanup projects or tutoring young children. Give a presentation describing these opportunities to the class.

15. **Math Practice** Find out how many people voted in the last local election. Compare this number to the total community population old enough to vote. Determine the percentage of eligible citizens who vote in your community.

16. **Civics and Economics** Find out how much people in your community pay in local property taxes. Compare the taxes to the services citizens receive in exchange. Do you think local tax rates are fair, or do you think they should be changed?

17. **Analyzing Visuals** Explain how this photo illustrates the idea of conflict between the different levels of government.

Standardized Test Prep

Test-taking Tips

Standardized tests often ask you to read a passage and answer questions about it. Read this description of a popular local-government program in Philadelphia and answer the sample question.

In an effort to help fight Philadelphia's daily battle with graffiti, Mayor Wilson Goode created the popular Mural Arts Program in 1984. This program identifies walls that are likely targets for graffiti. It then assigns artists to paint murals on them. Neighborhood residents participate in design and planning. These colorful scenes bring art to neighborhoods at no charge. They also give citizens contact with their local government. Today, hundreds of murals brighten the city's neighborhoods and depict their history.

TIP When more than one answer choice is an accurate statement from the passage, read the question again to see which choice is the best one.

Choose the letter of the best answer.

1. The Mural Arts Program is popular because
   A it was created by Mayor Wilson Goode.
   B it makes neighborhoods more attractive.
   C it employs artists.
   D it identifies likely targets for graffiti.

   TIP Reread the question. Think about the meaning of the word *popular.*

   The correct answer is **B.** All the statements are true, but the beautification of the neighborhoods is what makes people like the program.

2. Which is NOT a likely reason for citizens to be involved in planning the murals?
   A They will have to see the murals in their neighborhoods every day.
   B They take pride in how their neighborhood will look.
   C They want to learn to paint.
   D They want to see that their neighborhood's history is shown respectfully.

UNIT
5

Foundations of Economics

What's Ahead in Unit 5

In Unit 5 you will learn about economic systems. You will learn how the American economic system works and how it is a basic part of our free society. You will also learn about the role you play in our economy.

CHAPTER 13
What Is an Economy?

CHAPTER 14
Basics of Our Economic System

CHAPTER 15
Our Economy and You

Why Study Civics?

What is an economic system? How does our economy work? What role will you play in the economy? How will understanding the economy help you plan for the future? These are all questions that can be addressed by the study of civics.

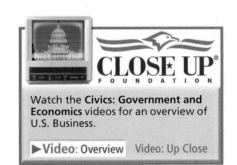

Watch the **Civics: Government and Economics** videos for an overview of U.S. Business.

▶**Video:** Overview   Video: Up Close

Standards for Civics and Government

National

The following National Standards are covered in this unit.

II. What are the foundations of the American political system?

B. What are the distinctive characteristics of American society?

C. What is American political culture?

D. What values and principles are basic to American constitutional democracy?

State

Go Online
PHSchool.com

For: Your state's Civics standards
Visit: PHSchool.com
Webcode: mpe5001

What's Ahead in Chapter 13

In this chapter you will read about economic wants, resources, and the decisions that must be made about using resources to satisfy wants. You will also find out about three different kinds of economic systems through which societies make these decisions.

SECTION 1
Why Societies Have Economies

SECTION 2
Basic Economic Decisions

SECTION 3
Three Types of Economies

TARGET READING SKILL

Sequence Understanding the sequence, or order, of events will help you remember how these events are related. As you read this chapter, you will use the skills of recognizing words that signal sequence and putting events in chronological order.

An outdoor market ▶

National | **Standards for Civics and Government** | **State**

The following National
Standards for Civics and
Government are covered
in this chapter:

II. What are the foundations
of the American political
system?

B. What are the distinctive
characteristics of American
government?

D. What values and principles
are basic to American constitutional democracy?

Active Citizen ▸ Civics in the Real World

"Guess what, Mike?" Jason exclaimed. "I got a job working at Rick's Bikes after school and on the weekends. I'll have money for movies and clothes, and I can start saving for a new computer."

Mike grinned. "That's great. I knew Rick would hire you. Let's go—hey, wait a second." He frowned. "If you take an after-school job can you stay on the soccer team?"

Josh's face fell. "I didn't think of that," he said. "I'd have to miss practice three times a week. And the games are all on Saturdays."

Josh has a problem. He wants to take a part-time job, but it means he'll have to give up his place on the soccer team. He has a tough decision to make.

Like Josh, societies have to balance their wants against their resources. To achieve this balance, they must make decisions. The system by which people in a society make decisions about how to use their resources to produce goods and services is called an economy.

Citizen's Journal   Do you think Josh should stay on the team, or should he give up soccer to take the job at Rick's Bikes? Which is more important, playing on the team or earning money? Explain your opinion in your journal.

Why Societies Have Economies

Reading Preview

Objectives

In this section you will

- Describe the characteristics of people's many wants and how resources satisfy wants.
- Describe
- Explain the steps of production to consumption.
- Determine how choices are made to satisfy wants.
- Discuss how scarcity affects economic choices.

Taking Notes

Make a diagram like the one below. As you read this section, complete the diagram with information about the main parts of an economy.

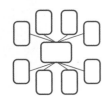

When we shop for food, such as the produce shown here, we are fulfilling a basic want.

▼

Key Terms

factors of production
capital

consumption
opportunity cost
scarcity

Main Idea

In an economic system, scarce resources are used to produce and distribute goods and services that satisfy people's needs and wants.

Target Reading Skill

Recognize Words That Signal Sequence Signal words, such as *at this time*, *soon after*, and *before*, point out relationships between ideas or events. As you read, look for signal words and phrases that help you understand the sequence of events.

In reading about Josh on page 349, you came across the basic economic facts of life: in any society, people must make choices about how to use their resources to produce goods and services to satisfy their wants. Notice that there are several elements to think about when looking at these economic facts—wants, resources, production of goods and services, and choices. By looking at how each of the elements is related to the others, you will gain a clearer understanding of what an economy is and why every society has one.

People's Many Wants

Everyone has wants. Our most basic wants are for food, clothing, and shelter. However, people are rarely satisfied to have just their basic wants met. People also want to be entertained, to be educated, and to have health care when they are sick. In fact, people have an almost endless number of wants.

Of course, your wants will differ from those of other people, depending on where you live and who you are. One important influence on your wants is your environment. If you live in Alaska, you will want to have warm clothes to wear and good heating for your house. In the hot weather of Phoenix, Arizona, these wants, of course, will be different.

Wants are also influenced by the societies in which we live and their cultures. Americans usually want to live in houses or apartments. For certain peoples in Mongolia, tents best fit their nomadic way of life.

Even when they live in the same environment and the same culture, different people want different things. Some people choose a vacation in the mountains, while others choose to go to the beach. You may favor white basketball shoes, while your best friend wants black ones.

People's wants can also change. Think of the toys you wanted when you were younger. How do they compare with the goods you want to have now?

Another important characteristic of wants is that many of them can be satisfied only for a short time. Do the jeans you wore last year still fit you, or do you need to buy a new pair? Understanding that many wants occur again and again is basic to learning what an economy is.

✔ Reading Check **List some of the factors that affect people's wants.**

Using Resources

The resources people have for producing goods and services to satisfy their wants are called **factors of production.** According to economists—the people who study how economies work—the three basic factors of production in an economy are labor, land, and capital.

Labor One factor of production, labor, includes time and energy. If Josh takes the job at Rick's Bikes, he will be using his time and energy to help sell bicycles. His labor will also include the knowledge and skills he uses in his job.

Satisfying Our Wants
People's wants are often shaped by where they live. **Contrast** *How do you think people's wants in both environments might differ? Why?*

Civics and Economics

Agriculture Farming is basic to the United States economy. Most of the early colonists were farmers, so farming has a long and important history in the United States.

The vast areas of the Midwestern plains allow the nation to grow far more food than Americans need. In 2003, American farmers grew over 40% of the world's corn and soybeans and 9% of its wheat. The United States is the world's leading agricultural exporter. More than $40 billion of agricultural products are exported yearly. Chief importers of American agricultural products are Japan, the European Union, Mexico, and Canada.

Analyzing Economics

Why do you think the nations and regions listed import agricultural products from the United States?

Land Another factor of production, land, is made up of the many natural resources that are needed to help produce goods and services. Such resources include soil, minerals, water, timber, fish and wildlife, and energy sources.

Capital Finally, there is the factor of production called capital. **Capital** is anything produced in an economy that is used to produce other goods and services.

Capital includes any tools, machines, or buildings used to produce goods and services. When goods such as tools and factories are used as capital, they are called capital goods. For example, tools for fixing bicycles and a computer for keeping track of sales are capital goods to the owner of Rick's Bikes.

Although it is not a factor of production, money is sometimes referred to as financial capital. Financial capital is money that is available for investing or spending.

✓ Reading Check How does land affect a society's economy?

Production to Consumption

From the Field to the Table A great deal of time, effort, and money go into the processes of production, distribution, and consumptionas these photos show.
Analyze Information *The second photo shows pasta being made in a factory. Which process does this step illustrate—production, distribution, or consumption?*

To produce the goods and services people want, the resources of labor, land, and capital must be combined in a process called production. That is why these resources are called factors of production. Farmers produce food by combining soil, water, and sunlight (land) with seeds and machinery (capital). They also use their knowledge, skills, time, and energy, as well as that of their workers (labor).

Production is followed by **distribution**, the process by which goods and services are made available to the people who want them. The truck that delivers bread to your market is part of the distribution process.

Finally, when goods and services have been produced and distributed, they are ready for consumption. **Consumption** is the act of buying or using goods and services.

Satisfying people's economic wants can be a very complex process. In our economy, millions of people work in hundreds of thousands of businesses that produce and distribute many different goods and services.

The steps in the process of satisfying wants are like links in a chain of activities. As you read the following description, look at the diagram of the want-satisfaction chain on pages 354–355.

Wants The process begins with a want. Suppose, for example, that you and some of your friends decide to get together one evening for a spaghetti dinner. Among the supplies that you will want to buy and cook is the pasta. The first link in this want-satisfaction chain, then, is your want for pasta.

Production The next link is made up of people who combine the resources of land, labor, and capital. In the case of your pasta, farmers use soil, water, seeds, farm machinery, and labor to produce wheat, which they sell to a grain-milling company. The company combines labor and machinery to turn the wheat into flour, which it sells to a pasta maker. The pasta maker adds other ingredients like salt and water and uses labor and machines to mix, roll, and cut the dough. This production process results in the pasta that you and your friends want.

Target Reading Skill
Sequence Reread the first four paragraphs on this page. Then, identify the signal words that help you understand the sequence of events being described.

Distribution However, your want is not yet satisfied. Once the pasta is made, it is sold to a grocery wholesaler who then sells and delivers it to a grocery store. This is the distribution link in the chain.

Consumption After the pasta has been distributed, you and your friends buy, cook, and eat it—the consumption link in the chain. At this point, you have achieved want satisfaction. However, your want may be satisfied only for the time being. If you decide you want to eat pasta another time, the chain will have to repeat itself. The want-satisfaction chain is arranged in a circle to show that the process of satisfying wants happens over and over again.

✔ Reading Check **How does production lead to distribution? How does distribution lead to consumption?**

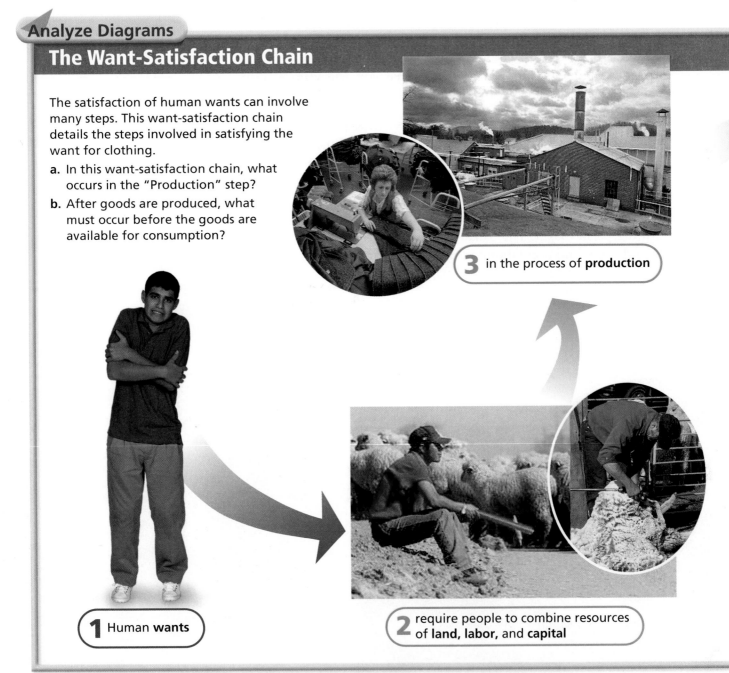

Analyze Diagrams

The Want-Satisfaction Chain

The satisfaction of human wants can involve many steps. This want-satisfaction chain details the steps involved in satisfying the want for clothing.

a. In this want-satisfaction chain, what occurs in the "Production" step?

b. After goods are produced, what must occur before the goods are available for consumption?

3 in the process of **production**

1 Human **wants**

2 require people to combine resources of **land, labor,** and **capital**

Making Choices

There are never enough resources to produce all the goods and services people want. As a result, people in all societies must make choices about which of their wants will be satisfied and which will not. These choices are economic choices. The process of making them is what an economy is all about.

Benefits One part of making an economic decision is looking at the benefits you will receive from each of your possible choices. Josh's benefits from the bike store job will include $150 a week. He will also gain work experience and the satisfaction of having money of his own.

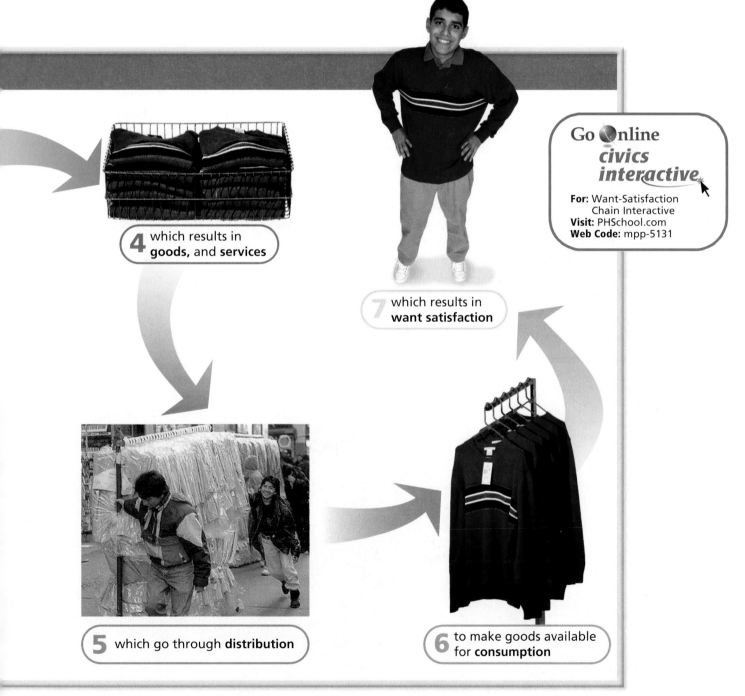

4 which results in **goods,** and **services**

7 which results in **want satisfaction**

5 which go through **distribution**

6 to make goods available for **consumption**

Go Online
civics
interactive

For: Want-Satisfaction Chain Interactive
Visit: PHSchool.com
Web Code: mpp-5131

Costs A second part involves looking at the costs of your choices. The major cost of any decision is giving up the benefits you would have received from the alternative. If Josh takes the job, for example, he will give up the benefits he would have received from using his time to play soccer.

Like Josh's decision, every economic decision has an **opportunity cost**, the benefit given up when scarce resources are used for one purpose instead of another. If Josh decides that the opportunity cost of taking the job would be greater than its benefits, then Josh should turn down the offer from Rick's Bikes.

✔ Reading Check **What factors must people balance when they want two things that are in conflict?**

Scarcity

Societies always face problems like Josh's. This problem is known as **scarcity**, which means that resources are always limited compared with the number and variety of wants people have. Scarcity is a problem in rich societies and poor ones. The idea of scarcity is not based on the total amount of resources in a society. It is based on the relationship between wants and the resources available to satisfy them.

The following example may help you understand scarcity. Japan does not have enough good farmland to grow all the food its people want. The United States has plenty of good farmland. However, some of the land that could be used to grow food is also in demand for factories, houses, and shopping malls. You can see that in both Japan and the United States, land resources are scarce compared with the ways people want to use them.

Limited Resources
Japan (left) is a small island nation with a very large population. There is very little land available for farming. The United States (right), however, has more land available for farming.
Draw Conclusions *How do you think the scarcity of farmland in Japan affects the prices that consumers in Japan pay for such things as produce?*

Each decision to use resources to produce one kind of good or service is, at the same time, a decision not to use the same resources to produce something else that people want. The farmer who grows wheat chooses to use the limited resources of land, labor, and capital to grow wheat instead of some other crop such as corn, oats, or barley.

In a large economy such choices are made by businesses as well as by individuals. For example, a clothing company that makes jackets and coats has a certain number of factories and workers. This company must make important decisions about how best to use these resources when making it products.

Governments also have to make choices. For example, how much of the federal government's resources should be used to build defense systems and how much to improve the schools? How much should be used to protect the environment and how much for the elderly?

Although the choices that individuals, businesses, and governments must make are different in many ways, they all have one thing in common. They involve making economic decisions about how to use resources to produce goods and services to satisfy wants.

▲ A company that makes cars has a limited number of factories, machines, and workers. That company will have to make choices about how many cars of each model to produce.

✔ Reading Check **Why do both rich and poor nations face the problem of scarcity?**

SECTION 1 Assessment

Key Terms

Use each of the key terms in a sentence that explains its meaning: factors of production, capital, consumption, opportunity cost, scarcity

Target Reading Skill

1. **Recognize Words that Signal Sequence** List words that helped you to understand sequence in the "Production to Consumption" section of the text.

Comprehension and Critical Thinking

2. **a. Recall** Describe some typical needs and wants.
   b. Categorize Which wants are influenced by friends and social status?

3. **a. Recall** What are the three factors of economic production?
   b. Determine Relevance Identify the factors of production at a local bakery.

4. **a. Describe** What steps must take place before you buy a box of pasta?
   b. Determine Relevance Choose an object that you want, such as a CD. Describe the steps in the want-satisfaction chain.

5. **a. Describe** What are the factors that affect an economic decision?
   b. Identify Alternatives How might Josh satisfy both his wants?

6. **a. Explain** How does the concept of scarcity apply to Josh's situation?

   b. Draw Conclusions What is the result of economic scarcity in a society?

Writing Activity

Suppose you have to choose between buying a new jacket and saving your money toward buy a used car when you get your license. List the economic factors that will affect your decision. Then make the decision and explain your choice.

> **TIP** Before you begin writing, make a list showing the benefits and costs of each option.

Basic Economic Decisions

Reading Preview

Objectives
In this section you will
- Understand that determining what and how much to produce is a basic economic choice.
- Explain why deciding how to produce goods and services is a second basic economic question.
- Understand that deciding who will get goods and services is a third basic economic decision.

Taking Notes
Make a diagram like the one below. As you read this section, complete the diagram with information about the three basic economic decisions.

Key Terms
quantity
technology

Main Idea
Basic economic decisions include what and how much to produce, how to produce it, and who will have the opportunity to consume it.

Target Reading Skill
Understand Sequence Remember that events follow one another in a cause-and-effect relationship. As you read this section of Chapter 13, look for the causes and effects that indicate a sequence of events.

Have you ever thought that a pizza is the result of economic decisions? A restaurant owner makes a choice to open a pizza business. The owner must decide how many pizzas to make in a day. He or she must also decide how many pizza ovens and other equipment to buy and how many people to hire to make the pizza and serve it to customers.

Like the owner of the pizza restaurant, people in any economy face major economic decisions. The three most basic decisions are

- Which goods and services should be produced, and how much of them?
- How should these goods and services be produced?
- Who will get the goods and services that are produced?

From the smallest neighborhood pizza parlor to the largest corporate boardroom, these decisions are being made every day in every part of the economy.

If this pizzeria is to succeed, the owner must make good decisions about what kinds of pizza to make and how many to make. ▶

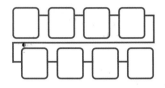

What and How Much?

In any economy, people must decide what to produce with the scarce resources they have. In our economy, the people who own or can get resources make this first major economic decision.

A farmer who owns land and machinery may decide to produce wheat instead of barley. You might decide to use a resource you own—your labor—to mow lawns instead of selling bicycles. Any decision about which goods or services to produce is based on a prediction of what people will want to consume.

As an owner of resources decides what to produce, he or she also decides the **quantity,** or amount, to produce. The amount of a good or a service that is produced will depend on a number of factors. For instance, farmers' decisions will be based on the amount of land they own or can rent, the amount of labor and machinery they can afford, and the amount of wheat or barley they think they can sell.

Citizen Profiles

Michael Dell Computers have always fascinated Michael Dell. While he was still in college, he realized that if he sold computers directly to customers, there would be no distributors and no retail stores involved in the sale. This meant that Dell could charge his customers less for a custom-made computer. He began selling his computers from his dorm room in college. Today, the Dell Computer Corporation employs thousands of people and is worth billions of dollars.

Citizenship
What economic choices did Dell make?

✔ Reading Check   **Who in our society decides what to produce?**

How to Produce Goods and Services

The second major economic decision is how to produce goods and services. In other words, in what way will land, labor, and capital be combined to produce goods and services?

Choices to Make Farmers who produce wheat must make several choices about how to do it. Should they plant all of their land with wheat or introduce some additional crops? Should they grow their crops using organic methods, or should they use conventional fertilizers and pesticides? Should they do all the work themselves, or should they hire workers to plant and care for the wheat? Should they rely more on workers or on machinery? Should they buy the farm machinery they use, or should they rent it? Should they manage the farm business themselves, or should they hire managers to oversee the work? In making decisions about how to produce, people usually want to choose the combination of resources that will be the least costly.

Companies that sell food products rely on "taste tests" in order to help them make important economic decisions about what kinds of products to make.▼

Technology and Production
Technology has had an enormous impact on production. In the early 1900s, Henry Ford developed the assembly line to speed up production (left). Today, robots and other technology (right) have speeded up the production process.
Identify Cause and Effect *What are some of the effects that technology has had on workers?*

Target Reading Skill

Understand Sequence Read the first sentence under the heading "The Role of Technology" at the top of the page. Note the cause-and-effect relationship indicated by the phrase "has led to." What other words in this section indicate cause and effect?

The Role of Technology In our economy, the desire to find the least costly way to produce goods and services has led to the growth of **technology**, or the practical application of science to commerce or industry. In the early 1800s, cloth makers began using power looms. Although the new looms cost a lot of money, they could produce cloth much faster than the old handlooms could. Therefore, the cost of producing cloth soon dropped.

Since those early beginnings, technology has played an increasingly important part in decisions that people make about how to produce goods and provide services. For example, researchers have developed seeds that produce larger crops. Advances in electronics have given us robots to use in factories. Computers keep records, make calculations, and speed up many jobs. The Internet allows businesses to sell products and services to a wide audience online.

✔ Reading Check **What is the relationship between production and technology?**

Who Gets What?

Deciding who get the goods and services that are produced is the third basic choice that must be made in an economy. In other words, people must find a way to decide how all the goods and services will be divided up. Wants are always greater than the resources available to satisfy them. Therefore, this choice is an important one and sometimes very difficult.

Choices to Make Should goods and services be divided equally among all people? Should people receive goods and services on the basis of what they say they want? Should a small group of people decide who is to receive which goods and services? Or should people who own more resources and produce more products get more goods and services than people who own and produce less?

The Role of Goals and Values Different societies have solved this problem in different ways, depending on their goals and values. A society that wants to achieve equality among its people might develop a system for sharing its products equally among its citizens, even if it means that some people worked harder than others for the same reward.

On the other hand, a society in which freedom is the highest value might solve the problem differently. It might let citizens compete freely among themselves to try to get the goods and services they want, even if it meant that some people got more than they needed while others got less.

The goals and values of a society have a great influence on how that society makes all three basic economic decisions. In the next section you will read about three different economic systems—traditional economies, command economies, and market economies. Societies have developed these three different systems for organizing their resources to produce and distribute the goods and services people want.

▲ Early settlers in Jamestown, Virginia, had to make the same basic economic decisions that we do today. However, their decisions reflected the needs and wants of their society, which was very different than our modern society.

✔ Reading Check   **What do a society's values have to do with its economy?**

SECTION 2 Assessment

Key Terms

Use the key term in a sentence that explains its meaning: technology

Target Reading Skill

1. **Understand Sequence** Explain the sequence of events that led to Michael Dell's success.

Comprehension and Critical Thinking

2. **a. Explain** Suppose you have just bought 100 acres of land. What is the first economic question you should ask yourself?

b. Draw Conclusions On what factors does the number of sweaters a factory owner produces depend?

3. **a. Describe** What choices must a smoothie stand owner make in determining how to produce smoothies.

b. Identify Main Ideas How might new technology affect a wheat farmer's decisions?

4. **a. Recall** How do people decide who will get what their economy produces?

b. Predict You will read about three different economic systems in the next section. Use the information in this section to predict their characteristics.

Writing Activity

Read the questions under "Choices to Make" on page 360. Write an essay in which you answer these questions. Explain the reasons behind your answers.

TIP Look at the U.S. economy as you answer the questions. How does the U.S. divide good and services among its citizens? Do you think this division of goods and services is fair? If not, how would you change it?

How to Analyze an Editorial

Editorials are newspaper articles that express a point of view. The writer of an editorial chooses a position on an important issue and makes an argument to support that point of view. Editorials express opinions based on facts.

Read the editorial below. Think about the author's opinion and the argument he or she has given. Does the editorial influence your opinion about the prevention of reckless driving among teenagers?

A Reckless Law

Our state senators should steer clear of the ill-conceived bill now before them, which would revoke the driver's license of any teenager found guilty of reckless driving.

Many community groups have campaigned for increasing penalties for driving recklessly. We have applauded their efforts to encourage safe driving among teens. However, the "reckless law" proposed by Senator Bellitt is not the most effective way to put an end to reckless driving.

Reckless drivers of all ages face severe consequences in our state. Even a first offense for reckless driving carries a stiff fine and often results in 10 license penalty points. (It only takes 15 points to lose a license).

Not only is the Bellitt bill reckless itself, but it would discriminate against drivers age 16–19. Why should a reckless driver who is one week short of his twentieth birthday be treated differently than all other adults? We already have punishments in place for reckless driving; perhaps now we should concentrate on preventing it in the first place.

Learn the Skill

To analyze an editorial, follow these steps:

① **Identify the writer's opinion.** Identify the issue that the author is concerned about.

② **Locate the evidence.** Look for facts the author uses to support his or her point of view.

③ **Think about the author's argument.** Is there enough evidence to support the argument? Do you agree or disagree?

Practice the Skill

① Read the editorial above. Write down the author's opinion.

② Write down the facts the author has given to support his or her opinion.

③ Decide whether you agree with the author's opinion. Discuss your response to the editorial with a classmate.

Apply the Skill

① Collect editorials from newspapers.

② Choose one that deals with an issue that is important to you.

③ Read the editorial carefully. Has your opinion about the issue changed? Has it become stronger?

Go **Online**
civics
interactive

For: Local Citizenship
Visit: PHSchool.com
Web Code: mpp-5132

Three Types of Economies

Reading Preview

Objectives

In this section you will

- Identify and discuss traditional economies.
- Identify and discuss command economies.
- Identify and discuss market economies.
- Discuss modern-day economics in China and the United States.

Key Terms

traditional economy	profit
command economy	invest
market economy	free enterprise
	capitalism
	mixed economy

Main Idea

Various types of economic systems include traditional economies, command economies, and market economies.

Target Reading Skill

Recognize Words That Signal Sequence Signal words point out relationships between ideas or events. As you read this section, look for words that signal sequence.

Taking Notes

Make a diagram like the one below. As you read this section, complete the diagram to compare and contrast command and market economies.

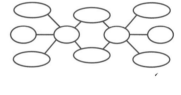

Most people do one kind of work. From the money they earn, they buy goods and services produced by other workers.▼

People do not make economic decisions all by themselves. Almost every economic task, from raising wheat to providing hospital services, requires that people work together. Also, people can rarely meet all their economic needs by themselves. Most people do one kind of work. They depend on the work of other people for most of the products and services that they use.

In human history, there have generally been three basic types of economic systems: traditional economies, command economies, and market economies. These systems are three different ways a society can organize production, distribution, and consumption to solve the economic problem of scarcity.

Traditional Economies

In a **traditional economy**, the basic economic decisions are made according to long-established ways of behaving that are unlikely to change. These customs are passed along from elders to youths. The family is the basic unit of the traditional economy. However, in societies with traditional economies, all members work together to support the society rather than just their families.

For example, a tribe of hunters may follow certain customs. They will make camp at the same places and hunt the same game year after year. The roles that fathers, mothers, daughters, and sons play as they help each other in the hunt remain the same over the years.

What to Produce Tradition answers the question of what and how much to produce. The people who belong to the tribe want to "produce" game. They want enough of it to feed the whole tribe.

How to Produce There are also customs that have to do with how to "produce" the game. Year after year, the tribe members use the same weapons and methods to hunt the game. They use the same methods to prepare and cook it.

Who Gets What is Produced The tribe's customs also determine who gets what is produced. When sharing the kill, each member might get an amount based on his or her role in the hunt. In another tribe, shares might be divided according to the number of members in a family.

Ownership of Resources People in a traditional economy usually own their own resources, such as land, tools, and labor. They have some freedom to make their own day-to-day decisions about when and how to use their resources. They may decide, for example, not to go on a hunt one day, but to gather fruit instead. They have little freedom, however, when it comes to making the basic economic decisions already set by tradition. As a result, there is very little change in the economy over time.

Societies with traditional economies are usually small. This way, fewer resources are needed and fewer goods need to be produced. Otherwise, the economy would not be able to support too large a society.

Today, few purely traditional economies remain in the world. A few societies in parts of Central and South America, Africa, and Asia still have economies that are mostly traditional.

✓ Reading Check   **What is the role of custom in a traditional economy?**

These hunters are part of the San tribe of Kalahari, Africa. In this traditional economy, they produce only what members of the tribe need. ▶

"I need some short-term economic stimulus."

ANALYZING Political Cartoons

Every economic system is subject to ups and downs. When a society's economy suffers, it becomes the responsibility of government to help stimulate economic growth

1. What do you think the girl is asking her father for? Explain your answer.

2. How does the cartoonist use humor in this cartoon?

Command Economies

In a **command economy**, the government or a central authority owns or controls the factors of production and makes the basic economic decisions. In such a system, the government usually has charge of important parts of the economy, such as transportation, communication, banking, and manufacturing. Farms and many stores are government-controlled. The government may also set wages and decide who will work at which jobs. The government, not private individuals, makes the major economic decisions.

Economic systems based on command principles have existed for thousands of years. From Egyptian pharaohs and medieval lords to communist nations such as the Soviet Union of the twentieth century, powerful rulers and governments have controlled the economies of their societies.

Government Decision Making In a command economy, a central planning group makes most of the decisions about how, what, and how much to produce. It is up to the central planning group to make sure that there are enough resources and workers to produce what is needed. The result is that only those products that the government chooses will be available for people to consume. In this type of economy, consumers have little or no power in determining what and how much gets produced.

Target Reading Skill

Recognize Words That Signal Sequence The word "result" shows a sequence: first a decision is made; then *as a result* products become available. As you read, look for more words that signal the order in which events take place.

Who Gets What In a command system, the decision of who gets what is produced depends on the goals and values of the central authority. A greedy dictator, for example, might choose to make himself and his friends rich. On the other hand, if the government's goal were to satisfy wants based on individual need, then each person might get food, clothes, and housing no matter how much or how little he or she produced.

✓ Reading Check **How much individual freedom exists in a command economy?**

Market Economies

The third kind of economic system is the **market economy**, a system in which private individuals own the factors of production and are free to make their own choices about production, distribution, and consumption. The economy of the United States is based on the market system.

In a market economy, all economic decisions are made through a kind of bargaining process that takes place in markets. A market is a place or situation in which buyers and sellers agree to exchange goods and services. A local farmers' market, a sporting goods store the New York Stock Exchange, and even the sign you posted in the neighborhood sandwich shop are all examples of markets.

In a market, the value of what you have to offer sets the value of what you can get. Therefore, no one person or group runs a market economy. Instead, everyone takes part in running it by freely making economic decisions.

Decision Making by Individuals In a market economy, people are free to decide how to use land, labor, and capital. They are also free to start their own businesses and to choose what jobs they want to do. The major economic decisions about what and how much to produce and how to produce it are made by individuals, not by a central government's command or by tradition and custom.

In a market economy, people who earn high wages for the work they do will be able to buy more goods and services than people who earn lower wages. People who own land and capital will also be able to afford more goods and services than people who do not.

Competition Competition plays an important part in a market economy. Producers compete to satisfy the wants of consumers. Workers compete for jobs. These individuals are all part of the process of making decisions in a market economy.

Making Economic Decisions
In a market economy, the wants of individuals like this American shopper play a major role in determining what will be produced.
Synthesize Information
What details in the photo indicate that the woman is a consumer in a market economy?

The Factors of Production

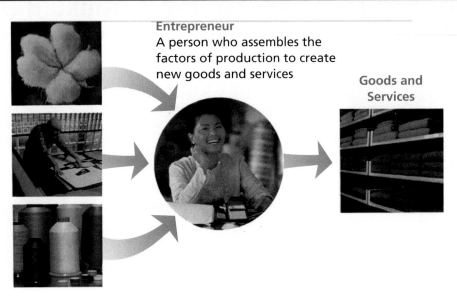

Land
All of the natural resources that are used to produce goods and services

Labor
Any effort a person devotes to a task for which that person is paid

Capital
Any human-made resources that used to create other goods and services

Entrepreneur
A person who assembles the factors of production to create new goods and services

Goods and Services

Interpreting Diagrams
An entrepreneur brings land, labor, and capital together to create goods and offer services.
Identify Central Issues *Give specific examples of land, labor, and capital involved in producing a jacket.*

Profit Seeking An incentive is the hope of reward that encourages a person to behave in a certain way. One of the chief incentives for people in a market economy is the potential to make a profit. **Profit** is the difference between what it costs to produce something and the price the buyer pays for it. In a market economy, people base their decisions about what and how much to produce largely on how much profit they think they will make.

The desire to make a profit also leads people to invest in a business. To **invest** means to use your money to help a business get started or grow, with the hope that the business will earn a profit that you can share.

Free Enterprise and Capitalism There are two other names for the market economy. One of these is free enterprise. The term **free enterprise** refers to the system in which individuals in a market economy are free to undertake economic activities with little or no control by the government.

The other name for the market system is capitalism. **Capitalism** is a system in which people make their own decisions about how to save resources as capital, and how to use their capital to produce goods and provide services. The term capitalism calls attention to the fact that in a market economy capital is privately owned.

✓ Reading Check   **What role does competition play in a market economy?**

Students Make a Difference

Michael Arriaga, a sophomore at Los Fresnos High School, in Los Fresnos, Texas, believes that volunteer services can help small communities meet the needs of its citizens.

As a member of his school's chapter of Family Career Community Leaders of America, Michael has worked to make a difference in other people's lives. He also works annually for the Feast of Sharing, a project that provides warm meals to poor and homeless people in his community.

Service Learning

How can you make a difference for the homeless in your community?

▲ Students can help make a difference by assisting people in need.

Modern-Day Economies

Describing economic systems as traditional, command, or market is useful for understanding the way people in different societies make economic decisions. In today's world, however, most countries have a **mixed economy,** an economy that is a mixture of the three basic systems. The People's Republic of China and the United States are two very different examples of mixed economies.

The Economy of China Before the late 1980s, the economy of China was a command economy. The central, one-party government had charge of the major resources and made the important economic decisions. The government of China made economic plans in which it set goals for which goods and how many of each would be produced during a certain period. These plans also set forth how resources were used in production.

In the late 1980s and 1990s, the Chinese government took steps toward creating a more mixed economy by adding some features of free enterprise to its economic system. In China's cities today, privately owned shops sell consumer goods, and new hotels and restaurants abound.

The Economy of the United States

The United States economy is considered a market—or free enterprise—system. Individuals and privately owned businesses own the factors of production. Business owners are free to compete with each other in the marketplace to produce and distribute any goods and services they think they can sell. Americans are also free to buy and consume any goods and services they want and can afford. The marketplace runs with very little government intervention.

However, there are elements of government control in our economy. As you have seen in earlier chapters, our government provides, or requires the economy to provide, certain services such as education, mail services, and an army and navy for defense. Government also provides such goods as highways and airports. Some citizens feel the government needs to be more involved in the economy. Others argue that the government should intervene less. In the following chapters, you will read about many other ways in which citizens have asked the government to help take charge of and guide the American economy and how the government has responded.

▲ San Francisco's busy downtown show's the economic success of the American free enterprise system.

✓ **Reading Check** How do the economies of China and the United States differ?

SECTION 3 Assessment

Key Terms

Use each of the key terms in a sentence that explains its meaning: traditional economy, command economy, market economy, profit, invest, free enterprise, capitalism, mixed economy

Target Reading Skill

1. **Recognize Words That Signal Sequence** Reread the section "Competition and Profit." List signal words from the section that indicate the sequence of events.

Comprehension and Critical Thinking

2. **a. Describe** Describe a traditional economic system.

   b. Link Past and Present Why are there so few traditional economies in the world today?

3. **a. Recall** Who answers the three basic economic questions in a command economy?

   b. Categorize What are some disadvantages of a command economy?

4. **a. Explain** What role do individuals play in a market economy?

   b. Determine Relevance What elements of a market economy do you see in your town or city?

5. **a. Explain** What is a mixed economy?

   b. Draw Inferences Why do most countries today have mixed economies?

Writing Activity

Both Russia and the Soviet Union once had centrally planned economies. Read more about these economies—past and present—online. Summarize what you have read in a well-organized essay that answers the question "Why did these economies change?"

Go Online PHSchool.com

For: Writing Activity
Visit: PHSchool.com
Web Code: mpd-5133

Synthesizing Information

When learning about a subject, you will often use information from many types of sources. Knowing how to synthesize, or put together, different pieces of information helps you draw conclusions. In the example below, a letter and a line graph describe the changes in attendance at a series of outdoor concerts held every year in the summertime.

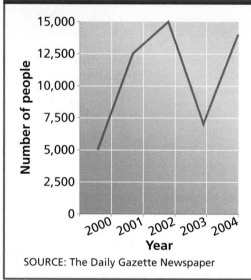

Attendance at the Summer Concert Series

Excerpt from a letter to potential advertisers from the director of the Summer Concert Series: "A review of the Summer Concert Series shows great success. In our second year, we more than doubled attendance. Growth continued to a high of 15,000 people in 2002. The terrible weather of the summer 2003 and the cancellation of two bands made that summer a disaster. But we recovered nicely in 2004. We are looking forward to continued growth in 2005."

SOURCE: The Daily Gazette Newspaper

Learn the Skill

Follow these steps to synthesize information:

❶ **Identify the sources.** Knowing the publication and the date of a graph, article, letter, or other text helps you evaluate information.

❷ **Identify key facts and ideas.** What are the main points you need to know?

❸ **Analyze the evidence.** Examine and compare the different types of evidence. Does the information in the text match the information in the graph?

❹ **Draw conclusions.** What conclusions can you draw from the combined evidence?

Practice the Skill

Study the text and graph and answer these questions:

❶ (a) Who wrote the letter? (b) What is the source of the information in the graph?

❷ What is the main point of the letter? What facts are given to support it?

❸ Describe what the data in the graph shows about changes in attendance over the years.

❹ What conclusion can you draw about the future of the Summer Concert Series?

Apply the Skill

Find an article in a newspaper or magazine that uses a graph or other form of illustration to further explain points made in the article. Describe how the two pieces of evidence work together.

Review and Assessment

Chapter Summary

Section 1
Why Societies Have Economies
(pages 350–357)

- People in a society have basic wants such as food, clothing, and shelter, and other important wants such as education and health care.

- A society combines its factors of production—labor, land, and capital—to produce the goods and services its citizens need and want.

- After goods are produced, they are distributed to people who want them. The purchase or use of these goods and services is called consumption.

- Because resources are limited, people must consider each option's opportunity costs and benefits as they decide which needs to satisfy.

- Scarcity results when a resource valued by society is not available in quantities high enough to satisfy the need for it.

Section 2
Basic Economic Decisions
(pages 358–361)

- A society must decide which goods and services to produce and in what quantity.

- People must decide how to produce those goods and services. The desire to bring down the costs of production often leads to improved production technology.

- Society must decide how the goods and services will be distributed among the people.

Section 3
Three Types of Economies
(pages 363–369)

- In traditional economies, people produce and distribute goods and services in the same way their ancestors always have done.

- In command economies, the leaders decide which goods and services to produce and how those goods will be distributed.

- In market economies, also known as free enterprise or capitalism, each individual decides what to produce, how to produce it, to whom to sell it, and how to invest the profits that result from the sale.

- Most modern economies are mixed economies that blend elements of traditional, command, and market economies.

Copy the chart below and use it to help you summarize the chapter.

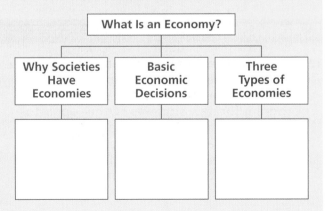

Go Online
PHSchool.com

For: Self-Text
Visit: www.PHSchool.com
Web Code: mpa-5133

Reviewing Key Terms

On a separate sheet of paper, write the term that makes each sentence correct.

1. The money left over after expenses have been met is called (capital, profit).

2. The disadvantages of an economic choice can also be called the (factors of production, opportunity cost).

3. (Scarcity, Technology) has played an increasingly important role in producing goods more cheaply.

4. The lack of sufficient resources to meet a society's needs is called (consumption, scarcity).

5. A (traditional economy, market economy) is one in which individuals compete for customers to get the best prices they can for their goods or services.

6. In a (command economy, mixed economy), both individual citizens and their government play roles in the production and distribution of goods and services.

7. The term (free enterprise, opportunity cost) describes a system in which individuals make their own economic decisions without interference from the government.

8. (Capital, profit) is anything produced in an economy that is used to produce other goods and services.

Comprehension and Critical Thinking

9. a. **Explain** Why do all economic choices have an opportunity cost?
   b. **Identify Main Ideas** Suppose you decide to go to the movies instead of studying for a test. What is the opportunity cost of your decision?
   c. **Determine Relevance** What factors of production are necessary to grow tomatoes for profit?

10. a. **Recall** What are three basic economic questions you should ask yourself if you want to open a restaurant?
    b. **Demonstrate Reasoned Judgment** Suppose you are starting a tutoring business. What questions should you ask yourself as you plan your business?
    c. **Identify Cause** Choose an example of a new technology and explain how it has resulted in new ways of producing goods or services.

11. a. **Describe** Describe the three basic types of economic systems.
    b. **Compare and Contrast** What are the main differences and similarities among the three systems?
    c. **Draw Conclusions** What does the fact that the United States has a free enterprise system suggest about American values?

Activities

12. **Skills Synthesizing Information** Does your school have a recycling program? A teacher appreciation day? A mentoring program for new students? Other opportunities to volunteer? Plan a story for your school newspaper that synthesizes text with charts, graphs, or photos. Explain how the images will fit with and add information to the text.

13. **Writing** Research an ancient society of your choice, such as Egypt or Rome. Write a narrative describing its economic system and evaluating the effectiveness of that system.

14. **Active Citizen** Suppose that you and your classmates want to earn money for a class trip to France. Make the necessary economic decisions. Present your plan and your budget to the class.

15. **Math Practice** Find out how many hours there are in one week. Subtract one-third for the time you spend sleeping. Then write down the number of hours you spend each week on all your activities (i.e., school, homework, sports, dance practice). What is the best use of the time left over?

16. **Civics and Economics** Discuss the advantages and disadvantages of a command versus a market system.

17. **Analyzing Visuals** Study the photo. What kind of economy is pictured? How do you know?

Standardized Test Prep

Test-Taking Tips

Standardized tests often ask you to answer questions about what you have read. Read the paragraph and answer the questions that follow.

> A market economy has always been basic to the United States. In 1776, the year of the United States' birth, Scottish philosopher Adam Smith published The Wealth of Nations, which clearly explained the benefits of competition and free enterprise. American journalist Robert Samuelson, who frequently writes about economics, wrote that "the market is not some magical process, but merely a system that allows trial and error—rewarding success and punishing failure—as a daily event."

Choose the letter of the best answer.

1. What does Samuelson think the market is?
   A a magical process
   B a system that allows trial and error
   C a success and a failure
   D a daily event

   The correct answer is **B**. All four phrases appear in the paragraph, but B matches what Samuelson says.

   TIP When all the answer choices appear in the text, reread the question to be sure you are choosing the answer that best matches what is being asked.

2. What would Adam Smith think of Samuelson's opinion about the market?
   A Smith would agree with Samuelson.
   B Smith would disagree with Samuelson.
   C Smith would feel that Samuelson did not understand the market.
   D Smith would laugh at Samuelson.

   TIP When a question asks for information not directly given in the passage, check each choice against the passage to see which inference is the most reasonable.

Basics of Our Economic System

What's Ahead in Chapter 14

In this chapter, you will learn how a market economy works and about the roles that business and labor play in a market economy.

SECTION 1
The Principles of Our Market Economy

SECTION 2
The Role of Business in the American Economy

SECTION 3
Labor in the American Economy

TARGET
READING SKILL

Cause and Effect In this chapter you will focus on the skill of cause and effect. This includes identifying cause and effect, recognizing multiple causes and understanding effects.

Workers assemble ▶
automobiles

National | **Standards for Civics and Government** | **State**

The following National Standards for Civics and Government are covered in this chapter:

II. What are the foundations of the American political system?

B. What are the distinctive characteristics of American society?

V. What are the roles of the citizen in American democracy?

B. What are the rights of citizens?

Active Citizen

Civics in the Real World

It is early summer. The farmer's market is buzzing with activity. Strawberries are in season and the sweet red berries have drawn Eric and his strawberry-loving buddies to the market. Farmers are selling strawberries in small paper or plastic baskets.

Eric walks around the market and notices that almost all the farmers are selling strawberries for the same price, $3.00 a basket. He sees a big crowd around one farmer. Getting closer, Eric notices this farmer is charging only $2.25 a basket. Nearby he notices a farmer who is charging $3.75 a basket for her strawberries. Eric is curious as to why she is charging more and walks up and asks her why her price is higher.

"These are organic strawberries," she answers. "I use organic fertilizer and no insecticides. It costs a little more so I have to charge more to make a profit. Try one. You'll see they taste better than other berries—and they are better for you as well."

Eric tastes a strawberry. Yum! It sure is tasty! Eric thinks about which berries to buy and how to make a choice. Choices like this one, he thinks, are what control a market economy. Farmers make choices about how to grow their berries and what to charge for them. Consumers make choices about how much to spend and who to buy from.

Citizen's Journal Which strawberries would you buy at the farmer's market? What reasons would you give for your decision? How would your decision be influenced if strawberries were your most favorite fruit? What if you didn't especially care about strawberries, but needed them for a fruit salad you were making?

The Principles of Our Market Economy

Reading Preview

Objectives

In this section you will

- Understand the circular flow of economic activity.
- Learn about supply and demand.

Taking Notes

Make a tree map like the one below. As you read the section, fill it in with information about circular flow and supply and demand.

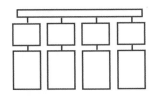

Key Terms

interest   market price
demand

Main Idea

A market economy works on a flow or exchange of labor, wages, capital, goods, and services, all regulated by laws of supply and demand.

Target Reading Skill

Recognizing Multiple Causes Sometimes an effect can have more than one cause. As you read, be aware of instances where many causes are described as coming together to produce a single effect.

In Chapter 13 you learned that the United States has a mixed economy that is based on the principles of a free enterprise, market system. In order to understand the American economy, then, it is important to take a closer look at the basic ways in which a market economy works.

The Circular Flow of Economic Activity

The Earth relies on a steady flow of water throughout the environment to remain healthy. Water falls as snow or rain to the ground where it collects in snowfields and rivers. Melting snow and rainwater flow through cities and across farmland to the oceans. From the oceans, water evaporates into the atmosphere, where it forms into raindrops or snow and returns to the Earth's surface. This flow of water powers the environment and allows life to flourish. In a similar way, a healthy market economy depends on a steady flow of resources, goods, and services.

Suppose that your bicycle has a flat tire. You walk your bike to the nearest bike shop that you know to be open that day. At the bike shop you hand the clerk four dollars and receive a new inner tube. This simple kind of exchange is repeated millions of times each day by millions of Americans.

Buying something, however, is only one kind of exchange. Suppose that you also work part-time for the bicycle shop. You exchange your labor for an hourly wage.

These two exchanges—money for an inner tube and work for wages—are connected because you buy inner tubes with the money you earn from working. By being part of both exchanges, you have created a "flow" of labor, inner tubes, and money. This is an example of the circular flow of economic activity.

Expanding the Circular Flow This example involves just you and one business. In real life, people exchange their labor to buy goods and services from many businesses. The entire American economy, however, is based on a circular flow that is very similar to the one involving you and the bike shop.

Think about every American business that produces goods or services. Together, all these businesses can be called producers. Then imagine all individuals in our society. The diagram on the next two pages shows how goods, services, labor, and money flow through the United States economy.

This circular flow diagram is not quite complete. Labor is only one resource that producers need to create goods. Producers need land and the raw materials found on the land. Producers also need capital, which includes tools and machines used in production.

Producers exchange a certain kind of payment for the use of land and capital. Rent is the payment for the use of land. **Interest** is the payment for the use of capital. The payment for the use of labor is called wages.

✓ Reading Check **What do workers get in exchange for their labor?**

Exchanges in the Circular Flow of Economic Activity
Work for hourly wages and money for a product are two exchanges in the circular flow of economic activity.
Draw Inferences *Where does a music store get money to pay its workers?*

Supply and Demand

Every market exchange brings together two sides. Like the bicycle store worker who uses wage income to buy a new tire, individuals in the marketplace can play different roles at different times. Producers and individuals act both as buyers and as sellers. Buyers and sellers exchange goods and services through a market. Markets determine how much will be produced in a free enterprise economy.

Markets also determine prices. In our free enterprise system, individuals are free to make choices about how to use resources to satisfy their needs. Producers compete with each other to sell goods and services to consumers.

When there is free competition among sellers and among buyers, a market works according to what are called the laws of supply and demand. These "laws" are not made by legislatures. They are descriptions of what happens when many people make choices in a free market.

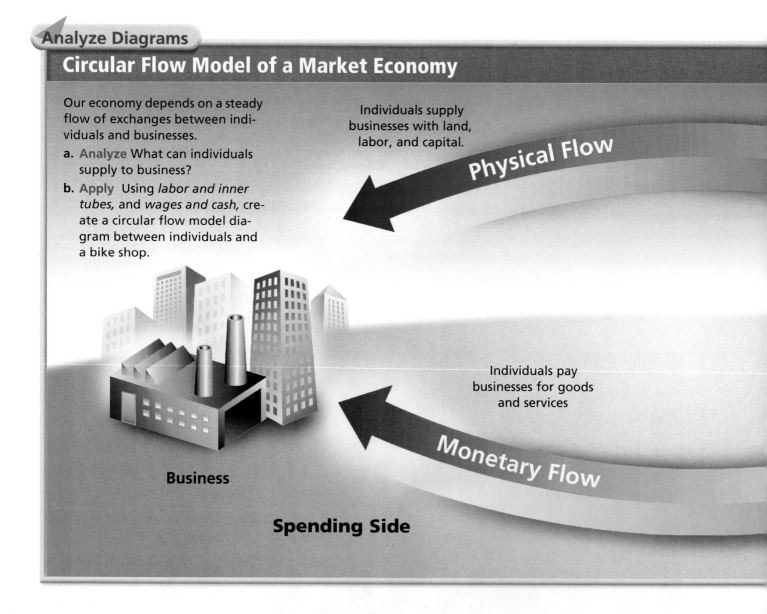

Analyze Diagrams

Circular Flow Model of a Market Economy

Our economy depends on a steady flow of exchanges between individuals and businesses.

a. **Analyze** What can individuals supply to business?

b. **Apply** Using *labor and inner tubes,* and *wages and cash,* create a circular flow model diagram between individuals and a bike shop.

Individuals supply businesses with land, labor, and capital.

Physical Flow

Individuals pay businesses for goods and services

Monetary Flow

Business

Spending Side

The Law of Demand At a farmer's market, people bought many strawberries from a farmer who was selling them for $2.25 a basket. In other words, people were demanding large amounts of strawberries at that price. **Demand** is the amount of a product or service buyers are willing and able to buy at different prices.

In deciding whether to buy an item, you balance its cost to you with the benefit you will receive from it. Will you enjoy the strawberries enough to pay 40 cents for them? Would the benefit be great enough for you to pay 80 cents? The lower the price of an item, the more likely you are to decide to buy it.

At a low price, more people will want strawberries, and more people will decide to buy more than one basket. In short, the quantity demanded by buyers will be high. At a high price, fewer people will decide to buy strawberries, and the quantity demanded will be low.

The way the law of demand works can be shown on a graph. The graph on the bottom of the next page shows what the quantity of strawberries demanded is likely to be at different prices. The demand is described by the line on the graph, called the demand curve.

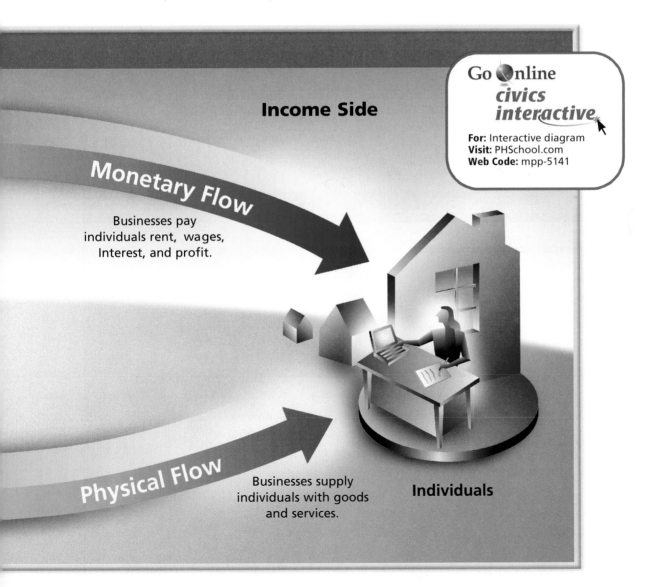

Income Side

Go Online
civics interactive

For: Interactive diagram
Visit: PHSchool.com
Web Code: mpp-5141

Monetary Flow

Businesses pay individuals rent, wages, Interest, and profit.

Physical Flow

Businesses supply individuals with goods and services.

Individuals

▲
Labor is one of many costs that producers must weigh.

The Law of Supply A producer, like a buyer, balances costs and benefits when making decisions. A producer's cost is determined by how much it costs to produce an item. The price a buyer pays for each item determines a producer's benefit. The higher the price a buyer is willing to pay for an item, the higher the benefit to the producer.

Supply is defined as the amount of a product that producers are willing and able to offer at different prices. When the price is high, more producers are willing to supply the product. In addition, each producer is willing to supply more of it. As a result, the amount supplied by producers as a whole will be high. When the price is low, fewer producers are willing to supply the product. The quantity supplied will be low.

The way the law of supply works for a particular product can also be shown on a graph. The graph below shows how supply, demand, and price relate for strawberries. One line on the graph below is a supply curve for strawberries. It shows what the quantity of strawberries is likely to be at different prices.

Supply and Demand How do prices get decided? The law of demand and the law of supply work together to determine the price of a product and the quantity offered. Price affects the amount demanded and the amount supplied in opposite ways. At higher prices, more of a product will be supplied but less will be demanded. At lower prices, less will be supplied but more demanded.

Analyze Graphs

Supply and Demand for Strawberries

The demand, the supply, and the price of strawberries are determined through a market. The graph shows how they relate.

1. **Analyze** How will a decrease in price effect the supply for strawberries?
2. **Calculate** At $0.20 a basket, how many baskets of strawberries could be sold and why?

The quantity supplied and the quantity demanded will tend to equal each other in an ideal market. This balance takes place at the market price. The **market price** is the price at which buyers and sellers agree to trade. If the demand and supply curves are placed on the same graph, the market price will be where the demand and supply curves intersect, or cross. The graph on the bottom of the previous page shows supply, demand, and market price.

Today, the market price for strawberries is 50 cents a basket. At this price, all the producers together are supplying about 1,000 baskets, and consumers are demanding about 1,000 baskets. A market price of 50 cents, however, does not prevent some farmers from charging less than the market price and other farmers from charging more.

If all the farmers raised their price for strawberries to 90 cents a basket, many buyers would decide the price was too high. Farmers would find they could not sell all their strawberries. They would have to lower their prices. If all other factors remained the same, the price would settle back to 50 cents a basket.

Other Influences Of course, demand can be influenced by factors other than price. For example, the demand for basic products, such as milk and penicillin, will not change very much when the price changes. People believe they need milk and medicine at almost any price.

Advertising, styles of fashion, and the way consumers perceive a certain product can affect the demand for that product. You might decide to buy a higher-priced pair of jeans, for instance, because that brand is more popular than a lower-priced brand.

Influencing Supply and Demand
Interactive displays and advertising help increase consumer demand for certain products, such as computers.
Draw Inferences *How can advertising affect demand for a product?*

✔ Reading Check **Why is the demand for milk not influenced much by its price?**

SECTION 1 Assessment

Key Terms
Use each of the key terms in a sentence that explains its meaning:
interest, demand, market price

Target Reading Skill
1. **Recognizing Multiple Causes** What factors affect the price of a product? List as many as you can.

Comprehension and Critical Thinking
2. **a. Recall** What kinds of resources do producers need to create goods and services?

b. Synthesize Information How are producers' payments for resources illustrated by the circular flow of the economy?

3. **a. Describe** What information do customers use when deciding whether or not to buy a product?
b. Analyze Information Why are some products such as milk and necessary medicines relatively unaffected by the laws of supply and demand?

Writing Activity
Think about a recent time when you bought a product. Reconstruct your decision-making process, and evaluate whether you made the right decision.

TIP Replay the shopping trip in your mind and make notes on your reactions. Look for critical decision-making moments when you considered such factors as the price of the good, the benefit you would receive from it, and how much money you had.

The Role of Business in the American Economy

Reading Preview

Objectives
In this section you will
- Learn about the role of the entrepreneur.
- Discuss how factors of production are used.
- Identify three models for owning a business.
- Learn about the rise of big business.

Taking Notes
Make a tree map like the one below. As you read the information, fill it in with information about the three types of business ownership.

Key Terms
entrepreneur
profit
sole proprietorship
partnership
corporation

Main Idea
In a market economy, goods and services are produced by privately owned businesses. Sole proprietorships, partnerships, and corporations are the three basic forms of private businesses.

Target Reading Skill
Understand Effects A cause makes something happen. An effect is what happens.

▲ Opening a business is a way many newcomers to the United States enter the economy.

Production and consumption are basic to any economy. As you have learned, people participate in production in order to be able to consume a variety of goods and services.

The production of goods and services is a complex process. In a market economy, most production is carried out by privately owned businesses. A business is any organization that combines labor, land, and capital in order to produce goods or services.

The Role of the Entrepreneur
Because businesses are vital to our economy, the people who start businesses play an important role. A person who starts a business is called an **entrepreneur (AHN truh preh NOOR)**.

An entrepreneur begins with an idea for a new product, a new way of producing something, or a better way of providing a service. The entrepreneur then raises money for capital goods to start the business.

By deciding to start a business, the entrepreneur is usually taking a major risk. If the business fails, he or she could lose all the money invested in it. If the business does well, however, he or she will make a profit. This **profit** will be the income earned by the business, minus the costs of the resources it uses. The hope of earning a profit—the profit motive—drives people to start businesses.

✓ Reading Check   **What motivates people in a capitalist economy to start a business?**

Using the Factors of Production

The three basic factors of production are labor, land, and capital. Many entrepreneurs are able to provide some of these factors of production themselves. They may provide their own land, labor, and capital to start their businesses.

Scott Sullivan, for example, is launching a small pie-baking business. He provides the labor by peeling and coring apples and baking the pies himself. He provides the capital by using his kitchen at home for preparing ingredients, baking the pies, and storing both new ingredients and fresh-baked pies. All he needs to buy, using money he has saved, are ingredients.

Payments for Resources Other entrepreneurs and business owners obtain the factors of production from other sources. Alice Ling is starting a larger pie-baking business. To set up a commercial kitchen, Alice borrows money from a bank. In exchange for this loan, she pays the bank interest. Alice's kitchen is located on land owned by someone else, to whom she pays rent. Finally, Alice hires workers as labor and pays them hourly wages. If she needs help in running her business, she will hire managers and pay them monthly salaries.

Through this example, you can see how businesses get each factor of production in exchange for a particular kind of payment. Some economists consider entrepreneurship to be a fourth factor of production in addition to land, labor, and capital. They point out that entrepreneurs provide ideas and take risks in return for payment in the form of profit.

✓ Reading Check **What cost is there to a business in borrowing capital?**

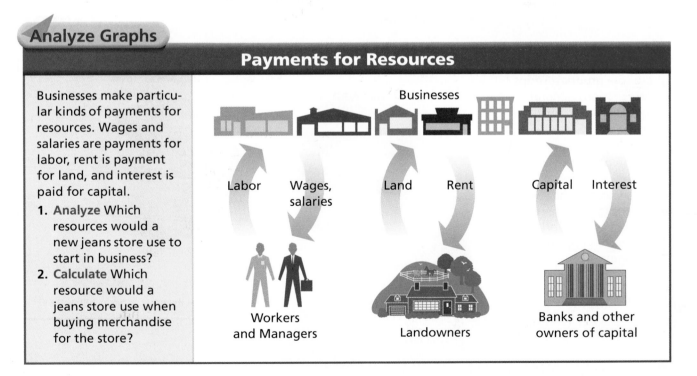

Analyze Graphs

Payments for Resources

Businesses make particular kinds of payments for resources. Wages and salaries are payments for labor, rent is payment for land, and interest is paid for capital.

1. **Analyze** Which resources would a new jeans store use to start in business?
2. **Calculate** Which resource would a jeans store use when buying merchandise for the store?

Businesses

Labor   Wages, salaries   Land   Rent   Capital   Interest

Workers and Managers   Landowners   Banks and other owners of capital

How Businesses are Owned

When entrepreneurs are planning their businesses, they must make an important decision. How will their businesses be owned? There are three basic types of business ownership in the United States: the sole proprietorship, the partnership, and the corporation. Each type has advantages and disadvantages.

The Sole Proprietorship Many entrepreneurs starting a small business, like Scott Sullivan, will establish a **sole proprietorship**, which is a business owned by an individual. Sole proprietorships are the most common form of business. About 70 percent of the businesses in this country are sole proprietorships. Most are small businesses such as restaurants, repair shops, and small groceries.

The advantages of a sole proprietorship are many. The owner, or sole proprietor, has the freedom to decide how to run the business. The profits belong to the owner alone. The owner also has the personal satisfaction of knowing that he or she made the business succeed.

There are also disadvantages of a sole proprietorship. First, the owner bears responsibility for all business debts. Second, it can be hard for one owner to borrow enough money to expand the business. Third, as a business grows, it becomes increasingly difficult for one owner to handle all responsibilities and decisions.

The Partnership A **partnership** is a type of business in which two or more people share ownership. Alice, for example, could set up her pie-baking business as a partnership if she knew someone who wanted to share the costs and help her run the business. In the United States, many law firms, medical groups, and accounting businesses are set up as partnerships.

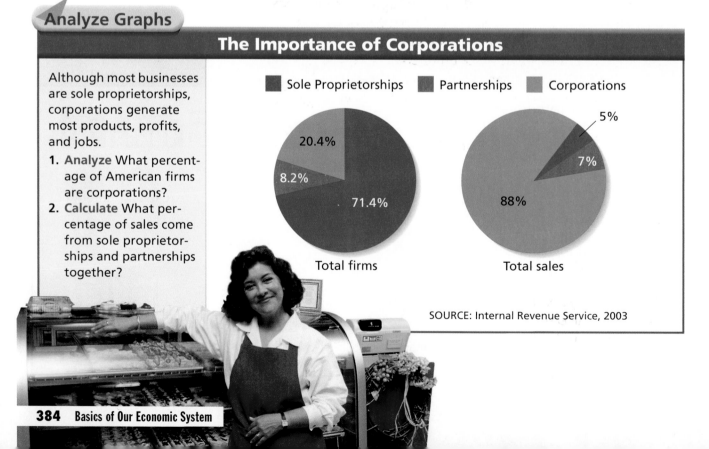

Analyze Graphs

The Importance of Corporations

Although most businesses are sole proprietorships, corporations generate most products, profits, and jobs.

1. **Analyze** What percentage of American firms are corporations?
2. **Calculate** What percentage of sales come from sole proprietorships and partnerships together?

■ Sole Proprietorships   ■ Partnerships   ■ Corporations

Total firms
- 71.4%
- 20.4%
- 8.2%

Total sales
- 88%
- 7%
- 5%

SOURCE: Internal Revenue Service, 2003

The advantages and disadvantages of a partnership are similar to those of a sole proprietorship. The main difference is that more than one person shares risks and benefits. An additional disadvantage of a partnership is the possibility of serious differences arising between the partners, which could damage or ruin the business.

The Corporation Sole proprietors and partners are personally responsible for the businesses they own. In contrast, a **corporation** is a business that is separate from the people who own it and legally acts as a single person.

More than one person shares the ownership of a corporation. The shares of ownership in a corporation are called its stock, and people who buy stock are called stockholders.

Many corporations sell stock to the public. By selling stock, a corporation raises the money necessary to start, run, and expand the business. Millions of Americans buy stock as an investment, because stockholders share a corporation's profits.

A corporation has unique advantages. It can raise large quantities of money to grow mainly through selling stock. Furthermore, stockholders are not responsible for the corporation's debts. If the corporation fails, a stockholder loses only the value of his or her stock.

Corporations also have several disadvantages. Corporations are more difficult and more expensive to start than other businesses. They are more limited by government regulations.

Corporations create most of the products, profits, and jobs in our economy. Although most large businesses are corporations, even some small businesses can benefit from a corporation's advantages.

> ✓ Reading Check **What is the most common form of business ownership in the United States?**

Citizen Profiles

Michael Bloomberg (born 1942) Michael Bloomberg began a career in financial services after he graduated from business school in 1966. He quickly rose to high levels at Solomon Brothers in New York City. However, he lost his position in 1981 when the company was sold. Bloomberg used his money and experience to start a company to organize the huge amounts of data produced on Wall Street. Soon, his company was bringing instant data from world financial markets to thousands of traders and investors. Looking for new challenges, Bloomberg turned to public service. Only a few months after the terrorist attacks of September 11, 2001, Bloomberg took office as mayor of New York City.

Citizenship
After achieving success, how did Bloomberg give back to the community?

The Rise of Big Business

Large businesses organized as corporations dominate our economy today. They make nearly 90 percent of the total sales in the American economy. However, large corporations did not always have such an important role in our economy.

In our country's early years, most businesses were small sole proprietorships. The economy was different. Many families were nearly self-sufficient, producing much of what they needed for themselves.

The Growth of Big Business
Sears, Roebuck and Co. started in Chicago in the late 1800s as a mail-order consumer catalog. **Draw Inferences** *What factors affected the growth of Sears?*

In the 1800s, however, new inventions and manufacturing methods spurred growth and industrialization. Factories sprang up, producing more goods at lower prices. People settled in cities, attracted by jobs in new industries.

People who lived in cities depended on businesses for goods and services, so businesses did well. Successful sole proprietors turned their businesses into corporations in order to grow. By the end of the 1800s, large corporations dominated the railroads, key manufacturing industries, and mining.

In the past 100 years, large corporations have become a major force in nearly every industry, from supermarkets and fast-food chains to computers and automobiles. Large corporations even own many of America's farms.

One reason large corporations have grown in importance is that they can produce goods and provide services more efficiently than smaller firms. Large firms can better afford the expensive machinery needed to produce more goods in less time. They also have the resources to do scientific research to develop new products and production methods.

In the future, large businesses organized as corporations will probably continue to grow in importance. However, sole proprietorships, partnerships, and small corporations will always have an important role to play in our economy.

✓ **Reading Check** **Why have large corporations grown in importance?**

SECTION 2 Assessment

Key Terms

Use each of the key terms in a sentence that explains its meaning: entrepreneur, profit, sole proprietorship, partnership, corporation

Target Reading Skill

1. **Understand Effects** What is the effect of new inventions and manufacturing methods on the American economy?

Comprehension and Critical Thinking

2. **a. Recall** What risk does an entrepreneur face?
   b. Draw Conclusions Why do you think people choose to start their own businesses?

3. **a. Recall** What are the three factors of production?
   b. Why do economists believe that entrepreneurship is also a factor of production?

4. **a. Describe** What are the three basic types of business ownership in the United States?
   b. Compare What are the advantages of a partnership over a sole proprietorship?

5. **a. Describe** Why might a sole proprietor turn a business into a corporation?
   b. Draw Inferences Why do you think banks are more likely to lend money to corporations than sole proprietors?

Writing Activity

Interview a business owner. Ask about their form of business ownership, what led them to start the business, and to describe events in the growth of the business. Write the results of your interview in a report.

TIP Write your questions in advance. If possible, show the questions to the business owner. Record the interview on a tape recorder or take careful notes. Show your report to the business owner to confirm its accuracy.

Debating the Issues

The debates in this feature are based on *Current Issues*, published by the Close Up Foundation. Go to **PHSchool.com**, Web Code mph-1025, to read the latest issue of *Current Issues* online.

Scientists have learned to alter plants to make them more resistant to insects and disease. Among the processes they use is genetic modification (GM). It can result in higher crop yields. Genetic modification changes the chemical structure of the plant. Some GM crops are created to resist pests and disease without the use of pesticides. Some people worry that genes from GM crops can cross to other plants and give weeds the same protections, causing unpredictable changes to the environment. Also, foods such as tomatoes, corn, and peas can look and taste different. These basic fruits and vegetables form the basis of canned soups, bottled sauces, and packaged foods. The federal government does not require that genetically modified foods be labeled. Therefore, American consumers have no way to know whether the food they buy is genetically modified.

Should Genetically Modified Foods Be Labeled?

YES	NO
• People have the right to know what they are eating. GM labels would allow them to make informed decisions about which foods to purchase.	• Farmers fear that most Americans will believe genetically modified foods are not healthy. If these foods were labeled, people would not buy them. This might a serious impact on the agricultural industry in this country.
• Member nations of the European Union already label foods. Their agricultural industries have not suffered.	• Studies have not proven that genetically modified foods are any more dangerous than organic ones. There is no need for "warning labels" on safe products.
• GM crops may be unsafe for the environment. Labeling GM food gives consumers the power to express their views by choosing alternatives.	

What is Your Opinion?

1. **Identify Bias** Which groups of people probably want GM labels? Which groups are against labeling? Why do you think so?

2. **Solve Problems** Propose a way to meet the needs of both sides of the genetic modification argument. How can the government protect both farmers and consumers? Explain.

3. **Writing to Persuade** Suppose that you are a farmer who grows GM crops, and Congress is currently debating legislation to require GM labels on all foods. Write your congressperson a letter in which you support or protest this legislation. Include specific arguments to convince him or her to vote your way.

Go Online
civics interactive
For: You Decide Poll
Visit: PHSchool.com
Web Code: mph-5142

Labor in the American Economy

Reading Preview

Objectives

In this section you will
- Describe the growth of wage labor.
- Discuss the rise of labor unions and learn about their history.
- Discuss today's labor force.

Taking Notes

Make a diagram like the one below. As you read the section, fill it in with information about the changing relationship between labor and business owners.

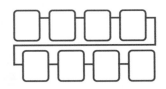

Young children were a big part of the labor force in the 1800s.
▼

Key Terms

labor unions
collective bargaining

boycott
strike

Main Idea

Industrialization changed the way Americans worked. Workers tried to form labor unions to improve their conditions, but business owners often opposed them. Today, labor unions are an important part of the economy.

Target Reading Skill

Identify Causes and Effects When you can identify the causes and effects of a situation, you can better understand the relationships among situations or events.

Labor, as you know, is one of the factors of production. However, labor is different from the other factors of production in that it is provided by human beings who care about their working conditions and the rewards they receive for their labor.

Workers have a built-in conflict with entrepreneurs and business managers. Workers and employers represent two sides of a free market trade in labor. On the one hand, business owners want to keep costs low and profits high. One way to do this is to keep wages low. Workers, on the other hand, want to earn the highest possible wages for their labor. This conflict has had an important impact on the American economic system.

The Growth of Wage Labor

Many Americans were farmers when our country was young. Most of what they needed they produced themselves. They could do this because they owned a productive resource—land.

Other Americans were skilled craftspeople, such as shoemakers and blacksmiths. Craftspeople either worked for themselves or for someone they knew. They also generally owned their own capital—the tools of their craft. Most Americans, therefore, had control over the conditions of their work.

Students Make a Difference

Naudereh Noori, a sophomore at Enloe Magnet School in Raleigh, North Carolina, believes that educating the public on cultural difference can strengthen a community.

Naudereh volunteers at two different institutions that educate people about different cultures. One is Exploris, a local Raleigh museum that exhibits works from different cultures. The other is Ten Thousand Villages, a non-profit store that sells crafts made from artisans who come from developing countries.

▲ Students can help make a difference by raising people's awareness of cultural differences.

Service Learning

How can you educate your community about cultural differences?

Deficit Budget Industrialization Creates Change Great changes began to occur in the 1800s. Improvements in farm machinery meant that farms needed fewer workers. New machinery and manufacturing methods led to rapid industrialization. Machines could produce more goods more cheaply than people making goods by hand.

Former craftspeople, farmhands, and new immigrants began to turn to wage labor to make a living. Wage laborers worked in mines, factories, and workshops. They owned no land or tools. Instead, they exchanged their labor for payments called wages.

Poor Working Conditions Many wage laborers had to accept whatever work was available at any wage or starve. Business owners took advantage of this situation by paying very low wages. If a worker complained, he or she could be fired.

The numbers of wage laborers grew steadily during the 1800s as factories increased in number. Most factory jobs were monotonous, low-paid, and dangerous. Wage laborers, many of them children, worked six days a week, 12 to 16 hours a day.

✓ Reading Check **In wage labor, who controls the working conditions, employers or workers?**

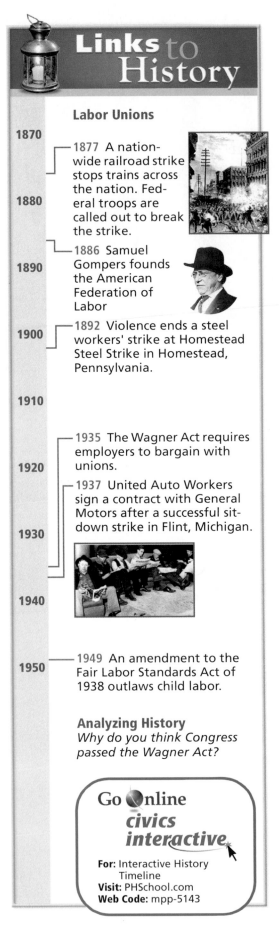

Labor Unions

1870

1877 A nation-wide railroad strike stops trains across the nation. Federal troops are called out to break the strike.

1880

1886 Samuel Gompers founds the American Federation of Labor

1890

1900

1892 Violence ends a steel workers' strike at Homestead Steel Strike in Homestead, Pennsylvania.

1910

1920

1935 The Wagner Act requires employers to bargain with unions.

1937 United Auto Workers sign a contract with General Motors after a successful sit-down strike in Flint, Michigan.

1930

1940

1950

1949 An amendment to the Fair Labor Standards Act of 1938 outlaws child labor.

Analyzing History
Why do you think Congress passed the Wagner Act?

The Rise of Labor Unions

Individual workers had little power over wages and working conditions. Workers began to realize that they could influence their employers only if they organized into groups fighting for common goals. As a result, workers began to form **labor unions**, which are organizations of workers that seek to improve wages and working conditions and to protect members' rights.

The first American unions formed in the 1790s. At the time, most Americans worked on farms or in small workshops in close contact with their employers.

The Industrial Revolution gradually brought many workers into large factories for the first time. New working conditions brought new needs for labor organization and representation before employers. By the early 1880s there were many small unions. Most were organized as trade unions, made up of workers in one particular trade such as carpentry or cigar making. These were generally skilled workers, whose jobs required some special knowledge.

The first important national union was The Noble Order of the Knights of Labor, which reached its height in 1886. The Knights of Labor tried to bring together the entire working class, both skilled and unskilled. However, these two groups of workers often disagreed, and finally the Knights of Labor broke up.

Soon after, a new union, the American Federation of Labor (AFL), gained power. The AFL united smaller trade unions, made up of only skilled workers, into a more powerful national organization. A goal of the AFL was to force employers to agree to participate in collective bargaining. **Collective bargaining** is the process by which representatives of the unions and business try to reach agreement about wages and working conditions.

The following years were a period of intense conflict between unions and business owners. Unions demanded an eight-hour day and higher wages. Owners were determined not to give in. They wished to protect their rights as entrepreneurs in a free market economy.

Labor's Weapons Unions used many methods to try to force employers to meet their demands. In a slowdown, workers stayed on the job but did their work much more slowly. In a sit-down strike, workers stopped working but refused to leave the factory, so the employer could not replace them with non-union workers. Sometimes union members would urge their members and the public to **boycott**, or refuse to buy, an employer's products.

The major weapon of the unions has been the strike. In a **strike**, workers refuse to work unless employers meet certain demands. Hundreds of strikes occurred between 1886 and 1920. Some of the most significant strikes were by textile, steel, and railroad unions.

The Weapons of Business Business owners responded to strikes in various ways. Typically they used strikebreakers, or "scabs." Scabs are non-union workers hired to cross a picket line to replace the striking workers and keep a factory or other business running. If union workers tried to keep strikebreakers from entering the factory, business owners often hired private police to stop them. These private police also broke up union meetings and bothered union members in other ways. Often the business owners had the support of local police or state militias. Violence broke out during some strikes, causing many deaths.

In lockouts, management refused to let union members enter the factory, and replaced them with scabs. Some employers forced workers to sign "yellow-dog contracts" in which they promised never to join the union. Finally, some employers circulated blacklists containing the names of union members and supporters, so that other employers would not hire them.

Conflict and Agreement
Striking workers block a driver from making deliveries (above, top). Employers and union leaders negotiate (above, bottom). **Draw Inferences** *Why do unions and businesses sometimes disagree on wages?*

Analyze Diagrams

Methods That Employers and Unions Use in Disputes

Union Tactics		Employee Tactics
Slowdowns		Strikebreakers
Sit-ins		Security Forces
Strikes		Lockouts
Boycotts		Yellow-dog Contracts
Demonstrations		Blacklists

Workers and businesses have used a number of tactics in disputes over wages and working conditions.
1. **Analyze** Which union tactics are more effective than others?
2. **Calculate** What are three ways that businesses have responded to strikes by workers?

Employers and union leaders often do not see eye-to-eye on every issue. This cartoon summarizes a disagreement in one round of negotiation.

1. Why does the union want more "moola," or money?
2. Describe the difference in tone between the phrases "profit maximization" and "moola." Why did the cartoonist chose these words?

"Gentlemen, nothing stands in the way of a final accord except that management wants profit maximization and the union wants more moola."

On Strike
Workers went on strike against companies in the garment industry in 1926.
Draw Inferences *How is picketing effective for workers on strike?*

Gains and Losses The weapons used by both labor and management were economic. Unions used sit-downs, slowdowns, boycotts, and strikes with the intent to interrupt production and reduce business profits. It was thought that by causing the employer to lose money through lost production, the employer would decide it would be less expensive to give in to worker demands and raise wages or improve conditions.

When employers used yellow-dog contracts, lockouts, blacklists, and strikebreakers, they took away union members' jobs and thus their ability to make a living. Many workers in the 1800s depended on weekly paychecks to feed their families and pay rent. They could not strike for more than a short amount of time without suffering from the loss of income. These tactics discouraged workers from trying to strike.

Labor unions won important victories by 1920. A few industries had reduced the working day to 8 or 10 hours. Wages had increased for some workers. The federal government had established the Department of Labor to protect the rights of workers. In spite of these gains, however, labor suffered many crushing defeats and broken strikes.

✓ Reading Check **What weapons did business use to respond to strikes?**

Labor Unions Since 1930

The government began to fully recognize the right of unions to exist and to strike by the 1930s. Congress passed the National Labor Relations Act, or Wagner Act, in 1935. It required employers to bargain with unions that represent a majority of a firm's employees. This act also outlawed several methods business owners had used to weaken unions. Employers could not set up "company" unions that would be friendlier to management than worker-led unions. They could not fire employees for union activity.

Later laws, such as the Taft-Hartley Act of 1947 and the Landrum-Griffin Act of 1959, put limits on the powers of unions and union leaders. However, the Wagner Act marked a turning point in the history of American labor. Unions felt that their rightful place in the American economy had finally been recognized.

Meanwhile, a new kind of union was gaining strength: the industrial union. An industrial union includes all workers in a particular industry—both skilled and unskilled. Soon, workers in such industries as steel, coal, and rubber had their own industrial unions representing American workers in all areas of the industry. Some industrial unions within the AFL formed the Committee of Industrial Organizations (CIO) in 1935. These unions were expelled from the AFL in 1938 and became independent as the CIO, which changed its name to the Congress of Industrial Organizations.

At first the AFL and the CIO were rivals, competing for members. The two unions united to form the AFL-CIO in 1955. Today, the AFL-CIO is the most powerful voice of organized labor in the United States. It has over 13 million members. Among its other activities, it plays an important political role by lobbying in Congress and working to elect pro-labor candidates to office.

Analyze Graphs

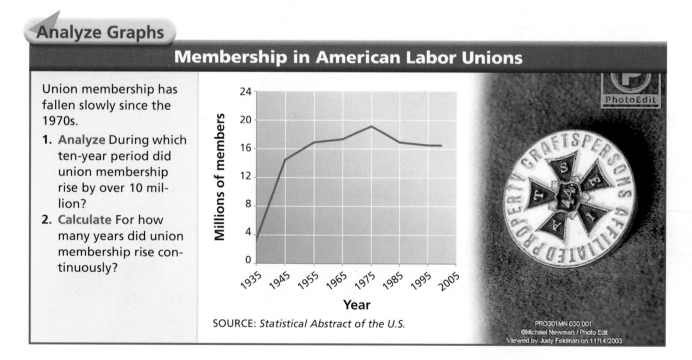

Membership in American Labor Unions

Union membership has fallen slowly since the 1970s.

1. **Analyze** During which ten-year period did union membership rise by over 10 million?
2. **Calculate** For how many years did union membership rise continuously?

SOURCE: *Statistical Abstract of the U.S.*

Labor's Accomplishments Unions have helped win fairer wages for workers since the early 1930s. They have been a major force in getting the government to pass laws creating social security, unemployment insurance, and a minimum wage. They have also worked for laws protecting workers' safety, banning child labor, and providing retraining for unemployed workers.

Today, only about one worker in seven is a union member. Union membership has declined in recent decades. Still, labor unions have played a key role in improving the lives of all workers.

Common Interests Unions today still go on strike and encourage boycotts. However, both workers and employers have learned to see their shared interests as well as their differences. Employers see that workers need safe working conditions. They also know that workers who are paid fairly produce more and are more likely to buy goods and services.

Unions, on the other hand, recognize that members' jobs depend on businesses making profits. They have seen that when wages rise too high, profits may decline. Then businesses may fail or move to other states or countries where labor costs are lower.

✓ Reading Check **Why is the Wagner Act an important law for labor?**

Today's Labor Force

As you have seen, the composition of the labor force—the number of people working at each type of job in the economy—has changed a great deal since the birth of our country. For example, farmers, who outnumbered any other kind of worker in 1776, today make up less than 3 percent of the American labor force. There are also more women in the labor force than ever before. Women have been entering the labor force in ever-increasing numbers since the 1940s.

Women in the Labor Force
Female workers rivet an airplane during World War II (below, left). Today, women perform many types of jobs, including work at a construction site (below, right).
Draw Inferences *Why do more women work today than in the 1940s?*

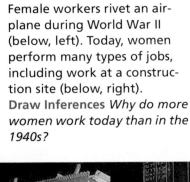

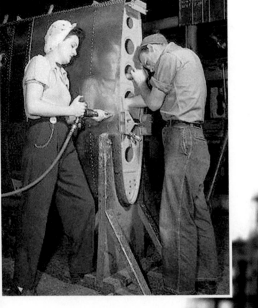

Another important change is the decline of manufacturing industries such as steel making. As a result, these industries are employing a decreasing percentage of America's workers.

At the same time, businesses that offer services have grown in importance. Service-oriented businesses, such as banks, insurance companies, and restaurants, now employ a large and growing majority of American workers. These businesses make up what is called the service sector of the economy.

The change in focus of our economy, from manufacturing to service, has caused many problems for workers. When a steel factory closes, for example, its workers do not always have the training to find new jobs in another industry. Furthermore, service-sector businesses are often located in different parts of the country than the factories that are closing. Americans, therefore, face personal and economic change as our country shifts from an industrial economy to a service economy.

✓ **Reading Check** **What has happened recently to manufacturing in America?**

▲ Some businesses open as other businesses close and let go of employees.

SECTION 3 Assessment

Key Terms

Use each of the key terms in a sentence that explains its meaning: labor unions, collective bargaining, boycott, strike

Target Reading Skill

1. **Identify Cause and Effect** What were some of the factors that caused Congress to pass the Wagner Act? What were the Act's effects?

Comprehension and Critical Thinking

2. **a. Explain** What advantages did farmers and craftspeople have over wage laborers?
   b. Synthesize Information How did new farm machinery and new methods of manufacturing affect workers?

3. **a. Recall** What was the American Federation of Labor?
   b. Draw Inferences Why do you think business owners resisted the demands of the AFL so strongly?

4. **a. Explain** How was the CIO different from the AFL?
   b. Make Generalizations Why do you think unions and employers have learned to identify common interests?

5. **a. Describe** How have manufacturing employment and service employment changed in recent years?
   b. Draw Inferences How do you think a town is affected when a large manufacturing plant that employs many people in that town closes?

Writing Activity

Using Internet resources, find out more about the issues that the AFL-CIO is campaigning for. Choose one issue that interests you. Write a brief summary of the position that the AFL-CIO takes on this issue. Give reasons for why you agree or disagree with this labor oganization's position on the issue.

Go Online
PHSchool.com
For: Journal Activity
Visit: PHSchool.com
Web Code: mpd-5143

Solving Problems

Historical events do not happen in isolation. They are the result of events that came before them and are linked to events that follow them. To understand an event, it is important to place it in the context of history. Studying events that preceded and helped cause other events can help you identify historical trends.

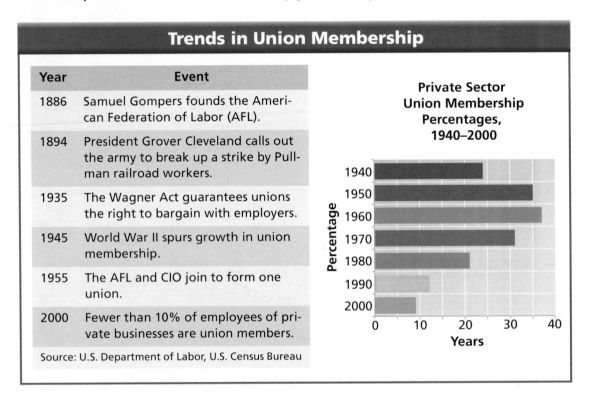

Trends in Union Membership

Year	Event
1886	Samuel Gompers founds the American Federation of Labor (AFL).
1894	President Grover Cleveland calls out the army to break up a strike by Pullman railroad workers.
1935	The Wagner Act guarantees unions the right to bargain with employers.
1945	World War II spurs growth in union membership.
1955	The AFL and CIO join to form one union.
2000	Fewer than 10% of employees of private businesses are union members.

Source: U.S. Department of Labor, U.S. Census Bureau

Private Sector Union Membership Percentages, 1940–2000

Learn the Skill

Follow these steps to identify historical trends:

❶ Examine the evidence. Identify key facts, issues, and dates.

❷ Look for connections among different pieces of evidence. What similarities or cause-effect relationships can you find? How are pieces of evidence related?

❸ Identify historical trends. What is the direction that these events are taking? What shifts in people's attitudes do they show?

Practice the Skill

Study the chart and graph above and answer these questions:

❶ (a) What events does the chart show? (b) What facts are shown in the graph?

❷ What event shown in the chart is reinforced by a fact on the graph?

❸ What trend can you see from the information in the graph?

Apply the Skill

Find a newspaper or magazine article that uses a graph of data collected over time to illustrate the points it is making. Examine the graph and the article closely and describe any trends you see.

CHAPTER 14

Review and Assessment

Chapter Summary

Section 1
The Principles of Our Market Economy
(pages 376–381)

- A market economy is a circular flow of goods, services, capital, and payments by producers such as wages and interest.

- The laws of supply and demand work together to determine the market price of a product and the quantity offered.

Section 2
The Role of Business in the American Economy
(pages 382–386)

- Entrepreneurs face the risk of losing their money and the possible reward of profit.

- The three factors of production are labor, land, and capital.

- The three basic forms of business ownership are sole proprietorships, partnerships, and corporations.

- The American economy today is dominated by large businesses organized as corporations.

Section 3
Labor in the American Economy
(pages 388–395)

- As a result of the growth of wage labor, workers began to form labor unions to gain more control over their working conditions.

- Labor unions participate in collective bargaining with employers over wages and working conditions.

- Labor unions use boycotts, strikes, and other tactics to achieve change.

TEN545PM 008 001

Copy the chart below and use it to help you summarize the chapter:

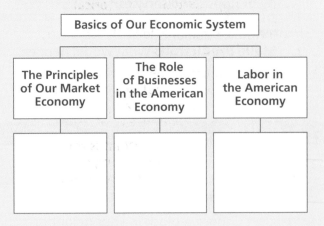

Basics of Our Economic System

The Principles of Our Market Economy	The Role of Businesses in the American Economy	Labor in the American Economy

Review and Assessment Continued

Reviewing Key Terms

Fill in the blank with one of the key terms from the list.

collective bargaining | partnership
interest | demand
corporation | entrepreneur
profit | boycott

1. The income earned by a business, minus the costs of the resources used, is its _____.

2. The amount of a product or service that customers are willing to buy is called _____.

3. The process by which employers and workers try to reach agreement on wages, working conditions, and other issues is called _____.

4. A person who starts a business is called a _____.

5. A weapon used by unions when they urge people not to buy their employer's products is called a _____.

6. When two or more people share ownership of a business, it is called a _____.

7. Payment for the use of capital is called _____.

8. A form of business ownership that sells shares to the public and legally acts as a single person is called a _____.

Comprehension and Critical Thinking

9. a. **Recall** In wage labor jobs, what do workers provide in return for wages?
   b. **Contrast** What do people need to buy goods and services? What do producers need to make goods and services?
   c. **Predict** What would happen to the circular flow of economic activity if a large number of people lost their jobs?

10. a. **Recall** In a free enterprise economy, what determines the price and availability of goods and services?
    b. **Draw Conclusions** How does price influence demand?
    c. **Make Predictions** What would happen to the price of a good if it was in short supply?

11. a. **Explain** Why do people buy stock in corporations?
    b. **Contrast** What advantages does a sole proprietorship have?
    c. **Contrast** What advantages does a corporation have over the other forms of business ownership?

12. a. **Explain** How did business owners take advantage of wage laborers after the industrialization of the 1800s?
    b. **Identify Cause and Effect** How did the growth of wage labor create the need for labor unions?
    c. **Draw Conclusions** Why do you think business owners had the support of the police or state militia in several strikes?

Activities

13. **Skills a.** Describe the historical trend that is shown by most of the points in the box. **b.** Which point does not fit the trend? Explain.

14. **Writing** Choose a block in your neighborhood or town and write a short essay about the businesses located there. In your essay, speculate about what form of business ownership each store or business uses.

1935
- The Wagner Act protects collective bargaining.
- The Social Security Act is passed.

1936
- United Auto workers stage a sit-down strike at a General Motors plant in Flint, Michigan.

1937
- Police attack a peaceful crowd in Chicago during a steel strike, killing 10 people and wounding 80.

398 Basics of Our Economic System

15. Active Citizen How has the labor force changed over the years? Ask parents or other adults to describe how their work experiences have been different from those of their parents and grandparents.

16. Math Practice If a state has 862,000 workers and 5% of those workers lose their jobs, how many people are out of work?

17. Civics and Economics Many businesses are required to comply with government regulations. Interview the manager of a local restaurant to find out what regulations the business must follow. Ask how the regulations help and hurt the business. Conclude your report by describing your opinion of the regulations as a customer.

18. Analyzing Visuals The map shows the location of Cones of Vermont Ice Cream shops in Vermont. If you were in Bristol, which would be the closest Cones of Vermont location?

Standardized Test Prep

Test-Taking Tips

The following text appears on a plaque outside the building in Flint, Michigan that was the site of a United Auto Workers strike.

> Starting December 30, 1936, this building was occupied for 44 days by striking members of the United Auto Workers. The strikers . . . asked for recognition of the union as sole bargaining representative for all hourly-rated employees of General Motors Corporation. Court injunctions [orders] and threats of eviction by both the sheriff of Genesee County and the Flint Police Department did not sway the strikers from their goal. An agreement was reached in Detroit on February 11, 1937, that changed the relationships between the company and its employees. The settlement led to complete unionization of the auto industry in ensuing years and added stability for the union and the company.

TIP Words like "led to" are good tips that the sentence is describing an effect.

Choose the letter of the best answer.

1. What was an effect of the agreement reached on December 11, 1937?
   A The police were banned from interfering in strikes.
   B The auto industry became unionized.
   C The workers promised never to stage a sit-down strike again.
   D The auto plant closed down.

   The correct answer is **B.**

2. What was the cause of the Flint sit-down strike?
   A General Motors' hiring of nonunion workers
   B a desire of the auto workers to get a raise
   C the demand that General Motors recognize the union
   D the agreement that led to unionization of the auto industry

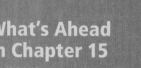
Our Economy and You

What's Ahead in Chapter 15

In this chapter, you will learn about personal money management. You will read about how to become a smart consumer and learn how to save money. You will also begin to think about how to plan for a career.

SECTION 1
Managing Your Money

SECTION 2
Spending and Saving

SECTION 3
Careers: Planning for the Future

TARGET READING SKILL

Clarifying Meaning In this chapter you will focus on the skill of clarifying meaning. To clarify meaning as you read, you will read ahead, paraphrase ideas, and summarize main points.

Shoppers at a music store

The following National Standards for Civics and Government are covered in this chapter:

II. What are the roles of the citizen in American democracy?

B. What are the rights of citizens?

C. What are the responsibilities of citizens?

Go Online
PHSchool.com

For: Your state's standards
Visit: PHSchool.com
Web Code: mpe-5151

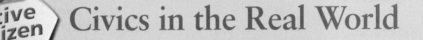

Active Citizen › Civics in the Real World

The following is a short segment from a radio talk-show called *Managing Your Money*. Kathy Clarke, a 24-year-old travel agent, called in to share her financial story with the talk-show host.

Kathy My trouble began when I started using credit cards just after I moved out of my parents' house and into my own place.

Host I gather that you used them a lot?

Kathy Yes. You name it, I bought it—new clothes, a color TV, some luggage. I kept telling myself that I needed the stuff I was buying, and that I could save later.

Host But later you had bills?

Kathy Right. At first I thought I could handle them because I was expecting a raise at work. But the raise never came. Now I'm stuck with a growing pile of bills. I'm really in a panic.

Kathy's story shows that people, acting as workers and consumers, make choices about money that dramatically affect their lives.

Citizen's Journal Suppose you were the host of *Managing Your Money*. What would you advise Kathy to do? Write a paragraph suggesting how she can get out of debt. When you have finished reading the chapter, reread your advice. Do you want to add anything to or change it?

Managing Your Money

Reading Preview

Objectives

In this section you will

- Learn to understand your income by knowing what you have.
- Discuss how to make financial choices.

Taking Notes

Make a diagram like the one below. As you read the section, complete the diagram with information connecting income, financial choices, and budgets.

Key Terms

fringe benefits
dividends
disposable income

fixed expenses
variable
  expenses

Main Idea

It is important to manage the money you earn so that you do not spend more than you have. You can keep track of your fixed and variable expenses and create a budget to help you.

Target Reading Skill

Read Ahead When you come to difficult or confusing passages in a text, reading ahead can help you understand. Section 1 contains charts and other graphic displays of information that illustrate the text. Sometimes, it may help to skip ahead to a graphic illustration and then go back to read the text it illustrates.

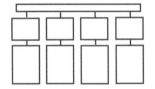

Responsible consumers must learn to manage the money they earn.▼

Learning how to manage your money involves several steps. You need to understand your income. You should know what your expenses will be. You should also determine what your goals and values are. Kathy Clarke got into trouble because she did not give enough thought to what her income and expenses were. Also, she did not understand credit well enough to see how using credit cards would affect her. Customers who charge their purchases with credit cards must pay their entire monthly bills or incur interest charges.

Making a budget, or a plan for spending and saving, can help you to set your goals and reach them. Kathy realizes that in order to pay the money she owes on her credit cards, she needs to come up with a plan for managing her money.

Income: Knowing What You Have

There are many forms of income. You can earn income directly by working. If you own stock in a corporation, or have money in a savings account, you can earn income from these sources. Gifts of money and money earned by renting or selling property are also income.

Earned Income The pay that people receive for their work is known as earned income. Earned income comes in several forms: salary, wage, commission, and bonus.

At the time Kathy got into debt, she was earning $27,000 per year at the travel agency. Kathy received a salary, or payment at regular intervals—$1,038.46 every two weeks, before taxes. After taxes, her income is less.

Others in Kathy's office are paid in different ways. Mark Aguilar, a college student, works part-time for a wage of $9 per hour. Mark's weekly income changes depending on how many hours he works. The more hours he works, the more money he earns.

Joe Pelligrino has been a travel agent for 20 years. In addition to his salary, he gets a commission, or a percentage of money taken in on sales. Joe's commission is 20 percent of his sales. If he sells five or more tours in a month, he also receives a bonus, extra income as a reward for excellent work.

Kathy decides to look at her salary to see what she is making per hour. She discovers that because she is working many extra hours each month, she is actually making a low wage. Based on this information, Kathy manages to convince her boss to give her a raise. She will now receive more money in each paycheck.

Analyze Charts

Types of Income

Type	Description	Advantages	Disadvantages
Salary	Employee receives a fixed payment at regular intervals	Guaranteed pay whether business thrives or is slow	No extra pay for extra hours worked
Wage	Employee paid by the hour	Paid for all time worked	May face loss of income if business is low and hours are cut back
Commission	Employee receives a percentage of the price of a good or service as payment for making the sale	Hard work rewarded with increased pay	Income not guaranteed; if business is slow, income could fall sharply
Bonus	Employee given additional money for excellent work performance	Good work rewarded with additional income	None
Piecework	Employee paid for each unit of a product he or she makes	Faster workers can make more money	Income can vary widely depending on work speed and availability of work

There are many diffent types of income that people can earn from working. The chart above shows these types of incomes, along with their advantages and disadvantages.

1. **Analyze** What are the advantages of a commission? What are the disadvantages?
2. **Apply** In your opinion, which form of income has the most important advantages? Explain.

Go Online
civics
interactive

For: Interactive Constitution
with Supreme Court Cases
Visit: PHSchool.com
Web Code: mpp-5151

The Supreme Court *Goldberg* v. *Kelly* (1970)

Why It Matters The question in this case is whether people receiving public assistance have the same legal rights as they would have in a court of law.

Background In 1969, John Kelly was unemployed and living with a disability in New York City. Kelly received public assistance because he was unable to work. Without warning, the state of New York cut off his benefits. Kelly had no work or money to support himself. Although the federal government provided money for pubic assistance, each state administered its own programs. A local organization helped Kelly sue New York and Jack Goldberg, New York City's commissioner for social services.

Kelly's lawyers argued that public assistance benefits were a right, not a privilege, and essential to Kelly's survival. As a result, they argued, New York was required to follow rules of due process guaranteed in the Fourteenth Amendment. Lawyers for New York argued that state officials had the right to terminate Kelly's benefits whenever they saw fit to do so.

The Decision The Court voted 7-2 in favor of Kelly. A majority of justices ruled that public assistance recipients could not be denied their benefits without a hearing and due process. Justice William Brennan wrote that Kelly was entitled by law to his benefits and that the Fourteenth Amendment guaranteed his rights. Furthermore, Kelly's right to due process was more important than the financial and administrative burden this placed upon New York State.

Understanding the Law

1. Why did John Kelly sue New York?
2. What significance do you think *Goldberg* v. *Kelly* holds for people who are not on public assistance?

Fringe Benefits In addition to salaries or wages, people often receive **fringe benefits,** or indirect payments for their work. Medical and dental care, sick leave, and paid vacation days are examples of fringe benefits provided for employees. These benefits mean that workers do not need to set aside part of their incomes to use for such purposes.

Other Income Kathy has a savings account at a local bank. She earns income in the form of interest on money in the account. People who own stock receive **dividends,** or payments from the profits of companies in which they own stock. People can also receive income from the sale or rental of their personal property, from gifts, and from money they inherit when a relative or friend dies.

Disposable Income To understand her income, Kathy starts her calculations using her new, higher salary. She adds the interest on her savings account. Then she subtracts what she pays in taxes. The result is her **disposable income**, the amount of money left after taxes have been paid. Once Kathy knows how much money she has, she can make some choices about what to do with it.

✓ Reading Check   **Why is it important to budget your money?**

Making Financial Choices

Choosing how to use your money involves making trade-offs, giving up one wish in order to satisfy another. To make these choices wisely, you must look at your disposable income and at your current and future needs.

Goals and Values The choices people make about money are based on their goals and values. Kathy's goal was to spend money on consumer goods. Consumer spending—buying clothes, a TV, and luggage—was more important to her than financial planning.

Some people choose to plan carefully in order to stay out of debt. Some plan to save for a particular goal, such as buying a house or going to college. Many people also choose to give money away. They may choose to give money to friends or family or people in need, or they plan to give to a cause or organization. All of these decisions reflect individual goals and values.

Kathy's credit card troubles have made her think about her values and her goals. She now sees the importance of good spending and saving habits. She knows she needs to take a look at her income and expenses and to make some decisions about what is most important.

Target Reading Skill

Read Ahead This page tells you that Kathy is going to budget her money. Look ahead at her budget, shown on page 407. Then return to this page and continue reading.

▲ Consumers must make important decisions when they spend their money so that they do not spend more money than they can afford.

Analyze Graphs

Median Credit Card Debt

Credit card debt is a very serious issue for consumers. This graph shows the median debt of credit card holders in the United States (the median is the middle number in a range of numbers).

1. **Analyze** In 1992, what was the median credit card debt?
2. **Apply** Between which two years did the median credit card debt increase the most?

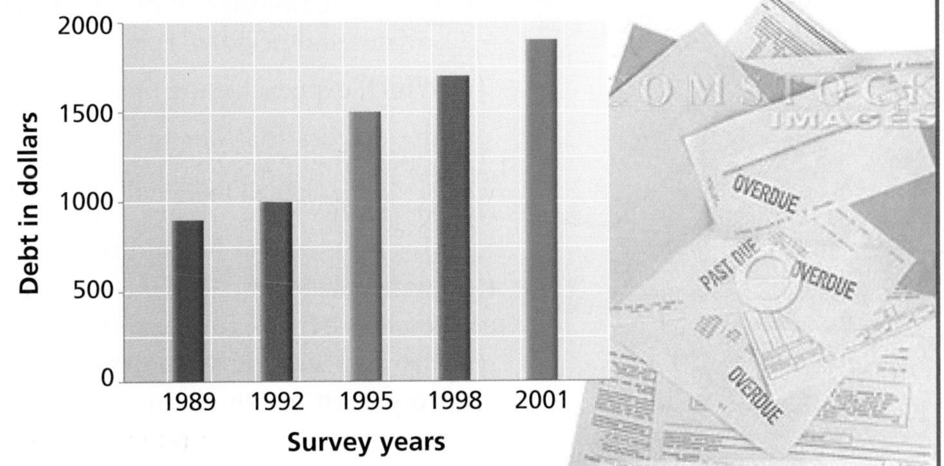

Debt in dollars

2000
1500
1000
500
0

1989   1992   1995   1998   2001

Survey years

SOURCE: Survey of Consumer Finances, 1989–2001

OVERDUE
PAST DUE   OVERDUE
OVERDUE
Royalty-Free Division

VARIABLE FIXED

Expenses
Consumers make many choices about how to spend their disposable income. People usually have more control over their variable expenses when creating budgets for their spending. **Categorize** *What are some other fixed expenses not mentioned on this page? Variable expenses?*

Making a Budget Making a budget is a good way to decide how you want to spend and save. It helps you to be sure you set aside enough money for the things you need. It also helps keep you from buying more than you can afford.

Armed with good information about her income and with clear financial goals, Kathy sets out to make her personal budget. To do this, she asks herself the following questions:

- What time period will my budget cover?
- How much income will I be making during this time?
- What will my expenses be during this time?
- How much money should I set aside for each expense, and for savings and personal spending?
- Which expenses must I pay first?

Kathy decides that her first budget will cover one month. With her new raise, her disposable income is $1,800 a month.

Next, Kathy looks at her expenses. Some are **fixed expenses**, expenses that have to be paid regularly, usually every month, such as rent and car payments. Unless Kathy moves into a cheaper apartment or sells her car, she cannot change those fixed expenses.

Kathy also has **variable expenses**, expenses that change from month to month. For Kathy, these variable expenses include food, clothes, entertainment, and her telephone bill. Cutting back on her variable expenses is a good way for Kathy to make progress in paying off her debt.

Finally, Kathy figures how much money she can save each month and how much she can put towards paying off her credit card debt. She then arrives at a budget for the month (right).

Making a budget gives Kathy a sense of confidence. She has taken responsibility of her finances and control of her spending. She has made the choice to plan her spending and saving.

If Kathy sticks to her current plan, she will be able to pay off her credit card debt. Her monthly payments of $205 will reduce her credit card balance without preventing her from paying necessary expenses such as rent and car insurance. In the future, her debt will be paid off and she will no longer need to set aside $205 a month. At that point she may want to take a new look at her budget. Budgets are not carved in stone. Whenever your income, expenses, or goals change, you can revise your budget as well to reflect these changes. Saving money and paying down debt in the short-term future will give you more options and choices in the future.

✔ Reading Check **Which of Kathy's monthly expenses are the most important? Which expenses are least important? Why?**

BUDGET	
rent	$750
car payment	$220
car insurance	$50
food	$180
personal (clothes, entertainment, etc.)	$120
utilities (electricity, gas, water)	$50
gasoline/transportation	$50
telephone	$50
savings	$125
credit card debt	$205
TOTAL	$1,800

Spending Money
A budget is a useful way for people to take more responsibility over their spending. **Identify Alternatives** *If Kathy wanted to save money each month, how could she reduce some of these expenses?*

SECTION 1 Assessment

Key Terms
Use each of the key terms in a sentence that explains its meaning: fringe benefits, dividends, disposable income, fixed expenses, variable expenses

Target Reading Skill
1. Read Ahead How did looking ahead at Kathy's budget help you understand the budget choices she made?

Comprehension and Critical Thinking
2. a. Explain How did Kathy's use of credit cards change her financial situation?

b. Predict What effect will Kathy's budget have on her financial situation?

3. a. Recall What are Kathy's sources of income?
b. Analyze Information How might Kathy raise her income?

4. a. Recall What are Kathy's basic monthly expenses?
b. Solve Problems How might Kathy lower her monthly expenses?

Writing Activity
Students at your school plan to put on a play. Create a budget for the play so the drama director will know how much money can be spent on costumes, sets, publicity, and other needs. Consider both expenses and sources of income.

TIP Interview a drama teacher before you begin writing. Remember that ticket sales, refreshments, and advertising can all generate income.

How to Be a Wise Consumer

We all are consumers—we buy everything from groceries to video games to cars. Many laws have been put into effect to protect consumers from unsafe products and unfair prices. Still, every day we must make decisions about which products to buy. One way to make wise choices when shopping is to compare items.

Look at the price, quantity, and quality of each item. By thinking before you buy, you could save yourself money or avoid unsafe products. Remember that advertisements are not always the most useful or accurate source of consumer information. Below, Helen Quincy helps her family choose the best car for them.

The Quincys had decided it was time for a new car, but they had no idea what kind they wanted to buy. Each person suggested a type of car: an SUV, a station wagon, a sedan, and a hybrid electric car. For a week, each member of the Quincy family did Internet research on the car he or she suggested. Helen had recommended the hybrid electric car, so she collected articles about it from consumer magazines and car manufacturers.

At the end of the week, each person reported to the family. Helen told them how hybrid cars work, their cost, gas mileage, and their benefits to the environment. Helen's brother reported that SUVs do not get as good gas mileage as does the hybrid electric car. Helen's argument for the hybrid car was fairly convincing. The family decided it was the car for them.

Next, they collected more information about the different brands of hybrid cars. They compared statistics about the performance, safety, and durability of the cars. By looking at these factors side by side, the Quincys could see which brand of hybrid car they wanted. Because it had been Helen's idea, they let her pick the color.

Learn the Skill

To be a wise consumer, follow these steps:

❶ **Find the unit price.** Divide the price of the item by the number of units in the item.

❷ **Compare the unit prices of different sizes of an item.**

❸ **Do research to compare brands.** Look for prices, size, a warranty, and features.

Practice the Skill

❶ Visit a grocery store and write down the size and price of three brands of cereal, laundry detergent, and juice.

❷ Calculate the unit price of each item.

❸ Which brand of each item would you buy?

Apply the Skill

❶ Choose an appliance or electronic device.

❷ Compare different brands by visiting stores or collecting information online. Make a chart to help you make comparisons.

❸ Write a short report explaining which brand you would choose and why.

Go Online
civics interactive

For: Local Citizenship
Visit: PHSchool.com
Web Code: mpp-5152

SECTION 2

Spending and Saving

Reading Preview

Objectives

In this section you will

- Learn about making spending decisions.
- Discuss how to make savings decisions.
- Learn about insurance.

Key Terms

warranty   time deposit
liquidity   insurance

Main Idea

People must consider major expenses carefully. Smart spending decisions include comparing prices and quality, resisting sales pressure, and buying only what the buyer can afford. People often keep liquid savings that are easy to access. Many other good investments can not be exchanged for cash as easily.

Target Reading Skill

Paraphrase This section contains vocabulary with which you may not be familiar. Sometimes it is easier to remember ideas if you rephrase them in simpler language. This is called *paraphrasing*. As you read this section, try paraphrasing difficult language in words you can easily understand.

Taking Notes

Make a diagram like the one below. As you read this section, complete the diagram with information about making the best use of your income.

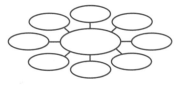

Which would you buy—an MP3 player (below) or a new printer?

Even after you have created a budget, however, your financial decisions are not over. You will have many choices to make about which goods and services to buy. You will also need to think about what savings plan will be the best for you. Your goals and values will affect your spending and savings decisions.

Making Spending Decisions

Mark Aguilar, the college student who works part-time in Kathy's office, has to make a spending decision. He is trying to decide between buying a portable MP3 player and a new printer.

Mark listens to a lot of music. He knows that a portable MP3 player is more convenient than his old CD player. However, his computer printer is old and breaks down often. He uses the printer for school work, so he needs a printer he can count on.

Values and Pressures Values have a strong influence on a person's decisions about what to buy. Mark is faced with a conflict in values. Music is important. However, he also values his education.

To decide between an MP3 player and a printer, Mark must also be aware of factors other than his values. All consumers face certain pressures to buy. Being aware of these pressures can help Mark to weigh whether or not they should influence his decision.

Law and the Real World

Lemon Laws: Protections for Car Buyers

You have just bought a new car, but six months later the thrill is gone. You have taken the car back to the dealer five times to fix a problem with the transmission. Did you buy a lemon? Does the law protect you?

- Lemon laws protect you if your new car cannot be repaired.
- Many states have lemon laws to protect the consumer from a defective product.
- You must keep all of your repair receipts and notify the maker of the car and the dealer of the recurring problems.
- With these records, many car manufacturers will replace your "lemon."
- If not, you may have to go to arbitration and explain what the problems are with the car.
- If you win, you will get a refund or a replacement car.

Applying the Law

1. What is arbitration?
2. Does your state have lemon laws?
3. Why have such laws been created?

Mark knows that his desire to buy an MP3 player is influenced by what his friends think. Most of his friends have MP3 players. Mark also realizes that salespeople and advertisements have an influence on him. Mark has learned that a common sales method is to make consumers think that items they now own are not good enough.

Finally, Mark makes a decision. He would like to have a portable MP3 player, but his printer is nearly past repair. If he does not replace it, he will not be able to do as good a job in school. Mark decides it is more important to buy a printer instead of an MP3 player.

Choosing What to Buy Once you have decided to buy an item, the next decision is which one to buy. Wise shoppers consider a variety of factors when making buying decisions. Considering the following factors can help you choose.

1. *Price.* Can you afford the product? Is its price about the same as the prices of other models of similar quality?
2. *Quality.* Will the product last? Is it well made? Does its quality match its price?
3. *Features.* Does the product have the features you need? Will you be paying for features you do not need?
4. *Warranty and Service.* Does the product have a **warranty**—a manufacturer's promise to repair it if it breaks within a certain time from the date of purchase? Will the store repair or replace the product or give you your money back if it breaks down?
5. *Sales/Discounts.* Can you buy the same product at a lower price at a discount store or a special sale?

When Mark goes shopping he thinks about all these factors. He talks to salespeople at several stores and compares printers that have similar prices. He reads ads in the local paper to see if any printers are on sale. He also goes to the library to look at consumer magazines which list and compare the major products, their features, and their prices.

Finally, Mark narrows his choices to two printers. Both are well made and have good warranties. One model costs about $200, the highest price that Mark had thought he would be willing to spend. The other model costs $300, but it has extra features.

Consumer Credit The salesperson suggests that Mark buy the more expensive printer. She tells him that he will not have to pay the whole price at once. He can make a down payment, only paying part of the price. Then he can finance the rest through a credit arrangement with the computer store.

This credit plan—getting a loan from the store to cover the rest of the printer's cost—sounds good to Mark. However, he finds out that he would be paying 20 percent interest on the borrowed money. If he takes a year to pay this money back, he will end up spending nearly $360 on the printer, once interest payments are added in. Mark decides to buy the less expensive printer to avoid the additional cost of credit.

In borrowing money for purchases, it is important to pay attention to the real cost of the item—the purchase price plus interest. Consumers often "shop" for a loan. Sometimes a bank loan will cost less than a store's credit plan. In that case, a person might choose to borrow money from a bank for the purchase rather than use the store's plan.

✓ Reading Check **What are the advantages and disadvantages to buying a less expensive item?**

Analyze Graphs

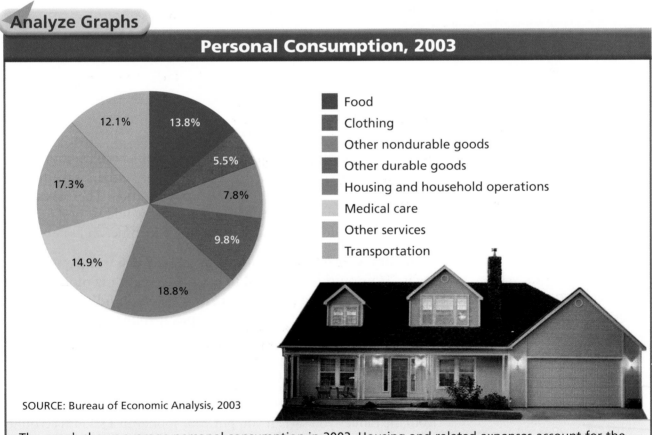

Personal Consumption, 2003

- Food
- Clothing
- Other nondurable goods
- Other durable goods
- Housing and household operations
- Medical care
- Other services
- Transportation

13.8%
5.5%
7.8%
9.8%
18.8%
14.9%
17.3%
12.1%

SOURCE: Bureau of Economic Analysis, 2003

The graph shows average personal consumption in 2003. Housing and related expenses account for the largest percentage of personal consumption.

1. **Analyze** What percentage of personal consumption was spent on transportation in 2003?
2. **Apply** Spending on housing, medical care, and food accounts for what percentage of personal consumption?

This cartoon presents a humorous look at household budgets and ways to save on spending.

1. What is happening in this cartoon?

2. What reason does the man give for letting go of the dog?

3. How does the cartoonist use humor to make his point?

"I'LL LAY IT OUT FOR YOU. WE'RE CUTTING BACK, AND WE NO LONGER NEED A DOG"

Making Savings Decisions

People save for all sorts of reasons. Some want to have money set aside in case of car trouble or a long illness. Others save to buy homes, to finance vacations, or to pay for education. There are many ways to save money. To decide which method would be best for you, think about the following factors: liquidity, income, and safety.

Liquidity One of the first questions to ask when you plan for saving is "How quickly do I need to be able to get at my money?" The ability to turn savings back into cash is called **liquidity**. Some savings plans are very "liquid." For example, if your money is in a savings account at a bank, you can withdraw your money immediately. If you have used your money to buy a house, you will not be able to use that money until you have sold the property.

Income Another factor to consider is the overall income you will earn from the money you save. If you put your money in a savings account, your income will be the interest you earn on your deposit. You can also earn income from money you have set aside in investments, such as a piece of land (which you can rent or sell) or stock in a corporation (which may return income from the company's profits).

Target Reading Skill

Paraphrase The text paraphrases the unfamiliar word "liquidity" with the phrase "the ability to turn savings back into cash." Read on to look for other new or difficult words. Replace them with easier ones.

Banks offer a number of savings plans, each with different possibilities for income. In general, banks pay higher interest rates on accounts that require you to leave your money in for a certain minimum amount of time. A **time deposit** is a savings plan with a set length of time that you must keep your money in the account. The bank charges a fee if you withdraw money early.

You can also earn income by buying bonds. Government bonds and bonds issued by corporations pay a fixed rate of interest. With bonds, as with savings accounts, you can know ahead of time what income your savings money will earn.

People whose main goal is to make as much income as possible are more likely to invest their savings than to put them in a bank. They may buy stocks or invest in mutual funds. A mutual fund is a collection of money from many small investors, which experts invest in stocks and bonds.

When you are thinking about a savings or investment plan, you will have to make a trade-off between income and liquidity. In general, the higher the interest rate on a savings plan, the longer you will have to leave your money on deposit. Investments in stock and real estate are usually hard to turn back into cash.

▲ People invest money in real estate—land and buildings—in the hope that its value will increase.

Analyze Charts

Common Savings Plans

Type	Description
Passbook savings	Pays a fixed interest rate; money can be withdrawn at any time.
Interest-bearing checking	Called NOW (Negotiable Order of Withdrawal) accounts; the owner can write checks on the account, which also earns interest.
Time deposit	Funds deposited for a set period of time; usually a penalty for early withdrawal. Interest rate dependent upon time limit on deposit.
Savings bond	Sold by the government. Common for bonds to be sold for half their full value, reaching their full value after a period of time.
Stock	Shares in corporations. Owners of stock sometimes earn income from dividends. They make profit when they sell their stock for a higher price than they paid for it.
Mutual fund	Pooled funds of investors, managed by professional. Funds usually invested in stocks and bonds.
Real estate	Purchase of land and/or buildings. Income earned from rent. Profit made when real estate is sold for a higher price than was paid for it.
Insurance	Investment can be made in an insurance policy such as life insurance. After a set number of years, some policies can be surrendered for cash value, plus interest.

There are a wide variety of savings plans to choose from. Each type has its own benefits and drawbacks.
1. **Analyze** What are two ways you can make money by investing in stocks?
2. **Apply** What is the main difference between a passbook savings plan and a time deposit plan?

The Health Insurance Industry Today, the United States spends far more on health care per person than any other nation. Health care is expensive because advances in medical science have led to more sophisticated treatments, technology, and medicines. As health care grows more expensive, so does the cost of health insurance. Health insurance companies spent an estimated $650 billion on health care in 2004, up from about $380 billion in 1998. Consumers pay the increased cost through higher premiums.

Analyzing Economics

If an insured person enjoys good health for an entire year, he or she will spend thousands of dollars for health insurance having never visited a hospital or used a prescription. Do you think this system works well? Why or why not?

Safety Of course you want your money to be safe. However, sometimes there is a trade-off between safety and income. Most deposits in banks and savings-and-loan companies are insured by the federal government. As long as your account does not have more than $100,000 in it, it is safe even if the bank or savings-and-loan fails. Government bonds are also considered safe investments. However, savings accounts and bonds have relatively low interest, and therefore low income.

In contrast, buying stocks in a corporation can be risky. In general, the more stock you own in a corporation, the riskier your investment is. If the corporation makes big profits, your share of those profits, called dividends, may be higher than the amount you could earn from a savings account. The price of the stock may go up, too, and you could make money by selling it. However, if the corporation has a bad year, you could lose money on your stocks.

Real estate investments involve a similar trade-off of safety against income. First, you must consider the amount of money you are investing. When you buy a house, for example, you must often take out a bank loan. You will have to pay interest on this loan. You will also have to pay taxes on your home. You may also need to renovate, or fix up, your house. All of these things will add to the amount of money you invest in your house. If the value of your house falls, you may lose some of the money you invested. If the value of your house rises, you may end up making money.

Savings and You You may find that a passbook savings account best meets your needs. It is safe. It is also liquid—you can get money whenever you need it. Not having your money tied up for long periods of time is probably more important to you at this stage in your life than earning higher interest.

However, your life will be changing and so will your financial needs. Your income and expenses will most likely increase. Your goals may change as well. You may decide you want to do some long-term financial planning. It is always possible to change your savings plan to suit these changes in your life.

✓ Reading Check   **What are the main reasons for and against investing in the stock market?**

Insurance

Most people find it impossible to save enough money to cover a serious emergency. In order to protect themselves, people buy **insurance**, a plan by which a company gives protection from the cost of injury or loss. In return, the insured person makes regular payments, called premiums, to the company.

Insurance is based on a simple idea. If many people pay some money into an insurance plan, all the money, taken together, will be enough to pay the large costs of the few people who will need it. Many kinds of insurance are available.

Health insurance plans are included in the fringe benefits of many working people. The government gives health insurance, through Medicaid and Medicare, to many people who cannot afford it, and to senior citizens.

Having insurance, like saving and investing, is a way to set aside money from current income in order to meet needs you may have in the future. Making decisions about insurance will be part of the way you manage your money as an adult.

✔ **Reading Check** **What is the purpose of insurance?**

Life Insurance
People buy life insurance to protect their families from loss of income should the insured person die

Property Insurance
Property Insurance protects houses, cars and other property. It pays to rebuild a house after a fire or replace a car after an accident.

Health Insurance
Health Insurance pays for all or part of the cost of doctors, hospitals and medicines.

Liability Insurance
Many people carry liability insurance, which is insurance that protects a person from the cost of damage or injury to others.

Types of Insurance
Insurance helps people cover the costs related to unforeseen events.
Contrast *What is the difference between property insurance and liability insurance?*

SECTION 2 Assessment

Key Terms
Use each of the key terms in a sentence that explains its meaning: warranty, liquidity, time deposit, insurance

Target Reading Skill
1. **Paraphrase** Choose three difficult sentences from the selection. Paraphrase them so that they are easier to read and remember.

Comprehension and Critical Thinking
2. **a. List** List the factors that affected Mark's decision to buy the $200 printer.

b. Evaluate Information Which printer do you think Mark should have bought? Why?

3. **a. Recall** What are the most important reasons to save money?

b. Compare and Contrast What are the advantages and disadvantages to having liquid savings?

4. **a. Identify** Describe the different types of insurance.

b. Make Generalizations Why do people consider insurance necessary?

Writing Activity
Millions of Americans have no health insurance. Most of them cannot afford private insurance. They do not qualify for government aid because they are too young or their incomes are not low enough. Write a newspaper editorial proposing a new health-insurance system that will cover everyone at a price all can afford.

TIP Find out about health-care systems in other industrialized nations. Compare their systems to the American system.

SECTION 3

Careers: Planning for the Future

Reading Preview

Objectives

In this section you will
- Think about careers and how to choose the best one for you.
- Learn to research careers that interest you.
- Learn about satisfying employers' expectations.

Taking Notes

Make a diagram like the one below. As you read the section, complete the diagram with information about careers and career research.

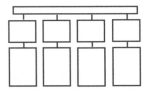

Key Terms

career
Occupational Outlook Handbook

Main Idea

There are many factors to consider in choosing a career. Researching a career will give you a good idea what your job prospects are. Understanding the expectations of your employer will help you be successful.

Target Reading Skill

Summarize When you summarize a text, you state its main ideas and key supporting details. Because summaries are shorter and more concise than the full text, they are good study aids.

In this chapter you have read about the importance of personal economic planning. You have learned about planning a budget and about making spending and saving decisions. Perhaps the most important planning you will do will be planning your **career**, the occupation for which you train and which you pursue as your life's work. How you choose to earn a living will affect all the other economic decisions you make in your life.

Thinking About Careers

Think for a moment about people who work in your community. In how many ways do people make a living? Then think of all the people in the United States who are working at different jobs. Some of these people have had the same job for their whole working lives. Others have had several different careers.

There are thousands of careers from which people can choose. Furthermore, as our economy changes, your career options can change. The demand for different kinds of jobs is always changing. Workers for a certain type of job may be in high demand for one year. However, demand for these jobs may fall in a later year. When you begin to think about careers, it will be helpful to know what the changes in our economy may mean for you. Thinking about what you will have to offer to the working world will also help you to choose a career.

The Changing Economy The economy of the United States is changing dramatically. Most Americans used to work in farming and factory jobs. Today, however, more than 70 percent of our work force performs service jobs.

New technology is also changing the career outlook. Computers, lasers, robots, and communication satellites are taking the place of some jobs and creating others. According to a recent report by the United States Department of Labor, high-tech industries will provide thousands of new jobs in the coming years.

> "Projections for the 1996–2006 period show high-tech and related employment growing more than twice as fast as employment in the economy as a whole."

Many of these new jobs demand a much higher level of education than farm and factory jobs did. In fact, an increasing amount of special training is needed for many careers, such as engineering, accounting, information technology, law, and medicine. Jobs in management and sales also call for education and training.

Asking Yourself Questions Evaluating your interests, talents, and personality can be an important step in finding your place in the job market. The school subjects you enjoy and do well in might give you some clues. What you like to do outside of school can also indicate things to look for in a career. Mark Aguilar's interest in music and in technology has led him to consider being a sound engineer.

Target Reading Skill
Summarize Take the first sentence of each paragraph in **The Changing Economy**. Combined into one new paragraph, these three sentences form a summary of this section of the text. As you continue reading, look for key sentences that you might use in a summary of the next section.

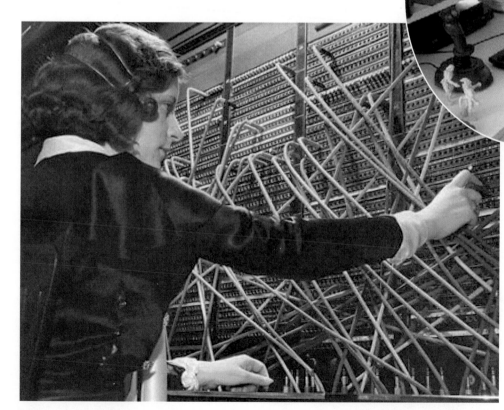

Technology and Careers
Advances in technology have had a huge impact on careers. A telephone operator from the early 1900s (left) might be shocked by how computers have changed our jobs today.
Make Generalizations *What are some of the ways in which technology has changed the workplace?*

Goals and Values Looking at your interests and abilities is an important part of thinking about careers. Thinking about your life goals and personal values also is an important part of a career search. Do you want to make a lot of money? Do you like a fast pace? Do you want to live in the country? Do you want your work to involve helping people? Answering these questions will help to guide your search by pointing you to careers that match your outlook on life and your personal goals. The more your career matches your interests and goals, the more satisfied you will be in your career.

✓ Reading Check **What are the important factors to consider when selecting a career?**

Analyze Graphs

Career Outlook, 2000–2010

Each year, the government projects job growth for different industries. Many service industries are expected to grow, while manufacturing industries are expected to decline.

1. According to the graph, by what percentage will the demand for child day-care services grow between 2000 and 2010?
2. Which industry is expected to decline the most between 2000 and 2010?

Child day care services

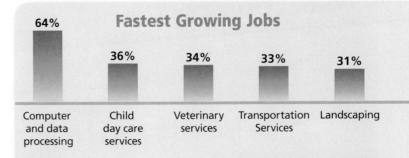

Fastest Growing Jobs

Job	Percentage
Computer and data processing	64%
Child day care services	36%
Veterinary services	34%
Transportation Services	33%
Landscaping	31%

Landscaping

Computer and data processing

Career Research

Once you have an idea of where your interests and abilities lie, you can begin to look at career fields. One way to learn about the possibilities is to do some research. If your parents or someone else you know works in a field that interests you, talk to them. Ask them about the work they do, the educational requirements for the job, and the potential for advancement.

The best way to research career fields is to read about them. Reading about career fields, the types of jobs they include, and the skills and abilities they require can help give you direction.

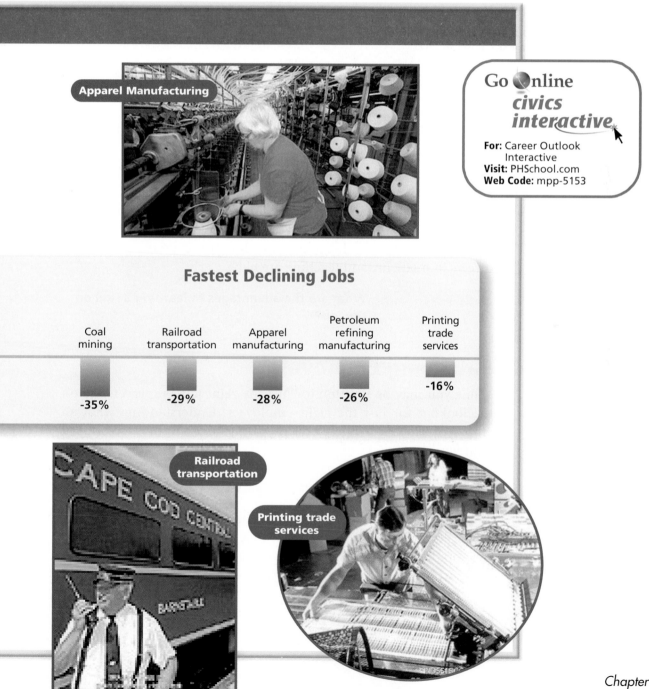

Apparel Manufacturing

Go Online
civics interactive
For: Career Outlook Interactive
Visit: PHSchool.com
Web Code: mpp-5153

Fastest Declining Jobs

Coal mining	Railroad transportation	Apparel manufacturing	Petroleum refining manufacturing	Printing trade services
-35%	-29%	-28%	-26%	-16%

Railroad transportation

Printing trade services

"Employment in occupations requiring at least a bachelor's degree is expected to grow 21.6 percent. Jobs requiring [higher-level degrees] will grow 24.1 percent [between 2000 and 2010]. Education is essential in getting a high-paying job. Air traffic controllers and nuclear power reactor operators are the only occupations of the 50 highest-paying that do not require a college degree."

Occupational Outlook Handbook, 2002–2003, published by the Bureau of Labor Statistics

Analyze Primary Sources
Why do you think highly-educated workers will be in greater demand than other workers in the future?

▲ The *Occupational Outlook Handbook* is published every two years. The handbook is designed to provide help to people make decisions about their future careers.

The library has information about careers. One example is the *Occupational Outlook Handbook*, a guide published by the Department of Labor Bureau of Labor Statistics. The handbook tells about hundreds of jobs, their requirements, and their future possibilities.

When you find a career field that interests you, try talking to someone who works in that field. Some questions you might ask are:

- What do you actually do in this job?
- What training and education does it require?
- What do you like most about your job? What do you like least?
- What job opportunities are available in this field now and in the future?
- What is the salary range for this job?
- Would I have to live in a certain region or city in order to get work in this field?

On-the-job experience can be a good way to find out whether or not a career is for you. Perhaps you can get a part-time or summer job in a field that interests you. You might work in an office, for example, to see what goes on day-to-day in a certain business. Many students volunteer in hospitals and day-care centers to see what careers in medicine and teaching are like.

✔ Reading Check   **What are the advantages to learning a skill on the job?**

Satisfying Employers

While you may be hunting for just the right job, employers are on the lookout for just the right employees. Understanding what an employer expects can help you prepare yourself to be successful in your work.

Three employers were asked what they expect from their employees. A personnel director at an aerospace company said:

"You have to know the basic skills of reading, writing, and calculating. I want someone who is willing to learn—both on the job and outside of it. Our business is changing very fast, and we need people who are willing to learn new things—new computer programs, new management ideas, new uses of metals. We provide training, but we can't teach unwilling learners."

A restaurant manager said:

"My customers come first. They are not always right, but I need to treat them as if they are, or else they won't come back. People who work for me have to understand this and be able to maintain a positive attitude no matter what customers say and do."

The manager of a photocopy sales and rental company said:

"People who work for me have to get engaged in the job. They need to know customers' names. They need to know whom we buy supplies and equipment from. I have had to fire people who didn't seem to care very much. You can't do a good job if you don't care."

Most employers say that they want employees with a positive outlook and a "can do" approach. Persistence and effort are two important qualities for making a successful career.

Doing career research can help you to feel more confident about your future. However, any decision you make today is not final. You will probably change career goals a number of times. In fact, most people change careers—or at least jobs within a career field—more than once. Planning a career is ongoing. It involves continuing to look at your interests, goals, skills, and experiences.

✓ Reading Check **At what point are career decisions final?**

Career Goals
Although this young woman's career goals will change, the skills that she learns from this after-school job will be helpful in the future.
Draw Inferences *Why do you think people's career goals change as they get older?*

SECTION 3 **Assessment**

Key Terms
Use each of the key terms in a sentence that explains its meaning: career, *Occupational Outlook Handbook*

Target Reading Skill
1. **Summarize** Summarize the section *Employers' Expectations*. Remember to include only the main ideas and key supporting details.

Comprehension and Critical Thinking
2. **a. Describe** How are new technologies changing the American economy and job market?

   b. Categorize List some jobs that demand a high degree of technical knowledge.
3. **a. Explain** Why is it a good idea to research a career?
   b. Make Decisions Which career interests you the most? Why does this career appeal to you?
4. **a. Recall** Why is it important to understand what an employer expects of you?
   b. Synthesize Information What are some characteristics that nearly all employers look for in their workers?

Writing Activity
Find the online version of the *Occupational Outlook Handbook*. You can search the handbook by specific jobs or general job categories. Research the career that interests you most. Then write a letter to yourself to be read 10 years in the future. Explain why a particular job interests you now and what the job prospects are for this career.

Go Online
PHSchool.com
For: Writing a Letter
Visit: PHSchool.com
Web Code: mpd-5153

Determining Relevance

As you search for information on a topic, you will encounter some items that are closer to the topic, or more relevant, than others. Read the two commentaries on the topic of inflation. Think about logical connections that exist between the topic and each piece of information.

Inflation and Savings

Inflation can cause serious damage to an economy. People who have saved money for their children's education or for retirement find that their money loses value over time. Suppose a family saved $15,000 for college when the price of a college education was $15,000 a year. After a few years of inflation, when a son or daughter is ready to go to college, a college education costs $25,000 a year. If they have made $3,000 in interest on their savings, they have $18,000 but are still $7,000 short of the amount of money they need.

Inflation Memories

Inflation was high when I was in middle school, but it never worried my friends or me. The team was good that summer and Hank broke the season home-run record for our league. That was the year Ruben pitched five no-hitters. We were all surprised when he didn't want to play professional ball. He played all through college, but he always wanted to be a reporter, not a ball player.

Learn the Skill

Follow these steps to determine if information is relevant:

❶ **Clarify the topic.** What is the topic? Restate the topic in your own words.

❷ **Examine the evidence.** Carefully examine the information you are presented with. What does it represent?

❸ **Determine the relevance.** How closely does the information relate to the topic?

Practice the Skill

Read the two articles above and answer these questions:

❶ State the topics of the articles in your own words.

❷ In what way is each article relevant or not relevant to the topic of inflation?

❸ If you were doing research on the topic of inflation, which article would be relevant? Explain.

Apply the Skill

Choose a school subject that interests you and type a keyword or two into a computer's Internet search engine. Evaluate two or three entries for their relevance to the topic. How did you determine the relevance of each entry?

CHAPTER 15

Review and Assessment

Chapter Summary

Section 1
Managing Your Money
(pages 402–407)

- Personal income comes from several sources, including salaries, fringe benefits, bonuses, commissions, dividends, and interest.

- Your fixed expenses and your variable expenses should not exceed your disposable income. It is best to budget your money so that you don't spend more than you can afford.

Section 2
Spending and Saving
(pages 409–415)

- Smart spending decisions include comparing different goods for price, quality, features, and a warranty.

- As you begin to save money, you should find a balance between liquid savings and time deposit savings that meets your needs.

- *Insurance* helps you pay for emergencies that might happen in the future.

- The Federalists' promise to add a bill of rights helped persuade people to support the Constitution. The Constitution was ratified by all 13 states in 1790.

Section 3
Careers: Planning for the Future
(pages 416–421)

- When choosing a career, look at several different factors. Think about your love of the subject or field, employment opportunities in that field, and how much you may earn in salary and benefits.

- Researching a career—by talking to people, consulting the Occupational Outlook Handbook, or gaining on-the-job experience—will help you make a smart career choice.

- The best way to keep a job is to meet your employer's expectations.

Copy the chart below and use it to help you summarize the chapter:

Our Economy and You

Managing Your Money	Spending and Saving	Careers: Planning for the Future

Review and Assessment Continued

Go Online
PHSchool.com
For: Self-Test
Visit: PHSchool.com
Web Code: mpa-5153

Reviewing Key Terms

Fill in each blank with one of the key terms from the list below.

liquidity	insurance
fixed expenses	warranty
variable expenses	disposable income
	fringe benefits
dividends	

1. _____ such as rent remain the same in each billing period.

2. A _____ is a guarantee that if a product fails to work properly within a given amount of time, the manufacturer will repair it free of charge.

3. Any money left over after you pay your taxes is called _____.

4. Many employers offer _____ such as health insurance and paid vacation time.

5. When companies earn profits, they pay _____ to their stockholders.

6. Liability, health, property, and life are four basic types of _____.

7. _____ such as telephone or grocery bills change from one billing period to the next.

8. _____ is the ability to turn savings back into cash.

Comprehension and Critical Thinking

9. a. **Identify** What is the most important reason to manage and budget your money?
   b. **Predict** What might happen if you don't budget your money?
   c. **Solve Problems** Describe the steps a person can take to get out of debt.

10. a. **Recall** What are different options for using savings to generate income?
    b. **Make Decisions** If you had to choose between renting an apartment or buying a house, which would you select? Why?

c. **Identify Effects** Describe the short-term and long-term effect of your decision in Question 15b on your savings.

11. a. **Recall** List the most important factors to consider when choosing a career.
    b. **Analyze Primary Sources** Reread the excerpt from the *Occupational Outlook Handbook* on page 420. What does the excerpt suggest about career choice?
    c. **Synthesize Information** Explain how getting an education is an investment in your future career.

Activities

12. **Skills a.** Which categories in the job market will see about 15% growth in the next few years? **b.** Is this graph relevant to a discussion of education and the job market? Explain.

13. **Writing** Think of a local business where you would like to work part-time. Write a letter to the owner or manager. Introduce yourself, explain why you want to work there, and describe the skills you can offer.

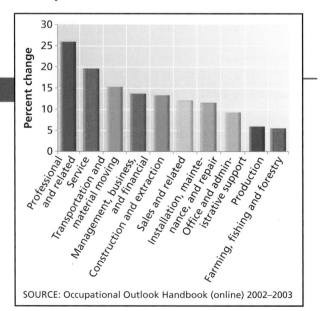

SOURCE: Occupational Outlook Handbook (online) 2002–2003

14. **Active Citizen** Lawyers sometimes take cases even if a client can't afford to pay fees. This is called *pro bono* work. Working in groups, put together a plan to persuade local doctors and hospitals to provide *pro bono* medical care for those who can't afford insurance.

15. **Math Practice** Create a monthly budget for yourself. Note your sources of income and your expenses. Are you spending more or less than you earn? How can you balance your budget?

16. **Civics and Economics** How much do you think it would cost a small business to hire a student as a part-time apprentice? Think about how many hours of work he or she should do.

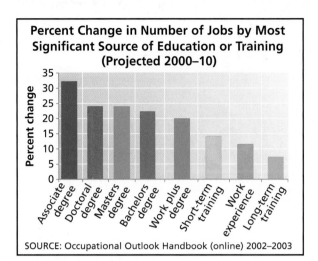

Percent Change in Number of Jobs by Most Significant Source of Education or Training (Projected 2000–10)

SOURCE: Occupational Outlook Handbook (online) 2002–2003

17. **Analyzing Visuals** Study the graph. What can you conclude about job growth and education over the next few years?

Standardized Test Prep

Test-Taking Tips

When you take a standardized test, you read passages and answer questions about them. Below is a passage about job opportunities in America. Read the passage and answer the questions that follow.

TIP When a primary source uses unfamiliar words, use the context to figure out the meaning.

Many factors have contributed to the increase in career opportunities for Americans. The service sector has been growing, opening up new jobs. Education, including college, is much more widely available. People are more willing to move to other parts of the country to find jobs they like. Finally, barriers based on race and gender have been breaking down. All these changes give Americans career options and opportunities not even dreamed of a hundred years ago.

Choose the letter of the best answer.

1. From the context, you can figure out that the word *sector* means

   TIP Go back to the excerpt and reread the sentence in which the word *sector* appears.

   A service
   B portion
   C jobs
   D opportunities

   The correct answer is **B**. If you made a circle graph of the economy, the service sector would be one "slice" of the graph.

2. All of the following are factors in the increase in career opportunities EXCEPT
   A the end of the 20th century.
   B the wider availability of education.
   C the decrease in racism and sexism.
   D people's willingness to move to find work.

UNIT
6

Government and the Economy

What's Ahead in Unit 6

In Unit 6 you will learn how government plays a vital role in our economic system. You will learn about the importance of money and about the banking system that manages it. Finally, you will learn about public finance at the federal, state, and local levels.

CHAPTER 16
Government's Role in Our Economy

CHAPTER 17
Money and Banking

CHAPTER 18
Public Finance

Why Study Civics?

What is the role of government in the economy? Why is money so important? What is the Federal Reserve System? How do your taxes pay for government? How does government at the federal, state, and local levels manage public monies? These are all questions that can be addressed by the study of civics.

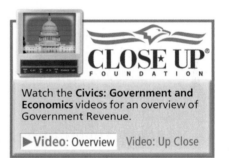

Watch the **Civics: Government and Economics** videos for an overview of Government Revenue.

▶**Video:** Overview   Video: Up Close

Standards for Civics and Government

National

The following National Standards are covered in this unit.

II. What are the foundations of the American political system?

B. What are the distinctive characteristics of American society?

C. What is American political culture?

D. What values and principles are basic to American constitutional democracy?

State

Go Online
PHSchool.com

For: Your state's Civics standards
Visit: PHSchool.com
Webcode: mpe6001

What's Ahead in Chapter 16

In this chapter you will learn about the government's role in the American economy. You will understand the actions the government takes and learn why it takes those actions.

SECTION 1
Government Intervention in the Economy

SECTION 2
Government's Efforts to Solve Economic Problems

SECTION 3
Managing the Economy

TARGET READING SKILL

Reading Process Before you begin reading, you should set a goal that will help you get to the end. Setting a personal goal will keep you interested and give you a stake in finishing each section. Asking questions, applying prior knowledge, and predicting what will come next are all ways to make a reading assignment more interesting.

Testing drug safety ▶

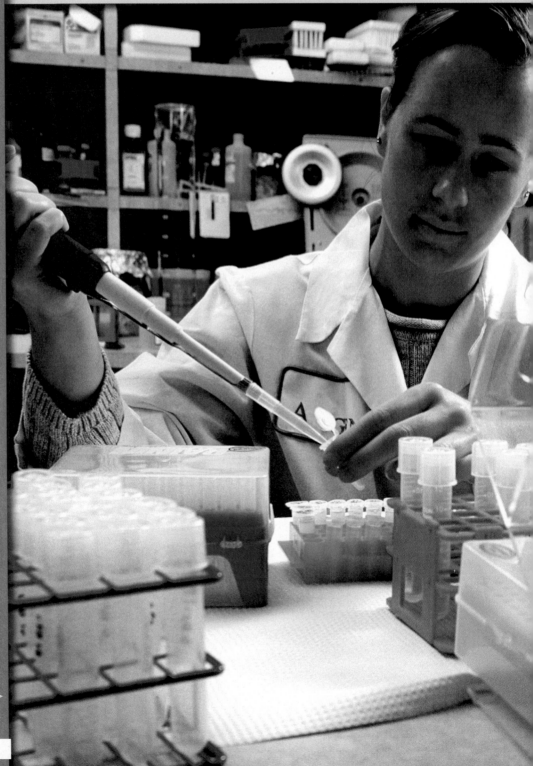

National **Standards for Civics and Government** | **State**

The following National Standards for Civics and Government are covered in this chapter:

I. What are civic life, poli-tics, and government?

B. What are the essential characteristics of limited and unlimited government?

III. How does the government established by the Constitu-tion embody the purposes, values, and principles of American democracy?

B. How is the national gov-ernment organized and what does it do?

Go Online
PHSchool.com

For: Your state's standards
Visit: PHSchool.com
Web Code: mpe-6161

Active Citizen

Civics in the Real World

Laura works in an electronics plant. She cleans manufactured parts by dipping them into a chemical solvent. As she gets ready to dip a new batch of parts, a man with a clipboard walks up to her work station.

"I'm from a federal agency that protects the safety of work-ers," he says. "May I ask you some questions?"

"Sure," replies Laura. "Go ahead."

"How do you feel when you work with this solvent?" asks the man.

"Well," Laura replies, "almost every day I get a headache—but it goes away pretty quickly. Sometimes, I feel dizzy, too. Some of the other people I work with complain about the same things."

Then Laura, who is curious, asks him why he is here. She finds out that his agency thinks that exposure to this solvent may increase workers' chances of getting cancer. Laura feels a sudden rush of fear.

The man explains that the federal government is thinking of making rules that require businesses to protect workers who use the solvent. "It's even possible," he says, "that the govern-ment will ban the solvent."

Citizen's Journal   Do you think the government should pass laws to protect workers like Laura, or should they leave it to the business owners to set their own rules? Write your opinion in your journal. Remember to support it with specific reasons.

Government Intervention in the Economy

Reading Preview

Objectives
In this section you will
- Discuss American values and economic goals.
- Identify the limits of free enterprise.
- Explain how governments correct and prevent economic problems.
- Explain the debate over government intervention in the economy.

Taking Notes
Make a diagram like the one below. As you read the section, complete the diagram with information about government intervention.

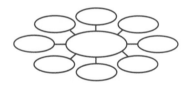

▲ Copyright laws protect intellectual property.

Key Terms
economic freedom

Main Idea
The government makes rules to ensure that businesses treat their competitors, employees, and customers ethically.

Target Reading Skill
Ask Questions Before you begin reading, look through Section 1. Read the headings and look at the photos. Write two or three questions that arise as you look at them. Read the section to find the answers to your questions.

The government plays many important roles in the American economy. It makes rules for how businesses should operate. It spends nearly $2 trillion each year. It also taxes individuals and corporations.

The federal government is the largest consumer in the economy. Millions of Americans work for the federal government, making it the country's biggest employer. How and why did government's role in our economy become so important?

American Values and Economic Goals

Individual freedom is one of the important basic values upon which our government is built. The framers of our Constitution believed that a basic right of citizens is **economic freedom**: the freedom to own property, to make a profit, and to make choices about what to produce, buy, and sell. In writing the United States Constitution, the framers envisioned a country with an economy based on a market system.

The framers wanted to make sure that the economy of the new nation would be strong and able to grow. The government would play an essential part. Therefore, Article 1, Section 8 of the Constitution gives Congress the power to coin money, collect taxes, borrow money, set up a postal service, build roads, and regulate commerce. In other words, Congress was to lay a foundation on which a market economy could flourish.

The Constitution also gives Congress and the states the power to make "ground rules" for a market economy. These rules include laws that protect private property against theft and laws that say how corporations may be set up. Once the foundations had been laid and the rules set, citizens expected the government to play only a small role in the economy.

✓ **Reading Check** **What did the Framers want to ensure for the new nation?**

The Need for Reform

Over time, Americans became increasingly aware that the free-enterprise system did not always serve the common good. The free-enterprise system has made the United States one of the wealthiest countries. It has also led to problems that cannot be solved by letting the market system work entirely on its own.

These problems have caused Americans to look to government for solutions. Below are six reasons why the government has become involved in our economy. Later in this chapter you will read more about these situations and what the government has done about them.

1. *Businesses have sometimes earned profits unfairly.* Some have driven competitors out of business or made secret agreements with competitors to fix prices at high levels. Businesses have also fooled consumers through false or misleading advertising.

2. *Working conditions have sometimes been unsafe and inhumane.* Workers have sometimes been badly treated. Some have been required to work long hours with low pay. Others have had to use dangerous machinery or chemicals without protection.

Child Labor
This photograph by Lewis Hines shows children working in a cotton mill in the early 1900s. Unsafe working conditions and the use of child labor led to increasing demands for government regulation.
Analyzing Primary Sources *What details in this photograph suggest unsafe working conditions?*

Civics and Economics

Labor Unions The first American labor unions formed to fight the terrible working conditions of factories in the 1800s. Workers banded together to bargain with employers for decent wages and working conditions. The labor movement reached its height in the 1940s. Today, about 16 million American workers of all kinds—from major-league baseball players to hotel cleaning staffs—belong to labor unions. This number represents about one in every seven workers. When employers and workers cannot reach an agreement, workers have the option to strike. Since this means business comes to a halt, both sides try to avoid strikes.

Analyzing Economics
1. What is the purpose of labor unions?
2. What advantages and disadvantages might there be to union membership?

Protecting the Environment
The Environmental Protection Agency (EPA) regulates businesses to protect the health of citizens and the environment. Here, EPA workers clean up the Fox River in Wisconsin.
Support a Point of View *What role should government play in protecting the environment?*

3. *Unsafe products have harmed consumers.* Foods have sometimes spread diseases. Medicines have worked incorrectly and made some people more sick. Household products have injured people and damaged their property. Toys have hurt children.

4. *Not all Americans have had economic security.* People who have lost their jobs or could not work due to sickness, injury, or old age have faced hunger and homelessness. Discrimination has made it hard for others to get jobs.

5. *The economy has been unstable.* Periods of economic slowdown have put many people out of work. Drought and flooding have caused farmers to lose their crops, land, and homes. Periods of inflation, when prices rise faster than incomes, have reduced the buying power of people's money.

6. *The environment has been damaged.* Businesses and consumers have polluted the air, water, and land. Many animals and plants have also been threatened.

Americans have called on the government to help solve each of these problems. As a result, various levels of the government have become increasingly involved in our market economy.

✓ Reading Check **Why has the government become involved in the economy?**

Safety First
Transportation Security Administration (TSA) employees screen baggage at Miami International Airport.
Draw Conclusions *Why do you think government took over baggage screening from private businesses following the 9/11 attacks?*

Methods Governments Use

What can governments do to correct or prevent economic problems? Local, state, and federal governments regularly take many actions to make changes in the way the economy works.

1. *Governments regulate businesses.* They can pass laws that set rules for business conduct. They can also set up regulatory agencies to enforce these laws.

2. *Governments make direct payments to individuals.* They can give money to people who need help to pay for food, shelter, medical care, and other basic needs.

3. *Governments own resources and produce goods and services.* They can own land, such as the national forests. They also can run businesses that promote the common good, such as providing hydroelectric power from a government-built dam.

4. *Governments help pay for important economic activities.* They can give money to a private business to help it provide an important product or service. For example, the federal government has given money to help farmers, airlines, and homebuilders.

5. *Governments control the amount of money they spend and the amount they receive in taxes.* Taxes take money from the economy, and spending puts it back. By controlling the flow of taxes and spending, governments can influence the economy.

6. *Governments make tax rules and collect special taxes.* They can change the tax rates on people's incomes. They can change taxes to reward some economic activities and punish others.

✓ Reading Check **Describe the relationship between taxes and the economy.**

Target Reading Skill

Ask Questions Note that the text under *Methods Governments Use* asks a question. As you continue reading, the text will answer the question. As you begin the next section, *The Debate Over Government Intervention*, ask yourself a question about it. Read on to find the answer.

Government Intervention

The market system alone does not always promote the common good. However, there is also a negative side to government intervention in the economy. Government regulations usually put some limits on individual freedom. They affect our freedom to buy and sell, to make a profit, and to do as we wish with our property.

In addition, Government intervention has a huge price tag. The taxes that pay for government programs take large parts of most citizens' incomes. In addition, the government does not always solve economic problems in the best way possible. People often complain that the government uses more time, more money, and more paperwork than necessary.

Because government intervention can both solve and cause problems, it often stirs great conflict. The question of how much to regulate business, for example, involves our most basic values. When freedom comes into conflict with equality and justice, as well as with the health of the public and the environment, people disagree about which values are more important to protect.

▲ The Trans-Alaska pipeline carries crude oil from the Arctic Circle to Valdez, Alaska. Construction of the pipeline required a great deal of cooperation among different government agencies and private businesses.

✓ **Reading Check** What are the major advantages and disadvantages of government intervention in the economy?

SECTION 1 Assessment

Key Terms

Use the following key term in a sentence that explains its meaning: economic freedom

Target Reading Skill

1. **Ask Questions** Write down the questions you asked when you previewed the section. If you didn't find the answers, where might you find them?

Comprehension and Critical Thinking

2. **a. Describe** Describe the government's economic powers.
   b. Analyzing Primary Sources Read Article 1, Section 8 of the Constitution (page 136). What do you think the Framers wanted the relationship of the government and the economy to be like?

3. **a. Recall** For what reasons was there need for reform in the American economy?
   b. Draw Inferences Why does the government find it necessary to intervene when these problems arise?

4. **a. Recall** What methods do governments use to respond to economic problems?
   b. Predict Do businesses welcome or oppose government intervention? Why?

5. **a. Explain** How might government intervention in the economy create conflict?
   b. Solve Problems What is the best solution to such a conflict?

Writing Activity

Make a poster for a class of younger students that will show how the government steps in to try to correct problems in the American economy.

> **TIP** Since your poster is aimed at children, remember to keep the language simple and to use visuals that will make the information clear and easy to understand.

Debating the Issues

CLOSE UP FOUNDATION

The debates in this feature are based on *Current Issues*, published by the Close Up Foundation. Go to **PHSchool.com**, Web Code mph-6161, to read the latest issue of *Current Issues* online.

The United States is a capitalist nation. Large corporations are privately owned and operated. In general, the government relies on these corporations to disclose their profits and losses honestly. But this does not always occur. The Enron Corporation declared bankruptcy in 2001, and thousands of innocent workers lost their entire lives' savings. This disaster has made many Americans call for tighter federal regulations on business.

Should the Government Impose Stricter Regulations on U.S. Corporate Practices?

YES

- Corporations are not in the business of serving the public interest. The major concern of corporations and their executives is to make profit. To protect the public interest, laws are required.

- By forcing business to act in more economically responsible ways, the public feels comfortable investing its money in company stock. The company in turn has more money to grow.

NO

- Self-interest will make corporations regulate themselves. No corporation or executive wants to be seen as dishonest. This provides a strong incentive for them to police themselves.

- It costs corporations a lot of money to change to meet government regulations. This heavy cost is passed on to the consumer. The economy is hurt as prices rise and consumers purchase from foreign corporations.

What is Your Opinion?

1. **Analyzing Information** Why would a corporation not report its profits and losses honestly?

2. **Identify Main Ideas** What do you think is the strongest argument in favor of stricter federal regulations on big business? Why?

3. **Writing to Persuade** You are a computer programmer in a major business corporation. You have been asked to speak to coworkers on the subject of government regulations affecting corporations like yours. Regulations include standards that require desk chairs that are not damaging to employees' posture and keyboards designed to prevent repetitive motion syndrome. Enforcing these regulations will increase the company's costs, and managers are considering hiring people in foreign countries to do your job. Write the speech you will give, urging your colleagues either to support or protest these regulations. Remember to give reasons to support your position.

Go Online
civics
interactive

For: You Decide Poll
Visit: PHSchool.com
Web Code: mpp-6161

Government's Efforts to Solve Economic Problems

Reading Preview

Objectives

In this section you will

- Discuss how the government ensures fair business practices.
- Describe how government regulations protect workers and consumers.
- Explain how government provides economic security, helps to maintain economic stability, and works to protect the environment.

Taking Notes

Copy the diagram below. As you read this section, complete the diagram with information about government's response to economic problems.

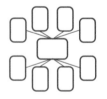

Key Terms

trust
monopoly
business cycle

monetary policy
fiscal policy

Main Idea

The federal government has come up with a variety of solutions to the problems created by a self-regulating free-enterprise system.

Target Reading Skill

Use Prior Knowledge When you already know something about a topic, that information will help you understand and absorb new information. Before you begin reading this section, glance through it to see if any of the illustrations, features, or vocabulary words look familiar. As you read, connect the new information with what you already know.

Economic problems raise a conflict in our basic values. On the one hand, we believe that individuals should have economic freedom. On the other hand, we believe that our economy should be fair and should promote the common good. Citizens have asked the government to solve problems while balancing freedom with fairness.

Ensuring Fair Business Practices

The free-enterprise system itself has no rules for how businesses should operate. Competition and supply and demand are supposed to keep prices fair. Many business owners in the late 1800s, however, learned how to get rid of competition and make bigger profits.

Many industries, including steel, oil, sugar, and meat, were no longer competitive by 1890. In some industries, all but one or two large corporations were forced out of business. Other industries were controlled by a **trust**, a group of several companies organized to benefit from the high prices they all agree to charge. A trust or a single corporation that controls a market has what is called monopoly power—the power to control prices in a market. A single business with monopoly power is often called a **monopoly**.

◄ The game Monopoly was first released in 1935. The object is to create a real estate monopoly in Atlantic City, New Jersey.

In the late 1800s, Americans became increasingly concerned about the unchecked power of big businesses.

1. What does the cartoonist use to represent monopolies in the cartoon? Why do you think the cartoonist chose this symbol?

2. Describe the action in the cartoon. How does the cartoonist view the American public? Explain your answer.

Controlling Monopolies Americans became angry about the growth of monopoly power during the late 1800s. People demanded reasonable prices and the chance for small businesses to compete in any market. Congress passed the Sherman Antitrust Act in 1890. This act outlaws agreements among companies that limit competition. The Clayton Antitrust Act was passed in 1914 to strengthen the Sherman Act. It outlaws many of the practices used by monopolies and trusts. The same year, Congress created the Federal Trade Commission to regulate companies.

Legal Monopolies The government does not always oppose monopoly power. Businesses that provide vital services, such as electricity, water, and local phone service, are often allowed to have legal monopoly power. Such a business is called a public utility.

Governments allow this because competition by many small businesses in these service industries can be inefficient. To keep utilities' prices fair, state and local governments often set the rates by law.

Banning False Advertising In 1938, Congress outlawed "unfair or deceptive practices" in product labeling and advertising. For example, ads may not claim that a medicine can cure a disease when in fact it contains only sugar and alcohol.

✓ Reading Check   **What did the Sherman and Clayton Antitrust Acts accomplish?**

Target Reading Skill
Use Prior Knowledge You may have read about the Sherman and Clayton antitrust acts in history class. What do you remember from what you already know that enriches your understanding of the section entitled "Controlling Monopolies?"

Upton Sinclair (1878–1968) devoted much of his career to publicizing the need for reform in the America of his day. He is best known for his novel *The Jungle* (1906). This was a blunt portrayal of the unsanitary conditions in the meat-packing industry in Chicago. His novel raised public anger and concern about the impurities in meat. President Theodore Roosevelt read the book and ordered an investigation into the meat industry. The Pure Food and Drugs Act and the Meat Inspection Act were passed that same year. Pure food legislation soon followed. Later in his career, Sinclair continued to expose corruption in politics, the oil industry, and journalism. In 1934, Sinclair unsuccessfully ran for governor of California.

Citizenship
How did Sinclair's novel lead to quick reform of the meat-packing industry?

▲ The Occupational Safety and Health Administration (OSHA) ensures worker safety. For example, OSHA requires employers to make sure that employees wear protective helmets when working in areas where there is a potential for injury from falling objects.

Protecting Workers and Consumers

The federal government began to take an active role in protecting workers in the 1930s. Beginning with the National Labor Relations Act of 1935 and the Fair Labor Standards Act of 1938, the government has passed laws to limit working hours, set minimum wages, and require employers to bargain with unions.

Safe Working Conditions Workplace dangers, such as toxic chemicals and disease-causing dust in the air, can threaten workers' health and lives. In the past, thousands of workers were injured or killed at work each year in accidents that might have been prevented. For more than 100 years, labor unions argued that business owners had a duty to make working conditions safe. Businesses did not always want to pay the extra costs of safe equipment.

The government stepped in and created the Occupational Safety and Health Administration (OSHA) in 1971. This agency sets and enforces safety and health standards in the workplace. Recently, OSHA set new standards for office workers to prevent injuries caused by typing and desk work.

Safe Products Since the early 1900s, several laws have been passed to protect consumers from unsafe and harmful food and drug products. A federal agency, the Food and Drug Administration (FDA), was created in 1927. The FDA sees that foods, cosmetics, and drugs are safe and labeled correctly. It requires that new drugs be tested before they go on the market.

The federal government created the Consumer Product Safety Commission (CPSC) in 1972. This government agency makes safety rules for products such as toys, tools, children's clothes, and household appliances. CPSC regulations ensure that clothing and other goods are unlikely to catch fire or injure consumers. If a product for sale has been found to be unsafe, CPSC can recall the product to protect people who have bought it.

✔ Reading Check   **How does the government protect workplace safety?**

Focus On

The Supreme Court

Go Online
civics interactive

For: Interactive Supreme
Court Case
Visit: PHSchool.com
Web Code: mpp-6162

Eldred v. *Ashcroft* (2003)

Why It Matters The issue at stake was the power of the federal government to extend the copyright on creative material such as songs, books and movies. A copyright is the ownership rights of the person or organization who creates something.

Background Congress passed the Copyright Extension Act in 1998. It extended copyrights by 20 years. Before this law, copyrights lasted for 50 or 75 years after an author's death. Congress acted in response to pressure from individuals and corporations that held copyrights due to expire. Eric Eldred was an online publisher who opposed the new law. Eldred sued the government, which was represented by U.S. Attorney General John Ashcroft. He argued that the purpose of copyright law was to eventually free copyrighted works to be used or adapted by others. Eldred argued the law would restrict free expression.

The Decision The Supreme Court ruled against Eldred and upheld the Copyright Extension Act. In the majority opinion, Justice Ruth Bader Ginsburg wrote that the Constitution gave the government wide leeway in dealing with copyrights. Ginsburg pointed out that the copyright law allowed for limited reproduction of copyrighted material and thus did not curb free expression.

Understanding the Law

1. What was Eric Eldred's objection to the Copyright Extension Act?
2. How does the case affect authors, composers, artists, and entertainment companies?

Providing Economic Security

In 1929, the United States fell into a long period of economic hardship called the Great Depression. Factories closed and banks failed. Within three years, 12 million people were out of work.

The United States was faced with what seemed to many to be the failure of the free enterprise system. In 1933, newly-elected President Franklin D. Roosevelt launched a series of government programs known as the New Deal. The New Deal programs were designed to get the economy moving again and help people in need.

The New Deal marked a turning point in our history. It greatly expanded the government's role in the economy. As a result, Americans became more likely to turn to the government to solve economic problems than they had been before.

▲ Franklin Delano Roosevelt's New Deal created agencies such as the Works Progress Administration (WPA), which put millions of unemployed people to work building bridges, roads, and public buildings. The WPA also provided work for artists. The mural above was painted by Victor Arnauff.

Social Security A major New Deal goal was to give Americans economic security. The Social Security Act, passed in 1935, provides a monthly payment to workers or their families to replace the income lost when a person retires, becomes injured, or dies. It also provides for unemployment insurance. Workers who lose their jobs receive payments while they look for new jobs.

Public Assistance Local, state, and federal governments have expanded their efforts to help people in need through public assistance programs. Public assistance helps poor families—not just people unable to work—by providing cash payments and various services. Food stamps, for example, make it possible for people with low incomes to buy groceries.

✓ Reading Check **What was the purpose of the New Deal programs?**

Maintaining Economic Stability

Economic instability has always been a part of the free enterprise system. The economy goes through what is called the business cycle, a repeated series of "ups" of growth and "downs" of recession. During a period of economic growth, businesses increase their production of goods and services. New jobs are created. Each period of growth is followed by a recession, or period of economic slowdown. In a recession, fewer goods are produced and unemployment increases.

Because Americans want a stable economy, government tries to "flatten out" the ups and downs of the business cycle. It uses two major methods to reach this goal: monetary policy and fiscal policy.

Monetary Policy The Federal Reserve System, also known as the Fed, is an independent agency of the government. One of its most important tasks is to regulate the money supply. The size of the money supply has a great influence on the health of the economy. Regulation of the money supply by the Federal Reserve System is called **monetary policy**. You will learn more about how the Federal Reserve controls the money supply in Chapter 17.

Fiscal Policy A government's decisions about the amount of money it spends and the amount it collects in taxes are called its **fiscal policy**. All governments have fiscal policies. However, the federal government's fiscal policy has a far greater effect on the economy than any state's.

Fiscal policy affects the economy because the role of the federal government as a spender and a taxer is so important. The federal government spends billions each year on highways, public assistance, and thousands of other products and services. Most of this money goes straight into the economy. Federal taxes take about 25 percent or more of most people's income.

Active Citizen / Students Make a Difference

When Marc Mallegni was 12 years old, he was rushed to the hospital for emergency surgery. What he remembered most about his stay was that there wasn't much for him to do.

The following year, Marc organized a toy drive for the pediatric department of Newton-Wellesley Hospital in Newton, Massachusetts. Marc has honed his fundraising abilities through the years. Soon, he was holding various fundraising events, engaging local businesses, and applying for grants. A junior now at Worcester Academy in Worcester, Massachusetts, Marc is already preparing for his next toy drive.

▲ Students can help make a difference by volunteering at a local hospital.

Service Learning

How can you make a difference for your local hospital?

If the economy is entering a recession, the government may cut tax rates. Then people can spend more of their incomes on goods and services. This increased spending will stimulate production and may bring the economy out of the recession. The same goal may be achieved if government increases its spending. Increased government spending will help to create more jobs, also giving people more money to spend.

✓ Reading Check **What is the difference between monetary policy and fiscal policy?**

Protecting the Environment

By the 1960s, years of pouring toxic wastes into the rivers, the lakes, and the air had begun to cause major environmental problems. Businesses were slow to take responsibility for the pollution they caused. They feared that trying to control or clean up their pollution would increase their costs.

Faced with growing citizen pressure, the government passed the Environmental Protection Act in 1970. This important law created the Environmental Protection Agency (EPA). The EPA controls pollution by making rules about what and how much can be dumped into our air, water, and soil.

▲ The Environmental Protection Agency (EPA) helps clean up sites when hazardous materials have been released into the environment. Here, EPA workers clean up a dioxin spill.

✓ Reading Check **Why was the EPA created?**

SECTION 2 Assessment

Key Terms
Use each of the key terms in a sentence that explains its meaning: trust, monopoly, business cycle, monetary policy, fiscal policy

Target Reading Skill
1. **Use Prior Knowledge** How did prior knowledge of the historical information in this chapter help your understanding of it?

Comprehension and Critical Thinking
2. **a. Recall** When does the government support monopolies?
   b. Categorize Give examples of monopolies that the government should support.

3. **a. Describe** What does the government do to protect workers?

   b. Draw Inferences What role do labor unions play in protecting workers?
   c. Draw Inferences Why did Congress need to create the CPSC?

4. **a. Recall** What important programs were begun as part of the New Deal?
   b. Support a Point of View Many Americans opposed the New Deal Programs. Why do you think they felt as they did?

5. **a. Describe** Describe the business cycle.
   b. Identify Cause Why does the business cycle work the way it does?

6. **a. Explain** What effect have business practices had on the environment?

   b. Predict What might the EPA do if businesses refused to obey its regulations?

Writing Activity
The CPSC publishes a list of products that have been recalled because of safety issues. Go to the recalls page on the CPSC Web site. Find three items related to your favorite outdoor sport. Write a paragraph per item explaining the hazard, and if a remedy is available to make those products safe.

Go Online
PHSchool.com
For: Writing Activity
Visit: PHSchool.com
Web Code: mpd-6162

Managing the Economy

Reading Preview

Objectives
In this section you will
- Discuss how the nation maintains its economic health.
- Understand how the federal budget works.
- Identify sources of federal income.

Key Terms
inflation
gross domestic
  product
federal budget
deficit
surplus
national debt

Main Idea
The federal government manages the economy by keeping track of its health and adjusting its performance. The government also decides how best to spend the public money it collects in taxes and fees.

Target Reading Skill
Predict By predicting what comes next, you give yourself a reason to keep reading. You want to see if your prediction is correct. As you read this section, look for questions raised in the text. Try to predict the answers. Read on to see if you were right.

Taking Notes
Make a diagram like the one below. As you read the section, complete the diagram to compare and contrast government income with government spending.

The federal government has taken on a role the framers of the Constitution could not have imagined. In addition to being the economy's biggest consumer and employer, the federal government has become the economy's chief manager. In its role as economic manager, the government must be responsive to the citizens of the United States.

The Nation's Economic Health

The federal government is constantly checking on the health of the economy. Government agencies track the number of people unemployed, the number of new jobs created, and the amount of money received from exports. Like a doctor taking a patient's pulse and blood pressure, the government needs to measure the economy's health before it can decide how to maintain and improve it.

Inflation One of the most closely-watched signs of the economy's health is the rate of inflation. **Inflation** is a general rise in the price level of goods and services. The rate of inflation describes how fast prices are rising. During a period of inflation, money loses its buying power. If your income stays the same while prices go up, you can afford to buy less and less. For this reason, inflation is one of the biggest worries of government, businesses, and consumers.

The rate of inflation is usually given as an annual percentage. If a set of goods cost $100 at one point, an annual inflation rate of 5 percent will increase the price of these goods to $105 over the course of a year.

Inflation is difficult to control. As prices rise, workers demand higher pay to keep up. Businesses then spend more on labor costs—and they raise their prices even higher so they can still make a profit. A high rate of inflation is dangerous to the economy because people become very nervous about the future and slow down the economic activity of the country.

The federal government mainly uses monetary policy to keep inflation in line. When the inflation rate gets too high, the Fed often raises interest rates.

Gross Domestic Product A major goal of government is to help the economy grow. Government measures the economy's growth by calculating the **gross domestic product (GDP)**. GDP is the total dollar value of all final goods and services produced within the country in a year.

Final goods are those that are complete and ready for sale. Goods used to make the final goods are not counted in the GDP because their values are included in the price of the final product. For example, the value of the plastic, glass, and steel used to make a car are included in the car's price.

A rising GDP, without rising prices, generally means that the economy is growing. A falling GDP means that the economy needs help, such as increased federal government spending.

√ Reading Check   **What causes inflation?**

Analyze Graphs

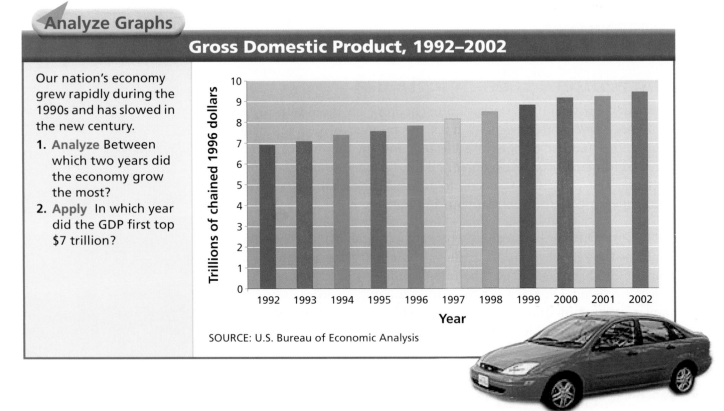

Gross Domestic Product, 1992–2002

Our nation's economy grew rapidly during the 1990s and has slowed in the new century.

1. **Analyze** Between which two years did the economy grow the most?
2. **Apply** In which year did the GDP first top $7 trillion?

SOURCE: U.S. Bureau of Economic Analysis

The Federal Budget for 2002: Spending $2.01 Trillion

The graph shows how the federal government spent the $2.01 trillion in its budget.

1. **Analyze** What percentage of this federal budget went to national defense?
2. **Calculate** Approximately how many times more does the government spend on benefit payments than on national defense?

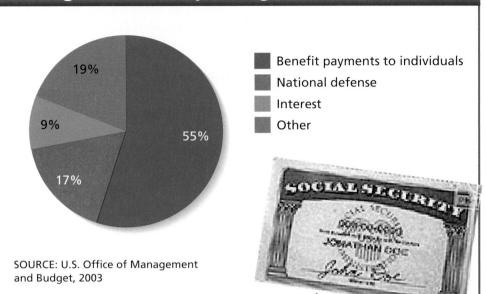

- Benefit payments to individuals
- National defense
- Interest
- Other

55%

19%

9%

17%

SOURCE: U.S. Office of Management and Budget, 2003

The Federal Budget

In 2002, the federal government spent $2 trillion. Much is spent on individuals for unemployment, medical care, and retirement. Money is also needed for other government functions, such as national defense and federal highways. Federal spending has a big effect on the economy.

Federal spending is planned ahead of time in great detail. The amount that each program, agency, department, and office will spend during a year is set by the federal budget. The **federal budget** is the government's plan for how it will raise and spend money. The budget estimates how much revenue will be received from taxes and how much money will be spent in a year.

The pie graph on this page shows the spending side of the federal budget for the year 2002. It is divided into the largest categories of expenditure. Benefit payments to individuals include social security payments and public assistance, such as food stamps. Interest is the money the government pays for using money that it has borrowed.

Although $2 trillion is a huge sum of money, the federal government faces the same problem that individuals and businesses face in our economy—scarcity. People want more goods and services from the government than the government is able to provide. As a citizen, when you vote for elected representatives, you help make decisions about the quantity and quality of goods and services that the government will provide.

✓ Reading Check **What does the federal government spend its money on?**

Target Reading Skill

Predict This page begins by asking a question. Predict the answer, then read on to see if you were right.

Federal Income and the National Debt

How does the federal government raise the money it spends? The federal government receives revenue, or income, from a variety of sources.

Income Taxes Governments at every level depend on taxes as a major part of their revenue. State and local governments receive most of their revenue from sales and property taxes. Most of the federal government's revenue comes from income taxes.

Individuals pay two kinds of federal tax on their incomes: personal income tax and social security tax. Your personal income tax is based on a percentage that increases as your income grows. In other words, the more money you earn, the greater the percentage of your income you pay in income tax.

Analyze Diagrams

Tax Deductions from Your Paycheck

Many paychecks use a chart format to show the taxes deducted from your earnings. Most paychecks show the amount of taxes deducted from the specific pay period as well as the total amount of taxes deducted that year. The circle graph below shows how the federal government raised $1.85 trillion in revenue.

a. Which tax accounted for the largest deduction from this paycheck?

b. What two types of taxes accounted for the largest majority of federal revenue?

The Federal Budget for 2002: Raising $1.87 Trillion

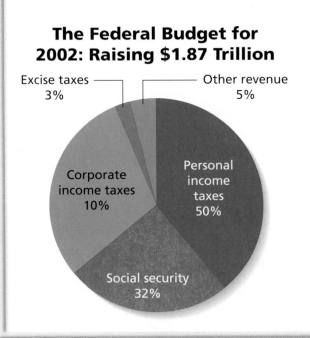

Excise taxes 3%
Other revenue 5%
Corporate income taxes 10%
Personal income taxes 50%
Social security 32%

State income tax

Pay Statement

Earnings	
Regular	450.00

NetGotham
525 Main Street
New York, NY 10028

Local income tax

Your social security tax is also based on a percentage of your income. However, this percentage does not vary according to income. Everyone pays the same rate of social security tax, except that any amount of income over $76,200, as of 2000, is not taxed.

Personal income taxes make up the single most important source of federal revenue. Your personal income tax goes to pay for a wide variety of government spending. Social security taxes pay for a specific kind of government spending—mainly the benefit payments established by the Social Security Act.

Social security and federal income taxes make up the largest part of most people's total tax bill. For this reason, income taxes are often the subject of conflict and debate.

Corporations must also pay income tax. Corporate income tax makes up about 10 percent of federal revenue.

Go Online
civics
interactive

For: Interactive Tax Diagram
Visit: PHSchool.com
Web Code: mpp-6163

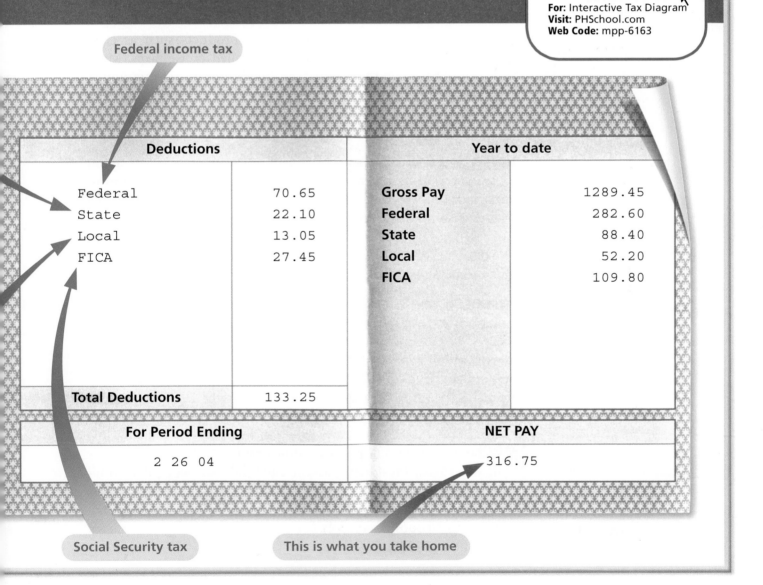

Federal income tax

Deductions		Year to date	
Federal	70.65	**Gross Pay**	1289.45
State	22.10	**Federal**	282.60
Local	13.05	**State**	88.40
FICA	27.45	**Local**	52.20
		FICA	109.80
Total Deductions	133.25		

For Period Ending	NET PAY
2 26 04	316.75

Social Security tax

This is what you take home

Annual Budget Surpluses and Deficits

During the 1900s, the government had 70 annual budget deficits. From 1998 to 2001, the federal government had a budget surplus.

1. **Analyze** Did the government have a budget surplus or deficit in 2002? What was the amount?

2. **Calculate** Approximately how many more times will the estimated budget deficit in 2004 be than the deficit in 1993?

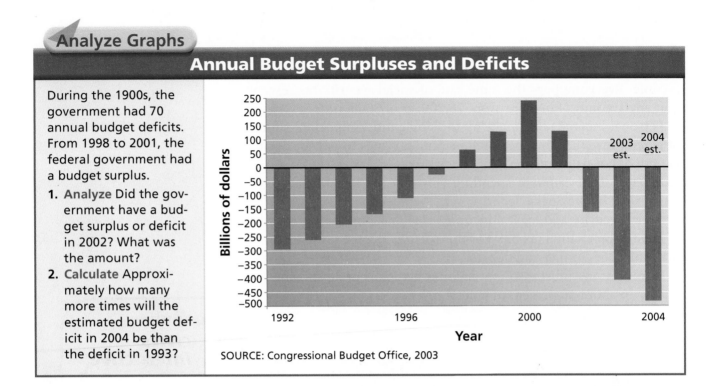

SOURCE: Congressional Budget Office, 2003

Excise Taxes Taxes charged on specific products such as cigarettes, alcohol, gasoline, and jewelry are called excise taxes. Many excise taxes have two main purposes. In addition to raising money, they are intended to regulate certain kinds of consumption. For example, the excise tax on liquor is designed to discourage drinking by making liquor more expensive.

Tariffs, Fees, and Sales The federal government collects about four percent of its revenue from various other sources. The most important of these are tariffs, fees, and sales of government-owned land or resources. Tariffs are taxes on imported products. Fees are charges to users of certain services, such as visitors to national parks. The resources the government may sell to make money include trees on national forest land.

Balancing the Budget The executive branch, Congress, interest groups, and the public all play a role in the federal budget-making process. Throughout much of our history, the government has spent more money than it has taken in. The federal government had its first budget deficit in 1792. A **deficit** is the amount by which government spending is greater than government income. Deficits occur when a government spends more money in a year than it takes in from taxes, tariffs, fees, and sales. To make up for a deficit, the government borrows money by selling bonds.

In the 1990s, President Clinton and Congress worked to limit government spending, with the goal of cutting the deficit. At the same time, strong economic growth led to an increase in the government's tax revenues. As a result, there was a federal budget surplus of $236 billion in 2000.

A **surplus** is the amount by which government income is greater than government spending. An economic recession, combined with tax cuts and increased government spending during the war on terrorism following the attacks on September 11, 2001, signaled a return to deficit spending.

The National Debt The total amount of money the government owes to lenders is called the **national debt**. The national debt grew sharply during the 1980s and early 1990s, when the government borrowed money to cover large budget deficits. The debt stood at $6.1 trillion at the end of 2002.

The size of the national debt worries many people. They worry that the national debt may threaten the government's ability to pay for programs and manage the economy.

Like any borrower, the federal government must pay interest on money it has borrowed. As the debt increases, the interest that must be paid on it takes a larger and larger bite out of our federal budget. By having to set aside money to pay interest on the debt, the government has less money to pay for new programs to promote the common good.

OUR NATIONAL DEBT:
$6,744,979,624,969.
YOUR *Family share* $ 73,620.
THE NATIONAL DEBT CLOCK

MON501RB 0SS 001
©Robert Brenner / Photo Edit
Viewed by Judy Feldman on 12/1/2003

▲ The National Debt Clock is located in New York City. This clock keeps constant count of the national debt and calculates the share of each family in the United States.

✔ Reading Check **Why does the government spend more than it can afford?**

SECTION 3 Assessment

Key Terms

Use each of the key terms in a sentence that explains its meaning: inflation, gross domestic product, federal budget, deficit, surplus, national debt

Target Reading Skill

1. **Predict** List one prediction you made while you read this section. Were you right? If not, why not?

Comprehension and Critical Thinking

2. **a. Explain** Why does the federal government watch the rate of inflation so closely?

   b. Solve Problems How can the government try to control inflation?

3. **a. Explain** What does it mean to say that the government faces the problem of scarcity?

   b. Identify Main Ideas How does the government deal with scarcity?

4. **a. Recall** What are the major sources of federal income?

   b. Identify Effect How can citizens affect how the government spends its money?

5. **a. Explain** Why did the national debt grow during the 1980s and early 1990s?

   b. Predict What will happen to the national debt in the next few years? Why do you think so?

Writing Activity

This section gives a very brief history of the national debt. Go online or to the library to read more about it. Write a one-page history of the national debt that expands on the information in this section.

TIP Organize your information in chronological order. Include interesting details such as names of specific individuals whose policies affected the debt and why they took the actions they did.

Evaluating Long-Term Effects

Important events can have both short-term and long-term effects. Short-term effects are evident soon after the event takes place. Long-term effects, however, may take many years to develop. The long-term effects of historical events can ripple through decades and still affect us today.

When Franklin D. Roosevelt was elected President in 1932, the nation was in the midst of the Great Depression. Roosevelt passed numerous economic programs, together known as the New Deal. These program were designed to restore the nation to prosperity.

An important New Deal program was the Social Security Act of 1935. It included a provision called Aid to Families with Dependent Children, which became known as welfare. For the first time, the federal government gave direct financial assistance to those who were out of work, as long as they had children under the age of 18. Welfare undoubtedly saved thousands of lives during Depression, when many found it impossible to find a job that would pay for groceries and rent.

By the 1980s, the amount of money the government spent on welfare payments had increased dramatically. In 1996, President Clinton passed a welfare reform act. New rules were put into place so that welfare recipients could only receive benefits for a limited number of months. The idea was that they would find work within that period. The number of people receiving welfare had been reduced by more than half by 2000.

Learn the Skill

Follow these steps to evaluate long-term effects:

❶ **Identify the short-term effects.** Determine the effects that resulted immediately, or soon after an event. These can be solutions to a problem, but they may also be new problems that arise from the event.

❷ **Identify the long-term effects.** Determine the consequences that develop over time. Look for changes that were set in motion by the event.

❸ **Evaluate the long-term effects.** How do the long-term effects continue to influence events and people? Are they positive or negative?

Practice the Skill

Read the passage and answer these questions:

❶ Identify one short-term effect of the welfare program. Is it positive or negative?

❷ Identify one long-term effect of the welfare program. Is it positive or negative?

❸ (a) How does welfare reform affect society today? (b) Are the long-term effects positive or negative? Explain.

Apply the Skill

Look through the front pages of the newspaper to find an important economic decision made recently by the federal government. Identify its short-term effects. Predict its long-term effects.

Review and Assessment

Chapter Summary

Section 1
Government Intervention in the Economy
(pages 430–434)

- The Framers of the Constitution tried to balance citizens' conflicting desires for economic freedom and economic security.

- The government intervenes to ensure that businesses obey regulations.

- Citizens debate government's role in the economy because they want as much freedom from government control as possible.

Section 2
Government's Efforts to Solve Economic Problems
(pages 436–442)

- To prevent trusts and monopolies from taking over entire industries, Congress passed antitrust acts.

- Congress protects workers by establishing minimum wage, maximum hours, and safety regulations.

- Congress protects consumers by establishing safety standards and mandatory testing for consumer goods.

- The New Deal of the Roosevelt administration began an era of substantial government involvement in the economy.

- The government uses fiscal and monetary policies to regulate the ups and downs of the business cycle.

- The government creates laws that protect the environment and enforces them through the Environmental Protection Agency.

Section 3
Managing the Economy
(pages 443–449)

- The government keeps an eye on inflation and the gross domestic product, two indicators of the economy's health.

- The government has a federal budget, which shows how its revenue, mainly individual and corporate tax dollars, is spent. The budget may run at a surplus, in which the government spends less money than it takes in, or a deficit, in which it spends more.

- Other sources of federal income include tariffs, sales, and excise taxes.

- Federal deficits lead to growth of the national debt.

Copy the chart below and use it to help you summarize the chapter.

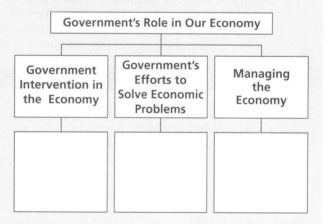

Government's Role in Our Economy

Government Intervention in the Economy	Government's Efforts to Solve Economic Problems	Managing the Economy

Review and Assessment Continued

Go Online
PHSchool.com

For: Self-Test
Visit: PHSchool.com
Web Code: mpa-6163

Reviewing Key Terms

On a separate sheet of paper, write the term that makes each sentence correct.

1. (A deficit, Inflation) occurs when the buying power of the dollar falls.

2. The (federal budget, gross domestic product) is the total value of goods and services the nation produces each year.

3. A government's (business cycle, fiscal policy) describes the decisions it makes about how to spend its income.

4. A (monopoly, trust) is a group of businesses that agree to charge high prices so they can all share the profits.

5. The government creates a budget (deficit, surplus) when it spends less money than it takes in.

6. The (gross domestic product, national debt) grows when the government borrows money to pay for spending programs it cannot afford.

7. When one business takes over an entire industry, it creates a (monopoly, trust).

8. Citizens hesitate to give the government too much power over the economy because they value their (economic freedom, fiscal policy).

9. The federal (business cycle, monetary policy) describes the regulation of the money supply.

Comprehension and Critical Thinking

10. **a. Explain** How did the government come to play an important role in the national economy?
    b. Identify Cause Why is there a debate over government intervention in the economy?
    c. Support a Point of View What role do you think the government should play in the economy? Explain.

11. **a. Describe** What effect did a lack of guarantees of worker safety have on the economy?
    b. Summarize Why did labor unions get involved in the fight for worker safety?

    c. Link Past and Present What can today's workers do if they feel they are not properly protected in the workplace?

12. **a. Explain** What are the three main aspects of the federal government's role as manager of the economy?
    b. Synthesize Information What is the connection between the federal government's role as economic manager and the national debt?
    c. Identify Alternatives What can the federal government do to pay down the national debt and to prevent it from growing in the future?

Activities

13. **Skills** Study the graphs of the federal budget on pages 445 and 446. **a.** How would a rise in the national debt for the next ten years affect the federal spending graph on page 445? **b.** What does this suggest about the long-term effects of deficit spending on the economy?

14. **Writing** You are a journalist investigating unsafe working conditions in a local factory. Write a short newspaper article explaining what the problems are, what changes need to be made, and who is responsible for making them.

Advertising Expenditures in the United States, 1776–2001 (in millions)

Year	Amount	Year	Amount	Year	Amount
1776	$0.2	1890	300	1985	94,750
1800	1	1900	450	1990	128,640
1820	3	1915	1,000	1995	160,930
1840	7	1940	2,110	1999	215,301
1850	12	1950	5,700	2000	243,680
1860	22	1960	11,960	2001	231,300
1867	40	1970	19,550		
1880	175	1980	54,780		

SOURCE: Advertising Age, 2002

15. **Active Citizen** Suppose that a local business refused to hire union workers or to allow its workers to unionize. Work with classmates to come up with a plan to organize the workers into a union.

16. **Math Practice** Ryan made $26,500 of taxable income in 2003 and paid 15% of his income in federal income tax. How much did he pay?

17. **Civics and Economics** You are the owner of a large factory. New legislation requires that you install additional pollution controls to make your factory cleaner. How might this affect your business?

18. **Analyzing Visuals** Study the table above. Why do you think advertising has grown so dramatically?

Standardized Test Prep

Test-Taking Tips

Standardized tests often ask you to answer questions about what you have read. Below is a paragraph about national defense spending. Read it, then answer the questions that follow.

TIP When the answer to a question is not given directly in the passage, read it carefully to help you make the correct inference.

> Upton Sinclair described his investigation of the meat-packing industry in a 1906 novel called *The Jungle*. To their horror, Americans learned that anything swept up off the factory floor was thrown into the sausage—such as dead rats with rat poison in their systems. Factories also commonly packed and shipped old, spoiled meat for sale. Shocked citizens demanded that the government take action. Congress promptly passed the Meat Inspection Act.

Choose the letter of the best answer.

1. Why did factories produce unsanitary meat products?

   TIP Apply the knowledge you acquired from this chapter about early business practices.

   A The American public turned a blind eye to factory conditions.

   B Meat inspectors announced that it was safe to eat rats.

   C The government specifically permitted these practices.

   D Factory owners were more interested in profits than public safety.

   The correct answer is **D**. Workers were under pressure from employers to help make as great a profit as possible.

2. Why did it take until 1906 for Americans to learn about the meat-packing industry?

   A Congress kept factory working conditions a secret.

   B Sinclair did not publish *The Jungle* until 1906.

   C Dead rats had never been used to make sausage until 1906.

   D Citizens ignored the industry.

17

Money and Banking

What's Ahead in Chapter 17

In this chapter you will read about money and how it functions in our economy. You will understand the services that banks provide. You will also learn about the Federal Reserve, its regulation of the banking industry, and its role in our national economy.

SECTION 1
Money

SECTION 2
Our Banking System

SECTION 3
The Federal Reserve System

TARGET READING SKILL

In this chapter you will focus on using context to help you better understand what you read. The context of a word includes the surrounding words and sentences that enable you to grasp meaning.

▶ Withdrawing money from a bank account

The following National Standards for Civics and Government are covered in this chapter:

I. What are civic life, politics, and government?

B. What are the essential characteristics of limited and unlimited government?

III. How does the government established by the Constitu-

tion embody the purposes, values, and principles of American democracy?

B. What does the national government do?

Go Online
PHSchool.com

For: Your state's standards
Visit: PHSchool.com
Web Code: mpe-6171

Active Citizen — Civics in the Real World

The United States Bureau of Engraving and Printing began printing paper money during the Civil War, when there was a shortage of coins. Here are some facts about United States money today:

• The Bureau of Engraving and Printing produces about 37 million paper bills a day worth nearly $700 million. It costs about 4.2 cents to produce each bill.

• The United States dollar is the most widely held type of money in the world. As of December 2002, there was $654 billion in circulation worldwide.

• The United States Secret Service was created in 1865 to combat counterfeiting of United States money. Today, the government estimates that 0.02 percent of United States bills in circulation are counterfeit.

• Paper bills wear out quickly from handling. The average life span of a $1 bill is about 18 months. A $10 bill lasts about 3 years, and a $20 bill lasts about 5 years. $100 bills, which are handled less often, last an average of eight and a half years.

Citizen's Journal Suppose you were in charge of designing a new $500 bill. Whose portrait would you put on the front of the bill? What would you put on the back of the bill? Explain your choices. How would you design the bill so it could not be counterfeited?

Money

Reading Preview

Objectives

In this section you will

- Examine the different functions of money.
- Explore the many characteristics of our money.
- Discuss the value of our currency.

Taking Notes

Make a diagram like the one below. As you read this section, complete the diagram with information about the functions, characteristics, and value of money.

Key Terms

bartering   currency

Main Idea

Money is essential to our economic system, and it provides consumers with a convenient and accurate means of paying for goods.

Target Reading Skill

Context Clues Context clues can help you understand words and ideas in the text. When you come across an unfamiliar word, you can often figure out its meaning by considering the surrounding words and sentences.

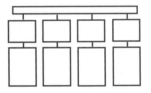

Money gives us a way to obtain the goods and services we need. ▶

Our market economy could not work without money. Like the blood in your body, money flows throughout our economic system, connecting and feeding all the vital parts.

Without money, we would have to rely on **bartering**—exchanging goods and services. Imagine that money did not exist. You have a TV that you would like to trade for a bicycle. You would need to find someone with the kind of bicycle you want who would be willing to trade it for your TV. Bartering still exists in some traditional economies, as well as informally in more developed parts of the world. For the most part, however, such trading would be inconvenient in today's economy.

The Functions of Money

Money has three basic functions no matter what kind of economy it is used in. When you go to the store to buy a bottle of water or a pen, why does the person behind the counter accept your money in exchange for real goods? After all, money is just some pieces of metal or paper. Your money is accepted because the owner of the store can spend it elsewhere to buy something he or she wants.

A Medium of Exchange Exchanging money for bottles of water, pens, and other goods and services is an everyday event. It illustrates the first and most basic function of money. Money is a medium of exchange between individuals in an economy.

A Standard of Value Money's second basic function is not as easy to see. Suppose you visit a shopping mall and discover a jacket on sale for $50. You know that this price is a "good deal," because you have checked the price of the same kind of jacket in other stores. You can compare the cost of the jacket in this store with its cost elsewhere because the price is expressed in the same way in every store—in terms of dollars and cents. Would it be as easy to know if the jacket was a good deal if one store sold it for three cows, and other stores were charging six sheep?

Prices stated in money terms provide a standard that allows you to compare values of goods and services. Income and profit can also be compared, which is the basis of the accounting system. By comparing income and profit, we are able to plan and make better economic decisions. The prices that you see every day reflect the second basic function of money. Money is a standard of value for goods and services.

A Store of Value The third function of money can be recognized when you decide to keep it instead of spending it. If you save money by hiding it in a dresser drawer or putting it in a bank, you are storing it for use in the future. Whether you save for emergencies, home repair, education, or health care, saving money can help you face your future with confidence. Saving shows the third basic function of money. Money serves as a store of value, allowing you to buy goods or services sometime in the future.

✔ Reading Check **In what way does money allow consumers to compare the values of goods and services?**

Storing Value
When we save up to buy an expensive item like a car, we are taking advantage of money's function as a store of value.
Draw Inferences *Why is money more efficient than barter when buying items of great value?*

Unlike this French fur trapper and Native American fisherman in Canada during the 1600s, we would find it hard to get what we want by barter alone. ▶

Changing Faces
The twenty-dollar bill has received a number of updates in recent years. Some are obvious; others cannot be seen by the naked eye. All are intended to make the bill harder to counterfeit.
Draw Inferences *How is counterfeiting dangerous to the economy?*

The Characteristics of Our Money

The coins and paper bills used as money in an economy are called **currency**. In the past, other kinds of objects have been used as money, such as salt, furs, grains, and gold. It is said that in Iceland several hundred years ago, three dried fish could buy a pair of shoes.

These kinds of money all worked well in the economies in which they were used. None of them, however, could function very well as money in our economy today. Each of them lacks one or more of the six characteristics that make our currency the ideal kind of money for our economy.

1. *Our money is generally acceptable.* If you tried to pay for a bottle of water with some salt, grain, or dried fish, would the clerk accept it? In our society, none of these goods can serve as a medium of exchange because they are not acceptable to everyone.

2. *Our money can be counted and measured accurately.* Consider the problem of pricing everything in terms of dried fish. One small dried fish might buy one hamburger. Two large dried fish might buy a T-shirt. This pricing is not an accurate way of establishing standard values of products, because dried fish vary widely in size. Imagine the arguments people would have over the size of the fish used as payment for a good.

3. *Our money is durable and not easily destroyed.* Dried fish, furs, and other objects used for money in the past did not always hold their value because they could be easily destroyed.

4. *Our money is convenient and easy to carry and use.* For hundreds of years, gold and silver in the form of standard-weight coins served as money all over the world. Unlike goods such as dried fish, gold and silver coins are durable and can be measured and counted accurately. However, gold and silver are not the ideal form of money in our economy because large amounts are very heavy and not easily transported.

5. *Our money is inexpensive to produce.* Today, gold and silver have a high value because they are expensive to find and mine.

6. *The supply of our money is easily controlled.* In a growing economy, there must be a continuous supply of money, with just the right amount available. It is difficult, however, to control gold and silver supplies to meet the demands for them. New discoveries of these metals are hard to predict.

✔ Reading Check **Why are gold and silver not ideal forms of currency today?**

The Value of Our Currency

The coins we use are generally made of a mixture of copper and nickel. The metal in each coin is worth less than the coin's face value. Our bills are just paper. Why, then, is this currency generally acceptable?

For the answer, look closely at a ten-dollar bill. On the side with Alexander Hamilton's picture on it, you will see the words, "This note is legal tender for all debts, public and private." This means that our money is money because the government says it is. The fact that our government stands behind our money gives us confidence that it will continue to have value in exchange for goods and services.

✔ Reading Check **Why is the metal used to make coins worth less than their face value?**

Legal Tender
The caption on the ten-dollar bill above means that it has been officially recognized as currency by the federal government.
Predict *What might happen if different cities or states started using their own currency instead of the U.S. dollar?*

SECTION 1 Assessment

Key Terms

Use each of the key terms in a sentence that explains its meaning: bartering, currency

Target Reading Skill

1. **Use Context Clues** Find the word *accurate* on page 458. If you did not know what the word meant, how would you figure out its meaning? How would you use context? What clues in the surrounding sentences would help you arrive at its meaning?

Comprehension and Critical Thinking

2. **a. Explain** How does money serve as a store of value?

   b. Make Predictions What might happen if our country returned to a system of bartering?

3. **a. Recall** What are some other kinds of objects used as currency in the past?

   b. Draw Inferences Why do you think the currency we use today is relatively inexpensive to produce?

4. **a. Describe** What are the coins we use today made from?

   b. Analyze Information Why would the knowledge that a government stands behind its national currency give consumers greater confidence?

Writing Activity

You have just returned from visiting a friend who lives in a region where bartering is the primary means for the exchange of goods. Write an essay that compares and contrasts the difference between bartering and using a standard currency to purchase items.

TIPS
• When you compare and contrast places, you should be clear in indicating which region you are describing.
• Be sure to include details about how the exchange of goods was similar in the two places and how it was different.

Our Banking System

Objectives

In this section you will

- Analyze the beginnings of banking.
- Discover the many different kinds of money used.
- Understand how bank services provide access to money.
- Discuss how the business of banking functions in our national economy.

Taking Notes

Make a diagram like the one below. As you read this section, complete the diagram with information about the development of Hiram Wakefield's bank.

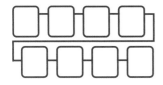

Key Terms

demand
deposit
money supply

loan
fractional reserve banking

Main Idea

Banks hold citizens' funds for safekeeping, enable them to pay for items using alternatives to currency, and give them short- and long-term loans. Banks enable citizens to participate more fully in the economy.

Target Reading Skill

Interpret Nonliteral Meanings
Sometimes language means something other than what it says on the surface, or it has nonliteral meanings. By considering the nonliteral words and phrases used to elaborate an idea, you may better understand its true meaning.

Even though the money we use in our economy is durable and convenient, it can be easily lost or stolen. To overcome this limitation of currency, societies have created banks. Banks help us to save money and to exchange it for goods and services safely and conveniently. In this way, banks help businesses and individuals manage their money.

The Beginnings of Banking

Merchants and goldsmiths in Europe created banks during the Middle Ages. Banks became necessary as more goods were exchanged and larger amounts of money were needed in the growing European economy.

In a similar way, banks sprang up as they were needed in the young United States. The following story about the creation of a bank in the 1860s is fictitious. However, it shows how banks developed over time into institutions that could meet the needs of consumers and producers in a modern economy.

Hiram Wakefield was a goldsmith in Denver, Colorado. When he heard about a gold strike near Gemstone City, 50 miles to the west, Hiram got excited about his own prospects. He knew he could be of service to the miners. He moved to the frontier town with his gold-weighing scale and his large safe. There he set up a new shop.

Soon Hiram's business was booming. Miners from the Gemstone City region brought their gold to be weighed, valued, and stored. When a miner brought in some gold for safekeeping, Hiram gave him a receipt that noted the value of that amount of gold. Then Hiram stored the gold in the safe.

The miners discovered that they could give any shopkeeper one of Hiram's receipts in exchange for the goods they wanted to buy. Business owners accepted these receipts because they could exchange them for gold if they wished.

Hiram further influenced the way his receipts were used in Gemstone City. He gave each miner both a receipt for the total value of the miner's gold stored in the safe and several "blank" receipts with which the miner could easily buy things. A miner completed a blank receipt by writing in a person's name and the amount of gold Hiram was to give to that person. The blank receipts became a form of money in Gemstone City.

Hiram soon discovered that miners only rarely came to exchange their receipts for all the actual gold they had on deposit in his safe. He also knew that some miners needed more gold than they had so they could buy supplies and continue to mine. Hiram decided, therefore, that he could safely lend some of the gold in his safe to miners who needed it. Miners who received these loans signed a note saying they would pay back the gold along with an added fee for borrowing it.

Hiram Wakefield had become the Gemstone City banker. His system of issuing blank receipts and loans is very similar to what banks do today.

✓ **Reading Check** **How does the story of Hiram Wakefield show how banks developed?**

Making A Deposit
An assayer judges the value of gold nuggets. These two Alaskan assayers ready a large quantity of gold for shipment. **Draw Inferences** *Why would miners choose to have others store their gold, and then to use their receipts for making purchases? Why not simply use the gold itself?*

$100,000.00 READY FOR SHIPMENT   PIONEER COS. OFFICE   NOME?

The Kinds of Money

When you think of money, you picture currency, such as quarters and dollar bills. Hiram Wakefield, however, had created a second kind of money: checks. Gold was cumbersome. The merchants of Gemstone City gladly accepted the miners' checks—the blank receipts Hiram gave them—in exchange for goods and services, just as if they were currency.

Checks Checks have all the characteristics of currency. They are generally accepted in exchange. By writing a specific amount on a check, a person states exactly how much money is to be paid. Although checks are not as durable as currency, the records banks keep for each check *are* durable. Checks are also easy to use and inexpensive to produce, and their supply can be controlled.

Checks can only exist in an economy if there are banks. In our economy, checks are used by people who have deposited money in a checking account at a bank. The money in a checking account is called a **demand deposit**. A person with a checking account can withdraw money from the bank "on demand" by writing a check.

Traveler's checks are a third kind of money we have in our economy today. Most traveler's checks are issued by banks. Printed on a traveler's check is the exact amount of money for which it can be cashed, usually $20, $50, or $100. Traveler's checks are accepted at most restaurants, hotels, and retail establishments around the globe.

Banks and the Money Supply Traveler's checks, demand deposits, and currency are the kinds of money that make up the money supply. The **money supply** is the total amount of money available for use as a medium of exchange. The money supply goes up and down. It does, however, stay within certain bounds. In September 2003, the money supply was about $8.7 trillion.

Modern Banks
Banks allow customers to write checks that draw upon the funds they have deposited. Checks are a form of currency accepted nearly as widely as coins and bills.
Draw Inferences *What might be the drawbacks of using checks instead of coins or bills?*

The Parts of the Money Supply, 2003

Kind of Money	Approximate Value (in billions)	Percent of Money Supply
Currency	$651	50.7%
Demand deposits (including all checking accounts)	$624	48.6%
Traveler's checks	$8	0.6%
Total	$1,283	100%

SOURCE: Federal Reserve Board, 2003

The majority of our nation's money supply is in currency.

1. **Analyze** In 2003, what was the total value of our money supply?
2. **Apply** How does the amount of money held in demand deposits make banks important to our nation's economy?

Look at the money supply table on this page. Almost 50 percent of our nation's money supply is in demand deposits. Knowing that demand deposits are managed by banks, you can see how important banks are to the economy. Banks not only hold a great deal of our currency, they also have a role in every transaction that is made using a check.

✔ **Reading Check** **How do checks differ from currency?**

Bank Services

Think back to the story of Hiram Wakefield. Hiram provided checking accounts for the miners, kept their gold safe, and made loans. Today, offering these same three services is the major function of banks in our economy.

Checking Accounts When Bill and Wilma Kowalski first got married, they opened a checking account at Central National Bank by depositing money there. They found that using checks instead of cash to pay for goods and to pay bills was an easy way to do business.

Using checks was also safe. Cash could be stolen. They knew that checks were useless to a thief because no one will accept a check unless it is written by the person whose name is printed on the check.

Bill and Wilma also liked the fact that the checks provided a good record of how they spent their money. Each month the bank sent a record of their cancelled, or paid, checks. It also sent a statement telling how much money was in their account.

Savings Accounts Bill and Wilma also decided to save for the future. They opened a savings account at Central National Bank because they knew it was a safe place to keep their money. Unlike their checking account, the Kowalskis' savings account was not a demand deposit. They could not withdraw the money on demand. The bank reserved the right to require advance notice of a large withdrawal.

However, the bank paid the Kowalskis for keeping their money in a savings account because they were in effect lending the bank money it could use for other purposes. The payment the Kowalskis received from the bank is called interest. This kind of interest is not the same as the payment for the use of capital you learned about in Chapter 14. Remember that capital is a factor of production. Interest, in this case, is the price the bank pays for use of someone else's funds.

People save for many reasons. The Kowalskis wanted to save for their daughter's college education and to have money in case of an emergency. Savings are an important source of funds in our economy. With savings funds, banks can make loans to help people in the economy buy goods and services and to help businesses produce goods and services.

Loans To make some extra money, Bill and Wilma began designing Web sites for local businesses. They soon got so many requests for their services that they decided to quit their jobs and start their own Web design business. Bill and Wilma developed a plan for their new business. They figured they needed to borrow $25,000 to buy computer equipment and software.

▲ People building homes often rely on bank loans. The loans are paid back with interest after the homes are built.

The Kowalskis presented their business plan to Marcia Slatterly at Central National Bank. Marcia approved a loan of $25,000. A **loan** is an amount of money borrowed for a certain time period. The borrower agrees to pay back the amount of money borrowed, plus a certain amount of interest.

The beginning of Bill and Wilma's business is the kind of story that takes place every day in banks throughout the United States. The homebuilder relies on bank loans for money for construction supplies. People take out loans to buy new cars or to put braces on their children's teeth. People who take out loans have decided that the benefit of having money now is greater than the cost of paying it back with interest later.

Civics and Economics

Women and Small Businesses A growing number of small businesses are owned and operated by women. According to the Center for Women's Business Research (CWBR), there were more 10.1 million privately held women-owned businesses in the United States in 2003. These businesses created 18.2 million jobs. They also contributed more than $2.3 trillion in sales to the economy. According to the CWBR, the number of privately held women-owned businesses grew by 11% between 1997 and 2002. This trend is expected to continue.

Analyzing Economics

1. Why do you think the number of privately held women-owned businesses has been increasing over the years?
2. How significant is the role played by women-owned business in our nation's economy?

In recent years, many companies have merged, creating one larger company with greater resources. Banks have been no exception. Small banks have been purchased by larger ones. In the cartoon at right, a man appears to have just had his loan application rejected.

1. What does the loan officer's advice imply?

2. What does the cartoonist seem to be saying about the current state of banking?

"Of course, you could try another bank, if there were any other banks."

By making loans, banks serve an important function. They help businesses make use of productive resources, which causes the economy to grow. When a business gets a loan, that business often creates more jobs by hiring new workers. Bill and Wilma, for example, may create after-school jobs for young programmers.

A business that gets a loan may also help other businesses grow. When Bill and Wilma buy computer equipment, the makers and distributors of the equipment will benefit.

✓ **Reading Check** **Why do banks pay customers who keep their money in savings accounts?**

The Business of Banking

Like other businesses in our economy, banks exist to make a profit. Most banks are corporations with stockholders who want a return on their investment. That is, they want their investment to grow, or become more valuable.

The largest source of revenue for most banks is interest on loans. The amount that banks pay customers in interest on savings accounts is less than the amount of interest that banks receive on loans. The difference between the amount paid out on savings and the interest paid to a bank by borrowers is a major part of a bank's income.

Insured Financial Institutions in the United States, 2003

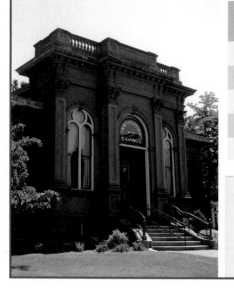

Type of Institution	Number	Total Value of Assets (in billions)
Banks	7,833	$7,485
Savings institutions	1,434	$1,438
Credit Unions	9,688	$557
Total	$1,283	100%

SOURCE: FDIC and National Credit Union Administration, 2003

Banks are only one type of important financial institution.
1. **Analyze** Which type of institution had the second-greatest total value of deposits in 2003?
2. **Apply** Why would the government want to insure these institutions?

Fractional Reserve Banking Making loans is perhaps the most important role of banks in our economy. Modern banking operates on the principle of fractional reserve banking. In **fractional reserve banking**, banks keep a percentage of checking and savings deposits in reserve. The rest of the money is available for loans and investments.

Hiram Wakefield knew that what a miner cared about was that he could get back the correct amount of gold for his deposit. He also learned that all the miners would not want all their gold at the same time. At any particular time some miners would withdraw their deposits and others would make new deposits. These withdrawals and new deposits were just about equal, so the total amount of gold in his safe stayed about the same.

Hiram found that he needed to keep only a fraction of the miners' total deposits in his vault to meet the demands for withdrawals. Therefore, he could loan out a certain amount of the gold in his vault as long as he kept—or reserved—enough gold to pay depositors who demanded it. Hiram was practicing fractional reserve banking.

When bankers learned that they needed to keep only a fraction of their money on hand, it was an important discovery. Until then, money just sat there, accumulating. Banks could now make the money they received from depositors do useful work instead of letting it sit in a dark vault. When the money deposited in banks is loaned to businesses and individuals, it helps those who need to borrow money. It also generates economic growth and creates an income for the bank in the form of interest payments on the loans. This exchange helps the bank to stay strong for its customers and the community it serves.

Other Financial Institutions Banks are only one type of financial institution. There are also savings institutions, which include savings and loan associations and mutual savings banks, and credit unions. Each type was created for a particular purpose. In recent years, savings institutions and credit unions have become more similar to banks.

Savings and loan associations were set up to accept savings deposits and make loans to families for buying land and houses. Today, most savings and loan associations also offer checking accounts, like banks.

A mutual savings bank is owned by its depositors, and any profits are paid to them. Mutual savings banks accept deposits, make loans, and allow checking accounts.

A credit union is a non-profit banking institution that serves only its members. The members often work for one organization such as a large company or a unit of government. Credit unions accept savings deposits and lend money. Credit unions also offer checking accounts called share drafts.

Credit Unions
Credit unions often serve members of large groups, such as the employees of a large company or the members of a large trade union.
Draw Inferences *Why would a credit union need a large number of members to be successful?*

✓ Reading Check **What is the largest source of revenue for banks?**

SECTION 2 Assessment

Key Terms

Use each of the key terms in a sentence that explains its meaning: demand deposit, money supply, loan, fractional reserve banking

Target Reading Skill

1. **Interpret Nonliteral Meanings** In your own words, rephrase the italicized portion of the sentence from page 466: "Banks could then make the money they received from depositors *do useful work* instead of letting it sit in a dark vault." Use your understanding of nonliteral meanings to help you arrive at your reformulation.

Comprehension and Critical Thinking

2. **a. Recall** When were banks first created?

   b. Draw Inferences Why would a bank's reputation enable it to make more money?

3. **a. Explain** How do regular checks differ from traveler's checks?

   b. Evaluate Information What is the money supply?

4. **a. Describe** Why might someone open both a checking account and a savings account?

   b. Draw Conclusions What are some of the reasons that people save money?

5. **a. Recall** How do banks profit when lending money to customers?

   b. Summarize Why does fractional reserve banking work?

Writing Activity

Alexander Hamilton, the first Secretary of the Treasury, proposed the establishment of a national bank. Go online and find out more about his reasons for supporting a national bank. Then write a paragraph or two in which you discuss Hamilton's views on the importance of a national bank.

Go Online
PHSchool.com
For: Writing Activity
Visit: PHSchool.com
Web Code: mpd-6172

How to Write a Letter to a Public Official

Public officials are elected in order to carry out the political goals of citizens. One way to participate in government is to let your elected representatives know how you feel about certain issues.

You can write a letter to convey your opinion about an issue. Your letter should state your views clearly and give reasons why you feel the way you do. Below, a concerned citizen asks her representative to take action on an issue.

2213 Essex Road
Castle City, CA 94320
August 28, 1994

The Honorable Carmen Mendoza
House of Representatives
Washington, D.C. 20515

Dear Representative Mendoza:

Last evening I saw you interviewed on the news. You said you were concerned about the lack of recreational facilities for teenagers in many areas. I share your concern. Unlike me, you can do much to solve this problem. You could propose a bill that provides federal funds to build such facilities.

Opponents of this bill might say that building such facilities would be very expensive. But what would be more expensive in the long run—abandoning many teens to a life of crime or providing an alternative to life on the streets? Many older people have testified that they were saved from the evils of street life by an opportunity to channel their energies into sports and other programs provided at recreational centers.

I have seen you express your concern on television. Now I would like to know what you plan to do about this problem.

Respectfully yours,
Cleotis Larkin

Learn the Skill

To write a letter to a public official, follow these steps:

❶ **Find out to whom you should write.** Do some research or call a few offices to find the best person to hear your comments.

❷ **Address the letter.** Follow the correct format for a letter.

❸ **Clearly state your purpose.** Provide reasons to back it up.

Practice the Skill

❶ Read the letter above. Find the writer's address, the receiver's address, the greeting, and the signature.

❷ Analyze the body of the letter. Did the writer convey her purpose clearly?

Apply the Skill

❶ Choose an issue that concerns you. Find out which public official handles that issue.

❷ Write a letter. Have a teacher or classmate read it over. Send it to the public official.

Go Online
civics
interactive

For: Local Citizenship
Visit: PHSchool.com
Web Code: mpp-6172

The Federal Reserve System

Reading Preview

Objectives

In this section you will

- Learn about the beginning of the Federal Reserve System.
- Understand the organization of the Federal Reserve System.
- Learn about the functions of the Federal Reserve System.
- Explore the delicate balance between money and the economy.

Key Terms

Federal Reserve System

Board of Governors recession

Main Idea

The Federal Reserve is an independent agency of the federal government. It regulates the banking industry and makes minor adjustments to balance the money supply and our economy.

Target Reading Skill

Use Context Sometimes the meaning of a word or phrase makes sense only in its context—the words, phrases, or sentences that surround it. By considering the meanings of these other words and phrases, you can make sense of the word or words you don't know.

Taking Notes

Make a diagram like the one below. As you read this section, complete the diagram with information about the Federal Reserve System and its roles.

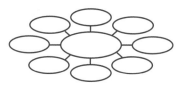

One important way in which the federal government affects the economy is to regulate the banking industry and the nation's money supply. It performs these functions through the Federal Reserve System.

The Federal Reserve System

Several times in the late 1800s and early 1900s, the economy stopped growing for a period of time. There was widespread hardship as businesses closed and workers lost their jobs.

During these periods, people who had money deposited in banks began to panic because they feared that the banks, too, would go out of business. They wanted all their money in cash. Because banks operated on the fractional reserve principle, many did not have enough money on hand to meet such a great and sudden demand. Some banks had to close down, and their customers lost all their money.

After one of these financial panics occurred in 1907, the public demanded that the government step in and make rules for how banks should operate. They also thought that the federal government should assist banks when they needed help.

Congress passed a bill in 1913, creating the Federal Reserve System, or "the Fed." This system became the central bank of the United States. The **Federal Reserve System** provides important services to United States banks and regulates their activities.

The Fed
The Federal Reserve System was created to oversee the United States banking industry and to keep it stable.

✓ **Reading Check** What helped bring about the creation of the Federal Reserve System?

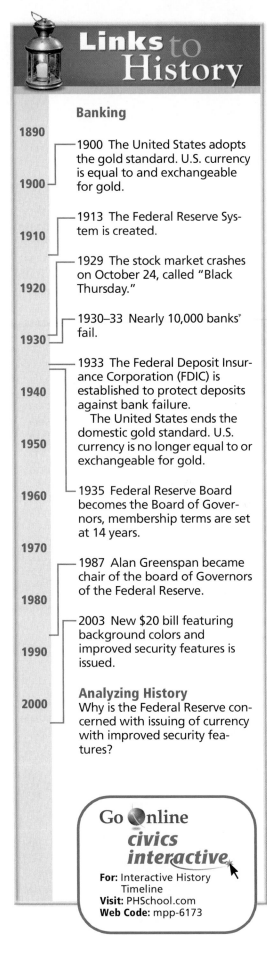

Banking

1890

1900

1900 The United States adopts the gold standard. U.S. currency is equal to and exchangeable for gold.

1910

1913 The Federal Reserve System is created.

1920

1929 The stock market crashes on October 24, called "Black Thursday."

1930

1930–33 Nearly 10,000 banks' fail.

1940

1933 The Federal Deposit Insurance Corporation (FDIC) is established to protect deposits against bank failure.
The United States ends the domestic gold standard. U.S. currency is no longer equal to or exchangeable for gold.

1950

1960

1935 Federal Reserve Board becomes the Board of Governors, membership terms are set at 14 years.

1970

1980

1987 Alan Greenspan became chair of the board of Governors of the Federal Reserve.

1990

2003 New $20 bill featuring background colors and improved security features is issued.

2000

Analyzing History
Why is the Federal Reserve concerned with issuing of currency with improved security features?

Organization of the Fed

The Federal Reserve System is an independent agency of the federal government. It remains beyond the reach of political influence so it can serve the needs of the nation as a whole.

Federal Reserve Districts The lawmakers who created the Federal Reserve System wanted to keep the central bank in touch with the business needs of the country. The economic problems of one region may be different from those of another. Therefore, Congress divided the United States into twelve geographic regions called Federal Reserve districts.

In each district there is a Federal Reserve Bank to supervise banking in that district and pay attention to the economic problems of that area. For example, the tenth district Federal Reserve Bank in Kansas City, which serves a farming region, is aware of the needs of farmers and of banks that make loans to farmers.

Running the Fed The most powerful people in the Fed are the seven members of the Board of Governors. They are appointed by the President for 14-year terms. The **Board of Governors** is responsible for running the Federal Reserve System as a whole.

✓ Reading Check **How does the Federal Reserve keep in touch with the business needs of the country?**

Functions of the Fed

The Federal Reserve Bank is not like any other bank. You cannot save money at the Federal Reserve; you cannot get a loan from the Fed. The Fed, however, is important to you and to the value of your money. It is often called "the bankers' bank."

The Fed supplies currency to banks. If a bank needs currency to pay customers who are making withdrawals, it orders currency from the nearest Federal Reserve Bank. Look at a dollar bill. At the top of the side with George Washington's picture are the words "Federal Reserve Note." Each Federal Reserve note comes from one of the twelve Federal Reserve Banks. The twelve districts in which these banks are located are shown on the map on the next page.

Federal Reserve Districts

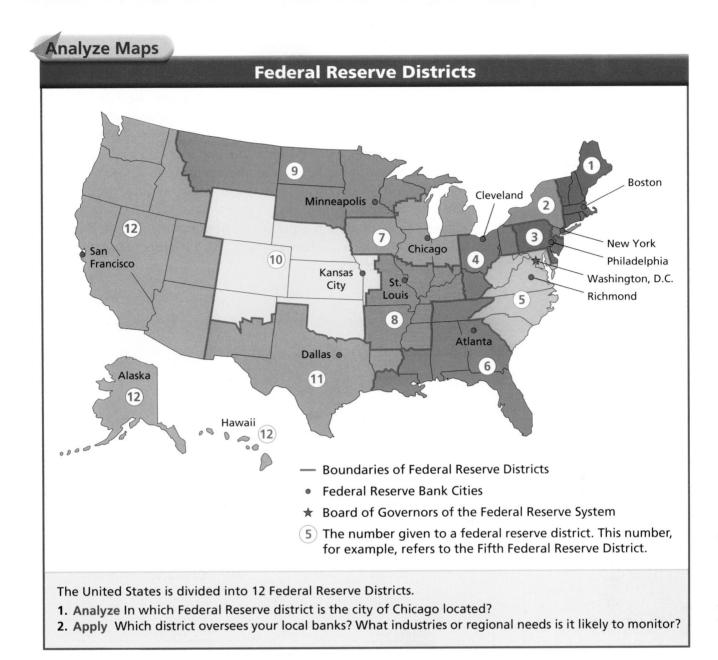

Boston
Cleveland
New York
Philadelphia
Washington, D.C.
Richmond
Minneapolis
Chicago
Kansas City
St. Louis
Atlanta
Dallas
San Francisco
Alaska
Hawaii

— Boundaries of Federal Reserve Districts
• Federal Reserve Bank Cities
★ Board of Governors of the Federal Reserve System
(5) The number given to a federal reserve district. This number, for example, refers to the Fifth Federal Reserve District.

The United States is divided into 12 Federal Reserve Districts.

1. **Analyze** In which Federal Reserve district is the city of Chicago located?
2. **Apply** Which district oversees your local banks? What industries or regional needs is it likely to monitor?

Serving as the Government's Bank The Federal Reserve performs many specialized services for the federal government. For example, it redeems food coupons and monitors special accounts, such as Treasury tax and loan accounts. In short, the Fed keeps the federal government's checking accounts. When people pay their taxes, the money is deposited in a government account at a Federal Reserve Bank. When the government pays for highways or airplanes, it writes checks on its Federal Reserve Bank accounts.

The Fed also keeps track of the federal government's debts. If the government borrows money, the lender—who may be an individual, a bank, or a business—receives a certificate called a government bond, bill, or note. This certificate tells how much money the government borrowed. The Federal Reserve System keeps records of all government bonds, bills, and notes.

Providing Services An important day-to-day job of the Fed is to collect and to clear checks. It has a mandate from Congress to pay and settle interbank payments. If you pay for your new clothes with a check, the clothing storeowner deposits the check in the store's bank. The store's bank then sends the check to the Fed, which sends it on to your bank. The Fed keeps the paper checks and sends electronic data to your bank to request payment. In this process, money is taken from your checking account and put into the clothing store's checking account.

This payments system is the largest in the world. In a year, the Fed will process billions of checks. These yearly transactions are valued at trillions of dollars.

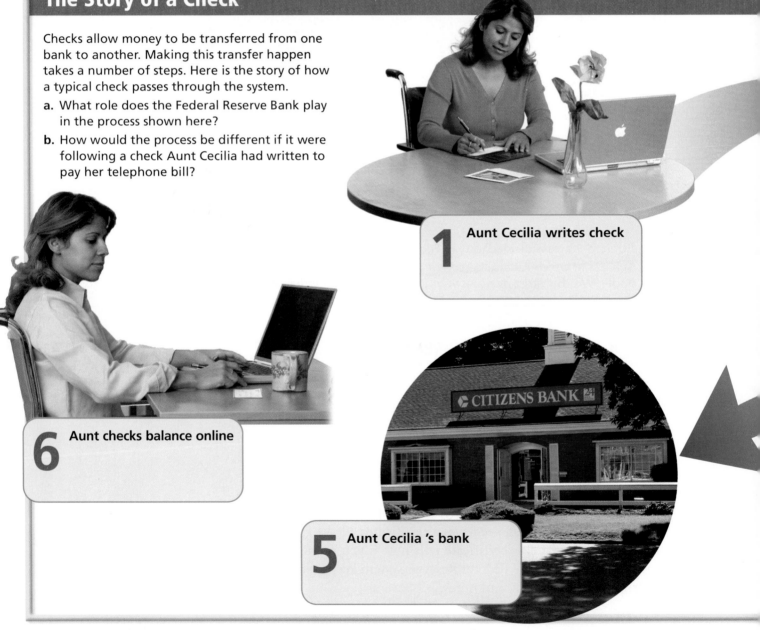

Analyze Diagrams

The Story of a Check

Checks allow money to be transferred from one bank to another. Making this transfer happen takes a number of steps. Here is the story of how a typical check passes through the system.

a. What role does the Federal Reserve Bank play in the process shown here?

b. How would the process be different if it were following a check Aunt Cecilia had written to pay her telephone bill?

1 Aunt Cecilia writes check

6 Aunt checks balance online

5 Aunt Cecilia 's bank

CITIZENS BANK

Regulating Banks The Federal Reserve governs the business of banking. One of the most important regulations sets a minimum on the amount of reserves a bank must keep on deposit with a Federal Reserve Bank. This rule ensures that banks will always have enough money available to meet the demand for withdrawals. The Fed has a staff of bank examiners who visit banks regularly to be sure they are following all the Fed's rules.

Congress has passed several laws to protect businesses and individuals doing business with banks. The Fed's job is to help put these laws into effect. One of the laws enforced by the Fed is the Truth in Lending Law. It requires banks and other financial institutions to tell you the full cost of borrowing money.

Go Online
civics
interactive

For: The Story of a Check Interactive
Visit: PHSchool.com
Web Code: mpp-6174

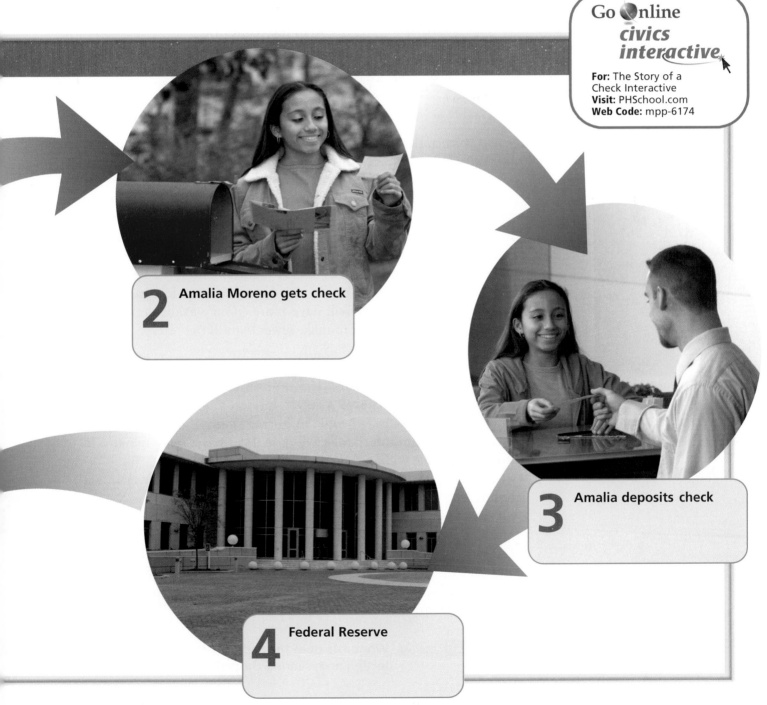

2 Amalia Moreno gets check

3 Amalia deposits check

4 Federal Reserve

Alan Greenspan (1926–) is described by some as the second most powerful man in America because of his ability to influence the U.S. economy. He is best known for his role as Chair of the Board of Governors of the Federal Reserve System. Greenspan was appointed chair of the Board of Governors in 1987. His position has been renewed by Presidents George H.W. Bush, Bill Clinton, and George W. Bush. Under Greenspan, interest rate adjustments were frequent, but usually small. He preferred to make minor adjustments in the economy's course rather than drive it in a new direction. As a result, some of Greenspan's terms as Fed chair witnessed the longest period of economic growth in the nation's history.

Citizenship

Why do you think both Republican and Democratic Presidents were willing to renew Greenspan's position as chair of the Fed?

Making Loans to Banks Banks sometimes need extra money. Usually this happens when bank customers want to borrow or withdraw large sums of money. The Fed will make loans to help out banks in these situations. Banks pay a special low rate of interest, called the discount rate, on funds borrowed from the Fed.

Controlling the Money Supply The most powerful job of the Fed is to regulate the nation's money supply—the amount available for spending. The size of the money supply has a great influence on the health of the economy.

The largest and most changeable part of the money supply is made up of demand deposits. The amount of money in demand deposits is directly affected by the amount of money that banks lend to individuals, businesses, and governments. Because of this relationship, the Fed can control the money supply indirectly—by influencing the amount of money banks can lend and the amount that individuals, businesses, and governments will choose to borrow. The Fed can use three different methods to influence the amount of money loaned by banks.

First, the Fed can change its reserve requirement. If the Fed lowers the reserve requirement, banks are obliged to keep less money on reserve at the Fed. They will have more money available to make loans. In contrast, banks can make fewer loans if the reserve requirement is raised.

Second, the Fed can change the discount rate. If the Fed lowers the discount rate, banks pay less interest on money they borrow. They can therefore charge a lower interest rate on loans. Lower interest rates encourage people to borrow more money. If the Fed raises the discount rate, banks will raise the interest rate on loans. In this case, people will tend to borrow less money.

Third, the Fed can buy and sell government bonds. Government bonds are certificates that the federal government issues in exchange for lending it money. A government bond can be bought or sold. It represents money owed to the holder of the bond certificate. If the Fed buys government bonds from banks, banks have more reserves and thus more money to lend. If the Fed sells government bonds to banks, banks pay for them from their reserves and thus have less money to lend.

✓ Reading Check **What role does the Federal Reserve play in collecting and clearing checks?**

Money and the Economy

The money supply is directly related to the amount of money people can spend in the economy. If the economy is healthy, spending is about equal to the economy's ability to produce goods and services.

When there is more money in the economy than there are goods and services to spend it on, increased demand for goods and services will make prices rise. A general rise in the prices of goods and services throughout the economy is called inflation. Inflation reduces the buying power of people's money. If your income stays the same, you can buy less because of inflation.

When there is less money in the economy than there are goods and services to spend it on, the demand for goods and services decreases. This situation can cause businesses to cut back on production. Such a slowdown in economic activity and production is called a **recession**. A recession results in lower production, lower profits for businesses, and increased unemployment.

Controlling the money supply is a delicate act. When prices begin to rise, the Fed may decide to discourage loans. With less money being loaned, spending slows and prices are less likely to rise. If a recession threatens to occur, the Fed will likely make it easier for banks to make loans. Increased lending will stimulate spending and increase production.

Inflation

Increase in demand for goods and services

Recession

Decrease in demand for goods and services

▲ The Fed controls the money supply to try to avoid inflation and recession.

✓ **Reading Check** Why does the Fed discourage loans when prices begin to rise?

SECTION 3 Assessment

Key Terms

Use each of the key terms in a sentence that explains its meaning: Federal Reserve System, Board of Governors, recession

Target Reading Skill

1. **Use Context** Find the word *panic* on page 469. Use context to figure out its meaning. What clues helped you?

Comprehension and Critical Thinking

2. **a. Describe** Before the existence of the Fed, what happened during financial panics?
   b. Draw Conclusions Why do you think the creation of a central bank was a solution to financial panics?
3. **a. Recall** Who runs the Fed?
   b. Evaluate Information Why is it important that the Federal Reserve is beyond the reach of political influence?
4. **a. Explain** What does the Fed do with the taxes paid annually?
   b. Summarize What are the three methods the Fed has to influence the amount of money loaned by banks?
5. **a. Describe** What happens when there is less money in the economy than goods and services to spend it on?
   b. Evaluate Information Why do the Fed's decisions to lower and raise interest rates affect the economy?

Writing Activity

You are a speechwriter for the Fed. Craft a speech for the chair of the Board of Governors explaining the need to lower interest rates to help stimulate the economy. Mention some of the economic reasons behind your decision.

TIP Your speech should consider arguments that could be made against lowering interest rates, and refute those arguments.

Solving Problems

Solving problems is a part of everyday life, both for individuals and for organizations. Many businesses succeed or fail depending on how well they identify and solve the problems facing them. The following passage describes one example.

> Joe wants to open his own seafood restaurant. He has worked as head chef at a well-known restaurant for many years. He is experienced, and many people who know of him would probably patronize his restaurant. He has found the perfect location for the restaurant by the harbor, but the land is expensive. He does not have enough money for it, but he does not want to pass up the perfect location either.
>
> Joe has given the matter a lot of thought. He could get a loan from the bank, but he would have to pay back the money with interest. He could look for investors to give him money, but then the investors would have a good amount of influence over the business. Finally, he could just open the restaurant in a different location where land is cheaper.

Learn the Skill

Follow these steps to learn problem-solving skills:

1. **Identify the problem.** Before you can solve the problem you have to identify it. State the problem clearly and simply in your own words.

2. **List possible solutions.** Most problems have more than one possible solution. List as many reasonable possible solutions as you can.

3. **Review the possible solutions.** Analyze each possibility. Examine the advantages and disadvantages of each one. Compare the advantages and disadvantages of each solution.

4. **Choose a solution.** Choose a course of action and explain why it is the best possible solution to the problem. Be prepared to discuss why the other options are not the best solution.

Practice the Skill

Read the passage above and answer these questions:

1. State the problem.

2. What possible solutions are given? Be sure to identify all the possible solutions.

3. What are some advantages and disadvantages of each solution?

4. Compare the advantages and disadvantages of each solution.

5. Which do you think is the best solution? Why?

Apply the Skill

Think of a problem facing your school or community. List all of the possible solutions to the problem you can think of. Then evaluate each one to determine which solution works best.

Review and Assessment

Chapter Summary

Section 1
Money
(pages 456–459)

- Money enables the functioning of our market economy, and it serves as a medium of exchange, a standard of value, and a store of value.

- Cultures without money rely on **bartering** to exchange goods.

- **Currency** is the coins and paper bills used as money. It is generally acceptable, can be counted and measured accurately, is durable, convenient, inexpensive to produce, and its supply is easily controlled.

- Our currency has value because it is officially recognized by our government.

Section 2
Our Banking System
(pages 460–467)

- Banking has existed since the Middle Ages to accommodate consumers who want to purchase goods and keep their resources in a safe place.

- Traveler's checks, **demand deposits,** and currency are the kinds of money that make up the **money supply.**

- Many bank customers have a checking account. They can use checks instead of cash. Some bank customers keep their cash reserves in savings accounts. Their banks pay them interest for lending the bank money. Other bank customers take out **loans** to finance homes, cars, and educations. Those customers pay interest on those loans. Interest on loans is the largest source of revenue for banks.

- Most modern banks operate on the principle of **fractional reserve banking.**

Section 3
The Federal Reserve System
(pages 469–475)

- The **Federal Reserve System** (or Fed) was created by Congress as an independent agency of the federal government in 1913. Its creation was partly in response to the financial panics of the early 1900s. The Fed provides services to banks and helps regulate the banking industry.

- The Fed is divided into 12 geographic regions called Federal Reserve districts. The Fed is run by a 7-member **Board of Governors.**

- The Fed supplies currency to banks, governs the business of banking, keeps the federal government's checking accounts, makes loans to banks, and collects and clears checks.

- The Fed balances the money supply. It tries to steer the national economy clear of prolonged periods of inflation and **recession.**

Copy the chart below and use it to help you summarize the chapter.

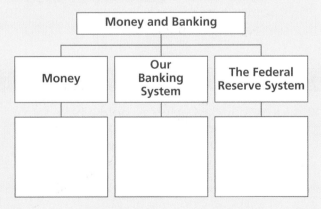

Go Online
PHSchool.com

For: Self-Test
Visit: PHSchool.com
Web Code: mpa-6173

Reviewing Key Terms

Fill in each blank with one of the key terms from the list below.

bartering   loan
currency   fractional reserve banking
demand   Federal Reserve System
  deposit   recession
money supply

1. Bank accounts that offer customers access to their money whenever they need it work on the _____ system.

2. Items such as coins, shells, bills, or beads that are used as money are referred to as _____.

3. A general slowdown in economic growth is called a _____.

4. Economic systems without money rely on the exchange of goods, called _____.

5. The _____ is the total of all currency available in an economy.

6. A bank that offers a _____ to a customer will expect it to be repaid with interest.

7. The _____ oversees the nation's banks.

8. The widespread adoption of _____ meant that more capital was available for economic growth.

Comprehension and Critical Thinking

9. a. **Describe** What are the three functions of money?
   b. **Evaluate Information** Why does our currency have value?
   c. **Summarize** What are the six characteristics of the money we use in our economy today?

10. a. **Recall** What are the three kinds of money in our economy?
    b. **Analyze Information** What are the advantages of depositing money in a savings account instead of hiding it somewhere?

    c. **Synthesize Information** How do loans made by banks help the economy to grow?

11. a. **Explain** How did financial panics lead to the formation of the Federal Reserve System?
    b. **Categorize** In what three ways can the Fed influence the money supply?
    c. **Draw Conclusions** Why is controlling the supply of money important?

Activities

12. **Skills** Your class wants to hold a bake sale to raise money for a class trip. You need $100 for supplies, but so far your class only has $75. **a.** What is the problem in this scenario? **b.** What are the possible solutions to this problem?

13. **Writing** You want to start a business that provides services, such as babysitting or bike repair. Before you start, it is wise to have a plan—a business plan. Choose a service that you could provide, then write a one-page business plan that describes your business. What service could you provide? Who would your customers be? How much money would you need for tools or equipment? How would you advertise?

14. **Active Citizen** Find out about the services and policies of a local bank. Answer these questions: Does the bank charge a fee for its checking accounts? What interest rate does it pay on savings accounts? Then compare your findings with others in your class. Which bank would you do business with?

15. **Math Practice** In 2002 there were $654 billion in paper currency in circulation. $458 billion of this was in $100 bills. What percentage of the U.S. currency in circulation is in the form of $100 bills?

16. **Civics and Economics** Why does today's currency serve our economy better than gold and silver coins could?

17. **Analyzing Visuals** Explain how the photograph above reflects the symbolic value of money.

Standardized Test Prep

Test-Taking Tips

Some questions on standardized tests ask you to analyze a reading selection. Study the passage below. Then follow the tips to answer the sample question.

TIP Sometimes more than one name is used in describing an organization. In this paragraph both "Board of Governors of the Federal Reserve" and "Governors" mean the same thing.

The Board of Governors of the Federal Reserve routinely confers with other government agencies, banking industry groups, the central banks of other countries and members of Congress. For example, they meet frequently with Treasury officials and the Council of Economic Advisers to help evaluate the economic climate and to discuss objectives for the nation's economy. Governors also discuss the international monetary system with central bankers of other countries. They are in close contact with the heads of the U.S. agencies that make foreign loans and transactions.

Pick the letter that best completes the statement.

1. Governors of the Federal Reserve
   A do not involve themselves in issues concerning other governments.
   B rarely meet with Treasury officials.
   C regularly interact with officials from other government agencies.
   D routinely confer with heads of state from other nations.

   The correct answer is **C**.

2. According to this passage, all of the following statements are true of the Board of Governors EXCEPT:
   A They regularly meet representatives of banking industry groups.
   B They meet only with heads of agencies that conduct domestic transactions.
   C They meet with the Council of Economic Advisers to discuss objectives for the nation's economy.
   D They discuss the international monetary system with central bankers of other countries.

Public Finance

What's Ahead in Chapter 18

In this chapter you will examine the government's role in the economy. You will learn how the government tries to maintain a stable economy. You will understand how federal, state, and local governments tax citizens, and what they spend this revenue on.

SECTION 1
Government and Economic Goals

SECTION 2
Paying for Government

SECTION 3
Government Policy and Spending

TARGET READING SKILL

Word Analysis One way to learn new words is to come across them in your reading. Word analysis helps you determine what a new word means. As you read this chapter, you will try out the skills of analyzing word parts and recognizing word origins.

Zakim Bridge, Boston ▶

National Standards for Civics and Government State

The following National Standards for Civics and Government are covered in this chapter:

III. How does the government established by the Constitution embody the purposes, values, and principles of American democracy?

B. How is the national government organized and what does it do?

C. How are state and local governments organized and what do they do?

Go Online
PHSchool.com

For: Your state's standards
Visit: PHSchool.com
Web Code: mpe-6181

Active Citizen Civics in the Real World

Deborah burst into the kitchen. "Look!" she cried. "My first paycheck!"

Noah and Rebecca stopped working and congratulated their sister. Deborah had recently started ushering at the local movie theater so that she could set aside some money for college.

"Let's see it!" said Noah. Deborah ripped open her pay envelope as he looked over her shoulder.

"Wait a minute," Deborah said. "This isn't the right amount of money I think it should be about fifty dollars more."

"Are you sure?" Rebecca took the check and looked at it carefully, turning it over. "Deborah, the check is right, You forgot about the taxes! See, here is where it shows the taxes taken out of your pay."

Deborah looked at her pay stub. It showed the number of hours she had worked, her total earnings for the week, and the deductions taken for taxes.

"That's almost a third of what I earned this week!" she exclaimed. "It's too much! What do I get for all that money?"

Noah laughed at her. "Our taxes help pay Dad's salary at the police department, don't forget! I know it seems like a lot, but we have to have taxes."

Citizen's Journal Do you know what citizens get in exchange for the taxes they pay? Make a list in your journal of the benefits to which taxes entitle us. As you read this chapter, you may want to add to your list or remove items from it.

Government and Economic Goals

SECTION 1

Reading Preview

Objectives

In this section you will
- Discuss the relationship between full employment and price stability.
- Study the government's role in the circular flow of economic activity.
- Investigate the process of national income accounting.

Taking Notes

Make a diagram like the one below. As you read this section, complete the diagram with information about the government's desire for a stable economy.

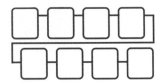

Key Terms

full employment
mixed economy
national income accounting
economic growth
inflation
deflation

Main Idea

The federal government plays an important economic role. It provides jobs, keeps prices stable, and taxes and spends in a pattern that stimulates economic growth.

Target Reading Skill

Recognize Word Origins A person's origin is his or her place of birth. A word origin includes its original language and meaning. For example, the word *economy* comes from two Greek words meaning "to manage a house." You can see the connection between managing money at home and doing the same thing on a national scale. When you recognize a word's origin, it helps you figure out what the word means.

During difficult economic times, the federal government has many ways to try to improve the economy. It can take action to achieve full employment and price stability. With government involved in the economy, it becomes an important part of the model of the circular flow of economic activity.

Full Employment and Price Stability

When prices are stable and employment is up, people generally feel positive about their future and their elected representatives. However, citizens become discouraged when businesses close, prices fluctuate, and unemployment rises. In bad economic times, citizens turn to their elected representatives. They want action.

The Employment Act of 1946 The American public grew concerned about unemployment at the end of World War II. Soldiers returning from the war needed jobs. Many people feared that this would lead the country into an economic depression, like the Great Depression that came before World War II. This situation prompted the Congress to pass the Employment Act of 1946.

The act states the government's intention to promote employment, production, and purchasing power. Let's examine three important ideas related to this Act.

The General Welfare The preamble to the Constitution states that one purpose of government is to "promote the general welfare." This means that the government is to serve the best interests of citizens. Through the Employment Act of 1946, the government assumed responsibility for people's general welfare by becoming committed to full employment with price stability.

Full Employment Unemployment is a problem that affects individuals and society. The lack of income disrupts families. It also affects business. One goal of our federal government is full employment. **Full employment** means that no person who wants to work should be out of a job. The economy should provide employment for any person who is willing and able to work.

Price Stability Suppose you go to the store with just enough money to buy a loaf of bread. When you get there, you discover that the price of bread is twice the amount of money you have. The fact that the price of bread has doubled may indicate that prices are no longer stable. The Employment Act of 1946 states that the Federal government will "promote maximum . . . purchasing power." If the prices of products increase significantly, your purchasing power is reduced. In this case, we no longer have price stability. The government uses its economic power to keep prices stable.

The Constitution also gives Congress and the states the power to make "ground rules" for a market economy. These rules include laws that protect private property against theft and laws that say how corporations may be set up. Once the foundations had been laid and the rules set, citizens expected the government to play only a small role in the economy.

✔ Reading Check　**What was the chief goal of the Employment Act of 1946?**

An Expanding Workforce Millions of American soldiers came home after World War II and needed jobs. Congress tried to help them by passing the Employment Act of 1946. **Summarize** *Why is widespread unemployment bad for the economy?*

Government and the Circular Flow

In Chapter 14 you learned about the circular flow of economic activity. You learned that individuals own the economic resources of land, labor, and capital. Individuals sell these resources to businesses in exchange for rent, wages, and interest. In turn, businesses use these resources to produce goods and services. Goods and services are then sold to individuals, completing the circular flow of economic activity.

The circular flow diagram in Chapter 14 represents what economists call the private sector of the economy. Since World War II, the government has become a big part of the economy. Many government actions affect the flow of resources through the economy. Now let's add government to the circular flow.

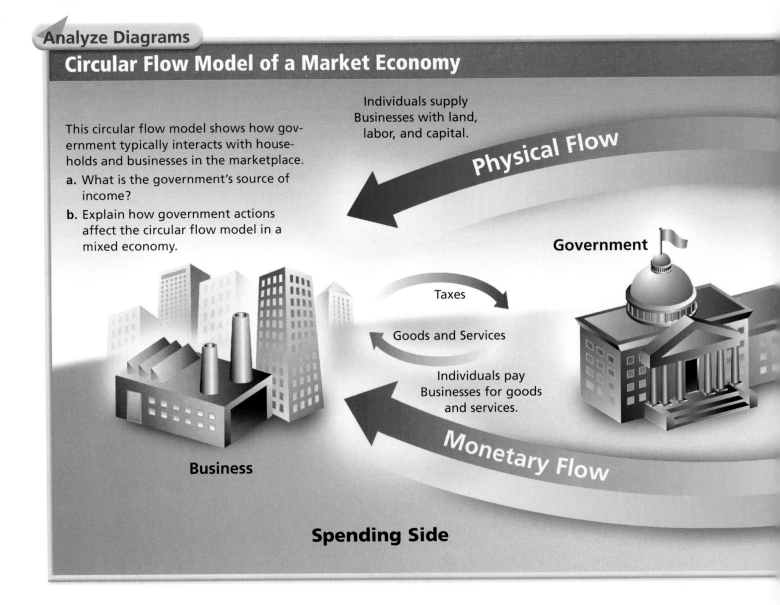

Analyze Diagrams

Circular Flow Model of a Market Economy

This circular flow model shows how government typically interacts with households and businesses in the marketplace.

a. What is the government's source of income?

b. Explain how government actions affect the circular flow model in a mixed economy.

Individuals supply Businesses with land, labor, and capital.

Physical Flow

Government

Taxes

Goods and Services

Individuals pay Businesses for goods and services.

Monetary Flow

Business

Spending Side

Adding Government to the Circular Flow In the circular flow diagram, the icon in the center labeled "Government" represents all levels of government. The federal government, state governments, and local governments all have the power to tax. At all levels, the government also provides goods and services. For example, the federal government provides national defense and interstate highways. State governments provide higher public education and state parks. Local governments provide public schools and libraries.

When we include the government in the circular flow of economic activity, we call this a mixed economy. A **mixed economy** includes the private sector (the market sector) and the public sector (government). Some of the best examples of mixed economies, such as France and Germany, are found in Europe.

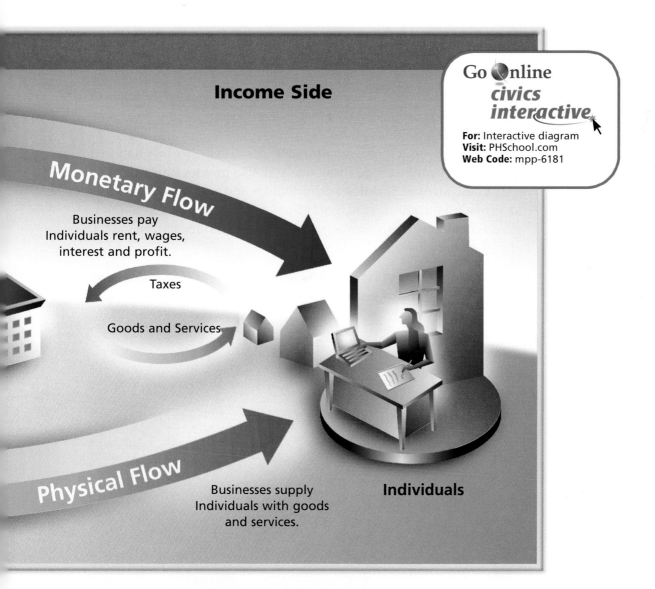

Income Side

Monetary Flow

Businesses pay Individuals rent, wages, interest and profit.

Taxes

Goods and Services

Physical Flow

Businesses supply Individuals with goods and services.

Individuals

Go Online
civics
interactive
For: Interactive diagram
Visit: PHSchool.com
Web Code: mpp-6181

Income Tax The first income tax in the United States was proposed during the War of 1812. However, this tax was never enforced. In 1861, a federal income tax was passed into law by the government. Two additional tax acts were passed in 1862 and 1864 to raise money for the Civil War. (Figures released after the Civil War show that 276,661 people actually filed tax returns in 1870. The country's population at this time was about 38 million.) Congress allowed the income tax laws to expire in 1872. In its place, lawmakers created tariff restrictions that served as a source of revenue for the United States until 1913. In 1913, the 16th Amendment was passed. It gave Congress the power to tax citizens on their income.

Analyze Economics

1. Why do you think the government proposed an income tax during wartime?
2. Do you think an income tax is a good idea? Why or why not?

Businesses Businesses pay federal and state taxes on their profits. (Profit is the money remaining after a business has paid all its costs.) Businesses also pay local property taxes on buildings and equipment they own. They pay taxes on the gasoline that they use to fuel cars and trucks needed for business. In turn, the government provides services such as transportation and police protection to businesses.

Individuals Almost all individuals in the United States pay taxes. The largest tax that individuals pay is the federal income tax. An income tax is paid based on wages or salaries earned by an individual in a year. Some states have a sales tax, a tax added to the price of a good or service sold. Sales taxes are paid by anyone who buys something. Sometimes, local governments in these states can charge their own additional sales tax on purchases. People who own their homes pay a local property tax. Property taxes are based in part on the value of any houses or other buildings on the site.

The federal government provides services such as national defense and health care to individuals. It also provides income support in the form of Social Security. State governments use tax funds to provide education, transportation, and judicial services. Local governments use tax revenue to provide education, citizen safety, and often hospital services.

✓ Reading Check **What role does the government play in the flow of economic activity?**

A Nation of Taxpayers
A postal employee accepts a last-minute tax return outside a post office in Washington, D.C. Most Americans who have incomes pay income taxes. **Summarize** *What services do Americans receive from the federal government in exchange for their taxes?*

Calculating GDP

Year	Goods and Services	Market Value
1	6 cars and 10 haircuts	(6 x $20,000) + (10 x $15) = $120,150
2	8 cars and 12 haircuts	(8 x $20,000) + (12 x $15) = $160,180
3	10 cars and 12 haircuts	(10 x $20,000) + (12 x $15) = $200,180
4	10 cars and 17 haircuts	(10 x $20,000) + (10 x $15) = $160,150

Suppose we have a simple economy that produces only cars and haircuts. Cars cost $20,000; haircuts cost $15.

1. **Analyze** By how much did the GDP go up in Year 2?
2. **Calculate** In Year 5, cars now cost $12,000. If the economy sells 15 cars and 15 haircuts in Year 5, what is the GDP?

National Income Accounting

Our nation keeps track of our overall income and spending in a process called **national income accounting**.

National income accounting includes data on how much businesses are producing. National income accounting also includes statistics on how much money Americans are earning and how much of that money is saved or invested.

The process of national income accounting allows us to understand what is happening in the overall economy. It allows us to measure changes in the economy from year to year. It also helps voters and government leaders decide on policies related to government spending and taxation.

Gross Domestic Product As you will recall from Chapter 16, the gross domestic product (GDP) is the total dollar value of all final goods and services produced and sold within the country in a year. GDP is a monetary measure. It accounts for a wide variety of goods and services in money terms.

Transactions that do not involve production are not included in the GDP. For example, Social Security payments to individuals are not included, because it does not involve production. Buying and selling stocks is not included, because these are merely exchanges of paper assets.

Also, the value of goods and services can only be counted once. If you sell a used set of headphones to a friend, for example, the value of this sale is not included in the GDP because the set of headphones was counted the first time it was sold—when you bought it from the store. Another example is the value of a car. The final price of a new car is included in the GDP. But the value of the engine, the upholstered seats, and the exterior trim are not, because their value is included in the final price of the car.

Target Reading Skill

Recognize Word Origins
The origin of the word *domestic* is the Latin word *domus*, meaning "house." Cats are called domestic animals because they live in houses. The term *gross domestic product* tells you that it deals with the home economy—the economy within the country.

Gross Domestic Product

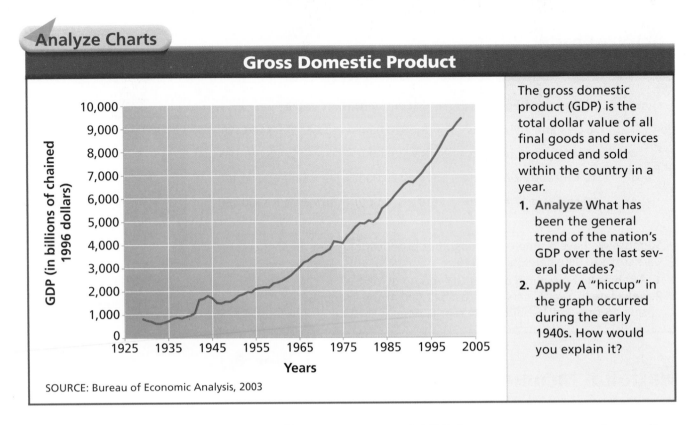

GDP (in billions of chained 1996 dollars)

Years

SOURCE: Bureau of Economic Analysis, 2003

The gross domestic product (GDP) is the total dollar value of all final goods and services produced and sold within the country in a year.

1. **Analyze** What has been the general trend of the nation's GDP over the last several decades?

2. **Apply** A "hiccup" in the graph occurred during the early 1940s. How would you explain it?

Spending, Income, and GDP In an economy, total spending must equal total income. That is, what is spent on this year's GDP becomes income to those who produced this year's GDP. For our purposes here, we will not include imports or exports.

Look at the circular flow diagram on pages 484-485. The spending side includes the dollar value of goods and services bought by individuals, businesses, and the government. The income side includes the dollar value of wages, salaries, investment interest, rents, and business profits.

The spending side and income side represent two diffent ways to determine the value of GDP. Suppose that a simple economy includes only Mrs. Green, Mr. Purple, Mrs. Blue, and Mr. Gray. These four individuals make or grow all the food, clothing, transportation, and books used in the economy each year. Nothing else is included in this simple economy.

Here is a possible calculation of GDP in this economy using income alone:

Mr. Green's income:	$35,000
Mr. Purple's income:	$21,000
Mrs. Blue's income:	$24,000
Mr. Gray's income:	$47,000
Total GDP:	**$127,000**

This is an example of how to determine the same economy's GDP by spending. Both systems should lead to the same total.

Food:	$11,000
Books:	$7,000
Clothing:	$39,000
Transportation:	$70,000
Total GDP:	**$127,000**

Policy Goals to Improve the Economy The GDP is a measure of the country's economic health. When the GDP increases from one year to the next without major increases in prices, we say we have had economic growth. **Economic growth** means an increase in the production of goods and services, which provides citizens with a higher standard of living. Economic growth is one goal of our economy. Policy makers use the GDP to tell whether we are reaching this goal.

Two other policy goals are full employment and price stability. Policy makers try to provide an economy in which anyone who wants to work can find work. Policy makers also try to avoid large increases or decreases in the overall price level. If the overall price level is increasing, we have **inflation**. If the overall price level is decreasing, we have **deflation**. Historically, inflation has been a major worry of policy makers in the United States. However, our country has not experienced strong inflation in the last 20 years. In the early 2000s, deflation returned as a major concern for the first time in many decades.

✔ Reading Check **Why is economic growth important?**

Job Seekers
To achieve economic growth, the economy must supply jobs for those who need them. **Analyze** *How does the government help provide jobs?*

SECTION 1 Assessment

Key Terms

Use each of the key terms in a sentence that explains its meaning: full employment, mixed economy, national income accounting, economic growth, inflation, deflation

Target Reading Skill

1. **Recognize Word Origins** Use your knowledge of the origin of the word *domestic* to define the word *domain*.

Comprehension and Critical Thinking

2. **a. Explain** Why is price stability important?

   b. Predict What might happen if the federal government decided not to ensure that prices remain stable?

3. **a. Explain** What does the phrase *circular flow of economic activity* mean?

   b. Identify Cause and Effect Why does the government tax businesses and individuals? What is the effect of the taxes?

4. **a. Describe** What is the relationship between the GDP and the economy?

   b. Identify Alternatives What are the best indicators of a thriving economy?

Writing Activity

You have just received your first paycheck from your first job, and you see that federal income tax has been withheld from your check. Write a letter to your penpal in Belgium explaining what the tax pays for in your country.

TIP Remember that your penpal does not understand the American system as well as you do. Be sure your explanation is very clear.

Recognizing Propaganda

Propaganda is an effort to spread certain ideas and shape public opinion. During wartime, for example, the United States government has urged the American people to join the armed forces, work in war industries, and pay for war. In both World War I and World War II, the government used propaganda to help heighten the need for support and motivate people to contribute to the war effort.

The poster shown here is one of the most famous examples of World War I propaganda.

Learn the Skill

Follow these steps to recognize propaganda:

1. **Identify the source.** Who produced the poster, article, or photograph you are reading or viewing? What do you know about that person or group's objectivity?

2. **Identify the topic.** What issue is being addressed? Note also the place, time, and circumstances surrounding the topic.

3. **Recognize propaganda techniques.** What approach does the material use to persuade? Patriotism is a common approach, as are exaggeration, sarcasm, and intimidation.

4. **Interpret the message.** Look for symbols. What point of view does the item reflect? How does it engage you emotionally instead of rationally?

Practice the Skill

Study the poster and answer these questions:

1. Who published the poster?

2. During what historical event was the poster published?

3. What propaganda techniques does the poster use? Explain.

4. What message does the poster convey?

Apply the Skill

Examine political advertisements during an election campaign. Interpret the ads for their objectivity and also for their use of propaganda techniques. Describe your findings.

Paying for Government

Reading Preview

Objectives

In this section you will

- Discuss tax fairness.
- Identify different types of income taxes.
- Examine the effects of taxes on individuals and the economy.

Key Terms

proportional tax
progressive tax
regressive tax
direct tax
indirect tax

Main Idea

Federal, state, and local governments tax citizens directly and indirectly.

Target Reading Skill

Analyze Word Parts When you come across an unfamiliar word, you can figure out what it means by breaking it up into parts. Words are made of roots, to which are added prefixes and/or suffixes. For example, the root word *govern* can take different suffixes to make the words *government* and *governor*.

Taking Notes

Make a diagram like the one below. As you read this section, complete the diagram with information about different kinds of income taxes.

E rin Neumann was excited. She was going to her first dance in a few days. She had saved $80 to buy a new outfit. The one she wanted cost exactly $80, and it fit perfectly.

Erin brought her savings to the local department store where she had seen her outfit on sale. She took the outfit off the rack and brought it to the sales clerk to buy. The sales clerk rang up the sale. The total was $84.80.

Erin was shocked. She protested, but the clerk reminded her about the 6 percent state sales tax. The 6 percent sales tax included a 5 percent state sales tax and an additional 1 percent county sales tax. For a purchase of $80, Erin had to pay another $4.80 in tax. Erin handed the clerk the $80 she had saved for the outfit plus $4.80 she had planned to spend on lunch after she had finished shopping.

Like Erin, people are often surprised and troubled by taxes. For the government to levy a tax, the tax must have one or more good characteristics. The government must impose taxes fairly. It also must consider the effects of taxes on the people who pay them.

A Seattle small-business owner protests a proposed new tax on coffee by evoking the Boston Tea Party. ▼

Tax Fairness

As citizens, we expect to receive goods and services from our government. We pay for those goods and services through taxes. You have probably heard people complain about taxes. Sometimes people say taxes are unfair or that their income, sales, or property taxes are too high. Yet citizens continue to want government goods and services.

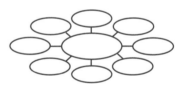

NO ON I-77! (espresso tax)
IT HURTS SMALL BUSINESS!

Indirect Benefits of Taxes
People who have no children in public schools do not receive a direct benefit from public education. However, they receive an indirect benefit, because society is better off with educated citizens.

Characteristics of a Good Tax It is the duty of all citizens and our elected leaders and government officials to understand the characteristics of a good tax. There are five characteristics of a good tax.

First, a good tax must be efficient or economical. The government should not spend too much money in order to collect the tax. If the cost of collecting the tax is too high compared to tax revenues, the tax is wasteful.

Second, the government must provide a good reason for imposing the tax. Taxpayers must know that their tax revenues will serve a purpose, even if they do not agree with every aspect of government spending.

Third, the tax must treat taxpayers fairly and equitably. You will read more about what might make a tax fair or unfair at the end of the section.

Fourth, the tax must be certain. Taxpayers must know when the tax is dues. Taxpayers also must know exactly how much they must pay and how to pay the tax properly. Finally, paying the tax should be simple and convenient for the taxpayer. A good tax is also convenient for the government to collect.

Benefits-Received Principle An important idea about tax fairness is the benefits-received principle. This principle states that the benefits of the tax should go to the people who pay the tax. The benefits-received principle shows that the tax on gasoline, for example, is a fair tax. The more gasoline a driver buys, the more miles he or she travels on government-provided highways. Therefore, the more gasoline taxes a driver pays, the more benefit he or she receives from using roads and highways.

Analyze Charts

Characteristics of a Good Tax

This word web shows the five characteristics of a good tax.
1. **Analyze** Why is it important that a tax be certain?
2. **Apply** How does the government ensure that taxes are economical?

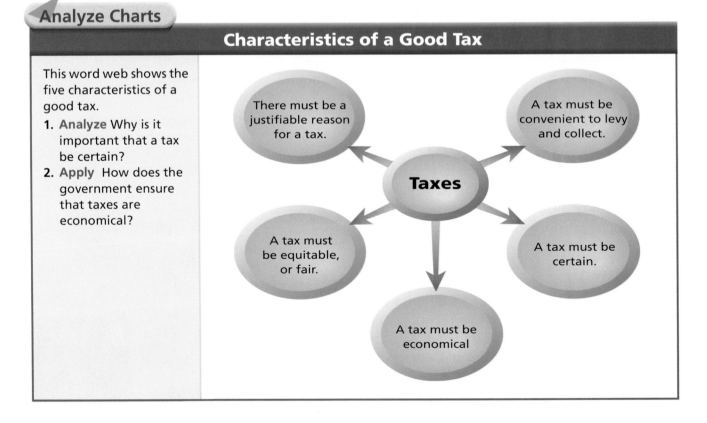

Taxes
- There must be a justifiable reason for a tax.
- A tax must be convenient to levy and collect.
- A tax must be equitable, or fair.
- A tax must be certain.
- A tax must be economical

Ability-to-Pay Principle The ability-to-pay principle of taxation means that a citizen should pay taxes in relation to his or her ability to pay. Usually, ability-to-pay relates to a person's income.

Suppose the Nelson family has an annual income of $100,000. The Neumann family has an annual income of $50,000. Is it fair that the Nelsons, who make $100,000 per year, pay the same dollar amount in income taxes as the Neumanns, who make half as much? Those who believe in the ability-to-pay principle of tax policy would say no. The Nelsons can afford to pay higher income taxes than the Neumanns.

✓ Reading Check **Who receives the benefits of a fair tax?**

Types of Income Taxes

An important question becomes how the ability-to-pay tax policy should be applied. There are three different ways of determining income taxes.

Proportional Tax A **proportional tax** requires each taxpayer to pay the same proportion, or percentage, of their income as taxes. Suppose the proportional rate of taxation is 15 percent. In our example, the Nelsons, who make $100,000 per year, would pay $15,000 in taxes. The Neumanns, who make $50,000, would pay $7,500 in taxes.

Progressive Tax A **progressive tax** takes a higher percentage of taxes from a person with a higher income than it does from a person with a lower income. The ability-to-pay principle of taxation states that people with higher incomes have a greater ability to pay taxes than people with lower incomes.

Suppose the progressive tax system states that people with $100,000 annual income pay 30 percent in income tax and that people with $50,000 annual income pay 20 percent in income tax. In our example, under a progressive tax system, the Nelsons would pay 30 percent of $100,000 in income taxes, or $30,000. The Neumanns would pay 20 percent of $50,000 in income taxes, or $10,000. The federal income tax is a progressive tax. Tax rates rise from 10 percent to 35 percent according to a taxpayer's income.

Law and the Real World

Taxing Your Internet Purchases

★ Online shopping is a convenient and efficient way for many people to buy some things.

★ Although online customers may pay for shipping, they do not pay local and state sales taxes for their purchases. Online companies do not collect sales taxes.

★ Stores at the local mall sell products to consumers and these businesses must collect sales taxes.

★ Local and state governments use sales taxes to fund such public needs as education, highways, police and fire protection, sewage systems, libraries, and courts of law. Some of this revenue is lost due to the popularity of internet shopping.

Applying the Law

1. What is a sales tax?
2. What do state and local governments do with this tax revenue?
3. Do internet companies receive any benefits from local governments and their services such as highways, police and fire protection?
4. What is a fair solution for the online companies, local stores, consumers, local and state governments?

Target Reading Skill

Analyze Word Parts Look at the words *progressive* and *regressive* on pages 493 and 494. The share the same root, *-gress*, but have different prefixes. *Gress* is from the Latin meaning "to step or go." *Pro* means "forward" and *re* means "backward." A progressive tax grows as it moves up the income ladder; a regressive tax grows as it moves down the income ladder.

Regressive Tax A **regressive tax** takes a larger percentage of tax on income from a person with a lower income than from a person with a higher income. A sales tax on food, clothing, and other everyday items is considered a regressive tax. A person with a lower income spends a higher percentage of his or her income on food, clothing, and other everyday items than a person with a higher income.

An example illustrates the impact of a regressive tax. Suppose both the Nelsons and the Neumanns spend $2,000 per month on food, clothing, and other everyday items. Each family spends $24,000 per year. Suppose also that the sales tax on these items is 5 percent in their state.

Both the Nelsons and the Neumanns will pay $1,200 per year in sales taxes. Five percent of $24,000 is $1,200 ($0.05 \times \$24,000$). However, this means that the Neumanns will spend 2.4 percent of their yearly income on sales taxes ($1,200 divided by $50,000). The Nelsons, on the other hand, will spend proportionately less of their yearly income on sales taxes. Their sales taxes represent only 1.2 percent of their yearly income ($1,200 divided by $100,000).

The Nelsons and the Neumanns spend the same amount on food, clothing, and other goods each year. The two families paid the same amount of sales tax. But the Neumanns paid a larger share of their income in the form of taxes, so this sales tax is a regressive tax.

✓ Reading Check   **What are the three types of income-tax systems?**

Analyze Graphs

Regressive Tax Summary

The Nelson and Neumann families are affected differently by sales tax.

1. **Analyze** What percent of their yearly income does each family spend on sales taxes?
2. **Apply** According to the principles of fair taxation, is this a fair tax?

Family	Nelson	Neumann
Annual Income	$100,000	$50,000
Annual Spending on Everyday Items	$1,200	$1,200
Five Percent Tax Paid	$24,000	$24,000
Sales Tax as Percent of Income	1.2%	2.4%

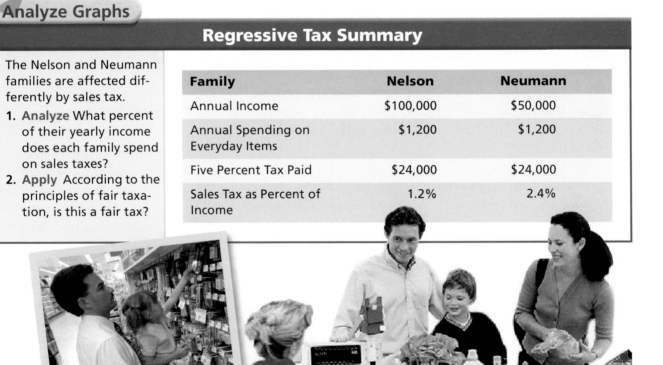

In this cartoon, a legislator is shown discussing a new bill he has authored with a woman at a Washington party.

1. What would the legislator's new bill do?

2. Does the legislator's behavior suggest that anything is unusual about his bill?

3. What do you think the cartoonist is saying about typical tax legislation?

"My bill isn't terribly controversial. It would provide modest tax breaks for people who don't really need them."

Effects of Taxes

The effect of taxation is perhaps one of the most controversial issues in the United States. A tax's effect is the economic consequence of paying the tax.

To truly understand a tax's effect, we must identify the kind of tax are we talking about. Is the tax direct or indirect? What is the impact of the tax?

Direct and Indirect Taxes A tax on income is called a **direct tax**. The person who pays the tax has no choice but to pay the tax. One person's income tax cannot be paid by another person. In our example, both the Nelsons and the Neumanns paid their income taxes directly.

An **indirect tax** generally ends up as part of the price a consumer pays for a product. A sales tax, like the tax Erin Neumann must pay, is an indirect tax. In the case of the new outfit, the government has imposed a retail sales tax on the product. The seller pays the tax to the government. This sales tax is then passed on to Erin, the buyer of the new outfit.

Many people are not aware of all of the indirect taxes they pay each day. This is because indirect taxes are included in the final price of the good and are not set apart. For example, each state charges an indirect tax on every gallon of gasoline sold to consumers. Few consumers realize how much of the cost of one gallon of gasoline is tax.

Pass It On
The impact of a tax is frequently passed on to consumers.
Explain *How may consumers choose not to pay a tax that is passed on as part of the cost of a good or service?*

Tax Impact The impact of a tax is the financial burden on the tax-payer.

The burden of the tax often does not fall on the business or individual who pays the tax to the government. For example, a coal producer in Montana may be taxed by that state on the coal removed from the ground. Suppose a Colorado power company buys the coal for generating electricity. The Montana coal producer adds the coal tax to the price of the coal sold to the Colorado power company. The power company then sells electricity and adds the coal tax to the price of electricity. Who ultimately bears the financial burden of the Montana coal tax? The consumers of the electricity in Colorado.

Many taxes imposed on businesses have an actual impact on the final consumer. Do you have a favorite restaurant? If the restaurant owner also owns the restaurant property, he or she must pay property tax. The restaurant owner includes this cost when deciding how much to charge for a meal. People who eat at this restaurant pay the cost of these taxes as part of their bill.

Tax impact is significant on people who buy a product, even if the price of the product continues to increase. Life-saving prescription drugs are a case in point. People with certain conditions such as diabetes must take certain drugs to stay alive. They have no choice but to pay higher prices for the drugs, even if taxes on the drugs increase.

✓ **Reading Check** **What is the difference between a direct tax and an indirect tax?**

SECTION 2 Assessment

Key Terms

Use each of the key terms in a sentence that explains its meaning: proportional tax, progressive tax, regressive tax, direct tax, indirect tax

Target Reading Skill

1. **Analyze Word Parts** Identify and define the prefixes in the following words: *progress, egress, congress.* Use your knowledge of the root *-gress* to help define these words.

Comprehension and Critical Thinking

2. **a. Explain** What is the benefits-received principle?

b. Draw Conclusions If someone pays a tax for which she gets no direct benefit, how might she benefit indirectly?

3. **a. Describe** What is the difference between regressive and progressive taxes?
b. Analyze Information Why are Americans taxed in proportion to their incomes?

4. **a. Explain** What effects do taxes have on individuals?
b. Predict What would happen if the tax system were abolished?

Writing Activity

Go online to the official website for your state. You should be able to find the state's budget. Write a report on the budget for the most recent year, explaining how much the state collected in taxes and how it spent the money. Evaluate the decisions made by the state legislature. Do you think the money should have been spent differently? Support your opinion.

TIP You may want to include graphs or charts in the report so readers can see at a glance how the money was spent.

Government Policy and Spending

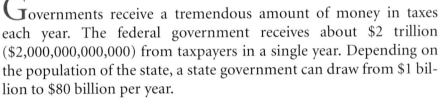

Reading Preview

Objectives
In this section you will
- Discuss spending policy goals.
- Identify and describe the types of government budgets.
- Explore the patterns of federal government spending.
- Explore the patterns of state and local government spending.

Key Terms
balanced budget
deficit budget
surplus budget
entitlement pro- grams

Main Idea
Governments try to develop budgets to spend their tax revenues in a way that will benefit the economy.

Target Reading Skill
Recognize Word Origins The Greek words *polis* and *polites* mean "city" and "citizens." Many words in our language come from these words. As you read this section, you will encounter a few of them.

Taking Notes
Make two diagrams like the one below. As you read this section, complete the diagrams with information that compares and contrasts federal government spending with state and local government spending.

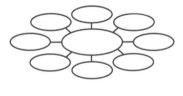

Cities must spend their money in ways that the public will support. Public parks are often popular with taxpayers.
▼

Governments receive a tremendous amount of money in taxes each year. The federal government receives about $2 trillion ($2,000,000,000,000) from taxpayers in a single year. Depending on the population of the state, a state government can draw from $1 billion to $80 billion per year.

These large sums of money are matched by equally large responsibilities, however. The federal government must defend, protect, and care for about 300 million Americans with its tax revenues. Proper use of the money requires careful planning and difficult decisions.

In order to spend tax revenue, the government must have goals that are acceptable to citizens. Government must also develop budgets that account for spending. Federal, state, and local governments have priorities for spending as well as historical spending patterns.

Spending-Policy Goals

If you buy a pizza, you can eat it all by yourself or share it. Similarly, you can make your own private decisions about what music you listen to and what movies you attend. Your buying decisions reflect your personal goals. People's personal buying decisions are private-sector decisions.

Public-sector decisions are buying decisions that are made by government. Public-sector decisions reflect public goals. Those are often goals that are agreed upon when we elect our representatives to city councils, state legislatures, and Congress.

The federal government works to keep the economy strong and stable. To do so, the government sets an economic stabilization policy. It reflects three economic goals:

1. To promote economic growth

2. To maintain stable prices

3. To ensure full employment

We promote economic growth because we wish to develop a higher standard of living. We maintain stable prices because we want to avoid inflation and deflation. We try to ensure full employment by seeking to provide suitable jobs for all citizens who are willing and able to work. The federal government develops its spending budget in response to the policy goals of economic stability.

Economic Stability
There are three main goals of government policies that promote economic stability. **Conclude** *Is one goal more important than the others?*

✔ Reading Check **What are the three main goals of the economic stabilization policy?**

Types of Government Budgets

Three types of federal government budgets influence the economy. They are balanced budgets, deficit budgets, and surplus budgets.

Balanced Budget A **balanced budget** requires that governments do not spend more than the tax revenues they receive. Most states and local governments require a balanced budget. This means that government officials must limit their spending according to the amount of tax revenue they receive. With some exceptions, these state and local governments cannot borrow money to spend more than this. When the economy weakens and tax revenues fall, state and local governments with balanced budget requirements often must cut spending. When individuals and businesses pay taxes, they give up money they might spend on other things. These taxes take funds out of the economic spending stream. Within a balanced budget, however, these funds are offset by an equal amount of government spending.

Deficit Budget With a **deficit budget**, a government spends more than the tax revenue it receives. To do so, the government must borrow money. It borrows money by selling government bonds to individuals, banks, and other financial institutions. Many investors are happy to lend money to the government. The federal government in particular is seen as a reliable borrower that will pay money back on time.

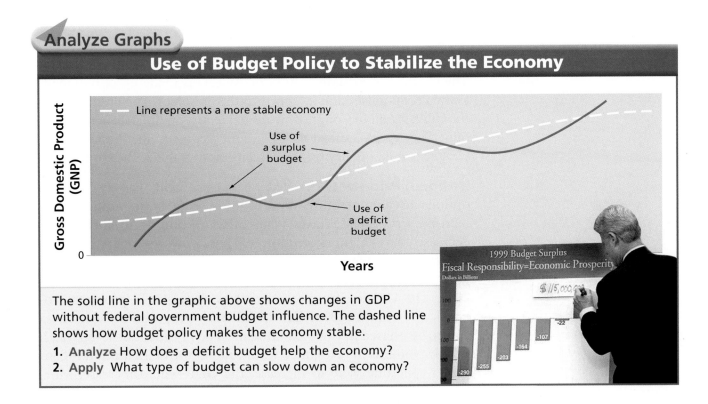

Use of Budget Policy to Stabilize the Economy

Gross Domestic Product (GNP)

- - - Line represents a more stable economy

Use of a surplus budget

Use of a deficit budget

0

Years

1999 Budget Surplus
Fiscal Responsibility=Economic Prosperity
Dollars in Billions

$ 115,050,60

The solid line in the graphic above shows changes in GDP without federal government budget influence. The dashed line shows how budget policy makes the economy stable.

1. **Analyze** How does a deficit budget help the economy?
2. **Apply** What type of budget can slow down an economy?

Surplus Budget A **surplus budget** occurs when government spends less than it receives in tax revenues. With a surplus budget, government spending does not offset tax revenues taken from individuals and businesses. This may not be all bad, especially if the economy is in a period of inflation. A surplus budget can help slow down an economy.

The federal government had surplus budgets for a few years in the late 1990s and early 2000s. Some of the surplus revenues were used to pay back money borrowed in earlier years. Many political leaders believed that surplus budgets were a sign that federal taxes were too high. As a result, these surplus budgets were followed by income tax cuts and business tax cuts.

Use of Budget Policy In chapter 16 you learned about the business cycle, which shows repeated "ups" and "downs" in the gross domestic product over time. The federal government can use its budget policy to help prevent major "ups" and "downs" in GDP.

During an "up" time, there may be inflation, an overall increase in prices. This would suggest that the government operate on a surplus budget by spending less than it receives in taxes. Spending less will slow down the GDP and bring down inflationary prices. In a "down" time, the government may operate a deficit budget by spending more than it receives in taxes. More government spending will stimulate the GDP and promote economic growth and employment.

Target Reading Skill
Recognize Word Origins
Look at the word *policy.* It contains most of the Greek word *polis.* A policy is a course of action taken by the government that affects how the cities and citizens are run. Read on to find other words that come from the Greek *polis.*

✓ Reading Check   **How can the government control the GDP?**

Federal Government Spending

The Council of Economic Advisors (CEA) is made up of nationally known economists, and it reports to the President. The President and the CEA submit to Congress an annual report on the state of the economy. The report is called the Economic Report of the President. The CEA also makes policy recommendations to stabilize the economy.

National Priorities The federal government has two policy options to help stabilize the economy. One policy option is to increase or decrease taxes. The other option is to increase or decrease government expenditures. These powerful policy tools can significantly influence the economy.

An example of the use of one of these policy tools occurred in 2003. The United States economy was sluggish. To promote economic growth, President George W. Bush proposed a series of tax cuts to be phased in over several years. The President believed that if people paid less in taxes, they would spend the extra money. If consumer spending were to increase, the GDP would increase. More jobs would then be created and economic growth would occur. It will take many years to know whether the tax cuts will achieve the goals that the President envisioned.

Federal Government Spending Pattern The federal budget is divided into two general categories—direct purchases of goods and services and transfer payments. Direct expenditures are for purchases of goods and services. Transfer payments are made to individuals for which no goods and services are produced. Included in transfer payments are Social Security and unemployment compensation.

Government Spending
Direct expenditures account for about one-third of the federal budget. The largest direct expenditure is for national defense (including the Coast Guard, below).
Evaluate Information *How do the federal government's expenditures reflect its values?*

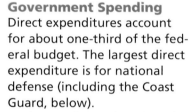

Analyze Charts

National Debt 1993 – 2003

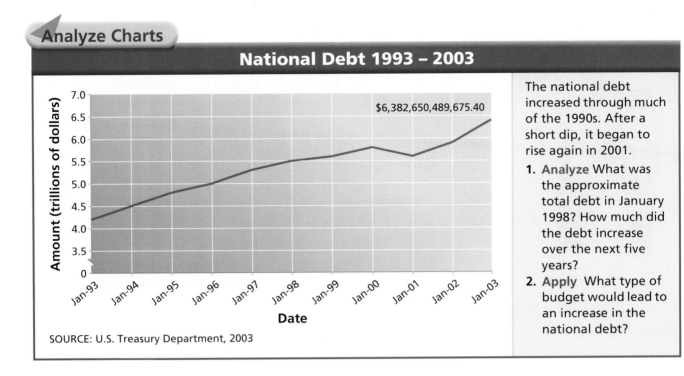

$6,382,650,489,675.40

SOURCE: U.S. Treasury Department, 2003

The national debt increased through much of the 1990s. After a short dip, it began to rise again in 2001.

1. **Analyze** What was the approximate total debt in January 1998? How much did the debt increase over the next five years?

2. **Apply** What type of budget would lead to an increase in the national debt?

Most of the transfer payments are for entitlement programs. **Entitlement programs** provide benefits to people who are entitled by law to receive them. The largest entitlement program is Social Security, which accounts for more than one-fifth of the federal budget. Other transfer payments include Medicaid and Medicare, unemployment assistance, and federal employees' retirement benefits.

Experts on the federal budget are concerned that these entitlement programs will increase significantly as the population continues to age. As people age, they become eligible for Social Security payments. They also require additional health care, often paid through Medicare and Medicaid. Our aging population creates pressure on the federal government to continue to increase transfer payments.

The National Debt The national debt is the total amount of money the federal government owes to lenders that own government bonds. The federal government can sell bonds to lenders if there is a deficit in the federal budget. The national debt was slightly less than 6.2 trillion dollars at the end of 2002. The Congressional Budget Office estimated that the national debt would exceed 8 trillion dollars by 2007.

Many people are concerned about the size of the national debt. Interest on the national debt must be paid. Interest on the debt in 2004 was about 176 billion dollars and will increase as the national debt increases. When federal policy makers decide on spending priorities, interest payments must be included. This reduces the amount of money available in the federal budget for other spending priorities.

A bond represents a debt—a promise to pay money back in the future with interest. Annual bond sales by the U.S. Treasury contribute to the national debt.

Draw Inferences *What would be the effect on the government if people were to stop buying the Treasury's bonds?*

✓ Reading Check   **Which is the largest entitlement program?**

Heather Thompkins is senior class president at South Summit High School in Kamas, Utah, and president of her school's chapter of Future Business Leaders of America. She volunteers for numerous organizations whose missions are to better the lives of abused and underprivileged children.

In addition to spending time with the children, she has mounted successful toy drives and numerous fund-raising events for organizations such as Art Kids, Children's Justice Center, Women's Peace House, Make-A-Wish Foundation, and Angel Tree.

▲ Students can help make a difference by improving the lives of less fortunate children.

Service Learning

How can you make a difference in the lives of underprivileged children in your community?

State and Local Government Spending

Most state and local governments are required by law to maintain balanced budgets. During a recession, state and local governments must cut spending because they have less tax revenue.

Spending Priorities of State and Local Governments Most state and local government expenditures are direct expenditures. Spending priorities relate closely to day-to-day demands of citizens. People want better schools, streets, highways, and hospitals.

If state and local governments suffer from reduced tax revenue, however, citizens become frustrated as a result of project cutbacks. Therefore, state and local government officials often find themselves in a continuing state of turmoil.

Historically, taxation and spending by the federal government was independent and separate from state and local government. However, in the past 50 years this pattern has changed. The states have turned to the federal government for assistance. And local governments have turned to their state governments for aid. These changes are reflected in the current revenue and spending patterns of state and local governments.

Revenue and Spending Patterns State and local government revenue comes from several kinds of taxes. Sales taxes and property taxes generally account for more than a third of state and local government revenue. State and local governments also receive revenue from individual income taxes and fees, such as automobile license fees. Some units of government impose taxes on personal property, gasoline, and use of recreation facilities.

Education accounts for more than a third of state and local government expenditures. Education spending includes universities and public schools. Significant spending is made on building and maintaining highways. Some states provide welfare assistance to citizens who need it. States and local government units pay for police and fire protection, water and sewage systems, garbage collection, local library and hospital facilities, and the judicial system.

State Spending
Oregon students rally to support a measure that would increase taxes to support education.
Draw Inferences *Why would people vote to increase their own taxes?*

✔ **Reading Check** **Give an example of a situation in which state and local governments might ask for outside assistance.**

SECTION 3 Assessment

Key Terms

Use each of the key terms in a sentence that explains its meaning: balanced budget, deficit budget, surplus budget, entitlement programs

Target Reading Skill

1. **Recognize Word Origins** Find one word in Section 3 besides *policy* that comes from the Greek word *polis.* Explain the connection between the two words. (HINT: look for this word on page 503.)

Comprehension and Critical Thinking

2. **a. Explain** What has to happen to the economy in order for citizens to enjoy a higher standard of living?
   b. Identify Effect How does a higher standard of living for citizens affect the government?

3. **a. Describe** How does the federal budget affect the economy?
   b. Recognize Points of View Why do you think have recent administrations chosen to operate on deficit budgets?

4. **a. Recall** What are the spending priorities of the federal government? On what does it spend the most money?
   b. Support a Point of View Do you think these spending priorities are in the best interest of the citizens? Why?

5. **a. Recall** What do citizens get in exchange for the state and local taxes they pay?
   b. Identify Cause Why do you think laws require state and local governments to operate on balanced budgets?

Writing Activity

Suppose you have a great-uncle who is nearing retirement age and wants to know more about Social Security. You have volunteered to find the information for him. Go to the Social Security Web site and find out what the qualifications are for receiving Social Security benefits. Write up a short summary of the qualifications that you can give to your great-uncle.

Go Online
PHSchool.com
For: Writing Activity
Visit: PHSchool.com
Web Code: mpd-6181

Debating the Issues

CLOSE UP FOUNDATION

The debates in this feature are based on *Current Issues*, published by the Close Up Foundation. Go to **PHSchool.com**, Web Code mph-6183, to read the latest issue of *Current Issues* online.

When President George W. Bush took office 2000, the country was experiencing an economic slowdown. The attacks of September 11, 2001, only worsened the economy. During the next few years, unemployment rose to new heights and the economy continued to decline. In the spring of 2003, the Bush administration pushed Congress to pass a series of sweeping new tax cuts in the hopes of stimulating economic growth.

Can Tax Cuts Stimulate Economic Growth?

YES

- Tax cuts mean that people will keep more of the money they earn. Consumers will have more money to spend on goods and services. An increase in demand for these goods and services will stimulate economic growth.

- When corporate taxes are cut, businesses can make greater profits. Also, as more consumers spend more money, there is greater demand for products and services. Companies will have to hire more workers to keep up with demand. Therefore, tax cuts will lead to job growth, which will help the economy to grow.

NO

- People do not always spend extra money from tax cuts the way the government expects them to. In difficult economic times, people are less likely to spend the extra money on new purchases. Instead, they may use the money to pay off debt or to protect in a savings account. This would not help to stimulate economic growth.

- Tax cuts usually result in reduced government services, especially for the poor. A tax cut leads to smaller government revenues. The government will have to cut spending, which means cuts to social welfare programs, education budgets, and military spending. This could have a negative impact on economic growth.

What is Your Opinion?

1. **Analyze Primary Sources** Use a library or the Internet to look up information about the Jobs and Growth Act of 2003. Outline the major provisions of the law.

2. **Predict** How can an increase in demand for goods and services result in economic growth? Is it possible that an increase in demand for goods and services would not lead to economic growth? Why or why not?

3. **Writing to Persuade** Suppose that you are a member of Congress who plans to vote on a bill that will cut taxes over the next several years. Write a press release explaining your vote to your constituents. Include specific reasons that will convince them that you made the right choice.

Go Online
civics interactive

For: You Decide Poll
Visit: PHSchool.com
Web Code: mpp-6182

Chapter Summary

Section 1
Government and Economic Goals
(pages 482–489)

- Beginning with the Employment Act of 1946, the federal government has tried to ensure full employment and price stability.

- The U.S. economy is called a mixed economy because services are provided by both the private and public sectors. Individuals give business labor; in return, business pays them wages. Business gives individuals goods and services; in return, individuals pay money. Individuals and businesses both pay taxes; in return, the government provides services.

- National income accounting lets us track the health of our economy. A healthy economy enjoys a period of economic growth. Unhealthy ones experience inflation or deflation.

Section 2
Paying for Government
(pages 491–496)

- Good taxes have five characteristics: they must be justifiable, equitable, certain, convenient, and economical.

- Proportional taxes charge everyone the same percentage of their income. Progressive taxes charge the wealthy more. Regressive taxes charge the poor more.

- Direct taxes include income taxes. Indirect taxes include sales taxes.

Section 3
Government Policy and Spending
(pages 497–503)

- The government tries to keep the economy stable by promoting economic growth, maintaining stable prices, and providing employment opportunities for all.

- Governments can operate on three kinds of budgets. In a balanced budget, spending equals revenue. In a surplus budget, revenue exceeds spending. In a deficit budget, spending exceeds revenue.

- The federal government can control the economy by raising or lowering taxes and by spending more or less on government programs. However, it must pay a certain amount of money each year toward entitlement programs and the national debt.

- State and local governments must operate on a balanced budget. They provide important local services like garbage collection and police protection.

Copy the chart below and use it to help you summarize the chapter.

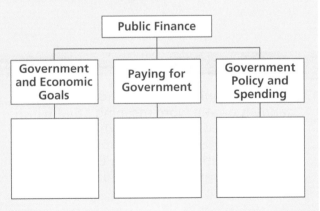

Review and Assessment Continued

Go Online
PHSchool.com
For: Self-Text
Visit: PHSchool.com
Web Code: mpa-6181

Reviewing Key Terms

Fill in the blank with the term that makes each sentence correct.

inflation   national income accounting
economic growth   entitlement programs
proportional tax   full employment
deficit budget   regressive tax
indirect tax   mixed economy

1. _____ describes a situation in which everyone who wants a job can find one.

2. When the government operates under a _____, its expenditures exceed its income.

3. During economic _____, prices go up and buying power goes down.

4. _____ occurs when the gross domestic product rises without a rise in prices.

5. A _____ makes poor people pay a higher percentage of their income than rich ones.

6. In a _____ system, everyone pays the same percentage of their income.

7. A _____ is one in which both privately-owned business and the government play roles.

8. _____ is the process by which the government keeps track of its overall budget.

9. An _____ offers a long-term, intangible return to the one who pays it.

Comprehension and Critical Thinking

10. a. **Explain** Why is full employment important to the economy?
    b. **Solve Problems** What can the government do to ensure full employment?
    c. **Determine Relevance** What relationship can you see between full employment and the GDP?

11. a. **Recall** Why does the government charge taxes on services?
    b. **Identify Bias** Who pays the most in taxes? Why?
    c. **Identify Alternatives** Design a tax system that you think is fair. Explain why it is fair.

12. a. **Describe** What are the three types of government budgets?
    b. **Identify Effects** What effect does a deficit budget have on the economy?
    c. **Draw Inferences** Why do you think the federal government is not required to operate on a balanced budget?

Activities

13. **Skills** Recognizing Propaganda a. *Propaganda* is a Latin word meaning "that which has multiplied or spread." Explain the connection between the word's origin and its current English definition. **b.** Explain how you can recognize propaganda when you come across it.

14. **Writing** A factory in your town has just closed, leaving 1,500 workers without jobs. Write a letter to the editor of a local paper, outlining what you think the government should do to help these people.

Selected State Income Tax Collections per Capita, 2001

Alabama	$471.29
California	1,293.13
Georgia	826.11
Iowa	646.16
Maryland	878.87
Massachusetts	1,552.31
Missouri	677.89
New Jersey	941.63
Ohio	730.27
South Carolina	523.93
Tennessee	34.51
Vermont	788.78
Virginia	1,005.38

Source: *NY Times Almanac 2003*, page 202.

15. **Active Citizen** How much are property taxes in your town? Using the Internet or contacting your local tax assessor's office, find out what the property tax rate is. How much tax would you pay if you owned a property worth $100,000?

16. **Math Practice** Find out the percentage of sales tax on items in your city or state. You want to buy an MP3 player that costs $159.99. How much will you have to pay in sales tax?

17. **Civics and Economics** Because the population is aging, more people are taking money out of Social Security while fewer people are paying money into it. This means the program will eventually run out of money. Make a plan for what the government should do to save Social Security.

18. **Analyzing Visuals** Study the table of selected state income taxes. Where do citizens pay the least tax? Where do they pay the most?

Standardized Test Prep

Test-Taking Tips

Standardized tests sometimes ask questions about vocabulary. Below is a paragraph about Federal Reserve Chair Alan Greenspan. Read the passage and answer the questions that follow.

TIP When you do not recognize a word, look at the context to get a sense of the meaning.

A mere word from Alan Greenspan can cause the stock market and the dollar to rise and fall. He once famously said: "If I seem unduly clear to you, you must have misunderstood what I said." His often cryptic testimony to Congress is seen as the most important assessment of the U.S. economic situation. During the late 1990s, he described the stock market as exhibiting an "irrational exuberance" as it continued to rise.

Choose the letter of the best answer.

1. Which is the best synonym for *cryptic?*

   A puzzling

   B inaccurate

   C clear

   D famous

   TIP Go back to the passage and look for context clues to the word *cryptic.*

   The correct answer is **A.** Greenspan describes his own testimony as unclear. The closest synonym is *puzzling.*

2. Which is the best synonym for *exuberance?*

   A craziness

   B dishonesty

   C growth

   D pleasure

The American Legal System

What's Ahead in Unit 7

In Unit 7 you will be considering the role laws play in our society. The first step will be to explore some of the basic purposes and origins of our laws. Then you will examine how the criminal and juvenile justice systems deal with people who are accused of breaking the law. Finally, you will read about the ways our civil justice system helps people to settle conflicts in an orderly manner.

CHAPTER 19
Laws and Our Society

CHAPTER 20
Criminal and Juvenile Justice

CHAPTER 21
Civil Justice

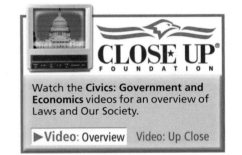

Why Study Civics?

Where do our laws come from? Why are the words law and order so often linked together? What is criminal law? What is civil law? What is a jury? These are all questions that can be addressed by the study of civics.

Watch the **Civics: Government and Economics** videos for an overview of Laws and Our Society.

▶Video: Overview   Video: Up Close

Standards for Civics and Government

National

The following National Standards are covered in this unit.

II. What are the foundations of the American political system?

B. What are the distinctive characteristics of American society?

C. What is American political culture?

D. What values and principles are basic to American constitutional democracy?

State

Go Online
PHSchool.com

For: Your state's Civics standards
Visit: PHSchool.com
Webcode: mpe7001

Laws and Our Society

CHAPTER

19

What's Ahead in Chapter 19

In this chapter you will read about the purpose of laws, the way laws are made, and the different types of laws.

SECTION **1**
Why We Have Laws

SECTION **2**
Where Our Laws Come from

SECTION **3**
Kinds of Laws

TARGET
READING SKILL

Comparison and Contrast
In this chapter you will focus on comparing and contrasting points about the different types of laws in the United States, the different reasons for these laws and the different places these laws are made.

► A police officer fingerprints a young child ►

The following National Standards for Civics and Government are covered in this chapter:

I. What are civic life, politics, and government?

B. What are the essential characteristics of limited and unlimited government?

III. How does the government established by the Constitution embody the purposes,

values, and principles of American democracy?

E. What is the place of law in the American constitutional system?

Active Citizen — Civics in the Real World

What is the purpose of laws? The novel *Lord of the Flies*, written by William Golding, provides a good example. In the book, a group of English schoolboys survive a plane crash and are stranded on a deserted island. They have no idea when help will arrive, so they must find a way to stay alive.

Put yourself in this story for a minute. What problems will you need to solve? How will decisions be made? Who will be the leaders? How will they be chosen? How much power should the leaders have? What will the responsibilities of each boy be?

A book like *Lord of the Flies* helps put in perspective the challenge faced by every group or society. It needs some rules or laws to follow. How those rules get made, and what kinds of rules they are, determines the kind of order and fairness in the group or society.

Citizen's Journal   In a survivor situation like *Lord of the Flies*, what do you think would be the most important tasks of the group in the beginning? How would you suggest the group make rules about those tasks? What kinds of rules would be necessary? What arguments would you advance to convince others about your choice of tasks and rules?

Why We Have Laws

Reading Preview

Objectives

In this section you will

- Discuss the need for order.
- Learn about the need to protect people's safety and property.
- Consider the need to protect individual freedoms and promote the common good.
- Discuss laws and morals.

Taking Notes

Make a diagram like the one below. As you read this section, complete the diagram with information about laws.

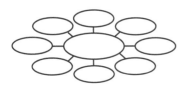

Key Terms

laws   civil disobedience
morals

Main Idea

Laws provide for order. They also protect people's safety, property, and individual freedoms, as well as promote the common good.

Target Reading Skill

Identify Contrasts One way to understand a collection of ideas is to examine the ways in which they are different from one another. When you look at these differences, you are contrasting the ideas.

Signs maintain order by reminding us about laws. ▼

You have many rules to follow. You follow one set of rules at school. You follow other rules when playing sports. Rules set standards. They also set penalties for failing to meet standards. A coach might have a rule that anyone who skips practice may not play in the next game.

Society also has rules that it expects all people to follow. These rules are enforced by governments and are called **laws.** An example is the law that requires drivers to stop at red lights. People who break this law usually must pay a fine.

Laws are the only rules that everyone has to follow. Your friend may have a family rule against playing loud music after 9:00 P.M. That rule applies only to her family, and her family decides what should be done if she breaks the rule. However, what if you broke a local law against playing loud music after midnight? You could be fined by your local government for disturbing the peace.

The Need for Order

One of the most basic purposes of laws is to bring order to society. One way laws bring order is by telling people what they may or may not do. Some of the most familiar do's and don'ts are traffic laws. Every driver must drive on the right side of the road and obey traffic signs. What would happen if people could drive on either side of the road? What if everyone tried to go through an intersection at the same time?

Laws also set standards in many areas. Some laws help make sure that supermarket scales, gasoline pumps, and other measuring devices are accurate. Others set standards for education, including courses of study and attendance requirements.

In many ways laws help bring order by telling people how something should be done. They tell how public officials should be elected, how evidence should be presented in trials, and how building permits should be obtained.

Laws also spell out the proper ways to settle serious conflicts. Suppose a bicycle rider runs into you, knocking you down and causing you to break your leg. You and your family ask the rider's family to pay your medical bills, but they refuse. Laws help bring order by providing peaceful ways of settling such conflicts in court.

✔ Reading Check **How do laws bring order to society?**

Protecting Safety and Property

Another purpose of laws is to protect people's lives and property. No society can run smoothly if people live in constant fear for their safety or for the security of their belongings.

Protecting People's Safety Laws protect people's lives. Therefore, physical attacks such as murder are against the law. These actions are punished by prison or even death.

Laws also protect the quality of people's lives. They especially look after the lives of people who are less able to protect themselves, such as children and elderly people. Laws hold parents responsible for the care of their children, including food, clothing, housing, and medical care. Laws help protect elderly people in many ways, such as guaranteeing retirement income and providing some low-cost medical care.

Crash Testing
Auto manufacturers are obligated by law to perform safety tests on their vehicles before they can be sold.
Draw Inferences *How does crash testing protect consumers?*

In this cartoon, one office worker (Asok) discusses with a co-worker (Dilbert) a revolutionary new computer program that Asok has created.

1. Which person seems more concerned about the effects of the new software?

2. Describe Asok's reaction to Dilbert's question.

Protecting People's Property What would happen if people were allowed to take anything that they wanted from each other? Laws against stealing are one way in which your property is protected. If your bike is stolen, the police will try to find your bike and arrest the thief so that he or she can be punished.

Laws also give you rights if your property is damaged. Suppose you lend a video game to a friend who spills juice onto it. He refuses to pay for the damage. Laws give you the right to take him to court. A judge may order him to pay for the damage.

Property also includes ideas and inventions. Ideas for a new cereal, a board game, a new style of skateboard, or a labor-saving invention for the home are the property of the person or company who thought of them. A person also owns any work of art, music, or literature that he or she creates.

Any creation or invention can be protected by law. Examples of this protection are all around you. Books, CDs, videotapes, and games display the copyright symbol: ©. Brand names have the ® symbol standing for "registered trademark." Patent numbers are stamped on many products, from sports shoes to computers. Copyrights, trademarks, and patents are all warnings that it is against the law to copy creations or inventions without permission.

✓ Reading Check   **What do laws against stealing protect?**

Protecting Freedom and Society

The Constitution names two other purposes of laws: to protect freedoms for individuals and to protect our society. Americans treasure individual freedoms. They also recognize that to protect individual rights, it is important to protect society as a whole.

Protecting Individual Freedoms Individual freedoms are protected by the Constitution—the highest law in the land. The Constitution, in the Bill of Rights, makes it illegal for the government to deny freedom of religion, freedom of speech, freedom of the press, and other basic freedoms.

The Constitution protects the basic rights and freedoms of individuals by limiting the government's power. The Constitution also guarantees, through the Fourteenth Amendment, that laws will be applied fairly and equally to all people.

Promoting the Common Good The Preamble of the Constitution declares that one of the goals of our government is to promote the general welfare. This means the common good of the people. Therefore, laws do not just protect the safety, property, and freedoms of each individual. They also protect society as a whole.

Some laws protect the environment and everyone's health. Laws limit air pollution. They also regulate the safety of the water we drink, the food we eat, and the products we use. Laws cover everything from how restaurants prepare food to how nuclear power plants get rid of their wastes.

Laws also make sure that help is given to people who need it. Laws set up unemployment insurance and job-training programs to help people who have little or no income. Laws allow the government to give aid to victims of floods and other disasters.

✓ Reading Check **How does the Constitution protect the basic rights and freedoms of individuals?**

Target Reading Skill
Identify Contrast As you read this page, contrast the government's need to protect individual freedoms with its need to protect the common good.

Environmental Standards Government regulations oversee the effects of industry on the environment—from smokestack emissions to nuclear-waste disposal. **Draw Inferences** *What purpose do environmental laws serve?*

Laws and Morals
The motto of the University of Pennsylvania, shown here in Latin, is "Laws without morals are in vain."

Laws and Morals

Most of us do not consciously think about the purposes of laws. However, we know that laws reflect many of the basic values and beliefs we share. Beliefs about what is fair and what is right or wrong are called **morals.** Most of us have similar morals. Our values and morals, rather than our laws, are the real glue that holds our nation together.

Most Americans obey laws because they want to. Theft and murder are against the law, but most people believe those actions are wrong anyway. Even if there were no laws, most people would never steal or commit murder. Laws are necessary so that the government can take action against people who do act wrongly.

What happens, though, if a law goes against your beliefs? In a situation like that, some people disobey the law. Breaking a law in a nonviolent way because it goes against personal morals is called **civil disobedience.**

People who take part in civil disobedience willingly accept the punishment for breaking the law. They follow their morals while recognizing the need for order in society. There could be no order if everyone decided to disobey certain laws but was unwilling to accept the punishments. If people want to change a law, our democratic government provides ways to do so.

✓ Reading Check **How do people's morals influence their regard for laws?**

SECTION 1 Assessment

Key Terms

Use each of the key terms in a sentence that explains its meaning: laws, morals, civil disobedience

Target Reading Skill

1. **Identify Contrasts** Reread the text for *Laws and Morals*. What is the difference between laws and morals?

Comprehension and Critical Thinking

2. **a. Recall** How do laws set standards?
b. Synthesize Information How do laws bring order to society?

3. **a. Describe** How does the law protect the quality of people's lives?
b. Summarize How does the law help protect people's ideas and artistic creations?

4. **a. Explain** What part of the Constitution protects individual freedoms?
b. Analyze How do laws that regulate restaurants protect customers and restrict the freedom of business owners?

5. **a. Explain** Why are laws necessary?
b. Make Generalizations Do you think that civil disobedience is a good way to get government to change a law?

Writing Activity

Is there a law that you disagree with? Write a short essay in which you explain your reasons for disagreeing with the law. Include logical, rational reasons why you think the law should be changed and provide your suggestions for change.

TIP Use comparison and contrast to help structure your essay. Contrast the current situation with what would happen should the law be repealed.

How to Analyze Television News Programs

Most Americans get information about local, national, and world events by watching the news on television. This means that television has a great influence on public opinion. When you watch the news, you should think critically about how information is presented to you.

A news program can make people think a certain way about issues. It could leave out important information without which you might think differently. Also, television news networks choose which stories to report and how much time to spend on them.

For a school project, Darius Heely is tracking the news. Every evening for the past two weeks he has watched the same news program. He sits by the television with his notebook in hand.

When the program starts, he gets his pencil and his stopwatch ready. For each story, Darius jots down the subject and records the time. He makes notes, such as whether a story was national or international, if it covered violent content, or if it seemed more like entertainment than news.

At the end of the program, Darius reads over the notes that he has taken. Sometimes he disagrees with how the news was presented by this program.

For the last part of his project, Darius will compare the news content over the whole two weeks. He will be able to see which stories were reported several days in a row and which got the most attention overall. By doing this, Darius will get a good idea of how the news shape what issues the public thinks about.

Learn the Skill

To analyze the news, follow these steps:

1 **Make a chart.** The columns should show the subject, length of time, location, and other notes.

2 **Watch the news.** Fill in the chart.

3 **Think about it.** What did you think was the most important story? Which was given the most emphasis? Were some less important than others? How long were most stories?

Practice the Skill

1 Watch the news with a friend or family member. Each of you should fill out a chart.

2 Decide which story you thought was the most important. Choose one thing you liked and one thing you didn't like about the program.

3 Compare your reactions with others.

Apply the Skill

1 With a group of classmates, read through a newspaper.

2 Plan a television news program with the stories from the newspaper.

3 Explain your group's decisions to the class.

Go Online
civics
interactive

For: Local Citizenship
Visit: PHSchool.com
Web Code: mpp-7191

Where Our Laws Come From

Reading Preview

Objectives

In this section you will

- Learn about laws made by legislatures.
- Discuss how judges' decisions and agency regulations affect laws.
- Understand how laws are organized.
- Learn how laws are changed.

Taking Notes

Make a diagram like the one below. As you read this section, complete the diagram with information comparing and contrasting statute and common law.

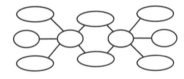

Key Terms

statutes   legal code
common law

Main Idea

Most laws come from legislatures. But other laws come from judges' decisions and regulations made by government agencies. Laws are collected in legal codes and constitutions.

Target Reading Skill

Compare and Contrast Comparing and contrasting can help you analyze likenesses and differences. When you compare you examine the likenesses. When you contrast you examine the differences.

Helmet laws are a response to rising numbers of cycling injuries. ▼

W here do our laws come from? Basically, they grow out of common values and beliefs in two ways: through rules written by legislatures and through decisions made by judges. Both of these sources of law have a long history. Both have played an important role in the development of American law.

Laws Made by Legislatures

When a certain need or problem arises, people often say that "there ought to be a law" to deal with it. If littering is a problem, your town or city council may pass a law setting a $500 fine for littering. Are too many people being injured in motorcycle accidents? Your state legislature may pass a law that riders must wear helmets. When the price of food goes up, Congress may pass a law increasing Social Security payments to the elderly.

All of these are **statutes**, written laws made by legislatures. The term statute usually refers to laws made by Congress or by state legislatures. Laws made by city or town councils are typically called ordinances.

In making laws, elected officials are guided by the morals, values, beliefs, and customs shared by most of the people served by the government. Laws passed by Congress reflect basic values shared by most Americans. Wherever you see the words *federal law* or *federal statute,* you know that everyone in the nation has to obey that law.

Laws passed by a state or local government, however, only apply within that state or local community. Since customs and beliefs in one place may differ from those in another, their laws may differ, too. For instance, one state may allow lotteries while another does not.

The relationship between laws and common beliefs has always been a close one. For example, in ancient Rome, where many people believed in witchcraft, statutes made it illegal for anyone to cast spells that would do harm. Laws against witchcraft were even found in the American colonies. Today we have no such laws.

Law and the Real World

What do students know about the law?

In a Law Day survey of 780 high school students conducted by the American Bar Association and Close Up Foundation, students answered eight-pages of questions about the law.

★ 90% knew that the Supreme Court has the power to declare laws unconstitutional.

★ 68% knew that a police officer did *not* need a warrant to search an automobile.

★ 61% knew that adults and students do *not* enjoy the same rights to free speech and free press.

★ 54% of students reported TV as their primary news source, 20% newspapers, 14% school, and 7% the Internet.

Extending the survey

1. Where do you get most of your information about the law?
2. Do you think these survey results would be the same for students in your class? in your school?

✔ **Reading Check** **From where do elected officials draw guidance when making laws?**

Other Effects on Law

Most laws are made by legislatures. When people talk about "laws," they are usually referring to statutes and ordinances. However, "obeying the law" also means obeying decisions made by judges. It includes complying with regulations made by government agencies.

Judges' Decisions Unlike legislatures, judges do not write laws. Instead, they wait for cases to come to them, and they decide each case based on laws that already exist. Those laws may be statutes and ordinances, or they may be earlier decisions made by judges.

American judges have inherited from England a strong tradition of being guided by earlier court decisions. Hundreds of years before the colonists came to America, a system of laws had developed in England. Some of these laws were statutes made by Parliament, the English legislature. However, the English people also relied greatly on **common law,** a body of law based on judges' decisions.

Target Reading Skill
Comparison and Contrast
How are federal and state laws alike and different?

Here is how common law worked. In making a decision on a case, an English judge would always consider general community customs and beliefs about what was fair. However, a judge would also need specific guidelines to follow in deciding each case. To find those guidelines, he looked at written records of how other judges had decided similar cases. If those decisions reflected the current beliefs of the community, the judge would follow them as a precedent, or guide.

Suppose, however, that community beliefs changed. Or perhaps a case came up that had no precedent. A judge would then make a new decision that reflected current beliefs and customs. The new ruling would set a precedent for future cases that involved similar circumstances and issues.

When the tradition of common law came to the United States, judges still followed many of the decisions of English judges. Conditions and customs were not always the same in the United States as in England, however. American judges needed to take this into consideration when making decisions. Therefore, some decisions of American judges began to reflect the unique aspects of life in the United States.

Under English common law, for example, it was illegal for a landowner to interfere with the natural flow of a stream. This law made sense in England. In the 1800s, Americans started using waterpower to run factories. American judges in some states, therefore, changed the common law ruling so that landowners could interfere with the flow of a stream by building dams to power factories. In this way, American law began to adapt itself to American society.

Setting Precedents
When deciding cases, judges are careful to investigate the precedents set in earlier decisions.
Predict *Are the precedents of common law 100 years from now likely to be the same as common-law precedents today? Why or why not?*

Regulations by Government Agencies When Congress and the state legislatures make statutes, those laws usually set very general requirements. Government agencies then spell out how those requirements are to be met. Suppose that Congress passes a law requiring school cafeterias to provide healthy lunches. Officials at the Department of Agriculture set regulations about what should be in those lunches. If schools do not follow those rules, they are breaking the law.

The Environmental Protection Agency (EPA) is another government agency that sets regulations to meet the requirements of laws pertaining to the environment. Congress and state legislatures have passed important anti-pollution laws for automobiles. The EPA is responsible for deciding how emission standards on cars should be carried out to meet the goals of the legislation. Car owners and manufacturers must abide by these standards.

Agency regulations are reviewed by the legislature that made the laws. Any regulations that do not carry out the laws are changed.

✓ Reading Check   **How has English law influenced American law?**

How Laws are Organized

As you might imagine, thousands of laws have been made over the years. They are organized in different ways. Some are organized as the foundation laws of government. Others are organized according to the areas they regulate.

Article 9 from the Code of Hammurabi:

If any one loses an article, and finds it in the possession of another: if the person in whose possession the thing is found says "A merchant sold it to me, I paid for it before a witnesses," and if the owner of the thing says, "I will bring witnesses who know my property," then shall the purchaser bring the merchant who sold it to him, and the witnesses before whom he bought it, and the owner shall bring witnesses who can identify his property. The judge shall examine their testimony . . . The merchant is then proved to be a thief and shall be put to death. The owner of the lost article receives his property, and he who bought it receives the money he paid from the estate of the merchant.

Analyzing Primary Sources
How was the punishment for theft different under the Code of Hammurabi than it is under American law?

The Code of Hammurabi
The laws of the Babylonian king Hammurabi were engraved into carved stones called *steles*.
Link Past and Present *How did the steles help Hammurabi maintain order?*

Legal Codes To help keep track of laws, lawmakers have organized many of them into legal codes. A **legal code** is a written collection of laws, often organized by subject. Traffic laws, for instance, are collected in your state's motor vehicle code. Laws relating to schools will be found in the state education code. Codes provide a way to organize laws so that they are up-to-date and easy for people to find.

Legal codes have a long history. One of the earliest codes was made almost 4,000 years ago when the Babylonian king Hammurabi collected the laws of his people. The Code of Hammurabi was carved on stone tablets. It contained almost 300 laws. Some of these ideas we share today, such as family laws and criminal laws.

In 621 B.C., a Greek citizen named Draco was chosen to write a code of law for the city-state of Athens. The punishment for many crimes was death. The code was so severe that the word *draconian* has come to mean an unreasonably harsh law. Draco's laws were the first written laws of Greece. These laws introduced the state's exclusive role in punishing persons accused of crimes, instead of relying on private justice.

Another ancient legal code was the Justinian Code, created under the orders of the Roman emperor Justinian. This collection of Roman laws influenced the development of laws in Europe and the United States.

Legal codes played a key role in the growth of American government. When the colonies were being formed, there was a need for order. Codes such as the *Laws and Liberties of Massachusetts* provided lists of laws that everyone could know and follow.

Constitutions Our United States Constitution and the constitutions of the states are also collections of laws. We do not usually think of constitutions as "laws" in the sense of rules or regulations, yet they include the basic rules by which our governments are run.

Constitutions tell how laws may be made and what the government can and cannot do. They also list the rights of citizens. As you know, state laws must follow the state constitution. Local, state, and federal laws must all follow the United States Constitution.

✓ Reading Check **How do constitutions affect laws?**

Changing the Law

In our country, citizens have the final say on all laws. Through elected representatives, we can add, change, or remove any law. Changes might be as major as amending the Constitution or as minor as doing away with a local ordinance.

As you have already seen, sometimes laws become out of date as beliefs, values, or customs change. People may also change their ideas about what is fair or reasonable. If the majority of the people disagree with laws, the government will usually change them. One example, of course, was the change in the laws about voting rights for women. The Eighteenth Amendment was passed in 1920 to make the sale of alcohol illegal, known as Prohibition. However, there was enough public opposition to Prohibition that the Twenty-first Amendment was passed in 1933 which repealed the earlier amendment. In short, the laws that last are those that are seen as fair, reasonable, and understandable by the majority of the people.

Prohibition
In the photograph above, a Federal agent is destroying illegal barrels of whiskey.
Draw Inferences *Why do you think government officials allowed photographs like this one to be taken?*

✓ Reading Check **What happens when a law becomes out of date?**

SECTION 2 Assessment

Key Terms

Use each of the key terms in a sentence that explains its meaning: statutes, common law, legal codes

Target Reading Skill

1. **Compare and Contrast** Compare and contrast statute law with common law.

Comprehension and Critical Thinking

2. **a. Recall** What are ordinances?
   b. Predict What do you think would happen if a law was passed that was offensive to a majority of citizens?

3. **a. Explain** What was the role of custom in common law?
   b. Draw Conclusions How do you think changes in technology affects common law?

4. **a. Recall** What was the importance of the Code of Hammurabi?
   b. Analyze Information What would be the effect if laws were not collected into legal codes?

5. **a. Describe** Why can constitutions be considered collections of laws?
   b. Draw Inferences Why do all state constitutions have to be in agreement with the U.S. Constitution?

6. **a. Explain** Why do legislatures review government regulations?
   b. Predict Since government agencies are part of the executive branch, what do you think happens to government regulations when the executive and legislative branches are controlled by different parties?

7. **a. Recall** What effect do changes in beliefs, values, or customs have on laws?
   b. Draw Inferences What changes do you think took place that resulted in the laws that gave women the right to vote?

Writing Activity

Write a brief essay about how the making of laws is a product of all three branches of government: legislative, executive and judicial.

TIP Make a list of what each branch of government contributes to the law-making process.

Kinds of Laws

Reading Preview

Objectives

In this section you will

- Learn about criminal law.
- Explore civil law.
- Discuss where criminal law and civil law meet.

Taking Notes

Make a diagram like the one below. As you read this section, complete the diagram with information about criminal and civil law and how they overlap.

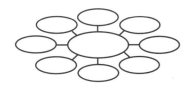

Key Terms

crime	misdemeanor
criminal law	civil law
felony	

Main Idea

The purpose of criminal law is to protect society as a whole. The purpose of civil law is to give people a way to solve disputes they cannot solve by themselves.

Target Reading Skill

Make Comparisons Comparing two or more situations enables you to see how they are alike. This understanding will help you to better understand the text as a whole.

Laws affect your life in many ways. Sometimes laws are so self-evident that following them is second nature. For instance, most people know that entering a business after closing hours could be considered breaking and entering, a criminal act punishable by law. Other times, though, laws are subtle or new and you may need to be reminded. You are reminded about laws even when you rent a DVD. Before the movie begins, a message in big letters appears on the screen:

> **WARNING**
>
> **Federal law provides severe civil and criminal penalties for the unauthorized reproduction, distribution, or exhibition of copyrighted motion pictures, videotapes, or video discs.**
>
> **Criminal copyright infringement is investigated by the FBI and may constitute a felony with a maximum penalty of up to five years in jail and/or a $250,000 fine.**

Why do you think the government might punish people for copying or selling DVDs? What does the warning mean by civil and criminal? You have probably heard the word felony, but what does it mean?

This section will explore the answers to these and other questions by looking at the two main types of law that affect you: criminal law and civil law.

Criminal Law

When people refer to "breaking the law," they are usually talking about crimes. A **crime** is any behavior that is illegal because the government considers it harmful to society. A crime may be an act, such as stealing. It may also be a failure to do something required by law, such as refusing to pay income taxes. In most cases, something cannot be a crime unless there is a specific written law against it. Each law must define a behavior and state how it may be punished. **Criminal law** refers to the group of laws that tell which acts are crimes, how accused persons should be tried in court, and how crimes should be punished.

The Purpose of Criminal Law The main purpose of criminal law is to protect society as a whole. Suppose that you catch a burglar leaving your home. The burglar returns your stolen property, and you agree not to tell the police. You might be satisfied just to get your property back. However, the government is not satisfied because it sees the burglar as a threat to the community's safety. That is why the act is a crime and must be reported.

What would happen if the government did not punish people who commit crimes? If stealing were not against the law, nothing would discourage some people from taking the property of others. Society would be harmed because everyone's property would be threatened. Suppose that people were allowed to copy and sell products made by businesses, such as videotapes. Society would be hurt because businesses could not make a fair profit.

Stolen Goods
This stolen car has been picked clean by the thieves who stole it.
Predict *What would happen if auto theft were not illegal?*

Penalties for Crimes Criminal laws must set fair and reasonable penalties. Some crimes deserve greater penalties than others. Also, most crimes have maximum and minimum penalties. This range allows people guilty of the same crime to receive different punishments, depending on the case. For instance, a first-time offender will probably receive a lighter penalty than someone who has committed many crimes. Sentencing guidelines try to ensure that different judges give similar punishments for crimes committed by people with similar criminal histories.

Crimes are divided into two categories: felonies and misdemeanors. A **felony** is a serious crime for which the penalty can be imprisonment for more than one year. Felonies include such crimes as kidnapping and murder. A **misdemeanor** is a less serious crime for which the penalty is often a fine. Littering and driving without a license are examples of misdemeanors.

Sources of Criminal Law In the United States, no individual government leader may make a law that a certain act is a crime. This is to make sure that too much power does not rest in the hands of one person.

When people talk about "the government" making an act a crime, they are referring to Congress, to state legislatures, or to local lawmakers such as city councils. At all three levels of government, criminal laws are passed, written down, and organized into codes.

Congress decides which types of behavior will be considered crimes everywhere in the United States. Each state legislature, though, can make its own criminal laws as long as they do not come into conflict with federal statutes or the Constitution.

Some types of behavior, such as gambling, may be illegal in one state but legal in another. Punishments may also differ. Drunk driving may be a felony in one state but a misdemeanor in another.

✓ Reading Check **What is the difference between a felony and a misdemeanor?**

Community Service
These non-violent offenders were sentenced to perform community service at a local food bank.

Civil Law

Criminal law includes all the laws that the government can punish people for breaking. **Civil law** is the group of laws that help settle disagreements between people.

The Purpose of Civil Law Civil law provides a way for people to settle disagreements in court if they cannot or will not settle them privately. In civil cases, the government will not automatically get involved, as it does with crimes. An individual or group involved in the conflict must first ask for help by suing, or taking the matter to court.

By providing a system of civil law, the government is in effect saying, "If you disagree with someone and think you have been treated unfairly, first try to work it out yourselves. If that fails, there are laws that judges and juries may use to help settle the conflict."

Suppose, for example, you buy a CD player that breaks down the first time you use it. Then, when you take it back to the store, the store owner refuses to replace the machine, saying that you must have broken it. Under civil law, you have the right to sue the owner. That is, you may file a complaint with a court stating why you think the owner has been unfair to you. Both you and the owner might then tell your stories to a judge or jury, who will make a decision based on rules of civil law.

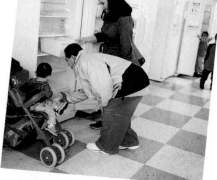

Bad Business
Civil law is intended to settle disagreements between two parties—such as buyers and sellers.
Contrast *When might a disagreement over a business transaction be covered by criminal law instead of civil law?*

Sources of Civil Law In criminal cases, the main question is, "Did the accused person commit a crime?" Judges and juries must compare the facts of the case with the statute that defines the crime. In civil cases, however, the main question is, "What is a fair way to settle this type of disagreement?" To answer that question, judges and juries often refer to earlier decisions that have been made in similar cases.

Decisions in civil cases may also be based on statutes. Most civil statutes sum up the unwritten laws on which judges have based their decisions over the years. For instance, in case after case judges have ruled that a seller has a duty to deliver goods and that a buyer must pay for them. Eventually, legislatures decided that this basic unwritten law should be spelled out as a written statute: "The obligation of the seller is to transfer and deliver and that of the buyer is to accept and pay in accordance with the contract."

Some civil statutes are collected and organized into legal codes. In fact, the example just mentioned comes from the Business and Commerce Code, which includes many laws that protect consumers.

Target Reading Skill
Making Comparisons
Compare the source of civil law with the source of common law.

✔ Reading Check **What is the purpose of civil law?**

How Criminal and Civil Trials Interact

Go Online
*civics
interactive*

For: Interactive Trial
Diagram
Visit: PHSchool.com
Web Code: mpp-7193

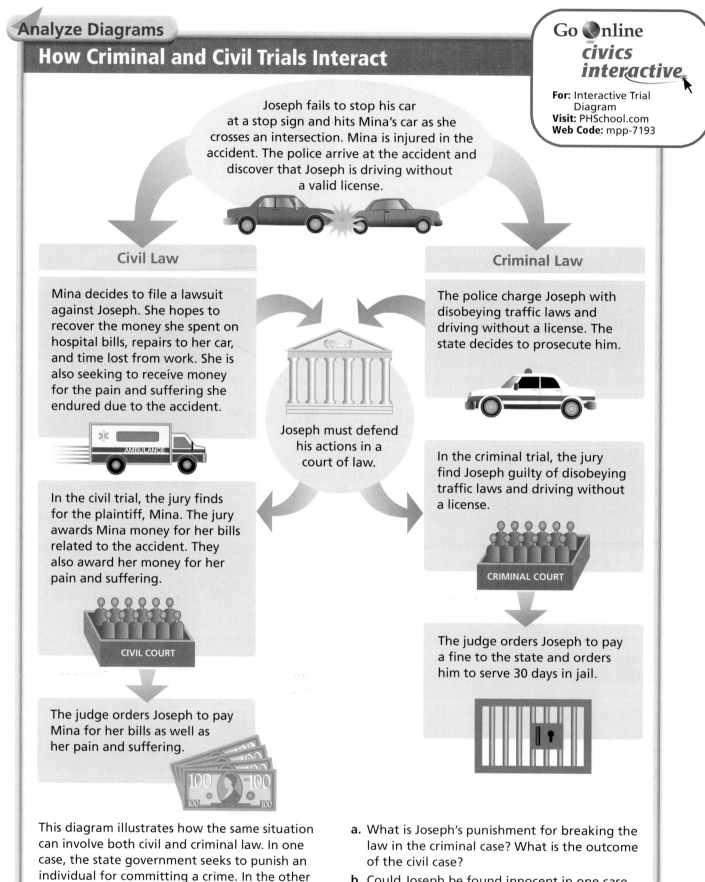

Joseph fails to stop his car at a stop sign and hits Mina's car as she crosses an intersection. Mina is injured in the accident. The police arrive at the accident and discover that Joseph is driving without a valid license.

Civil Law

Mina decides to file a lawsuit against Joseph. She hopes to recover the money she spent on hospital bills, repairs to her car, and time lost from work. She is also seeking to receive money for the pain and suffering she endured due to the accident.

In the civil trial, the jury finds for the plaintiff, Mina. The jury awards Mina money for her bills related to the accident. They also award her money for her pain and suffering.

CIVIL COURT

The judge orders Joseph to pay Mina for her bills as well as her pain and suffering.

Criminal Law

The police charge Joseph with disobeying traffic laws and driving without a license. The state decides to prosecute him.

In the criminal trial, the jury find Joseph guilty of disobeying traffic laws and driving without a license.

CRIMINAL COURT

The judge orders Joseph to pay a fine to the state and orders him to serve 30 days in jail.

Joseph must defend his actions in a court of law.

This diagram illustrates how the same situation can involve both civil and criminal law. In one case, the state government seeks to punish an individual for committing a crime. In the other case, two private parties seek to resolve a conflict arising from the crime.

a. What is Joseph's punishment for breaking the law in the criminal case? What is the outcome of the civil case?

b. Could Joseph be found innocent in one case but guilty in the other case? Why or why not?

Where Criminal Law and Civil Law Meet

Criminal law gives government the power it needs to protect society as a whole by taking action against individuals and organized groups that commit crimes. Civil law provides a way for individuals or groups within society to settle their conflicts in an orderly manner. Both types of laws help bring order to society and protect people's rights.

Sometimes situations involve both criminal and civil law. Suppose a drunk driver who has no insurance accidentally hits a woman out for an evening stroll, severely injuring her. Criminal law protects society by punishing the driver for drunk driving. However, it does not require the driver to pay the injured woman's medical bills. That is where civil law enters the picture. If the driver refuses to pay, the injured woman can sue. Under civil law, a court can force the driver to pay.

Think back to the warning that appears on DVDs. Every year, hundreds of criminals are caught with illegally copied DVDs and prosecuted. Criminal law protects society by fining or imprisoning a person who illegally copies and sells a company's DVDs. However, punishing the criminal does not completely solve the company's problem. It has lost money it could have earned by selling DVDs itself. Under civil law, the company can ask a court to force the criminal to pay the company the amount lost in sales.

✔ Reading Check **What is the role of civil law in a case of injury resulting from drunken driving?**

SECTION 3 Assessment

Key Terms

Use each of the key terms in a sentence that explains its meaning: crime, criminal law, felony, misdemeanor, civil law

Target Reading Skill

1. **Make Comparisons** Compare the role of criminal law with the role of civil law in the drunk-driving case described on this page. What do they have in common?

Comprehension and Critical Thinking

2. **a. Recall** Why might two people guilty of the same crime receive different sentences?

   b. Draw Inferences How does criminal law help prevent crime?

3. **a. Recall** What is the main question to be decided in civil trials?

   b. Draw Conclusions In criminal cases, the government pursues its case immediately upon discovery of a crime. Why do you think civil law requires one party to sue in court before the government gets involved?

4. **a. Explain** How does criminal law protect society?

   b. Contrast How are civil law cases different from criminal law cases?

Writing Activity

The U.S. Department of Justice helps individuals and communities that have problems with violations of federal laws. Visit the Department of Justice's web site to find out what services it provides to people who believe they have been the victims of civil-rights law violations. Write a brief report that explains what you found on the web site.

Go Online PHSchool.com

For: Report
Visit: PHSchool.com
Web Code: mpd-7193

Skills for Life ✓

Summarizing

Summarizing documents helps you make sure you understand the information they contain. When you summarize, you should pick out the key points of information and understand the connections between them.

The passage below discusses the many legal changes brought about by the Supreme Court in the 1960s.

Throughout the 1950s and 60s, the Supreme Court became very active in social justice. Headed by Chief Justice Earl Warren, the "Warren Court" made numerous decisions that helped redefine society in the United States.

The Warren Court is perhaps best known for its decision to outlaw segregation in public schools. In the case of *Brown* v. *Board of Education of Topeka*, the Court ruled that "separate but equal" facilities violated the civil rights of African Americans. Other cases followed, and eventually segregation was banned in all public facilities. The Warren Court played a key role in the advancement of the Civil Rights Movement.

The Court's decisions brought about other social changes as well. In 1963, the Court declared prayer in the public schools to be unconstitutional and sparked a debate that continues today. It also secured the constitutional rights of accused persons. In *Miranda* v. *Arizona*, the Court ruled that a person arrested must be read his rights, or else his confession would be inadmissible in court. It also ruled that a state lawyer must be appointed to any accused person who could not afford one.

Learn the Skill

Follow these steps to summarize information:

❶ **Identify the main idea.** Look for the main idea, which states the purpose of the passage. The main idea is often found in the first sentence.

❷ **Look for details.** Details such as facts, explanations, examples, or descriptions will support the main idea.

❸ **Restate the main idea.** Use your own words to restate the main idea.

❹ **Choose important details.** Select details that most strongly support the main idea to include in your summary. Condense the information into a few sentences.

Practice the Skill

Read the passage above and answer these questions:

❶ Which sentence states the main idea?

❷ (a) What were some of the Warren Court's rulings? (b) What changes occurred as a result of those decisions?

❸ State the main idea in your own words.

❹ Select the two most important details to include in a summary of this passage.

Apply the Skill

Summarize a magazine or newspaper article about an issue you are interested in. Be sure to restate the main idea and include important details in your summary.

CHAPTER 19 Review and Assessment

Chapter Summary

Section 1
Why We Have Laws
(pages 512–516)

- Laws provide order, protect people's safety, property, individual freedoms, and promote the common good.

- Laws reflect the morals of a society.

- Some people commit civil disobedience to protest a law that is against their personal morals.

Section 2
Where Our Laws Come From
(pages 518–523)

- Statutes are laws made by legislatures.

- Judges' decisions, based on common law, are also part of the law-making process.

- Laws are collected into legal codes.

- Laws are based on the rules set out in constitutions.

- Government agencies make the regulations that provide the details of a law's content.

- People change laws when the beliefs upon which the laws are based change.

Section 3
Kinds of Laws
(pages 524–529)

- The purpose of criminal law is to protect society from the effects of crime.

- The penalties for the same felony or misdemeanor can differ.

- The purpose of civil law is to resolve disputes.

Copy the chart below and use it to help you summarize the chapter.

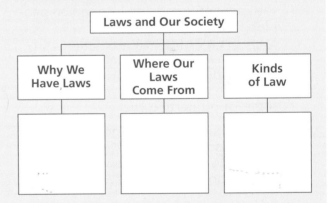

Go Online
PHSchool.com
For: Self-Test
Visit: PHSchool.com
Web Code: mpa-7193

Reviewing Key Terms

Choose the best term to complete each of the following sentences.

crime   felony
civil law   statutes
misdemeanor   criminal law
common law   civil disobedience

1. Law that is based on past judges' decisions is called _____.

2. Laws passed by legislatures are called _____.

3. A serious crime for which punishment can be imprisonment for more than a year is called a _____.

4. The group of laws that helps settle disputes between people is called _____.

5. Breaking a law because it goes against a person's morals is called _____.

6. Harmful behavior that is against the law is called a _____.

7. The group of laws that defines which acts are illegal is called _____.

8. A less serious crime for which a fine is often the penalty is called a _____.

Comprehension and Critical Thinking

9. a. **Recall** How do laws provide for the common good?
   b. **Contrast** How can laws that provide for the common good also infringe on people's freedoms?
   c. **Support a Point of View** Community zoning laws regulate what can be built on individuals' property. How do these laws both support and conflict with the rights of property owners?

10. a. **Recall** Which branch of government is most responsible for making laws?
    b. **Predict** What would happen if state constitutions and state laws did not have to conform to the United States Constitution?
    c. **Link Past and Present** What beliefs do you think were behind denying the vote to women?

11. a. **Explain** How are criminal laws made?
    b. **Contrast** How is civil law different from criminal law?
    c. **Synthesize Information** Can the federal government make criminal laws on any matter? Explain.

Activities

12. **Skills** **Summarizing** Write two sentences that summarize the main points of the paragraph.

13. **Writing** Find news of a criminal trial in an article from a newspaper, magazine, or the Internet. Write a brief summary in which you outline the main issues involved in the case.

In the early 1200s, King John of England imposed crushing taxes on his subjects, enforcing them ruthlessly. He also administered justice according to his whim. In 1215 a group of barons demanded a charter, or official document, that outlined their rights. They took up arms and forced the king to sign this document, which became known as the Magna Carta, or Great Charter. The Magna Carta was one of the first documents to guarantee certain civil liberties. The United States Constitution shows ideas that come directly from the Magna Carta.

14. **Active Citizen** Is there an issue in your school or community you would like to change? Identify the issue, your reasons for changing it, and whom you should approach to start the process of change.

15. **Math Practice** When the population of the United States was about 285 million people, there were about 2 million Americans in prison. What percentage of residents in the United States was in prison at that time?

16. **Civics and Economics** In many states, retails stores cannot legally stay open on Sundays as long as they can on other days. How does this restriction affect the economy? Why do you think states continue to keep these restrictions?

17. **Analyzing Visuals** In a short paragraph, explain how successful this photograph is in portraying the dangers of child labor.

Standardized Test Prep

The graph below shows how many people were in the correctional system in the United States from 1985 to 2000. Read the graph, then answer the questions that follow.

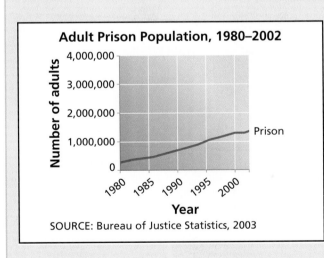

Adult Prison Population, 1980–2002

SOURCE: Bureau of Justice Statistics, 2003

1. The graph shows
   A the number of men in prison.
   B the number of women in prison.
   C the number of people in prison.
   D the number of people convicted of crimes in each year.

   The title of the chart tells you the answer is **C**.

   TIP To understand graphs, it is important to read everything that accompanies them carefully. Read the title to understand the topic of the graph. Graphs sometimes will also further define terms that appear on them. Be sure to double-check the information as you read it.

2. The number of people in prison in 2000 was about
   A 500,000.
   B 1 million.
   C 1.5 million.
   D 2 million.

Criminal and Juvenile Justice

What's Ahead in Chapter 20

In this chapter you will study the problem of crime in our society. You will learn about how the criminal justice system deals with people accused of breaking the law.

SECTION 1
Crime in American Society

SECTION 2
The Criminal Justice System

SECTION 3
The Juvenile Justice System

TARGET READING SKILL

Sequence When you list events in sequence, you put them in chronological order. Putting events in order will help you remember how they are linked. As you read this chapter, you will try out the skills of recognizing words that signal sequence and putting events in chronological order.

◀ A Neighborhood Watch community

National | National Standards for Civic Government | **State**

The following National Standards for Civics and Government are covered in this chapter.

III. How does the government established by the Constitution embody American democracy?

D. What is the place of law in the American system?

V. What are the roles of the citizen in American democracy?

D. What traits are important to American constitutional democracy?

Go Online
PHSchool.com

For: Your state's standards
Visit: PHSchool.com
Web Code: mpe-7200

Active Citizen

Civics in the Real World

Kate slammed the front door behind her. "It's only me," she called as she ran into the family room to drop her schoolbooks on the table. The she noticed something. "Mom, where's the DVD player?" she called.

Kate's mother saw the empty space next to the television set and said, "Kate, I think we've been robbed! Quick, run and see if anything is missing from upstairs. I'll call the police."

Kate saw right away that her computer was gone. Their mother's jewelry had also been stolen.

An officer arrived soon after. He made a list of the stolen items, then went through the house with them. "Looks like this is how the burglar got in," he said, examining the broken lock on the kitchen door. "Make sure you get a locksmith out here right away."

"Will I get my computer back?" asked Kate.

"We'll do our best," answered the officer. "But don't count on it. We don't recover many stolen items. And many burglars aren't caught."

Citizen's Journal Have you ever had anything stolen from you or someone you know? Write a short paragraph about this experience. How did you feel when you discovered the theft? Did you contact the police, and if so, what did they do about it? How was this situation finally resolved?

Crime in American Society

Reading Preview

Objectives

In this section you will

- examine the problem of crime in the United States.
- identify and describe the types of crimes.
- discuss the causes of crime.

Taking Notes

Make a diagram like the one below. As you read this section, complete the diagram with information about the various categories of crime.

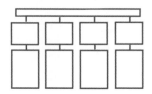

Key Terms

assault
battery
burglary

embezzlement
treason
terrorism

Main Idea

Thousands of crimes are committed in the United States each year. The crimes, their causes, and what people think the system should do about it vary widely.

Target Reading Skill

Understand Sequence Remember that events follow one another in a cause-and-effect relationship. As you read this section, look for the causes and effects that indicate a sequence of events.

Barred windows are a sign that neighbors are afraid of crime. ▼

A jogger is mugged in the park. A four-year-old is kidnapped from his front yard. A bank president flees the country, having stolen millions of dollars from depositors. These are the kinds of crimes that you hear about all too often on the news. Crime is a major problem in the United States today.

The Problem of Crime

Crime touches many Americans every year. According to the Federal Bureau of Investigation (FBI), there were more than ten million property crimes and nearly one-and-a-half million violent crimes in 2000. Crime costs people, businesses, and governments billions of dollars every year. Many Americans consider crime to be one of the most important problems facing our nation today.

Some places have more crime than others. In general, there is more crime in urban areas than there is in suburban or rural communities. In addition, poor neighborhoods often have more crime than wealthy ones.

Crime makes people afraid. When people are frightened, they change their way of life. They put extra locks on their doors and do not go out at night. They become suspicious of strangers. As the problems caused by crime worsen, everyone in society suffers.

✓ Reading Check **Which parts of the country tend to have higher crime rates, cities or suburbs?**

The Types of Crimes

Crime is a problem for all Americans. Serious crimes fall into several major groups: crimes against people, crimes against property, white-collar crimes, victimless crimes, and crimes against the government.

Crimes Against People Acts that threaten, hurt, or end a person's life are crimes against people. They are also called violent crimes. Murder, rape, and assault are examples of violent crimes. **Assault** is placing someone in fear without actual physical contact. If physical contact occurs, as with a weapon or a foot, the crime is called **battery**.

Killing someone is known as homicide. When a killing is intentional and the killer has no legally recognized excuse, it is called murder. A killing that happens by accident or in a fit of anger is called manslaughter. Not all killings are crimes. Killing someone in self-defense is not against the law, if such an act is the only way to save your life.

Crimes Against Property Crimes against property happen more often than any other crimes. Most involve stealing. There are three kinds of stealing.

Larceny is taking anything of value that belongs to another person without using violence. Shoplifting and stealing a car are both acts of larceny.

Robbery is a special kind of stealing. A robber takes something of value from another person by force or by threat of violence. Robbery is therefore both a crime against property and a crime against a person.

When a person breaks into a building and plans to do something illegal inside, that person is committing **burglary**. Burglary is a crime against property. It may or may not involve stealing.

Other kinds of crimes against property include arson and vandalism. Arson is the act of setting fire to someone's property on purpose. Vandalism is purposely damaging property. Breaking windows and painting graffiti on walls are examples of vandalism.

Kinds of Crime
Crimes against people include assault and homicide. Crimes against property include theft and arson.
Support a Point of View *Do you feel that all the categories listed are of equal seriousness? Why or why not?*

White-Collar Crime White-collar crimes are nonviolent crimes by office workers for personal or business gain. One white-collar crime is fraud, or taking someone else's property or money by cheating or lying. Another is **embezzlement**, stealing money that has been trusted to your care. If a bank employee put money from other people's bank accounts into his or her own account, it is embezzlement. Stealing company secrets and not paying taxes are white-collar crimes.

Each year, Americans file their federal income tax returns. The Internal Revenue Service makes sure that taxpayers fill out the forms correctly and do not cheat.

1. What is happening in this cartoon?

2. Do you think the man made a major mistake on his return or did he attempt to cheat the government by not paying his taxes? Explain.

"Now, this over here, this is why you're going to have to go to jail."

Victimless Crimes Drug use and gambling are known as "victimless crimes," acts that hurt primarily the people who commit them. Our society calls them crimes because they go against common values.

Should there be laws against acts that do not hurt any innocent people? Some people say that such laws limit the freedom of individuals. Others argue that such acts really do hurt innocent people. They warn that gamblers and drug users are a bad influence, that their families suffer, and that they often turn to violent crime to pay for their habits.

Crimes Against the Government Crimes against the government include treason and terrorism. **Treason** is the betrayal of one's country by helping its enemies or by making war against it. **Terrorism** is a crime in which people or groups of people use, or say they will use, violence in order to get what they want from the government or society. The terrorist bombing of a federal government office building in Oklahoma City in 1995 caused the death of 169 people. On September 11, 2001, terrorists crashed commercial airliners into the World Trade Center in New York and the Pentagon near Washington, D.C. These attacks killed about 3,000 people.

✓ Reading Check   **Who are the victims of "victimless" crimes?**

The Causes of Crime

In the United States, millions of crimes are committed each year. People disagree about what causes crime. All of the reasons below have been suggested as contributing to the problem.

Poverty Poverty and unemployment are closely connected to crime. When people cannot earn enough money to support themselves and their families, they may feel that society does not work well for them. These people are more likely to break the law.

Social Change and Changing Values New technology and changes in the economy are bringing about great changes in the United States. Many Americans must learn new job skills or move to different parts of the country. Values are changing, too. In the process, some people lose their sense of right and wrong.

Poor Parenting Some studies show that an unhappy family life can make a person much more likely to break laws. Children whose parents hurt or neglected them may suffer great emotional pain. Some find it hard to control their behavior as adults.

Drug Abuse Many crimes committed each year are drug-related. The people who commit them are under the influence of drugs, are stealing to support a drug habit, or are selling drugs. Many people think that solving the drug-abuse problem in our society will also help solve the crime problem.

Target Reading Skill
Understand Sequence Note the heading **The Causes of Crime**. That tells you that each crime listed is an effect of one or more of these causes. In the sequence of events, the cause comes first and the effect comes next.

Analyze Charts

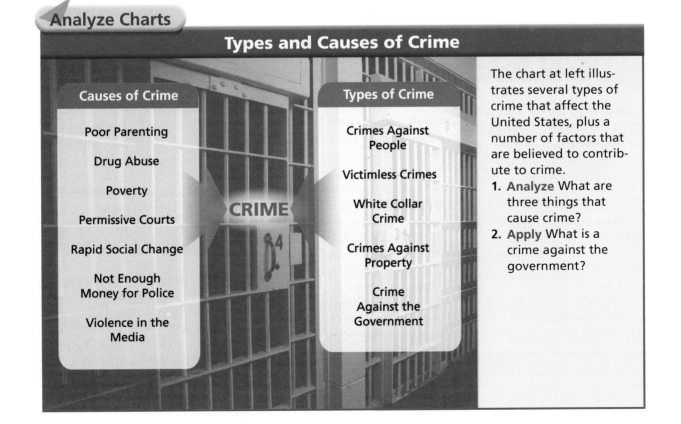

Types and Causes of Crime

Causes of Crime

- Poor Parenting
- Drug Abuse
- Poverty
- Permissive Courts
- Rapid Social Change
- Not Enough Money for Police
- Violence in the Media

CRIME

Types of Crime

- Crimes Against People
- Victimless Crimes
- White Collar Crime
- Crimes Against Property
- Crime Against the Government

The chart at left illustrates several types of crime that affect the United States, plus a number of factors that are believed to contribute to crime.
1. **Analyze** What are three things that cause crime?
2. **Apply** What is a crime against the government?

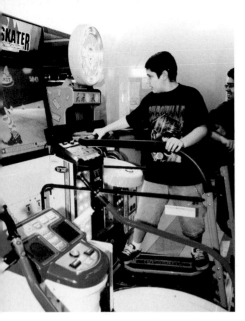

Video Violence
The debate continues about how much the violence in video games influences people to become violent.
Support a Point of View *Do you feel that violent images in television, films, and video games should be controlled by the government?*

Permissive Courts Some people place much of the blame for crime on the way our courts treat criminals. Too few criminals are sent to prison, they say. Many receive short sentences. Some are let go on technicalities. Some people also feel that those criminals who do go to prison are given parole too soon, and that they will go right back to committing crimes.

Not Enough Money for Police Crime will not be reduced, say many people, until the chances of getting caught are much higher. More money, they argue, should be given to police departments so that more police officers can be hired. Police officers also need the latest technology and equipment to help them fight crime.

Violence in the Media Every day, millions of children and adults watch violent acts on television, in movies, and in computer games. Many people believe that the more violence that people see, the more desensitized they become to violence. They fear that watching a great deal of violence causes people to be more violent themselves.

No Single Cause These and many other aspects of our modern society have been blamed for causing crime. People do not agree about which of these causes are most important. Experts do agree that no single cause can explain our crime problem.

✓ Reading Check **What is the connection between crime and poverty in the United States?**

SECTION 1   Assessment

Key Terms

Use each of the key terms in a sentence that explains its meaning:
assault, battery, burglary, embezzlement, treason, terrorism

Target Reading Skill

1. **Support a Point of View** Summarize the sequence of events that leads to the police officer coming to Kate's house (page 535).

Comprehension and Critical Thinking

2. **a. Explain** Why is crime such a serious problem in the United States?

   b. Identify Cause and Effect What effect does the high crime rate have on our society?

3. **a. Recall** What are the major categories of crime?

   b. Support a Point of View In your opinion, which crimes are the most serious? Which are the least serious? Explain.

4. **a. Recall** List three possible causes of crime.

   b. Analyze Information In your opinion, what is the chief cause of crime in the United States? Explain.

Writing Activity

Choose one of the categories of crime describe in this section. Look up the statistics for your state in this category over the past decade. Note whether the crime rate is falling or rising. Write a report in which you try to account for the change in the crime rate over time.

> **TIP** Reread "The Causes of Crime" in Section 1. Think about other causes of crime as you write your report. How have changes in laws or society affected the causes of crime?

Identifying Bias

To evaluate evidence correctly, you need to be able to identify whether the evidence is objective or biased. Objective information simply contains facts. However, readers must interpret those facts to find any bias that lies behind them. For example, what bias might the author of a primary source have felt toward the topic he or she wrote about? What biases does a government's decision indicate? It is important to detect bias, as this may undermine the validity of the evidence.

> To the Editor:
>
> The justice system in our state is in need of serious reform. Criminals are spending too little time in prison for committing the most violent crimes. Murderers are released after 10 years in prison or less. Kidnappers receive just a few years in prison.
>
> I have seen the effects of lenient sentences firsthand. My brother suffered at the hands of a violent criminal who attacked him one September evening. My brother spent weeks recovering, but the criminal got a slap on the wrist—just two years in prison.
>
> We must get tough on violent criminals. Giving them short sentences and letting them out early puts all of us at risk. We need to punish the criminals for what they've done. We need to keep them locked away from law-abiding Americans.
>
> —Jim Overcroft

Learn the Skill

Follow these steps to identify bias:

❶ **Identify main ideas.** What is the main point of the evidence?

❷ **Identify the source.** Who created the evidence? Whose decisions and actions does it report?

❸ **Identify bias.** What bias or biases do these actions and decisions indicate?

Practice the Skill

Study the letter above and answer these questions:

❶ What is the main idea of the letter?

❷ Is the letter biased or objective? Explain.

❸ (a) Whose actions and decisions are reflected in the letter? (b) What are those decisions?

❹ What bias or biases can you find in the letter?

Apply the Skill

Find a newspaper or magazine article about a criminal trial. Read the article carefully and describe any signs of bias that you find.

The Criminal Justice System

Reading Preview

Objectives

In this section you will

- describe the arrest and pre-trial process.
- learn about going to trial.
- learn about correctional institutions.
- discuss challenges facing the criminal justice system.
- analyze proposals for fighting crime.

Taking Notes

Make a diagram like the one below. As you read this section, complete the diagram with information about the sequence of events that leads from arrest to imprisonment.

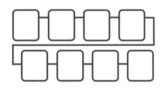

▲
The process of penalizing lawbreakers begins with an arrest.

Key Terms

probable cause
warrant
bail
indictment
arraignment
plea bargaining
parole

Main Idea

When an adult is arrested , he or she goes through a specific process. The process includes arraignment, indictment, trial, and sentencing or acquittal.

Target Reading Skill

Recognize Words That Signal Sequence Signal words point out relationships between ideas or events. Words and phrases such as *at this time, soon after,* and *before* tell you the order in which these steps take place.

The criminal justice system faces a challenge. It must protect society against those who break the law. It must also protect the rights of people accused of crimes. Americans often disagree about how to balance these responsibilities.

The Arrest and Pre-Trial Process

In order to make sure that people's rights are protected, there are many steps to be taken in deciding whether a person is guilty of a crime. To follow those steps, suppose that Jack Jones broke into an electronics store and stole portable MP3 players.

The Arrest Jack Jones enters the criminal justice system when he is arrested by a law enforcement official. To arrest Jack, the police must have **probable cause**, a good reason to believe that a suspect has been involved in a crime. If the police see Jack commit the crime, or if someone reports that Jack has committed the crime, then the police have probable cause.

A person can also be arrested if the police have a warrant for his or her arrest. A **warrant** is a legal paper, issued by a court, giving police permission to make an arrest, seizure, or search. To get a warrant the police must give evidence to a judge.

During the arrest, the officers must tell Jack that he has the constitutional right to remain silent and to have a lawyer present during questioning. This is part of the Miranda warning.

After the arrest, Jack is taken to a police station. The police record Jack's name, the time of the arrest, and the charges, or reason for the arrest. At this time, Jack has the right to make a phone call to a lawyer or to a friend who can arrange for a lawyer. Then he is placed in a jail cell.

The case is given to a prosecuting attorney, or prosecutor. In the state court systems, the prosecutor will be the district attorney (DA) or an attorney on the DA's staff. The prosecutor will lead the government's case against Jack Jones. If the prosecutor decides that the case against Jack is too weak, the charges may be dropped, and the suspect released.

The Preliminary Hearing On the day of his arrest or soon after, Jack appears in court for a preliminary hearing. The suspect, Jack Jones, is now called the defendant. At this hearing, the prosecutor must show the judge that a crime has been committed, and that there is enough evidence against Jack to go ahead with the case. The judge may decide to dismiss the case if the prosecutor cannot show that there is enough evidence that Jack committed the crime.

If the crime could lead to a prison sentence, Jack has a right to the help of a lawyer, or attorney. If he does not have enough money to pay for a lawyer, the court will appoint one at this hearing. The lawyer may be either a private attorney whom the government will pay for representing Jack or a public defender. Public defenders are lawyers who work full time for the government defending criminal suspects who cannot afford to pay. The defendant's lawyer is called the defense attorney.

Target Reading Skill
Recognize Words That Signal Sequence As you read these paragraphs, look for signal words or phrases such as *during, after, at the same time,* and *then.* These words clarify the order in which the steps happen.

Analyze Graphs

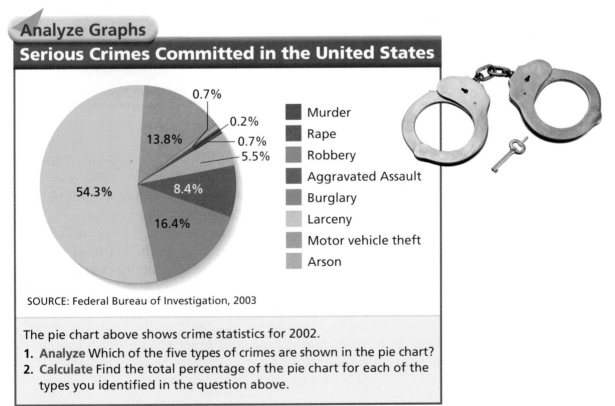

Serious Crimes Committed in the United States

0.7%
0.2%
0.7%
5.5%
13.8%
54.3%
8.4%
16.4%

- Murder
- Rape
- Robbery
- Aggravated Assault
- Burglary
- Larceny
- Motor vehicle theft
- Arson

SOURCE: Federal Bureau of Investigation, 2003

The pie chart above shows crime statistics for 2002.
1. **Analyze** Which of the five types of crimes are shown in the pie chart?
2. **Calculate** Find the total percentage of the pie chart for each of the types you identified in the question above.

Go Online
civics
interactive

For: Interactive Constitution
with Supreme Court cases
Visit: PHSchool.com
Web Code: mpp-7202

Gideon v. *Wainwright* (1963)

Why It Matters The case established that every person accused of a crime has a right to a lawyer.

Background In 1961, Clarence Gideon, an unemployed 40-year-old man, was accused of breaking into a Florida pool room and was arrested. He asked the court for a lawyer, saying he had no money to hire one himself. The judge refused, saying that under Florida law, only people accused of a capital crime (a crime in which the death penalty was a possible punishment) could have a lawyer appointed by and paid for by the court. Gideon claimed that under the Sixth Amendment he was entitled to a lawyer even though he could not afford to hire one.

Gideon did his best in representing himself at the trial, but he was convicted and sentenced to five years in jail. From jail, Clarence Gideon wrote a letter to the U.S. Supreme Court in pencil appealing his conviction. The case reached the Supreme Court in 1963.

The Decision The Supreme Court voted unanimously in favor of Gideon, saying that the Sixth Amendment did guarantee Gideon the right to a lawyer. The Court said in denying Gideon the right to counsel (a lawyer), the State of Florida had denied him due process of law, a violation of his rights under the Fourteenth Amendment. The Court's decision overturned Gideon's conviction for burglary.

Understanding the Law

1. Why did the Florida judge deny Gideon a lawyer?
2. How did the Gideon case help assure that people would receive a fair trial?

In either a misdemeanor or felony case, the defendant may enter a plea of guilty, not guilty, or a plea of "no contest" at this first court hearing. (In a "no contest" plea, a defendant does not admit committing the crime, but accepts the punishment anyway.)

At this first appearance in court, the judge may set bail. **Bail** is money that a defendant gives the court as a kind of promise that he or she will return for the trial. If the defendant does not return, the court keeps the bail. The judge may also simply let the defendant go on his or her "own recognizance." This means that the defendant is considered to be a good risk to appear at the trial. If the judge decides the defendant is dangerous to society, the defendant can be held in jail without bail.

Grand Jury The Constitution says that a grand jury must review cases involving serious federal crimes. Some states use grand juries, too. The grand jury is a group of from 16 to 23 citizens. Their job is to decide if there is probable cause for believing that the defendant committed the crime. The grand jury acts as a check on the government. It protects the rights of the individual, making sure there is enough evidence against him or her.

The grand jury may either return an **indictment** [in DITE ment]—a formal charge against the accused—or refuse to indict. A defendant who is indicted must appear in court for a felony **arraignment** [uh RAIN ment], a court hearing in which the defendant is formally charged with a crime and enters a plea of guilty, not guilty, or no contest. If the defendant pleads guilty, no trial is needed. If the defendant pleads not guilty, the defense attorney will take the next step.

Pretrial Motions If Jack Jones has pleaded not guilty to the charges against him, there are important steps, called pretrial motions, that may be taken before the actual trial begins.

One of the most important motions is to keep evidence from being presented in court. Sometimes the defense attorney may say that the police got the evidence through an illegal search. If the judge rules that key evidence cannot be used in the trial for this reason, the prosecution may have to drop the charges. This rule protects the constitutional rights of the accused. But it may result in people who have actually broken the law being set free.

Plea Bargaining Most criminal cases never go to trial. The main reason these cases do not go to trial is that the defendant pleads guilty. A trial is not needed.

If a defendant knew that he had broken the law and that the evidence against him was strong, he might want to make a deal with the prosecutor. Making such a deal is called **plea bargaining**, agreeing to plead guilty in exchange for a lesser charge or a lighter sentence. As a result of plea bargaining, the defendant gets a milder punishment than he or she would probably have received in a trial. Meanwhile, the government saves the cost of a trial.

✓ Reading Check **Why would a defendant agree to engage in plea bargaining?**

Appearing in Court
A judge speaks to a defendant and his attorney during a trial. Once a defendant enters a plea, the judge may set a bail amount for the defendant.

Going to Trial

Suppose that, after all of these steps, Jack's case makes it to trial. What happens in the courtroom?

Jury Selection Citizens are called to serve on the jury. They are questioned either by attorneys on both sides of the case or by the judge. The purpose of the questioning is to determine who will listen carefully to the evidence and then make up their minds fairly. Sometimes many people must be questioned before a group of jurors is selected.

The Trial The rights granted by the Constitution determine how a trial is run. The trial must be speedy and public. The defendant—Jack—has the right to call witnesses and to question witnesses called by the prosecution. He has the right to be present in the courtroom, but he does not have to answer questions. The purpose of the trial is to decide whether Jack is innocent or guilty.

Analyze Diagrams

Criminal Law: From Arrest to Conviction

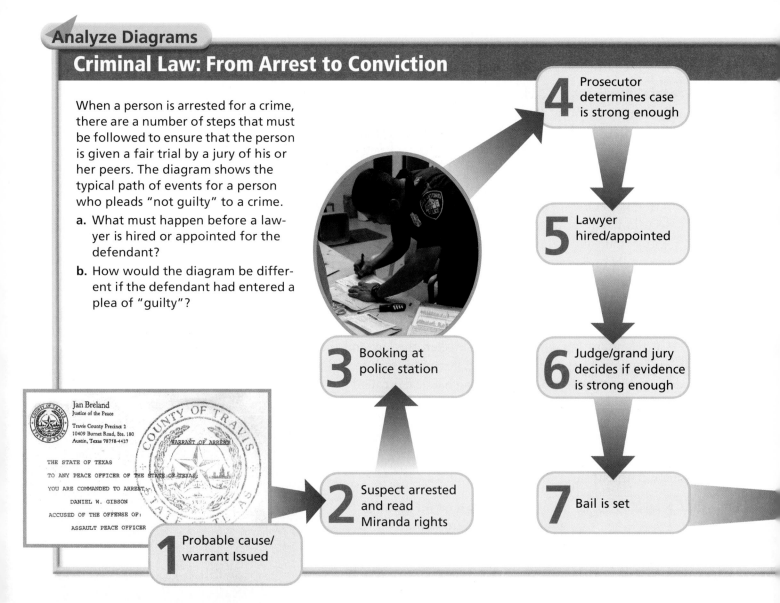

When a person is arrested for a crime, there are a number of steps that must be followed to ensure that the person is given a fair trial by a jury of his or her peers. The diagram shows the typical path of events for a person who pleads "not guilty" to a crime.

a. What must happen before a lawyer is hired or appointed for the defendant?

b. How would the diagram be different if the defendant had entered a plea of "guilty"?

1 Probable cause/ warrant Issued

2 Suspect arrested and read Miranda rights

3 Booking at police station

4 Prosecutor determines case is strong enough

5 Lawyer hired/appointed

6 Judge/grand jury decides if evidence is strong enough

7 Bail is set

Usually, statements made by witnesses are the most important evidence in a trial. A witness may be a person who saw the crime take place. A witness may also be the defendant, the victim, or anyone who knows anything about the defendant, the victim, or the crime.

The attorneys in the trial each call their own witnesses, asking them questions in court. After one attorney questions a witness, the other attorney may question that same witness.

At the end of the trial, the attorneys for each side make closing arguments. The judge then gives directions to the jury and sends it out to make its decision.

A jury must decide if the defendant is guilty beyond a reasonable doubt. If they have any doubts about the defendant's guilt, they must find the defendant 'not guilty.' If the jury cannot agree, it is called a 'hung jury,' and the case may be tried again before another jury.

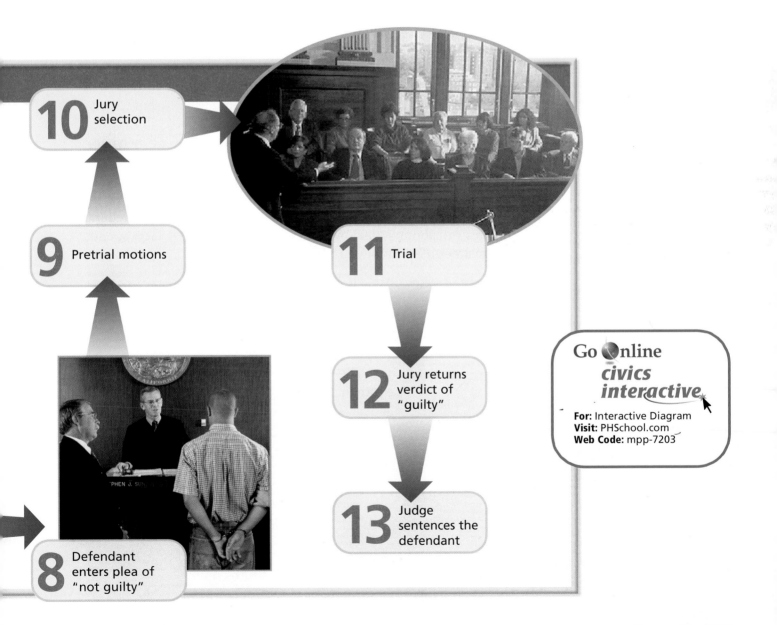

10 Jury selection

9 Pretrial motions

11 Trial

12 Jury returns verdict of "guilty"

13 Judge sentences the defendant

8 Defendant enters plea of "not guilty"

Go Online
civics interactive
For: Interactive Diagram
Visit: PHSchool.com
Web Code: mpp-7203

Sentencing If Jack is found guilty or pleads guilty, the final step in the courtroom is sentencing. Sentencing is deciding how the defendant will be punished.

The law generally sets the maximum and minimum sentences for each crime. Sometimes the judge has the power to decide the exact sentence within that range. The judge considers the severity of the crime, and the criminal record, age, and attitude of the offender. For example, the judge may give a first-time offender who regrets the crime a lower sentence.

Sometimes, however, a judge must follow sentencing guidelines. These provide a narrower range of sentences, based on the nature of the offense and the defendant's criminal history.

✔ Reading Check **Whom do attorneys for both sides call as witnesses in a trial?**

Correctional Institutions

Having been convicted, Jack now enters the corrections system. He may be sentenced to a community treatment program, a jail, or a prison.

Cities and counties run jails. They hold people waiting for trial. People convicted of misdemeanors may also serve time in a jail. Both state and federal governments run prisons. People convicted of serious crimes, such as murder and robbery, are usually sent to prisons. In prison they are called inmates.

An inmate's time in prison may be lowered for good behavior. Letting an inmate go free to serve the rest of his or her sentence outside of prison is called **parole**. A group called a parole board decides whether to let inmates go before their sentences are over.

In 2001, there were more than 1.4 million state and federal inmates and about 700,000 inmates in local jails. Our society spends a large amount of money running jails and prisons.

✔ Reading Check **Why would the criminal-justice system parole a criminal?**

Addressing the Jury
An attorney tries to convince the jury to believe his argument. The final decision on a defendant's guilt or innocence belongs to the jury, not to the judge.
Draw Inferences *What might happen if an attorney had the facts of a case on his side but was unable to make clear, persuasive arguments?*

Challenges Facing the System

Our criminal justice system is challenged by the number of people it must deal with each year. There were more than 9.1 million arrests in the United States in 1999, and another 9.1 million in 2000. In many courts, there are not enough judges and other court employees to handle all the people waiting for trial

In the last decade, nearly every state has increased the number of youth under 18 who are processed by adult criminal courts rather than by juvenile courts. This growing population of young defendants and prisoners presents unique challenges to the entire criminal justice system. Lawyers, judges, probation officers, and corrections officials are encountering new problems and looking for guidance in how to deal with them.

Prisons are also overcrowded. The number of people in prison nearly doubled between 1990 and 2001. New prison construction has not kept pace with the growing prison population. A 1999 Department of Justice report stated that state prisons housed up to 17 percent more inmates than they were designed to hold. Federal prisons housed 32 percent beyond their capacities.

Parole
A parole board interviews an inmate. Parole boards have the ability to let prisoners go before their sentences are complete.
Make Inferences *What factors do you think would influence a parole board when it makes its decision about a specific inmate?*

✔ **Reading Check** How has the American correctional system kept up with rising prison populations?

Analyze Charts

Populations of State Prisons

Largest Prison Population			
State	**Prison Population**	**% Women**	**% Men**
California	162,317	6.2%	93.8%
Texas	162,003	8.1%	91.9%
Florida	75,210	6.1%	93.9%
New York	67,065	4.5%	95.5%
Michigan	50,591	4.5%	95.5%
Smallest Prison Populations			
New Hampshire	2,451	5.9%	94.1%
Maine	1,900	4.7%	95.3%
Vermont	1,863	7.1%	92.9%
Wyoming	1,737	9.6%	90.4%
North Dakota	1,112	9.3%	90.7%
SOURCE: Bureau of Justice Statistics, 2003			

The chart at left compares the five states with the largest populations of state prison inmates with the five states with the smallest prison populations.

1. **Analyze** How does a state's overall population affect its ranking by size of prison population?

2. **Calculate** What is the average percentage of women in the prison population in these states?

Proposals for Fighting Crime

Because of public pressure, Presidents, governors, and mayors have been giving top priority to fighting crime. These leaders have many ideas about how to solve our crime problem. However, few of them agree. What a person thinks is the best solution to crime often depends on what he or she sees as the major cause of crime.

Preventing Crime Many people think we should work hardest at keeping crimes from taking place at all. There are several ways to help prevent crime, including neighborhood watch programs.

Meanwhile, many people favor broader ways of preventing crime. They want to attack what they see as the root causes of crime: poverty and other social problems.

Being Tougher on Criminals Others believe that the best way to fight crime is to be harder on criminals. Congress and some states have passed laws calling for mandatory sentences—punishments that are set by law and that a judge must give no matter who the defendant is or the reason for the crime. In some states, for example, anyone who uses a gun while carrying out a crime must be sent to prison.

Many people also favor the death penalty, or capital punishment, as a sentence for serious crimes such as murder. The death penalty, however, has many opponents. Some people point out that innocent people have been wrongly convicted of murder. They feel that the possibility that the government might execute an innocent person makes the death penalty unjust. The Supreme Court, however, has upheld state laws allowing the death penalty.

Citizens Get Involved
In neighborhood watch communities, neighborhoods look out for each other's property and report problems quickly to the police. An organization called the Guardian Angels works in many urban areas, keeping a lookout for criminal activity.

Rehabilitation Rehabilitation is the process of trying to teach prisoners how to live useful lives when they get out. Unfortunately, rehabilitation is not working very well. A large number of inmates break laws again after they are released. Many people, however, say that rehabilitation programs can be improved and become an important way of fighting crime.

Some rehabilitation programs go on within prison. Inmates may get counseling that helps them understand and change the way they act. Educational and job-training programs are also a part of prison rehabilitation.

Rehabilitation may continue after the time in prison is over. Some ex-prisoners live in 'halfway houses,' group homes for people who are returning to life outside prison. There they get support and help. They can test new skills in a job that brings in a steady income. Some people believe that skills and job training can reduce the number of former inmates who commit crimes again.

Inmate Job Training
A prison inmate in Ohio trains a puppy to become a guide dog for blind people as part of a rehabilitation program. **Make Inferences** *Why would job training for prison inmates help to fight crime?*

✔ Reading Check **What are the arguments for and against the death penalty?**

SECTION 2 Assessment

Key Terms

Use each of the key terms in a sentence that explains its meaning: probable cause, warrant, bail, indictment, arraignment, plea bargaining, parole

Target Reading Skill

1. **Recognize Words That Signal Sequence** Review the story of Jack Jones' arrest and trial. Point out some signal words and explain what they told you about the order of events.

Comprehension and Critical Thinking

2. **a. Describe** What is a grand jury? In what kinds of cases is one summoned?
   b. Contrast Judges and grand juries can keep a case from going to trial. Why is the grand jury necessary?

3. **a. Recall** Who selects the jurors for a trial?
   b. Draw Inferences Why might someone who has been the victim of a robbery not be seated in a jury in a robbery case?

4. **a. Recall** How are prisons and jails different?
   b. Draw Conclusions Some people advocate putting more criminals into community treatment programs instead of jail. They claim that it makes better economic sense. What might be their reason for believing this?

5. **a. Describe** How did the number of people in prison change during the 1990s?
   b. Synthesize Information Laws imposing tough mandatory sentences on criminals became increasingly popular in the 1980s and 1990s. How

might this have contributed to prison overcrowding?

6. **a. Recall** What are the three major ways of fighting crime?
   b. Make Decisions Which of the three do you think is the most effective? Why?

Writing Activity

Police must repeat the Miranda warning when they arrest someone. Look up the Miranda warning online. Write a brief history of what the Miranda warning is, where it got its name, and why the law requires it.

Go Online PHSchool.com
For: Writing Activity
Visit: PHSchool.com
Web Code: mpd-7203

The Juvenile Justice System

Reading Preview

Objectives

In this section you will

- discuss the history of juvenile courts.
- describe juvenile court procedure.
- consider possibilities for strengthening juvenile justice.

Taking Notes

Make a diagram like the one below. As you read this section, complete the diagram with information about the juvenile court procedure from arrest to sentencing.

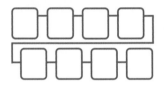

Key Terms

delinquent   status offender

Main Idea

The juvenile justice system was especially designed for troubled youths younger than 18. This system involves a different process and different penalties than the adult criminal justice system.

Target Reading Skill

Recognize Words That Signal Sequence In Section 2 you practiced identifying words that tell you the order in which events occur. Continue looking for signal words as you read this section.

Until the late 1800s, children accused of crimes were treated like adults. They were thrown in jails with hardened criminals and given long prison terms if they were found guilty.

Some people objected to this harsh treatment of young offenders in courts and prisons. They argued that young people need special treatment. About 100 years ago, a group of reformers set out to create a separate justice system for juveniles, or young people.

Juvenile Courts

Juvenile courts are state courts set aside for young people. Their goal is to help juveniles in trouble, not to punish them. The first juvenile court was opened in Illinois in 1899.

Most states say that a juvenile is a person under the age of 18, although a few states set the age at 16 or 17. A youth thought to have broken a criminal law is brought before a juvenile court. A juvenile who is found guilty of a crime is called a **delinquent**.

Children may also have to appear in juvenile court if they are charged with running away, disobedience, or truancy—skipping school without permission. These acts are not crimes. They are against the law only for young people. A youth who is found guilty of one of these acts is called a **status offender**. A status offender is a youth who is judged to be beyond the control of his or her parents or guardian.

✓ Reading Check   **Why was the juvenile court system created?**

Students Make a Difference

Laurel Olsen, a senior at Evergreen Academy in Hackensack, New Jersey, understands that a safe community means keeping the channels of communication open between police departments and the people they serve.

At her town's police department, Laurel participates in an internship program. She is learning how law enforcement works not only to ptotect the law, but also to educate communities on police matters. "On my first day, for example, I was part of a dual-community task force being set up to investigate complaints of domestic violence, as well as informing the public of resources available in those situations."

Service Learning

How can you make a difference with your local police department?

▲ Students can help make a difference by becoming involved with their local police to make their communities safer.

Juvenile Court Procedure

Suppose Jenna Williams, a 16-year-old girl, is arrested for shoplifting makeup. The steps she goes through are different from the ones for an adult charged with the same crime.

Arrest and Intake When Jenna is arrested, the police now have the power to decide what to do with her. They might return her to her parents or give her case to a social service agency, an organization that helps children and families.

In Jenna's case the police do not send her home. Jenna has been charged with shoplifting before, and she has a history of running away from home. For these reasons, the police take her to a county detention home, or juvenile hall.

Next, Jenna goes through an informal court process called 'intake,' to decide if her case should be sent to juvenile court. A social worker asks Jenna questions and looks at her past record and family situation. Almost 25% of all cases are dismissed and the juvenile is sent home or directed to a social service agency. Because of Jenna's past record, however, the social worker sends her case to the next step in juvenile court.

Target Reading Skill

Recognize Words That Signal Sequence The word *procedure* in the heading on this page is a signal word. A procedure is a series of steps that are followed in a given situation. As you read this section, look for the signal words that will help you put the steps in chronological order.

The Initial Hearing At the initial hearing the judge must be convinced that a law was broken and that there is good evidence that the young person was the one who did it. If there is not enough evidence, the juvenile is sent home.

The judge hearing Jenna's case decides that there is probable cause to believe that Jenna stole the makeup. The judge sends Jenna back to juvenile hall.

The Adjudicatory Hearing The third step, the adjudicatory hearing, takes the place of a trial. It is not public, and there is no jury. The young person, however, may have an attorney.

Jenna has an attorney appointed by the court. After the hearing, the judge makes a decision. In this case the judge finds Jenna to be a delinquent.

The Dispositional Hearing At the next step, the dispositional hearing, the judge decides on the sentence. The judge considers the youth's school situation, family, and past behavior.

The judge then decides on a sentence. Should the youth be sent to a state institution for juveniles, placed in a group home or community treatment program, or put on probation? Probation is a kind of sentence in which a person goes free but must be under the supervision of a court official called a probation officer.

Aftercare The purpose of juvenile aftercare is to help young people after they have been released from an institution. Each youth is given a parole officer who can give advice and information about school, jobs, and other needed services.

✓ Reading Check   **What steps does Jenna go through in the juvenile justice system?**

Starting Over
A parole officer helps juvenile offenders find educational and employment help so that they can avoid future trouble with the law.
Contrast *How might the experience of a juvenile offender who has been released from an institution differ from an adult who has been released from prison?*

Strengthening Juvenile Justice
Some people think that the juvenile justice system has been a big disappointment. They see overworked judges who make quick decisions without much knowledge of children or families. Others say that the system is too easy on young criminals. Still other people have argued that juvenile courts should be done away with altogether. It is in the best interests of a young defendant, they say, to go to trial in a criminal court. There the defendant's rights to due process have much stronger protections.

Community-Based Programs There are many successful programs for juvenile offenders. One is the community residential treatment center. Youths live in small group homes instead of being locked up in a large state institution. There, psychologists and social workers help them learn to get along better with other people in their lives and learn to change their behavior. Youths also continue their educations, so that they are better prepared for life on the outside.

Diversion Programs Many programs attempt to nip crime in the bud. They educate youths and show them possibilities other than crime.

Some delinquent youths take part in tough wilderness programs. The idea of these programs is that people's self-esteem grows as they find that they can do difficult tasks. In the wilderness, youths may discover that they have the power within them to change the way they act and to affect the world around them in positive ways.

Keeping Kids from Becoming Criminals A large percentage of adults convicted of crimes were youths when they first got in trouble with the law. Instead of being rehabilitated, they went on to commit more crimes. Therefore, the better our society is at preventing juvenile crime, the fewer adults the criminal justice system will have to deal with.

Community-Based Programs
A juvenile offender in Texas helps to sort relief supplies as part of a probation program.

✓ Reading Check **Describe the flaws people have found in the juvenile justice system.**

SECTION 3 Assessment

Key Terms
Use each of the key terms in a sentence that explains its meaning: delinquent, status offender

Target Reading Skill
1. **Recognize Words That Signal Sequence** Reread the section "Juvenile Court Procedure." List signal words from the section that tell you the order in which the steps of the procedure occur.

Comprehension and Critical Thinking
2. **a. Recall** What offenses would bring a youth before a juvenile court?

   b. Make Generalizations Why is it in the state's interest to make special laws that apply only to young people?

3. **a. Describe** What happens to a juvenile offender after the adjudicatory hearing?

   b. Compare and Contrast How is this like what happens to an adult criminal after trial? How is it similar?

4. **a. Recall** How does the system try to rehabilitate juvenile offenders?

   b. Evaluate Information Do you think the juvenile justice system punishes and helps young offenders adequately? Explain.

Writing Activity
Do you think that the juvenile justice system provides appropriate punishment for today's crimes? Use library or internet sources to find out more about sentences handed down to juvenile offenders. Write a newspaper editorial expressing your views.

TIP You might compare the juvenile-court penalties with the seriousness of the crimes youths commit today. This is a good place to begin an argument for or against reform.

Debating the Issues

CLOSE UP® FOUNDATION

The debates in this feature are based on *Current Issues*, published by the Close Up Foundation. Go to **PHSchool.com**, Web Code mph-7201, to read the latest issue of *Current Issues* online.

Each state court system has its own rules for dealing with juvenile offenders. The maximum age for juveniles differs from state to state. The penalties and punishments for juvenile criminals are less harsh than those for adults. The court system tries to provide mentors, jobs, and other help for youths.

Should the U.S. Court System Try Juveniles as Adults?

YES

- A crime such as murder is no less serious if the person who commits it is under a certain age. Violent young people should be punished in accordance with the seriousness of the crimes they commit.

- The juvenile court system was designed to deal with petty crime. Today, teen offenders commit serious violent crimes. They should be tried by the adult courts, which were designed to deal with those crimes.

- It is more important to protect law-abiding citizens than it is to worry about the rights of lawbreakers. If juvenile offenders are harshly punished, communities will be safer for the innocent.

NO

- Juveniles are too young to understand fully the consequences of their actions. They cannot reason like adults. It is unfair to punish them as adults.

- Putting young people into prison with violent adult criminals would only harm them further. Prisons are dangerous places for the young.

- The adult court and prison systems are already overtaxed. Adding in juvenile offenders would not result in greater justice for anyone. Instead, the government should spend money on education and rehabilitation programs that will help reform young criminals to become good adult citizens.

What is Your Opinion?

1. **Identify Main Ideas** Should the courts take an offender's age into consideration when assessing punishment? Why or why not?

2. **Support a Point of View** Should the government set a nationwide minimum age at which children can be tried as adults? Why or why not?

3. **Writing to Persuade** Nathaniel Abraham was 11 years old on October 29, 1997, when he killed someone. Under a 1997 Michigan law, a child of any age may be tried as an adult for severe crimes. Write an editorial for your school newspaper, arguing that Abraham should or should not have been tried as an adult. Give specific reasons for your position.

Go Online
civics interactive

For: You Decide Poll
Visit: PHSchool.com
Web Code: mpp-7201

20 Review and Assessment

Chapter Summary

Section 1
Crime in American Society
(Pages 536–540)

- Thousands of crimes are committed in the United States each year.

- Serious crimes fall into the following major groups: crimes against people such as assault and battery, crimes against property such as burglary and larceny, white-collar crime such as fraud and embezzlement, "victimless" crimes such as drug use and gambling, and crimes against the government such as treason and terrorism.

- The crime rate is high for many reasons, among which are poverty, underfunded police departments, and drug addiction.

Section 2
The Criminal Justice System
(Pages 542–551)

- Probable cause or a warrant are required to arrest a suspect. When a suspect is arrested, he or she is jailed, and a preliminary hearing is held, at which time bail may be set. An arraignment may also take place before trial.

- A trial may never happen if the suspect engages in plea bargaining. If a trial does take place, it will happen before a jury selected by the attorneys for both sides of the case.

- Those convicted of crimes may enter community treatment programs, jails, or prisons.

- The criminal justice system is challenged by a lack of judges and of adequate space for prisoners. It cannot parole prisoners fast enough to make room for the incoming population.

- The three main solutions to the problem of crime are prevention, tougher sentencing, and rehabilitation.

Section 3
The Juvenile Justice System
(Pages 552–555)

- The juvenile justice system classifies young people convicted of crimes as either delinquents or status offenders.

- If someone 18 or under is arrested, he or she is detained in juvenile hall, interviewed by a social worker, given an initial hearing, given an adjudicatory hearing, and if found guilty, sentenced.

- Instead of going to prison, many juvenile offenders are sentenced to community service or diversion programs.

Copy the chart below and use it to help you summarize the chapter.

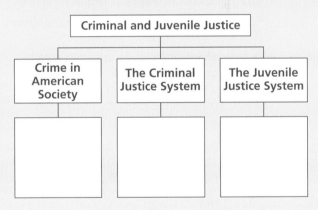

Review and Assessment Continued

Go Online
PHSchool.com
For: Self-Test
Visit: PHSchool.com
Web Code: mpa-7204

Reviewing Key Terms

Fill in the blank with the term that makes each sentence correct.

1. A youth judged to be beyond his or her parents' or guardians' control is called a(n) _____.

2. The person who broke into Kate's house and stole her computer committed _____.

3. _____ is a white-collar crime that involves stealing funds with which your company has entrusted you.

4. If the judge thinks a defendant will not come back for trial, he or she may refuse to set _____.

5. In order to arrest a suspect or search his or her property, the police must apply to a judge for a(n) _____.

6. A criminal may be allowed out of prison on _____ if he or she has behaved well and seems unlikely to commit another crime.

7. Confessing guilt in exchange for a lesser jail sentence is an example of _____.

8. A person who harms another with a weapon commits the crime of _____.

9. A(n) _____ is a formal charge that a person has committed a crime.

10. A(n) _____ is the hearing in which that formal charge is made.

Comprehension and Critical Thinking

11. a. **Recall** What are the broad, general causes of crime?
    b. **Determine Relevance** Choose one of the causes you listed and explain its relationship to the crime rate.
    c. **Identify Effects** Explain how crime itself can be the cause of further crime. Give specific examples.

12. a. **Explain** How do people try to prevent crimes from occurring?
    b. **Demonstrate Reasoned Judgment** Do you think these methods are effective? Why or why not?

    c. **Identify Alternatives** What do you think is the most effective way to prevent crime? Explain.

13. a. **Describe** What kind of sentence is a juvenile offender likely to get?
    b. **Contrast** How is this different from the kind of sentence an adult criminal might get?
    c. **Support a Point of View** What kinds of sentences do you think are reasonable and constructive for juvenile offenders? Explain.

Activities

14. **Skills** Read the passage to the right and answer the questions. **a.** What is the main idea of the passage? **b.** Can you detect any bias? Explain.

15. **Writing** Go online to read about the October 2002 sniper killings in the Washington, D.C. area. Compare and contrast how the criminal justice system handled the two defendants. Do you think the youth should have been tried as an adult? Explain.

> We must do something about reducing or getting rid of mandatory minimum prison sentences for first time offenders of minor, non-violent crimes. It is simply ridiculous. This would definitely help reduce prison overcrowding and the cost to taxpayers.

16. **Active Citizen** Work with classmates to design a program to prevent crime in your neighborhood. Present your ideas to the class for discussion.

17. **Math Practice** Suppose you want to go to law school. Choose a school and find out what its tuition charges are. Assume that you can pay for half the tuition and have to borrow the rest. How much debt will you have when you graduate?

18. **Civics and Economics** Some law schools help graduates repay their student loans if they take relatively low-paying jobs in the public sector. What long-term impact should this policy have on the U.S. economy? Explain.

19. **Analyzing Visuals** How does this photo illustrate a problem facing the American criminal justice system? Suggest a way that problem can be solved and why you think it is a good solution.

Standardized Test Prep

Test-Taking Tips

Standardized tests often ask you to answer questions about what you have read. Read the paragraph and answer the questions that follow.

TIP When all the answer choices are accurate statements, check the question again to see which one it indicates.

Since 1920, the term *white-collar* has been used to describe those who work at desks, because they dressed formally in white shirts and ties. Even though today's dress standards are more casual, people still refer to office workers as white-collar workers. *Blue-collar* describes the soft blue work shirts once worn by manual laborers; this term has been in use since 1946. During the 1970s, some people used the term *pink-collar* to describe jobs traditionally taken by women, such as nurse and switchboard operator. That term has since fallen out of favor.

Choose the letter of the best answer.

1. Why did the term *white-collar* come into use?
   A All workers wore white collars during the 1920s.
   B Office workers wore white collars during the 1920s.
   C Nursing was a job traditionally done by women in the 1920s.
   D People began using the term *blue-collar* during the 1940s.

   The correct answer is **B.** All four statements are true, but only choice B relates to the question asked.

2. Why did blue-collar workers avoid wearing white shirts?
   A Dress standards have become more casual.
   B Manual laborers are male and men always wear blue.
   C White shirts get dirty too easily.
   D Only office workers are allowed to wear white.

21

Civil Justice

What's Ahead in Chapter 21

In this chapter you will read about how the civil justice system works to solve conflicts between parties in a peaceful, lawful way.

SECTION 1
The Role of Civil Law

SECTION 2
Civil Procedure

SECTION 3
Choices in Civil Justice

TARGET READING SKILL

In this chapter you will focus on the skill of identifying cause and effect. Understanding causes and effects can help you understand the relationships among situations or events. This skill includes recognizing multiple causes and understanding effects.

Court case in progress ▶

The following National Standards for Civics and Government are covered in this chapter:

I. What are civic life, poli-tics, and government?

B. What are the essential characteristics of limited and unlimited government?

III. How does the government established by the Constitu-tion embody the purposes, values, and principles of American democracy?

E. What is the place of law in the American constitu-tional system?

Go Online
PHSchool.com

For: Your state's standards
Visit: PHSchool.com
Web Code: mpe-7211

Active Citizen — Civics in the Real World

It never fails to bring kids running: the music of an ice cream truck in a suburban neighborhood on a hot summer day, Kids being kids, the excitement sometimes results in more than a nice cold ice cream pop.

A few years ago, in Ohio a five-year old boy named Tommy came running for the ice cream truck with his money in his hand. He raced into the street without looking both ways and was hit by an oncoming car.

Tommy was taken to the hospital with serious injuries. Tommy's parents first concern was for his health. But they also began to think about who was responsible for Tommy's injuries and who should pay. According to Tommy's parents, both the driver of the car that struck him and the ice cream truck driver were responsible. The driver of the car had hit Tommy. And the ice cream truck was parked in a dangerous location that caused the accident.

Neither driver accepted reasonability for the accident. Both claimed Tommy had run out into the street without warning and had not crossed in the crosswalk. When neither driver would accept responsibility, Tommy's parents feared they would have to go to court.

Citizen's Journal Suppose you were on the jury of the case in which Tommy's parents are suing both drivers. Who do you think was responsible? Who should pay? Was it just a tragic accident, with neither driver to blame? Write a brief paragraph in which you outline your view of the case.

The Role of Civil Law

Reading Preview

Objectives

In this section you will

- Learn about the principles of civil law.
- Discuss some types of civil cases.
- Explore the wide range of civil cases.

Taking Notes

Make a diagram like the one below. As you read this section, complete the diagram with information about civil law cases.

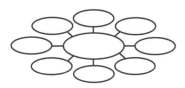

Key Terms

lawsuits	equity
compensation	injunction
damages	contracts

Main Idea

The purpose of civil law is to solve dispute between people or organizations. There are many different types of civil cases including personal injury, property, domestic relations, probate, and housing cases.

Target Reading Skill

Recognizing Multiple Causes A cause makes something happen. Sometimes events can have more than one cause.

Our civil justice system helps people settle conflicts according to the rules of civil law. In a typical year, Americans file more than a million **lawsuits,** or cases in which a court is asked to settle a dispute. Some people who file lawsuits believe that someone has injured them physically. Others believe that someone owes them money. Some think that their rights have been violated.

People who file lawsuits usually have two things in common. They believe that they have been harmed. And they want the courts to do something about it. Our civil justice system is based on the idea of responsibility. Civil trials are one way to make people take responsibility for the harm they have caused others.

A civil case, like a criminal case, always has a plaintiff and a defendant. In a criminal case, the plaintiff is always the government. The defendant is the person or persons accused of a crime. In a civil case, the plaintiff is usually an individual. The defendant may be an individual, a group, a business, or even a government body. For instance, a person may sue the maker of a product that does not work.

Principles of Civil Law

Civil law has different purposes than criminal law. Criminal law protects society by punishing people who break the law. The main purpose of civil law is to settle disagreements fairly. Civil courts depend on two main principles for settling conflicts: the principle of compensation and the principle of equity.

Compensation Under civil law a person has a right to **compensation**, or being "made whole" for harm caused by another person's acts. Suppose someone damages your bicycle, and you have to pay $45 to get it repaired. The person refuses to pay you back, so you decide to take him or her to court. The judge rules that the person must give you $45. This money is not a fine because it is not meant to be a punishment. Instead it is called **damages**, money that is paid in an effort to make up for a loss.

Sometimes the payment of damages completely makes up for a loss. For instance, if you get the $45 you paid to repair your bike, you are where you were before the bike was damaged.

In many cases, though, the payment of damages cannot completely make up for the harm done. An example would be money a court gives to a person left paralyzed by an auto accident. The money will not make the person able to walk again. Instead, it is an effort to soften the effects of the injury.

Equity Not every problem can be settled by the payment of money. Sometimes courts rely on **equity**, the use of general rules of fairness to settle conflicts. Suppose that potentially harmful fumes are coming from a nearby factory. Forcing the factory owners to pay money to everyone in town will not stop the terrible smell. The dispute between the owners and the community has to be settled in a different way.

Under the rules of equity, a court may issue an **injunction**, an order to do or not do a certain act. For instance, a court could order the factory to keep the harmful fumes from escaping. Unlike damages, which make up for past injuries, an injunction prevents future harm.

✓ Reading Check **What is the main purpose of civil law?**

Damages
If the drivers of these two cars cannot agree on who should pay for the damage caused to their vehicles, a civil suit may be necessary.
Draw Inferences *Why would the police need to examine the accident scene if no crime had been committed?*

Some Types of Civil Cases

Many civil cases are personal injury cases. Personal injury cases can involve both physical and mental suffering. In some cases, such as those involving plane crashes, survivors may seek compensation for emotional stress. Also, relatives of a person killed in an accident may receive payments for mental suffering if the death was caused by someone else's carelessness.

In addition to personal injury cases, there are many other types of civil cases. These include property cases, consumer cases, housing cases, domestic relations cases, and probate cases.

Property Cases People often want payment for damage to their property. A car owner might sue a repair shop if the car comes back with a new dent. A homeowner might sue a neighbor whose tree fell over and damaged the homeowner's roof.

Before going to court, a person should carefully consider whether it is fair to blame someone else for the damage. If the case comes to trial, the plaintiff must prove that the defendant did the damage either on purpose or out of carelessness.

Another common type of property case involves charges of trespassing. In many trespassing cases, a plaintiff is trying to prove that the defendant knowingly and wrongfully crossed over his or her land. Property owners do have rights, of course, and signs saying "Private Property—Keep Out" are quite common. However, laws also protect people who have good reasons for crossing someone's property. For example, the person who reads your gas meter is not trespassing.

Property cases may be settled through compensation or through equity. Payment of money, for instance, may make up for damage to a person's roof. However, courts usually settle trespassing cases through equity. A court may issue an injunction ordering a defendant to stay off the plaintiff's land in the future.

Asserting Your Rights
Property owners place "No Trespassing" signs on the edges of their lands to prevent people from entering their property.
Make Predictions *Why would exceptions from trespassing lawsuits be made for some people?*

In this cartoon, a group of people listen to a deceased family member's will. A will is a document describing what to do with a dead person's property.

1. What seems to be the general reaction of the people listening to the will?

2. Who do you think the wife is in the cartoon? Explain.

3. Why do you think the man left his wife's couch to his cat?

"...AND TO MY CAT, WILHELM, I LEAVE MY WIFES BEST COUCH!"

Consumer Cases "This computer you sold me broke down just one week after I took it home," declared Sharon. "I want my money back."

What happens if a product does not work as it was supposed to? What can consumers do if they are misled by an advertisement or by a salesperson? What guarantees must come with products you buy?

These questions and many others related to consumers' rights are covered in a collection of laws called the Uniform Commercial Code, which was created in 1940. These laws were put together to help clean up legal issues concerning interstate commerce. It took over ten years to draft the Uniform Commercial Code and another fourteen years to get the laws into place across the country.

Many of the laws that make up the Uniform Commercial Code set basic rules for **contracts**, legal agreements between buyers and sellers. The buyer promises to pay for a product or service, and the seller agrees that it will meet certain standards. Conflicts arise when either a buyer or a seller says that the other has not lived up to the contract.

In Sharon's situation, for instance, if the computer store does not settle the problem, she may decide to sue the store. If the court finds that Sharon is not to blame, it may order the store to repair or replace the computer for free. In this way, the law protects Sharon's rights as a consumer.

Landlord-Tenant Disputes
A woman cleans up the mess after a flood in her home (above). In such cases, a tenant may demand that her landlord pay for the damage to her possessions—a dispute that may have to be resolved in housing court (right).
Draw Inferences *Why might a landlord be responsible for water damage to a tenant's property?*

Housing Cases Suppose that you live in an apartment building where the landlord refuses to repair some broken stairs. Do you have a legal right to do something about it?

Housing cases involve relationships between landlords and tenants. When you rent an apartment or a house, you usually sign a lease, an agreement stating the rights and responsibilities of the landlord and the tenant. In a lease, the tenant agrees to pay rent every month. The landlord agrees to keep the rental unit safe and in good repair.

Under civil law, a tenant and a landlord may take certain steps if either one believes that the other has not lived up to the lease. In some situations tenants can pay for needed repairs and take the cost out of the rent. If apartment conditions are allowed to become unlivable, tenants have the right to end their leases and move out without paying rent.

On the other hand, landlords who meet their responsibilities can force tenants to leave for not paying rent or violating other terms of the lease. In cases of housing law, the courts must consider the rights and responsibilities of both landlords and tenants.

Domestic Relations Cases Cases that concern family relationships are called domestic relations cases. Most domestic relations cases relate to divorce. The problems in divorce cases are often complicated and emotional. How will the couple divide up their property? Who will have custody of the children? Who will support them? In a divorce case, there are seldom easy answers.

Probate Cases Disagreements can also arise over how to divide up the property of a friend or relative who has died. Such cases are called probate cases.

Sometimes there is no will, a document that tells what is to be done with the dead person's property. Usually, however, probate cases involve questions about whether the will can be trusted. Is the signature real? Was the person who made the will unfairly influenced or not thinking clearly? In probate cases, it may take years for the court to decide how to divide the property.

✓ Reading Check   **What type of civil case would involve dividing the property of someone who died?**

Target Reading Skill
Recognizing Multiple Causes What are some reasons for bringing a probate case to court?

The Wide Range of Civil Cases

Civil courts can find ways to settle any type of disagreement. In some cases, such as property damage, the courts use compensation. Others, such as probate cases, are usually settled through equity. Sometimes courts use a combination of compensation and equity. For instance, a person who dumps trash on your land may have to pay you back for the cost of removing it. In addition, the court may issue an injunction ordering the person never to dump trash there again.

Regardless of how civil cases are settled, they all have something in common. Their goal is to make a fair settlement and to place the responsibility where it belongs.

✓ Reading Check   **What is the goal of the settlement of all civil law cases?**

SECTION 1   **Assessment**

Key Terms

Use the following key term in a sentence that explains its meaning: lawsuits, compensation, damages, equity, injunction, contracts

Target Reading Skill

1. **Recognize Multiple Causes** What are some of the causes of civil lawsuits?

Comprehension and Critical Thinking

2. **a. Recall** What type of case would child custody come under?
   b. Contrast How is compensation different from equity?

3. **a. Explain** What is the Uniform Commercial Code? What types of cases use the Uniform Commercial Code as a guideline?
   b. Draw Inferences Why do you think probate cases can take so long to settle?

4. **a. Recall** Civil cases can involve what area of people's lives?
   b. Draw Conclusions How does civil law protect a part of the freedoms we enjoy? Explain your answer.

Writing Activity

Find a newspaper article about a civil suit. Write a brief summary of the case. Make sure you identify the main issues of the case and who is suing whom.

TIP When reading your newspaper article, look for topic sentences that give you the main idea. Also look for names that will identify the parties in the case.

How to Analyze a News Article

Newspapers are a very important source of news. They often include statistics or other facts, as well as quotes from public officials.

Unlike newspaper editorials, which express opinions, news articles report the facts of a story. Reporters strive to write their articles without bias—they try to report all sides of an issue fairly. As you read the following newspaper article, look carefully to see how objective it is.

By Jonathan Thomas
Towne Crier News Staff Writer

WASHINGTON, D.C., March 4—Andrew Jackson walked up to the Capitol building in Washington, D.C., today to take the oath of office and deliver his inaugural address. The new President mounted a horse and rode to the White House for a reception.

Normally such events are closed to the public. However, the new President wanted no one turned away, and in their excitement, the mob overturned furniture, knocked down waiters, and spilled food and drinks on the rugs and fine furniture. At one point, Mr. Jackson was pinned against the wall, and it was necessary for a number of men to make a barrier around him with their bodies.

Quick-thinking servants set out bowls of punch on the White House lawn. As the crowd of supporters rushed out of the White House to drink their fill, our President of the People made his escape through a window. He spent the first night of his presidency at a nearby hotel.

This party gives us a clue as to the kind of man we have elected President. "King Mob" now rules our fine nation.

Learn the Skill

To analyze a news article, follow these steps:

1 Determine what the article is about. Every news article should answer the questions of who, what, where, when, and why.

2 Define the main idea of the story.

3 Find facts that support the main idea.

4 Look for the author's opinion. Does the author remain objective?

Practice the Skill

1 Summarize the article above.

2 List three details the writer uses to support the main idea.

3 How does the writer feel about President Jackson? How can you tell?

Apply the Skill

1 Collect three newspaper articles about the same topic.

2 Find the main idea of each article.

3 Look for hints of the authors' opinions.

4 Compare and contrast how the three articles approach the topic.

Go Online
civics interactive

For: Local Citizenship
Visit: PHSchool.com
Web Code: mpp-7211

Civil Procedure

Reading Preview

Objectives
In this section you will
- Learn about preparing for a civil trial.
- Discuss juries and verdicts in civil trials.
- Understand problems in the civil courts.
- Appreciate the need for alternatives.

Key Terms
complaint   discovery
answer   subpoena
summons   deposition

Main Idea
Civil procedure includes a process of filing papers and obtaining evidence. A judge decides most civil trials. Juries generally only decide compensation cases. Civil trials are expensive and time-consuming, and many cases are settled before coming to trial.

Target Reading Skill
Understand Effects A cause makes something happen. An effect is what happens as a result of the cause.

Taking Notes
Make a diagram like the one below. As you read this section, complete the diagram with information about the sequence of events in a civil lawsuit.

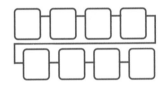

Civil procedure is the process used to take a case through the civil justice system. The federal and state courts have rules about how a disagreement must be brought to trial. The purpose of these rules is to settle disputes in a fair and orderly way.

Preparing for a Civil Trial

Think back to the accident described at the beginning of this chapter. Tommy's parents thought that one or both of the drivers were responsible. The parents hired a lawyer. The lawyer tried to get either of the two drivers to pay the medical bills. When that failed, she advised the parents to go to court.

Court Filings A civil lawsuit begins with a **complaint**, a legal document that charges someone with having caused harm. The complaint is filed with a court. It describes the problem and suggests a possible solution—damages, equity, or both. By filing a complaint against each driver, Tommy and his parents became the plaintiffs.

The defendant's written response to a complaint is called an **answer**. In the answer the defendant will either admit or deny responsibility. For example, the driver whose car hit Tommy may blame Tommy for not using the crosswalk and the ice cream truck driver for parking in a dangerous place. The driver of the ice cream truck, meanwhile, may blame both Tommy and the driver of the car.

Serving a Summons
When a civil complaint is filed against someone, the defendant is informed by being given a summons.

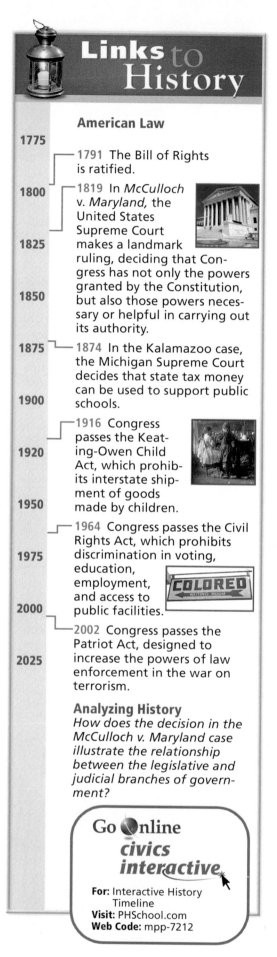
American Law

1775

— 1791 The Bill of Rights is ratified.

1800

— 1819 In *McCulloch v. Maryland,* the United States Supreme Court makes a landmark ruling, deciding that Congress has not only the powers granted by the Constitution, but also those powers necessary or helpful in carrying out its authority.

1825

1850

1875 — 1874 In the Kalamazoo case, the Michigan Supreme Court decides that state tax money can be used to support public schools.

1900

— 1916 Congress passes the Keating-Owen Child Act, which prohibits interstate shipment of goods made by children.

1920

1950

— 1964 Congress passes the Civil Rights Act, which prohibits discrimination in voting, education, employment, and access to public facilities.

1975

2000

— 2002 Congress passes the Patriot Act, designed to increase the powers of law enforcement in the war on terrorism.

2025

Analyzing History
How does the decision in the McCulloch v. Maryland case illustrate the relationship between the legislative and judicial branches of government?

Go Online
civics
interactive

For: Interactive History Timeline
Visit: PHSchool.com
Web Code: mpp-7212

The defendant learns about the civil lawsuit when he or she receives a copy of the complaint and a **summons,** an order to appear in court. The summons is usually delivered by a court employee through certified mail. Next, the defendant is permitted to tell the court his or her side of the story.

Obtaining Evidence The next step is for the parties—the two sides in the lawsuit—to gather evidence. Each party has a right to know any information relevant to the trial, including information held by the other party. The process of gathering evidence before a trial is known as **discovery.**

The purpose of discovery is to make sure that the plaintiff, defendant, and lawyers know of any evidence that might be presented at the trial. Unlike movie or television courtroom dramas, there are no "surprise witnesses" in a real civil or criminal trial.

One method of discovery is a **subpoena (suh PEE nuh),** a court order to produce a witness or document. Suppose a plaintiff was injured when her car's brakes failed. She might ask for a subpoena ordering the carmaker to provide written records of factory brake tests.

Information may also be gathered by asking questions. The record of answers to questions asked of a witness before a trial is called a **deposition (dep uh ZISH uhn).** A court reporter is present at the interview and writes down what the witness says. Lawyers use depositions to find out what witnesses will say in court. The lawyer representing Tommy and his parents, for instance, might get depositions from both drivers and from neighbors who saw the accident.

Questions can also be mailed to a person, who must then answer them in writing. Written questions are often used to get detailed or technical information concerning the case. Both depositions and written answers must be truthful. They are given under oath, just like testimony during the trial itself.

✔ Reading Check   **What is civil procedure?**

Juries and Verdicts in Civil Trials

Once the evidence has been gathered, the parties are ready for the trial to begin. As in criminal trials, witnesses are questioned, evidence is presented, and a judge makes sure that the trial proceeds in an orderly manner. However, there are some important differences between criminal and civil trials.

First of all, there is usually more at risk in a criminal trial. Someone convicted of a crime can be sentenced to jail or prison and may even be sentenced to death. Therefore, the defendant has the right to a jury. The verdict must be based on the unanimous vote of a group of citizens.

Parties in a civil case run less risk. They do not always have the right to a jury. Under the Constitution, federal courts must allow juries in civil cases that involve more than $20. However, most civil cases are heard in state and local courts, where the minimum amount is usually over $2,000. Juries are used mostly for compensation cases. They are rarely used in equity cases. In most civil trials, both parties may agree to have a judge decide the case without a jury.

A jury in a civil trial is often made up of twelve people. In some states, though, there can be as few as six jurors, if both parties agree. The jury does not always have to reach a unanimous decision. Agreement by three-fourths of the jury is enough for a verdict in some states.

The Burden of Proof Verdicts in civil cases are based on a less difficult burden of proof than in criminal cases. In a criminal case, the government must prove the defendant's guilt "beyond a reasonable doubt." In civil cases, the plaintiff must prove the case only "with a preponderance [greater weight] of the evidence." This means that the courts decide which side has presented the more convincing and reasonable evidence.

✓ Reading Check **In state and local courts, what is the minimum amount for a jury trial?**

Civil Juries
Many states do not require unanimous jury verdicts in civil cases.
Make Generalizations *Why do you think a state would decide that a three-fourths agreement by a jury is enough to make a decision in a civil case?*

Civil Cases in U.S. District Courts, 1988–2002

Of all the civil cases begun each year, very few of them are actually seen by a jury, or even decided by a judge. Most of them end before a trial can take place.

1. **Analyze** What has been the general trend of the number of cases going to trial each year?
2. **Apply** Why do you think an increasing number of plaintiffs would decide to settle their cases before going to trial?

Year	Cases Begun	Non-Jury Trials	Jury Trials
1988	239,000	5,422	4,329
1989	233,500	5,128	4,010
1990	217,900	4,772	3,829
1991	207,700	4,390	3,579
1992	226,900	4,378	3,410
1993	226,165	4,245	3,322
1994	236,391	4,380	2,987
1995	248,335	4,249	2,801
1996	269,132	4,401	2,646
1997	272,027	4,491	2,380
1998	256,787	4,125	2,148
1999	260,271	4,737	3,795
2000	259,517	4,529	3,404
2001	250,907	3,533	2,980
2002	274,841	3,365	2,650

SOURCE: Judicial Business of the United States, 2003

Target Reading Skill

Understand Effects Thousands of civil suits are filed every year. What does this passage say is the effect of these suits?

Problems in the Civil Courts

Tommy and his parents were happy when their trial was over. The jury decided that the ice cream truck driver was at fault because his truck had blocked the view of oncoming traffic. The jury awarded the family enough money to pay Tommy's medical bills. Still, the process had taken two years and had been expensive.

Court Delays Lawsuits often take a long time to settle. There are not enough judges to handle the growing number of cases being filed. Between 1960 and 2002, federal district courts had nearly a 400 percent increase in cases. More than 400 new judgeships were created during that time, but the courts have not been able to keep up with their workload. Someone filing a lawsuit may wait weeks or months before a judge has time to hear the case.

Once the trial starts, it can take a while to settle. The average federal lawsuit takes less than a year. However, as of 2002 there were a little over 34,000 federal cases that were three or more years old. Delays in state courts are sometimes much longer.

One cause of delay is the time it takes to gather evidence. Also, selecting a jury can take a long time. In addition, court rules make it possible for lawyers to delay trials in ways that will help their side.

High Costs Trials are often expensive. For many civil trials, people need the help of lawyers who understand the law and know how to prepare cases. Lawyers' fees make up much of the cost of most civil cases.

In some cases, the lawyers are paid by the hour. The fees add up when there is a great deal of evidence to gather and study, and many hours to spend in court. In personal injury cases, the lawyer's fee is often a large percentage of the money awarded by the judge or jury. Other costs include filing fees for court papers and payments for expert witnesses, such as doctors. There is also the cost in time and inconvenience to the parties themselves.

The Need for Alternatives Most lawsuits never make it to trial. Plaintiffs often drop cases if they think they have little chance of winning. Sometimes the high cost of a trial will cause parties to settle out of court.

The judge and lawyers involved in a case may strongly encourage the parties to find other ways of settling the conflict. In some states, courts will not even hear certain types of cases, such as those involving child custody, unless the parties have already tried to settle the conflict out of court.

In recent years, more and more people have been looking for ways of settling conflicts more quickly and cheaply. In the next section, you will explore some of the methods they have used.

✓ Reading Check **Why do plaintiffs drop cases before trial?**

Expert Witnesses
Expert witnesses give testimony about specialized fields, such as medicine or engineering. They are paid for their time spent reviewing the details of a case. They are also paid for the time they spend testifying before the courts.

SECTION 2 Assessment

Key Terms

Use each of the key terms in a sentence that explains its meaning: complaint, answer, summons, discovery, subpoena, deposition

Target Reading Skill

1. **Understanding Effects**
   What are the possible financial effects of filing a civil lawsuit?

Comprehension and Critical Thinking

2. **a. Recall** What begins a civil lawsuit?
   b. Draw Conclusions Why are there no surprise witnesses in a civil trial?

3. **a. Describe** What kinds of civil cases are usually decided by juries?
   b. Contrast How is the burden of proof different in a civil trial than in a criminal trial?

4. **a. Describe** How do the costs of a trial effect whether a case goes to trial?
   b. Draw Inferences Why do you think some judges will not hear child custody cases unless the parties have tried to settle out of court first?

Writing Activity

Recall an argument you had with a friend or family member that you resolved satisfactorily. Write a short summary of what caused the argument, and the process you used to settle it.

TIP In recounting the argument and settlement, identify each cause and effect in the process in a bulleted list. Use each bullet point as the starting point for a paragraph.

Choices in Civil Justice

Objectives

In this section you will

- Discuss avoiding civil trials.
- Learn about cutting the cost of civil trials.
- Understand the debate over large awards.
- Appreciate the decision to sue or not to sue.

Taking Notes

Make a diagram like the one below. As you read this section, complete the diagram with information about the civil justice system.

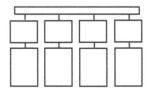

Key Terms

mediation   small claims
arbitration   court

Main Idea

There are many alternatives to going to trial including using a mediator, arbitrator, private judge, or referee. Small claims court and other institutions help cut the cost of civil trials.

Target Reading Skill

Identify Cause and Effect Determining causes and effects can help you understand the relationship between two events or situations.

Many people go to court without being aware of the time and cost involved in a civil trial. Often they do not know about other ways to settle conflicts peacefully. There are several methods of settling disagreements without a civil trial. Even when people do have to go to court, they can find ways to save time and money.

Avoiding Civil Trials

There are a number of ways to keep from going to trial. One possibility, of course, is for the people to discuss the problem themselves and come to an agreement. If they cannot reach an agreement, they can bring in a third person to help them settle the conflict. There are three main methods for doing this: mediation, arbitration, and "rent-a-judge" programs.

Making the Call
One alternative to bringing a case to trial is to get a referee—a third party who will make a recommendation to the judge.
Summarize *Why would the parties in a civil case wish to avoid going to trial?*

Students Make a Difference

Melinda Sebastian, a sophomore at Tappan Zee High School in Orangeburg, New York, believes that the best way to learn about the court system is to participate in Youth Court.

In the town of South Orangetown, New York, the Youth Court deals with teens that commit crimes. The Youth Court hopes to help troubled teens change their behavior by trying the crime before a court of the teens' peers. Melinda's roles change with every arraignment. She has been a judge, defense attorney, prosecutor, bailiff, and clerk.

▲ Students can help make a difference by learning more about our legal system.

Service Learning

How can you make a difference for troubled teenagers in your community?

Mediation Major league baseball players went on strike in 1994. After months of negotiations, players and team owners finally came to an agreement with the help of mediation.

Mediation is a process by which people agree to use a third party to help them settle a conflict. The third party, called a mediator, does not make a decision. Instead, mediation is a way to bring people together so that they can settle their own disagreement. The mediator listens to both sides and helps them reach a compromise.

In many states there are programs that train people to be mediators. Many mediation programs are sponsored by city or county courts, while others are run as private businesses. Mediation programs handle a variety of problems, including child custody, housing, and consumer problems.

Mediation can also be used to settle conflicts between students. Schools in many states have successful mediation programs. Students in elementary schools as well as in junior and senior high schools act as official "conflict managers," helping their fellow students end disputes.

For mediation to work, both sides must be willing to compromise. No one is legally required to obey an agreement reached by mediation.

Arbitration People who want a conflict settled "once and for all" often turn to **arbitration**, the use of a third person to make a legal decision that is binding on all parties. The arbitrator listens to both sides and makes a decision that each party is required by law to obey.

Arbitration almost always costs less than a civil trial. It is considerably faster to use arbitration rather than go to trail. The arbitrator is usually an expert on the subject in dispute. Therefore, it takes less time to settle a case.

Arbitration has become so successful that today the federal government and more than 40 states have laws requiring that arbitrators' decisions be obeyed. Many courts will make arrangements for people to use arbitration. In certain conflicts involving public employees, such as firefighters or police officers, federal and state laws actually require arbitration.

Analyze Diagrams

Alternatives to a Civil Trial

Because civil trials can involve a great deal of time and money, a number of alternatives have developed to settle disputes and disagreements between people.

a. How do mediation and arbitration differ?

b. Which of these alternatives do you think is less expensive than going to trial? Which do you think are quicker than going to trial? Explain your answers.

Mediation

In mediation, an impartial third party works with both sides to help them reach an agreement. The agreement, however, is not legally binding.

Arbitration

In arbitration, a third party listens to both sides. The arbitrator then makes a decision, which is legally binding.

Private Judges

People can hire a private judge to listen to both sides and decide their case.

Private Judges People can settle conflicts through private judges. Using this method, the two sides hire a person to hear and decide their case. This process is sometimes called "rent-a-judge."

Referees Another alternative is using a referee. A judge can appoint a referee, who is usually a lawyer. In some places, when two sides agree to the use of a referee, they give up their right to a jury trial. In the end, though, a judge makes the final decision in the case.

Mock Trials Even after both sides in a conflict have filed court papers, they may change their minds and decide not to go to trial. In some cases this change of mind comes as a result of a "mock trial," a preview of how the case would probably be settled if a trial were held.

A mock trial has been described as a "trial on fast-forward" because there are no witnesses, and no evidence is presented. Instead, the lawyers for each side summarize their case before a jury, which then gives an unofficial verdict. Both sides get a good idea of what the result would be if a real trial were held. They are often able to reach a compromise without having to spend months in court.

✔ Reading Check   **What do mediators do?**

Target Reading Skill
Identify Cause and Effect
How does the availability of mediation, arbitration and other alternatives help reduce the number of civil cases?

Referees

A referee is a third party appointed by a judge to listen to both sides of the case. The referee advises the judge, who makes the final decision.

Go Online
civics interactive

For: Interactive Alternatives to Trial
Visit: PHSchool.com
Web Code: mpp-7213

Mock Trials

A mock trial allows both sides to see what the outcome of a trial might be. This way, they can decide whether to go to court or to settle out of court.

Civics and Economics

Asbestos was an important building material because it was fireproof. Its use was popularized in World War II shipbuilding and then in the vast housing and building boom that followed the war. In the 1970s people who had worked with asbestos began coming down with cancer and respiratory diseases. Legal research found that the principal manufacturer of asbestos had known about the dangerous qualities of the material and suppressed that information. Lawsuits followed with thousands of workers filing claims each year as they came down with the disease. The manufacturer went bankrupt due to the claims. The federal government stepped in to create a fund to compensate stricken workers and their families.

Analyzing Economics
Why do you think the manufacturer suppressed information about the health consequences of asbestos?

Going to Trial
Sometimes a case is best served by going to trial, despite the time and expense it may require.
Summarize *Why would one or both sides in a case desire to bring the case to trial instead of choosing a speedier, cheaper option?*

Cutting the Cost of Trials

Although conflicts can often be settled out of court, there are still good reasons for having civil trials. Sometimes one or both sides are unwilling to compromise or to accept an arbitrator or referee. Perhaps they want to make sure that the verdict or settlement can be legally enforced in any state. Often a plaintiff thinks that he or she can get a better settlement by going to trial. In such situations, a civil trial may be the only solution. A trial, however, does not always have to involve a lot of time and money. There are ways to cut the cost of a trial.

Small Claims Court When people have a conflict over a small amount of money, they have a good chance of getting a quick, inexpensive trial if they use a special kind of court. **Small claims court** is a civil court that people use when the amount of money they want to recover is small, usually not more than $3,000.

Some examples of small claims court cases involve breach of contract, property damage, auto accidents, personal injury, and bad debt. You must be 18 years or older to bring an action to small claims court. If you are under the age of 18, your parent or guardian may file a claim on your behalf. Most small claims courts are part of larger city or county courts. They are one answer of how to cut the high cost of taking a case to court.

In small claims court, the whole trial may take less than an hour. The costs are not much more than the filing fee—which is usually less than $100 in most states. Usually there are no lawyers or juries. Instead, both parties tell their stories directly to the judge. Either side can bring witnesses, but there are no formal rules for questioning them. The judge either decides the case on the spot or mails the decision to the parties in a day or two.

Prepaid Legal Plans Even when a dispute involves too much money to qualify for small claims court, the costs of going to trial can still be reduced. One method is prepaid legal plans, which are like insurance policies. For a fixed fee, these plans cover almost all of the costs of going to court, no matter how high.

Storefront Law Offices Another trend in low-cost legal services is the "storefront law office." Storefront law offices provide legal services for low prices. These offices are often located in convenient places such as shopping malls.

Thinking Small
Rather than using a large, traditional law firm, some people choose to obtain legal help through smaller 'storefront' firms with set prices.
Predict *Are storefront firms likely to take on large or complicated cases? Why do you think so?*

LINCOLN-HERNDON LAW OFFICES

Traditional lawyers generally charge their clients by the hour at rates that can range from $100 to $400 per hour or more. Storefront offices usually have a printed "menu" of set prices for specific services, such as preparing legal papers. For example, the cost to prepare a simple will might be $150. Because customers know the total fee for services ahead of time, they can shop around and compare prices before selecting a lawyer.

✓ Reading Check   **Who decides cases in small claims court?**

The Debate over Large Awards

Betty Bullock was a lifelong smoker. After decades of smoking, she developed lung cancer, which spread throughout her body. She sued the company that produced her preferred brand of cigarettes for damages.

Betty's lawyers argued that the company was well aware of the dangers associated with cigarette smoking and had begun concealing this information as far back as the 1950s. They charged that the company did this through a campaign of misinformation, whether through advertising or other means. The lawyers for the company argued that Betty knew of the health risks associated with cigarettes. They argued that she had been repeatedly warned of these risks by her doctor. In 2002, a jury awarded her over $28 billion in damages—the largest verdict ever in an individual product-liability case.

Large awards in civil law suits are the subject of major public debate. Some people argue that such awards are needed to make up for serious losses. They also argue that the largest awards are usually paid by those who can afford to pay them: insurance companies and large businesses.

Other people argue that in the long run, the average American consumer bears the burden of large awards. To cover their costs, businesses raise prices. Insurance companies raise the rates they charge to their customers.

Top Civil Cases Awards in 2002

Awards by juries in civil cases have gotten steadily larger in recent years. This is especially true in cases where a consumer or a group of consumers is suing a corporation. Debate continues over whether or not this increase is good or bad for American consumers.

1. **Analyze** Which of these cases were least likely to have been brought by a consumer or group of consumers?

2. **Apply** How do these large awards affect the American economy?

Award	Type of Case
$28,000,000,000	Fraud, product liability
$2,225,000,000	Personal injury
$520,770,000	Unfair competition
$505,000,000	Breach of contract, unfair competition
$500,200,000	Breach of contract
$276,000,000	Breach of contract, fraud
$270,050,000	Personal injury
$261,700,000	Breach of contract
$225,000,000	Product liability
$185,090,000	Fraud

SOURCE: National Law Journal, 2003

Also, some services are no longer provided because the cost of insurance is too high. For instance, many public swimming pools no longer have diving boards. Some schools do not allow certain "high-risk" sports, such as pole vaulting. Others no longer take students on field trips.

Both sides in the debate think that awards should be fair and reasonable. However, the question of what is fair and reasonable is often hard to answer. As the debate continues, a number of efforts have been made to limit the size of awards.

First of all, judges usually have the power to reduce the amount of an award made by a jury. Mrs. Bullock's award, for instance, was later reduced to about $29 million. Laws have been passed that limit awards in certain types of cases. Under federal law, for example, airlines do not have to pay more than $2,500 per person for lost baggage, no matter how much it was worth. Another federal law limits the amount of damages a person may collect when injured by an accident at a nuclear power plant.

"No-fault" auto insurance plans are another way for companies to avoid large awards. Under these plans, people hurt in auto accidents do not sue the person responsible for their injuries. Instead, their medical bills are paid directly by their own insurance companies. In many cases, this means that the parties do not have to go to court.

✓ Reading Check **What can a judge do about a large award voted by a jury?**

Choosing Not to Sue
Opposing parties meet with an arbitrator, choosing not to take their case to trial.
Draw Inferences *Why would parties choose to use an arbitrator rather than a mediator in a disagreement?*

To Sue or Not to Sue?

As you have seen, the civil justice system is burdened with many cases. Civil trials are often long and costly. People may have to wait months before their trial can start. Once the trial has begun, months or even years may pass before the case is finally settled.

In short, people involved in a conflict should think carefully about what is the best way to settle it. Going to court may be the best solution in some cases. However, many judges and lawyers agree that people should first explore whether other methods might work. In many cases, going to court may be the last, not the first, resort.

✓ **Reading Check** **What is one reason people should try to settle before going to trial?**

SECTION 3 Assessment

Key Terms

Use each of the key terms in a sentence that explains its meaning: mediation, arbitration, small claims court

Target Reading Skill

1. **Identify Cause and Effect** What are two effects of rising damage awards in civil lawsuits?

Comprehension and Critical Thinking

2. **a. Recall** What does a referee do?
   b. Contrast How is arbitration different from mediation?

3. **a. Recall** What is the usual limit for small claims courts?
   b. Evaluate Information What are the advantages and disadvantages of storefront law offices?

4. **a. Describe** How does no-fault auto insurance work?
   b. Analyze How have large jury awards affected public pools and school sports?

5. **a. Recall** Why should people think of going to court to settle a dispute as a last resort?
   b. Make Predictions What kinds of cases do you think would be most difficult to resolve out of court?

Writing Activity

Write an article summarizing recent noteworthy jury awards in civil cases. Be sure to point out why the awards were significant— were they the first to be awarded in such a case? The largest? The smallest?

For: Article
Visit: PHSchool.com
Web Code: mpd-7213

Finding Main Ideas and Supporting Details

When reading information of any kind, it is crucial to identify the main idea, or topic, and the important details that support it. Finding the main idea and supporting details helps you better understand what you are reading in order to think critically about it.

Read the following excerpts from The Declaration of Independence.

> The history of the present King of Great Britain is a history of repeated injuries . . . all having in direct object the establishment of an absolute Tyranny over these States. To prove this, let Facts be submitted to a candid world.
>
> He has refused his Assent to Laws the most wholesome and necessary for the public good.
>
> He has forbidden his Governors to pass Laws of immediate and pressing importance . . .
>
> He has dissolved Representative Houses repeatedly, for opposing . . . his invasions on the rights of people . . .
>
> He has obstructed the Administration of Justice, by refusing his Assent to Laws . . .
>
> He has kept among us in times of peace, Standing Armies, without the Consent of our legislature.

Learn the Skill

Follow these steps to identify the main idea and supporting details:

❶ Find the main idea. What is the passage about? The first sentence often contains the main idea.

❷ Restate the main idea in your own words. Putting the main idea in your own words helps you better understand it.

❸ Look for details. Find facts, descriptions, and examples that tell more about the main idea.

❹ Make connections. Understand how the details support and expand the main idea.

Practice the Skill

Read the excerpts from The Declaration of Independence and answer these questions:

❶ What is the main idea in your own words?

❷ How can you tell what the main idea is?

❸ Identify details that support the main idea.

❹ How do the details relate to the main idea?

Apply the Skill

Choose a heading in Chapter 21. Read the text under the heading and identify the main idea and supporting details of that section.

Review and Assessment

Chapter Summary

Section 1
The Role of Civil Law
(pages 562–567)

- Civil lawsuits decide arguments between two parties. In civil lawsuits, people have a right to compensation for damages they have suffered. Equity, or general rules of fairness, is used to decide cases.

- Among the types of cases are those involving property, consumer issues (frequently including contracts), housing, domestic relations, and probate cases.

- In addition to awarding damages, the court can issue an injunction to order a party in a suit to do or stop doing a certain action.

Section 2
Civil Procedure
(pages 569–573)

- A civil case begins with the filing of a complaint. The complaint generates a summons to the defendant. The defendant files an answer to the complaint.

- The obtaining of evidence is called discovery. Among the methods of discovery are the subpoena and deposition.

- Only civil cases involving compensation are usually heard by juries.

- The high cost and backlog of cases provide an incentive to attempt to settle cases before they come to trial.

Section 3
Choices in Civil Justice
(pages 574–581)

- Several methods exist for avoiding civil trials, including mediation, arbitration, and private judges.

- In cases where the conflict is over a small amount of money, the expense of a large trial can be avoided by going to small claims court.

- Awards by juries continue to grow. Some people feel that these awards are justified by the losses suffered by the plaintiffs. Others argue that the awards are destructive, because their costs ultimately get passed on to consumers.

- The best way to settle a dispute is not always by bringing a civil lawsuit. Plaintiffs should consider their options carefully before going to court.

Copy the chart below and use it to help you summarize the chapter.

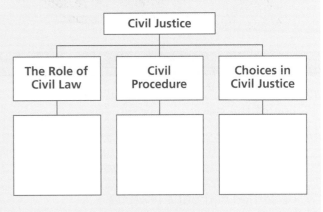

Review and Assessment Continued

Go Online
PHSchool.com

For: Self-Test
Visit: PHSchool.com
Web Code: mpa-7213

Reviewing Key Terms

Fill in each blank with one of the key terms from the list below.

discovery   summons
arbitration   deposition
compensation   mediation
small claims court   lawsuit

1. Making up for harm caused by another person's acts is called _____.

2. An order to appear in court is called a _____.

3. Questioning a witness before a trial is called a _____.

4. The use of a third party to make a binding decision is called _____.

5. A case in which a court is asked to settle a dispute is called a _____.

6. A process in which people agree to use a third party to help them settle a dispute is called _____.

7. The process of gathering evidence before trial is known as _____.

8. A special court used for settling disputes about small amounts of money is called _____.

Comprehension and Critical Thinking

9. a. **Recall** What two principles do civil courts use for settling cases?
   b. **Analyze** How does civil law hold people responsible for their actions?
   c. **Draw Inferences** Why is civil law looked upon as a last resort for settling disputes?

10. a. **Recall** How does a defendant know they are being sued?
    b. **Analyze** Why do you think the burden of proof is lower in civil cases than criminal cases?
    c. **Demonstrate Reasoned Judgment** What process do you think is most useful in settling cases out of court?

11. a. **Recall** How does arbitration work?
    b. **Analyze** Why do you think juries give large awards?
    c. **Draw Conclusions** How do large awards impact society as a whole?

Activities

12. **Skills** Read the story at right. Make a timeline of the story.

13. **Writing** Place yourself in the role of a mediator in the story. Write an analysis of what happened. Where do you think responsibility lies? How could the dispute be settled without a lawsuit?

One day, Theo goes over to Charlie's house. He and Charlie are going to practice skateboard tricks in Charlie's driveway. Theo's little cousin Hughie is there, too, because Theo has to look after him. Before long Charlie and Theo go inside to get water. Seven-year-old Hughie picks up Theo's skateboard and tries a trick. He falls badly and has to be taken to the emergency room. He has a broken collarbone.

Hughie's parents are furious. They decide to sue Charlie's parents for allowing children to do dangerous activities without supervision. They want Charlie's parents to pay Hughie's medical bills.

14. **Active Citizen** Why do you think it is important to serve as a juror in civil and criminal trials?

15. **Math Practice** A jury awards an accident victim $6,240,000. The judge reduces the award by 60%. How much is the final amount?

16. **Civics and Economics** Write a letter to the editor that expresses your views about the cost of lawsuits and the availability of other means of settling disputes.

17. **Analyzing Visuals** Look at the photo to the right. If this accident resulted in a civil trial, who would most likely be the defendant in the case? Why?

Standardized Test Prep

Test-Taking Tips

Some questions on a standardized test will ask you about details and the sequence or order in which events take place. Read the following interview with a witness to an auto accident and answer the questions below.

Witness A

"You know this is a dangerous corner. There's a big shrub right on the corner that hides the view of traffic coming up the hill. So I was standing across the street. First, I saw the gold minivan coming to a stop directly across from me. I took a sip of my coffee. Then I saw this little red sportscar coming through the intersection and down-shifting to get up the hill. Next, I saw the gold mini-van starting to turn left into the path of the sports car. Pow!"

TIP Look for details that give concrete information. Look for sequence words like *first, next, then.*

Choose the letter of the best answer.

1. Where was the witness standing in relation to the intersection where the accident took place?
   A Down the hill
   B Up the hill
   C Across the street
   D Behind the shrub

   The answer is **C.** The question asks about where the witness was located during the accident.

2. Which is the correct sequence of events reported by the witness?
   A Sip of coffee, red sportscar charging up the hill, gold minivan stops, Pow!
   B Red sportscar charging up hill, gold minivan stops, sip of coffee, Pow!
   C Sip of coffee, Pow!, red sports car charging up hill, gold minivan stops
   D Gold minivan stops, sip of coffee, red sportscar, Pow!

UNIT
8

People Make a Difference

What's Ahead in Unit 8

In Unit 8 you will take a look at ways in which Americans, as a group and as individuals, make a difference in government. You will see how people can play their citizen roles through political parties, through voting and running for public office, and through helping solve problems that face out society.

CHAPTER 22
Political Parties in Our Democracy

CHAPTER 23
Voting and Elections

Active Citizen

Why Study Civics?

What is a political party? How are presidential candidates chosen? How does voting help you participate in our democracy? How do candidates for office try to influence your vote? These are all questions that can be addressed by the study of civics.

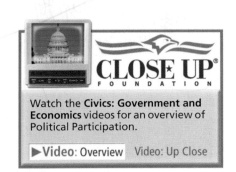

Watch the **Civics: Government and Economics** videos for an overview of Political Participation.

▶**Video**: Overview   Video: Up Close

Standards for Civics and Government

National

The following National Standards are covered in this unit.

II. What are the foundations of the American political system?

B. What are the distinctive characteristics of American society?

C. What is American political culture?

D. What values and principles are basic to American constitutional democracy?

State

Go Online
PHSchool.com

For: Your state's Civics standards
Visit: PHSchool.com
Webcode: mpe8001

22 Political Parties in Our Democracy

What's Ahead in Chapter 22

In this chapter you will learn how political parties function and how they help government and citizens. You will read about the two-party system in the United States and how both parties nominate candidates for public office.

SECTION 1
The Role of Political Parties

SECTION 2
Our Two-Party System

SECTION 3
Choosing Candidates

TARGET READING SKILL

In this chapter you will focus on the skill of clarifying meaning to help you better understand what you read. Clarifying meaning includes reading ahead, rereading, paraphrasing and summarizing.

Democratic National ▶ Convention

National National Standards for Civic Government | **State**

The following National Standards for Civics and Government are covered in this chapter.

II. What are the foundations of the American political system?

B. What are the distinctive characteristics of American society?

C. What is American political culture?

D. What values and principles are basic to American constitutional democracy?

Go Online
PHSchool.com
For: Your state's standards
Visit: PHSchool.com
Web Code: mpe-8221

Active Citizen Civics in the Real World

"Hey Tony! Happy birthday! How does it feel to be 18?" asked Marta.

"I don't know," Tony replied. "No real difference, I guess."

"Well, at least you can go register to vote," Marta said.

"Sure, but to tell the truth I don't know the first thing about it," said Tony. "I don't know where or how to register. And I really don't know who to vote for."

"You can just go over to Town Hall and sign up, Tony. But are you going to register as a Republican or a Democrat?"

"Beats me! What did you do, Marta?"

"I registered as a Republican because my parents are Republicans. Plus Karen Consolo is our neighbor and she was elected to the City Council as a Republican. I helped out on her campaign."

"Hmm. Well, my Mom is a Democrat and my Dad is a Republican. Every year around election time, they just agree to disagree. I guess I am going to have to find out more about what each party stands for before I register, Marta."

"Well, good luck, Tony—and happy birthday again!"

Citizen's Journal Think about registering to vote when you turn 18. How can you prepare yourself now for deciding if you would like to join one of the political parties? How will you find out where each party stands on the issues that are important to you?

The Role of Political Parties

Reading Preview

Objectives

In this section you will
- Learn about how parties help government.
- Discuss how parties help citizens.

Taking Notes

Make a diagram like the one below. As you read this section, complete the diagram with information about the role of political parties.

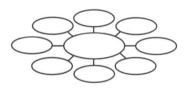

Key Terms

political party   planks
nominate   canvass
platform

Main Idea

Political parties bring people together who share similar political ideas. Political parties select candidates, provide leadership, and set goals for political action.

Target Reading Skill

Reread or Read Ahead Rereading and reading ahead are strategies that can help you understand words and ideas in the text. If you do not understand a certain passage, reread it to look for connections among the words and sentences. It might also help to read ahead, because a word or idea may be clarified further on.

Bumper stickers ▼

People want many things from government. They want their rights protected. They want to feel secure against poverty and unemployment. They want to be treated fairly in business, at work, and in the courts. They want a clean environment. Many want government to pass laws or to pay for specific programs that they believe are important, such as education for the handicapped, product safety, gun control, or finding a cure for cancer.

Alone, an individual may feel powerless to make his or her wants, needs, and ideas known. Acting together, however, groups of people can often have a greater effect.

On a larger scale, people form groups called political parties in order to influence government. A **political party** is an organization of citizens who wish to influence and control government by getting their members elected to office. Party members share similar ideas about what they want government to do. If a party can put enough of its members into office, that party can have a major effect on the policies of the government. Parties play a key role in government and provide opportunities for citizens to take part in the political process.

How Parties Help Government

Parties help government at the local, state, and national levels in a number of ways. They select candidates for many public offices. They set goals for the government and provide leadership to reach those goals. Political parties also keep an eye on each other.

Selecting Candidates Political parties **nominate,** or name candidates to run for public office. Parties take the responsibility for finding and nominating qualified candidates.

There are about a half million elected positions in the local, state, and national governments of the United States. Some public offices, especially in local government, are nonpartisan. This means that the candidates do not declare themselves to be members of a political party when running for office. For example, seats on school boards and town boards are often nonpartisan.

However, most offices are partisan. The candidates for these offices run as members of political parties. If elected, they try to carry out the party's programs.

Setting Goals A political party establishes positions on issues and sets goals for government. Each party has a **platform,** a statement of a party's official stand on major public issues. The platform is made up of **planks,** position statements on each specific issue in a party's platform. Party members who are elected to office often turn these planks into government programs.

Providing Leadership Parties help provide day-to-day leadership in government. Leadership is necessary to make the laws and carry out the programs that citizens want. Party members in Congress select majority and minority floor leaders and whips to provide leadership in making laws. Parties work in much the same way in state legislatures, too.

Political parties also provide leadership in the executive branch of government. The political party of the executive is referred to as the party "in office." The executive often appoints loyal members of the party in office to high government posts. They are then in a position to help shape government programs and policies.

Target Reading Skill
Read Ahead Keep reading to see how political parties keep an eye on each other. How do they monitor each other?

Strength in Numbers
Members of political parties work together to put the candidates they support into office.
Identify Cause and Effect *What purposes do you think political rallies like this one serve?*

Parties as "Watchdogs" Political parties also play an important "watchdog" role in government. After an election, the party not in power makes sure that the public knows when the party in power is not living up to its promises.

Parties keep tabs on the behavior of members of the other party. They are eager to report any wrongdoing. The watchdog function of parties makes sure that members of the party in power are honest and hard working.

✓ Reading Check How do parties play a "watchdog" role in government?

How Parties Help Citizens

Parties also help citizens fulfill their responsibilities in our democracy. Parties help citizens make their voices heard. They also inform citizens and provide ways for them to participate.

Citizens' Voice in Government Political parties provide a way for citizens to be heard. Edie Stevenson, the county chairperson of her political party, describes her experience:

"When I accepted the job as county chair, few people in our county were aware of what the party stood for. So we wrote short statements of our policies on such topics as education and the environment. Then we held a series of community meetings. The people who came really spoke up about what was most important to them. We rewrote some of our statements based on what we learned about people's concerns. Our candidates discovered that the meetings were a good way to keep up on what people around here want from government."

Edie's experience shows that at the local level parties give citizens a voice. At the state and national levels, party members help hammer out the party platform, debating and deciding on the issues.

Speeches and Handshakes Campaigns give candidates (such as Elizabeth Dole, left, and Harry Truman, right) the chance to meet directly with the voters.
Make Generalizations *Why is it important for candidates to have contact with large numbers of citizens when campaigning?*

Students Make a Difference

At age ten, Matthew R. Green-field was asked by a neighbor to pass out literature for the Democratic Party in his hometown of Fair Lawn, New Jersey. He soon found himself attending council meetings.

By age 15, Matthew was interning for the Democratic campaign chairman for New Jersey's state legislature. The following year, Matthew was a page in the U.S. House of Representatives, working daily on the floor of Congress. Today, Matthew serves as the municipal youth liaison of the Fair Lawn Democratic Organization

▲ Students can help make a difference by helping educate voters so they can make informed decisions on election day.

Service Learning

How can you make a difference for your chosen political party?

Informing Citizens Edie's party helped provide citizens in her county with information—facts, figures, and party stances on various important issues. Parties also inform citizens by sending out mailings and giving information to newspapers, radio, and television. They provide quick responses to new issues so voters will know where the party stands.

Parties inform citizens by arranging meetings with candidates. Party members and volunteers also **canvass**, or go door-to-door handing out information and asking people which candidates they support. Often, the party will give volunteers a list of voters who are most likely to welcome a visit and listen to what they have to say. Parties do not always have enough volunteers to visit people who rarely vote or who strongly disagree with the party.

Parties canvass and provide information in order to encourage people to vote for their candidates. By making information available to voters, parties can also help simplify political decision-making. If a voter agrees with a party's point of view, he or she can vote on the basis of the party. People who agree with a party's positions on the issues often feel comfortable supporting most of the party's candidates.

Pitching In
Political parties need the help of many volunteers to get their messages out at election time. **Draw Inferences** *Why would a person volunteer their time for a political campaign?*

Involving Citizens Parties provide citizens with many ways to get involved in the political process. To be successful, a party needs the help of many people, especially at election time. Campaign volunteers write letters and pamphlets and send them to voters. They raise money and hold events at which candidates can meet voters. They make phone calls and canvass neighborhoods. On election day, volunteers remind people to vote and may even drive them to the polls.

As a citizen, it is both your right and responsibility to participate in government. Working through a party is one way to play your citizen role.

✓ Reading Check   **Why do parties canvass and provide information to voters?**

SECTION 1 — Assessment

Key Terms

Use the following key term in a sentence that explains its meaning: political party, nominate, platform, planks, canvass

Target Reading Skill

1. **Reread or Read Ahead** How did rereading help you better identify the different ways political parties provide leadership?

Comprehension and Critical Thinking

2. **a. Recall** How do political parties keep watch over one another?

   b. Draw Inferences Why do you think parties monitor one another's activities?

3. **a. Explain** How do volunteers help political parties?

   b. Draw Inferences How might party activity at the local level affect a party's national policy?

Writing

Suppose you are going to interview a local politician about a current controversial issue. Choose an issue that is important to you. Then prepare a list of questions to determine how the view of this politician and his or her party is different from the view of the other major party.

> **TIP** Read your local paper or local Web sites to find a controversial issue in your community. Be sure you understand both sides of the issue when preparing your list of questions.

Our Two-Party System

Reading Preview

Objectives

In this section you will

- Discuss a brief history of political parties.
- Understand the role of third parties.
- Explore the characteristics of today's parties.
- Explore the characteristics of today's parties.
- Learn about changes in party strength.

Key Terms

precincts
patronage
straight ticket
split ticket
independent
voter

Main Idea

The Democratic and Republican parties each have their own particular views. However, a change in government does not result in big changes in policy, since both parties' views are not that far apart.

Target Reading Skill

Paraphrase A paraphrase is restating information in one's own words. It is different than a summary, which involves restatement of important ideas and details in the correct order.

Taking Notes

Make a diagram like the one below. As you read this section, complete the diagram with information about the development of political parties in the United States.

Political parties are not mentioned in the Constitution. In fact, George Washington feared that conflict between parties might destroy the new democracy. He warned against "the baneful [harmful] effects of the Spirit of Party" in his 1796 farewell address.

However, even at the birth of our nation, Americans were dividing into groups. One group supported a strong central government (Federalists) and another feared it (Anti-Federalists). The first political parties arose out of these differences over the role of government.

A Brief History

Alexander Hamilton was President Washington's Secretary of the Treasury. He led the first political party, the Federalist Party. The Federalists, who wanted a strong national government, had the support of merchants and bankers. The party's power declined in the early 1800s.

The rival of the Federalists was the Democratic-Republican Party, led by Thomas Jefferson. This party opposed a strong national government. It supported the power of the individual states. Farmers and frontier settlers supported the Democratic-Republican Party. The party became known as the Democratic Party in 1828.

The Whig party organized in 1834. The Whigs opposed the policies of Andrew Jackson, the Democratic president at the time. The Whigs and the Democrats remained rivals until the early 1850s.

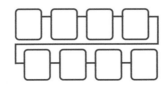

Alexander
Hamilton

Thomas
Jefferson

Party Symbols
The elephant and donkey are symbols of the Republicans and Democrats, respectively.

Democrats and Republicans Our current two-party system emerged in 1854. In that year the Republican Party was born. It replaced the Whigs as a major party. It was formed by groups opposed to slavery. The Republican Party supported business interests and at first was purely a party of the North.

Abraham Lincoln became the first Republican President in 1860. The Republican Party remained the majority party from the Civil War until the Great Depression of the 1930s. It dominated both the presidency and the Congress during those years.

A major shift in party power began in 1932. Franklin D. Roosevelt, a Democrat, was elected President that year. Roosevelt's New Deal programs were designed to bring the country out of the depression. Power shifted back and forth between Democrats and Republicans during the second half of the twentieth century.

✓ Reading Check   **Who was the founder of the Democratic-Republican Party?**

The Role of Third Parties

For almost all of American history, presidential elections have been dominated by two parties at a time. But third parties do arise, especially during presidential election years. Sometimes a third party forms to support a cause or idea. When the Republican Party formed in opposition to slavery, it was a third party to the Democrats and the Whigs.

Third parties sometimes form to back a candidate, often one who splits from a main party. Former President Theodore Roosevelt failed to win the Republican nomination for President in 1912. Roosevelt formed the Progressive, or "Bull Moose," party. The Bull Moose Party disappeared after Roosevelt lost the election.

In nationwide elections, third-party candidates face many problems. It may be difficult to get on the ballot because election laws in many states favor the two major parties. People often hold back from giving money because they doubt that a third-party candidate can win. Also, people sometimes think that voting for its candidate would be wasting their vote. However, in state and local elections, third-party candidates frequently win offices.

The Importance of Third Parties Third-party candidates rarely win major elections. But they still play an important role in American politics. A third-party candidate can change the outcome of an election by drawing votes away from one of the main parties. In the 2000 election, Green Party candidate Ralph Nader won many votes that probably would have gone to the Democratic candidate, Al Gore. As a result, Republican George W. Bush won the very close election.

Third parties can also play a key role by bringing up new ideas or pressing for action on certain issues. In the 1992 election, independent candidate Ross Perot made the national debt a major issue. This forced the Republican and Democratic candidates to talk about the problem more directly. Perot got 19 percent of the popular vote. It was the strongest showing for a third party presidential candidate in 80 years. Perot hoped to transform this support into a permanent political party. He formed the Reform Party in 1995. Perot ran as the Reform Party's candidate for President in 1996, receiving 8 percent of the vote. However, Perot left politics after that election, and his party soon lost much of its national influence.

✓ Reading Check **How did Ross Perot influence the election of 1992?**

Characteristics of Today's Parties

What do the major parties stand for? Generally, the Democratic Party believes that the federal government should take responsibility for many social programs, such as aid to the poor. Democrats are more likely than Republicans to support tax increases to pay for these programs. The Democratic Party is also more likely to support labor unions.

The Republican Party generally supports reducing the power of federal government. Republicans tend to believe that state and local governments, as well as non-government organizations, should take more responsibility for social programs.

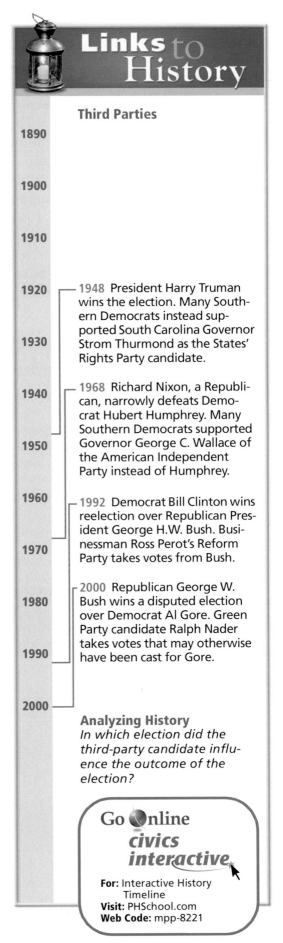

Links to History

Third Parties

1890

1900

1910

1920

1948 President Harry Truman wins the election. Many Southern Democrats instead supported South Carolina Governor Strom Thurmond as the States' Rights Party candidate.

1930

1968 Richard Nixon, a Republican, narrowly defeats Democrat Hubert Humphrey. Many Southern Democrats supported Governor George C. Wallace of the American Independent Party instead of Humphrey.

1940

1950

1960

1992 Democrat Bill Clinton wins reelection over Republican President George H.W. Bush. Businessman Ross Perot's Reform Party takes votes from Bush.

1970

2000 Republican George W. Bush wins a disputed election over Democrat Al Gore. Green Party candidate Ralph Nader takes votes that may otherwise have been cast for Gore.

1980

1990

2000

Analyzing History
In which election did the third-party candidate influence the outcome of the election?

Go Online
civics
interactive

For: Interactive History Timeline
Visit: PHSchool.com
Web Code: mpp-8221

Political Parties Are Similar When you look at the two parties you can see differences. However, when the party in office changes, we do not usually have a radical change in government policies. Why not? The answer lies in the fact that, in many ways, our two major political parties are similar.

The two political parties have different historical traditions and see the role of government differently. However, the parties, like the American people they represent, hold the same basic beliefs and values.

Furthermore, in order to win elections, both parties need broad support. Each party tries to attract members from a broad spectrum of people—rich and poor, white collar and blue collar, rural and urban. Each party also tries to attract the votes of the large number of voters who are not strongly committed to either party. To keep the support of all these different groups, both parties typically avoid taking extreme stands on issues.

Analyze Diagrams and Charts

Political Parties in the United States

Political parties in our country take different stands on various issues, as do citizens. The political spectrum diagram shows the general range of political opinions that people hold. The charts show the major agendas of the Democratic and Republican parties, as well as information about major third parties.

a. How do the Democratic and Republican parties differ on the role of the government in the nation's economy?

b. Based on the information in the diagram and charts, where do you think the Democratic Party falls on the political spectrum? The Republican Party? The Constitution Party? Explain your reasoning.

Democratic Party

- favors government regulation of the economy; supports organized labor

- favors higher taxes for high income earners and a redistribution of tax revenue to programs for the poor

- favors keeping welfare in place for the poor and disadvantaged

- favors school funding initiatives that create competitive public schools

The Political Spectrum

LEFT ←

Radical
Favors extreme change to create an altered or entirely new social system.

Liberal
Believes that government must take action to change economic, political, and ideological policies thought to be unfair.

SOURCES: New York Times Almanac, Federal Election Commission

Party Organization The Democratic and Republican parties are also similar in the way they are set up. Both parties have local, state, and national organizations. These organizations work independently of each other. In other words, there is no single authority making decisions for the whole party.

Individual members at the local level are the most important part of any party. These members do the job of getting the party's candidates elected. Each community is divided into **precincts**, or voting districts. Precincts are made up of generally fewer than 1,000 voters who all vote at the same polling place. In each precinct, each party has a chairperson or captain who organizes volunteers to try to get as many party members as possible to vote.

Parties at the local level elect members to city and county committees. These committees may recommend candidates for office and are responsible for running local campaigns.

Go Online
civics interactive

For: You Decide Poll
Visit: PHSchool.com
Web Code: mpp-8222

Republican Party

- favors less governmental intervention in the economy; supports restricting organized labor

- favors lower taxes and breaks for high income earners to encourage business investment and economic growth

- favors cutting back welfare benefits in order to foster initiative for welfare recipients to find work

- favors school funding initiatives that allow for parental choice, including school vouchers for private schools

Major Third Parties

Party	Issues
Constitutional Party (1992–present)	anti gun control, anti tax, protectionist
Green Party (1985–present)	environmental protection
Independent Party (1992–present)	political reform
Labor Party (1996–present)	protecting the rights of workers
Libertarian Party (1971–present)	individual liberty, economic freedom

CENTER ⟶ RIGHT

Moderate
Holds belief that fall between the liberal and conservative views, usually including both.

Conservative
Seeks to keep in place the economic, political, and social structures of society.

Reactionary
Favors extreme change to restore society to an earlier, more conservative state.

Mark Hanna (1837–1904) Mark Hanna was a wealthy Cleveland industrialist. He invented the modern political campaign. William McKinley was a Republican Congressman from Ohio who supported high tariffs to protect American industries. Hanna devoted his organizational skills and money to help William McKinley advance his political career. Thanks to Hanna's help, McKinley was elected governor of Ohio. Hanna organized more than a thousand campaign workers nationwide for McKinley's presidential campaign in 1896. It was the first professional national political campaign and resulted in McKinley's election.

Citizenship
Why do you think Hanna helped McKinley?

Each party is also organized at the state level. Most states have party committees, each with a chairperson. At state conventions, party leaders write the state party platform and nominate candidates for office. Party leaders also raise money and help with candidates' campaigns.

Once every four years, each party holds a national convention. At the convention, delegates write the national party platform and nominate the candidates for President and Vice President.

The national convention has become an important part of the presidential campaign, not just a meeting of party activists. Millions of Americans watch the conventions on television. Political parties use their conventions to present their message and their candidates to voters.

Between national conventions, the national committee keeps the party running. During election years, the national committee helps the candidates for President and Vice President run their campaigns. It also works to elect members of Congress and to raise funds for the party.

Target Reading Skill

Paraphrase Restate the section under the heading **Supporting a Party** in your own words. Try to do it in 25 or fewer words.

✓ Reading Check **What takes place at the national party conventions?**

Supporting a Party

Membership in a political party is not like membership in a club. You do not need to pay dues or attend meetings. All you need to do is think of yourself as a member. In some states, you can officially declare your party when you register to vote. Even so, you are free to vote for any party's candidates in general elections and to change your party registration whenever you wish.

How do you decide what party to support, or whether to support a party at all? Your views on issues influence which political party you support. If you take a strong stand on an issue, you are more likely to back a party that shares your view. Also, if you like certain candidates and agree with their opinions, you may be attracted to their party. The views of family, friends, co-workers, and teachers may also influence you. If people you respect support a party, you, too, may choose to back that party.

✓ Reading Check **How might your views on a certain issue influence which party you would support?**

Changes in Party Strength

Parties depend for their strength on their ability to elect their candidates. In order to be successful in elections, parties must have dedicated members to work on campaigns. Historically, political parties have maintained their strength through a combination of three elements: (1) a system of patronage, (2) a central role in election campaigns, and (3) voter loyalty.

Patronage The system in which party leaders do favors for loyal supporters of the party is called **patronage**. Today, some patronage is still possible, especially at high levels. For example, the President often appoints loyal party members to cabinet positions. However, many people now get government jobs through the civil service system. As a result, the patronage system has decreased, though there are still 2,000 federal appointments as well as many state and local ones.

Parties in Campaigns The parties' role in campaigns has also changed. In earlier times, candidates for office worked within the party. They depended on party support in their campaigns to inform voters about their candidacies.

Today, although party support is still a tremendous help, candidates can more easily strike out on their own. They can raise their own campaign funds and run a campaign apart from the party. They can buy television ads and print their own pamphlets. When candidates are less dependent on party help, they may be less bound to support the party's programs. Candidates are more free to publicly disagree with their party leaders.

Balance of Power
Republican Senator Jim Jeffords of Vermont left the Republican Party and joined the Democrats in 2001. The Democratic Party suddenly had control of the Senate.
Make Inferences *How do you think the voters of Vermont responded to Jeffords' change of party affiliation? Why?*

Party Identification in the United States, 1952–2000

This chart shows the percentage of voters who identify with the two major parties and the percentage of independents.

1. **Analyze** Which group shows the biggest gain of support between 1972 and 1988?

2. **Apply** How did this group's share change between 1988 and 2000, and which other group was most likely affected by the change?

Year	Democrats (%)	Independents (%)	Republicans (%)
1952	48.6	23.3	28.1
1956	45.3	24.4	30.3
1960	46.4	23.4	30.2
1964	52.2	23.0	24.8
1968	46.0	29.5	24.5
1972	41.0	35.2	23.8
1976	40.2	36.8	23.0
1980	41.7	35.3	23.0
1984	37.7	34.8	27.6
1988	35.7	36.3	28.0
1992	35.8	38.7	25.5
1996	39.3	32.9	27.8
2000	34.8	41.0	24.2

SOURCE: National Election Studies, University of Michigan

Voter Loyalty A third change that has weakened political parties is a change in voter loyalty. Only 40% of people now vote a **straight ticket**. Voters now tend to base their decisions on the appeal of a particular candidate or issue rather than on party loyalty. Many people now vote a **split ticket**, the practice of voting for candidates of more than one party on the same ballot.

As a result of split-ticket voting, parties can no longer count on a certain core of party votes in an election. In 2002, for example, Oregon voters re-elected Republican Senator Gordon Smith. But they elected a Democrat, Ted Kulongoski, as Oregon's governor.

One reason for declining voter loyalty is that many Americans choose their party membership and their preferred candidates for different reasons. For example, many Americans in southern states are registered Democrats because their families and hometowns have strong historic loyalties to the Democratic Party. Southern ties to the Democratic Party date back to the early 1800s. In many rural areas, all local and county officials are Democrats.

However, many of these registered Democrats regularly support Republican candidates for Congress and the Presidency. They find that the Republican Party's national platform more closely represents their conservative views.

Kentucky, a historically Democratic state, illustrates this pattern. In 2002, 60 percent of Kentucky's voters were registered Democrats, and Democrats controlled the lower house of the state legislature. That year, both of Kentucky's senators and five of its six representatives in the House were Republicans. Kentucky voters had strongly supported Republican candidate George W. Bush for President in 2000.

A recent poll found that 31 percent of American voters considered themselves Democrats. Some 31 percent considered themselves Republicans. How do the rest of the voters think of themselves? About 38 percent are **independent voters**, people who do not support a particular political party. This number is highest among young voters. However, a certain percentage of independent voters "leans" toward one party or the other.

Some observers claim that the influence of political parties is weakening—that "the party is over." Others believe that our two-party system will stay in place, but that the parties will change in response to changing times.

Split Tickets
New York Governor George Pataki (left), a Republican, shakes hands with New York State Attorney General Eliot Spitzer (right), a Democrat. **Make Inferences** *Why do you think voters are increasingly likely to vote for split tickets?*

✓ Reading Check **Check How does split-ticket voting affect candidates for office?**

SECTION 2 Assessment

Key Terms
Use each of the key terms in a sentence that explains its meaning: precincts, patronage, straight ticket, split ticket, independent voter

Target Reading Skill
1. **Paraphrase** Paraphrase the passage entitled *Voter Loyalty* on pages 602 and 603.

Comprehension and Critical Thinking
2. **Recall** What event contributed to the Republican Party becoming the majority party?
3. **a. Recall** What third party did Theodore Roosevelt lead?

b. Analyze Information What disadvantages does a third-party candidate have?
4. **a. Recall** What are the general beliefs of the Republican and Democratic Parties?
b. Draw Conclusions What prevents either political party from adopting an extreme position on an issue?
5. **a. Recall** What three elements have parties used to maintain their strength?
b. Demonstrate Reasoned Judgment How would you expect patronage appointments to affect the efficiency of government?

Writing
Do your political beliefs align more closely with the Democratic or the Republican Party? Visit both parties' Web sites to learn their positions on three issues that are important to you. Determine which party's positions most closely match yours. Then write a one-page flyer to convince others to support that party. Be sure to outline clearly the party's position on your three issues.

Go Online
PHSchool.com
For: Political Party Web sites
Visit: PHschool.com
Web Code: mpd-8222

Debating the Issues

CLOSE UP FOUNDATION

The debates in this feature are based on *Current Issues*, published by the Close Up Foundation. Go to **PHSchool.com**, Web Code mph-8222, to read the latest issue of *Current Issues* online.

A candidate for political office in the United States has no limits on what he or she may spend on an election campaign. Those who spend more will reach more potential voters because they can travel to more places, broadcast more ads, and pay more staffers. Corporations, labor unions, and individuals can donate money, within certain limits, to political parties and candidates. In practice, the rules allow those who donate the most to have the greatest political influence.

Should Further Limits Be Placed on Campaign Contributions?

YES	NO
• Current laws give the wealthy far more political influence than the middle class or the poor. This corrupts our democratic system of government, in which all votes should count equally.	• Donating money to a candidate who will represent your views is a form of free speech. Limiting campaign contributions therefore violates free speech.
• In a system where the candidate with more money usually wins the election, candidates for reelection have to spend a lot of time raising funds. This distracts them from the work the voters elected them to do.	• Many people believe that the news media are too conservative. Others believe that they are too liberal. Campaign finance laws should not limit contributions from those who feel that the media suppress their views.
• When huge donations help elect candidates, the candidates are under pressure to represent the donors' interests. They may not feel able to vote according to their own beliefs once they have accepted money.	• The best way to reform campaign finance laws is to force donors promptly to publish their names and the amounts of money they donate to candidates. This will ensure that everyone knows whose interests each candidate represents.

What Is Your Opinion?

1. **Summarize** What are the strongest arguments for and against limiting donations? (You may outline arguments not listed above.)

2. **Predict** Suppose that Congress were to ban all donations. Instead, the federal government would give candidates equal amounts of money to spend on campaigns. Predict the consequences. Explain your answer.

3. **Writing to Persuade** Suppose that you are a Supreme Court justice. In a case before you, one side argues that political donations are a form of free speech. The other side insists that money is not speech. Write an opinion giving your view. Include specific reasons that will persuade readers to agree.

Go Online
civics
interactive

For: You Decide Poll
Visit: PHSchool.com
Web Code: mpp-8223

Choosing Candidates

Reading Preview

Objectives

In this section you will

- Discuss nominating candidates.
- Learn about choosing presidential candidates.

Key Terms

self-nomination
write-in candidate
caucus

direct primary
closed primary
open primary

Main Idea

Many political candidates nominate themselves or are chosen at party conventions. Presidential candidates are nominated at national conventions after a series of primaries or caucuses in individual states.

Target Reading Skill

Summarize When you summarize, you review and state the main points in the correct order. Summarizing what you read is a good technique to help you understand and study.

Taking Notes

Make a diagram like the one below. As you read this section, complete the diagram with information about the events that lead to the nomination of a candidate.

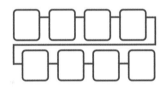

The most important role of political parties is nominating the candidates who will run for office. Parties play an important part in deciding who our political officials will be based on their nominations. Taking a look at the nominating process for candidates in general, and for presidential candidates in particular, is a good way to see parties in action.

Nominating Candidates

Suppose you want to run for office. The first step is to declare that you intend to run. After that, the nominating process may be simple or complex, depending on the office.

The simplest way to become a candidate is **self-nomination**, which means declaring that you are running for office. Self-nomination is possible for many local offices. A self-nominee usually pays a small fee called a filing fee, as do other declared candidates. Another type of self-nominated candidate is a **write-in candidate**, one who asks voters to write his or her name on the ballot.

For some offices, a candidate may need to file a nominating petition. A number of voters must sign the petition saying that they support the nomination. Then the candidate pays the filing fee and begins the campaign. For other offices, candidates are chosen by delegates at party meetings called conventions. Parties hold local, state, and national conventions.

Candidates use convention speeches to win the support of convention delegates. However, they must avoid making promises that will win the support of some delegates while losing the support of other delegates whose opinions differ.

1. What is this delegate promising?
2. What do you think the cartoonist is saying about politicians and their campaign promises?

"And if I'm elected I promise to go with the flow."

A few states select candidates or choose delegates to conventions at a caucus. A **caucus** is a meeting of party leaders to discuss issues or choose candidates. In earlier days, caucuses put great power in the hands of a few party leaders because the meetings were closed to ordinary members. Today a few state and local caucuses are still held, but they are very different. Most caucuses are open meetings.

Primaries Most candidates for state and federal office are now chosen in a direct primary. A **direct primary** is an election in which members of a political party choose candidates to run for office in the name of the party. The candidate with the most votes is then that party's nominee in the general election.

Most states use one of two kinds of direct primary: closed or open. A **closed primary** is a primary in which a voter must be registered as a party member and may vote only in that party's primary. Only Democrats may vote in the Democratic primary to choose Democratic candidates, and the same is true for Republicans. Voters registered as independent cannot vote in a closed primary. An **open primary** is a primary in which voters do not need to declare a party before voting, but may vote in only one party's primary.

✓ Reading Check   How are most candidates for state and federal office now chosen?

Choosing Presidential Candidates

The primaries that receive the most attention take place every four years to select the parties' candidates for President. Anyone over 35 years old and born in the United States may run for President. Realistically, a candidate needs to be well known, to have experience in government, and to be able to raise enough money for the campaign.

Most presidential candidates from the major parties have held elected office before seeking the nomination for President. Since World War II, 80 percent of Republican and Democratic candidates for President have been senators or governors. Also, since 1900, every President who has wanted to run for reelection has gained his party's nomination.

Paying for a Primary Campaign In the presidential primaries, candidates raise much of their money from individuals. Federal laws, however, say that individuals may give only $2,000 to each candidate per election. Once candidates have raised at least $5,000 in each of 20 states, they can receive an equal amount from the federal government, up to a total of almost $31 million. Primary elections and general elections count as separate elections under federal fundraising laws.

Civics and Economics

In a democracy, anyone who meets certain basic requirements can run for office. In reality, however, it takes huge amounts of money to run a political campaign. Candidates spend much of their time fundraising.

Many political campaigns start with party primaries. Candidates, in effect, have to wage two campaigns—one to get the nomination and another to win the election. To pay for these campaigns, candidates must gain the support of large groups of people with lots of money. Many such organizations, including corporations, labor unions, and other interest groups, will donate to candidates who will support their positions on key issues.

Analyzing Economics
Why is fundraising so important to political campaigns?

Target Reading Skill

Summarizing Summarize the section under the heading **Choosing Delegates**. Be sure to include the main idea from each paragraph.

Choosing Delegates Delegates to the national nominating conventions are chosen in one of two ways. They may be chosen through a presidential preference primary election. Or they may be chosen through a statewide caucus or convention process.

In a preference primary, voters show which candidates they prefer by voting either for the candidates themselves or for the delegates who support that candidate. In most primary states, delegates must promise to support a certain candidate at the national convention. In states without primaries, delegates are chosen by caucus or state convention.

In January or February of a presidential election year, candidates traditionally begin the race in New Hampshire, a primary state, and Iowa, a caucus state. Iowa and New Hampshire are relatively small states, so candidates have the opportunity to meet voters one by one. Many voters in these two states feel they have a responsibility to the rest of the nation to weigh their choices carefully before voting. Nominees begin visiting these states months before the first votes are cast or caucus is held. How well a candidate does in these early tests will affect his or her ability to raise money and attract voters in later primaries and caucuses. As the process continues, some candidates drop out and others gain strength.

Conventions
Delegates gather every four years to select a party's presidential nominee.
Summarize *What other purposes do conventions serve?*

National Conventions In a presidential election year, the parties hold their national conventions. At each convention, the delegates debate and discuss the candidates. They listen to speeches, vote on the nominations, and hammer out the party platform.

Because of the primaries, almost all delegates are "pledged" to a candidate before the convention begins. Usually only one vote is needed to choose the candidate. Once the candidate for President has been chosen, the delegates most often approve that candidate's choice for Vice President.

Another task of the national convention is to approve the party platform. A committee writes the platform with advice from party leaders, including the candidates. Each plank is carefully worded to appeal to the widest possible audience. The delegates debate and finally approve a platform.

The convention winds up with acceptance speeches from the presidential and vice presidential candidates. These speeches are meant to bring the party together after months of primaries and four grueling days of discussions and disagreements. The next step to gaining office will be the election campaign, leading up to the presidential election in November.

✔ Reading Check **How are delegates chosen for the national nominating conventions?**

Balloons and Confetti
Conventions are often a celebration of a party's core values—a way to unify party members after the primary season ends.
Make Inferences *What do you think is the purpose of televising the national conventions?*

SECTION **3** Assessment

Key Terms

Use each of the key terms in a sentence that explains its meaning: self-nomination, write-in candidate, caucus, direct primary, closed primary, open primary

Target Reading Skill

1. **Summarize** Summarize the section entitled *Nominating Candidates* on pages 605 and 606.

Comprehension and Critical Thinking

2. **a. Describe** What does a candidate need to do with a nominating petition?

b. Contrast How is a caucus different from a primary?

c. Determine Relevance Why are the Iowa caucuses and New Hampshire primary important?

3. **a. Explain** Who can run for President?

b. Analyze Information Why do you think candidates who fare poorly in early primaries rarely get the nomination for President?

c. Predict Why might a candidate who barely succeeded in the primary elections face difficulties in the general election?

Writing

You are a journalist for your local paper. Write an editorial providing voters some guidance about the qualities to look for in a candidate for office. Be sure to include the qualities that are objectionable in a candidate.

> **TIP** Be sure to provide your reasons for each of the qualities you list.

Comparing and Contrasting

As you learn about a subject, you should compare and contrast information to understand similarities and differences. Using a chart helps you organize information so that you can compare and contrast it easily.

The statements in the following chart are adapted from the Democratic and Republican party platforms of 2000. As you read the information, look for similarities and differences in the two parties' positions.

Selected Party Platform Statements

Democratic Party	Republican Party
"We believe in making child care more affordable."	"We advocate choice in child care."
"Democrats believe that in building upon record-breaking prosperity and growth we must not leave any community behind . . ."	"Budget surpluses are the result of overtaxation of the American people. The tax system threatens to slow, and perhaps to reverse, economic expansion."
"America needs public schools that compete with one another, not private school vouchers that drain resources from public schools."	"We endorse the principle of expanding parental choice and encouraging competition . . ."

Learn the Skill

Follow these steps to compare and contrast information:

❶ **Identify the topic.** This is the main idea, or the subject of similarities and differences. What is being compared and contrasted?

❷ **Identify similarities.** How are the items being compared alike? List these in a chart.

❸ **Identify differences.** How are the items different? List these in the chart.

❹ **Analyze the information.** Are the items being compared more similar or more different? How might the similarities influence outcomes? How might the differences create problems?

Practice the Skills

Look at the chart above and answer these questions:

❶ What is being compared?

❷ Identify one important similarity.

❸ Identify one important difference.

❹ Make a generalization about the two political parties. Base your generalization on the information in the chart.

Apply the Skill

Look through the front page section of the newspaper. Find an issue on which the Republicans and Democrats in Congress, or any pair of Democratic and Republican candidates running against one another for the same office, disagree. Use a graphic organizer to compare and contrast the two politicians' viewpoints.

Review and Assessment

Chapter Summary

Section 1
The Role of Political Parties
(Page 590–594)

- Political parties help government by nominating candidates and setting goals by adopting platforms with planks on specific issues. They also provide leadership and act as watchdogs on the party in power.

- Political parties help citizens by distributing information through canvassing and other means and by involving them as volunteers.

Section 2
Our Two-Party System
(Pages 595–603)

- The two-party system stretches back to the early years of the United States when Alexander Hamilton led the Federalist Party and Thomas Jefferson led the Democratic-Republican Party

- Third-party candidates influence election results and focus attention on issues.

- The Democratic and Republican Party are similarly organized down to the local precinct level.

- The role of patronage has been reduced but still plays a role in party politics.

- There has been a growth in independent voters and split ticket voting and a movement away from straight ticket voting.

Section 3
Choosing Candidates
(Pages 605–609)

- Candidates can use self-nomination or become write-in candidates in order to run for office. Political parties may also hold primary elections or caucuses to select candidates.

- For selecting a presidential nominee, some states use direct primaries, with some states having open primaries and others, closed primaries.

Copy the chart below and use it to help you summarize the chapter.

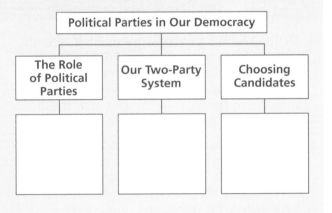

Political Parties in Our Democracy

The Role of Political Parties	Our Two-Party System	Choosing Candidates

Go Online
PHSchool.com
For: Self-Test
Visit: PHSchool.com
Web Code: mpa-8221

Reviewing Key Terms

Fill in the blank with one of the key terms from the list.

platform   patronage
caucus   planks
closed primary   canvass
split ticket   self-nomination

1. The system in which party leaders do favors for loyal party supporters is called _____.

2. A meeting of party leaders to choose a nominee for office is called a _____.

3. The practice of voting for candidates of more than one party on the same ballot called voting a _____.

4. A statement of a party's official stand on public issues is called a _____.

5. To _____ is to go door-to door asking voters which candidate they support.

6. Candidates use _____ when they declare they are running for office.

7. A party's position statement on a specific issue is called a _____.

8. A primary in which only voters registers as members of one party are allowed to vote is called a _____.

Comprehension and Critical Thinking

9. a. **Recall** How do political parties help citizens?
   b. **Analyze** How do political parties help make American democracy work?
   c. **Make Predictions** What would government be like if there were no political parties?

10. a. **Explain** How can a third-party candidate influence the result of an election?
    b. **Identify Cause and Effect** What causes the views of two major parties to remain somewhat similar?

c. **Link Past and Present** How have the differences between the the two major parties continued from their founding until today?

11. a. **Describe** How do primaries work?
    b. **Draw Conclusions** How are primaries a more democratic way of choosing candidates than caucuses?
    c. **Draw Inferences** Now that television has become an important advertising medium, how has the entire nominating process become less democratic?

Activities

12. **Skills** Make a Venn diagram. Fill it in with information comparing and contrasting the views of the Federalist and Democratic-Republican parties. What views did they share? Use the Internet to research these two political parties.

13. **Writing** Choose one of the major parties and write a brief essay about what you know. Include a list of questions. Then, use newspapers, magazines, or online resources to answer your questions.

Party rivalry has been part of American history from the very beginning. James Madison, who is recognized as the "Father of the Constitution," and Alexander Hamilton worked hard to assure its ratification. Both contributed to the work known as The Federalist. But Madison soon broke with Hamilton on certain issues. Together, Thomas Jefferson and Madison founded the Democratic-Republican Party to oppose Hamilton's Federalist Party.

14. **Active Citizen** Choose an issue you are concerned about. It could be a national or international issue, a state or local one, or one dealing with matters at your school. Write a letter to your elected representative expressing your concern, your views and request the representative to respond to your concerns.

15. **Math Practice** There are 142,600 votes cast in an election between Candidate A and Candidate B. Candidate A won the election with 51.5% of the votes. How many votes did Candidate A receive?

16. **Civics and Economics** You are a speech-writer for a candidate for governor of your state. Your candidate is running against the current governor. In the last few years unemployment has grown in your state. Write an outline for a speech in which your candidate uses the rise in unemployment to his or her advantage.

17. **Analyzing Visuals** What is the main idea of this cartoon? Explain your answer.

Standardized Test Prep

Some questions on standardized tests will ask you to read and analyze charts and graphs. The pie chart below shows the result of the election of 1860, in which Abraham Lincoln won the presidency in a four-way struggle. In that election the Democratic Party split along regional lines. The Northern Democrats nominated Senator Stephen Douglas. The Southern Democrats nominated John Breckenridge. Use the chart to answer the questions below.

TIP Be sure to read the title to graph to know what information it is showing.

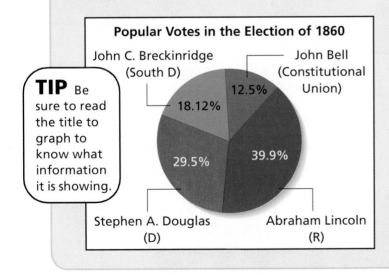

Popular Votes in the Election of 1860

John C. Breckinridge (South D) — 18.12%
John Bell (Constitutional Union) — 12.5%
Stephen A. Douglas (D) — 29.5%
Abraham Lincoln (R) — 39.9%

Choose the letter of the best answer.

1. The candidate who received the fewest popular votes was
   A Lincoln
   B Douglas
   C Breckenridge
   D Bell

   The answer is **D**.

2. Which of the following is a true statement?
   A Douglas received the fewest popular votes
   B Breckenridge was second in popular votes.
   C The combined Democrats received more than 50% of the popular votes.
   D Lincoln received more than 50% of the popular vote.

23

Voting and Elections

What's Ahead in Chapter 23

In this chapter you will read about how voting gives citizens a voice in government. You will read about how candidates and interest groups work to influence how you vote. You will also understand how political campaigns are organized.

SECTION 1
Being a Voter

SECTION 2
Influencing Your Vote

SECTION 3
Campaigning for Office

TARGET READING SKILL

Reading Process When you give yourself a focus for reading, you improve your concentration and comprehension. The reading process includes the skills of setting a purpose, previewing and predicting, previewing and asking questions, and previewing and using prior knowledge.

Voters at a polling place ▶

National **Standards for Civics and Government** **State**

The following National Standards for Civics and Government are covered in this chapter.

V. What are the roles of the citizen in American democracy?

C. What are the responsibilities of citizens?

D. What dispositions or traits of character are important to the preservation and

improvement of American constitutional democracy?

E. How can citizens take part in civic life?

Go Online
PHSchool.com

For: Your state's standards
Visit: PHSchool.com
Web Code: mpe-8231

Active Citizen Civics in the Real World

Ian was cooking dinner when his mother came home from work. She walked into the kitchen with a big smile on her face.

"Hey Mom! What's up? You sure look like you had a good day."

"I did! I filed my papers to run for city council," she said.

"No kidding! Hey Mom, that's great! Good for you! Soon I'll be able to tell all my friends I've got pull at City Hall. My mom's going to be running this town!"

Ian's mother laughed. "Slow down there, kiddo. The election hasn't happened yet. And there are already five other candidates in the race from our district."

"Sure, Mom. But I'm sure you can win this. And you can count on my help, too. I know it's a lot of work to run for office."

"Thanks, Ian. And now that you've turned 18, I'll be able to count on your vote as well."

"Hey, Mom, I said I would help you in your campaign. That's no promise about voting for you." Ian smirked into the saucepan he was stirring. "I've got to check out the other candidates and make sure you're the best one for the job." He and his mother both burst out laughing.

Citizen's Journal Suppose someone you know is running for office. Based on what you have learned so far, what is one piece of advice you would give that person? Why do you think this advice would be helpful?

Being a Voter

Reading Preview

Objectives

In this section you will

- Understand general elections.
- Explore the basics of voting.
- Learn about becoming an informed voter.

Taking Notes

Make a diagram like the one below. As you read the section, complete the diagram with information about voting.

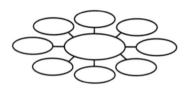

Key Terms

general election registration

Main Idea

Elections give citizens a voice in government. To vote, you need to register and then go to a designated polling place on election day.

Target Reading Skill

Set a Purpose When you set a purpose for reading, you give yourself a focus. This means you identify the reason you are reading the passage. Before you read this section, look at the headings and visuals to see what the section is about. Then set a purpose for reading the section.

Even now, you have the chance to play several of a citizen's roles. You go to school, you obey laws, and you may do volunteer work. Soon, you will be old enough to play the most important citizen role in a democracy: the role of voter.

General Elections

Voters take part in two kinds of elections: primary elections and general elections. In a primary election, members of political parties nominate candidates. A **general election** is an election in which voters make final decisions about candidates and issues.

About half a million federal, state, and local offices are filled in general elections. These offices include everything from President of the United States to a member of a town council.

In many states, counties, and cities, voters in a general election are asked to vote on certain ballot measures. These measures include initiatives, referendums, and recalls. They give each voter a voice in deciding what laws should be passed, how the government should raise money, and who should be removed from office.

In a typical general election, several hundred proposals for new laws, constitutional amendments, and new taxes appear on state ballots. For example, citizens in California were asked in 2002 to vote on seven proposals, ranging from state grants for after-school programs to penalties for voter fraud.

✓ Reading Check **What happens in a primary election?**

▲ Polling places are where people vote.

The Basics of Voting

In order to vote in the United States, you must be a citizen at least 18 years of age. As you learned in Chapter 7, African Americans and women could not vote until they gained full citizenship. In 1868, three years after the Thirteenth Amendment abolished slavery, Congress passed the Fourteenth Amendment, which gave African Americans full citizenship. Still, citizenship did not guarantee African Americans the right to vote in some states, so Congress passed the Fifteenth Amendment, which stated that the right to vote could not be denied on the basis of race and color. After years of struggle, women finally gained full citizenship and the right to vote when Congress passed the Nineteenth Amendment in 1918.

In addition, you must be a resident of the state in which you will vote. Not everybody who meets these qualifications can vote. In most states, prison inmates and people who are mentally incompetent are not allowed to vote.

Registration The process of signing up to be a voter is called **registration**. Registration was introduced in the late 1800s. It was meant to stop voter fraud, such as the same person voting more than once.

In a few states, voters may register at the polling place when they go to vote. In most states, you must register several weeks ahead of time. Many cities and towns set up registration tables in libraries, church basements, and shopping centers.

Each state makes its own laws about voter registration. In most states, local governments run the elections. They set the rules on voter registration and operate the polling places.

Voting—When and Where An act of Congress set the Tuesday after the first Monday in November as the day for federal congressional and presidential elections. Most elections for state offices take place at the same time.

Primary elections and elections for local governments may take place at any time, but most are in the spring. Special elections may be held at any time to choose candidates to finish the terms of officeholders who have died, resigned, or been recalled.

Voting takes place at polling places. As a registered voter, you are assigned to a polling place near where you live. Each polling place serves a voting district or precinct. Your polling place may be a nearby school or church.

"Motor Voter" Registration

States with "motor voter" laws allow people to register to vote when applying for or renewing their drivers' licenses. **Predict** *Why would such laws be successful in getting more of a state's population registered to vote?*

Target Reading Skill

Setting a Purpose Before reading the section **How to Cast a Vote**, scan the headings and visuals to set a purpose for reading.

How to Cast a Vote On entering the polling place, you check in with an election official, who looks up your name to see that you are registered to vote there. Local election units within each state set up the ballot. As a result, there are different ways to cast a vote. You may pull a lever on an election machine, mark an X on a paper ballot, punch a hole in a card, or make your choice on a touchpad.

If you cannot get to your polling place, you can have an absentee ballot sent to you. In this case, you mark your ballot and then mail it in.

There is some debate over the varying kinds of voting methods. Some methods are considered to be easier and more accurate than others. The 2000 presidential election illustrated this point. Some of the Florida voters were given a "butterfly ballot," in which they punched out a hole to cast their votes. These ballots were confusing because of the way the boxes were lined up next to the candidates' names.

Analyze Diagrams and Graphs

Voting Methods in the United States

These images show the variety of voting methods used in elections around the country. The graph below shows the percent of each method is used.

a. What is the difference between the punch card and paper ballot methods?

b. Which voting method is used the most? What are some possible drawbacks to this voting method?

Voting Methods Around the United States, 2002

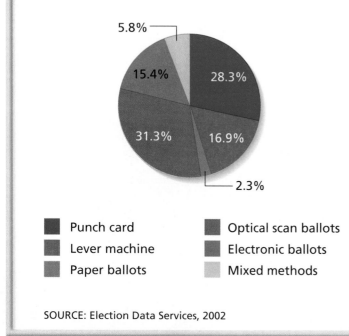

5.8%

15.4%

28.3%

31.3%

16.9%

2.3%

- Punch card
- Lever machine
- Paper ballots
- Optical scan ballots
- Electronic ballots
- Mixed methods

SOURCE: Election Data Services, 2002

1 **Paper Ballots** Voters mark their choices on a paper ballot.

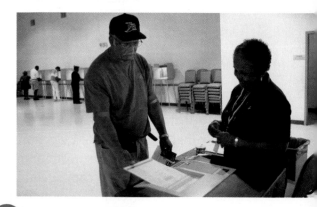

2 **Optical Scan Ballots** Voters mark their choices on a special ballot. Then, the ballots are fed through an optical scanner which reads and records each vote.

After the election, many of these voters feared that they misread the ballot and voted for the wrong candidate by mistake. In addition, the hole-punch method was found to be inaccurate when voters didn't punch all the way through the ballot. This election was extremely close. President George W. Bush won by about 500 votes out of some 10 million votes cast in Florida. A confusing ballot may have affected the outcome of the election.

States are investigating new methods of voting. Oregon became the first state to conduct an election totally by mail-in ballots in 2000. States are also looking into the use of the Internet for voting. Whatever methods they may choose, states must pay careful attention to the possible drawbacks of the method they choose to use.

✓ **Reading Check** **When is election day for federal and state offices?**

Go Online
civics
interactive

For: Interactive Diagram
Visit: PHSchool.com
Web Code: mpp-9231

3 **Punch Card** Voters mark their choices by corresponding punching holes in a ballot.

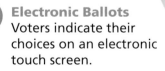

4 **Lever Machine** Voters use a voting machine and move a lever to indicate their choices.

5 **Electronic Ballots** Voters indicate their choices on an electronic touch screen.

The Supreme Court

Go Online
civics interactive
For: Interactive Constitution with Supreme Court Cases
Visit: PHSchool.com
Web Code: mpp-8232

Bush v. *Gore* (2000)

Why It Matters The issue at stake was a controversial recount in the 2000 U.S. presidential election and who would become President of the United States.

Background The 2000 presidential election pitted U.S. Vice President Al Gore, a Democrat, against Texas Governor George W. Bush, a Republican. As the election results were counted, it became clear that the vote would be very close and that the results in Florida would decide the election. Bush was initially declared the winner; however, reports of widespread problems with ballots soon called the results into question.

Gore's supporters sued the state of Florida for a recount. Bush's supporters sued to prevent it. To add to matters, Florida's election laws set an unchangeable deadline for announcing the final results. Therefore, the recount had to be begun quickly. The Florida Supreme Court decided in favor of Gore. Bush appealed to the U.S. Supreme Court.

The Decision The U.S. Supreme Court, in a 5–4 decision, stated that the Supreme Court of Florida had violated the U.S. Constitution when it ordered the recount only in certain districts. The Supreme Court also ruled that shifting methods of vote counting had already tainted the recount. Both of these, it said, violated the equal-protection guarantees of the Fourteenth Amendment. The court then said that there was no way to hold an acceptable recount by the final election deadline and ordered the recounts stopped. This effectively named Bush the winner. The Court's decision remains a highly controversial moment in the Court's history.

Understanding the Law

1. Why was the Supreme Court's involvement in the 2000 elections significant?
2. Why did George W. Bush's supporters oppose the Florida recount?

Becoming an Informed Voter

To vote wisely, you must become an informed voter. You should find out all you can about the candidates. What are their qualifications? Where do they stand on important issues?

You can get the answers to these questions from many sources. The candidates can tell you how they stand on the issues. Public service organizations with no ties to political parties, such as the League of Women Voters, often put out excellent information. You can also count on newspapers to write stories on the candidates' records, backgrounds, and stands on the issues.

You can also learn about the candidates through television news and live speeches. By watching televised debates, you can see how they answer questions and handle themselves in a tough situation.

Ballot Measures You should also learn about ballot measures. Having a complete picture of a ballot measure is very important. For example, at first glance you might vote against a 25-cent-per-gallon rise in the tax on gasoline because it would make gasoline more expensive. However, if the money raised by the tax would pay for a highway that would shorten your drive to work by 10 miles, you might change your mind. Some states send information on ballot measures to all registered voters.

Why Vote In recent years, only about half of all eligible citizens have actually voted in presidential elections. Sometimes people think their vote cannot possibly affect the final outcome of an election. How, they ask, can my one vote make a difference in a presidential race in which more than 90 million people vote?

Elections are almost never won by 1 or by even 100 votes. However, the 2000 presidential election came down to only about 500 votes in the deciding state of Florida. In the end, a very small part of the population determined the outcome of the race.

Furthermore, even if your candidate loses, your vote still matters. Through the ballot box you announce where you stand on the issues. You state what kind of representatives you want. By casting your vote you perform an important civic duty. You take part in the process of deciding who will lead our government and what policies those leaders will follow.

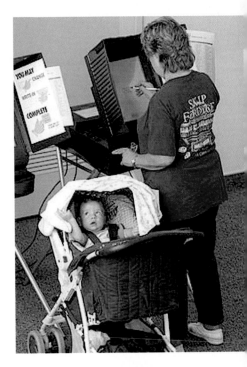

Making Voting Easier
A voter tries out an electronic voting system, designed to make elections easier to organize and to participate in.

✔ Reading Check **About what fraction of eligible voters vote in presidential elections?**

SECTION 1   Assessment

Key Terms
Use the following key term in a sentence that explains its meaning: general election, registration

Target Reading Skill
1. Set a Purpose How did you describe the purpose you set for reading the section "How to Cast A Vote"?

Comprehension and Critical Thinking
2. a. Recall What types of ballot measures give citizens a direct role in deciding which laws get passed?

b. Contrast How are general elections different from primary elections?

3. a. Explain Who makes election laws about voter registration?

b. Draw Inferences How does voter registration stop voter fraud?

4. a. Describe What does the League of Women Voters do?

b. Solve Problems If only half the eligible voters vote in an election and the winning candidate wins with a bare majority of the votes, about what percentage of eligible voters elected the candidate to office?

Writing Activity
Why is it significant that only half of eligible voters vote in elections? Write a letter to the editor in which you express your views about this issue.

TIP Make an outline of your views. Devote a paragraph to each point you make in your essay.

Influencing Your Vote

Reading Preview

Objectives

In this section you will

- Learn about messages from the candidates.
- Understand the reasons for messages from interest groups.
- Learn about recognizing propaganda techniques.
- Explore how news media report the elections.

Taking Notes

Make a diagram like the one below. As you read the section, complete the diagram with information about the factors that influence voters.

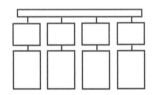

Spreading the Word
Candidates for office rely on a number of methods to get their messages to voters.

Key Terms

direct mail   propaganda
media bias

Main Idea

Candidates use many different methods to influence voters, including advertising, direct mail, bumper stickers and personal appearances. Interest groups also campaign for candidates and issues they favor. The media also influences voters by the way it covers elections.

Target Reading Skill

Preview and Predict Making predictions about your text helps you set a purpose for reading and remember what you read. Before you begin, preview the section by looking at the headings, the visuals, and anything else that stands out. Then make a prediction about the subject of the text.

The television screen shows a man walking down a quiet, tree-lined street holding the hands of his two young children. An announcer says, "Bob Kane has lived in our city all his life. He graduated from our public schools. His children attend those schools. He knows your problems and he knows what you want." Another television ad shows an empty jail cell. A frightened voice says, "What Bob Kane has done puts criminals back in our neighborhoods—not here, where they belong."

Before an election, you will hear many campaign messages. Each will try to influence how you vote. Some will give you information. Others, like these TV ads, will try to play on your fears and other feelings. You should be aware that you cannot always trust what campaign ads say.

Messages from the Candidates

Candidates have many different methods to try to get voters to vote for them. Depending on the office for which they are running and the number of votes they must win, they may shake your hand in person or buy thousands of dollars' worth of television advertising time. As a voter, you should know about the many ways candidates try to get their messages to you.

Posters, Bumper Stickers, and Leaflets In the months before election day, you will see posters and stickers plastered on lampposts, billboards, windows, and car bumpers. People running for office want to make their names known to the voters.

To give voters a better picture of the person behind the name, candidates use leaflets and flyers. Such leaflets give short biographical sketches of the candidates and tell where they stand on the major issues.

Personal Appearances Candidates running for a town council usually campaign in a personal way. They ring doorbells and hold neighborhood meetings, bringing their messages to citizens through conversations and speeches to small groups.

Even in elections for state and national offices, candidates appear in person to spread their messages among the voters. Your chance to meet someone running for state or national office usually comes at huge political rallies in public parks or auditoriums or at neighborhood political meetings.

Direct Mail One of the best ways to get the attention of voters is by mail. Candidates can use **direct mail**, a way of sending messages to large groups of people through the mail. Direct mail allows candidates to target voters who have special interests. For example, a candidate can send a message to senior citizens promising to support higher Social Security payments.

The Internet More and more American voters are using the Internet to gather political information. Web sites from global news sources and special interest groups have been available to Internet users for years, and have only become more numerous as Internet use soars.

In 2000, politicians first took notice of the Internet as an important communications tool. Then President Bill Clinton and Vice President Al Gore began posting papers on various Web sites devoted to the Democratic Party and political discourse. Other politicians were soon following suit. It then became standard practice for politicians to have a Web site of their own.

Yet, it wasn't until 2003 and the run-up to the Democratic race for the 2004 presidential candidacy that the full power of the Internet as a campaign took came to light. Through his use of chat rooms, Weblogs ("blogs"), which are like daily diaries posting campaign updates that people can respond to, Web sites devoted to his campaign, and carefully composed campaign e-mail messages sent by a network of supporters to friends and family, Former Vermont Governor Howard Dean was able to get his message out to a large Internet community. As a result of his efforts, he not only raised millions of dollars for his campaign through Internet donations, but shot to the top of the Democratic field. Other candidtaes have learned from his experience.

Handouts
Candidates produce a variety of materials to influence voters during campaigns.
Contrast *What advantages do buttons offer to candidates over leaflets? What advantages do leaflets have over buttons?*

Advertisements in the Media Candidates for state and national office reach very large numbers of voters. They have found that one of the best ways to get their message out is through advertisements in the **media**—television, radio, newspapers, magazines, and the internet.

Since television time and newspaper space is so expensive, political ads are usually short and simple. They often give very little in the way of information. Instead, they try to grab your attention and to focus on a candidate's personality rather than qualifications and abilities.

Often, political advertisements take a negative stance toward a candidate's opponents. They may focus on the opponents' failures or other weaknesses. But these kinds of ads tell you very little about the candidate who sponsors the ad. However, using the media can be very expensive. A full-page advertisement in a major newspaper costs thousands of dollars. The cost of a few minutes on television can cost hundreds of thousands of dollars. Many media ads depend on slogans, such as "Building a Better Tomorrow" or "It's Morning in America."

For these reasons, TV and newspaper ads are not a good source of information about what a candidate would do if elected. They rarely say much, for example, about how a candidate plans to fight the drug problem or improve the economy. However, some of these ads do tell voters what stands the candidates have taken on major issues.

✔ Reading Check   **How can direct mail help candidates?**

PACs Get Involved
During an election, political action committees often place advertisements supporting the candidates they feel will best serve their group's specific interest.
Summarize How else do PACs influence elections?

Messages from Interest Groups

Interest groups also put out their share of direct mail and media ads. Interest groups want to help elect candidates who agree with their views and to defeat candidates who do not. Interest groups also work to pass or defeat ballot measures. Interest groups try to achieve their election goals in two other ways. They endorse, or lend their names in support of, candidates and ballot measures. They also give money to campaigns.

The largest interest groups have political action committees (PACs) whose job is to carry out these election activities. PACs often work very hard for or against ballot measures. For example, when a recent ballot measure in Oregon asked voters to decide if people who want to buy guns should be subject to background checks, Handgun Control, Inc. campaigned in support of the measure while the National Rifle Association worked to defeat it.

PACs also give large sums of money to campaigns for state and national office. United States senators running for re-election in 2002 received an average of $860,000 each from PACs.

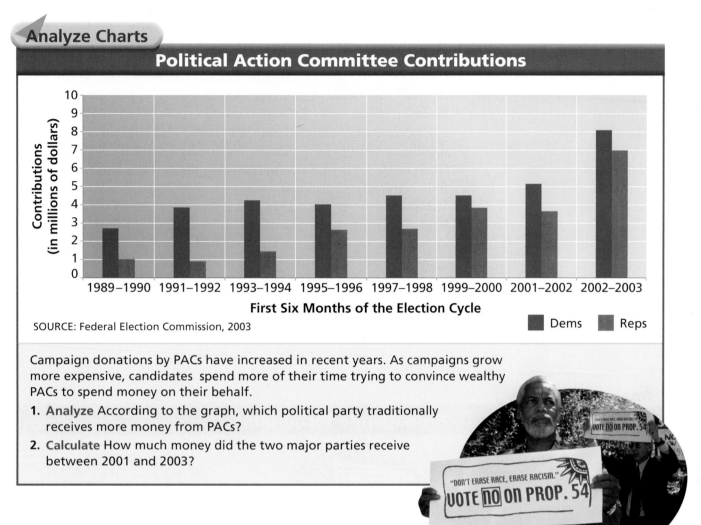

Analyze Charts

Political Action Committee Contributions

Contributions (in millions of dollars) vs. **First Six Months of the Election Cycle**

SOURCE: Federal Election Commission, 2003

■ Dems ■ Reps

Campaign donations by PACs have increased in recent years. As campaigns grow more expensive, candidates spend more of their time trying to convince wealthy PACs to spend money on their behalf.

1. **Analyze** According to the graph, which political party traditionally receives more money from PACs?
2. **Calculate** How much money did the two major parties receive between 2001 and 2003?

Since the early 1970s, the number of PACs in the United States has grown from about 600 to more than 4,000. Some PACs get their money from the people they represent—union members, employees of businesses, and corporation stockholders. Others use direct mail to find people who agree with their views and will send them large sums of money. The success of both methods of raising money has given PACs a strong voice in campaigns.

Federal law limits the amount that PACs may give to each candidate. However, there are few rules for how much PACs may spend on running their own campaigns.

Many people believe that PACs have too much influence on the outcome of elections. They charge that the "special interests" that PACs represent are gaining too much power in government. Each interest group represents only a small percentage of Americans, or cares about only one issue, they say. Through PACs, however, interest groups can have a voice in who will hold office and make decisions on important issues that affect everyone in the United States.

Although some people want limits placed on what PACs can do, other people are opposed to such limits. They argue that PACs are simply using their First Amendment right to free speech.

✓ Reading Check **What are PACs?**

Chapter 23 **625**

Recognizing Propaganda Techniques

Candidates and interest groups all have the same goal: to influence the way you think. A message that is meant to influence people's ideas, opinions, or actions in a certain way is called **propaganda**.

Propaganda can include lies, but it can also contain truthful—or mostly truthful—information. A message is called propaganda when it tells only one side of the story, distorts the truth, or appeals mostly to people's feelings.

Messages from candidates and PACs make use of many different kinds of propaganda. Six of the most common propaganda techniques used by candidates are described in the chart below.

When reading and listening to political messages, be aware of the kinds of propaganda techniques that might be at work. Recognizing them will help you decide how to act on the messages.

✓ Reading Check   **What is the goal of interest groups?**

Analyze Diagrams

Propaganda Techniques

Glittering Generalities
Use words and phrases that sound appealing and that everyone agrees with.
Example: "I stand for freedom and the American way."

Card Stacking
Use only those facts that support your argument.
Example: "My opponent voted against raising Social Security." (You do not mention that she vote no because the proposed increase was too small.)

Plain Folks
Tell voters that you are just like them—an ordinary person with similar needs and ideas.
Example: "I've lived in this city all my life. My children go to the same schools as your children."

Name Calling
Attach negative labels to your opponent.
Example: "He's soft on crime."

Bandwagon
Appeals to desire to follow the crowd.
Example: "Polls show that more than 80 percent of voters support me."

Transfer
Connect yourself to a respected person, group, or symbol.
Example: "Remember what Abraham Lincoln said . . ."

Candidates use a variety of techniques to try to influence voters.

1. **Analyze** What would be another example of the bandwagon technique?
2. **Apply** Which technique would be most effective in a presidential primary? Why?

ANALYZING Political Cartoons

In the cartoon at right, a candidate for office is speaking to a pair of sheep.

1. Does this scene take place early or late during the candidate's campaign?

2. How is the timing of the scene significant to what is taking place?

3. What do you think the cartoonist is trying to say about political candidates?

LAST-MINUTE CAMPAIGN STOP

How News Media Report the Elections

The media also put out their own information about candidates and issues. This information comes in two forms: editorials and news reporting. In their editorials, the media give their opinions. News reporting, on the other hand, is supposed to stick to the facts.

Election News Election news reports give information about what a candidate says and does. Even though news reports give facts, not opinions, they can present these facts in ways that favor one candidate over another.

For the most part, the news media usually try not to show **bias**, or a favoring of one point of view. However, reporters, news directors, and editors have their opinions, likes, and dislikes.

How can you spot bias in news reporting? Bias can show when stories about one candidate are given more time or space or better placement than stories about other candidates. If you were running for class president, how would you feel if a story about you got 10 lines on page 6 of the school newspaper, while your opponent was given half of the front page?

Another sign of bias is when the media play up the negative side of one candidate's personality or behavior. They may run stories about a candidate's bad temper or a divorce that took place years ago. Such stories, though they may not be lies, can give voters a bad impression of the candidate and influence the way they vote.

Target Reading Skill
Preview and Predict Preview the section **How News Media Report the Elections** by scanning the headings and visuals. Then make a prediction about the subject matter of the text.

Opinion Polls The news media also present the results of opinion polls. Polls can show which candidate voters favor at a certain time, why they like that candidate, and what issues they think are most important.

The basic idea behind a poll is that you do not have to talk to every person in a group to find out what the outcome of that group's vote will be. A poll asks questions of a sample, or small part, of the group. The answers given by the people in the sample are then taken to stand for how the whole group would answer if everyone were asked.

Polling works only if the people are chosen at random. This helps make sure that the views of the people in the sample will stand for those of the whole group. Most of the major national polls use random sampling and ask fair questions. Most experts agree that polls are not always accurate, but polls can give a sense of how the public thinks.

However, not all polls reported in the news are based on random samples. A poll that gets answers from only certain kinds of people may not be very accurate. Such polls include those in which people mail in answers to lists of questions in magazines, visit Web sites, or call in their answers by telephone.

Some people think that polls should not be used. They believe that polls can change the results of elections. They point to voters who say they will vote for a certain candidate mainly because that candidate is leading in the polls. In other words, those voters will jump on the candidate's bandwagon.

Also, some voters may decide whether to vote or not based on the results of opinion polls. Studies suggest that if the polls show a huge gap between candidates, some people believe that the leading candidate will win, and they do not bother to vote.

Political Polling
Polls help candidates find out how well their campaigns are doing.
Summarize *How can inaccurate polls have a negative effect on the political process?*

The Impact of Television Today, many voters receive most of their information by watching the television news. Television has had a big impact on the way people see the candidates, understand the issues, and cast their votes.

Critics charge that television has made election issues seem unimportant because it covers the more exciting activities of the candidates, rather than paying attention to the major issues. These people also say that to make election news exciting and appealing, television tries to reduce campaign stories to 20-second "sound-bites" that catch viewers' attention but give little or no information.

Television has also had a powerful impact on the way candidates run their campaigns. They make their messages short and simple to fit easily on the television news. They also plan campaign activities that will look good on TV.

Overall, television has created a new kind of political candidate. A person running for high office today must come across well on the screen. This "television" candidate, by and large, must be good looking, have a compelling personality, and be at ease in front of the camera. Otherwise, he or she may face a tough time in an election.

Even though network news is not always the best source of facts about the candidates and issues, good sources do exist. Public television and special network programs provide fuller coverage, but people have to seek these alternatives out.

Camera-Ready Candidates
The debates between John F. Kennedy and Richard Nixon in 1960 were the first presidential debates to be televised. Modern campaigns rely more and more on television to sway voters.
Make Generalizations *What have voters lost as campaigns have become more reliant on television?*

✓ Reading Check **How do polls influence voter behavior?**

SECTION 2 Assessment

Key Terms

Use each of the key terms in a sentence that explains its meaning: direct mail, media, propaganda, bias

Target Reading Skill

1. **Preview and Predict** What parts of the content of "How News Media Report the Elections" did your prediction *not* include?

Comprehension and Critical Thinking

2. **a. Describe** Describe four methods candidates use to reach voters.

   b. Identify Cause and Effect How do advertisements in the media create a need to raise money?

3. **a. Explain** Why do interest groups participate in elections?

   b. Analyze Information Why do some people think that PACs have too much influence in government?

4. **a. Recall** What is propaganda?

   b. Draw Conclusions Why do you think candidates and interest groups use propaganda in election campaigns?

5. **a. Describe** What is the difference between news reporting and editorials?

   b. Identify Cause and Effect How has television influenced politics and a candidate's chances of success?

Writing Activity

Choose a local or national issue that is in the news. Write a statement about the issue that uses propaganda techniques.

TIP Make an outline before you begin writing. Organize your information under major headings. This will help you eliminate unnecessary information and keep your report concise.

How to Conduct an Interview

Americans hold a variety of views on important issues. Conducting an interview is one way to find out what people think about an issue.

The interview below is from a student newspaper. As you read, pay attention to the questions asked and how the answers reveal the feelings of the person being interviewed.

Reporter: What made you decide to become a principal?

Principal Kennedy: Being an administrator was the job that seemed to take in all of the things I love doing—working with kids and parents, teaching teachers, and solving problems.

Reporter: Why is a good education so important for young people?

Principal Kennedy: The education a person receives as a youngster is one of the most important influences on their future. Without a good education, a person would have a hard time finding a good job. A good education also helps you learn to respect people from all walks of life.

Reporter: What is one of the biggest challenges facing students today?

Principal Kennedy: Budget cuts in education present a big challenge. With less money, some schools won't be able to provide students with the resources necessary for a good education.

Learn the Skill

To conduct a successful interview, follow these steps:

❶ **State the purpose.** Tell the person being interviewed the purpose of the interview.

❷ **Ask relevant questions.** Ask only questions that relate to the topic of the interview. Ask for clarification when an answer is not clear. Also, be prepared to ask follow-up questions.

❸ **Take notes.** To the extent that you can, write down exactly what the person says. Or, you may want to record the interview on an audiotape. Be sure to ask for permission to record from the person you are interviewing.

Practice the Skill

❶ With the class, brainstorm a list of possible interview topics related to school.

❷ Write three questions related to the topic chosen by the class.

Apply the Skill

Interview a student in your school who is not a member of your class. Summarize the result and present your findings to the class.

Go Online
civics interactive

For: Local Citizenship
Visit: PHSchool.com
Web Code: mpp-8233

Campaigning for Office

Reading Preview

Objectives

In this section you will

- Explore planning and running a campaign.
- Learn about financing a campaign.
- Explain who wins an election.
- Learn about the electoral college.

Key Terms

campaign manager
campaign press
  secretary

incumbent
electors

Main Idea

A political campaign requires organization, staff and money. In a presidential election voters send electors to the Electoral College, who then elect the President.

Target Reading Skill

Preview and Ask Questions
Before you read a section, preview the headings and visuals to see what the section is about. Write one or two questions about what you see that will help you understand or remember what you read in the section. Then read and find the answers to your questions.

Taking Notes

Make a diagram like the one below. As you read the section, complete the diagram with information about what is involved in planning and running a campaign.

I n the movie *The Candidate*, actor Robert Redford plays a man running for Congress. At one point the candidate says that he wants to "go where I want, say what I want, do what I want." His campaign advisor then writes a message on a matchbook and pushes it toward the candidate. The message reads, "You lose."

Campaigning for a major office is not something a person does alone. It is a highly organized, tightly controlled activity. Presidential campaigns take a great deal of planning and money. But all campaigns share a common goal—to get the candidate elected. Most use the same techniques to work toward that goal.

Planning and Running a Campaign

By the November general election, a major-party candidate has passed several hurdles. He or she has won primary elections and caucuses and has been nominated by his or her party at its national convention. The candidate has chosen a running mate, raised money, and built up an organization. Much work, however, still lies ahead.

A great deal of thought, planning, and hard work by many people goes into a presidential campaign. Staff members work with the candidate to plan and carry out the campaign. Thousands of workers work long hours stuffing envelopes, making telephone calls, and ringing doorbells. The candidate's party contributes money and people. The final success or failure of the campaign depends on the organization as a whole.

The Work of Many People
A campaign's success depends on many people in addition to the candidate.

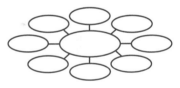

The following is an excerpt from a 1980 campaign brochure for Ronald Reagan, entitled "Let's Make American Great Again."

"We can solve our problems ... But we must have wise and experienced leadership from the President of the United States. Of all the candidates, only Ronald Reagan has the proven leadership we need. He will not try to solve our problems with empty promises. He will not rely on bigger government with more spending. That hasn't worked. The answer is better government, and Ronald Reagan can provide it."

Analyzing Primary Sources
Based on the title and content of the brochure, what do you think was Reagan's campaign strategy?

Campaign Organization Besides the candidate, the most important person in a campaign is the campaign manager. The **campaign manager** helps plan the broad outlines of the campaign: where to go, what issues to talk about, and what image of the candidate to put forth. The manager also guides the work of other members of the staff, such as fundraisers, speechwriters, and media advisors.

The manager keeps in touch with the people who run the campaign across the country. These lower-level managers are in charge of the thousands of volunteers who handle the day-to-day campaign work that is needed to win the election.

Finally, the manager is in charge of the workers who plan for the candidate to appear at meetings, picnics, and rallies. These "advance people" make sure that the candidate has big crowd on hand.

Finding Out What the Public Thinks

A successful campaign must keep its finger on the pulse of the American public. What issues should the candidate be talking about? A presidential campaign usually has its own opinion poll taker who finds the answers to such questions.

The poll taker finds out which issues the voters think are important. Polls can also show the impact of the campaign in different parts of the country and among different groups of voters.

Managing and Using the Media Candidates for President are followed by planeloads and busloads of people from the media. The **campaign press secretary** makes certain that the news shows the candidate in the best light. The press secretary tells reporters about public appearances and gives them copies of speeches and policy positions.

Meeting the Candidate
Campaign workers often organize informal events for voters to get to know the candidate

Active Citizen

Students Make a Difference

Nathaniel Weixel, a senior at Marlborough High School in Marlborough, Massachusetts, believes knowledge of government begins at the local level.

Nathaniel has worked on both state and local campaigns, attending rallies and handing out campaign literature. As reporter and editor of his school's newspaper, Nathaniel strives to educate his peers on the importance of politics in their lives, writing about issues that concern them and their community. When there are elections, he takes the time to publicize them.

▲ Students can help make a difference by helping inform voters about candidates' position on the issues.

Service Learning

How can you help make people in your community more aware of the importance of voting?

The press secretary also helps make sure that the media is on hand when the candidate is "making news." A television news report on a candidate's visit to a children's hospital will be seen by thousands of people. Such media coverage is a good source of free publicity for the candidate.

One way for national candidates to get their message across to the public is by advertising in newspapers and on radio and television. A campaign hires media advisors to create ads for the media. Such ads, especially television ads, can have a major impact on a campaign.

Media people have learned that saying bad things about the other candidate can sometimes work better than saying nice things about their own. They also know that it is often best to focus on image and style rather than issues and ideas.

Some critics say that this approach amounts to little more than "packaging and selling" the candidates. It is up to you, the voter, to view these ads carefully and to pay attention to the propaganda techniques being used.

✔ Reading Check   **Who is the person in charge of a political campaign?**

Campaigns And Money In a democracy, each vote is supposed to be equal. But many people are concerned that the huge amounts of money required for campaigns for high office have changed the nature of our democracy. Critics point to the number of millionaires serving in the U.S. Senate and House. They point to the great influence wielded by PACS, which often support candidates who will act in ways that support their business or interest. Many politicians claim that they are not influenced by the people who raise money for them. But since almost every politician runs for reelection, it is hard to think they could ignore those who raised funds for their initial election.

Analyzing Economics
What do you think would happen if candidates were only allowed to spend the same amount of money?

Changing the Rules
Senator John McCain of Arizona became known as a crusader for reform of campaign finance laws.
Synthesize Information *Why would people feel that the way candidates raise money for their campaigns would need changing?*

Financing a Campaign

People who run for President and for other national and state offices have one thing in common—they need a lot of money. As Tip O'Neill, former Speaker of the House of Representatives, once said, "There are four parts to any campaign. The candidate, the issues of the candidate, the campaign organization, and the money to run the campaign with. Without money you can forget the other three." In 1998, for example, major party candidates for the Senate spent an average of nearly $4 million each.

Candidates for local, state, and national office get most of their money from individuals. Many candidates for national and high state office also get money from political parties and PACs.

Campaign Finance Law Several laws outline the rules for how campaigns for federal office can be paid for. No one person may give more than $2,000 to a candidate. Candidates must report the name of anyone who has given them more than $200, so that the public can know where the money is coming from. Congress set up the Federal Election Commission (FEC) to carry out these and other rules.

Citizens may give $3 of their taxes each year to a presidential campaign fund. Every election year, the FEC offers money from this fund to each of the major candidates for the presidency. Once presidential candidates accept these public funds, they cannot accept or spend money from any other sources.

FEC rules allow a PAC to give up to $5,000 to a presidential candidate in the primary elections. However, in the general election, candidates who have accepted public tax money may not take money from PACs. This rule does not keep PACs from spending as much as they like on their own campaigns in support of candidates.

Criticism of Campaign Financing Many people complain that elections cost too much money. They say the high cost of running for office keeps many good people from running at all. If costs continue to rise, will only the wealthy—and candidates backed by wealthy individuals and groups—be able to run and win?

Some groups, however, would like to go further. They want to have all campaigns paid for entirely with public funds so that candidates do not have to raise funds privately.

✓ **Reading Check** **What is the maximum amount that a voter can contribute to a candidate?**

Incumbent and Challengers
Incumbent President George Bush was defeated in 1996 by his challenger, Bill Clinton. Clinton won re-election in 1996.

Who Wins an Election?

It is a goal of our democracy to elect people who will be our best leaders and decision makers. Being a good leader and being able to make good decisions, however, are not all it takes to win an election. As you have seen, it is also important to look good on television, be well organized, have a good campaign team, and be able to raise a lot of money, especially if you are running for national office. It also helps to have the backing of either the Democratic or Republican party.

One other factor is also very important. An **incumbent**, someone who already holds the office for which he or she is running, has a very good chance of winning. Incumbents win re-election far more often than they lose. During the 2002 elections, for example, 390 incumbent members of the House of Representatives ran for re-election—and 383 of them won.

An incumbent has a name that voters know and a record to point to. Unless an incumbent has made major mistakes, a challenger usually faces a hard battle with only a small chance of winning. However, incumbents are not unbeatable. About one-quarter of all incumbent presidents have lost re-election. John Adams was the first incumbent president to lose re-election when he lost to Thomas Jefferson in 1800. Since World War II, three incumbent presidents have lost re-election. In the 1976 presidential elections, incumbent Gerald Ford lost to Jimmy Carter. President Carter would later lose to Ronald Reagan in the presidential election of 1980. In the 1992 elections, incumbent President George H.W. Bush lost to Bill Clinton.

✔ Reading Check   **What advantages does an incumbent have over a challenger?**

Electoral Votes by State, 2004

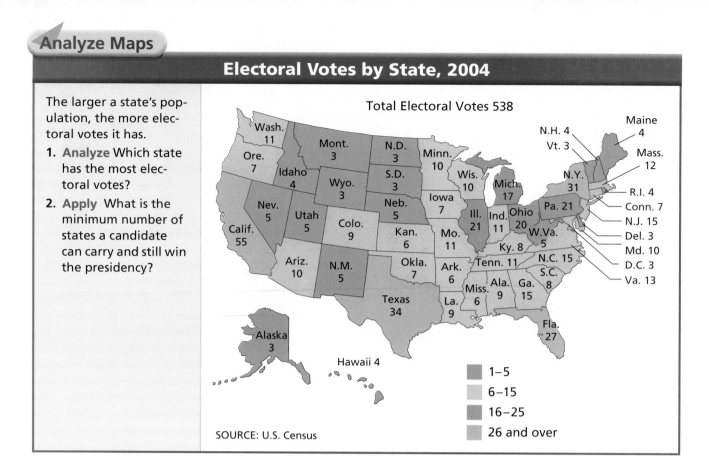

The larger a state's population, the more electoral votes it has.

1. **Analyze** Which state has the most electoral votes?

2. **Apply** What is the minimum number of states a candidate can carry and still win the presidency?

Total Electoral Votes 538

SOURCE: U.S. Census

- 1–5
- 6–15
- 16–25
- 26 and over

The Electoral College

When you vote for President, do you choose the candidate directly? No. You actually elect people called **electors,** people who promise to cast votes for the candidate selected by voters. As set down in the Constitution, the President is chosen by votes in the Electoral College.

How the Electoral College Works Each state has the same number of electors as it has members of Congress. Iowa, for example, has 5 representatives and 2 senators. It has 7 electors. The Electoral College has 538 electors, each with one vote.

Before the presidential election, each political party in every state draws up a list of electors who promise to vote for the party's presidential candidate. On election day, when you vote for a certain candidate, you are really voting for that candidate's team of electors.

On election night, the whole nation waits to find out which states each candidate has "won." "Winning" or "carrying" a state, means that a candidate's whole team of electors has won in that state. That winning team then has the right to cast their electoral votes in the Electoral College.

A few weeks after the election, the official electoral voting takes place in each state. An elector is not required by law to vote for the candidate to whom he or she is pledged, but nearly all do. The votes are then counted in Congress. To win, a candidate needs an absolute majority of electoral votes—270 or more.

Target Reading Skill

Preview and Ask Questions Before you read the section **How the Electoral College Works,** preview the headings and visuals to see what the section is about. Write one or two questions that will help you understand or remember what you read in the section. Then read and find the answers to your questions.

The 2000 Election and the Electoral College

Over the years, many people have charged that the "winner-take-all" method of awarding electoral votes from each state is not fair. They point out that candidates have gotten less than a majority of the votes nationwide but, by winning enough large states, have still been elected President. In 2000, for example, Al Gore received about 500,000 more popular votes than George W. Bush. However, Bush was elected President with 271 electoral votes to Gore's 267.

In most cases, however, the person who gets the majority of popular votes also gets the majority of electoral votes. George W. Bush won the presidency after being awarded Florida's 25 electoral votes in a bitterly contested vote recount that was eventually settled by the Supreme Court. He is only the fourth president in history to reach the White House without winning the popular vote.

The drama of the 2000 election made many American political leaders question whether the Electoral College system is worth keeping, however. It is likely that Congress will continue to examine and debate methods of improving our electoral system.

The Electoral Colelge
Al Gore speaks to reporters. Usually, the Electoral College vote echoes the results of the popular vote. When it did not do so in 2000, many Americans wondered why it was still used.

✓ Reading Check   **What made the 2000 Presidential election unusual?**

SECTION 3 Assessment

Key Terms

Use each of the key terms in a sentence that explains its meaning: campaign manager, campaign press secretary, incumbent, electors

Target Reading Skill

1. Preview and Ask Questions What questions did you ask when previewing the section "How the Electoral College Works"?

Comprehension and Critical Thinking

2. a. Explain What is the role of a campaign's poll-taker?

b. Summarize How do campaigns use the media?

3. a. Recall Why are candidates required to report the name of contributors who give more than $200?

b. Analyze Information How can PACs support candidates without directly giving them money?

4. a. Describe In addition to being a good leader, what else does a candidate need to win elections?

b. Make Predictions How does the great number of incumbents who get reelected to the House of Representatives influence government?

5. a. Explain How are a state's electoral votes determined?

b. Analyze Information Does the Electoral College emphasize the individual vote, or lessen its importance?

Writing Activity

Find out the election results in your state and county in the most recent Presidential election. Write a brief essay that summarizes those results.

Go Online
PHSchool.com

For: Writing Activity
Visit: PHSchool.com
Web Code: mpd-8233

Making Decisions

You make decisions every day. Some decisions are harder to make than others. A reliable method for decision-making can help you make the choices that are best for you.

Karen is the Student Council President. She needs to choose one person to be the head of an important committee. She has the choice of two well-qualified fellow students.

Michael is captain of the soccer team, a singer with the jazz band, president of the Community Service Club, and one of the most popular students in school. He does everything well and gets along with everybody. One potential problem with Michael is that he sometimes is not available and misses meetings because of his busy schedule. However, Michael really wants the job and will be disappointed if he does not get it.

Lawrence is quiet and one of the smartest kids in school. He is not as active in extracurricular activities or as popular as Michael. However, he has impressed Karen with his accurate observations about people. Lawrence always seems to have studied the issues and is prepared with new ideas. He is not overly busy and could give the committee job his full attention. Lawrence will probably not expect to be chosen, since Michael is so much more popular. Still, the school would greatly benefit from his energy and intelligence, and he would benefit from getting more involved in school activities.

Who should Karen choose?

Learn the Skill

Follow these steps to help you make decisions:

1. **Identify the problem.** What are the issues that need resolving? What is your goal?

2. **Identify the facts.** What information do you need to make an informed decision?

3. **List options.** What are the choices?

4. **Predict consequences.** What could be the results of the decision you make? Identify the pros and cons of each option.

5. **Make the decision.** Review your options, examine the facts, consider the possible consequences, and choose the option that works best.

Practice the Skill

Read the passage above and answer these questions:

1. What is Karen's goal?

2. What information does Karen have to help her make the decision?

3. Identify the choices that Karen has.

4. What consequences might result from Karen's decision?

5. Who should Karen choose? Why?

Apply the Skill

Use the steps to make a decision you have been facing. Explain your choice.

Review and Assessment

Chapter Summary

Section 1
Being a Voter
(pages 616–621)

- A general election is an election in which voters make final decisions about candidates and issues.

- Voting in an election requires registration and then showing up at the polls on Election Day. In recent years about half of all eligible citizens have voted in presidential elections.

- To vote wisely, one must become an informed voter.

Section 2
How Candidates and Groups Try to Influence Your Vote
(pages 622–629)

- Candidates use various methods, including direct mail, to get their message out to voters.

- Interest groups form PACs to influence voters.

- Candidates use propaganda to influence the outcome of elections.

- The media play a significant role in elections. Voters need to be alert to occasional bias shown by the media.

Section 3
Campaigning for Office
(pages 631–637)

- The campaign manager and campaign press secretary are two of the most important staff members of a political campaign.

- Fundraising is critical to a successful political campaign.

- Incumbents have many advantages in an election.

- Electors in the Electoral College actually elect the President.

Copy the chart below and use it to help you summarize the chapter.

```
              Voting and Elections
        ┌───────────┬─────────────────┬──────────────┐
                          How
                       Candidates
       Being a        and Groups Try    Campaigning
        Voter          to Influence       for Office
                         Your Vote
      ┌────────┐      ┌────────────┐    ┌───────────┐
      │        │      │            │    │           │
      └────────┘      └────────────┘    └───────────┘
```

Go Online
PHSchool.com

For: Self-Test
Visit: PHSchool.com
Web Code: mpa-8233

Reviewing Key Terms

Fill in the blank with one of the key terms from the list.

bias   direct mail
electors   general election
propaganda   incumbent
media   campaign manager

1. A message meant to influence people's ideas or actions in a certain way is called _____.

2. An election in which voters make final decisions about candidates and issues is called a _____.

3. The person in charge of a political campaign is called a _____.

4. A way of sending messages to large groups of voters is called _____.

5. When a news article favors one candidate or point of view over another, it is displaying _____.

6. Newspapers, television, radio and magazines are all part of the _____.

7. The person who holds an office is called the _____.

8. The people in the Electoral College who actually elect the President are called _____.

Comprehension and Critical Thinking

9. a. **Explain** What do voters actually decide in a general election?
   b. **Check Consistency** Why do you think there is no law that requires all eligible citizens to vote?
   c. **Make Predictions** What do you think it would take to get more people to vote in presidential elections?

10. a. **Describe** Where do PACs get their funds?
    b. **Draw Conclusions** Why has raising money has become so important in political campaigns?

c. **Make Predictions** What could be done to improve how candidates communicate with voters?

11. a. **Explain** Why is the campaign press secretary an important person in a campaign?
    b. **Demonstrate Reasoned Judgment** What should you keep in mind when you see campaign statements and advertisements?
    c. **Analyze Information** How do the actions of political campaigns help and hurt the people's desire for good government?

Activities

12. **Skills** Read the passage at right. Who do you vote for and why? Explain your decision.

13. **Writing** What qualities would you look for in a candidate? Write a brief essay in which you identify the important qualities a candidate should have and some qualities that would cause you to not vote for a candidate.

You are voting in your first election. Candidate A is the incumbent. You agree with everything Candidate A says, but his behavior while in office has made you concerned about his honesty and ability to think independently. He seems to support the position of the party every time. Candidate B is very different. You agree with some of her positions, but strongly disagree with some others. She strikes you as honest, intelligent and eager to do the job.

14. **Active Citizen** How easy is it to register to vote in your state? Call your local Board of Elections and research the process of registering to vote. Then make a poster that shows how and where to register to vote.

15. **Math Practice** There are 74,600 people who are eligible to vote for mayor. 36,883 votes are cast. What percentage of the eligible voters voted?

16. **Civics and Economics** A commission is trying to get more young people registered to vote. After voting, young people will be invited to a big party with well known bands. Write an essay that analyzes how successful you think that idea would be and any possible ethical conflicts it might raise.

1992 Presidential Election

Clinton (Democrat)
Bush (Republican)

17. **Analyzing Visuals** What generalizations can you make about the states that Bush won in the 1992 election?

Standardized Test Prep

Test-Taking Tips

Some questions on standardized tests will ask you to read and analyze information that is presented on a chart.

TIP In answering such questions, double-check the information you have pulled from the chart to make sure you are reading from the correct column.

Year	Percentage of Voting-Age Population that Voted
1952	61.6
1956	59.3
1960	62.8
1964	61.9
1968	60.9
1972	55.2
1976	53.5
1980	52.8
1984	53.3
1988	50.3
1992	55.1
1996	49.0
2000	51.3

SOURCE: Federal Election Commission

Choose the letter of the best answer.

1. In what year was the voter participation the highest?
   A 1968
   B 1960
   C 1952
   D 1992

   The correct answer is **B**.

2. Which of the following is a true statement?
   A A Voter participation was highest in 1972 and 1976.
   B Voter participation increased from 1952 to 2000.
   C Voter participation decreased from 1952 to 2000.
   D Voter participation was lowest in the election of 1988.

UNIT
9

The United States and the World

What's Ahead in Unit 9

This unit will introduce you to the world beyond the borders of the United States. You will study our nation's foreign policy. You will also learn about nations and how they relate to each other.

CHAPTER 24
American Foreign Policy

CHAPTER 25
One Nation Among Many

Active Citizen

Why Study Civics?

What is foreign policy? How can good relations with other countries help preserve global peace? What is meant by the global economy? What does it mean to be a citizen of the world? These are all questions that can be addressed by the study of civics.

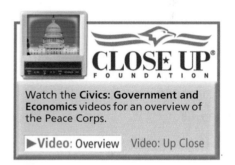

CLOSE UP®
FOUNDATION

Watch the **Civics: Government and Economics** videos for an overview of the Peace Corps.

▶**Video: Overview**   Video: Up Close

Standards for Civics and Government

National

The following National Standards are covered in this unit.

II. What are the foundations of the American political system?

B. What are the distinctive characteristics of American society?

C. What is American political culture?

D. What values and principles are basic to American constitutional democracy?

State

Go Online
PHSchool.com

For: Your state's Civics standards
Visit: PHSchool.com
Webcode: mpe9001

24

American Foreign Policy

What's Ahead in Chapter 24

In this chapter you will learn what foreign policy is and how it is made. You will also read about how our foreign policy has changed over time to reflect the changing role of the United States in the world.

SECTION 1
What Is Foreign Policy?

SECTION 2
Making Foreign Policy

SECTION 3
Foreign Policy in Action

TARGET READING SKILL

Main Idea The main idea of a text is the most important point to remember. Note the main ideas to make sure you understand what you read. As you read this chapter, you will practice the skills of identifying stated and implied main ideas and of identifying supporting details.

International trade is an ▶ important part of American foreign policy.

The following National Standards for Civics and Government are covered in this chapter.

IV. What is the relationship of the United States to other nations?

B. How do the domestic politics and constitutional prin- ciples of the U.S. affect its relations with the world?

C. How has the U.S. influenced other nations, and vice versa?

Go Online
PHSchool.com
For: Your state's standards
Visit: PHSchool.com
Web Code: mpe-9240

Active Citizen — Civics in the Real World

It is September 12, 2001—the day after Saudi terrorists hijacked four jet planes and slammed two of them into the World Trade Center and another into the Pentagon, killing thousands. Heroic passengers on the fourth plane forced it to crash before it reached its intended target; everyone aboard was killed. Throughout the country, Americans remain in a state of shock, horror, and mourning. Many look to the government to explain what has happened and to reassure them that they are safe.

One by one, men and women enter a room and take seats around a table. Several of them are wearing military uniforms hung with medals. Finally, the President arrives. He greets the people gathered in the room. They are the members of the National Security Council.

The President begins by asking each member of the council to update him on the actions they have taken to protect the country from further attacks. The remainder of the meeting is spent discussing both short- and long-term plans for the nation's security. In the face of this sudden crisis, the President and the Security Council must act quickly and carefully as they decide how to respond to the attacks, both militarily and diplomatically, both at home and abroad.

Citizen's Journal Suppose you were a member of the President's National Security Council. How would you suggest fighting the war on terrorism, both at home and overseas? Defend your position.

What Is Foreign Policy?

Reading Preview

Objectives

In this section you will
- Summarize the goals of foreign policy.
- Identify and describe the tools of foreign policy.

Taking Notes

Make a diagram like the one below. As you read this section, fill it in with information about the goals and tools of foreign policy.

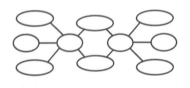

Key Terms

aggression   foreign aid
deterrence   sanctions
diplomacy   intelligence
summit meeting

Main Idea

To achieve important foreign-policy goals, the United States uses tools such as diplomacy, foreign aid, and intelligence.

Target Reading Skill

Identify Stated Main Ideas Writers often state their main ideas in plain words. As you read the section, look for main ideas that are plainly stated.

Threat Advisories
The national threat advisory keeps Americans aware of the danger posed by terrorist organizations.

O ne of the mostly important duties of any government is making a plan for relating to other nations. This plan is called a foreign policy. A government's foreign policy is a plan that outlines the goals it hopes to meet in its relations with other countries. Foreign policy also sets forth the variety of ways these goals are to be met.

Goals of Foreign Policy

The United States has many foreign-policy goals. The United States wants to protect citizens' safety. It seeks to promote prosperity. In addition, it strives to work for peace and democracy in other countries.

National Security Government leaders naturally try to protect the interests of their country. Acting in the national interest involves making sure the nation is safe. National security, or the ability to keep the nation safe from harm, is the chief goal of American foreign policy. Because war is the greatest danger to any nation, national security mainly focuses on the threat of war. American leaders generally work to avoid war in their quest to protect national security. However, there are cases in which leaders consider war to be unavoidable.

Stop Terrorism Terrorists use violence to intimidate or coerce societies or governments. American foreign policy works to stop terrorism in order to keep the nation safe. It also works to safeguard American interests overseas.

World Peace A second goal of American foreign policy is to get countries to work together as a way to prevent war. Wars anywhere can be a threat to people everywhere. People fear that other countries may be drawn into the fighting.

Trade Increasing trade is a third goal of United States foreign policy. Trade is good for the United States economy. Trade creates markets for American goods and services, earning profits for our businesses. It also brings us goods from other countries.

Human Rights and Democracy Another goal of American foreign policy is to encourage all countries to respect the human rights of freedom, justice, and equality. Americans believe that democracy is the best way to protect human rights. Thus, the US tries to help other nations as they try to form or keep democratic governments.

Countries in which human rights are denied can be a threat to world peace. When citizens are denied human rights, wars are likely to break out, and other countries may be drawn in. Encouraging human rights and democracy is also a way to meet our foreign policy goals of peace and security.

✓ Reading Check **What are the foreign-policy goals of the United States?**

Analyze Graphs

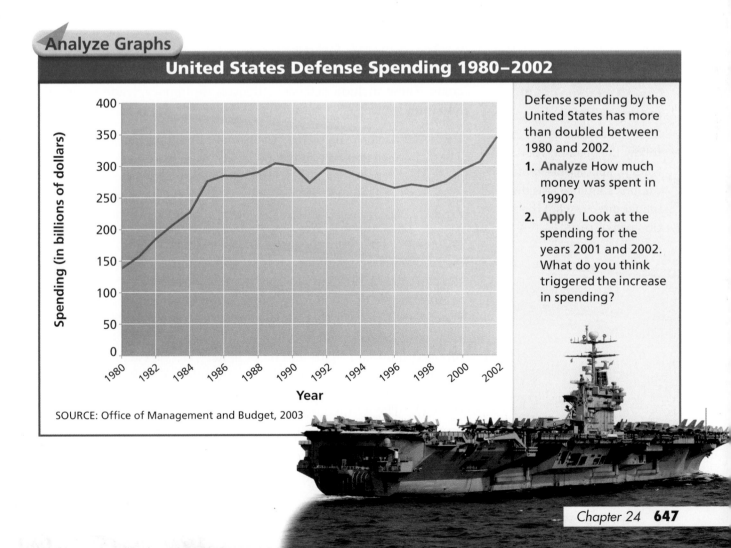

United States Defense Spending 1980–2002

Defense spending by the United States has more than doubled between 1980 and 2002.

1. **Analyze** How much money was spent in 1990?
2. **Apply** Look at the spending for the years 2001 and 2002. What do you think triggered the increase in spending?

SOURCE: Office of Management and Budget, 2003

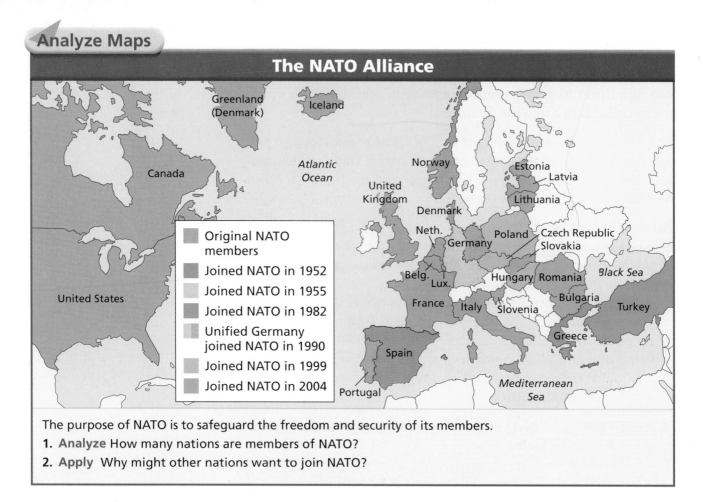

Analyze Maps

The NATO Alliance

Greenland (Denmark)

Iceland

Canada

Atlantic Ocean

Norway

Estonia
Latvia
Lithuania

United Kingdom

Denmark

Neth.

Poland

Czech Republic
Slovakia

Germany

United States

Legend:
- Original NATO members
- Joined NATO in 1952
- Joined NATO in 1955
- Joined NATO in 1982
- Unified Germany joined NATO in 1990
- Joined NATO in 1999
- Joined NATO in 2004

Belg.
Lux.

France

Hungary

Romania

Black Sea

Italy

Slovenia

Bulgaria

Turkey

Spain

Greece

Portugal

Mediterranean Sea

The purpose of NATO is to safeguard the freedom and security of its members.

1. **Analyze** How many nations are members of NATO?
2. **Apply** Why might other nations want to join NATO?

Tools of Foreign Policy

The United States uses several tools to achieve its foreign policy goals. These include defense, alliances, diplomacy, trade measures, and intelligence.

Defense Defense helps the government maintain national security. The American military is the means by which we defend ourselves against **aggression**, an attack or threat of attack by another country. A key part of United States foreign policy has been **deterrence**, keeping a strong defense to discourage aggression by other nations.

Alliances The United States forms military, political, and economic alliances with other countries. One military alliance is NATO, the North Atlantic Treaty Organization.

An example of a political alliance is the Organization of American States (OAS), made up of countries in North, Central, and South America. The OAS helps its members work together peacefully. The OAS also reports on human rights and helps to keep elections fair and honest.

The United States is a member of several economic alliances. One is the Organization for Economic Cooperation and Development (OECD). The 27 members of the OECD agree to help each other's economic well-being through trade. They also work together to aid developing nations.

Target Reading Skill

Identify Stated Main Ideas Read the two sentences that follow the heading **Tools of Foreign Policy**. Note that the first sentence tells the reader directly what the section will discuss.

Diplomacy Diplomacy is the relations and communications carried out between countries. When nations disagree, they send representatives called diplomats to talk about the issues.

The United States also uses diplomacy to accomplish certain complex tasks such as building canals or space stations. Alliances and trade agreements are also made through diplomacy. Diplomacy often results in formal agreements known as treaties.

Usually, diplomacy is carried out by members of the Department of State. Sometimes, however, there is a **summit meeting**, a meeting at which the President talks about important issues with heads of other governments.

Foreign Aid Another tool used to achieve foreign policy goals is **foreign aid**, a program of giving military and economic help to other countries. After World War II, the United States gave aid to European countries to help them rebuild factories, farms, cities, and homes destroyed in the war. Since the end of World War II, the United States has given or loaned almost $500 billion in foreign aid to more than 100 countries.

Foreign aid can support American policy goals by strengthening governments and political groups that are friendly to the United States. Economic aid takes many forms. The United States might help pay for a hospital, or a dam to control floods or produce electricity. Aid might be loans or grants to help a country start a new industry. Foreign aid helps national economies to grow and is seen as a way to reduce the chance of revolution and war.

Americans disagree about foreign aid. Some say that helping other countries is our duty as a rich and powerful country. They say that if we do not give aid, poorer nations will turn to other governments—governments that are not necessarily friendly to the United States—for help.

Those who oppose aid do so for two main reasons. Some say that we should solve problems at home first and not send so much money out of the country. Other critics say that the kind of aid we give sometimes helps governments that violate human rights. Just because a group is friendly to the United States, they say, is not a good reason to give it money and weapons.

Trade Measures Another tool of foreign policy is trade measures, or the terms under which the United States trades with other countries. One trade measure is a quota, which states how much of a foreign product can be sold in the United States. Another measure is a tariff, a tax on foreign products sold in the United States.

Helping Other Countries Foreign aid—in the form of military and economic assistance—is a powerful tool for meeting foreign-policy goals. **Summarize** *Why might some Americans oppose providing aid to other governments?*

U.S. Secretary of State Colin Powell (left) meets with Australian Foreign Minister Alexander Downer (right).
▼

Homeland Security
Tom Ridge (second from left) was the nation's first Secretary of Homeland Security. The Department of Homeland Security oversees several of the government's intelligence-gathering groups.
Draw Inferences *Why is it important to have our nation's intelligence-gathering agencies working closely together?*

Another foreign policy tool is **sanctions**—measures to stop or limit trade with another nation in order to change its behavior. For example, the United States disapproved of the underground nuclear tests conducted by Pakistan and India in 1998. The United States imposed economic sanctions on both nations.

The United States has two goals in regulating trade with other countries. One is to get other countries to buy American goods. The other is to get our trading partners to support us in other foreign policy goals.

Intelligence Information about another country and what its government plans to do is called **intelligence**. Most countries work hard to gather intelligence in order to help them meet the goal of national security.

The Central Intelligence Agency (CIA) and other agencies gather information. The CIA focuses mostly on countries it thinks might be unfriendly, and tries to learn what the governments of these countries intend to do. It also tries to predict how these governments will react to what the United States does.

Other agencies also gather intelligence, especially intelligence concerning terrorism. The Department of Homeland Security receives and analyzes terrorism-related reports from the CIA, Federal Bureau of Investigation (FBI), National Security Agency, and other intelligence agencies.

✓ Reading Check **Describe one important tool of American foreign policy.**

SECTION 1 Assessment

Key Terms
Use the following key term in a sentence that explains its meaning: aggression, deterrence, diplomacy, summit meeting, foreign aid, sanctions, intelligence

Target Reading Skill
1. **Identify Stated Main Idea** Identify the main idea of the section headed "Goals of Foreign Policy."

Comprehension and Critical Thinking
2. **a. Explain** Why does the U.S. have foreign-policy goals?

   b. Check Consistency Are these goals always consistent with one another? Explain.
3. **a. Recall** What types of alliances does the United States form with other nations?
   b. Demonstrate Reasoned Judgment Why is it important that the United States form international alliances?

Writing Activity
Choose one of the international alliances mentioned in this section. Write a report in which you identify its most important member nations and describe its current

activities. Evaluate the important of membership in this alliance to American foreign policy.

> **TIP** Make an outline before you begin writing. Organize your information under major headings. This will help you eliminate unnecessary information and keep your report concise.

Making Foreign Policy

Reading Preview

Objectives

In this section you will

- Describe the role of the executive branch in making foreign policy.
- Examine the role of Congress in making foreign policy.
- Explain how private groups and citizens can affect foreign policy.

Key Terms

National Security Council
National Security Advisor

Main Idea

The President, Congress, interest groups, and individual citizens all play roles in shaping American foreign policy.

Target Reading Skill

Identify Supporting Details Supporting details give further information about the main idea. As you read Section 2, find the main idea and identify the supporting details.

Taking Notes

Make a diagram like the one below. As you read this section, complete the diagram with information about how U.S. foreign policy is shaped.

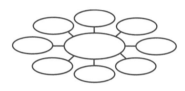

Condoleeza Rice (right), National Security Advisor to President George W. Bush.

▼

Sarah was upset. She had learned that whales might become extinct because they were being hunted. Every year there were fewer and fewer whales left.

The International Whaling Commission (IWC) had banned whaling in the 1980s. However, Iceland, whose economy depended on whaling, refused to go along with the ban. Sarah decided to write her member of Congress in hopes that the government might enforce the ban.

Sarah is only one person, but she hopes to affect American foreign policy. Like Sarah, many people and organizations have ideas about America's relations with other countries. They want the government to take action to help achieve their goals.

Who decides how the United States should behave toward other countries? Many people both inside and outside of government play a role in foreign policy.

The Executive Branch

The Constitution gives the President the responsibility for making foreign policy. Many departments and agencies of the executive branch get involved in foreign-policy decisions.

The President The President shapes foreign policy both as commander in chief of the armed forces and as the nation's chief diplomat. The President sets defense policies, meets with leaders of other countries, and makes treaties and executive agreements. The President also appoints ambassadors.

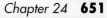

Secretary of Defense Donald Rumsfeld (left) is the head of the Defense Department and is responsible for the United States' military.

The President does not make foreign policy decisions alone. In the case of Iceland and whaling, the President might begin by asking the chief of staff to look into the matter. The chief of staff would then discuss the matter with other members of the White House staff. Once the White House staff has discussed it, the chief of staff asks the Secretary of State for information and perhaps some recommendations.

The Department of State The Department of State advises the President on foreign policy. It also carries out foreign policy. The Secretary of State works closely with the President and represents the United States in many diplomatic meetings. The Secretary is assisted by experts on different parts of the world, such as the Middle East or Europe, and by experts on foreign policy.

The Department of State also has nearly 16,000 officials working in other countries. These officials are known as foreign service officers. They include ambassadors, who represent our country in embassies, or diplomatic offices, around the world. They also include consuls, who help American businesspeople and travelers abroad.

The Department of Defense The Department of Defense also plays a part in making foreign policy. It advises the President on matters such as which weapons to make and where to place military bases and troops.

The United States Navy has bases in Iceland. The Secretary of Defense could warn the President that if trade were cut off, Iceland might close these bases.

The National Security Council The **National Security Council** (NSC) advises the President on the country's safety. The NSC includes the President and Vice President and the secretaries of state and defense. The President calls a meeting of the NSC when American security seems in danger.

The President's **National Security Advisor** is the director of the NSC. He or she would consider how changing our trade policy with Iceland could affect NATO and our bases.

Other Executive Departments and Agencies The President may seek help from other executive departments and agencies. In the whaling case, the Department of Commerce played an important role. One division of the Department of Commerce is responsible for protecting marine mammals and representing the United States on the International Whaling Commission.

✓ Reading Check   **Describe the President's role in setting foreign policy.**

Role of Congress

Although the President plays the major role in making and carrying out foreign policy, Congress also has some power over foreign policy. The Senate has the power to approve or reject treaties. The Senate must approve the President's choices for the diplomatic corps. Furthermore, only Congress can declare war.

The executive and legislative branches sometimes have conflicts over foreign policy. In 1999 President Clinton clashed with the Senate over the Comprehensive Test Ban Treaty—a treaty to prohibit nuclear weapons tests worldwide. Clinton urged senators to ratify the treaty, saying it would help prevent the spread of nuclear weapons. Republican senators, however, argued that the agreement would weaken national security. The Senate voted to reject the treaty.

Several congressional committees are important in making foreign policy. Those most directly involved are the Senate Foreign Relations Committee, the House International Relations Committee, and the Armed Services committees in both houses. These committees hold hearings and write and study bills that affect our relations with other countries.

✔ **Reading Check**   **Describe Congress' role in setting foreign policy.**

ANALYZING Political Cartoons

The Korean War of the early 1950s did not have universal support in the United States. As the war became more unpopular, the Republicans and the Democrats struggled to avoid paying the political costs.

1. What do the tub, the ocean, and the frightened man represent?
2. What do you think the cartoonist was trying to say about the behavior of the political leadership?

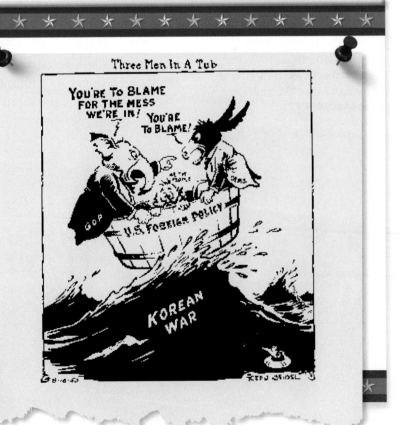

Civics and Economics

World Trade The United States exports and imports far more goods and services than any other nation. The United States exported goods and services worth more than $781 billion in 2000. It also imported more than $1.25 trillion of goods and services that year.

Many American policy-makers are concerned about the nation's negative trade balance, or trade deficit. A trade deficit indicates that other nations do not buy as many American goods as Americans buy imported goods.

Analyze Economics

1. Why is the American government concerned about the trade deficit?
2. What might the government do to convert the trade deficit to a trade surplus?

Labor Unions and NAFTA President Bill Clinton signed the 1994 North American Free Trade Agreement, which changed many aspects of trade among the United States, Mexico, and Canada.
Make Inferences *Why might American labor unions have opposed NAFTA?*

Role of Private Groups

Private organizations and individuals can also shape foreign policy. Many groups have special interests that are affected by foreign policy. These groups want to have a voice in what that policy will be.

Business Groups Businesses that trade with other nations have a direct interest in foreign policy. During the whaling controversy, environmental organizations convinced several major American restaurant chains to boycott Icelandic fish. This action hurt Iceland's economy, causing Iceland's leaders to rethink their whaling policy.

Labor Groups Labor groups want to protect American jobs. They try to get executive branch policymakers and members of Congress to protect those jobs by limiting or taxing certain imports and by putting pressure on our trading partners to buy more American products.

Political Groups Many other organizations try to affect foreign policy. The United States is home to people of diverse backgrounds, some of whom try to shape policy toward areas of the world they care about. For example, many Cuban Americans who fled Cuba's government have influenced American policy towards that country. Although the United States recently eased its policy of restricting trade and travel to Cuba, the strong support of Cuban Americans has kept the basic policy in place.

Individual Citizens Individuals can also play a role in foreign policy. Americans who keep up with international news, and who study, travel, or work abroad, learn about foreign countries and our government's policies toward them. Being better informed helps citizens make better decisions on foreign policy. It also helps citizens make better decisions about cadidates for election.

There are many ways that citizens who care about foreign policy can make a difference. Running for office or voting for a candidate who shares your views are two important ways. Working for a private organization with a focus on foriegn-policy issues is another way to let your voice be heard. Letting your senator or representative know what you think about the issues is another way. Members of Congress want to know how citizens feel about matters of foreign policy, especially if an issue puts American troops in harm's way.

In the whaling matter, Iceland agreed to go along with the International Whaling Commission's ban on whaling. It decided not to risk losing the American market for its fish. In this case, citizens' groups and individuals played an important role in getting our government to put pressure on Iceland. That pressure encouraged Iceland to change its own policy.

Americans Abroad
A Peace Corps volunteer helps to fight tuberculosis in Bolivia. **Predict** *How is this volunteer's experience likely to shape her opinions on American foreign policy?*

✓ Reading Check   **How can an interest group affect foreign policy?**

SECTION 2 Assessment

Key Terms
Use each of the key terms in a sentence that explains its meaning:
National Security Council,
National Security Advisor

Target Reading Skill
1. **Identify Supporting Details** Identify the major details that support the statement that many American groups and individuals play roles in shaping foreign policy.

Comprehension and Critical Thinking
2. **a. Describe** What is the Department of State's role in shaping foreign policy?

   b. Categorize What are the roles of the other government departments?
3. **a. Recall** Which congressional committees play important foreign-policy roles?

   b. Determine Relevance Why is it important for Congress to have some power over setting foreign policy?
4. **a. Describe** What kinds of private groups try to affect foreign policy?

   b. Support a Point of View Do you think it is a good idea for private groups to affect foreign policy? Why?

Writing Activity
Research a foreign-policy issue that interests you. Write a short summary outlining the major points of the issue. In your summary, be sure to explain who the majot influencers are on the development of the foreign policy.

TIP Make sure you understand the roles played by the executive branch, Congress, and private groups in creating the foreign policy you are writing about.

Debating the Issues

CLOSE UP

The debates in this feature are based on *Current Issues*, published by the Close Up Foundation. Go to **PHSchool.com**, Web Code mph-9241, to read the latest issue of *Current Issues* online.

The United States has actively promoted democracy abroad since the end of World War II. After the war, Marshall Plan aid helped to stabilize the democratic governments of Europe. Throughout the Cold War, the United States made every effort to stop the spread of communism. In recent years, the United States has sent troops to help restore democracy and human rights in areas such as Afghanistan and Iraq.

Should U.S. Foreign Policy Focus on Promoting Democracy and Human Rights Overseas?

YES	NO
• "Liberty and justice for all" is an ideal on which the United States was founded. Helping other nations achieve this ideal is a moral obligation.	• Some people in other nations regard the United States with suspicion and hostility. For its own safety, the United States should not interfere with another nation's government or its treatment of its people.
• The United States is one of the wealthiest and most powerful nations in the world, but not always one of the best-liked. Promoting democracy and human rights in other nations will gain the United States much-needed international allies.	• The United States has no right to impose its own culture and values on other nations that have not invited outside interference.
• When one nation abuses the rights of its people, the rights of all people are threatened. The United Stateswill strengthen its own security as it helps other people claim their natural rights.	• The United States must consider economic and political issues when dealing with human rights issues. If a nation is a political ally or trade partner, our government should use diplomacy only to help that nations' people claim their rights.

What is Your Opinion?

1. **Identify Effect** Suppose the United States cut off trade with a nation because of its domestic human-rights abuses. What would be the effects of this decision? Explain.

2. **Identify Main Ideas** What are the strongest arguments for and against promoting democracy and human rights abroad? Why?

3. **Writing to Persuade** Suppose that you are the President of the United States. You want to send troops to help a democratic African nation in its struggle with a neighboring dictatorship. Write a short, informal speech you will make at a Cabinet meeting to persuade your Cabinet to support your position.

Go Online
civics
interactive

For: You Decide Poll
Visit: PHSchool.com
Web Code: mpp-9241

Foreign Policy in Action

Reading Preview

Objectives
In this section you will
- Discuss the history of American foreign policy through World War II.
- Learn about the Cold War.
- Study regional challenges to American foreign policy.
- Describe how American policy is leading the war on terrorism.

Key Terms
isolationism   containment
neutrality   détente

Main Idea
American foreign policy has changed over time, and will continue to change in response to international events and the actions of other nations.

Target Reading Skill
Identify Implied Main Ideas Writers don't always state their main ideas directly. Sometimes they imply them, leaving the reader to infer the most important points. As you read this section, identify main ideas and think about what the writer is suggesting rather than stating outright.

Taking Notes
Make a diagram like the one shown. As you read this section, complete the diagram with information about the changes in American foreign policy over time.

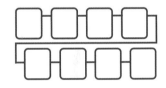

James Monroe, President from 1817–1825, used the Monroe Doctrine to help isolate the United States from European affairs. ▼

The role that the United States plays in the world is continually changing. At times we have followed **isolationism**, a foreign policy that seeks to limit our relations with other countries as much as possible. During other periods, the United States has tried to meet its goals by taking an active part in affairs around the world.

Foreign Policy Through World War II

In its early years, the United States had a largely isolationist foreign policy. A farming country with very little industry, we had just fought a costly war for independence. President George Washington believed that the young country could not afford to take part in European alliances and wars.

Isolationism Washington chose a position of **neutrality**, a policy of not taking sides in wars between other countries. This neutrality kept the United States out of war. It also allowed America to continue to trade with both sides in a war.

Staying isolated was not easy. European countries were expanding into Latin America, competing with our economic interests and threatening American security. President James Monroe responded to the threat with the Monroe Doctrine in 1823. He warned European nations not to create more colonies in the western hemisphere. Monroe promised that in return, America would stay out of European affairs. Monroe saw this position as a way to protect American interests and stay isolated from Europe.

War Over Cuba
Americans were outraged over Spain's interference with American interests in Cuba. The United States gained control over Cuba after winning the Spanish-American War. **Synthesize Information** *How did the Monroe Doctrine lead to the Spanish-American War?*

Expansion The policy of isolationism was again tested as Americans began to move west, seeking more land. Expansion forced the United States into contact—and sometimes conflict—with Mexico, France, Spain, Great Britain, and Russia, which held claims to the lands the American s desired.

Meanwhile, American businesses were expanding across the Pacific, beginning to trade with Japan, China, and other Asian countries. The United States built military bases in Hawaii and the Far East to protect this trade and prevent European countries from setting up colonies.

American business also expanded into Central and South America. The policy of isolationism did not apply to that part of the world, which the United States, still following the Monroe Doctrine, viewed as being in its own backyard. Many times, the United States sent its armed forces into Latin America. Most often, the goal was to protect economic interests or national security.

World War I and the Return to Isolationism World War I forced the United States to change its policy of isolationism toward Europe. At first, President Woodrow Wilson took a position of neutrality. But German aggression caused Congress to declare war in 1917. President Wilson said that the goal in entering the war was to make the world "safe for democracy." He believed that this would be the "war to end war," leading to lasting world peace.

After the war, Wilson helped found the League of Nations, a new organization intended to help keep peace. However, Congress was eager to return to isolationism. It refused to approve American membership in the League.

World War II: The End of Isolationism

The League of Nations failed to keep peace. Within 20 years the world was again at war. When World War II began in Europe, the United States tried to stay out of it. When the Japanese bombed the American navy at Pearl Harbor, Hawaii, in 1941, the United States declared war.

When the war ended in 1945, the United States was the richest and most powerful country in the world. It believed it could play a key part in keeping world peace. American leaders met with Soviet and European leaders to make a peace plan. The United States also helped to found the United Nations, an international organization you will learn more about in the next chapter.

✓ **Reading Check** **What caused the United States to abandon its policy of isolationism?**

The Pearl Harbor Attack
The Japanese bombed Pearl Harbor on December 7, 1941 (top). President Franklin D. Roosevelt (bottom) responded by asking Congress to declare war on Japan and on its allies. The United States had entered World War II.
Identify Cause and Effect *What did Pearl Harbor and World War II teach the United States about its policy of isolationism?*

The Cold War

The end of World War II marked the end of the belief that the United States should try to stay out of conflicts between other nations. After World War II, American leaders saw that our own national security went hand-in-hand with global security. Trouble anywhere in the world could mean trouble for the United States. Therefore, the goal of world peace took center stage in foreign policy.

Containment After World War II, many Americans thought that the Soviet Union and the spread of communism were the main dangers to peace. The Soviets took control of several Eastern European countries. When Soviet-backed Communists tried to take over Greece and Turkey, President Harry Truman sent American military aid to help those countries defend themselves.

Truman's action was the beginning of a new foreign policy of **containment**, a policy of using military power and money to prevent the spread of communism. At first, the government's main tool of containment was providing economic aid. The United States hoped to strengthen the economies of European countries so that they could hold out against Soviet aggression.

Later, the United States came to depend military strength and deterrence to support the policy of containment. The Cold War was fought with words and warnings, and sometimes confrontation. The Cuban missile crisis and the wars in Korea and Vietnam are examples of confrontations that grew out of the effort to contain the spread of communism.

Cooperation By the mid-1960s, it was clear the Soviet Union was gaining nuclear strength nearly equal to that of the United States. In the 1970s, there was a period of **détente** (day TAHNT), or a loosening of tensions between the United States and the Soviet Union. The superpowers turned to treaties and diplomacy to ease the tensions caused by the military buildup. Through the 1980s, leaders continued to see that depending on military strength alone would not guarantee national security. Even though both the United States and the Soviet Union continued building up arms, the spirit of cooperation grew.

The End of the Cold War As the 1980s gave way to the 1990s, the improving relationship between the superpowers was overshadowed by some breathtaking events. Communist governments fell in Poland and other Eastern European countries. Then the Soviet Union itself began to fall apart. Suddenly, the ground on which forty-five years of American foreign policy had been built had shifted greatly. Americans could no longer picture the world as a cold-war battleground, with Communist nations united against democracies.

In the mid-1980s, Soviet leader Mikhail Gorbachev undertook reforms aimed at improving the economy. These reforms loosened some government controls over the economy and encouraged some private business. Gorbachev also announced a policy of openness between government and citizens. Gorbachev's policies gave the people of the Soviet Union a taste of freedom—and they wanted more. Citizens grew impatient with the slow pace of change. Nationalist feelings erupted among the diverse peoples of the 15 Soviet republics.

The Fall of the Wall
The Berlin Wall divided democratic West Germany from Communist-ruled East Germany from 1961 to 1989. The East German government opened the wall in 1989. **Summarize** *How did American foreign policy change after the fall of the Communist governments of Eastern Europe?*

Students Make a Difference

Cassandra Katsiaficas, a senior at Watertown High School, in Watertown, Massachusetts believes that knowledge of international affairs is necessary to make informed decisions.

Cassandra decided to organize the first symposium on international affairs ever held at her school. Today, Cassandra is working with school administrators to create a human rights club. She hopes to hold more symposiums and discussion groups on foreign policy.

▲ Students can help make a difference by becoming more involved in issues related to their schools.

Service Learning

How can you make a difference at your school by helping students to become more aware of the world around them?

By the end of 1991, every Soviet republic had declared its independence and the Communist central government had been dissolved. The Soviet Union ceased to exist.

As an independent nation, Russia began making the transition from communism to democracy and a market economy. Relations between Russia and the United States continued to improve. Reflecting the new spirit of cooperation, the United States began helping its longtime rival with economic aid.

Eastern Europe Dramatic changes took place in Eastern Europe as well. Hungary declared itself an independent republic in 1989. Voters in Poland elected the first non-Communist government in the region since World War II. Communist leaders in Czechoslovakia gave up power after masses of citizens marched in the streets. In 1989, the people of Germany broke down the Berlin Wall, a hated symbol of the Cold War that had been built to keep East and West Germans apart.

The United States began helping the nations of Eastern Europe establish democratic governments and market economies. Three former Communist nations (the Czech Republic, Poland, and Hungary) were invited to join NATO in 1999.

Relations with China Some observers of the startling events in Eastern Europe and the Soviet Union spoke of the "death of communism." However, the world's most populous country—China—was still ruled by a communist government.

More American businesses are setting up shop in China, and many goods that were once made in the United States are now made in China. Trade has increased between China and the United States. However, China's treatment of its own citizens has hurt relations between the two countries. Americans were outraged when Chinese troops crushed a student-led democratic movement in June 1989, killing hundreds of protestors in Beijing's Tiananmen Square.

There has been debate over how to react to these human rights violations. Should we punish China by cutting off diplomatic relations and trade? Or should we maintain such contacts as ways of influencing Chinese leaders?

✓ Reading Check **Why did the Soviet Union seem like a threat to the United States?**

Analyze Diagrams

American Foreign Policy

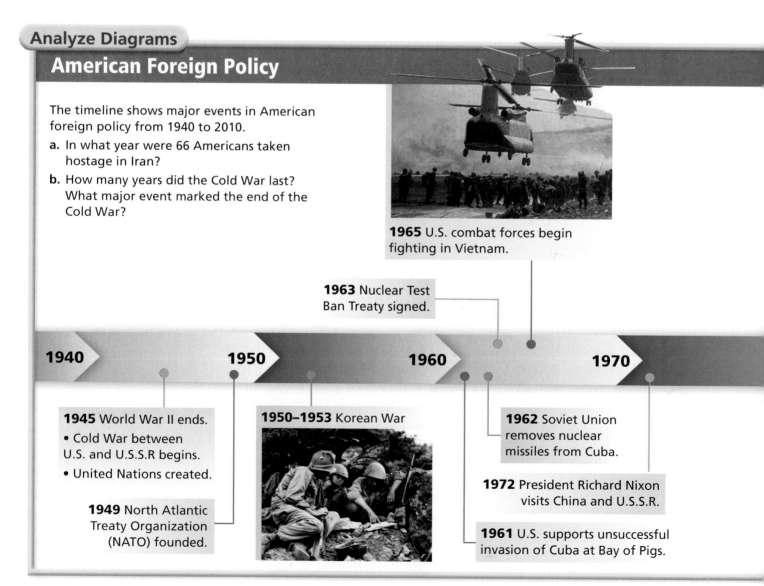

The timeline shows major events in American foreign policy from 1940 to 2010.

a. In what year were 66 Americans taken hostage in Iran?

b. How many years did the Cold War last? What major event marked the end of the Cold War?

1965 U.S. combat forces begin fighting in Vietnam.

1963 Nuclear Test Ban Treaty signed.

1940   **1950**   **1960**   **1970**

1945 World War II ends.
• Cold War between U.S. and U.S.S.R begins.
• United Nations created.

1949 North Atlantic Treaty Organization (NATO) founded.

1950–1953 Korean War

1962 Soviet Union removes nuclear missiles from Cuba.

1972 President Richard Nixon visits China and U.S.S.R.

1961 U.S. supports unsuccessful invasion of Cuba at Bay of Pigs.

Today's Challenges

The United States faces changes in economic power around the world. As other countries have gained strength, American leaders have had to rethink their policies. American leaders also have to make foreign policy fit the issues and needs of different regions in the world.

Economic Challenges Japan has become a great economic power. While the United States buys many Japanese products, Japan buys far fewer American goods and services. An important goal of foreign policy is to balance this trade. Meanwhile, China's rapidly growing economy is making it a strong force in international trade.

The European Union (EU) is breaking down trade barriers between its member nations. This alliance gives the countries of the EU power to compete with the United States.

Another source of economic power outside the United States is the oil-rich countries. Foreign policy toward the Middle East will continue to be greatly affected by our need for oil.

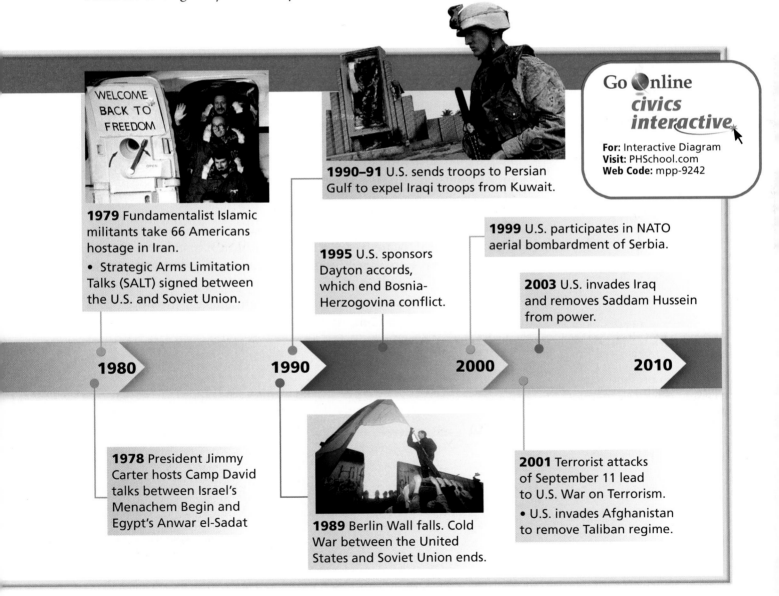

Go Online
civics interactive

For: Interactive Diagram
Visit: PHSchool.com
Web Code: mpp-9242

1990–91 U.S. sends troops to Persian Gulf to expel Iraqi troops from Kuwait.

1979 Fundamentalist Islamic militants take 66 Americans hostage in Iran.
• Strategic Arms Limitation Talks (SALT) signed between the U.S. and Soviet Union.

1995 U.S. sponsors Dayton accords, which end Bosnia-Herzogovina conflict.

1999 U.S. participates in NATO aerial bombardment of Serbia.

2003 U.S. invades Iraq and removes Saddam Hussein from power.

1980   **1990**   **2000**   **2010**

1978 President Jimmy Carter hosts Camp David talks between Israel's Menachem Begin and Egypt's Anwar el-Sadat

1989 Berlin Wall falls. Cold War between the United States and Soviet Union ends.

2001 Terrorist attacks of September 11 lead to U.S. War on Terrorism.
• U.S. invades Afghanistan to remove Taliban regime.

WELCOME BACK TO FREEDOM

Madeleine Albright (1937–) became the first woman ever appointed as Secretary of State. Prior to her appointment as secretary, she was the United States ambassador to the United Nations. It was here that she gained worldwide respect for her tough defense of American foreign policy regarding Iraq and the Kosovo crisis in Serbia. Her exceptional work at the UN led President Bill Clinton to appoint her as the 64th Secretary of State.

Citizenship
How did Albright gain worldwide respect at the United Nations?

Challenges in Latin America During the Cold War the United States used aid, diplomacy, and military intervention to stop the spread of communism in Latin America. By the early 1990s most Latin American countries were governed by fragile democracies. What is the best way for the United States to support these democratic governments and help their economies?

Challenges in Eastern Europe The standard of living in Eastern Europe remains well below that in Western Europe. Wars in Bosnia and Serbia have left serious ethnic divisions that will need to be healed. Three former Soviet states— Ukraine, Kazakhstan, and Belarus—still have nuclear weapons, and their economies are lagging. Should we try to help these countries and, if so, how?

Challenges in the Middle East This region has a long history of religious and political conflict. Violence broke out once again between Israelis and Palestinians in 2000. When Ariel Sharon was elected Israel's prime minister in 2001, he took a much tougher stance on negotiating peace with the Palestinians than the previous prime minister had. It will take a great effort to overcome the history of conflict in the region.

Challenges in Africa Many African nations are among the poorest in the world. Many also suffer from political instability. During the 1990s, civil wars raged in Sudan, Rwanda, the Congo Republic, and Algeria, leaving hundreds of thousands dead. The new democracy in South Africa appears to be a bright star on the horizon. It faces a challenge, though, in expanding economic opportunity for black South Africans.

North Korea presents challenges to American foreign policy. North Korea is a secretive Communist dictatorship that avoids contact with the outside world. ▶

Foreign policy questions for Africa are similar to those for other parts of the developing world. Should the United States become involved? What actions will promote peace, economic growth, and democracy?

✓ **Reading Check** What foreign-policy challenges does the United States face today?

Leading the War on Terrorism

The United States emerged from the Cold War as the world's strongest economic and military power. The threat from another superpower no longer exists, but in its place is the threat of terrorism. After the terrorist attacks on New York and the Pentagon on September 11, 2001, the United States vowed to work with allies throughout the world to halt future terrorist attacks and to stop the flow of money to terrorist organizations.

While Americans may debate how best to fight the threat of terrorism, most agree that returning to a policy of isolation is not a workable foreign policy in an interdependent and dangerous world. Neither is relying on economic or military power. Foreign policy decisions are likely to be more difficult, now that the enemy is no longer easy to identify. However, the end of the superpower conflict has removed a major barrier to cooperation. The United States can now begin to establish a new role.

✓ **Reading Check** What effect has terrorism had on foreign policy?

Aid Sent Abroad
Sending humanitarian aid to Iraq is a significant part of United States foreign policy towards the Middle East.
Make Inferences *Why would sending humanitarian aid to Iraq be a useful policy?*

SECTION 3   Assessment

Key Terms

Use each of the key terms in a sentence that explains its meaning: isolationism, neutrality, containment, détente

Target Reading Skill

1. **Identify Implied Main Ideas** Reread the section about World War I. What do Wilson's words imply about German aggression?

Comprehension and Critical Thinking

2. **a. Recall** What was the purpose of American isolationism?
   b. Identify Bias How could the United States reconcile the Monroe Doctrine with its own

invasions of Latin American nations?

3. **a. Describe** How did the United States try to combat the spread of communism?
   b. Draw Inferences Why did the Cold War not become a military conflict?

4. **a. Explain** In which region do we face our most serious foreign-policy challenge?
   b. Predict How will the United States rise to this challenge? Explain.

5. **a. Explain** When did the war on terrorism begin?
   b. Synthesize Information How is the war connected to America's status as the world's only superpower?

Writing Activity

Americans disagree about the UN's role in world affairs and about whether the United States should be subject to UN authority. Visit the UN website and read about its goals and activities. Then write an editorial stating your position on U.S. membership in the UN and the role you think the United States should play in the UN.

Go Online
PHSchool.com
For: Writing Activity
Visit: PHSchool.com
Web Code: mpd-9243

Predicting Consequences

Making predictions about the consequences of our actions can help us make decisions that will have positive effects in the future. One way to practice this skill is to look at past events and see how they affected events that followed. The following passage describes the changes that occurred after President Thomas Jefferson completed the Louisiana Purchase in 1803.

The American colonies had won independence from Britain, but France still controlled parts of North America. In 1803, President Thomas Jefferson bought all of France's land from the Mississippi to the Rocky Mountains. In one year, the territory of the young United States doubled.

Jefferson sent Meriwether Lewis and William Clark to explore and survey the Louisiana Purchase. Within a few years, Americans were packing up and heading out West to claim land. However, much of this land was already inhabited by Native American tribes. Conflicts frequently arose between the settlers and the Indians. As more and more people spilled across the plains, they pushed the United States boundary westward.

Within a few decades, American settlements had reached the West Coast. The Louisiana Purchase had sparked a chain of events that would eventually form the 48 contiguous states, but which would permanently alter the population of North America in the process.

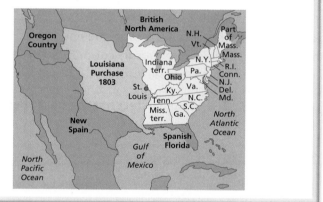

Learn the Skill

Follow these steps to predict consequences:

❶ **Identify what has happened.** What events or developments have taken place? What problems or conflicts can you see?

❷ **Analyze Information.** What facts are available? What conclusions can you draw?

❸ **Predict future consequences.** How do you think present events will affect the future?

Practice the Skill

Read the passage above and answer these questions:

❶ How did the Louisiana Purchase change the United States in 1803?

❷ What events happened after the Louisiana Purchase?

❸ Which consequences of the Louisiana Purchase were positive? Which were negative?

❹ What circumstances today can be considered consequences of the Louisiana Purchase?

Apply the Skill

Use news magazines, Web sites, and newspapers to gather information about an important current event. Assemble facts about the event and then predict how the event will affect the future.

Review and Assessment

Chapter Summary

Section 1
What Is Foreign Policy?
(pages 646–650)

- The United States uses its foreign policy to promote its own national security, increase fair trade, and encourage the spread of democracy and the recognition of human rights for people.

- Achieving the foreign policy goals of the United States requires curbing aggression everywhere. The United States uses foreign aid, military deterrence, and diplomacy to keep armed conflict from arising in the first place. American leaders gather intelligence about nations and organizations that may threaten stability. They also hold summit meetings with the leaders of other nations. They may even impose sanctions against nations that disagree with our policies.

Section 2
Making Foreign Policy
(pages 651–655)

- The President sets foreign policy, deals directly with heads of state, and makes treaties with other nations. He is advised in this role by the National Security Council (and its director, the National Security Advisor), among others.

- Congress has the power to declare war. Congress must approve or reject any treaty with another nation.

- Interest groups and individuals can petition the government to vote and set foreign policy in accordance with their views.

Section 3
Foreign Policy in Action
(pages 657–665)

- In its early years, the United States practiced a policy of isolationism, specifically warning other nations not to colonize the western hemisphere. It tried to maintain neutrality in the affairs of the Eastern Hemisphere.

- Two world wars in Europe drew the United States into international affairs.

- During the Cold War, the Soviet Union tried to spread communism and the United States tried to reinforce democracy. Initially, American policy attempted containment of communism, but later a state of détente was achieved with the communist nations.

- Since the Cold War, some Asian and Middle Eastern nations have risen to positions of great economic power. Today, the United States faces numerous challenges over where and whether to take part in international affairs.

Copy the chart below and use it to help you summarize the chapter.

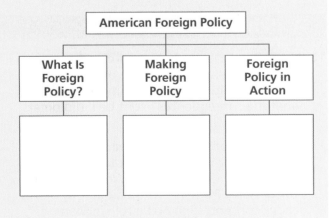

American Foreign Policy

What Is Foreign Policy?	Making Foreign Policy	Foreign Policy in Action

Review and Assessment Continued

Go Online
PHSchool.com
For: Self-Test
Visit: PHSchool.com
Web Code: mpa-9244

Reviewing Key Terms

On a separate sheet of paper, write the term that makes each sentence correct.

1. A policy of avoiding contact and conflict with other nations is called (isolationism, neutrality).

2. Information about the plans of foreign governments is called (détente, intelligence).

3. (Détente, diplomacy) involves communication between nations.

4. During the Cold War, the United States feared Soviet (aggression, sanctions) in Eastern Europe.

5. When one nation disagrees with the policies of another, it can impose economic (deterrence, sanctions).

6. (Containment, foreign aid) was a policy used in order to try to stop the spread of communism during the Cold War.

7. When a nation practices (diplomacy, neutrality), it refuses to support either side in a war between other nations.

8. The term (détente, intelligence) refers to an easing of tension between the superpowers as the Cold War drew to a close.

Comprehension and Critical Thinking

9. a. **Explain** Why does the United States want to promote human rights and democracy abroad?
    b. **Predict** How can the United States promote democracy abroad?
    c. **Make Inferences** Which kinds of governments are likely to infringe on human rights? Why?

10. a. **Explain** Who makes American foreign policy?
    b. **Compare and Contrast** Which individual or groups plays the most important role in making foreign policy? Explain.

    c. **Identify Effects** What effect does foreign policy have on domestic policy? Explain.

11. a. **Describe** What were the advantages and disadvantages of American isolationism?
    b. **Identify Cause** What caused the United States to abandon isolationism?
    c. **Support a Point View** Is isolationism possible in today's world? Explain.

Activities

12. **Skills** Read the passage at right and answer the questions. **a.** Predict some of the consequences of diplomatic immunity. **b.** Predict what the consequences might be if diplomats did not enjoy immunity.

13. **Writing** Choose one of the leaders mentioned in Section 3 of this chapter—George Washington, James Monroe, Woodrow Wilson, or Harry Truman. Write a biography of this leader, concentrating on his role in shaping and executing the foreign policy of his nation.

To help foreign relations run smoothly, nations have agreed on the concept of "diplomatic immunity." This means that a diplomat cannot be arrested by the country in which he or she serves. An embassy is treated as part of the nation it represents; police or soldiers of the host nation cannot go into the embassy unless invited. Packages sent home by diplomats cannot be seized or searched.

14. **Active Citizen** Choose a foreign-policy issue. Write a letter to your congressional representatives, outlining your views and urging them to vote for or against pending legislation that deals with this issue.

15. **Math Practice** You read that African nations are among the world's poorest. In 2000, the per capita income in the Congo was $600; in Burundi, it was $720; in Niger, it was $1000. Divide each of these numbers by 12 to find the monthly income in these nations. (In comparison, the annual per capita income in the United States was $29,500.)

16. **Civics and Economics** How does promoting stability in other nations serve the economic needs of the United States?

17. **Analyzing Visuals** What is the American soldier doing in this photo? Why do you think the U.S. military would support his actions?

Standardized Test Prep

Test-Taking Tips

Standardized tests often ask you to answer questions about what you have read. Read the paragraph and answer the questions that follow.

> After World War II, the armies of the United States, the United Kingdom, France, and the Soviet Union divided Germany and its capital Berlin into four sectors. Each nation was to help rebuild its section of Germany. The Soviets quickly imposed communism on East Germany and East Berlin, while West Germany and West Berlin began to return to prosperity and democracy. Thousands of East Germans fled to West Berlin. The Soviets were determined to put a stop to this. In the early morning hours of August 13, 1961, they began to build a high, thick wall between East and West Berlin.

Choose the letter of the best answer.

1. Why did the Soviets build the Berlin Wall?
   A They wanted to protect East Germans from attack.
   B They wanted West Germans to stay out of East Berlin.
   C They wanted East Germans to stay in East Germany.
   D They wanted to make Germany a Soviet republic.

   > **TIP** Read the question, then check the passage to find the answer.

   The correct answer is **C**. The passage says that the Soviets wanted people to stop leaving East Germany.

2. Which is the best synonym for the word *imposed?*
   A forced
   B gave
   C imprisoned
   D built

One Nation Among Many

What's Ahead in Chapter 25

The United States is one nation among many others. You will learn how nations differ, why conflicts occur, and what brings peace. Finally, you will see how developments in technology and the global economy are bringing many nations closer together.

SECTION 1
The Nations and the World

SECTION 2
Relations Among and Within Nations

SECTION 3
The Challenge of Interdependence

TARGET
READING SKILL

Comparison and Contrast Comparing and contrasting includes recognizing and using signal words, making comparisons, identifying contrasts, and identifying similarities and differences.

Flags of the ▶
world's nations

The following National Standards for Civics and Government are covered in this chapter.

I. What are civics life, politics, and government?

D. What are alternative ways of organizing constitutional governments?

IV. What is the relationship of the U. S. to other nations and to world affairs?

A. How is the world organized politically?

B. How do the domestic politics and constitutional principles of the U. S. affect its relations with the world?

Go Online
PHSchool.com

For: Your state's standards
Visit: PHSchool.com
Web Code: mpe-9251

Active Citizen — Civics in the Real World

March 7, 2003. The 20 members of the United Nations Security Council listen to a report by Hans Blix, the leader of the United Nations team that has been inspecting Iraq for evidence of nuclear weapons. Blix states that the Iraqis have been cooperating up to a point, and he feels that the team needs more time to finish its work.

The United States and Britain want to cease inspections and set an immediate deadline for Iraq to disarm. France disagrees. The French feel that the inspections are producing good results and should continue. Russia and China indicate support for the French position. These are the permanent members of the council and their votes are the most important. Each position has some support among the other 15 member nations.

A negative vote by any of the permanent members means that a resolution will not pass and the UN will take no action. Knowing that France would vote against a resolution to give Iraq a deadline for disarming, the US and Britain decide to act independently. Within weeks of Blix's report, American and British soldiers attack Iraq.

Citizen's Journal The UN has no authority to act without the consent of its members, or to force its members to act on any particular situation. Do you think the UN should have these powers? Write the answer in your journal. Explain your position.

The Nations and the World

Reading Preview

Objectives

In this section you will
- Define what a nation is.
- Explore the different histories of nations.
- Discuss the process of economic development.

Taking Notes

Make a diagram like the one below. As you read this section, complete the diagram with information about the important differences between developed and developing nations.

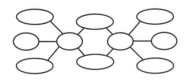

Key Terms

sovereignty
nationalism
colony

standard of living

Main Idea

Nations can be classified as former colonial powers, former colonies, developed nations, or developing nations.

Target Reading Skill

Identify Contrasts When you contrast two types within the same category, you observe the characteristics that make them different.

Suppose that you are an astronaut looking back at the earth from far out in space. From space, you see the earth as a small globe, the shared home of more than six billion human beings. Now, look at the map of the world on pages 728–729 of this book. The map shows the nations of the world and the borders that divide them. An astronaut cannot see these nations. Nevertheless they are of great importance to the people living inside their borders.

What Is a Nation?

A nation is a group of people who share a language, a history, and an identity. By this definition, there may be more than one people within the borders of a country who call themselves a nation."

In the eyes of the world, though, a group of people needs more than a sense of unity in order to be called a nation. It must form a political unit with a well-defined territory and a government that has authority over the people living there.

One new nation is Andorra, located in the Pyrenees Mountains between France and Spain. The people of Andorra consider themselves to have their own identity that is neither French nor Spanish. In early 1993 they adopted their own constitution. Andorra, with a population of only 62,000 people, became a new nation.

Characteristics of Nations Every nation has three basic characteristics. First, it has a territory with borders. The borders define the land area of the nation. Second, a nation has a government. Third, a nation has **sovereignty**, the power to make and carry out laws within the nation's borders. The government also has the power to deal with other nations. Having sovereignty means, for example, that a nation can regulate trade with other nations and decide who may enter its territory.

National Interest All nations have a duty to protect the interests of the nation as a whole. Each nation has an interest in protecting itself from outside attack. It is also in each nation's interest to build a strong economy and to preserve order through its legal system.

To look after its national interest, a nation must have power. National power takes many forms. Some nations gain power because they have valuable natural resources, military strength, or strong economies.

Nationalism People within a nation often feel a sense of **nationalism**, a pride in their shared history and a loyalty to their nation. Culture, language, religion, and political tradition can contribute to nationalism. Governments often try to stir feelings of nationalism through holidays, slogans, songs, and pledges.

✓ Reading Check **List the three basic characteristics that all nations share.**

The Different Histories of Nations

Although nations have many similarities, they also have differences. Some nations are rich, while others are poor. Nations have different climates, landscapes, languages, and religions.

One of the most important ways in which nations differ is in their histories. Some nations, such as China, have existed for thousands of years. Others, such as some of the nations in Africa, are less than 50 years old.

Big and Little
The tiny nation of Andorra (left) is a relatively isolated region high in the mountains. Mexico (right) is home to millions of people, with many busy urban areas.
Compare *What basic characteristics do these two nations share?*

Target Reading Skill

Identify Contrasts Note the phrase *by contrast* in the third paragraph. This phrase tells you that the writer is going to note differences between the two groups. Read on to find out what those differences are.

Colonies and Colonial Powers In the past, many nations in the Americas, Africa, and Asia were colonies. A **colony** is a territory ruled by a more powerful nation called a colonial power. Colonial powers wanted colonies to supply crops and natural resources. Colonies were also a source of cheap labor.

A few colonies, such as the 13 American colonies and Australia, were settled by people from the colonial power. In their rush to get land, the newcomers killed or pushed aside the native peoples. In time, these peoples became a small minority in their own lands.

In most colonies, by contrast, the native peoples remained in the majority. Under colonial rule, however, their traditional ways of life were upset. A colonial power often forced its own language, religion, and laws on its colonies.

Analyze Maps and Diagrams

Nations Around the World

The map and diagram provide information about selected countries around the world.

a. Which country shown has the largest population? The smallest?

b. What generalizations about each country's economy can you make from the information about cars and telephones?

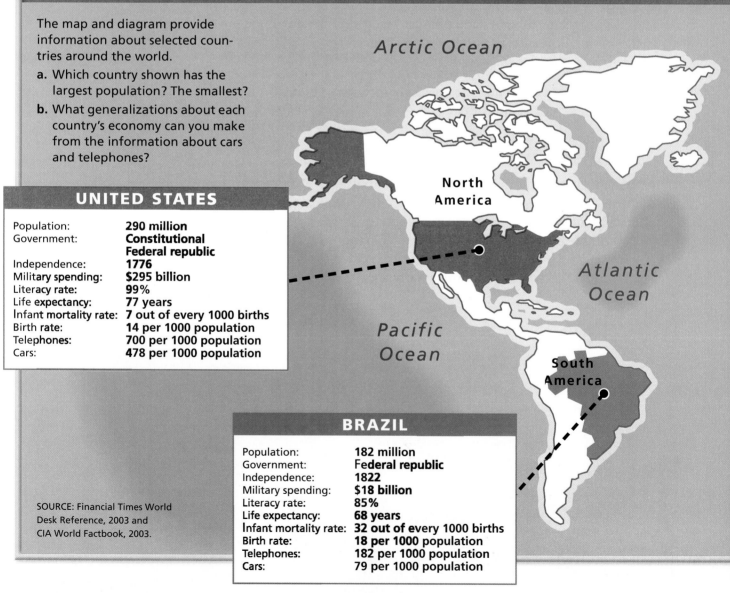

UNITED STATES

Population:	**290 million**
Government:	**Constitutional Federal republic**
Independence:	**1776**
Military spending:	**$295 billion**
Literacy rate:	**99%**
Life expectancy:	**77 years**
Infant mortality rate:	**7 out of every 1000 births**
Birth rate:	**14 per 1000 population**
Telephones:	**700 per 1000 population**
Cars:	**478 per 1000 population**

SOURCE: Financial Times World Desk Reference, 2003 and CIA World Factbook, 2003.

BRAZIL

Population:	**182 million**
Government:	**Federal republic**
Independence:	**1822**
Military spending:	**$18 billion**
Literacy rate:	**85%**
Life expectancy:	**68 years**
Infant mortality rate:	**32 out of every 1000 births**
Birth rate:	**18 per 1000 population**
Telephones:	**182 per 1000 population**
Cars:	**79 per 1000 population**

Independence After the 13 American colonies declared their independence in 1776, people in colonies all over the world have fought to free themselves. Most colonies in Latin America gained independence in the early 1800s. More than 80 colonies in Africa, Asia, and the Middle East became independent nations after World War II.

Some former colonies, such as the United States, have become strong and wealthy nations. However, many have not had that good fortune. Colonization usually had negative consequences for the colonies themselves. Therefore, most colonies were not prepared for nationhood after they achieved independence.

✓ Reading Check   **Why did some nations of the world become colonial powers?**

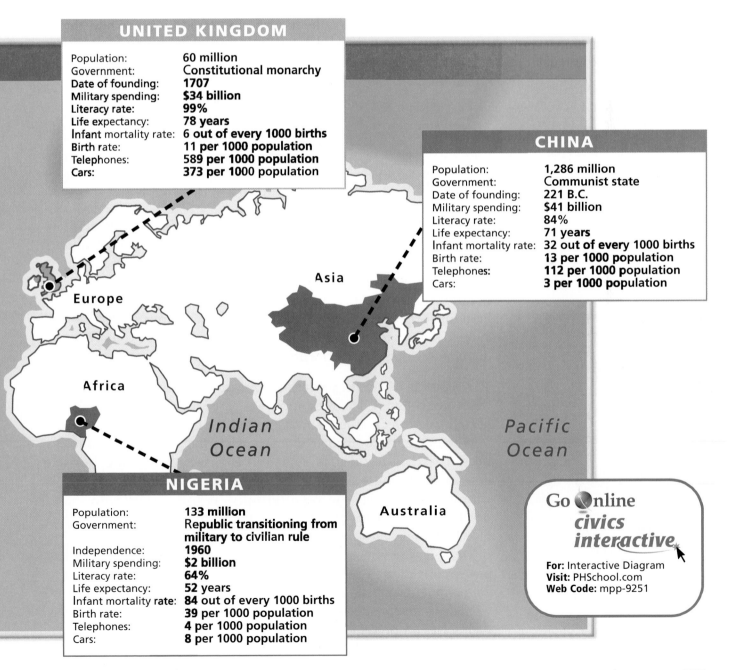

UNITED KINGDOM

Population:	**60 million**
Government:	**Constitutional monarchy**
Date of founding:	**1707**
Military spending:	**$34 billion**
Literacy rate:	**99%**
Life expectancy:	**78 years**
Infant mortality rate:	**6 out of every 1000 births**
Birth rate:	**11 per 1000 population**
Telephones:	**589 per 1000 population**
Cars:	**373 per 1000 population**

CHINA

Population:	**1,286 million**
Government:	**Communist state**
Date of founding:	**221 B.C.**
Military spending:	**$41 billion**
Literacy rate:	**84%**
Life expectancy:	**71 years**
Infant mortality rate:	**32 out of every 1000 births**
Birth rate:	**13 per 1000 population**
Telephones:	**112 per 1000 population**
Cars:	**3 per 1000 population**

Europe

Asia

Africa

Indian Ocean

Pacific Ocean

Australia

NIGERIA

Population:	**133 million**
Government:	**Republic transitioning from military to civilian rule**
Independence:	**1960**
Military spending:	**$2 billion**
Literacy rate:	**64%**
Life expectancy:	**52 years**
Infant mortality rate:	**84 out of every 1000 births**
Birth rate:	**39 per 1000 population**
Telephones:	**4 per 1000 population**
Cars:	**8 per 1000 population**

Go Online
civics
interactive

For: Interactive Diagram
Visit: PHSchool.com
Web Code: mpp-9251

Law and the Real World

Democracies Around the World

The 21st century can be seen as an age of global democracy. An annual Freedom House survey places countries in categories of "Free" and "Not Free." Free countries are those with a minimum level of democracy. This global standard for democracy requires a country to have free, open, and fair elections. In Not Free countries, there are no free elections, and limited political rights or civil liberties for the inhabitants.

Thirty years ago, about 35% of the world's population lived in "Free" countries. Today, that number has increased to 44%. Of the people living in "Not Free" countries, about 60% live in the People's Republic of China. The move toward democracy has been most dramatic in Latin America, Central and Eastern Europe, and the Asia-Pacific region.

Applying the Law

1. What is the difference between Free and Not Free countries?
2. What trend can you identify in nations being considered Free or Not Free?

Economic Development

When people describe the nations of the world today, they often divide them into two groups: "developed nations" and "developing nations." These two groups of nations differ mainly in their **standard of living**, or the number and kinds of goods and services people can have.

The Developed World The developed nations are all heavily industrialized. They depend on factories and modern technology to turn out a wide range of goods and services. Most of their citizens live in towns and cities, and many of them work in service jobs. While the developed nations have only about 20 percent of the world's population, they have more than three quarters of the world's annual income.

The developed world has a relatively high standard of living. While there is poverty, hunger, and homelessness in nearly all developed nations, the poor are a minority of the population.

The Developing World In contrast, most people in the developing world are poor. Many are hungry. In some places poor soil and lack of rain make it hard for people to grow food. Some developing nations do not have enough jobs for those who need work.

Another reason people in developing nations are poor is that it is hard for them to get an education. Many poor nations do not have enough schools for their children. About a quarter of the young children in developing countries do not attend school.

The Results of Having Been Colonies Most developing nations were once colonies. Their resources were used to increase the wealth of colonial powers rather than to improve life in the colony.

When colonies won their independence, they had weak economies. They had few people trained in engineering, banking, business, or government service. In addition, the new nations were left with economies that had been set up to export resources to the developed world. Changing those economies to meet the basic needs of their own people proved very difficult.

Many new countries also faced political problems. The colonial powers had created some colonies that included groups of people with different languages, religions, and histories. Once such colonies won their independence, these groups sometimes fought among themselves for power.

▲
Since gaining its independence from Britain in 1947, India has become a major new power in the global economy.

Economic Development The poorer nations are working to develop their economies. They have been aided in this huge task by the developed nations. There are also international organizations concerned with economic development in poor countries. However, many nations are still poor, and the gap between rich and poor nations has narrowed very slowly.

South Korea Today
South Korea has made great improvements in the standard of living of its citizens.

Some nations have had great success. One of them is South Korea. In 1963, the per capita gross domestic product (GDP) of South Korea was about $80. In other words, if the value of the goods and services produced in South Korea in 1963 had been divided among all South Koreans, each person would have received $80. By 1980, South Korea was becoming a worldwide exporter of manufactured goods, from cars and steel to shoes and clothing. Its economy grew stronger and stronger. By 2002, its GDP had reached over $19,000 per person.

Economic development has improved life for many people in developing nations. Even so, 800 million people in the world, or about one person in seven, go to bed hungry every night. One challenge facing us in the years ahead is to help developing nations meet the basic needs of their people.

✓ Reading Check   **What is the most important difference between developing and developed nations?**

SECTION 1 **Assessment**

Key Terms
Use the following key term in a sentence that explains its meaning: sovereignty, nationalism, colony, standard of living

Target Reading Skill
1. **Identify Contrasts** Contrast the characteristics of developed and developing nations.

Comprehension and Critical Thinking
2. **a. Define** What is a nation?
   b. Draw Inferences What role does nationalism play in a nation's actions and decisions?

3. **a. Describe** Describe the relationship of a colonial power to a colony.
   b. Analyze Information Why did colonial powers often leave their colonies poorly prepared for nationhood?
4. **a. Explain** Why are most former colonies part of the developing world today?
   b. Check Consistency How did some former colonies become developed nations?

Writing Activity
Look at a map of the continent of Africa. Choose any African nation that interests you. Write a newspaper article about this nation. Give its history, including when it was colonized, by which country, when and how it won its independence, and whether it is a developed or developing nation today.

TIP A current almanac is a good place to begin your research.

How to Express Your Views

Government institutions and policies have a great impact on citizens' daily lives. You may sometimes disagree with the way the government has handled an issue, or you may have a suggestion for solving a public problem.

There are many ways you can share your views with government officials. Mia Renatti was upset by her city's plan to tear down her school and build a new one. As you read about Mia, think about what issues you might want to speak out about.

Mia Renatti lives in one of the oldest neighborhoods in her city. She attends the same school that her older sisters, her father, and her grandmother attended. She lives just down the street from the school and grew up playing on its playground.

Mia was very upset when the city announced that it was considering tearing down the school and completely rebuilding it. Mia didn't think a whole new building was necessary. She thought about the different ways she could convince her neighborhood to fight the new school.

Mia decided she could reach out to other concerned citizens by speaking at a public school board meeting. She thought about all the reasons why her school was important to her and about how expensive the long-term construction project would be.

The day of the meeting came, and Mia was very nervous. But she knew that many people in the audience felt the way she did. She delivered her speech, and everyone applauded. At the end of the meeting, the school board decided that it would be best to preserve the old school.

Learn the Skill

To express your views publicly, follow these steps:

1. **Identify a local issue.**

2. **Find out what government bodies are involved.** Do some research on the issue to find out what offices handle it and how they have an impact on the issue.

3. **Decide the best way to express your opinion.** Write a letter to one of the government offices, attend a city council meeting, or speak with your neighbors.

Practice the Skill

1. With a partner, research a community issue.

2. Contact relevant local organizations to receive information.

3. Send a letter to one organization expressing your views on the issue.

Apply the Skill

1. Prepare a short speech about the issue you have researched.

2. Hold a "city council meeting" in class and deliver your speech.

Go **Online**
civics
interactive

For: Local Citizenship
Visit: PHSchool.com
Web Code: mpp-9252

Relations Among and Within Nations

Reading Preview

Objectives

In this section you will

- Identify the types of conflict that arise among nations.
- Explore competition among nations.
- Discuss the Cold War and its aftermath.
- Examine cooperation among nations.

Key Terms

communism   balance of power
Cold War

Main Idea

Nations can fight or they can get along peacefully together. Conflicts can bring trade embargoes or wars.

Target Reading Skill

Make Comparisons Comparing two or more events can help you see their similarities. As you read this section, think about the international conflicts it describes, and what those conflicts have in common.

Taking Notes

Make a diagram like the one below. As you read this section, complete the diagram with information about types of conflict and cooperation between nations.

Nations come into conflict and competition. They also must cooperate. Unfortunately, conflict and competition have shaped human history far more than cooperation has.

In the 20th century alone, there were two major world wars and dozens of smaller ones. Many of these "small wars" were civil wars. Others were conflicts between nations.

Types of Conflict

If you look in any daily newspaper, you will likely find a story about conflict within a nation or among nations somewhere in the world. Conflict is a struggle for something that two or more of them want, such as land or power.

At the root of most conflicts is one group's belief that another group opposes its interests. A conflict may have one major cause, but there will probably also be others. Experts have identified four major causes of conflict within or between nations: (1) conflict over beliefs and values, (2) territorial and environmental conflict, (3) racial and ethnic conflict, and (4) conflict over political power.

✓ **Reading Check** What are two major sources of conflict among or within nations?

The Cost of War
Thousands died in a civil war in Bosnia during the 1990s. Here, a man digs a grave in the capital city of Sarajevo.

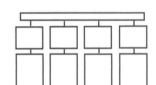

Types of Conflict

These four types of conflict describe most of the sources of civil unrest in the modern world. They may lead to violence among the different nations or even within the borders of a single nation.

1. **Apply** Which of these types of conflict can be seen in the world today? Give examples of each type you list.
2. **Analyze** Which of these conflict types do you think would be most difficult for United Nations peacekeeping forces to solve? Why?

Conflict Over Beliefs and Values

Conflict may arise because of differing views on what is right or wrong. There may be disagreement about the role of government in society, or over how businesses should be owned

Conflict Over Political Power

This kind of conflict is about who makes decisions for a group of people. It may be a struggle to gain political power, or a protest or rebellion against a government that abuses its power.

Racial and Ethnic Conflict

Conflict can occur between different racial or ethnic groups when one thinks it is superior, or because of long-term hatred.

Territorial and Environmental Conflict

Disputes may arise over the control and use of land, water, oil, and other natural resources.

Competition Among Nations

Nations compete economically through trade. Although such competition can benefit nations by causing companies to improve the way they do business, it can harm international relations if one nation believes that another is being unfair. A country may try to help its own farmers by refusing to buy farm products from another country. That country, in turn, may react by refusing to buy products from the first country. Both nations are hurt because trade decreases.

Nations also compete for military power. After World War II, the United States and the Soviet Union competed in a dangerous arms buildup. Today there is concern about the arms buildup in nations like North Korea and China. Such buildups can increase tension, which in turn leads to conflict.

✓ Reading Check **What are the possible consequences of international competition?**

The Cold War and Its Aftermath

Conflict and competition between the United States and the Soviet Union had a great impact on the world for more than 40 years. The superpower rivalry created tensions that no nation could escape. It forced people to live in fear of nuclear war in the United States, the Soviet Union, and many other nations.

The Beginnings of the Conflict The United States and the Soviet Union were uneasy allies during World War II. By 1945, they were the two most powerful nations in the world. But after the war, conflict arose between them. They could not agree on the future of Germany and Eastern Europe. By 1949, the Soviet Union had set up Communist governments in Poland, Hungary, Bulgaria, Romania, Czechoslovakia, and East Germany. Under **communism**, the central government owns and controls the economic resources. These nations were known as "satellites" of the Soviet Union.

Conflict between the United States and the Soviet Union was over more than territory. It was mainly a clash between two ideas about what was good for the world: communism and a state-controlled economy, or democracy and the free market. It was also a conflict between two military superpowers viewing each other as a danger to its national interest.

The Growing Conflict The growing superpower conflict became known as the **Cold War**, a struggle much like a real war but with no armed battles directly between the United States and the Soviet Union. Instead, it was fought with words, warnings, and an arms buildup. The Cold War was also fought indirectly as the United States and the Soviet Union became involved on opposing sides of conflicts in Korea and Vietnam.

To protect their interests, the United States and the nations of Western Europe formed the North Atlantic Treaty Organization (NATO) in 1949. The goal of NATO was to protect the security and freedom of member nations by political and military means. According to the treaty signed by ten countries in Western Europe, the United States, and Canada, an attack against one member country was an attack against all of them.

In 1955, the Soviet Union and the Eastern European nations formed the Warsaw Pact alliance. The alliance was the Soviet equivalent to NATO. Each alliance built up its military power under a unified military command. Several times the Cold War led to the brink of nuclear war.

Links to History

The Cold War

1940

1945

1950

1955

1960

1965

1970

1975

1980

1985

1990

1945 Soviet army marches into Berlin; the German capital city falls. Soviet Union, United States, Great Britain, and France divide Berlin and Germany into four zones of occupation.

1953 More than 300,000 East Germans flee to West Berlin and then to West Germany.

1961 Soviet-controlled East Germany divides Berlin with the Berlin Wall.

1963 U.S. President John F. Kennedy tells a crowd of Germans in Berlin that the Wall proves the failure of the Soviet system.

1985 Mikhail Gorbachev become Soviet leader; begins to ease away from old Communist policies.

1989 The Berlin Wall falls.

1991 The Soviet Union breaks up into independent republics; the Cold War ends.

Analyzing History
Germans have preserved a part of the Berlin Wall as a museum and historic site. Why would they want to remember it?

Go Online
civics
interactive

For: Interactive History Timeline
Visit: PHSchool.com
Web Code: mpp-9253

Target Reading Skill

Make Comparisons On page 680 you read that a nation's belief that its interests are threatened is the root of all conflicts. How is this belief common to the conflicts of the era?

"Hot" Wars The Cold War broke into several "hot" wars between Soviet and American allies. North Korea, backed by the Soviet Union and China, invaded South Korea in 1950. The United States and its allies helped South Korea fight off the attack.

The Cold War turned hot again in Vietnam. The United States sent hundreds of thousands of troops to South Vietnam between 1964 and 1973. The United States wanted to prevent Communists from taking over the South Vietnamese government. Despite American efforts, the Communist government of North Vietnam took over all of Vietnam in 1975.

The United States and the Soviet Union were on opposite sides of conflicts in Ethiopia, Afghanistan, and Nicaragua. However, at no time did Americans and Soviets actually fight each other, nor were nuclear weapons used.

The Cold War Ends In the 1970s the United States and the Soviet Union began to find ways to cooperate. During this period, the two superpowers signed treaties to slow down the arms race. They increased trade with each other.

Stunning political changes began to unfold in the Soviet Union and Eastern Europe in late 1989. One by one the nations of Eastern Europe rid themselves of communist, one-party rule. They began to switch to free market economies. The Warsaw Pact was dissolved. The Soviet Union unraveled as its states called for independence and its economy stalled. In 1991, the Soviet Union ceased to exist and the Cold War ended. Today, the nations of Eastern Europe and the former states of the Soviet Union are working to build up their economies and govern themselves. Some nations have had more success than others.

✔ Reading Check **Who were the nations on the opposite sides of the Cold War?**

The End of the Soviet Union
Boris Yelstin (left, raised arm) became the first elected leader of post-communist Russia. In Czechoslovakia (right), crowds filled the public spaces to celebrate the end of communist rule there.
Draw Inferences *How did the collapse of the Soviet Union affect the rest of the world?*

The Supreme Court

Crosby v. National Foreign Trade Council (2000)

Why It Matters The issue at stake is the role states may play in regulating foreign trade and foreign affairs.

Background The Asian nation of Burma, sometimes called Myanmar, was ruled by a brutal military dictatorship in the 1990s. The Massachusetts legislature passed a law that forbade the state from buying goods from companies that did business in Burma. Both the legislature and governor favored the law because they wanted to influence events in Burma. State officials thought that if enough states were to forbid trade, they could pressure the Burmese generals to change their policy.

The National Foreign Trade Council, a private organization of businesses that favors free trade between nations, sued to have the Burma law overturned. The other named party in the suit was Stephen Crosby, the Massachusetts Secretary of Administration and Finance. In its suit, the Council argued that the law was unconstitutional because foreign policy was a federal issue, not a state one. The case reached the U.S. Supreme Court in 2000.

The Decision The U.S. Supreme Court voted unanimously against Massachusetts and declared the Burma Law unconstitutional. In two different majority opinions, the Court agreed with the National Foreign Trade Council's argument that the law was an intrusion of state power into foreign affairs, which the Constitution reserved for the federal government.

Understanding the Law

1. Why did Massachusetts pass the Burma law?
2. What was the main issue in the case?

Cooperation Among Nations

Much of the cooperation among nations has been through military alliances. However, nations also cooperate economically.

Cooperation in Trade Many nations have formed regional trade organizations to break down trade barriers. One of the oldest is the European Union (EU). In 1999, eleven EU countries gave up their currencies and adopted the euro as a single currency.

The Association of Southeast Asian Nations (ASEAN), the Organization of American States (OAS), and the Organization of African Unity (OAU) are other examples of regional organizations that promote cooperation. In 1993, Congress passed the North American Free Trade Agreement (NAFTA), which lowered trade barriers between Canada, Mexico, and the United States.

Doctors Without Borders Doctors Without Borders spent more than $40 million on its emergency and medical programs and other services in 2002. Doctors Without Borders charges its patients no fees. Therefore, it must depend on individual and corporate donors. Private contributions to the organization totaled more than $43 million in 2002. These donations enable Doctors Without Borders to fight disease in Africa, to provide proper nutrition and sanitation in refugee camps, and to provide emergency care to civilians living in or near zones of international combat.

Analyze Economics

1. Why does Doctors Without Borders refuse to charge its patients fees?
2. Why is there a need for an organization like Doctors Without Borders?

Cooperation in Providing Aid With the end of the Cold War, the United States and other industrialized nations decided as a group to help Russia and the other countries of the former Soviet Union. The aid was to pay for importing food, dismantling nuclear weapons, and promoting democratic and free market reforms.

Nations also worked together to help refugees from the 1994 civil war in Rwanda. More than one million people had fled the country. People had little food, drank contaminated water, and lived in filthy surroundings. Thousands died from disease. Many governments—including the United States—came to their aid.

In December 2003, a devastating earthquake leveled the city of Bam, Iran, killing over 50,000 people and injuring more than 15,000. Up to 40 nations rushed to the city's aid.

The United States was one of the first nations to aid in humanitarian relief efforts. The United States sent emergency supplies, organizational aid, a field hospital that treated more than 700 patients in four days, and emergency personnel to aid in the search and rescue of earthquake victims The United States also temporarily lifted aid restrictions imposed on Iran since 1979. This permitted Americans to donate private funds to earthquake relief in Iran.

Cooperation in Promoting Peace During the Cold War, international conflict was managed through a **balance of power,** the threat that one superpower's military strength might be used against the other's. Some experts claim that this balance of power helped keep peace.

Today, we are witnessing new paths to peacemaking. Peace may be promoted through cooperation among nations, the influence of a respected person, the act of a nation not involved in a dispute, or the economic pressures of many nations acting together. The following examples illustrate some of these possibilities.

A United States soldier helps an Iraqi girl following the Iraq War in 2003.

▼

- **North Korea** In late 1993 and early 1994, North Korea refused to allow international inspectors to observe withdrawal of fuel rods from a nuclear reactor. Officials were concerned that the North Koreans would use the fuel rods to make nuclear weapons. In August 1994, former President Jimmy Carter succeeded in getting North Korea to announce a freeze of its nuclear arms program. In the years that folowed, North Korea agreed to limit its arms production in exchange for economic aid from the United States and other nations. However, North Korea has recently begun to reestablish its nuclear program. Nations around the world have started to put pressure on North Korea to end its nuclear program.

- **The Middle East** A near-permanent state of conflict has existed between Israel and nearby Arab states and the Palestine Liberation Organization (PLO). The world held little hope for peace in the Middle East. In 1993 the foreign minister of Norway, a nation not involved in the crisis, held secret discussions with Israel and the PLO. Since that time, Israel and the PLO have signed several peace agreements, but obstacles to a lasting peace have not been overcome. Still, the United States, the European Union, and key countries of the Middle East are striving towards a permanent solution to the regional conflict.

The End of Apartheid
A South African displays his new voter ID card during South Africa's first post-apartheid election.

- **South Africa** From the late 1940s until the 1990s, South Africa practiced apartheid, a policy of denying its nonwhite citizens political and economic equality. During the 1980s, the United States and other nations cut off most trade with South Africa. These protests pressured the government to do away with apartheid and allow free elections. South Africans of voting age voted in the country's first free nationwide election in 1994. Nelson Mandela, a black leader imprisoned for 27 years under apartheid, was elected President.

✓ Reading Check **In which three areas do nations work together?**

SECTION 2 Assessment

Key Terms
Use each of the key terms in a sentence that explains its meaning: communism, Cold War, balance of power

Target Reading Skill
1. **Make Comparisons** Identify and describe common characteristics of Cold War-era conflicts.

Comprehension and Critical Thinking
2. **a. Recall** What is at the root of every international conflict?
   b. Determine Relevance Conflicts can exist within a nation as well as between different nations. Which of the conflicts described in this section exist today with the United States? Explain.
3. **a. Describe** What makes nations compete with one another?
   b. Predict What would happen if nations did not compete?
4. **a. Explain** What was the cause of the Cold War?
   b. Identify Effect What long-term effects did the Cold War have on the nations of the world?
5. **a. Describe** How do nations work together to promote peace?
   b. Demonstrate Reasoned Judgment What motivates nations to work together to promote peace outside their own borders?

Writing Activity
The Cuban Missile Crisis was a point of great tension during the Cold War. President John F. Kennedy and Soviet premier Nikita Khrushchev knew that their nations stood on the brink of nuclear war. Do some research about the crisis. Describe the actions taken, the decisions, made, and the outcome.

TIP Organize your information in chronological order. This will give your narrative a logical structure with a beginning, middle, and end.

The Challenge of Interdependence

Reading Preview

Objectives

In this section you will

- Learn about the United Nations.
- Explore the work of non-governmental organizations.
- Discuss the impact of these organizations.

Taking Notes

Make a diagram like the one below. As you read this section, complete the diagram with information about the main activities of the United Nations.

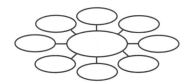

Key Terms

peacekeepers   bureaucracy

Main Idea

The United Nations provides a way for the nations of the world to work together to solve global problems. Other private organizations also work to solve problems.

Target Reading Skill

Identify Contrasts When you contrast two things, you observe their different characteristics. As you read this section, note the differences among the duties and powers of the various United Nations divisions.

How do people from different countries work together to solve problems facing the world? In many cases, representatives from two or more countries meet to talk about problems. International economic conferences and summit meetings of world leaders are examples of such meetings. However, as nations have grown more interdependent, permanent organizations have also been set up to deal with the world's problems.

In this section you will look at the role of the largest organization of governments, the United Nations. You will also see how private groups are helping to solve global problems.

The United Nations

The United Nations (UN) has 189 member nations—almost every nation in the world. Its constitution is the United Nations Charter. It sets forth the rules and purposes of the UN. The UN was created in 1945 at the end of World War II. Its goals are to preserve world peace, to promote justice, and to encourage international cooperation. The headquarters of the UN has been New York City since 1951.

The UN has six major divisions: the Security Council, the General Assembly, the Secretariat, the Economic and Social Council, the International Court of Justice, and the Trusteeship Council. As you will see, in some ways the UN is like a national government. However, it is not a "super-government." It does not have sovereignty over its member nations.

Security Council The most powerful arm of the UN is the Security Council. It has power to take action to keep the peace and help settle conflicts that break out.

The Security Council had five permanent members at the end of World War II: the United States, the Soviet Union, Great Britain, China, and France. They were the five most powerful countries at the end of World War II. Russia now holds the Soviet seat. Ten other members are elected to two-year terms by the General Assembly. For an action to be approved, nine votes out of fifteen are needed.

When the UN was created, none of the "Big Five" countries wanted to give up any of its power. Therefore, each has veto power in the Security Council. If a proposal is vetoed by one of the "Big Five," it is defeated. It does not matter how many members voted for the proposal.

When a war breaks out, the Security Council may send a force of peacekeepers to the trouble spot. **Peacekeepers** are members of the military whose job is usually to help settle conflicts and maintain order in a region. The Security Council may also ask member nations to stop trading with the warring countries or perhaps to break diplomatic relations with them.

General Assembly Every member nation has a vote in the General Assembly. Nations may discuss problems anywhere in the world there. The General Assembly also decides how the UN will spend its money.

The General Assembly cannot make laws. It can only make resolutions, or recommendations. However, General Assembly resolutions can lead to international agreements. For instance, more than 160 nations signed the Montreal Protocol—an agreement to end the production of certain ozone-depleting chemicals.

The United Nations building in New York City houses the meetings of the General Assembly. Kofi Annan became the Secretary General in 1997▶

The Security Council, the most powerful arm of the United Nations, cannot take action without the support of all five Permanent Members. If any one decides to veto a Security Council resolution, the resolution is defeated.

1. Whose offices are behind the door shown in the cartoon?
2. What do you think the cartoonist is trying to say about the United Nations Security Council?

Secretariat To carry out its daily tasks, the UN needs a **bureaucracy**, or a structure of departments staffed by nonelected government officials. People from more than 150 countries work in the UN bureaucracy, called the Secretariat. They translate documents, prepare reports, and provide services to UN councils and agencies. The Secretariat has 25,000 workers in New York and in UN offices in Geneva, Vienna, Nairobi, Rome, and the Hague in the Netherlands.

Economic and Social Council The Economic and Social Council works to improve standards of living. The Council has representatives from 54 countries. It works closely with a number of UN agencies, such as the United Nations Educational, Scientific, and Cultural Organization (UNESCO).

UNESCO supports education, science, art and culture, and communications. It has helped developing nations set up radio stations and newspapers. It runs scientific projects that study Earth's crust, atmosphere, and water supply. UNESCO also sets up exchanges of teachers and students between countries so that people of different nationalities can learn about each other's cultures.

In addition to agencies, the Council works with UN committees, like the United Nations Children's Fund (UNICEF). The goal of UNICEF is to give food and health care to needy children throughout the world.

The International Court of Justice
The judicial branch of the UN is the International Court of Justice. Often called the World Court, it is made up of 15 judges from 15 different countries. The judges, elected by the General Assembly and the Security Council, hear cases on international disputes. The "Big Five" countries have permanent seats on the Court.

World Court judges work with a growing body of international law. Like common law, it is made up of long-standing customs, such as allowing freedom of travel on the seas. Treaties, UN declarations, and World Court decisions are also part of international law.

The judges' decisions are by majority vote. However, a country does not have to accept what the Court decides. Only 62 countries have agreed to accept all Court rulings. The United States does not accept all the Court's decisions as binding. As countries become more interdependent, though, the Court may play a growing role in getting them to settle conflicts peacefully.

The Trusteeship Council When the UN was formed after World War II, there were still some territories that did not have governments. It set up the International Trusteeship System to help govern these territories until they were ready to become independent nations. The UN Charter that set up the system assigned the supervision of the trust territories to the Trusteeship Council, which was made up of the 5 permanent members of the Security Council. The Charter authorized the Trusteeship Council to analyze and discuss reports on the key social, political, economic, and social advances in the trust territories. The Charter also called for the Trusteeship Council to make periodic missions to the regions under its supervision.

In 1994, the tiny Pacific island of Palau gained its independence. It was the last remaining trust territory. Some of the countries that were once trust territories are Somalia, Burundi, Rwanda, and Papua New Guinea. Today, all 11 trust territories have either gained independence or have become parts of other nations. Therefore, the Trusteeship Council suspended operation.

✓ Reading Check **Identify and describe one of the six major divisions of the United Nations.**

Primary Sources

" ...the United Nations in the next century [has] three key priorities for the future: eradicating [getting rid of] poverty, preventing conflict, and promoting democracy . Only in a world that is rid of poverty can all men and women make the most of their abilities. Only where individual rights are respected can differences be channeled politically and resolved peacefully. . . . individual self-expression and self-government [must] be secured, and freedom of association [must] be upheld."

—UN Secretary-General Kofi Annan, accepting the 2001 Nobel Peace Prize

Analyzing Primary Sources
What can the United Nations do to achieve these three goals?

National Leader on Trial
Former Yugoslav president Slobodan Milosevic is brought before a World Court tribunal, charged with war crimes in Croatia, Bosnia, and Kosovo. **Demonstrate Reasoned Judgment** *Why do you suppose the United States might refuse to accept rulings of the World Court as binding?*

Active Citizen

Students Make a Difference

Jessica Rimington's civic involvement began in sixth grade in Massachusetts when she joined Roots and Shoots, an environmental and humanitarian program established by the Jane Goodall Institute. "Through this program, I have learned the value of community service."

Jessica attended the Children's Earth Summit in South Africa. Back in her hometown, she has established a youth council, where students work to make a difference in their local environment.

Service Learning

How can you help protect environmental resources in your area?

▲ Students can help make a difference by learning more about environmental issues that impact their communities.

Nongovernmental Organizations

Private nongovernmental organizations (NGOs) also work on global problems. They meet many challenges, from protecting human rights to working for arms control.

Some NGOs protect political and economic rights. For example, the Red Cross helps victims of war and natural disaster. A wide variety of organizations work on issues such as protecting human rights and combating hunger and disease.

Private groups also deal with other global problems. For example, a group called Doctors Without Borders provides medical care to war and disaster victims worldwide. Doctors Without Borders was awarded the Nobel Prize in 1999.

Many Americans have become involved in groups that are trying to solve world problems. What these people share is an awareness that "global issues" and "local issues" are becoming one and the same.

✓ Reading Check **What is one example of a nongovernmental organization? What does it do?**

The Impact of Organizations

For organizations to succeed in their attempts to solve global problems, countries have to be willing to work together. However, there is a limit to what each country is willing to give up. Nations are not likely to give up any of their political power.

It is not surprising, then, that the UN has had trouble stopping conflicts. When a war breaks out, UN peacekeeping forces are sent only if both sides agree. A dispute can come before the World Court only if the parties involved agree.

Countries are most willing to work together when it does not mean giving up power. For this reason, the UN and other worldwide organizations have had some of their greatest successes dealing with economic, rather than political, problems. Teams of experts teach farmers better ways of preparing fields and raising crops. International agencies help countries build dams and railroads, start businesses, and enter into world trade.

Countries tend to cooperate best in smaller, regional organizations, such as NATO and the Organization of African Unity. Members of such groups usually have more in common than do members of worldwide organizations like the UN. As countries gain more experience in working together, though, and as people's awareness of the world's problems increases, the countries of the world may become more willing to turn to worldwide organizations to help them solve global problems.

Keeping the Peace
These British soldiers are part of a United Nations peacekeeping force in Cyprus.
Summarize *Why is the UN more successful in solving economic problems than political or military ones?*

✓ Reading Check **What obstacles are in the way of international cooperation?**

SECTION 3 **Assessment**

Key Terms
Use each of the key terms in a sentence that explains its meaning: peacekeepers, bureaucracy

Target Reading Skill
1. **Identify Contrasts** What are the major differences in the duties of the UN's six divisions?

Comprehension and Critical Thinking
2. **a. Recall** Which nations are permanent members of the UN Security Council?

   b. Analyze Information Do these five nations fairly represent the interests of all the world's nations? Explain.
3. **a. Describe** What do nongovernmental organizations do?

   b. Draw Inferences Why don't governments do the work of nongovernmental organizations?
4. **a. Explain** Why is it difficult for the UN to maintain peace between conflicting nations?

   b. Make Predictions How might the UN play a stronger role in world affairs?

Writing Activity
Visit the United Nations website. Write a newspaper article describing one aspect of the UN's activities.

Go Online
PHSchool.com
For: Writing Activity
Visit: PHSchool.com
Web Code: mpd-9253

Determining Patterns and Distributions of Maps

Maps can illustrate many different types of information. A distribution map, for example, combines political, economic, or social information with geographic information. Study the map below.

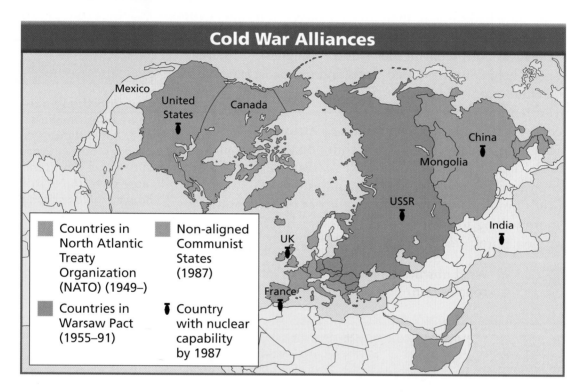

Cold War Alliances

Mexico
United States
Canada
China
Mongolia
USSR
India
UK
France

- Countries in North Atlantic Treaty Organization (NATO) (1949–)
- Non-aligned Communist States (1987)
- Countries in Warsaw Pact (1955–91)
- Country with nuclear capability by 1987

Learn the Skill

Follow these steps to determine patterns and distribution on a map:

1 Read the title. The map title summarizes the information shown on the map. In distribution maps, the title often indicates where people or things are located.

2 Study the map key. The key identifies what the colors or symbols on the map represent.

3 Determine patterns. Note which groups or things are predominant in different areas.

4 Analyze the information. Combine what you know about the subject with the information shown on the map to draw conclusions or make predictions.

Practice the Skill

Study the map above and answer these questions:

1 What does the map title tell you about the map?

2 (a) Which region did the Soviet Union control? (b) Which region or regions was allied with the United States?

3 Which nations had nuclear capability as of 1987?

Apply the Skill

Find a map in your textbook. Pose three questions about the map that apply the skills on this page. Trade maps and questions with a partner and answer the questions.

CHAPTER 25

Review and Assessment

Chapter Summary

Section 1
The Nations and the World
(pages 672–677)

- A nation is a geographical area within recognized borders. It has a government and sovereignty over its people. Nationalism gives citizens a sense of group identity.

- Former colonial powers are today's developed nations, with thriving economies and a high standard of living.

- Former colonies are today's developing nations, with widespread poverty.

Section 2
Relations Between and Within Nations
(pages 679–685)

- Nations come into conflict when they have opposing interests, often based on conflicts over beliefs, politics, territory, or ethnicity.

- Nations compete economically and militarily to gain the greatest wealth and security for their people.

- The Cold War (1940s–1991) was a conflict between the United States and Soviet Union and their allies over the spread of communism. The two superpowers maintained a balance of power that kept most regional conflicts from turning into larger wars.

- Nations often cooperate over issues of trade and social welfare and in attempts to build a peaceful world. Wealthy nations often lend money to developing nations.

Section 3
The Challenge of Interdependence
(pages 686–691)

- The six major divisions of the United Nations bureaucracy work to bring about international peace.

- The UN has only as much authority as its member states give it. For instance, it can only send in peacekeepers if all sides of a conflict agree to their presence.

- Many private organizations give medical and other aid to all nations without discrimination.

- Nations hesitate to work together if it means giving up control of their own futures, but often cooperate within regions.

Copy the chart below and use it to help you summarize the chapter.

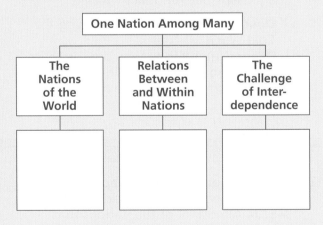

Go Online
PHSchool.com

For: Self-Test
Visit: PHSchool.com
Web Code: mpa-9253

Reviewing Key Terms

On a separate sheet of paper, write the term that makes each sentence correct.

1. (Nationalism, Sovereignty) is the pride people take in their nation's history, language, and culture.

2. A (colony, sovereignty) is a nation or territory under the rule of a foreign nation.

3. The Economic and Social Council of the United Nations works to raise the (balance of power, standard of living) in the nations of the world.

4. (Communism, Nationalism) is a system of government that does not allow for private property or privately-owned businesses.

5. The breakup of the Soviet Union in 1991 brought an end to the (balance of power, Cold War).

6. The power to make and carry out laws within one's nation is called (bureaucracy, sovereignty).

7. (Bureaucracy, Balance of power) is a general term for a large administrative structure of offices and the officials who work there.

8. The (balance of power, standard of living) between the United States and the Soviet Union prevented either nation from attacking the other directly.

Comprehension and Critical Thinking

9. a. **Recall** What made Andorra declare itself an independent nation?
   b. **Recognize Points of View** What might make a people call themselves a nation, even without recognized borders, a government, or sovereignty?
   c. **Link Past and Present** What effects would a past history as a colony have on a present-day republic?

10. a. **Describe** What happened during the Cold War?
    b. **Draw Conclusions** Why did the United States and the Soviet Union begin to slow down the arms race during the 1970s?

c. **Predict** Might there ever be another Cold War? Why?

11. a. **Explain** What powers do member nations have in the United Nations?
    b. **Identify Bias** Why does the Security Council have so few members compared to the total number of UN member nations?
    c. **Identify Effects** What might happen if all UN member nations had votes on the Security Council?

Activities

12. **Skills a.** According to the map, what nations gained their independence before 1945? **b.** Almost all of the nations that gained their independence between 1955 and 1964 are located in the same general area. Why do you suppose that is?

13. **Writing** Write an essay describing what you think is the greatest challenge to the effectiveness of the United Nations. Describe a way that the UN might meet this challenge.

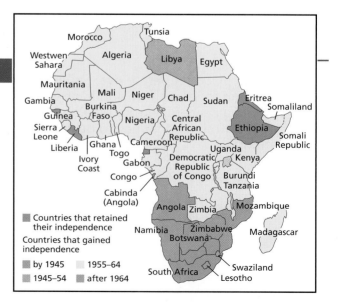

■ Countries that retained their independence

Countries that gained independence

■ by 1945   1955–64
■ 1945–54   ■ after 1964

14. **Active Citizen** Go online to visit a nongovernmental organization that provides aid worldwide. Find out how to volunteer to work abroad with populations in need of care. What kinds of work could you do? Which nations offer opportunities for volunteer work?

15. **Math Practice** A total of $52.1 billion was invested in all of East Asia in 2000. China was the recipient of the most foreign investment in any single nation, a total of $38.4 billion. How much money did this leave for the rest of East Asia?

16. **Civics and Economics** Why would countries want to invest in foreign nations? Explain.

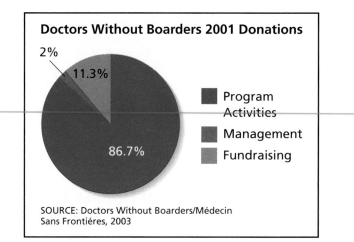

Doctors Without Boarders 2001 Donations

2%
11.3%
86.7%

Program Activities
Management
Fundraising

SOURCE: Doctors Without Boarders/Médecin Sans Frontiéres, 2003

17. **Analyzing Visuals** Study this circle graph. Draw a conclusion about the organization based on the graph.

Standardized Test Prep

Test-Taking Tips

Sometimes a standardized test will ask you to analyze a primary source. Below is an excerpt from UN Secretary-General Kofi Annan's speech accepting the 2001 Nobel Prize. Read the excerpt and answer the questions that follow.

"It [the United Nations] is the nearest thing we have to a representative institution that can address the interests of all states, and of all peoples. Through this universal, indispensable instrument of human progress, states can serve the interests of their citizens by recognizing common interests and pursuing them in unity. . . . the Nobel Committee wishes . . . to proclaim that the only negotiable route to global peace and cooperation goes by way of the United Nations."

Choose the letter of the best answer.

1. Which of the following is a synonym of *proclaim*?

   A say

   B deny

   C agree

   D understand

   TIP Substitute each of the choices for the word *proclaim* in the excerpt's final sentence until you find one that makes sense.

   The correct answer is **A**. The Nobel Committee has made a statement, so *say* is the best synonym of *proclaim*.

2. Why does Annan feel that the UN is indispensable?

   A because it has the world's most powerful army

   B because it allows nations to meet and work together in peace

   C because it has awarded him the Nobel Prize

   D because it ensures world peace

Reference Section

Historical Documents 697

Personal Finance Handbook 706

Landmark Supreme Court Cases 718

Presidents of the United States 724

World Map 728

United States Map 730

Profile of the Fifty States 731

Glossary 732

Spanish Glossary 740

Index 748

Acknowledgments 767

The Magna Carta

The Magna Carta established a significant constitutional principle—that the power of the highest leader in the land can be limited by the law. In the early 1200s, King John of England imposed crushing taxes on his subjects. He also administered justice according to whim rather than the law. In 1215 a group of barons demanded their rights. They took up arms and forced the king to sign a document that became known as the Magna Carta, or Great Charter.

No `scutage' or `aid' [tax] may be levied in our kingdom without its general consent, unless it is for the ransom of our person [the king], to make our eldest son a knight, and (once) to marry our eldest daughter. . . .

To obtain the general consent of the realm for the assessment of an `aid' - except in the three cases specified above - . . . we will cause the archbishops, bishops, abbots, earls, and greater barons to be summoned individually by letter. . . to come together on a fixed day . . . and at a fixed place.. . .

No free man shall be seized or imprisoned, or stripped of his rights or possessions, or outlawed or exiled, or deprived of his standing in any other way, nor will we proceed with force against him, or send others to do so, except by the lawful judgment of his equals or by the law of the land. . . .

The barons shall elect twenty-five of their number to keep. . . the peace and liberties granted and confirmed to them by this charter.

If we, our chief justice, our officials, or any of our servants . . . transgress [break] any of the articles of the peace or of this security, and the offence is made known to four of the said twenty-five barons, they shall come to us [the king]. . . to declare it and claim immediate redress [righting the wrong]. If we. . . make no redress within forty days, . . .the four barons shall refer the matter to the rest of the twenty-five barons, who may . . . assail us [work to change the king's behavior] in every way possible, with the support of the whole community of the land, by seizing our castles, lands, possessions, or anything else . . . , until they have secured such redress as they have determined upon. Having secured the redress, they may then resume their normal obedience to us [the king]. . . .

Both we and the barons have sworn that all this shall be observed in good faith and without deceit. . . . Given by our hand in the meadow that is called Runnymede, between Windsor and Staines, on the fifteenth day of June in the seventeenth year of our reign.

Mayflower Compact

In November 1620, a group of Pilgrims waited aboard the *Mayflower*, which was anchored off the coast of Massachusetts. The men in the group signed a plan of self-government for the colony they would establish. This document was later called the Mayflower Compact.

IN THE NAME OF GOD, AMEN. We, whose names are underwritten, the Loyal Subjects of our dread Sovereign Lord King James, by the Grace of God, of Great Britain, France, and Ireland, King, Defender of the Faith, &c [etc.]. Having undertaken for the Glory of God, and Advancement of the Christian Faith, and the Honour of our King and Country, a Voyage to plant the first Colony in the northern Parts of Virginia; Do by these Presents, solemnly and mutually, in the Presence of God and one another, covenant [make an agreement] and combine ourselves together into a civil Body Politick [group of people under a government], for our better Ordering and Preservation, and Furtherance of the Ends aforesaid: And by Virtue hereof do enact, constitute, and frame, such just and equal Laws, Ordinances, Acts, Constitutions, and Officers, from time to time, as shall be thought most meet and convenient for the general Good of the Colony; unto which we promise all due Submission and Obedience. IN WITNESS whereof we have hereunto subscribed our names at Cape-Cod the eleventh of November, in the Reign of our Sovereign Lord King James, of England, France, and Ireland, the eighteenth, and of Scotland the fifty-fourth, Anno Domini; 1620.

The Federalist, No. 10

1787, the struggle for ratification began. Between October 1787 and May 1788, essays urging ratification began appearing in New York newspapers. The essays were published anonymously. The identities of the writers were later revealed: Alexander Hamilton, John Jay, and James Madison. In this excerpt, James Madison argues the benefits of a federal republic.

. . . The two great points of difference between a democracy and a republic are: first, the delegation of the government, in the latter [a republic], to a small number of citizens elected by the rest; secondly, the greater number of citizens, and greater sphere of country, over which the latter may be extended.

The effect of the first difference is. . . to refine and enlarge the public views, by passing them through the medium of a chosen body of citizens, whose wisdom may best discern the true interest of their country, and whose patriotism and love of justice will be least likely to sacrifice it to temporary or partial considerations. . . .

In the first place, it is to be remarked that, however small the republic may be, the representatives must be raised to a certain number, in order to guard against the cabals [plottings] of a few; and that, however large it may be, they must be limited to a certain number, in order to guard against the confusion of a multitude. . . .

By enlarging too much the number of electors [voters], you render the representatives too little acquainted with all their local circumstances and lesser interests; as by reducing it too much, you render him . . . too little fit to comprehend and pursue great and national objects. The federal Constitution forms a happy combination in this respect; the great and aggregate interests being referred to the national, the local and particular to the State legislatures. . . .

James Madison

The Monroe Doctrine

President James Monroe declared a new policy in his address to Congress in December 1823. This policy became known as the Monroe Doctrine. The purpose of the Monroe Doctrine was to end European interference in the Western Hemisphere.

. . . [T]he American continents . . . are henceforth not to be considered as subjects for future colonization by any European powers. . . .
In the wars of the European powers . . . we have never taken any part, nor does it comport [agree] with our policy to do so. It is only when our rights are invaded or seriously menaced that we resent injuries or make preparation for our defense. . . . We . . . declare that we should consider any attempt on their part to extend their system to any portion of this hemisphere as dangerous to our peace and safety. With the existing colonies or dependencies of any European power we have not interfered and shall not interfere. But with the Governments who have declared their independence and maintain it, and whose independence we have . . . acknowledged, we could not view any interposition [interference] for the purpose of oppressing them, or controlling in any other manner their destiny, by any European power in any other light than as the manifestation of an unfriendly disposition toward the United States. . . .

Our policy in regard to Europe . . . remains the same, which is, not to interfere in the internal concerns of any of its powers; to consider the government de facto as the legitimate government for us; to cultivate friendly relations with it, and to preserve those relations by a frank, firm, and manly policy, meeting in all instances the just claims of every power, submitting to injuries from none. . . .

The Seneca Falls Declaration

Elizabeth Cady Stanton and Lucretia Mott organized the first American women's rights convention. The convention took place in Seneca Falls, New York, In 1848. The delegates to the convention demanded that the rights of women be respected by American society. The delegates issued their demands in a document based on the Declaration of Independence. It was signed by 68 women and 32 men.

We hold these truths to be self-evident: that all men and women are created equal; that they are endowed by their Creator with certain inalienable rights; that among these are life, liberty, and the pursuit of happiness; that to secure these rights governments are instituted, deriving their just powers from the consent of the governed. Whenever any form of government becomes destructive of these ends, it is the right of those who suffer from it to refuse allegiance to it, and to insist upon the institution of a new government, laying its foundation on such principles, and organizing its powers in such form, as to them shall seem most likely to effect their safety and happiness. Prudence, indeed, will dictate that governments long established should not be changed for light and transient causes. . . . But when a long train of abuses . . . evinces [indicates] a design to reduce them under absolute despotism [tyranny], it is their duty to throw off such government, and to provide new guards for their future security. Such has been the patient sufferance of the women under this government, and such is now the necessity which constrains them to demand the equal station to which they are entitled. . . . To prove this, let facts be submitted to a candid world. . . .

He has never permitted her to exercise her inalienable right to the elective franchise [the vote].

He has compelled her to submit to laws, in the formation of which she had no voice. . . .

He has made her, if married, in the eye of the law, civilly dead.

He has taken from her all right in property, even to the wages she earns. . . .

He has monopolized nearly all the profitable employments, and from those she is permitted to follow, she receives but a scanty remuneration [pay]. . . .

He has denied her the facilities for obtaining a thorough education, all colleges being closed against her. . . .

Now, in view of this entire disfranchisement of one-half the people of this country, their social and religious degradation--in view of the unjust laws above mentioned, and because women do feel themselves aggrieved, oppressed, and fraudulently deprived of their most sacred rights, we insist that they have immediate admission to all the rights and privileges which belong to them as citizens of the United States.

Susan B. Anthony (center), Elizabeth Cady Stanton (right), and other nineteenth century suffragists.

Abraham Lincoln

The Emancipation Proclamation

In January 1863, the midst of the bloody Civil War, President Abraham Lincoln issued the Emancipation Proclamation. The Proclamation declared that all enslaved people held within Confederate territory would be freed. In reality, the Proclamation did not immediately free anyone. However, it paved the way for the Thirteenth Amendment, which abolished slavery in the United States.

. . . [O]n the first day of January, in the year of our Lord one thousand eight hundred and sixty-three, all persons held as slaves within any State or designated part of a State, the people whereof shall then be in rebellion against the United States, shall be then, thenceforward, and forever free. . . . .

That the Executive will, on the first day of January . . . designate the States and parts of States, if any, in which the people . . . shall then be in rebellion against the United States; and the fact that any State, or the people thereof, shall on that day be. . . represented in the Congress of the United States by members chosen thereto at elections wherein a majority of the qualified voters of such State shall have participated, shall . . . be deemed conclusive evidence that such State, and the

people thereof, are not then in rebellion against the United States. . . .

And by virtue of the power, and for the purpose aforesaid, I do order and declare that all persons held as slaves within said designated States, and parts of States, are, and henceforward shall be free; and that the Executive government of the United States, including the military and naval authorities thereof, will recognize and maintain the freedom of said persons.

And I hereby enjoin upon the people so declared to be free to abstain from all violence, unless in necessary self-defence; and I recommend to them that, in all cases when allowed, they labor faithfully for reasonable wages.

And I further declare and make known, that such persons of suitable condition, will be received into the armed service of the United States . . . .

And upon this act, sincerely believed to be an act of justice, warranted by the Constitution, upon military necessity, I invoke the considerate judgment of mankind, and the gracious favor of Almighty God. . . .

The Gettysburg Address

On November 19, 1863 President Abraham Lincoln gave a short address at the dedication of a cemetery for the Union war dead. In his speech, Lincoln not only honored the war dead. He also expressed his view that the Civil War was a fight to save the Union and to establish freedom for all under the law.

Four score and seven years ago our fathers brought forth, upon this continent, a new nation, conceived in liberty, and dedicated to the proposition that "all men are created equal"

Now we are engaged in a great civil war, testing whether that nation, or any nation so conceived, and so dedicated, can long endure. We are met on a great battle field of that war. We have come to dedicate a portion of it, as a final resting place for those who died here, that the nation might live. This we may, in all propriety do. But, in a larger sense, we can not dedicate—we can not consecrate—we can not hallow, this ground. The brave men, living and dead, who struggled here, have hallowed it, far above our poor power to add or detract. The world will little note, nor long remember what we say here; while it can never forget what they did here.

It is rather for us, the living, we here be dedicated to the great task remaining before us—that, from these honored dead we take increased devotion to that cause for which they here, gave the last full measure of devotion—that we here highly resolve these dead shall not have died in vain; that the nation, shall have a new birth of freedom, and that government of the people by the people for the people, shall not perish from the earth.

Soldiers' National Cemetery, Gettysburg National Military Park

Fort McHenry Battle Flag, the original "Star-Spangled Banner."

Star-Spangled Banner

During the War of 1812, Francis Scott Key watched the American victory over the British in the Battle of Baltimore. Key published his impressions of the victory as a poem to be sung a popular British melody. Although the song was popular, it was not until 1931 that Congress made the song the national anthem.

Oh, say can you see, by the dawn's early light,
What so proudly we hailed at the twilight's last
    gleaming?
Whose broad stripes and bright stars, through the
    perilous fight,
O'er the ramparts we watched, were so gallantly
    streaming?
And the rockets' red glare, the bombs bursting in air,
Gave proof through the night that our flag was still
    there.
O say, does that star-spangled banner yet wave
O'er the land of the free and the home of the brave?

On the shore, dimly seen through the mists of the
    deep,
Where the foe's haughty host in dread silence reposes,
What is that which the breeze, o'er the towering steep,
As it fitfully blows, half conceals, half discloses?

Now it catches the gleam of the morning's first beam,
In full glory reflected now shines on the stream:
'Tis the star-spangled banner! O long may it wave
O'er the land of the free and the home of the brave.
And where is that band who so vauntingly swore
That the havoc of war and the battle's confusion
A home and a country should leave us no more?
Their blood has wiped out their foul footstep's
    pollution.
No refuge could save the hireling and slave
From the terror of flight, or the gloom of the grave:
And the star-spangled banner in triumph doth wave
O'er the land of the free and the home of the brave.

Oh! thus be it ever, when freemen shall stand
Between their loved homes and the war's desolation!
Blest with victory and peace, may the heaven-rescued
    land
Praise the Power that hath made and preserved us a
    nation.
Then conquer we must, when our cause it is just,
And this be our motto: "In God is our trust."
And the star-spangled banner in triumph shall wave
O'er the land of the free and the home of the brave

The Pledge of Allegiance

An editor named Francis Bellamy wrote and published the Pledge of Allegiance in 1892. President Dwight Eisenhower encouraged Congress to add the words "under God" in 1954.

I pledge allegiance to the flag of the United States of America and to the republic for which it stands, one nation under God, indivisible, with liberty and justice for all.

Americans recite the Pledge of Allegiance.

The American's Creed

William Tyler Page wrote "The American's Creed" as part of a nationwide contest in 1917. The American's Creed is a brief summary of American political faith. It was accepted by the House of Representatives on April 3, 1918.

I believe in the United States of America as a government of the people, by the people, for the people; whose just powers are derived from the consent of the governed; a democracy in a republic; a sovereign Nation of many sovereign States; a perfect union, one and inseparable; established upon those principles of freedom, equality, justice, and humanity for which American patriots sacrificed their lives and fortunes.I therefore believe it is my duty to my country to love it, to support its Constitution, to obey its laws, to respect its flag, and to defend it against all enemies.

Patriotic Americans come from a variety of backgrounds.

John F. Kennedy's Inaugural Address

John F. Kennedy became President durring turbulent times. The Cold War raged between the United States and the Soviet Union. The threat of nuclear destruction terrified millions. The civil rights movement was in full force. It was a time of great danger and great promise. In his inaugural address on January 20, 1961, President Kennedy called Americans to action.

John F. Kennedy delivers his inaugural address.

. . . The world is very different now. For man holds in his mortal hands the power to abolish all forms of human poverty and all forms of human life. And yet the same revolutionary beliefs for which our forebears fought are still at issue around the globe—the belief that the rights of man come not from the generosity of the state, but from the hand of God. . . .

Let every nation know, whether it wishes us well or ill, that we shall pay any price, bear any burden, meet any hardship, support any friend, oppose any foe, in order to assure the survival and the success of liberty.

This much we pledge—and more.

To those old allies whose cultural and spiritual origins we share, we pledge the loyalty of faithful friends. United, there is little we cannot do in a host of cooperative ventures. Divided, there is little we can do—for we dare not meet a powerful challenge at odds and split asunder. . . .

Finally, to those nations who would make themselves our adversary, we offer not a pledge but a request: that both sides begin anew the quest for peace, before the dark powers of destruction unleashed by science engulf all humanity in planned or accidental self-destruction. . . .

Let us never negotiate out of fear. But let us never fear to negotiate.

Let both sides explore what problems unite us instead of belaboring those problems which divide us. . . .

Let both sides seek to invoke the wonders of science instead of its terrors. Together let us explore the stars, conquer the deserts, eradicate disease, tap the ocean depths, and encourage the arts and commerce. . . .

In the long history of the world, only a few generations have been granted the role of defending freedom in its hour of maximum danger. I do not shrink from this responsibility—I welcome it. I do not believe that any of us would exchange places with any other people or any other generation. The energy, the faith, the devotion which we bring to this endeavor will light our country and all who serve it—and the glow from that fire can truly light the world.

And so, my fellow Americans: ask not what your country can do for you—ask what you can do for your country.

My fellow citizens of the world: ask not what America will do for you, but what together we can do for the freedom of man. . . .

"I Have a Dream" Address

More than 200,000 demonstrators gathered in Washington, D.C., on August 28, 1963, for the March on Washington for Job and Freedom. A number of civil rights groups had planned the march. They wanted to show the nation that there was a gap between the American ideals of democracy and the everyday experiences of African Americans. During this march, Dr. Martin Luther King, Jr., delivered a powerful speech about his vision of freedom and equality.

But there is something that I must say to my people who stand on the warm threshold which leads into the palace of justice. . . . Let us not seek to satisfy our thirst for freedom by drinking from the cup of bitterness and hatred. We must forever conduct our struggle on the high plane of dignity and discipline. . . . [M]any of our white brothers, as evidenced by their presence here today, have come to realize that their destiny is tied up with our destiny and their freedom is inextricably bound to our freedom. We can not walk alone.

And as we walk, we must make the pledge that we shall march ahead. We cannot turn back. There are those who are asking the devotees of civil rights, "when will you be satisfied?"

We can never be satisfied as long as the Negro is the victim of unspeakable horrors of police brutality. . . . We can never be satisfied as long as a Negro in Mississippi cannot vote and a Negro in New York believes he has nothing for which to vote. . . .

I say to you today, my friends, that in spite of the difficulties and frustrations of the moment I still ave a dream. It is a dream deeply rooted in the American dream.

I have a dream that one day this nation will rise up and live out the true meaning of its creed:"We hold these these truths to be self evident, that all men are created equal."

I have a dream that one day on the red hills of Georgia the sons of former slaves and the sons of former slaveowners will be able to sit down together at the table of brotherhood.

I have a dream that one day even the state of Mississippi, a desert state sweltering with the heat of injustice and oppression, will be transformed into an oasis of freedom and justice.

I have a dream that my four little children will one day live in a nation where they will not be judged by the color of their skin but by the content of their character. I have a dream today. . . .

When we let freedom ring, when we let it ring from every village and every hamlet, from every state and every city, we will be able to speed up that day when all of God's children, black men and white men, Jews and gentiles, Protestants and Catholics, will be able to join hands and sing in the words of the old Negro spiritual:

"Free at last! Free at last! Thank God Almighty, we are free at last!"

Martin Luther King, Jr.

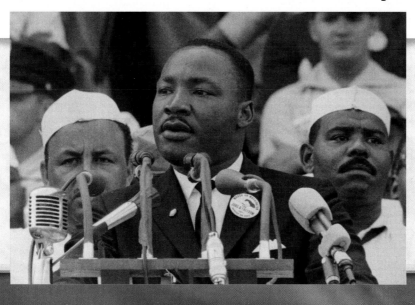

Creating a Budget

A tiny drip from your bathtub faucet can send thousands of gallons of water down the drain each year. Your money can dribble away, too.

An $8 pizza, a $12 pair of sunglasses, $20 at the movies—they don't seem like much at the time. But a lifetime pattern of careless spending can be painful, even ruinous. Money problems can cause stress, wreck personal relationships, and trap people in jobs they don't like just so they can pay their bills. What a way to live your life!

Start a better way. Budget your money.

Calculate Income Versus Spending

Budgeting begins simply with writing how much money you receive and how much you spend. Try these steps:

Four Steps to Successful Budgeting

1. Make a list of your earnings like the one below right. Then calculate your total monthly income.

2. For one month, keep a record of everything you spend money on, from car payments to candy bars. You can jot down each purchase on a scrap of paper, and toss all the scraps in a shoebox. Or carry a small notebook to list items and amounts.

3. At the end of the month, organize the records of your purchases into categories such as food, clothing, entertainment, car payments, and so on. Find the total for each category.

4. On a sheet of paper or on a computer spreadsheet, make a list similar to the one on the next page. Fill in the expenditures and the amounts. Then calculate your total monthly spending.

This record of your income and spending can be very revealing. Do you have a little money left over at the end of the month? Or do you spend more than you earn? Experts recommend that you put about 10 percent of your income into savings. If you have very little left over—or worse, if you spend more than you earn—it's time to create a budget.

Living Within Your Budget

Look at your expenditures and find areas in which you can cut spending. For instance, buy a frozen pizza from the grocery store instead of ordering take-out. Get together at friends' houses instead of at the mall. Shop end-of-season clothing sales. And be careful with automatic teller machines! ATMs make it too easy to drain your bank account.

Fill in the first two columns of a chart like the one on the next page. Then in the third column, enter the reduced amounts you think you can spend. Keep cutting until you can reserve 10 percent of your earnings as savings. This is your new **budget,** a plan for saving and spending.

If you have a difficult time staying within your budget, enlist a friend or family member to review your expenditures each week to help keep you on track. Distinguish between "needs" and "wants." Try not to rationalize impulse buying. After all, you'll only be kidding yourself.

My Earnings	
SOURCE	**MONTHLY INCOME**
Restaurant job	$392
Computer tutoring	$68
Baby-sitting	$20
TOTAL	**$480**

My Spending and Saving Plan

MONTHLY EXPENDITURE	CURRENT EXPENSES	BUDGET
Car		
Payment	$120	$120
Insurance	$42	$42
Gasoline	$27	$14
Maintenance (estimated)	$30	$30
Food		
Lunches at school	$58	$35
Snacks	$34	$20
Movies		
Theater	$28	$7
Rentals	$4	$8
Clothes		
Shoes	$16	$7
Other clothes	$39	$25
Savings for school trip	$50	$50
Magazine subscription	$5	$0
CDs	$24	$12
Gifts	$0	$35
Savings	$0	$48
Emergencies	$0	$27
TOTALS	**$477**	**$480**

Costs such as car payments are fixed.

Bike or carpool instead of driving. Savings: one tank of gas a month.

Cut out chips at lunch. Savings: $23 a month! (It's healthier, too.) Even better: Pack a lunch.

Items such as new clothes are optional expenses. Wear last year's shirt for one more season.

Borrow magazines from friends or the library. Savings: $5 a month

By cutting expenses, you can set aside money for savings, holiday gifts, and emergency needs.

Check Your Understanding

1. **Key Terms** Why is it important to create a **budget**?
2. **Review** Reread the suggested ways for saving money, and brainstorm others to add to the list.

Opening and Managing a Checking Account

If your piggy bank is bursting, consider opening a checking account.

Before banks dotted every streetcorner in America, some people stuffed their money under the mattress for safekeeping. It wasn't very safe.

Today virtually everyone has access to a bank. It's a safe place to store your money, and it offers conveniences such as check writing, electronic banking, and interest on your money.

Choosing a Bank

The most common types of bank accounts are checking and savings. If you plan to take money out of your account frequently, you probably need a checking account. Savings accounts and other savings options are discussed on page 506.

Opening a checking account is fairly easy. First you'll need some kind of identification, such as a driver's license or a pay stub. You'll also need a Social Security number. (If you don't yet have a Social Security number, you can apply on-line at the Web site of the Social Security Administration.) Finally, you'll need at least a small sum of money to deposit when you open your account.

How to Choose a Checking Account

☐ Do I have to keep a **minimum balance,** or amount of money, in the account to avoid fees?
☐ Is there a monthly fee? How much is it?
☐ Will I be charged check writing fees?
☐ How many checks can I write per month?
☐ Will the bank return my canceled checks each month or keep them on file?
☐ Will I be charged ATM fees?
☐ What other fees are associated with this account?

It pays to shop around for the best checking account. Although the interest that most banks pay on checking accounts ranges from little to none, other features, such as fees, vary widely. The chart above lists some of the criteria to consider when selecting a checking account.

Keeping Records

When you open an account, you'll receive a checkbook that includes sequentially numbered checks and a **check register,** a booklet in which you'll record your account transactions. You'll make your life a lot easier if you decide from the start to be a good recordkeeper. Every time you write a check, make a deposit, or use an ATM, take a few seconds to jot it down in your check register.

You won't believe how glad you'll be that you have your own records of your financial business. For example, if you earn money, the Internal Revenue Service could ask at any time to see

ITEM NO. OR TRANS. CODE	DATE	TRANSACTION DESCRIPTION	SUBTRACTIONS AMOUNT OF PAYMENT OR WITHDRAWAL (-)	√ T	(-) FEE IF ANY	ADDITIONS AMOUNT OF DEPOSIT OR INTEREST (+)	BALANCE	
		RECORD ALL CREDITS AND CHARGES THAT AFFECT YOUR ACCOUNT					246	30
							-45	99
#383	9/5	Scott's Sporting Goods Gym shoes	-45 99				200	31
			-20 00				-20	00
WD	9/9	ATM withdrawal - movies					180	31
			-24 88				-24	88
#384	9/10	CD Superstore Birthdays-Kate+Sierra				+185 86	155	43
							+185	86
Dep.	9/16	Deposit - paycheck					341	29
							-10	00
#385	9/21	Lake Forest High School yearbook deposit	-10 00				331	29
							-11	18
#386	9/22	Kelly's Flower Shop Get-well bouquet-Nana	-11 18				320	11
						+127 07	-127	07
Dep.	9/30	Deposit - paycheck					447	18
							-5	00
Fee	9/30	Checking acc't fee	-5 00				442	18
						+12 00	+12	00
Dep.	10/2	Deposit Babysitting Rebecca					454	18
							-7	25
#387	10/8	Sam's Market Food for hunger drive	-7 25				446	93
			-400 00				-400	00
Trans.	10/10	Transfer to savings account				+195 04	46	93
							+195	04

Journey of a Personal Check

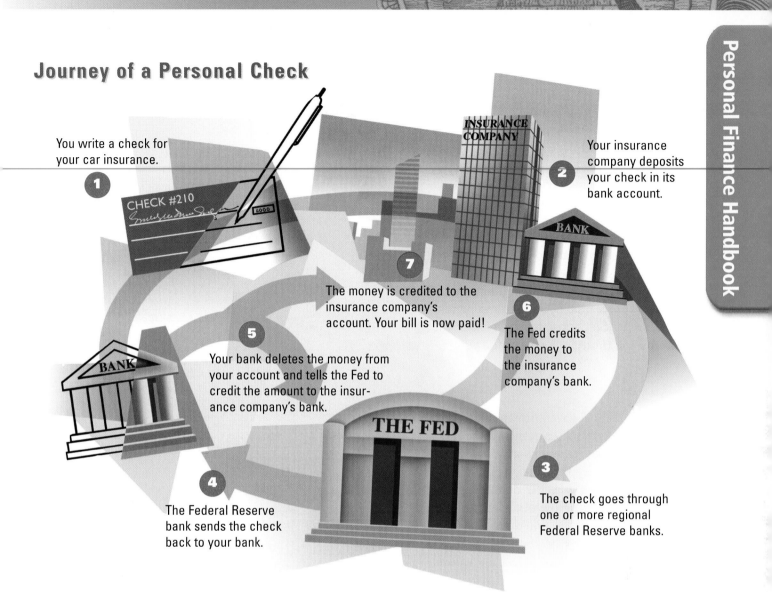

You write a check for your car insurance.

1

CHECK #210

Your insurance company deposits your check in its bank account.

2

INSURANCE COMPANY

BANK

7

The money is credited to the insurance company's account. Your bill is now paid!

6

The Fed credits the money to the insurance company's bank.

5

Your bank deletes the money from your account and tells the Fed to credit the amount to the insurance company's bank.

BANK

THE FED

4

The Federal Reserve bank sends the check back to your bank.

3

The check goes through one or more regional Federal Reserve banks.

your financial records for the past three years. Also, your bank could make a mistake. Bank records are rarely wrong, but it does happen. The ATM receipt you shoved in your wallet is your proof that you withdrew $50, not $500!

Balancing Your Checkbook

Each month you'll receive a statement, a record of your checking account activity during the last month. It lists deposits, withdrawals, ATM transactions, interest paid, and fees charged. Any checks you wrote that were cashed during the month may be returned to you in the statement, although some banks keep the originals in storage. The diagram above shows where your check goes before it is returned to you.

It's extremely important to balance your checkbook every month. That means comparing the transactions in the bank statement to your own records to make sure they agree. Most statements have a worksheet on the back to help you balance your account in a few easy steps. If you have any trouble balancing your checkbook, someone at your bank's local branch office can assist you.

Check Your Understanding

1. **Key Terms (a)** How is your account balance different from your **minimum balance? (b)** Why is it a good idea to use a **check register?**

2. **Evaluate** If you were going to open a checking account today, which criteria listed above would be most important and least important to you? Why?

Saving and Investing

It's never too early to prepare for your financial future, whether that means holiday shopping, next year's vacation, college, or retirement.

Paving the way to a sound financial future involves more than getting a job and living within a budget. Managing your money also involves saving and investing. How much you save and how much you invest depends on the lifestyle you choose for yourself in the present and the lifestyle you plan for your future.

Saving

Why do you need to save your money? While you might have enough earnings to meet your daily expenses, saving is a way to make sure you have money for special purchases and future expenses, whether planned or unplanned. The box below outlines the main types of bank or credit union accounts for saving money. The box on the next page provides questions to help you select an account.

Passbook

			21163347	
Always verify entry before leaving window				
DATE	DEPOSIT	INTEREST	WITHDRAWAL	BALANCE	TELLER
				$100.00	5454
01 18JUN02	$100.00			$100.06	INT
02 15JUL02		$.06		$100.14	INT
03 15AUG02		$.08		$100.21	INT
04 15SEP02		$.07		$100.27	INT
05 15OCT02		$.06		$100.34	INT
06 17NOV02		$.07		$100.37	INT
07 15DEC02		$.03		$100.42	INT
08 15JAN03		$.05		$100.46	INT
09 15FEB03		$.04		$100.50	INT
10 15MAR03		$.04		$100.54	INT
11 15APR03		$.04		$100.58	INT
12 15MAY03		$.04			

Notify us of change of address
Report loss of passbook immediately

				$100.62	INT
13 15JUN03		$.04		$100.66	INT
14 15JUL03		$.04		$165.66	5463
15 04AUG03			$65.00		
16					
17					
18					
19					
20					
21					
22					
23					
24					

THANK YOU

Types of Accounts

Banks offer several ways for you to save your money. Each account has different features and restrictions.

Savings Accounts It's a good idea to use a **savings account** for savings that you may need to use within a short period of time. When you deposit money in a savings account, your bank or credit union will record deposits, withdrawals, fees, and any **interest** earned by your account. The interest rate is the rate of interest an account will earn on funds deposited for a full year.

Money Market Accounts A money market deposit account (MMDA) will let you save and write a limited number of checks. It usually earns higher interest than a savings account, but also usually requires a higher minimum balance and has more fees. MMDAs have a variable interest rate, which can be a benefit or a drawback depending on whether rates move up or down.

Time Deposits A **time deposit**, such as a certificate of deposit (CD), offers a guaranteed interest rate for a fixed period of time. In general, the longer the term, the higher the interest rate. Most banks will charge you a high penalty fee if you withdraw from the CD account before the term expires, or "matures." Open a CD account only if you think you won't need access to that money during the term of the CD.

How to Choose

a Savings Account

Deposits and withdrawals
- ❑ What is the minimum balance?
- ❑ When can I make my first withdrawal?
- ❑ How many deposits and withdrawals am I allowed to make each month?
- ❑ Am I limited in the dollar amount of my withdrawals?
- ❑ What are the penalties for early withdrawal?
- ❑ Can I use an automated teller machine (ATM) to make deposits and withdrawals?

Interest
- ❑ What is the interest rate?
- ❑ Is it compounded? How frequently?
- ❑ What is the minimum balance required to earn interest?
- ❑ When is the interest paid?

Fees
- ❑ What fees apply?
- ❑ What is the minimum balance needed to avoid fees?
- ❑ Do certain transactions carry penalty fees?
- ❑ What ATM fees apply?

Truth in Savings The **Truth in Savings Act** is a federal law that requires banks to provide you with certain information about the accounts they offer, including
- annual percentage yield—the amount of interest you will earn on a deposit
- interest rates
- fees and other charges that apply
- features, such as the minimum balance needed to avoid fees

Use this information to help you choose the bank and the type of account that is best for you.

Investing

Saving is a great way to plan for your future. Many experts advise saving 10 percent of your earnings annually. While keeping your money in a savings account is safe, investing your money can give your dollars the opportunity to grow. Bonds, stocks, and mutual funds are among the many investment options available to you.

Bonds A **bond** is an IOU issued by a corporation or by the government as a way for them to borrow money. When you buy a bond, you buy the right to receive a fixed amount of money at some future date as well as an annual interest payment. The face value of the bond is the fixed amount agreed upon. Corporate bonds can be risky, depending on the financial health of the firm. If the firm goes bankrupt, it won't be able to pay what it owes you. Government bonds are more secure because the government is unlikely to declare bankruptcy.

Government bonds can be purchased through your bank and are available in small denominations. Interest earned is subject to federal tax, but not state or local taxes. They are a secure investment, although the return is low compared to other types of investment.

A word about interest rates Interest rates are expressed as percentages and indicate the rate of interest an account will earn on funds deposited for a full year. Interest is compounded when it is added to your principal. In effect, compound interest is interest on interest.

Stocks A popular form of investment, **stock** represents ownership in an organization. If a firm issues and sells 10,000 shares of stock, and you purchase 1,000 of them, you own 10 percent of the firm. By purchasing a corporation's stock, you are buying the right to receive a fraction of its profit.

The two potential benefits from owning stock are dividends and capital gains. **Dividends** are portions of a corporation's profit paid to stockholders. **Capital gain** is the profit you make if you can sell your stock for more than you paid for it. Not all stocks pay dividends. Some companies reinvest their profits, rather than pay out dividends. Such "growth" stocks are attractive to investors because they expect the stock price to increase as the company grows.

Stock is available in two forms: **common stock** and **preferred stock**. Preferred stock earns dividends fixed at an annual rate, whereas any dividends earned by common stock are dependent on market fluctuations. Preferred shareholders are paid dividends before common shareholders.

Corporate stocks are bought and sold on stock markets. Most investors rely on the services of a stockbroker to purchase stock. You'll want to compare reputations, transaction fees, insurance, and services of various brokerage firms before you choose one. Many people rely on the advice of a professional financial advisor or investment advisor when choosing stock. Make sure you check an advisor's credentials.

Stocks are riskier than bonds, because stock price is based on the expectation of profit. If the firm turns out to be less profitable than expected, dividends will be smaller than expected and the market price of shares may decrease. You may find yourself selling your shares for less money than you paid for them.

Experts warn that if you get into the stock market, you should be prepared to ride the ups and downs. Sometimes you will win, and sometimes you will lose. And don't go into the stock market

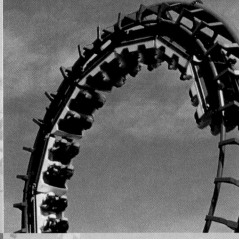

On October 27, 1997, the Dow plummeted a record 554 points, leading the New York Stock Exchange to halt trading for the rest of the day.

The longest bull run—period in which stock prices rise without interruption—lasted from 1949 until 1957.

The Dow exceeded 3,000 points for the first time in 1991. By January 2000, it attained an all-time high of over 11,000 points, only to drop sharply after the September 11, 2001, terrorist attacks.

Comparing Investment Options

Type of investment	Income generated	Growth potential	Risk level
Bonds	very steady	little or none	low risk
Common stock	variable	good	high risk
Preferred stock	less variable than common stock	good	moderate risks

to make a quick profit for something crucial, like school tuition. If you do, the stock could take a tumble right at the time you need to sell it, and you could lose all of your investment.

Mutual Funds You might choose to invest your money in a **mutual fund,** which is an investment in an investment company. Investment companies sell stock in their mutual funds. Instead of producing a product or service, however, they take the money they receive for their stock and invest it in the stocks and bonds of other corporations. The mutual fund will combine the money you invest with that of other investors in order to make substantial investments in other companies.

A major benefit of investing in a mutual fund is that it provides instant diversification to your portfolio. This means that the money you invest in a mutual fund is spread out among all the different companies in which the mutual fund invests its money.

Mutual funds include stocks of varying risk levels. There are three categories of mutual funds:

- *Money market funds* are short-term, low risk investments. The money you invest will be used to make short-term loans to businesses or the government. (Do not confuse money market funds with money market deposit accounts, which are described on page 506.)
- *Bond funds* are, as the name implies, investments in bonds. They usually have higher potential yields than money market funds, but they are also riskier.
- *Stock funds,* though riskiest, offer the highest potential returns. As long-term investments, they perform better than money market funds and bond funds.

As with any investment, you must do your homework before you commit to a mutual fund. Even though a professional money manager will control your investment, mutual funds are not without risk.

Risk Versus Payout You have many options when it comes to investing your money. What you choose depends on what rate of return you'd like on your money and how much risk you are willing to accept. You also need to consider the length of your investment, the ease of making the transaction, and any tax burdens the investment may carry. In general, the safer the investment, the lower the return. High-risk investments have the potential for high returns because investors demand higher rates of return to compensate for the risk they face.

Despite stock tips, hype about hot stocks or "sure things," you should not approach investing as if you were a gambler in a casino. Informed decisions and careful planning are your best strategies for successful investment.

Check Your Understanding

1. **Key Terms (a)** What is the difference between a **bond** and a **stock? (b)** How does a **dividend** differ from a **capital gain? (c)** Explain the difference between **common stock** and **preferred stock. (d)** What makes a **mutual fund** an attractive investing option?

2. **Identifying Alternatives** Think about your future financial needs. Are you planning to buy a car? Do you need money for an apartment deposit or college tuition? Use the information on these pages to design a savings and investment plan that will help you reach your goals.

Credit and Debt

Credit gives extra punch to your purchasing power;
but reckless handling of credit can bury you in debt.

Seems like everyone wants to lend you money. Each year, credit-card companies bombard American consumers with alluring offers of easy money. "Congratulations—you are qualified to receive $10,000!" "You will not be turned down!" "Why postpone your dreams? Apply today."

Why do they want to lend you money? Because that's how they make money. Banks and other financial institutions lend money to both businesses and consumers. Borrowers, in return, pay fees, and those fees can be hefty. If you must borrow—for a car, for college, or for other expenses that you lack the cash to cover—learn how to borrow wisely.

Are You Credit Worthy?

Loans, credit cards, and other methods of deferred payment are known as **credit**. For a bank or other institution to extend you credit, it must be confident that you will repay all the money you borrow, plus any additional interest and fees. You, on the other hand, must understand what you're getting into before you sign on the dotted line.

Creditors, the folks who lend you money, aren't going to give you money just on your word. They are going to ask many questions about your financial past and demand evidence of your financial health to determine if you are able and willing to pay them back.

The Four Cs Creditors look for *capacity, capital, character,* and *collateral* when judging your credit worthiness. *Capacity* is your ability to repay the debt. Creditors will want to know where you work, how long you've worked there, and how much money you make. They will also want to know how much you spend.

Capital is your regular income plus the money in your savings and checking accounts.

Character is your willingness to repay your debts. Creditors will obtain a record of your past borrowing, your bill-paying habits, and your ability to live within your means. Much of this information they will obtain from an organization called a **credit bureau.** If you fail to maintain a good **credit rating,** you will find it very difficult to obtain credit. Creditors will also look for signs of stability in your life. How long have you lived at your current address? How often have you moved in the past few years? Do you own or rent your home?

Don't let the **credit card monster consume you!**

Some loans require **collateral,** which is property used to secure a loan. If you default on the loan or fail to repay it, the creditor takes ownership of the collateral. Often the item that the loan is used to purchase serves as collateral. This is usually the case with car loans and home mortgages. If you fail to keep up with your car payments, you may find yourself walking to work.

Four Steps to Establishing Credit

1 **Maintain savings and checking accounts.** While these are not credit, they can be used to show that you know how to manage your money. You can use your canceled checks to prove that you pay bills promptly.

2 **Get a department-store charge card.** Store cards, which can be used only to make purchases from that particular retailer, are usually easier to obtain than bank credit cards or other forms of credit. Responsible use of a store charge card can help you establish good credit.

3 **Use your bank deposits as collateral for a credit card.** Your limit, or the maximum amount you're allowed to borrow, would not exceed the amount of your deposits.

4 **Have someone with good credit cosign your credit application.** A cosigner agrees to pay your debt if you fail to do so. With a cosigner, you can use someone else's good credit to establish your own.

Information Creditors Can't Use The federal government has passed laws protecting consumers from being discriminated against when applying for credit. The Equal Credit Opportunity Act forbids creditors from using age, gender, marital status, race, color, religion, national origin, or public assistance income when establishing your credit worthiness. Nor can creditors discriminate against you for exercising certain rights, such as filing a billing error notice with a creditor.

Maintaining Good Credit As you begin to make purchases with loans and credit cards, credit might seem to you like free money, but it's not. When you borrow money from a financial institution, you are, in effect, renting money. Eventually you have to pay it all back, along with interest and fees, called **finance charges.** Finance charges can be quite expensive and add up rapidly. If you're not paying attention, you can quickly lose control of your debt.

Making late payments, missing payments, or borrowing more than you can pay back will damage your credit history. A poor credit history can haunt you for seven years or more. If you are irresponsible with your credit card, you're going to have a hard time financing that new car you plan to buy.

To maintain good credit, you need to develop good credit behavior. Don't overborrow or overspend, make sure you pay your bills promptly, and protect your credit cards from loss or theft. It is also crucial for you to understand the different forms of credit available to you and how their finance charges are calculated. That way, you can make sound decisions that will keep you out of financial hot water.

Types of Credit

Different forms of credit are suited to different purposes. You know that you shouldn't use your credit card to pay for a new car. And you wouldn't take out a loan to pay for dinner and a movie on Friday night. There is much more you need to know, however, about credit.

Loans Loans come in two forms: single-payment loans and installment loans. Single-payment loans are short-term loans paid off in one lump sum. Installment loans, on the other hand, are repaid at regularly scheduled intervals, or installments, usually monthly. Each installment payment is for the same amount. Each payment is applied to both the principal (the amount borrowed) and the interest (the fee for borrowing the

money). Although you pay the same number of dollars each month, at first, more of the payment goes toward interest than principal. An automobile loan is an example of an installment loan. (See "Buying a Car" on pages 520–521.)

Loans that require collateral are called secured loans. Loans that don't require collateral are called unsecured loans. Credit for these loans, also known as signature loans, is based on the borrower's references and credit rating. A Guaranteed Student Loan is an example of an unsecured loan.

Credit Cards One of the most popular forms of credit in the United States today is the credit card. It is a form of open-ended, or revolving, credit. A credit card lets you borrow money on an ongoing basis, up to a prearranged limit, to buy goods and services. Any amount you pay back you are able to reborrow.

Many people find credit cards more convenient than cash. You can order movie tickets, buy clothes, pay for a meal, or just about anything else

using a credit card. Bank cards such as Visa and MasterCard are the most widely accepted.

As a cardholder you receive a monthly bill and are required to pay at least some portion of the balance (the amount you owe) each month. Annual fees, interest rates, and other charges vary greatly among credit card issuers, so you should carefully compare the terms of several card offers before making any commitments. Some nonprofit organizations on the Internet offer listings of good credit card deals and guidance in applying for them.

Another form of credit is a travel and entertainment (T&E) card. It is similar to a credit card, but the borrower is required to pay the total amount owed each month. Because you pay your debt in full each month, you aren't charged interest. Usually you are required to pay an annual membership fee. American Express and Diners Club are popular travel and entertainment cards.

Finance Charges and Terms

As a borrower, you pay for the privilege of borrowing money. Interest is the primary fee for borrowing money. Just as a bank will pay you interest to use your money, you must pay your creditors to use theirs. A creditor, however, may charge you additional fees. The total dollar amount you pay to use credit is called the finance charge. It includes interest and other fees that may apply.

Annual Percentage Rate An important number for you to understand when applying for credit is the **annual percentage rate (APR)**. The APR tells you what your credit will cost. It is the finance charge expressed as an annual rate. Comparing the annual percentage rates, rather than the interest rates, offered by lenders is a good way to compare loans. Be sure you understand how your lender calculates the APR for the credit cards you are considering.

Pay your bill in full by the due date and pay no finance charge.

The APR for this card is fairly high. See if you can find a lower one.

Pay your bill on time to avoid late fees.

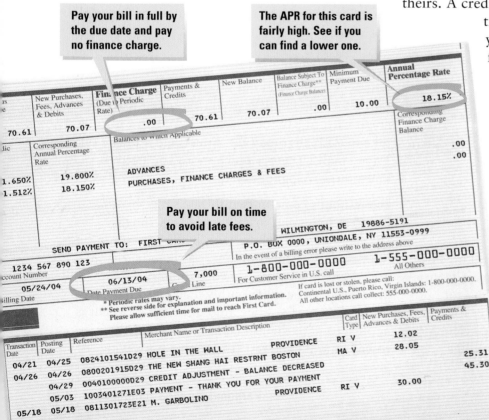

Comparing APR

EXAMPLE a $100,000, 30-year home mortgage

	Plan A	Plan B
Interest rate	7.5%	7.5%
Points	0	2.0
Other closing costs	$1,500	$1,000
APR	7.6527	7.8046

Comparing Terms on an Installment Loan

EXAMPLE a $13,500 loan with 12.5% interest

	3-year loan	5-year loan
Number of monthly payments	36	60
Amount of each payment	$451.62	$303.72
Total interest paid	$2,758.32	$4,723.20

Terms Another important factor to consider is the term, or length, of your loan. For example, if you arrange to pay for your new car in three years rather than five, your monthly payments will be higher, but in the end, you will pay less interest.

How to Choose
a Credit Card

When selecting a credit card, be sure you understand all the terms of the credit-card offer before you make a commitment.

What is the APR? You may want to choose the card with lowest APR, especially if you carry a balance on your account.

Is the APR fixed or variable? A fixed APR will stay the same. A variable APR will rise and fall as the prime rate or other economic indicator changes.

What is the periodic rate? The periodic rate is the interest rate that is applied to your account balance each billing period.

How are finance charges computed? Most creditors use your average daily balance to determine the finance charge. The average daily balance is calculated by adding up all daily balances and dividing them by the number of days in a billing period.

Is there a grace period? Many creditors will charge you no interest if you pay your bill in full before the due date.

What fees does the creditor charge? Many credit cards charge an annual membership fee, as well as fees for late payments, cash advances, or exceeding the credit limit.

Know Your Rights Credit card issuers and other lenders are required by **Truth in Lending laws** to disclose certain information. Institutions extending loans must tell you the exact finance charge on your loan. Credit card issuers must disclose monthly interest rates, the APR, and the method of finance charge calculation.

The Fair Credit Reporting Act protects you from errors on credit reports issued by credit bureaus. You are entitled to know the reason for any negative activity on your report and to have any errors corrected. Similarly, the Fair Credit Billing Act lets you dispute and correct billing information.

If you find yourself in debt and subject to debt collection, be aware that debt collectors must ensure the accuracy of the bill in question and allow you to dispute the bill if you believe it to be in error. Debt collectors may not threaten, harass, or otherwise abuse you in pursuit of the debt.

Check Your Understanding

1. **Key Terms (a)** Name two types of **credit** and explain how they are different. **(b)** How does **collateral** discourage borrowers from defaulting on a loan? **(c)** How do the Equal Credit Opportunity Act and **Truth in Lending laws** protect consumers?

2. **Analyzing Information** Analyze the credit card offers your household receives in the mail or that you see advertised. Make a chart comparing their features and finance charges. Identify and explain which credit card is the best deal.

Landmark Supreme Court Cases

Over the course of the nation's history, many Supreme Court cases have shaped the way that the United States Constitution is interpreted. These pages provide summaries of some of the most significant Supreme Court rulings in United States history.

Go Online
School.com

For: More Supreme Court Cases
Visit: PHSchool.com
Webcode: mph-1011

Brown v. Board of Education of Topeka (1954)

Significance: This case began the process of school desegregation in the United States. It overturned Plessy v. Ferguson (1896). That case had allowed "separate but equal" facilities for African Americans.

Background: Linda Brown was a 10-year-old African American girl living in Topeka, Kansas. Her neighborhood school was for whites only. Brown could not attend it. Plessy v. Ferguson let cities and towns have segregated schools as long as the services offered were "equal." Brown claimed this system violated the Equal Protection Clause. The lower courts ruled against Brown because the schools for blacks and whites were about the same. Brown appealed to the U.S. Supreme Court.

Decision: A unanimous Supreme Court agreed with Brown. It ruled that school segregation denied her equal protection of the laws. The Court found that separate schools were unequal even if they had similar buildings, books, and teachers. Segregation suggested that African Americans were inferior. Therefore, segregation did not give them all the benefits they would get in an integrated school.

Dred Scott v. Sandford (1857)

Significance: This case supported the interests of slave owners. It favored property rights over human rights. This case increased the tensions in the United States that led to the Civil War.

Background: Dred Scott was an enslaved African American. His slaveholder had taken him from a state that allowed slavery to a territory that did not. The Missouri Compromise of 1820 had ruled that the territory could not allow slavery. Scott sued his slaveholder for his freedom. He claimed that by living on free soil he had become a free man. The lower courts ruled against him. Scott appealed to the U.S. Supreme Court.

Decision: The Supreme Court ruled 7 to 2 that the Missouri Compromise was unconstitutional. The Court ruled that the compromise deprived slaveholders of their "property" without just compensation. Congress therefore had no power to exclude slavery from any part of the United States.

Engel v. Vitale (1962)

Significance: This case shows the Court's commitment to separation of church and state. Many Americans favor some form of prayer in school. The Supreme Court received intense criticism for its decision in this case.

Background: The New York State Board of Regents recommended that school districts require a morning prayer. The prayer did not favor any particular religion. However, it did express a belief in God and asked for God's blessing. The parents of ten students claimed the Regents' Prayer was unconstitutional. The state trial court and Court of Appeals ruled that the prayer was lawful as long as students did not have to join in praying if they or their parents objected. The parents appealed to the U.S. Supreme Court.

Decision: The Supreme Court ruled 6 to 1 (with 2 judges not participating) that State governments cannot write or recommend prayers for students. The Regents' Prayer did not favor one particular religion. However, it still expressed governmental support for a belief in God. The prayer therefore violated the Establishment Clause of the First Amendment.

In Re Gault (1966)

Significance: Juvenile criminal cases used to be handled with few due process safeguards. This case guaranteed juvenile defendants some of the same due process guarantees that apply to adults.

Background: Gerald Gault was 15 years old. He was arrested for making harassing phone calls to a neighbor. At that time, Arizona had an informal procedure for handling juvenile crimes. Gault's parents were not notified. He was not given a lawyer. He did not have a chance to question the neighbor in court. Gault was assigned to a juvenile detention facility for six years, until he turned 21. The maximum sentence for an adult would have been a $50 fine and two months in jail. Gault's lawyers filed a writ of habeas corpus. It was denied by the trial court and by the state Supreme Court. The U.S. Supreme Court took the case for review.

Decision: The Supreme Court ruled in Gault's favor. "Neither the Fourteenth Amendment nor the Bill of Rights is for adults alone." Juveniles are entitled to notice of charges against them and to have the involvement of their parents. Juveniles are entitled to notification of the right to counsel. They have the opportunity for cross-examination at the hearings. They also should have adequate safeguards against self-incrimination.

Gibbons v. Ogden (1824)

Significance: This case strengthened Congress's power to regulate any interstate activity. It also paved the way for federal regulation of national businesses, such as broadcasting and oil pipelines.

Background: Ogden and Gibbons each operated steamboats in New York Harbor. They ran ferries between New York City and New Jersey. Ogden had a monopoly license from the New York State Legislature. Gibbons was licensed for "the coasting trade" under a 1793 federal law. Ogden sued to enforce his monopoly. The trial court ordered Gibbons to stop running his ferry. Gibbons appealed. He argued that Congress had the power to regulate interstate commerce and that the states could not interfere.

Decision: The Supreme Court ruled in favor of Gibbons. Under the Interstate Commerce Clause, Congress has the full and exclusive power to regulate interstate commerce. The states do not have that power.

Gideon v. Wainwright (1963)

Significance: This case guaranteed court-appointed counsel to poor persons facing a state felony charge. It expanded the right of criminal defendants to have a fair trial. It gave defendants access to a defense attorney, even if they were too poor to pay for one themselves.

Background: Clarence Earl Gideon was tried for breaking and entering. He could not afford a lawyer to represent him. He asked the judge to appoint one. The trial judge refused his request. Gideon was convicted. He was sentenced to five years in prison. Gideon appealed to the U.S. Supreme Court. He argued that he had been unconstitutionally denied counsel.

Decision: With no dissent, the Supreme Court created the "Gideon Rule" requiring the states to appoint counsel for all poor persons on trial for a felony. The Court granted Gideon a new trial since he had not been given counsel. On retrial, a court-appointed attorney represented Gideon. He was found not guilty.

Heart of Atlanta Motel, Inc. v. United States (1964)

Significance: This case confirmed the power of Congress to prohibit discrimination in all activities affecting interstate commerce. It allowed Congress to take a leading role in enforcing equal rights. At that time, many states were not willing to do so themselves.

Background: The Heart of Atlanta Motel refused to rent rooms to African Americans. However, Title II of the Civil Rights Act of 1964 prohibited places of "public accommodation" from discrimination based on customers' race, sex, color, religion, or national origin. The Heart of Atlanta Motel challenged the constitutionality of this provision. The Motel argued that hotels were purely local. Therefore, they could not be regulated under the Interstate Commerce Clause. The motel lost before a three-judge federal court. It appealed to the Supreme Court.

Decision: A unanimous Supreme Court ruled against the motel. It ruled that motels could be regulated under the Interstate Commerce Clause. The Court noted that the motel was located within ready access to two interstate highways. The motel advertised in national media. It was also a center for conventions of out-of-state guests.

Katz v. United States (1967)

Significance: This case changed the interpretation of a "search" under the Fourth Amendment. Previously, there had to be a physical intrusion or seizure. Katz recognized that the electronic age required a new approach to privacy.

Background: In 1965, Charles Katz called his bookie from a public telephone booth in California. The FBI had hidden a recording device in the booth. Katz was arrested and charged with interstate gambling. He argued that the recordings were illegal. The FBI had not had a warrant. The trial court concluded that a warrant was not necessary because the phone booth was a public place. Katz was convicted. The Court of Appeals upheld his conviction. Katz then asked the U.S. Supreme Court to review his case.

Decision: The Supreme Court ruled in Katz's favor 7 to 1. "[T]he Fourth Amendment protects people, not places. What a person knowingly exposes to the public, even in his own home or office, is not a subject of Fourth Amendment protection. . . . But what he seeks to preserve as private, even in an area accessible to the public, may be constitutionally protected."

Korematsu v. United States (1944)

Significance: This case shows that government actions based on race or national origin may be allowed in wartime. However, the ruling in Korematsu has troubled jurists and civil libertarians. It suggests that basic civil rights can give way to prejudice and hysteria.

Background: Japanese forces bombed Pearl Harbor in 1941. Afterward, U.S. military commanders ordered people of Japanese ancestry removed from a large area of California. Toyosaburo ("Fred") Korematsu refused to obey the order. He was arrested and convicted. He lost in the Court of Appeals. Korematsu then appealed to the U.S. Supreme Court. He challenged the constitutionality of the deportation order.

Decision: With three Justices dissenting, the Supreme Court ruled that the deportation order was lawful. They upheld Korematsu's conviction. The Court ruled that restrictions that apply to a single racial group must be given the "most rigid scrutiny." However, it found a "pressing public necessity" for the order because it was impossible to segregate out the loyal from the disloyal persons.

Lemon v. Kurzman, (1971)

Significance: This case dealt with state interactions with religious institutions. The case resulted in a test to determine whether those interactions are constitutional.

Background: This case was a group of three cases from Pennsylvania and Rhode Island. Those cases concerned public assistance to private schools, including religious schools. Pennsylvania paid teachers' salaries and paid for textbooks in religious schools. Rhode Island paid 15% of the salaries of private school teachers. A federal court found Rhode Island's program unconstitutional; another federal court found Pennsylvania's grants were legal. The U.S. Supreme Court agreed to hear the cases.

Decision: A unanimous Supreme Court ruled that the states' aid to religious schools violated the Constitution. The Court created a three-part test. "First, the statute must have a secular legislative purpose; second, its principal or primary effect must be one that neither advances or inhibits religion . . . ; finally, the statute must not foster an excessive government Entanglement with religion." Both states failed the third part of this test.

Mapp v. Ohio (1961)

Significance: This case said that a state could not use evidence from an illegal search at the trial of a criminal defendant. Police would therefore have an incentive to follow the law. But the decision was controversial because it allowed criminals to go free if police broke the law.

Background: Cleveland police searched Dollree Mapp's home looking for a fugitive. They did not find the fugitive. But they did find illegal materials. However, the search violated the Fourteenth Amendment because the police did not have a search warrant. Mapp appealed her conviction for unlawful possession. She argued that the government should not be allowed to use improperly obtained evidence against her. The Supreme Court of Ohio ruled against Mapp. She appealed to the U.S. Supreme Court.

Decision: The Supreme Court decided in Mapp's favor. Almost 50 years earlier, the Court had established the "exclusionary rule." This rule prohibited the use of illegally obtained evidence in federal criminal prosecutions. The Mapp decision extended this exclusionary rule to the states. It made provisions of the Bill of Rights apply to the states through the Fourteenth Amendment.

Marbury v. Madison (1803)

Significance: This case established the principle of judicial review. Judicial review is the power of the courts to review statutes and to invalidate those that violate the Constitution. This power made the Supreme Court the final decision maker on legal matters. It also established the Court as a fully equal branch of the government.

Background: William Marbury was a judge appointed at the end of President Adams's administration. His commission was not delivered before President Jefferson took office. Secretary of State James Madison refused to deliver it to him. Marbury sued Madison in the Supreme Court to force him to deliver the commission.

Decision: Chief Justice Marshall indicated that President Adams's signature on the commission completed Marbury's appointment. Marbury was therefore entitled to receive the commission. However, the Constitution provides that "the Supreme Court shall have original jurisdiction in all cases affecting ambassadors, other public ministers and consuls, and those in which a state shall be a party. In all other cases, the Supreme Court shall have appellate jurisdiction."

Marbury's case did not qualify for original jurisdiction. The law that authorized him to sue in the Supreme Court was therefore unconstitutional. As a result, Chief Justice Marshall ruled that the Court could not give Marbury the order he sought. Marshall used this case to establish the principle that the Supreme Court had the power to invalidate a law of Congress if the law conflicted with the Constitution.

McCulloch v. Maryland (1819)

Significance: This case established that Congress is not limited to the powers expressly granted it in the Constitution. It also helped pave the way for the stronger national government that emerged after the Civil War.

Background: Congress chartered a national bank in 1816. Two years later, Maryland passed a law taxing any bank not chartered by the State of Maryland. When the state tried to impose the tax on the national bank, James McCulloch, the cashier, refused to pay. Maryland claimed that Congress did not have the power to create a national bank. McCulloch claimed Maryland did not have the power to tax a bank created by Congress.

Decision: The Supreme Court ruled unanimously that Congress had the power to create a national bank. The Constitution does not mention a bank. However, the "necessary and proper" clause of the Constitution authorizes Congress to do things that assist it in performing its assigned role in the federal government. A state could destroy the national bank by taxing it. Since the federal government is supreme under the Constitution, Maryland did not have the power to tax the bank.

Miranda v. Arizona (1966)

Significance: This case created the now famous "Miranda warnings" to help insure that criminal suspects would not coerced by the police. The opinion was one of the most controversial rulings during Chief Justice Earl Warren's tenure.

Background: Miranda was arrested for kidnapping and assault. In custody, he signed a full confession. But he did not consult a lawyer. After conviction, he appealed. He claimed that the confession was obtained illegally. The Supreme Court of Arizona upheld his conviction. It noted that Miranda had never requested counsel. Miranda appealed to the U.S. Supreme Court.

Decision: By 5 to 4 vote, the Supreme Court ruled in Miranda's favor. Chief Justice Warren wrote: "Prior to any questioning, the person must be warned that he has a right to remain silent, that any statement he does make may be used as evidence against him, and that he has a right to the presence of an attorney, either retained or appointed."

NAACP v. Alabama (1958)

Significance: This case recognized that the privacy of membership lists may be necessary to preserve freedom of association.

Background: An Alabama court ordered the National Association for the Advancement of Colored People (NAACP) to produce its membership lists. The NAACP refused. The Alabama court held the NAACP in contempt of court and fined it $100,000. After the state Supreme Court declined to review the decision. Then the NAACP asked the U.S. Supreme Court to hear the case.

Decision: The Supreme Court ruled in favor of the NAACP. Individual members have a Fourteenth Amendment right to free association. By demanding the membership list, Alabama discouraged this free association. It also interfered with their privacy. Alabama did not have the strong justification that would be necessary to allow this intrusion.

New Jersey v. T.L.O. (1985)

Significance: This case shows the flexibility of the Fourth Amendment, balancing the privacy rights of students with the schools' need to keep order.

Background: "T.L.O." was a 14-year-old New Jersey high school student caught smoking in the restroom. She claimed that she did not smoke at all. Then the vice-principal demanded to see her purse. He opened the purse and saw cigarettes and rolling papers. Searching further, he found marijuana and other items suggesting that she was selling drugs. In juvenile court, she was found to be a delinquent. The New Jersey Supreme Court reversed that decision. It held that the search of the purse was unreasonable. The U.S. Supreme Court agreed to hear the case.

Decision: The Supreme Court ruled against T.L.O. The Fourth Amendment does apply to searches by public school officials. However, school officials do not need the level of "probable cause" that police must have for a search. School officials are not required to get a search warrant when they reasonably believe the law has been broken. However, the search must be justified by legitimate suspicion. It must also relate to violations of school rules or policies.

Plessy v. Ferguson (1896)

Significance: This case gave states the right to require that public facilities be segregated. The case became known for the concept of "separate but equal" facilities. The 1954 case Brown v. Board of Education overruled this case.

Background: A Louisiana statute required that blacks and whites travel in separate railway carriages. Herman Plessy was arrested after refusing to move from the whites' coach to the blacks' coach. He said he was seven-eights white and one-eighth black. Plessy sued the judge of the criminal court, John Ferguson, to prevent his trial. The state Supreme Court ruled that the law was constitutional and denied Plessy's suit. The U.S. Supreme Court then reviewed the case.

Decision: The Supreme Court ruled that the Louisiana statute was a legitimate exercise of the state's police powers. The majority rejected the argument that segregation gave African Americans inferior status. In dissent, Justice Harlan wrote, "If evils will result from the commingling [integration] of the two races upon public highways. . . , they will be infinitely less than those that will surely come from state legislation regulating . . . civil rights upon the basis of race."

Roe v. Wade (1973)

Significance: This case made abortion a legal procedure and affected the laws of nearly all the states. The decision remains highly controversial today.

Background: Texas law prohibited abortions except to save the pregnant mother's life. "Roe" was a Texas resident who sought an abortion. She brought a class action against the district attorney to challenge the constitutionality of the law and block its enforcement. A three-judge district court declared the law unconstitutional. She appealed to the Supreme Court followed.

Decision: The Supreme Court ruled that the Fourteenth Amendment protected the right to privacy. It ruled that the right to seek an abortion was part of the right of privacy. The decision also noted that there were different levels of state interest for regulating abortion in the second and third trimesters of pregnancy to protect the woman's health and the potentiality of human life. The Court therefore gave the states greater right to regulate or restrict abortions later in the pregnancy.

Schenck v. United States (1919)

Significance: This case created the "clear and present danger" exception to the First Amendment. It showed that speech may be limited if it poses an actual danger.

Background: During World War I, Congress passed the Espionage Act of 1917. This act made it a crime to actively oppose the war or hinder the war effort. Charles Schenck and others sent pamphlets to men who had been called for military service urging them to resist the draft. They were charged with violating the Act and were convicted. They appealed to the U.S. Supreme Court. They argued that the Act violated their First Amendment right of free speech.

Decision: The Supreme Court upheld the convictions. Although the pamphlets would normally have been protected speech, speech in times of war is not unlimited. "The most stringent protection of free speech would not protect a man in falsely shouting fire in a theatre and causing a panic." Speech can be restricted when it creates a "clear and present danger."

Tinker v. Des Moines Public Schools (1969)

Significance: Tinker showed that students have the right to express opinions in school so long as they do not disrupt education. Schools may not punish students for expressing politically unpopular ideas.

Background: The Tinker children and other students wore black armbands to school to protest the Vietnam War. They were sent home from school. Their fathers sued, but the District Court ruled that the school had not violated the Constitution. The Court of Appeals upheld the District Court's ruling. Tinker appealed to the Supreme Court.

Decision: In a 7-to-2 decision, the Supreme Court ruled that the students had the right to wear armbands to school. The Court affirmed students' First Amendment rights: "It can hardly be argued that either students or teachers shed their constitutional rights to freedom of speech or expression at the schoolhouse gate."

United States v. Nixon (1974)

Significance: This case established that the President is not above the law. The courts have the power to order the President to produce tapes or documents for review.

Background: In 1974, seven associates of President Richard Nixon were indicted for their roles in the break-in at the Democratic Party's campaign headquarters in the Watergate hotel in Washington. Nixon himself was named as an unindicted co-conspirator. The Special Prosecutor asked the District Court to order Nixon to turn over certain tapes. These tapes related to the meetings at which the break-in had been discussed. Nixon claimed executive privilege. He asked that the subpoena be withdrawn. The lower court denied his request. He asked for a ruling from the Supreme Court.

Decision: The Supreme Court unanimously ruled that no person—not even the President—is above the law. The President does have a general interest in confidentiality. But that interest would not be harmed if a federal judge reviewed the evidence to determine its relevance to an ongoing federal criminal prosecution.

Weeks v. United States (1914)

Significance: This case is the Supreme Court's first use of the "exclusionary rule." This rule prohibits the federal government from using illegally obtained evidence against a criminal defendant at trial.

Background: A U.S. marshal entered Freemont Weeks' home without a search warrant. He searched the house and found illegal lottery slips. Weeks argued unsuccessfully that this evidence should not be used at his trial. He was convicted. Weeks argued before the U.S. Supreme Court that the search violated the Fourth Amendment and that his conviction therefore should not stand.

Decision: The Supreme Court ruled in favor of Weeks. The marshal needed a search warrant to enter the house. Instead, he acted illegally and in violation of the Constitution. "If letters and private documents can thus be seized and held and used in evidence against a citizen accused of an offense, the protection of the 4th Amendment, declaring his right to be secure against such searches and seizures, is of no value, and, so far as those thus placed are concerned, might as well be stricken from the Constitution."

Wesberry v. Sanders (1964)

Significance: This case created the "one man, one vote" rule. It required that the congressional districts within each state be approximately equal in population.

Background: Georgia's Fifth Congressional District had two to three times the population of some other districts in the state. Voters in the Fifth District sued. They claimed that this difference in population meant that they had proportionally less influence in Congress. A District Court ruled that the imbalance was a "political question." It declined to order the state to change the district boundaries. The plaintiffs then appealed to the U.S. Supreme Court.

Decision: The Supreme Court ruled that the district boundaries violated the Constitution. "The command of Art. I, § 2 that Representatives be chosen 'by the People of the several States' means that, as nearly as is practicable, one man's vote in a congressional election is to be worth as much as another's."

Presidents of the United States

1

George Washington
(1732–1799)
Years in office: 1789–1797
No political party
Elected from: Virginia
Vice Pres.: John Adams

2

John Adams
(1735–1826)
Years in office: 1797–1801
Federalist
Elected from: Massachusetts
Vice Pres.: Thomas Jefferson

3

Thomas Jefferson
(1743–1826)
Years in office: 1801–1809
Democratic Republican
Elected from: Virginia
Vice Pres.: Aaron Burr

4
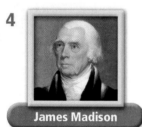
James Madison
(1751–1836)
Years in office: 1809–1817
Democratic Republican
Elected from: Virginia
Vice Pres.: George Clinton,
Elbridge Gerry

5

James Monroe
(1758–1831)
Years in office: 1817–1825
National Republican
Elected from: Virginia
Vice Pres.: Daniel Tompkins

6
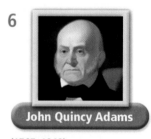
John Quincy Adams
(1767–1848)
Years in office: 1825–1829
National Republican
Elected from: Massachusetts
Vice Pres.: John Calhoun

7

Andrew Jackson
(1767–1845)
Years in office: 1829–1837
Democrat
Elected from: Tennessee
Vice Pres.: John Calhoun,
Martin Van Buren

8
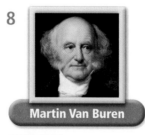
Martin Van Buren
(1782–1862)
Years in office: 1837–1841
Democrat
Elected from: New York
Vice Pres.: Richard Johnson

9
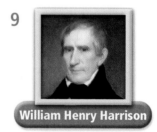
William Henry Harrison
(1773–1841)
Years in office: 1841
Whig
Elected from: Ohio
Vice Pres.: John Tyler

10

John Tyler
(1732–1799)
Years in office: 1789–1797
No political party
Elected from: Virginia
Vice Pres.: John Adams

11
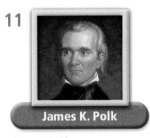
James K. Polk
(1795–1849)
Years in office: 1845–1849
Democrat
Elected from: Tennessee
Vice Pres.: George Dallas

12
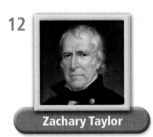
Zachary Taylor
(1784–1850)
Years in office: 1849–1850
Whig
Elected from: Louisiana
Vice Pres.: Millard FIllmore

13
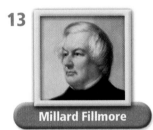
Millard Fillmore
(1800–1874)
Years in office: 1850–1853
Whig
Elected from: New York
Vice Pres.: none

14

Franklin Pierce
(1804–1869)
Years in office: 1853–1857
Democrat
Elected from: New Hampshire
Vice Pres.: William King

15
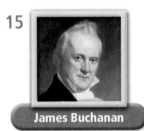
James Buchanan
(1791–1868)
Years in office: 1857–1861
Democrat
Elected from: Pennsylvania
Vice Pres.: John Breckinridge

16
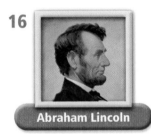
Abraham Lincoln
(1809–1865)
Years in office: 1861–1865
Republican
Elected from: Illinois
Vice Pres.: Hannibal Hamlin,
Andrew Johnson

17
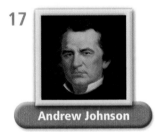
Andrew Johnson
(1808–1875)
Years in office: 1865–1869
Republican
Elected from: Tennessee
Vice Pres.: none

18

Ulysses S. Grant
(1822–1885)
Years in office: 1869–1877
Republican
Elected from: Illinois
Vice Pres.: Schuyler Colfax,
Henry Wilson

19

Rutherford B. Hayes
(1822–1893)
Years in office: 1877–1881
Republican
Elected from: Ohio
Vice Pres.: William Wheeler

20

James A. Garfield
(1831–1881)
Years in office: 1881
Republican
Elected from: Ohio
Vice Pres.: Chester A. Arthur

21

Chester A. Arthur
(1830–1886)
Years in office: 1881–1885
Republican
Elected from: New York
Vice Pres.: none

Presidents of the United States

22 Grover Cleveland

(1837–1908)
Years in office: 1885–1889
Democrat
Elected from: New York
Vice Pres.: Thomas Hendricks

23 Benjamin Harrison

(1833–1901)
Years in office: 1889–1893
Republican
Elected from: Indiana
Vice Pres.: Levi Morton

24 Grover Cleveland

(1837–1908)
Years in office: 1893–1897
Democrat
Elected from: New York
Vice Pres.: Adlai Stevenson

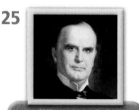

25 William McKinley

(1843–1901)
Years in office: 1897–1901
Republican
Elected from: Ohio
Vice Pres.: Garret Hobart,
Theodore Roosevelt

26 Theodore Roosevelt

(1858–1919)
Years in office: 1901–1909
Republican
Elected from: New York
Vice Pres.: Charles Fairbanks

27 William Howard Taft

(1857–1930)
Years in office: 1909–1913
Republican
Elected from: Ohio
Vice Pres.: James Sherman

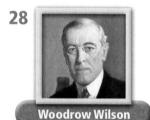

28 Woodrow Wilson

(1856–1924)
Years in office: 1913–1921
Democrat
Elected from: New Jersey
Vice Pres.: Thomas Marshall

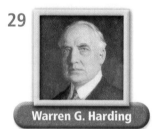

29 Warren G. Harding

(1865–1923)
Years in office: 1921–1923
Republican
Elected from: Ohio
Vice Pres.: Calvin Coolidge

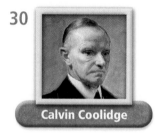

30 Calvin Coolidge

(1872–1933)
Years in office: 1923–1929
Republican
Elected from: Massachusetts
Vice Pres.: Charles Dawes

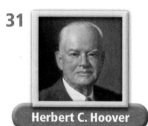

31 Herbert C. Hoover

(1874–1964)
Years in office: 1929–1933
Republican
Elected from: New York
Vice Pres.: Charles Curtis

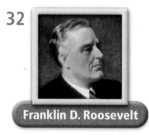

32 Franklin D. Roosevelt

(1882–1945)
Years in office: 1933–1945
Democrat
Elected from: New York
Vice Pres.: John Garner, Henry
Wallace, Harry S. Truman

33 Harry S Truman

(1884–1972)
Years in office: 1945–1953
Democrat
Elected from: Missouri
Vice Pres.: Alben Barkley

34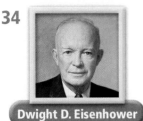

Dwight D. Eisenhower

(1890–1969)
Years in office: 1953–1961
Republican
Elected from: New York
Vice Pres.: Richard M. Nixon

35

John F. Kennedy

(1917–1963)
Years in office: 1961–1963
Democrat
Elected from: Massachusetts
Vice Pres.: Lyndon B. Johnson

36

Lyndon B. Johnson

(1908–1973)
Years in office: 1963–1969
Democrat
Elected from: Texas
Vice Pres.: Hubert Humphrey

37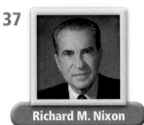

Richard M. Nixon

(1913–1994)
Years in office: 1969–1974
Republican
Elected from: New York
Vice Pres.: Spiro Agnew,
Gerald R. Ford

38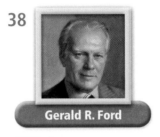

Gerald R. Ford

(1913–)
Years in office: 1974–1977
Republican
Elected from: Michigan
Vice Pres.: Nelson Rockefeller

39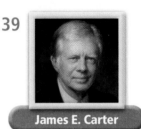

James E. Carter

(1924–)
Years in office: 1977–1981
Democrat
Elected from: Georgia
Vice Pres.: Walter F. Mondale

40

Ronald W. Reagan

(1911–)
Years in office: 1981–1989
Republican
Elected from: California
Vice Pres.: George H.W. Bush

41

George H.W. Bush

(1924–)
Years in office: 1989–1993
Republican
Elected from: Texas
Vice Pres.: J. Danforth Quayle

42

William J. Clinton

(1946–)
Years in office: 1993–2000
Democrat
Elected from: Arkansas
Vice Pres.: Albert Gore, Jr.

43

George W. Bush

(1946–)
Years in office: 2001–
Republican
Elected from: Texas
Vice Pres.: Richard Cheney

*Died in office
**Assassinated
***Resigned

Presidents of the United States

World Map

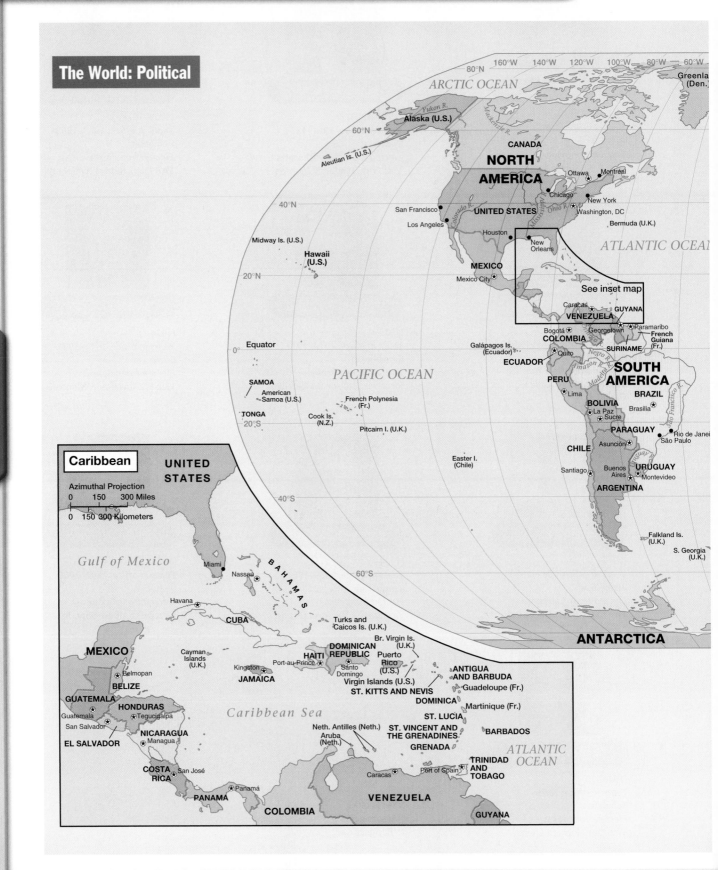

The World: Political

ARCTIC OCEAN

Greenla
(Den.)

Yukon R.
Alaska (U.S.)

60°N

Aleutian Is. (U.S.)

CANADA

NORTH AMERICA

Ottawa · Montréal

· Chicago

· New York

40°N

San Francisco ·

Colorado R. **UNITED STATES**

Washington, DC

Mississippi R. *Ohio R.*

Bermuda (U.K.)

ATLANTIC OCEAN

Los Angeles ·

· Houston

Midway Is. (U.S.)

New Orleans

20°N

Hawaii (U.S.)

MEXICO

Mexico City ⊛

See inset map

Caracas ⊛ **GUYANA**

VENEZUELA

Bogotá ⊛ Georgetown Paramaribo
COLOMBIA **French Guiana (Fr.)**

0° Equator

Galápagos Is. (Ecuador)

Negro R. **SURINAME**

⊛ Quito **ECUADOR**

Amazon R. **SOUTH AMERICA**

PACIFIC OCEAN

PERU

Madeira R.

SAMOA

· Lima

BRAZIL

American Samoa (U.S.)

French Polynesia (Fr.)

BOLIVIA
· La Paz ⊛ Brasília
⊛ Sucre

São Francisco R.

TONGA

Cook Is. (N.Z.)

20°S

Pitcairn I. (U.K.)

PARAGUAY

Asunción ⊛

Rio de Janei
São Paulo ·

CHILE

Easter I. (Chile)

Santiago ⊛

Buenos Aires ⊛ **URUGUAY**
Montevideo

ARGENTINA

40°S

Falkland Is. (U.K.)

S. Georgia (U.K.)

60°S

ANTARCTICA

Caribbean

Azimuthal Projection

0   150   300 Miles

0   150 300 Kilometers

UNITED STATES

Gulf of Mexico

Miami ·

B A H A M A S

Nassau ⊛

Havana ⊛

CUBA

Turks and Caicos Is. (U.K.)

Br. Virgin Is. (U.K.)

DOMINICAN REPUBLIC

MEXICO

Cayman Islands (U.K.)

Kingston ⊛

HAITI

Port-au-Prince

Santo Domingo ⊛

Puerto Rico (U.S.)

ANTIGUA AND BARBUDA

Guadeloupe (Fr.)

Belmopan ·

JAMAICA

Virgin Islands (U.S.)

BELIZE

ST. KITTS AND NEVIS

DOMINICA

Martinique (Fr.)

GUATEMALA

HONDURAS

Caribbean Sea

ST. LUCIA

Guatemala ⊛

Tegucigalpa ⊛

San Salvador ·

NICARAGUA

Neth. Antilles (Neth.)
Aruba (Neth.)

ST. VINCENT AND THE GRENADINES

BARBADOS

EL SALVADOR

Managua ⊛

GRENADA

ATLANTIC OCEAN

COSTA RICA

San José ⊛

Caracas ⊛

Port of Spain ⊛ **TRINIDAD AND TOBAGO**

· Panamá

PANAMA

COLOMBIA

VENEZUELA

GUYANA

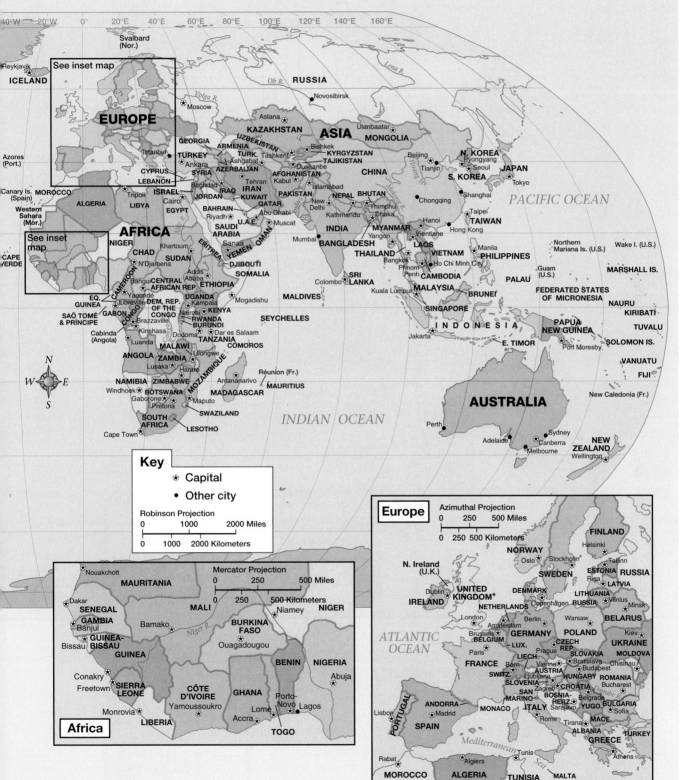

United States Map

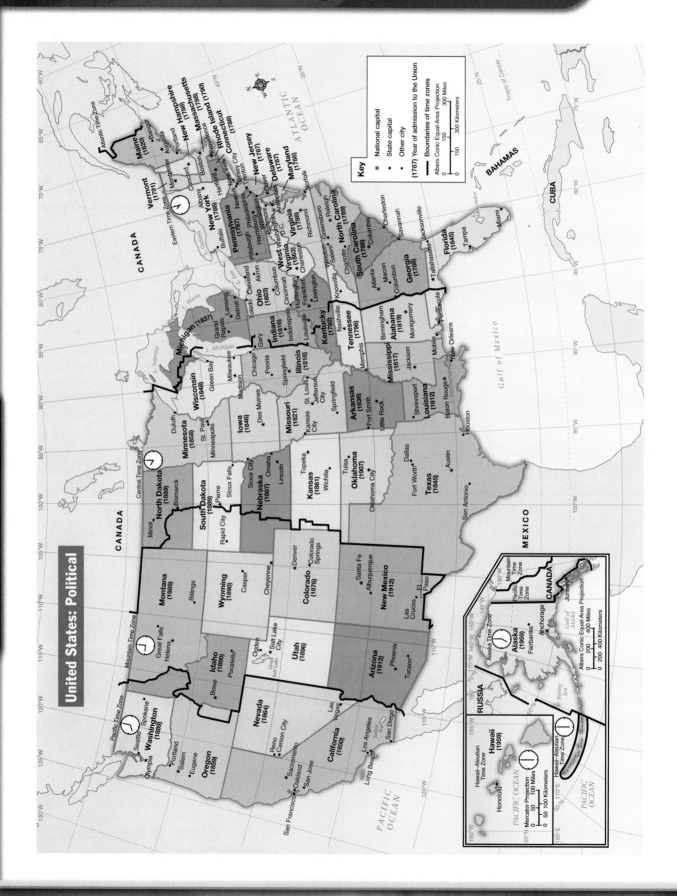

United States: Political

Key

- ⊛ National capital
- ★ State capital
- • Other city
- (1787) Year of admission to the Union
- ━━ Boundaries of time zones

Albers Conic Equal-Area Projection

0   150   300 Miles
0   150   300 Kilometers

Profile of the Fifty States

State	Capital	Entered Union	Population (2000)	Population Rank	Land Area (Square Miles)	Land Area Rank
Alabama	Montgomery	1819	4,447,100	23rd	51,705	29th
Alaska	Juneau	1959	626,932	48th	591,004	1st
Arizona	Phoenix	1912	5,130,632	20th	114,000	6th
Arkansas	Little Rock	1836	2,673,400	33rd	53,187	27th
California	Sacramento	1850	33,871,648	1st	158,706	3rd
Colorado	Denver	1876	4,301,261	24th	104,091	8th
Connecticut	Hartford	1788	3,405,565	28th	5,018	48th
Delaware	Dover	1787	783,600	45th	2,044	49th
Florida	Tallahassee	1845	15,982,378	4th	58,664	22nd
Georgia	Atlanta	1788	8,186,453	10th	58,910	21st
Hawaii	Honolulu	1959	1,211,537	42nd	6,470	47th
Idaho	Boise	1890	1,293,953	39th	83,564	13th
Illinois	Springfield	1818	12,419,293	5th	56,345	24th
Indiana	Indianapolis	1816	6,080,485	14th	36,185	38th
Iowa	Des Moines	1846	2,926,324	30th	56,275	25th
Kansas	Topeka	1861	2,688,418	32nd	82,277	14th
Kentucky	Frankfort	1792	4,041,769	25th	40,409	37th
Louisiana	Baton Rouge	1812	4,468,976	22nd	47,751	31st
Maine	Augusta	1820	1,274,923	40th	33,265	39th
Maryland	Annapolis	1788	5,296,486	19th	10,460	42nd
Massachusetts	Boston	1788	6,349,097	13th	8,284	45th
Michigan	Lansing	1837	9,938,444	8th	58,527	23rd
Minnesota	St. Paul	1858	4,919,479	21st	84,402	12th
Mississippi	Jackson	1817	2,844,658	31st	47,689	32nd
Missouri	Jefferson City	1821	5,595,211	17th	69,697	19th
Montana	Helena	1889	902,195	44th	147,046	4th
Nebraska	Lincoln	1867	1,711,263	37th	77,355	15th
Nevada	Carson City	1864	1,998,257	35th	110,561	7th
New Hampshire	Concord	1788	1,235,786	41st	9,279	44th
New Jersey	Trenton	1787	8,414,350	9th	7,787	46th
New Mexico	Santa Fe	1912	1,819,046	36th	121,593	5th
New York	Albany	1788	18,976,457	3rd	49,108	30th
North Carolina	Raleigh	1789	8,049,313	11th	52,669	28th
North Dakota	Bismarck	1889	642,200	47th	70,703	17th
Ohio	Columbus	1803	11,353,140	7th	41,330	35th
Oklahoma	Oklahoma City	1907	3,450,654	27th	69,956	18th
Oregon	Salem	1859	3,421,399	29th	97,073	10th
Pennsylvania	Harrisburg	1787	12,281,054	6th	45,308	33rd
Rhode Island	Providence	1790	1,048,319	43rd	1,212	50th
South Carolina	Columbia	1788	4,012,012	26th	31,113	40th
South Dakota	Pierre	1889	754,844	46th	77,116	16th
Tennessee	Nashville	1796	5,689,283	16th	42,144	34th
Texas	Austin	1845	20,851,820	2nd	266,807	2nd
Utah	Salt Lake City	1896	2,233,169	34th	84,899	11th
Vermont	Montpelier	1791	608,827	49th	9,614	43rd
Virginia	Richmond	1788	7,078,515	12th	40,767	36th
Washington	Olympia	1889	5,894,121	15th	68,138	20th
West Virginia	Charleston	1863	1,808,344	38th	24,231	41st
Wisconsin	Madison	1848	5,363,675	18th	56,153	26th
Wyoming	Cheyenne	1890	493,782	50th	97,809	9th

Sources: World Almanac, Statistical Abstract of the United States, U.S. Census Bureau

Glossary

Pronunciation Key

Certain glossary terms and other words have been respelled in the text and in this glossary as an aid to pronunciation. The small capital letters mean that the first syllable should be spoken with a minor stress. The large capital letters mean that the last syllable should be spoken with a major stress. The vowel sounds shown by the letters ah, uh, eh, and oo in the respelling correspond to the vowel sounds in the pronunciation key below.

Pronounce	as in	Pronounce	as in
a	hat	j	jet
ah	father	ng	ring
ar	tar	o	frog
ay	say	ō, oh	no
ayr	air	oo	soon
e, eh	hen	or	for
ee	bee	ow	plow
eer	deer	oy	boy
er	her	sh	she
ew	new	th	thick
g	go	u, uh	sun
i, ih	him	z	zebra
ī	kite	zh	measure

A

administration A team of executive branch officials appointed by each President (page 249)

affirmative action Steps to counteract the effects of past racial discrimination and discrimination against women (page 199)

aggression An attack or threat of attack by another country (page 648)

alien A citizen of one country that lives in another country (page 57)

ambassadors Official representatives to foreign governments (page 244)

amendment process The way in which changes are added to the Constitution (page 160)

amendments Changes, such as changes to the Constitution (page 128)

answer A defendant's written response to a complaint (page 569)

Anti-Federalists People who opposed ratification of the Constitution because they feared that a strong central government would endanger people's liberties. (page 121)

appeal To ask a higher court to review a decision and determine if justice was done (page 269)

appellate jurisdiction (a-PEL-et JOO-ris-DIK-shun) A court's authority to hear an appeal of a decision by another court (page 269)

apportioned Divided among districts (page 299)

arbitration The use of a third party to make a legal decision that is binding on all parties (page 576)

arraignment (uh-RAIN-ment) A court hearing in which the defendant is formally charged with a crime and enters a plea of guilty, not guilty, or no contest (page 545)

assault Placing someone in fear without actual physical contact (page 537)

B

baby boom The dramatic rise in the number of births in the United States that occurred between 1946 and 1964 (page 7)

bail Money that a defendant gives the court as a kind of promise that he or she will return for the trial (page 544)

balance of power The threat that one superpower's military strength might be used against the other's (page 684)

balanced budget When a government does not spend more than the tax revenues it receives (page 498)

bartering Exchanging goods and services for other goods and services without the use of money (page 456)

battery Harming someone through physical contact, as with a weapon or a fist (page 537)

beliefs Certain ideas that people trust are true (page 18)

bias Favoring a particular point of view over another (page 627)

bicameral (bī-KAM-er-uhl) Two-house, as in a legislature with two houses (page 116)

bill A proposed law (page 213)

bill of attainder A law that convicts a person of a crime without a trial (page 221)

Bill of Rights A list of citizens' rights, specifically the first ten amendments to the American Constitution (page 160)

blended families Families made up of adults and their children from previous marriages (page 34)

board A group of people who manage the business of an organization (page 321)

Board of Governors Seven people appointed by the President for 14 year terms who are responsible for running the Federal Reserve System as a whole (page 470)

bonds Certificates that people buy from the government, which agrees to pay back the cost of the bond, plus interest, after a set period of time (page 302)

boycott To refuse to buy a certain company's products (page 390)

budget A plan for raising and spending money (page 219)

bureaucracy (byoo-RAH-kru-see) An organization of government departments, agencies, and offices (pages 249, 688)

burglary The act of breaking into a building with plans to do something illegal (page 537)

business cycle A repeated series of "ups" of growth and "downs" of recession (page 440)

C

Cabinet An important group of policy advisors to the President, made up of the executive department heads and a few other officials (page 253)

campaign manager A person who helps plan the broad outlines of a campaign: where to go, what issues to talk about, and what image of the candidate to put forth (page 632)

campaign press secretary A person who makes certain that the news shows the candidate in the best light (page 632)

candidate A person running for office (page 66)

canvass (KAN-vuhs) To go door-to-door handing out information and asking people which candidates they support (page 593)

capital Anything produced in an economy that is saved to be used to produce other goods and services (page 352)

capitalism Another name for a market economy; a system in which people make their own decisions about how to save resources as capital and how to use their capital to produce goods and services (page 367)

career The occupation for which you train and which you pursue as your life's work (page 416)

case studies Descriptions of situations or conflicts, the issues involved, and the decisions made (page 173)

caucus A meeting of party leaders to discuss issues or choose candidates (page 606)

census An official count of the population made every ten years to find out how many representatives each state should have and to forecast the demand on the different services governments provide (pages 17, 215)

charter A document giving permission to create a government, and providing a plan as to how that government should work (pages 84, 323)

checks and balances The system that gives each of the three branches of government ways to limit the powers of the other two (page 131)

circuit courts Another name for the courts of appeals (page 272)

citizen A person with certain rights and duties under a government; a person who by birth or by choice owes allegiance, or loyalty, to a nation (page 56)

civil disobedience Breaking a law in a nonviolent way because it goes against personal morals (page 516)

civil law The group of laws that help settle disagreements between people (page 527)

closed primary An election in which a voter must be registered as a party member and may vote only in that party's primary (page 606)

cloture (KLÔ-chur) An agreement by three-fifths of the members of the Senate to end the debate on a bill and allow a vote on it (page 231)

Cold War A struggle much like a real war but with no armed battles between the United States and the Soviet Union (page 681)

collective bargaining The process by which representatives of the unions and business try to reach agreement about wages and working conditions (page 390)

colony A territory ruled by a more powerful nation called a colonial power (page 674)

command economy An economic system in which the government or a central authority owns or controls the factors of production and makes the basic economic decisions (page 365)

common good The well-being of all members of society (page 65)

common law A body of law based on judges' decision (page 519)

communism A system under which the central government owns and controls the economic resources (page 681)

compact A written agreement to make and obey laws for the welfare of the group (page 99)

Political campaign volunteers canvass in a neighborhood.

The coins and bills we use are our nation's **currency.**

compensation A person's right to being "made whole" for harm caused by another person's acts (page 563)

complaint A legal document that charges someone with having caused harm (page 569)

concurrent powers Powers shared by the federal and state governments (page 129)

congressional district The area that a member of the House represents (page 215)

constituents (kun-STICH-oo-ents) The people a member of Congress represents (page 212)

consumer A person who uses, or consumes, goods and services to satisfy his or her wants (page 42)

consumption The act of buying or using goods or services (page 353)

containment A foreign policy of using military power and money to prevent the spread of communism (page 659)

contracts Legal agreements between buyers and sellers (page 565)

convention Assembly (page 161)

corporation A business that is separate from the people that own it and legally acts as a single person (page 385)

councils of governments Groups of local and state government officials that work together to meet regional needs (page 336)

courts of appeals Courts that handle appeals from lower federal district courts (page 272)

crime Any behavior that is illegal because the government considers it harmful to society (page 525)

criminal law The group of laws that tell which acts are crimes, how accused persons should be tried in court, and how crimes should be punished (page 525)

currency The coins and paper bills used as money in an economy (page 458)

D

damages Money that is paid in an effort to make up for a loss (page 563)

defendant The party who answers a complaint and defends against it in a court case (page 267)

deficit The amount by which government spending is greater than government income (page 448)

deficit budget When a government spends more than the tax revenues it receives (page 498)

deflation A decrease in the overall price level (page 489)

delinquent A juvenile who is found guilty of a crime (page 552)

demand The amount of a product or service buyers are willing and able to buy at different prices (page 379)

demand deposit The money in a checking account (page 462)

democracy A system of government in which the power is shared by all the people (page 48)

demography The study of the size, growth, and distribution of human populations (page 4)

deposition (dep-uh-ZISH-uhn) The record of answers to questions asked of a witness before a trial begins (page 570)

détente (day-TAHNT) Loosening of tensions between the United States and the Soviet Union (page 660)

deterrence Keeping a strong defense to discourage aggression by other nations (page 648)

dictatorship A government controlled by one person, called a dictator, who usually takes power by force, rather than by inheriting it (page 47)

diplomacy The relations and communications carried out between countries (page 649)

direct democracy A form of government in which laws are made directly by the citizens (page 91)

direct mail A way of sending messages to large groups of people through the mail (page 623)

direct primary An election in which members of a political party choose candidates to run for office in the name of the party (page 606)

direct tax A tax on income (page 495)

discovery The process of gathering evidence before a trial (page 570)

discrimination The unfair treatment of a group of people compared with another group (page 14)

disposable income The amount of money left after taxes have been paid (page 405)

diversity Differences (page 8)

dividends Payments from the profits of companies in which a person owns stock (page 404)

domestic policy Plans for dealing with national problems (page 245)

double jeopardy (JEP-ur-dee) Being placed on trial twice for the same crime (page 168)

due process of law A process by which the government must treat accused persons fairly according to rules established by law (page 168)

E

economic freedom The freedom to own property, to make a profit, and to make choices about what to produce, buy, and sell (page 430)

economic growth an increase in the production of goods and services, which provide citizens with a higher standard of living (page 489)

economy A system of producing and distributing goods and services to fulfill people's wants (page 41)

electors People who promise to cast votes for the candidate selected by voters (page 636)

embezzlement Stealing money that has been trusted to your care (page 537)

eminent domain (EM-ih-nehnt do-MAYN) The power of the government to take private property for public use (page 167)

entitlement programs Benefits paid by the government to people who are by law entitled to them (page 501)

entrepreneur (AHN-truh-preh-NOOR) A person who starts a business (page 382)

equal protection Principle whereby everyone is to be treated fairly, but not necessarily the same (page 197)

equality The condition of everyone having the same rights and opportunities (page 19)

equity The use of general rules of fairness to settle conflicts (page 563)

excise tax (EK-sîz taks) A charge on certain goods, such as alcoholic beverages, gasoline, and tobacco (page 302)

exclusion laws Laws passed to prohibit further immigration from a particular country or region. Especially laws passed in 1882 and 1907 targeting Chinese and Japanese immigrants. (page 16)

executive agreements Agreements with other countries that do not need Senate approval (page 244)

executive branch The branch of government responsible for executing or enforcing the laws (page 240)

executive privilege The President's right to keep some information secret from Congress and the courts (page 256)

F

factors of production The resources people have for producing goods and services to satisfy their wants (page 351)

family The most basic social institution in any society (page 34)

federal budget The government's plan for how it will raise and spend money (page 445)

Federal Reserve System (the Fed) The central bank of the United States which provides services to banks, regulates their activities, and controls the nation's monetary policy (page 469)

federalism The division of powers between the states and the federal, or national, government (pagess 129, 295)

Federalists People who supported ratification of the Constitution because they supported a strong federal, or national, government. (page 120)

felony A serious crime for which the penalty can be imprisonment for more than one year (page 526)

filibuster (FIL-ih-BUS-ter) The use of long speeches to prevent a vote on a bill in the Senate (page 231)

fiscal policy A government's decisions about the amount of money it spends and the amount it collects in taxes (page 441)

fixed expenses Expenses that remain the same from month to month (page 406)

floor leaders The chief officers of the majority and minority parties in each house who guide the bills that their party supports through Congress (page 225)

foreign aid Programs giving military and economic help to other countries (page 649)

foreign policy Plans for guiding our nation's relationships with other countries (page 244)

fractional reserve banking A system of banking whereby banks keep a percentage of checking and saving deposits in reserve, leaving the rest available for loans and investments (page 466)

free enterprise The system in which individuals in a market economy are free to undertake economic activities with little or no control by the government (page 367)

freedom The ability to make the choices you want and act upon them (page 21)

freedom of speech The right to express one's opinions publicly (page 172)

freedom of the press The right to publish newspapers, magazines, and other materials without government restriction (page 172)

fringe benefits Indirect payments for work (page 404)

full employment A goal of the federal government whereby any person who wants and is able to work should be able to find a job (page 483)

G

general election An election in which voters make final decisions about candidates and issues (page 616)

grant Money given by the federal and state governments to local communities (page 333)

Great Compromise The plan agreed to during the writing of the Constitution that created the House of Representatives, in which each state was given votes based on its population, and the Senate, in which each state was given equal votes (page 116)

gross domestic product (GDP) The total dollar value of all final goods and services produced and sold in the country in a year (page 444)

H

heritage The traditions passed down from generation to generation (page 84)

home rule The right of cities and counties to write their own charters (page 337)

I

immigrants People who move from one country to make their homes in another (page 10)

impeach When a majority of the members of the House of Representatives accuse the President or other high government officials, such as a federal judge, of serious wrongdoing (pages 131, 220, 301)

income tax A tax on what individuals and businesses earn (page 302)

incumbent Someone who already holds the office for which he or she is running. This gives him or her a very good chance of winning. (page 635)

independent voter People who do not support a particular political party (page 603)

indictment (in-DITE-ment) A formal charge against an accused person (page 545)

indirect tax A tax paid by a seller and then passed on to the buyer through a higher price (page 495)

inflation A general rise in the prices of goods and services throughout the economy (pages 443, 489)

initiative The process by which citizens can propose laws (page 300)

injunction A court issued order to do or not to do a certain act (page 563)

insurance A plan by which a company gives protection from the cost of injury or loss (page 415)

intelligence Information about another country and what its government plans to do (page 650)

interest Payment for the use of capital (page 377)

interest groups Groups of people who work together for similar interests or goals (page 213)

intergovernmental revenue Money given by one level of government to another (page 333)

invest To use money to help a business get started or grow, with the hope that the business will earn a profit that you can share (page 367)

isolationism A foreign policy that seeks to limit our relations with other countries as much as possible (page 657)

item veto The power to reject particular parts, or items, of a bill (page 307)

J

judicial action commissions Official government bodies that handle situations in which judges might not be doing their job well (page 312)

judicial activism An effort by judges to take an active role in policymaking by overturning laws relatively often (page 283)

judicial restraint An effort by judges to avoid overturning laws and to leave policymaking up to the other two branches of government (page 283)

judicial review The Supreme Court's power to overturn any law that it decides is in conflict with the Constitution (page 276)

jury of peers A group of ordinary citizens who hear a court case and decide whether the accused person is innocent or guilty (page 62)

justice Fairness; the idea that every person deserves to be treated fairly (page 22)

L

labor unions Organizations of workers that seek to improve wages and working conditions and to protect members' rights (page 390)

laws Rules that are created and enforced by governments (page 512)

lawsuits Cases in which a court is asked to settle a dispute (page 562)

legal code A written collection of laws, often organized by subject (page 522)

legislature A group of people chosen to make laws (page 84)

lieutenant governor A state official second in rank to the governor (page 309)

liquidity The ability to turn savings back into cash (page 412)

loan An amount of money borrowed for a certain time period (page 464)

lobbyists People who represent interest groups (page 213)

M

market A place or situation in which an exchange of goods or services takes place, such as stores, shops, or stock exchanges (page 42)

market economy An economic system in which private individuals own the factors of production and are free to make their own choices about production, distribution, and consumption (page 366)

market price The price at which buyers and sellers agree to trade (page 381)

media Television, radio, newspapers, magazines, and the Internet (page 624)

mediation A process by which people agree to use a third party to help them settle a conflict (page 575)

misdemeanor A minor crime for which the penalty is often a fine (page 526)

Missouri Plan A method of choosing judges whereby the governor appoints a judge from a list prepared by a commission and then voters cast a vote as to whether they can stay in office or not (page 311)

mixed economy An economy that is a mixture of the characteristics of two or more of the three basic economic systems (pages 368, 485)

monarchy A form of government in which all or most of the power is in the hands of one individual, the monarch. The monarch's authority is hereditary. (page 47)

monetary policy Regulation of the money supply by the Federal Reserve System (page 441)

money Anything that is generally accepted as payment for a good or service (page 42)

money supply The total amount of money available for use as a medium of exchange (page 462)

monopoly A single business with the power to control prices in a market (page 436)

morals Beliefs about what is fair and what is right or wrong (page 516)

municipality A government that serves people who live in an urban area (page 323)

N

national debt The total amount of money the government owes to lenders (page 449)

national income accounting The tracking by the federal government of all the income and spending happening in the overall economy (page 487)

National Security Advisor The director of the National Security Council (page 670)

Naturalized citizens taking an oath.

National Security Council (NSC) A group of officials that advise the President on matters of the country's safety (page 652)

nationalism Pride people feel in their shared history and a loyalty to their nation (page 673)

natural rights Rights that people are born with and that no government can take away, such as the rights of life, liberty, and property (page 94)

naturalized To have gone through the process of becoming a citizen. Naturalization is a process which applies to a person not born a citizen of the United States. (page 56)

neutrality A foreign policy of not taking sides in wars between other countries (page 657)

nominate When a political party selects and names a candidate to run for public office (page 591)

O

Occupational Outlook Handbook A guide published by the Department of Labor Bureau of Labor Statistics detailing hundreds of jobs, their requirements, and their future possibilities (page 420)

open primary An election in which voters do not need to declare a party before voting, but may vote in only one party's primary (page 606)

opinion A written statement by a court explaining the reasons for a decision (page 280)

opportunity cost The benefit given up when scarce resources are used for one purpose instead of another (page 356)

ordinances Local laws (page 321)

original jurisdiction A court's authority to hear a case first (page 269)

P

parole Letting an inmate go free to serve the rest of his or her sentence outside of prison (page 548)

partnership A type of business in which two more people share ownership (page 384)

patriotism The demonstration of love and devotion to one's country (page 49)

patronage The system in which party leaders do favors for loyal supporters of the party (601)

peacekeepers Members of the military whose job is usually to help settle conflicts and maintain order in a region (page 687)

plaintiff An individual or a group of people who bring a complaint against another party in a civil case (page 267)

planks Position statements on each specific issue in a party's platform (page 591)

platform A statement of a party's official stand on major public issues (page 591)

Voters at a polling place for a **referendum.**

plea bargaining When a defendant agrees to plead guilty in exchange for a lesser charge or a lighter sentence (page 545)

pocket veto A way in which the President can veto a bill by pocketing, or keeping and not signing, the bill for ten days, during which Congress ends its session (page 228)

political parties An organization of citizens who wish to influence and control government by getting their members elected to office (page 590)

political socialization The process of learning how to behave politically (page 49)

poll tax A fee to vote (page 190)

precedent A guideline for how similar cases should be decided in the future (page 268)

precincts Voting districts (page 599)

president pro tempore (pro-TEMP-puh-ree) An officer who presides over the Senate when the Vice-President is absent. [Also known as president pro tem.] (page 224)

price The amount a person must pay for a good or service (page 42)

probable cause A good reason to believe that a suspect has been involved in a crime (page 542)

profit The difference between what it costs a business to produce something and the price the buyer pays for it (pages 367, 382)

progressive tax A tax system whereby the percentage of a person's income he or she pays in taxes increases with the more income he or she has (page 493)

propaganda A message that is meant to influence people's ideas, opinions, or actions in a certain way (page 626)

property tax A tax on land and buildings (page 332)

proportional tax A tax system whereby each taxpayer is required to pay the same proportion, or percentage, of their income as taxes (page 493)

prosecution A government body that brings a charge against a defendant who is accused of breaking one of its laws (page 267)

public policy Government response to public issues (page 294)

Q

quantity Amount (page 359)

R

racism The belief that members of one's own race are superior to those of other races (page 15)

ratification Approvl, as in of an amendment to the Constitution (pages100, 120)

recall A process for removing elected officials from office (page 300)

recession A slowdown in economic activity and production (page 475)

referendum The process by which a law proposed or passed by a state legislature is referred to the voters to approve or reject (page 300)

registration The process of signing up to be a voter (page 617)

regressive tax A tax that takes a higher percentage from the income of a person who has a low income than from a from a person who has a higher income (page 494)

representative People who are chosen to speak and act for their fellow citizens in government (page 58)

republic A government in which citizens elect representatives to make laws (page 92)

reserved powers Powers that the Constitution neither gives to Congress nor denies to the states (page 129)

revenue Income (page 302)

rule of law The concept of a government of laws (page 61)

rules Specific expectations about what our behavior should be (page 31)

S

sales tax Charges on purchases of goods and services, usually a percentage of the price (page 302)

sanctions Measures to stop or limit trade with another nation in order to change its behavior (page 650)

scarcity The problem that resources are always limited in comparison with the number and variety of wants people have (page 356)

segregation Separation, as in separation of one racial group from another, especially in public places such as hotels, schools, restaurants, and trains (page 197)

self-nomination Declaring yourself as a candidate for public office (page 605)

separation of church and state The situation in which government may not favor any religion or establish an official state religion (page 164)

Glossary

separation of powers Dividing government power among legislative, executive, and judicial branches (page 94)

service job A job in which a person makes a living by providing a service for other people (page 6)

small claims court A civil court that people use when the amount of money they want to recover is small, usually not more than $3,000 (page 578)

social institutions Systems of values and rules that determine how our society is organized. Five major institutions in our society are the family, religion, education, the economy, and government. (page 33)

social roles Roles that people play in real life (page 69)

socialization (soh-shul-i-ZAY-shun) The process of learning how to participate in a group; learning to accept the values in a group and learning the rules for behavior within it (page 31)

sole proprietorship A business owned by an individual (page 384)

sovereignty The power to make and carry out laws within a nation's borders (page 673)

Speaker of the House The presiding officer of the House of Representatives (page 224)

split ticket The practice of voting for candidates of more than one party on a ballot (page 602)

standard of living The number and kinds of goods and services people can have (page 676)

status offender A youth who is judged to be beyond the control of his or her parents or guardian (page 552)

statutes Written laws made by legislatures (page 519)

straight ticket The practice of voting for candidates of only one party on a ballot (page 602)

strike When workers refuse to work unless employers meet certain demands (page 391)

subpoena (suh-PEE-nuh) A court order to produce a witness or a document (page 570)

suffrage The right to vote (page 190)

summit meeting A meeting at which that President talks about important issues with heads of other governments (page 649)

summons An order to appear in court (page 570)

Sunbelt A region of the United States whose climate is dominated by warm weather. This area includes states such as Georgia, Florida, Texas, and Arizona. (page 5)

surplus The amount by which the government's income is greater than government spending (page 448)

surplus budget When a government spends less than the tax revenues it receives (page 499)

T

technology The practical application of science to commerce or industry (page 360)

terrorism Crimes in which people or groups of people use, or say they will use, violence in order to get what they want from the government or society (page 538)

Three-Fifths Compromise The plan agreed to during the writing of the Constitution that counted each slave as three fifths of a person when a state's population was calculated (page 117)

time deposit A savings plan with a set length of time that money must be kept in the account and a penalty for withdrawing early (page 413)

traditional economy An economic system in which the basic economic decisions are made according to long-established ways of behaving that are unlikely to change (page 363)

treason Betraying one's country by helping its enemies or by making war against it (page 538)

treaties Formal agreements with other countries (page 255)

trust A group of companies organized to benefit from the high prices they all agree to charge (page 436)

tyranny Abuse of power (page 89)

U

unitary system A system of government in which practically all political power lies with a central government (page 295)

utilities Services needed by the public, such as water, gas, and electricity (page 327)

V

values Standards of behavior; guidelines for how people should treat each other (page 18)

variable expenses Expenses that change from month to month (page 406)

W

warrant A legal document, issued by a court, giving police permission to make an arrest, seizure, or search (page 542)

warranty A manufacturer's promise to repair a product if it breaks within a certain period of time from the date of purchase (page 410)

witnesses People who have seen events related to a crime or who have special information that may help determine the guilt or innocence of a person on trial (page 63)

write-in candidate A candidate whose name does not appear on a ballot but who asks voters to write his or her name in as their choice (page 605)

Z

zoning Local rules that divide a community into areas and tell how the land in each area can be used (page 331)

Spanish Glossary

A

administration/administración Equipo de funcionarios del poder ejecutivo designados por cada presidente (pág. 249)

affirmative action/acción afirmativa Medidas para contrarrestar los efectos de la discriminación racial y la discriminación contra las mujeres que ocurría en el pasado (pág. 199)

aggression/agresión Ataque o amenaza de ataque de otro país (pág. 648)

alien/extranjero Ciudadano de un país que vive en otro (pág. 57)

ambassadors/embajadores Representantes oficiales de los gobiernos extranjeros (pág. 244)

amendment process/proceso de enmienda La manera en que se agregan cambios a la Constitución (pág. 160)

amendments/enmiendas Cambios, como los cambios a la Constitución (pág. 128)

answer/respuesta Respuesta escrita de un demandado a una reclamación (pág. 569)

Anti-Federalists/Antifederalistas Personas que se oponían a la ratificación de la Constitución porque creían que un fuerte gobierno central pondría en peligro las libertades de las personas (pág. 121)

appeal/apelación Solicitar a un tribunal superior que revise una decisión y determine si se hizo justicia (pág. 269)

appellate jurisdiction/jurisdicción de apelación Autoridad de un tribunal para escuchar la apelación de una decisión tomada por otro tribunal (pág. 269)

apportioned/prorrateado Dividido entre distritos (pág. 299)

arbitration/arbitraje El uso de un tercero para tomar una decisión legal que es obligatoria para todas las partes (pág. 576)

arraignment/acusación Audiencia en un tribunal en la cual el demandado es acusado formalmente de un crimen y se declara culpable, inocente o sin disputa (pág. 545)

assault/asalto Causar temor a alguien sin incurrir en contacto físico (pág. 537)

B

baby boom/generación de la posguerra (baby boom) El notable aumento en el número de nacimientos que ocurrió en los Estados Unidos entre 1946 y 1964 (pág. 7)

bail/fianza Dinero que un demandado entrega a un tribunal como promesa de que regresará para el juicio (pág. 544)

balance of power/equilibrio de poderes La amenaza de que la fuerza militar de una superpotencia podrá utilizarse contra la fuerza militar de otra (pág. 684)

balanced budget/presupuesto equilibrado Cuando un gobierno no gasta más que los ingresos tributarios que recibe (pág. 498)

bartering/trueque Intercambio de bienes y servicios por otros bienes y servicios, sin utilizar dinero (pág. 456)

battery/agresión Lesionar a una persona mediante contacto físico, por ejemplo, con un arma o con los puños (pág. 537)

beliefs/creencias Ciertas ideas que las personas consideran verdaderas (pág. 18)

bias/parcialidad Favorecer un punto de vista en particular sobre otro (pág. 627)

bicameral/bicameral De dos cámaras, como una legislatura con dos cámaras (pág. 116)

bill/proyecto de ley Una ley propuesta (pág. 213)

bill of attainder/decreto de proscripción y confiscación Ley que condena a una persona sin juicio (pág. 221)

Bill of Rights/Declaración de Derechos Lista de los derechos de los ciudadanos, específicamente las diez primeras enmiendas de la Constitución de los Estados Unidos (pág. 160)

blended families/familias combinadas Familias compuestas por adultos y sus hijos de matrimonios anteriores (pág. 34)

board/junta Grupo de personas que administran los negocios de una organización (pág. 321)

Board of Governors/Junta de Gobernadores Siete personas responsables de la dirección del Sistema de la Reserva Federal, designadas por el presidente para ejercer su cargo durante períodos de 14 años (pág. 470)

bonds/bonos Certificados que la gente compra al gobierno, el cual se compromete a pagar su costo, más intereses, después de un período determinado (pág. 302)

boycott/boicot Rehusarse a comprar los productos de cierta empresa (pág. 390)

budget/presupuesto Un plan para recaudar y gastar dinero (pág. 219)

bureaucracy/burocracia Una organización de departamentos, agencias y oficinas del gobierno (pág.s 249, 688)

burglary/hurto El hecho de entrar ilegalmente en un edificio con el propósito de hacer algo ilegal (pág. 537)

business cycle/ciclo de negocios Serie repetida de "alzas" de crecimiento y "bajas" de recesión (pág. 440)

C

Cabinet/Gabinete Un grupo importante de asesores políticos del presidente, integrado por los directores de los departamentos ejecutivos y algunos otros funcionarios (pág. 253)

campaign manager/director de campaña Una persona que ayuda a planificar las pautas generales de una campaña: adónde ir, de qué temas hablar y qué imagen debe presentar el candidato (pág. 632)

campaign press secretary/secretario de prensa de campaña Persona que se asegura de que las noticias presenten al candidato de la mejor manera (pág. 632)

candidate/candidato Persona que busca ser elegida para ejercer un cargo público (pág. 66)

canvass/solicitación Ir de puerta en puerta, entregando información y preguntando a la gente qué candidatos apoyan (pág. 593)

capital/capital Cualquier cosa producida en una economía que se guarda para producir otros bienes y servicios (pág. 352)

capitalism/capitalismo Otro nombre que se le da a la economía de mercado; un sistema en el cual las personas toman sus propias decisiones acerca de cómo guardar sus recursos como capital y cómo utilizar su capital para producir bienes y servicios (pág. 367)

career/carrera La ocupación para la cual uno se capacita y que ejerce como trabajo en la vida (pág. 416)

case studies/estudios de casos Descripciones de situaciones o conflictos, los asuntos en cuestión y las decisiones tomadas (pág. 173)

caucus/reunión electoral Reunión de los líderes de un partido para analizar asuntos o seleccionar candidatos (pág. 606)

census/censo Recuento oficial de la población, realizado cada diez años, para determinar cuántos representantes debe tener cada estado y pronosticar la demanda de los distintos servicios provistos por los gobiernos (pág.s 17, 215)

charter/carta constitucional Documento que otorga permiso para crear un gobierno y establece un plan para el funcionamiento de dicho gobierno (pág.s 84, 323)

checks and balances/controles y equilibrio El sistema que concede a cada una de los tres poderes del gobierno maneras de limitar los poderes de las otras dos (pág. 131)

circuit courts/tribunales de circuito Otro nombre para los tribunales de apelación (pág. 272)

citizen/ciudadano Persona con ciertos derechos y obligaciones bajo un gobierno; una persona que por nacimiento o decisión propia debe su lealtad a una nación (pág. 56)

civil disobedience/desobediencia civil Infringir las leyes de manera no violenta porque se oponen a la moral de una persona (pág. 516)

civil law/derecho civil Conjunto de leyes que ayuda a resolver desacuerdos entre personas (pág. 527)

closed primary/elección primaria cerrada Elección en la cual un votante debe estar registrado como miembro del partido y sólo puede votar en la elección primaria de dicho partido (pág. 606)

cloture/clausura de debate Acuerdo de tres quintas partes de los miembros del Senado para poner fin al debate de un proyecto de ley y permitir que se vote sobre dicho proyecto de ley (pág. 231)

Cold War/Guerra Fría Lucha, similar a una guerra real, pero sin batallas armadas, entre los Estados Unidos y la Unión Soviética (pág. 681)

collective bargaining/negociación colectiva El proceso mediante el cual los representantes de los sindicatos y las empresas intentan llegar a un acuerdo sobre salarios y condiciones de trabajo (pág. 390)

colony/colonia Territorio gobernado por una nación más poderosa, llamada poder colonial (pág. 674)

command economy/economía de mando Sistema económico en el cual el gobierno o la autoridad central posee o controla los factores de producción y toma las decisiones económicas básicas (pág. 365)

common good, the/bien común, el El bienestar de todos los miembros de la sociedad (pág. 65)

common law/derecho consuetudinario Conjunto de leyes basadas en las decisiones de jueces (pág. 519)

communism/comunismo Sistema en el cual el gobierno central posee y controla los recursos económicos (pág. 681)

compact/pacto Acuerdo escrito para elaborar y obedecer leyes para el bienestar del grupo (pág. 99)

compensation/compensación El derecho de una persona a resarcirse de los daños provocados por las acciones de otra persona (pág. 563)

complaint/demanda Documento legal que acusa a alguien de haber causado daños (pág. 569)

concurrent powers/poderes concurrentes Poderes compartidos por los gobiernos federal y estatal (pág. 129)

congressional district/distrito del congreso El área que representa un miembro de la Cámara de Representantes (pág. 215)

constituents/electorado Las personas representadas por un miembro del Congreso (pág. 212)

consumer/consumidor Persona que usa o consume bienes y servicios para satisfacer sus deseos y necesidades (pág. 42)

consumption/consumo El acto de comprar o utilizar bienes o servicios (pág. 353)

containment/contención Política extranjera que consiste en emplear la fuerza militar y el dinero para evitar la difusión del comunismo (pág. 659)

contracts/contratos Acuerdos legales entre compradores y vendedores (pág. 565)

convention/convención Asamblea (pág. 161)

corporation/corporación Una empresa que es independiente de sus propietarios y que funciona legalmente como una sola persona (pág. 385)

councils of governments/consejos de gobiernos Grupos de funcionarios de gobiernos locales y estatales que colaboran para satisfacer las necesidades regionales (pág. 336)

courts of appeals/tribunales de apelaciones Tribunales que se encargan de las apelaciones de los tribunales federales de distrito de menor nivel (pág. 272)

crime/delito Cualquier comportamiento que es ilegal porque el gobierno lo considera perjudicial para la sociedad (pág. 525)

criminal law/derecho penal Conjunto de leyes que establece qué acciones constituyen delitos, cómo juzgar a los acusados en un tribunal y cómo castigar los delitos (pág. 525)

currency/moneda Los billetes y monedas utilizados como dinero en una economía (pág. 458)

D

damages/indemnización por daños y perjuicios Dinero que se paga con el propósito de resarcir una pérdida (pág. 563)

defendant/demandado La parte que responde a una demanda y se defiende de ella en un caso ante un tribunal (pág. 267)

deficit/déficit El monto por el cual los gastos del gobierno exceden sus ingresos (pág. 448)

deficit budget/déficit presupuestario Cuando un gobierno gasta más de los ingresos tributarios que recibe (pág. 498)

deflation/deflación Una reducción en el nivel general de precios (pág. 489)

delinquent/delincuente Persona que se ha encontrado culpable de un crimen (pág. 552)

demand/demanda Cantidad de un producto o servicio que los compradores quieren y pueden comprar a distintos precios (pág. 379)

demand deposit/depósito a la vista El dinero en una cuenta corriente (pág. 462)

democracy/democracia Sistema de gobierno en el cual el poder es compartido por todo el pueblo (pág. 48)

demography/demografía El estudio del tamaño, el crecimiento y la distribución de las poblaciones humanas (pág. 4)

deposition/declaración El registro de las respuestas a las preguntas hechas a un testigo antes de que comience un juicio (pág. 570)

détente/détente Relajamiento de las tensiones entre los Estados Unidos y la Unión Soviética (pág. 660)

deterrence/disuasión Mantener una defensa sólida para desalentar las agresiones de otros países (pág. 648)

dictatorship/dictadura Gobierno controlado por una sola persona, llamada dictador, que por lo general asume el poder por la fuerza, en lugar de heredarlo (pág. 47)

diplomacy/diplomacia Las relaciones y comunicaciones entre países (pág. 649)

direct democracy/democracia directa Forma de gobierno en la cual las leyes son elaboradas directamente por los ciudadanos (pág. 91)

direct mail/correo directo Una manera de enviar mensajes a grandes grupos de personas a través del correo (pág. 623)

direct primary/votación primaria directa Elección en la cual los miembros de un partido político eligen candidatos para ocupar cargos públicos en nombre del partido (pág. 606)

direct tax/impuesto directo Un impuesto sobre los ingresos (pág. 495)

discovery/revelación El proceso de obtención de pruebas antes de un juicio (pág. 570)

discrimination/discriminación El trato injusto de un grupo de personas en comparación con el trato que recibe otro grupo (pág. 14)

disposable income/ingresos disponibles El dinero que sobra después de pagar impuestos (pág. 405)

diversity/diversidad Diferencias (pág. 8)

dividends/dividendos Pagos de las ganancias de las empresas en las cuales una persona tiene participación propietaria (pág. 404)

domestic policy/política nacional Planes para tratar de resolver problemas nacionales (pág. 245)

double jeopardy/procesamiento por segunda vez Ser juzgado dos veces por el mismo delito (pág. 168)

due process of law/debido proceso legal Proceso mediante el cual el gobierno debe tratar de manera justa a los acusados, conforme a reglas establecidas por la ley (pág. 168)

E

economic freedom/libertad económica La libertad de tener propiedades, obtener ganancias y elegir lo que se produce, compra y vende (pág. 430)

economic growth/crecimiento económico Incremento en la producción de bienes y servicios que proporciona a los ciudadanos un nivel de vida mejor (pág. 489)

economy/economía Sistema de producción y distribución de bienes y servicios para satisfacer los deseos y las necesidades de los individuos (pág. 41)

electors/electores Personas que prometen votar por el candidato seleccionado por los votantes (pág. 636)

embezzlement/desfalco Robar el dinero que le ha sido confiado a uno (pág. 537)

eminent domain/dominio eminente Capacidad del gobierno para tomar propiedades privadas para uso público (pág. 167)

entitlement programs/programas de adjudicación Beneficios pagados por el gobierno a quienes por ley tienen derecho a ellos (pág. 501)

entrepreneur/empresario Persona que inicia una empresa (pág. 382)

equal protection/protección igualitaria Principio mediante el cual todas las personas deben ser tratadas de manera justa, aunque no necesariamente de la misma manera (pág. 197)

equality/igualdad La condición de que todos tienen los mismos derechos y oportunidades (pág. 19)

equity/equidad El uso de reglas generales de imparcialidad para resolver conflictos (pág. 563)

excise tax/impuesto sobre el consumo Cargo sobre ciertos bienes, como las bebidas alcohólicas, la gasolina y el tabaco (pág. 302)

exclusion laws/leyes de exclusión Leyes aprobadas para prohibir más inmigración de un país o región en particular. En particular se refiere a las leyes aprobadas en 1882 y 1907 para los inmigrantes chinos y japoneses. (pág. 16)

executive agreements/acuerdos ejecutivos Acuerdos con otros países que no requieren la aprobación del Senado (pág. 244)

executive branch/poder ejecutivo La rama del gobierno responsable de ejecutar o hacer cumplir las leyes (pág. 240)

executive privilege/privilegio ejecutivo Derecho del Presidente a ocultar cierta información al Congreso y los tribunales (pág. 256)

F

factors of production/factores productivos Los recursos que las personas tienen para producir bienes y servicios para satisfacer sus deseos y necesidades (pág. 351)

family/familia La institución social más básica de cualquier sociedad (pág. 34)

federal budget/presupuesto federal Plan del gobierno para recaudar y gastar dinero (pág. 445)

Federal Reserve System (the Fed)/Sistema de la Reserva Federal ("Fed") El banco central de los Estados Unidos, que proporciona servicios a bancos, regula sus actividades y controla la política monetaria del país (pág. 469)

federalism/federalismo La división de poderes entre los estados y el gobierno federal o nacional (pág.s 129, 295)

Federalists/federalistas Personas que apoyaban la ratificación de la Constitución porque favorecían un sólido gobierno federal o nacional (pág. 120)

felony/delito mayor Crimen grave que puede ser castigado con encarcelamiento por más de un año (pág. 526)

filibuster/obstrucción parlamentaria El uso de largos discursos para evitar la votación sobre un proyecto de ley en el Senado (pág. 231)

fiscal policy/política fiscal Decisiones de un gobierno sobre la cantidad de dinero que gasta y la cantidad que recauda en impuestos (pág. 441)

fixed expenses/gastos fijos Gastos que no cambian de un mes a otro (pág. 406)

floor leaders/líderes parlamentarios Los principales funcionarios de los partidos mayoritarios y minoritarios de las cámaras, que guían los proyectos de ley apoyados por sus partidos en el Congreso (pág. 225)

foreign aid/ayuda exterior Programas que otorgan ayuda militar y económica a otros países (pág. 649)

foreign policy/política exterior Planes para conducir las relaciones de nuestra nación con otros países (pág. 244)

fractional reserve banking/sistema bancario de reserva fraccionaria Sistema bancario en el cual los bancos mantienen en reserva un porcentaje de los depósitos a cuentas corrientes y de ahorros, dejando el resto disponible para préstamos e inversiones (pág. 466)

free enterprise/libre empresa Sistema en el cual los individuos de una economía de mercado tienen la libertad de emprender actividades económicas con un control nulo o mínimo del gobierno (pág. 367)

freedom/libertad La capacidad de tomar las decisiones que uno quiere y de llevarlas a cabo (pág. 21)

freedom of speech/libertad de expresión El derecho de una persona a expresar públicamente sus opiniones (pág. 172)

freedom of the press/libertad de prensa El derecho a publicar periódicos, revistas y otros materiales sin restricciones gubernamentales (pág. 172)

fringe benefits/prestaciones complementarias Pagos indirectos por trabajo (pág. 404)

full employment/empleo total Una meta del gobierno federal, en la cual cualquier persona que quiere y puede trabajar debe ser capaz de conseguir empleo (pág. 483)

G

general election/elecciones generales Elecciones en las cuales los votantes toman decisiones finales acerca de candidatos y asuntos (pág. 616)

grant/subvención Dinero entregado por el gobierno federal y estatal a las comunidades locales (pág. 333)

Great Compromise/Gran Acuerdo El plan acordado durante la redacción de la Constitución que creó la Cámara de Representantes, en la cual cada estado recibió un número de votos según su población; y el Senado, en el que cada estado obtuvo igual número de votos (pág. 116)

gross domestic product (GDP)/producto interno bruto (PIB) El valor monetario total de todos los bienes y servicios finales producidos y vendidos en el país en un año (pág. 444)

H

heritage/herencia cultural Las tradiciones transmitidas de generación en generación (pág. 84)

home rule/autonomía El derecho de las ciudades y condados a escribir sus propias cartas constitucionales (pág. 337)

I

immigrants/inmigrantes Personas que se mudan de un país a otro para formar allí su hogar (pág. 10)

impeach/impugnar Cuando la mayoría de los miembros de la Cámara de Representantes acusa al Presidente o a otros funcionarios gubernamentales de alto rango, como un juez federal, de transgresiones graves (pág.s 131, 220, 301)

income tax/impuesto sobre la renta Impuesto sobre lo que ganan las personas y empresas (pág. 302)

incumbent/titular Una persona que ya ocupa el cargo público para el cual se está postulando. Esto le da buenas oportunidades de ganar. (pág. 635)

independent voter/votante independiente Persona que no apoya a un partido político en particular (pág. 603)

indictment/acusación Cargo formal en contra de una persona acusada (pág. 545)

indirect tax/impuesto indirecto Impuesto que paga el vendedor, quien luego lo transfiere al comprador en la forma de un precio más alto (pág. 495)

inflation/inflación Aumento general de los precios de bienes y servicios en la economía (pág.s 443, 489)

initiative/iniciativa de ley El proceso mediante el cual los ciudadanos pueden proponer leyes (pág. 300)

injunction/requerimiento judicial Orden emitida por un tribunal para realizar o no realizar determinada acción (pág. 563)

insurance/seguro Plan mediante el cual una empresa ofrece protección contra el costo de una lesión o pérdida (pág. 415)

intelligence/inteligencia Información acerca de otro país y lo que piensa hacer su gobierno (pág. 650)

interest/interés Pago por el uso de capital (pág. 377)

interest groups/grupos de interés Grupos de personas que colaboran para satisfacer ciertos intereses o alcanzar determinadas metas (pág. 213)

intergovernmental revenue/ingresos interguberna-mentales Dinero entregado por un nivel del gobierno a otro (pág. 333)

invest/invertir Utilizar dinero para que una empresa inicie operaciones o crezca, con la esperanza de que la empresa obtendrá ganancias que puedan compartirse (pág. 367)

isolationism/aislacionismo Política exterior que busca limitar lo más posible nuestra relación con otros países (pág. 657)

item veto/veto parcial El poder de rechazar partes específicas, o artículos, de un proyecto de ley (pág. 307)

J

judicial action commissions/comisiones de actuación judicial Organismos oficiales del gobierno que se encargan de situaciones en las que los jueces tal vez no estén realizando bien su trabajo (pág. 312)

judicial activism/activismo judicial Esfuerzo de los jueces para asumir un papel más activo en la elaboración de políticas, al revocar leyes con relativa frecuencia (pág. 283)

judicial restraint/moderación judicial Esfuerzo de los jueces para evitar la revocación de leyes y dejar la elaboración de políticas en manos de los otros dos poderes del gobierno (pág. 283)

judicial review/revisión judicial Poder de la Suprema Corte para revocar cualquier ley que en su opinión entre en conflicto con la Constitución (pág. 276)

jury of peers/jurado de iguales Un grupo de ciudadanos ordinarios que escuchan un caso en un tribunal y deciden si la persona acusada es inocente o culpable (pág. 62)

justice/justicia Imparcialidad; la idea de que cada persona merece ser tratada de manera justa (pág. 22)

L

labor unions/sindicatos laborales Organizaciones de trabajadores que buscan mejorar los salarios y proteger los derechos de sus afiliados (pág. 390)

laws/leyes Reglas creadas y ejercidas por los gobiernos (pág. 512)

lawsuits/demandas judiciales Casos en los cuales se solicita que un tribunal resuelva una disputa (pág. 562)

legal code/código legal Conjunto de leyes escritas, por lo general organizadas por tema (pág. 522)

legislature/legislatura Grupo de personas elegidas para elaborar leyes (pág. 84)

lieutenant governor/vicegobernador Funcionario estatal que es segundo en rango después del gobernador (pág. 309)

liquidity/liquidez La capacidad de convertir ahorros de nuevo a efectivo (pág. 412)

loan/préstamo Dinero que se presta durante un período determinado (pág. 464)

lobbyists/cabilderos Personas que representan grupos de interés (pág. 213)

M

market/mercado Lugar o situación donde tiene lugar un intercambio de bienes o servicios, como tiendas, talleres o bolsas de valores (pág. 42)

market economy/economía de mercado Sistema económico en el cual los individuos privados son propi-etarios de los factores productivos y tienen la libertad de tomar sus propias decisiones sobre producción, distribu-ción y consumo (pág. 366)

market price/precio de mercado Precio por el cual los compradores y vendedores llegan al acuerdo de comerciar (pág. 381)

media/medios de comunicación Televisión, radio, peri-ódicos, revistas e Internet (pág. 624)

mediation/mediación Un proceso por el cual las per-sonas convienen en utilizar los servicios de un tercero para resolver un conflicto (pág. 575)

misdemeanor/delito menor Delito menor que usual-mente se castiga con una multa (pág. 526)

Missouri Plan/Plan de Missouri Método de selección de jueces en el cual el gobernador designa al juez a partir de una lista elaborada por una comisión y los votantes votan para determinar si puede o no ocupar el cargo (pág. 311)

mixed economy/economía mixta Economía que com-bina las características de dos o más de los tres sistemas económicos básicos (pág.s 368, 485)

monarchy/monarquía Forma de gobierno donde la totalidad o la mayor parte del poder está en manos de una sola persona, el monarca. La autoridad del monarca es hereditaria. (pág. 47)

monetary policy/política monetaria Regulación de la oferta monetaria del Sistema de la Reserva Federal (pág. 441)

money/dinero Cualquier cosa que se acepte generalmente como pago de un bien o servicio (pág. 42)

money supply/oferta monetaria La cantidad total de dinero disponible para usarse como medio de intercambio (pág. 462)

monopoly/monopolio Una sola empresa que tiene el poder de controlar los precios en el mercado (pág. 436)

morals/moral Creencias acerca de lo que es justo y lo que es bueno o malo (pág. 516)

municipality/municipalidad Gobierno que sirve a las personas que viven en un área urbana (pág. 323)

N

national debt/deuda nacional El monto total del dinero que el gobierno debe a sus acreedores (pág. 449)

national income accounting/contabilidad de ingresos nacionales El control que el gobierno federal hace de todos los ingresos y gastos que ocurren en la economía en general (pág. 487)

National Security Advisor/Asesor de Seguridad Nacional El director del Consejo de Seguridad Nacional (pág. 670)

National Security Council (NSC)/Consejo de Seguridad Nacional Grupo de funcionarios que asesora al Presidente sobre asuntos de seguridad del país (pág. 652)

nationalism/nacionalismo Orgullo que la gente siente por la historia que comparte y lealtad a su nación (pág. 673)

natural rights/derechos naturales Derechos con los que nacen las personas y que ningún gobierno puede quitarles, como el derecho a la vida, la libertad y la propiedad (pág. 94)

naturalized/naturalizado Que ha pasado por el proceso requerido para convertirse en ciudadano. La naturalización es un proceso que se aplica a las personas que no son ciudadanos de los Estados Unidos por nacimiento. (pág. 56)

neutrality/neutralidad Política exterior de no tomar partido en guerras entre otros países (pág. 657)

nominate/nominar Cuando un partido político selecciona y designa un candidato que se postulará para un cargo público (pág. 591)

O

Occupational Outlook Handbook/Manual de Ocupaciones Guía publicada por la Oficina de Estadísticas Laborales del Departamento del Trabajo, donde se detallan cientos de trabajos, sus requisitos y sus posibilidades futuras (pág. 420)

open primary/elección primaria abierta Elecciones en las cuales los votantes no tienen que declarar un partido antes de votar, pero sólo pueden votar en la elección primaria de un partido (pág. 606)

opinion/opinión Declaración escrita de un tribunal donde se explican las razones de una decisión (pág. 280)

opportunity cost/costo de oportunidad El beneficio al cual se renuncia cuando se utilizan recursos escasos para un fin en lugar de otro (pág. 356)

ordinances/ordenanzas Leyes locales (pág. 321)

original jurisdiction/jurisdicción original Autoridad de un tribunal para ser el primero en escuchar un caso (pág. 269)

P

parole/libertad condicional Cuando se permite que un recluso quede libre para cumplir el resto de su condena fuera de prisión (pág. 548)

partnership/sociedad Empresa que es propiedad de dos o más personas (pág. 384)

patriotism/patriotismo Demostración del amor y la devoción de una persona por su país (pág. 49)

patronage/patrocinio Sistema en el cual los líderes de los partidos hacen favores a los partidarios leales del partido (pág. 601)

peacekeepers/fuerzas de paz Miembros de las fuerzas armadas cuyo trabajo usualmente consiste en resolver conflictos y mantener el orden en una región (pág. 687)

plaintiff/demandante Persona o grupo de personas que presentan una demanda en contra de otra parte en un caso civil (pág. 267)

planks/puntos de programa Declaraciones de la posición sobre temas específicos en la plataforma de un partido (pág. 591)

platform/plataforma Declaración de la posición oficial de un partido acerca de asuntos públicos importantes (pág. 591)

plea bargaining/acuerdo de sentencia Cuando un demandado acepta declararse culpable a cambio de un cargo o sentencia menor (pág. 545)

pocket veto/veto indirecto Manera en que el presidente puede vetar un proyecto de ley al guardarlo o no firmarlo durante diez días, plazo en el cual el Congreso termina su sesión (pág. 228)

political parties/partidos políticos Organización de ciudadanos que desean tener control e influencia en el gobierno, al lograr que sus miembros sean elegidos a cargos públicos (pág. 590)

political socialization/socialización política Proceso de aprendizaje del buen comportamiento político (pág. 49)

poll tax/impuesto de capitación Cuota que debe pagarse para votar (pág. 190)

precedent/precedente Pauta sobre la manera en que deben decidirse casos similares en el futuro (pág. 268)

precincts/precinto Distritos de votación (pág. 599)

president pro tempore/presidente interino
Funcionario que preside el Senado cuando el vicepresidente está ausente. [También se conoce como presidente pro tem.] (pág. 224)

price/precio Cantidad que una persona debe pagar por un bien o servicio (pág. 42)

probable cause/causa razonable Una buena razón para creer que un sospechoso ha estado implicado en un delito (pág. 542)

profit/ganancia La diferencia entre lo que le cuesta a una empresa producir algo y el precio que el comprador paga (pág.s 367, 382)

progressive tax/impuesto progresivo Sistema tributario en que el porcentaje de los ingresos que una persona paga por concepto de impuestos aumenta a medida que aumentan sus ingresos (pág. 493)

propaganda/propaganda Mensaje cuyo propósito es influir de cierta manera en las ideas, opiniones o acciones de las personas (pág. 626)

property tax/impuesto predial Impuesto sobre terrenos y edificios (pág. 332)

proportional tax/impuesto proporcional Sistema tributario en el cual cada contribuyente debe pagar la misma proporción o porcentaje de sus ingresos como impuestos (pág. 493)

prosecution/fiscalía Organismo del gobierno que presenta cargos en contra de un demandado acusado de infringir una de sus leyes (pág. 267)

public policy/política pública Respuesta del gobierno a los asuntos públicos (pág. 294)

Q

quantity/cantidad Monto (pág. 359)

R

racism/racismo La creencia de que los miembros de la raza a la que uno mismo pertenece son superiores a los miembros de otras razas (pág. 15)

ratification/ratificación Aprobación, como en el caso de una enmienda a la Constitución (pág.s 100, 120)

recall/revocación Proceso para destituir de sus cargos a los funcionarios electos (pág. 300)

recession/recesión Una desaceleración de la actividad y producción económicas (pág. 475)

referendum/referendo Proceso mediante el cual una ley propuesta o aprobada por una legislatura estatal es remitida a los votantes para que éstos la aprueben o rechacen (pág. 300)

registration/empadronamiento Proceso para registrarse como votante (pág. 617)

regressive tax/impuesto regresivo Impuesto que toma un mayor porcentaje de los ingresos de quienes tienen ingresos más bajos que de las personas con ingresos más altos (pág. 494)

representative/representante Persona elegida para hablar y actuar en el gobierno en nombre de sus conciudadanos (pág. 58)

republic/república Gobierno en el cual los ciudadanos eligen representantes para elaborar las leyes (pág. 92)

reserved powers/poderes reservados Poderes que la Constitución no concede al Congreso ni niega a los estados (pág. 129)

revenue/rentas Ingresos (pág. 302)

rule of law/Estado de Derecho El concepto de un gobierno basado en leyes (pág. 61)

rules/reglas Expectativas específicas acerca de cuál debe ser nuestro comportamiento (pág. 31)

S

sales tax/impuesto sobre ventas Cargos sobre las compras de bienes y servicios; por lo general es un porcentaje del precio (pág. 302)

sanctions/sanciones Medidas para detener o limitar el comercio con otra nación, con el fin de cambiar su comportamiento (pág. 650)

scarcity/escasez El problema que se tiene cuando los recursos siempre son limitados en comparación con el número y la variedad de deseos y necesidades de las personas (pág. 356)

segregation/segregación Separación, como en la separación de un grupo racial de otro, especialmente en lugares públicos como hoteles, escuelas, restaurantes y trenes (pág. 197)

self-nomination/autonominación Declararse uno mismo como candidato para un cargo público (pág. 605)

separation of church and state/separación de la iglesia y el Estado Situación en la cual el gobierno no puede favorecer a ninguna religión ni establecer una religión oficial del Estado (pág. 164)

separation of powers/separación de poderes División del poder del gobierno entre los poderes legislativo, ejecutiv y judicial (pág. 94)

service job/empleo de servicio Empleo en el cual una persona se gana la vida proporcionando un servicio a otras personas (pág. 6)

small claims court/tribunal de reclamaciones de menor cuantía Tribunal civil que la gente utiliza cuando el importe monetario que quiere recuperar es pequeño, por lo general no mayor que $3,000 (pág. 578)

social institutions/instituciones sociales Sistemas de valores y reglas que determinan cómo está organizada nuestra sociedad. Las cinco principales instituciones de nuestra sociedad son la familia, la religión, la educación, la economía y el gobierno. (pág. 33)

social roles/funciones sociales Funciones que las personas representan en la vida real (pág. 69)

socialization/socialización Aprendizaje del comportamiento en grupo; aprender a aceptar los valores de un grupo y aprender las reglas de comportamiento dentro del grupo (pág. 31)

sole proprietorship/propiedad individual Empresa que pertenece a una sola persona (pág. 384)

sovereignty/soberanía El poder para elaborar y aplicar leyes dentro de las fronteras de una nación (pág. 673)

Speaker of the House/Presidente de la Cámara de Representantes El funcionario que preside la Cámara de Representantes (pág. 224)

split ticket/lista dividida La práctica de votar por candidatos de más de un partido en la misma boleta (pág. 602)

standard of living/nivel de vida El número y el tipo de bienes y servicios que pueden tener las personas (pág. 676)

status offender/infractor juvenil Joven a quien se considera fuera del control de sus padres o tutores (pág. 552)

statutes/estatutos Leyes escritas elaboradas por las legislaturas (pág. 519)

straight ticket/lista directa La práctica de votar por candidatos de un solo partido en la misma boleta (pág. 602)

strike/huelga Cuando los trabajadores se rehúsan a trabajar si los patrones no satisfacen ciertas demandas (pág. 391)

subpoena/citación Orden de un tribunal para presentar un testigo o documento (pág. 570)

suffrage/sufragio El derecho al voto (pág. 190)

summit meeting/reunión cumbre Reunión en la cual el presidente habla de asuntos importantes con los jefes de otros gobiernos (pág. 649)

summons/emplazamiento Orden de comparecer ante un tribunal (pág. 570)

Sunbelt/Franja del sol Región de los Estados Unidos donde predomina el clima cálido. Esta región comprende, entre otros, los estados de Georgia, Florida, Texas y Arizona. (pág. 5)

surplus/superávit El monto por el cual los ingresos del gobierno exceden sus gastos (pág. 448)

surplus budget/superávit presupuestario Cuando un gobierno gasta menos que los ingresos tributarios que recibe (pág. 499)

T

technology/tecnología La aplicación práctica de la ciencia en el comercio o la industria (pág. 360)

terrorism/terrorismo Delitos en los que personas o grupos de personas usan, o dicen que usarán, la violencia para obtener lo que quieren del gobierno o la sociedad (pág. 538)

Three-Fifths Compromise/Acuerdo de Tres Quintas Partes El plan acordado durante la redacción de la Constitución mediante el cual se contaba a cada esclavo como tres quintas partes de una persona al calcular la población de un estado (pág. 117)

time deposit/depósito a plazo Plan de ahorros en el que se establece un período determinado durante el cual el dinero debe permanecer en la cuenta, así como una penalización por retirar el dinero antes de que termine el plazo (pág. 413)

traditional economy/economía tradicional Sistema económico en el cual las decisiones económicas básicas son tomadas conforme a patrones de comportamiento que han estado en vigor mucho tiempo y que tienen poca probabilidad de cambiar (pág. 363)

treason/traición Traicionar al propio país ayudando a sus enemigos o luchando en una guerra contra él (pág. 538)

treaties/tratados Acuerdos formales con otros países (pág. 255)

trust/consorcio Grupo de empresas organizadas para beneficiarse de los altos precios que convienen en cobrar (pág. 436)

tyranny/tiranía Abuso del poder (pág. 89)

U

unitary system/sistema unitario Sistema de gobierno en el cual prácticamente todo el poder político está en manos de un gobierno central (pág. 295)

V

values/valores Normas de comportamiento; pautas de cómo la gente debe tratar a los demás (pág. 18)

variable expenses/gastos variables Gastos que cambian de un mes a otro (pág. 406)

W

warrant/orden judicial Documento legal, emitido por un tribunal, que autoriza a la policía realizar un arresto, decomiso o cateo (pág. 542)

warranty/garantía Promesa de un fabricante de reparar un producto si se descompone dentro de un período determinado a partir de la fecha de compra (pág. 410)

witnesses/testigos Personas que han visto acontecimientos relacionados con un delito o que poseen información especial que puede ayudar a determinar la culpabilidad o inocencia de una persona enjuiciada (pág. 63)

write-in candidate/candidato elegible para recibir votos por inserción Candidato cuyo nombre no aparece en la boleta pero que pide a los votantes que escriban su nombre como el candidato que eligen (pág. 605)

Z

zoning/zonificación Reglas locales que dividen una comunidad en áreas y estipulan cómo deben emplearse los terrenos de cada área (pág. 331)

Index

Note: Entries with a page number followed by a *c* indicate a chart, graph, or diagram on that page; *m* indicates a map; and *p* indicates a picture.

A

abortion, 283
absentee ballot, 618
accused, rights of the, 168–169, 168*p*, 169*p*
ACLU. *See* American Civil Liberties Union
Adams, John, 91, 97, 105, 277, 284*c*, 635
Adams, John Quincy, 263, 284*c*
adjudicatory hearing, 554
administration, 249
adobe, 4*p*
adoption, 34
advertising, 437
affirmative action, 199*p*, 200*p*, 201–202
Afghanistan, 669*p*, 682
AFL-CIO, 393
Africa, 664–665
    colonies in, 675
    nations of, 673
    traditional economy of, 364
African Americans, 12*c*, 12*m*, 14–15, 14*p*, 15*c*, 15*p*
    abolishment of slavery and, 186–189, 188*p*, 189*m*
    affirmative action and, 199–202
    Brown v. *Board of Education of Topeka*, 530
    in Congress, 219*p*, 224*p*, 237*c*
    population, 17
    segregation and, 197–199, 197*p*, 198*p*
    on Supreme Court, 278, 278*p*
    voting rights of, 189–190, 189*p*, 190*p*, 617
aggression, 648
agriculture, 352
Agriculture, Department of, 252*c*, 521, 521*p*
Aid to Families with Dependent Children, 450
airport security, 297, 297*p*
Alabama
    Electoral College electors, 636*m*
    state constitution, 296*m*
Alaska
    economic wants in, 350
    Electoral College electors, 636*m*
    state constitution, 296*m*
    Trans-Alaska pipeline, 434*p*
    utilities in, 330
Albright, Madeline, 664*p*
Algeria, 664
alien, 57
alliances, 648, 649
ambassadors, 126, 244, 652
amendments, 128
    examples of, 186–194, 187*c*
    process of changing, 160–161, 161*c*
    See also individual amendments
American Civil Liberties Union (ACLU), 176
American Federation of Labor (AFL), 390
American mosaic, 11, 11*p*
American Nazi Party, 175–178, 175*p*
American Revolution. *See* Revolutionary War
Americans with Disabilities Act (1990), 21
Andorra, 672, 673*p*
Angel Island, 16
Annan, Koffi, 687*p*, 689, 695
Anthony, Susan B., 191
Anti-Federalists, 120, 121–122, 126, 160, 595. *See also* Federalists
apartheid, 685
appeal, 269, 280*c*–281*c*

appeals court, 269–270, 270, 271, 272, 273*m*
appellate jurisdiction, 269
apportionment, 299
arbitration, 576, 576*p*, 581*p*
Archer, Bill, 232
Arizona
    economic wants in, 350
    Electoral College electors, 636*m*
    Hispanic Americans in, 14
    state constitution, 296*m*
    in the Sunbelt, 5
Arkansas
    Electoral College electors, 636*m*
    state constitution, 296*m*
armed forces, 46
arraignment, 545
arrests, 542–543, 546*c*–547*c*, 553
arson, 537, 543*c*
Arthur, Chester A., 250*c*, 284*c*
Articles, Constitutional, 125–128, 127*c*
Articles of Confederation, 99–100, 99*p*, 101, 112, 116*c*, 122
asbestos, 578
Ashcroft, John, 439
Asia, 364, 675
Asian Americans, 12*c*, 12*m*, 15*c*, 16
    affirmative action and, 199
assault, 537, 543*c*
assembly, freedom of, 165
assembly line, 360*p*
assessors, 321
Association of Southeast Asian Nations, 683
Atlanta, Georgia, 498*p*
atomic bomb, 244
attorney general, state, 309
Attorney General, U.S., 253
Australia, 674
automobiles
    emission standards, 521
    lemon laws and, 410
    production, 357*p*, 360, 360*p*, 374*p*
    safety laws, 513, 513*p*

B

baby boomers, 7
Babylonia, 522
bail, 169, 169*p*, 544
Bakke, Allan, 200–201
balance of power, 684
balanced budget, 498
ballot measures, 621
ballots, 618
bankruptcy, 435
banks and banking, 254*p*
    business of, 465–466, 466*c*
    checking accounts, 462, 463, 472, 472*c*–473*c*
    demand deposit, 462, 474
    Federal Reserve System and, 473, 474
    fractional reserve banking, 466
    history of, 460–461, 461*p*
    loans, 464–465, 465
    money supply and, 462–463, 463*c*
    purpose of, 460
    regulation of, 473
    savings accounts, 464
    savings plans, 413, 413*c*, 414
    services of, 463–465
    time line, 470
    See also financial institutions

bar graphs, 24*c*
barter system, 42, 456
battery, 537
Bayeux Tapestry, 322*p*
Belarus, 664
beliefs, 18, 519
Bellamy, Francis, 55
benefits, 355
Berlin Wall, 660*p*, 661, 681
bias, 627
bicameral legislature, 116, 299
Big Dig, 340*p*
bill of attainder, 221
Bill of Rights, English, 93, 93*c*, 162
Bill of Rights, U.S., 121, 162*c*–163*c*, 515, 570
    interpreting the, 172–180
    Madison and, 160–162
    need for, 160
    protections in, 163–170
    purpose of, 163
    See also individual amendments
bills, 125, 213, 300
    become laws, 225–226, 227*c*
    compromise, 232
    in Congress, 223, 225–226, 227*c*
    reporting, 230
blacklists, 392
Blair, Tony, 48*p*
blended families, 34
Blix, Hans, 671
block grants, 303, 333
Bloomberg, Michael, 385, 385*p*
BLS. *See* Bureau of Labor Statistics
Board of Governors, Federal Reserve, 470
boards, county, 321
Bollinger, Lee, 200
bonds, 302, 413, 413*c*, 414, 474
borders, 673
Borel, Clarence, 571
Bork, Robert, 262
Bosnia, 664
Boston, Massachusetts, 480*p*
boycotts, 390, 391*c*, 392
Brandeis, Louis, 272, 272*p*
Braun, Carol Moseley, 219*p*
breaking and entering, 524
Brennan, William, 404
Breyer, Stephen, 272*p*, 284
Broward County, Florida, 321*p*
Brown, Willie, Jr., 334, 334*p*
Brown v. *Board of Education of Topeka*, 198–199, 198*p*, 268, 530
Buchanan, James, 284*c*
budgets
    of Congress, 219
    direct purchases, 500, 500*p*
    federal, 445, 445*c*, 448, 448*c*
    personal, 406–406
    President and the, 246, 251
    tax revenues and, 498–499, 499*c*
    transfer payments, 500–501
    types of, 498–499, 499*c*
building codes, 329
Bulgaria, 681
Bull Moose Party, 596, 597
Bullock, Betty, 579, 580
Bureau of Engraving and Printing, 455
Bureau of Labor Statistics (BLS), 5, 420
bureaucracy, 249, 688
Burger, Warren, 283, 283*p*
burgesses, 84, 85, 85*p*
burglary, 537, 543*c*
Burma, 683

Burundi, 689
Bush, George H.W., 232, 284*c*, 285, 635*p*
Bush, George W., 126*p*, 242*p*, 245*p*, 251*p*, 253, 255*p*, 284*c*, 339, 500, 504*p*, 652*p*
    election of 2000, 597, 620, 637
    Iraq War and, 219, 219*p*, 671
    USA Patriot Act and, 49
Bush v. *Gore* (2000), 620
business cycle, 440–442, 499
businesses
    banks, 465–466, 466*c*
    Congress and, 218
    entrepreneurs, 382–384, 382*p*
    foreign policy and, 654, 654*c*
    government regulation of, 433, 435
    labor unions and, 388–392, 391*p*
    minimum wage law and, 229–233, 229*p*, 231*c*, 231*p*, 232*p*, 233*p*
    ownership, 384–385, 384*c*
    regulation of, 234
    rise of big, 386, 386*p*
    taxes and, 377, 486, 496
    women-owned, 464
butterfly ballot, 618–619
buyers, 378–381, 380*c*
Byrd, Richard, 242*p*

C

Cabinet, 253
California
    congressional representatives, 215
    court cases and, 313
    elections in, 616
    Electoral College electors, 636*m*
    gold in, 16
    Hispanic Americans in, 14
    prison population, 549*c*
    Proposition 209, 201, 300–301, 300*p*
    recall vote, 300–301, 300*p*
    state and local governments, 337
    state constitution, 296*m*
campaign finance law, 634, 634*p*
campaign manager, 632
campaign press secretary, 632–633
campaigns
    candidates messages, 622–624, 622*p*, 623*p*
    citizens and, 66, 592–594
    contributions to, 604
    fundraising, 607, 625, 625*c*
    opinion polls, 628
    organization of, 632
    planning and running, 631–633, 631*p*, 632*p*, 633*p*
    political parties and, 601, 634
    presidential, 607–609, 607*p*
    propaganda techniques, 626, 626*c*
    use of media in, 624, 629, 629*p*, 632–633
Canada, 683
candidates, political
    campaigns and, 631–633, 631*p*, 632*p*, 633*p*
    citizens becoming, 66
    fundraising, 607, 625, 625*c*
    messages from, 622–624, 622*p*, 623*p*
    nominating, 605–606
    presidential, 607–609, 607*p*
    selecting, 591, 591*p*
canvass, 593
capital, 352, 484
    circular flow of economic activity and, 376–377, 378*c*–379*c*, 484–486, 484*c*–485*c*, 486*p*
    as factor of production, 383, 383*c*
    See also money

capital punishment, 550
capitalism, 367
Capitol Building, 186*p*
careers
    choosing, 416–418
    economy and, 416
    outlook for, 418*c*–419*c*, 420, 420*p*
    researching, 419–420, 420*p*
    technology and, 417, 417*p*
Carter, Jimmy, 241*p*, 259*p*, 263, 284*c*, 635, 684
case studies, 173–178
categorical grants, 303
Catholics, 12
caucus, 606, 608
CEA. *See* Council of Economic Advisors
census, 17, 215, 299
Census Bureau, U.S., 129, 199
Central America, 364, 658
Central Intelligence Agency (CIA), 650
charter, 84, 323
Chase, Salmon P., 284*p*
checking accounts, 462, 463, 472, 472*c*–473*c*
checks and balances, 129, 130*c*, 131, 221, 241, 259, 284
child custody, 566, 573
child labor, 388*p*, 389, 390, 431*p*
China, 658, 673, 680
    foreign policy and, 662, 663
    immigration from, 16
    in United Nations, 687
Church of England, 88
CIA. *See* Central Intelligence Agency
circuit courts, 272, 273*m*
circular flow, 376–377, 378*c*–379*c*, 484–486, 484*c*–485*c*, 486*p*
cities, 323–326, 323*p*, 324*c*, 325*p*
citizens
    becoming, 19*p*, 54*p*, 186
    definition of, 56–57
    duties of, 58, 60–64, 62*c*–63*c*
    naturalization process, 54*p*, 56–57, 57*c*
    political parties and, 592–594
    responsibilities of, 65–67, 66*p*, 67*p*
    rights of, 59, 99, 221, 285
    role of, 74–75
    voting and, 620–621
    See also social roles
citizenship, 86–87, 86*m*–87*m*
    giving up, 57
city manager, 325
civics
    economics and, 5, 74, 167, 199, 217, 251, 279, 337, 377, 414,
        432, 464, 486, 525, 545, 578, 607, 634, 654, 684
civil cases, 267, 267*p*, 572*c*
    types of, 564–567
civil disobedience, 516
civil laws, 527–529, 527*p*
    principles of, 562–563
    role of, 562–567
Civil Rights Act (1964), 21, 570
civil rights laws, 21, 199, 570
civil rights movement, 21*p*, 184*p*, 207*p*
civil service system, 254, 601
civil trial
    avoiding, 574–577, 574*p*, 576*p*, 577*p*
    awards in, 579–580, 580*c*
    burden of proof, 571
    cost of, 578–579, 579*p*
    juries and verdicts in, 570–571
    preparing for, 569–570, 569*p*
    problems in, 572–573
Clayton Anti-Trust Act (1914), 234, 437
Cleveland, Grover, 284*c*
Clinton, Bill, 220, 232, 232*p*, 243*p*, 257, 284*c*, 450, 597, 623, 635*p*,
    653, 654*p*

closed primary, 606
cloture, 231
Coast Guard, U.S., 500*p*
Code of Hammurabi, 522, 522*p*
codes, 329
Cold War, 656, 659–662, 660*p*, 662*p*, 681–682, 681*p*, 682*p*, 684
collective bargaining, 390
Collin, Frank, 175*p*
colonies, 674–675, 676
    laws of, 519–520
Colorado
    Electoral College electors, 636*m*
    state constitution, 296*m*
    taxes in, 496
command economies, 365–366
Commerce, Department of, 252*c*, 257, 652
commission plan, 326
commissioners, 321
Committee of Industrial Organizations, 393
Committees of Correspondence, 96
common good, 65, 74, 431, 515
common law, 519–520
Common Sense (Paine), 97, 97*p*
communism, 659, 681, 682, 692*m*
community service, 67, 67*p*
community treatment programs, 548, 555
compact, 99
compensation, 563, 563*p*, 564, 567, 571
competition, 366, 436
complaint, 569
Comprehensive Test Ban Treaty, 653
comptroller, 309
concurrent powers, 129
conference committees, 226
conflict manager, 575, 576*p*
conflicts, 679, 680*c*, 681–682. *See also* wars
Congo Republic, 664
Congress, U.S.
    amendment process, 160–161, 161*c*
    under Articles of Confederation, 99
    benefits, 217
    bills in, 223, 225–226, 227*c*
    budget of, 219
    checks and balances, 221
    commerce and, 218
    committees of, 225–226, 227*c*
    Electoral College, 636–637, 636*m*, 637*p*
    floor leaders, 225
    foreign policy and, 653, 653*p*
    grants for states, 303
    growth of, 224*c*
    impeachment and, 220
    income tax and, 486
    interest groups and, 213
    joint sessions, 210*p*
    lawmaking and, 212–213, 225–226, 227*c*, 229–233
    leadership of, 224–225
    majority party, 224, 591
    members of, 212–217, 213*p*, 214*p*, 215*p*, 216*c*, 237*c*
    minority party, 224, 591
    nonlegislative powers of, 220–221, 220*c*
    organization of, 125–126, 223–228, 223*p*, 224*c*, 225*p*, 226*p*,
        227*c*, 228*p*
    political parties and, 213
    powers of, 170, 218–220, 218–221, 219*p*, 220*c*, 221*p*
    President and, 241, 243, 244, 245, 255–256
    requirements, 217
    salaries, 217
    slavery and, 188
    statutes, 519
    taxes and, 486, 219
    trade and, 100

veto and, 245
War Powers Resolution, 219
See also House of Representatives, U.S.; Senate, U.S.
Congress of Industrial Organizations (CIO), 393
congressional districts, 215–216, 216*c*
Connecticut
Electoral College electors, 636*m*
Great Compromise and, 116
ratification of the Constitution and, 123*c*
state constitution, 296*m*
conscientious objector, 61
constituents, 212, 214
constitution, state, 313
Constitution, U.S., 313, 522
amending the, 128, 160–161, 161*c*, 186–194, 187*c*
articles of, 125–128, 127*c*, 221, 271
Articles of Confederation and, 116*c*
Bill of Rights, 515
death penalty and, 169
economy and, 430
elastic clause, 220
federalism, 129
powers of Congress, 218–221
Preamble, 124–125, 218, 515
ratification of, 120, 121, 121*p*, 123, 123*c*, 128
as rules of government, 48
state government and, 127, 295
supremacy of, 128
Supreme Court and the, 196–197
See also individual amendments
Constitutional Convention, 113–115, 113*p*, 118, 171*c*
constitutional monarchy, 48
Constitutional Party, 599*c*
constitutions, 99, 296*m*, 522
consuls, 652
consumer credit, 411
Consumer Product Safety Commission (CPSC), 253, 438
consumers, 42
cases regarding, 565
finanancial choices and, 405, 409–415
how to be wise, 408
lemon laws, 410
personal consumption, 411*c*
protection of, 438
consumption, 352–354, 352*p*, 353, 353*p*, 354
containment, 659
contracts, 565
Coolidge, Calvin, 250*c*, 284*c*
copyright, 430*p*, 439, 514, 524, 529
Copyright Extension Act (1998), 439
corporation, 384*c*, 385–386, 386*p*, 435, 436
correctional institutions, 548–549, 549*c*
council-manager plan, 325
Council of Economic Advisors (CEA), 500
councils of governments, 336
county government, 320–321, 320*p*, 321*p*
Court of Appeals for the Federal Circuit, 272
Court of Claims, 273
Court of Customs and Patent Appeals, 273
court of final appeals, 270, 273
courts, 127
Congress and, 220
crime and, 540
laws and, 266
members of the, 268
parties in the conflict, 267
purpose of, 267–268
role of, 172–173
trial by jury, 169
types of cases, 267
See also federal courts; juvenile courts; state courts; Supreme Court, U.S.

covered wagons, 322*p*
Cox, Archibald, 262
CPSC. *See* Consumer Product Safety Commission
credit, 411
credit unions, 466*c*, 467, 467*p*
crime, 525–526, 525*p*, 526*p*, 529
causes of, 539–540, 539*c*, 540*p*
fighting, 550–551
proble of, 536
types of, 537–538, 537*p*, 538*p*, 539*c*, 543*c*
criminal cases, 267
criminal justice system
arrests, 542–543, 546*c*–547*c*
correctional institutions, 548–549, 549*c*
pre-trial process, 543–545, 546*c*–547*c*
sentencing, 548
trials in the, 546–548, 546*c*–547*c*
criminal law, 525–526, 525*p*, 526*p*, 529
Crosby, Stephen, 683
***Crosby* v. *National Foreign Trade Council* (2000),** 683
cruel and unusual punishment, 169
Cuba, 260, 658*p*, 659
Cuban Americans, 654
Cuban Missile Crisis, 260, 659
culture, 14
currency. *See* money
Currier & Ives, 82*p*
Czech Republic, 661, 682*p*
Czechoslovakia, 661, 681

D

damages, 563, 563*p*
Davis, Gray, 300–301
Dean, Howard, 623
death penalty, 169, 550
debates
campaign contributions, 604
food labeling, 387
foreign policy, 656
government regulation of corporations, 435
illegal immigrants, 335
juveniles tried as adults, 557
privacy issues, 222
term limits, 286
debt
credit card, 405*c*
national, 449, 449*p*
Declaration of Independence, 582
creation of, 97–98, 98*p*
text of, 106–109
Declaration of Rights (Virginia), 162*p*
defendant, 267, 543, 544, 547, 562, 569, 571
Defense, Department of, 251, 252*c*, 647*c*, 652
defense attorney, 543
deficit budget, 448, 448*c*, 498, 499*c*
deflation, 489
Delaware
Electoral College electors, 636*m*
ratification of the Constitution and, 123*c*
state constitution, 296*m*
delegated powers, 126, 129
delegates, selecting, 608
delinquent, 552
Dell, Michael, 359*p*
Dell Computer, 359
demand, law of, 378–381, 380*c*
demand deposit, 462, 474
democracy
of ancient Greece and Rome, 91, 91*p*, 92
definition of, 48
global, 676

influences on, 91–93, 93*c*
spread of, 647
See also direct democracy
Democratic Party, 219*p,* 247
balance of power and, 601*p*
characteristics of, 597–600, 598*c*
history of, 595
national convention, 588*p*
platform of, 610
symbol of, 595
use of Internet, 623
voter loyalty and, 602–603
Democratic-Republican Party, 595
demography, 4
deposition, 570
Des Moines, Iowa, 174–175, 174*p*
détente, 660
deterrence, 648
developed nations, 676, 677
developing nations, 676, 677
Dickinson, John, 100*p*
dictatorship, 47. *See also* communism
diplomacy, 649
direct democracy, 91, 322
direct expenditures, 502
direct mail, 623, 624–625
direct primary, 606
direct purchases, 500, 500*p*
direct tax, 495
discovery, evidence, 570
discrimination, 14, 200–201, 432
diseases, 16
disposable income, 405
dispositional hearing, 554
distribution, 353
district attorney, 543
district courts, 271, 572–573, 572*c*
diversion programs, 555
divorce, 566
DNA tests, 169
Doctors Without Borders, 684, 690
Dole, Elizabeth, 592*p*
domestic policy, 245
domestic relations cases, 566
double jeopardy, 168, 270
Douglas, William O., 286, 286*p*
Downer, Alexander, 649*p*
Draco, 522
draconian, 522
Dred Scott case, 188, 188*p,* 196, 285
driver's license, 312
Driver's Privacy Protection Act, 312
drug use and abuse, 538, 539
drunk driving, 529
due process of law, 168, 169, 404

E

earned income, 403
earthquakes, 684
East, migration from the, 5
East Germany, 660*p,* 661
Eastern Europe, 661, 664, 681, 682
Eckhardt, Christopher, 174–175, 174*p*
economic activity
circular flow, 376–377, 378*c*–379*c,* 484–486, 484*c*–485*c,* 486*p*
government and, 433
Economic and Social Council, United Nations, 688
economic choices, 355, 356, 357, 375, 405
See also financial choices
economic decisions, 358, 360–361
in economic systems, 366*p*
goals and values, 361

producing goods and services, 359–360
economic development, 676–677, 677*p*
economic freedom, 42–44, 42*c,* 430
economic growth, 489, 489*p,* 504
Economic Report of the President, 500
economic resources, 484
economic stabilization, 440–442, 498, 498*c,* 500
economic systems
command economies, 365–366
market economies, 366–367, 366*p,* 367*c*
mixed economy, 368–369
traditional economies, 363–364, 363*p,* 364*p*
economics
budgets and, 498–499, 499*c*
business ownership, 384–385, 384*c*
capital, 352
census and, 129
circular flow, 376–377, 378*c*–379*c,* 484–486, 484*c*–485*c,* 486*p*
civics and, 5, 74, 167, 199, 217, 251, 279, 337, 377, 414, 432, 464, 486, 525, 545, 578, 607, 634, 654, 684
consumption, 353, 353*p,* 354
deflation, 489
distribution, 353
entitlement programs, 501
factors of production, 351–352, 383, 383*c*
full employment, 482–483
gross domestic product, 487–488, 488*c,* 489
inflation, 443–444, 489, 499
labor, 351
land, 352
local government spending, 502–503
market price, 381
national debt, 501, 501*c*
national income accounting, 487–488, 487*c,* 488*c*
price stability, 482–483, 489
production to consumption, 352–354, 352*p,* 353, 353*p*
profit, 382
scarcity, 356
spending policies, 497–498, 497*p,* 500–501, 500*p,* 501*c*
state budgets and, 309
state government spending, 502–503, 503*p*
supply and demand, 378–381, 380*c*
tax cuts and, 504
values and goals, 430–431
wants, 350–351, 351*p,* 353
economy
after Revolutionary War, 100–101
agriculture and, 352
business cycle, 440–442
careers and the, 416
characteristics of, 42
Constitution and, 430
definition of, 41
fairness and the, 44
goods and services, 41, 44
government intervention in, 431–434, 431*p,* 432*p,* 433*p,* 434*p*
gross domestic product, 444, 444*c*
inflation, 443–444, 489, 499
labor and the, 388–395
minimum wage law, 229–233, 229*p,* 231*c,* 231*p,* 232*p,* 233*p*
monetary policy, 444
money supply and the, 475
national debt, 449, 449*p*
recession, 475
service sector, 395
as a social institution, 32–33, 32*p*
Edelman, Marian, 247*p*
editorials, 50, 362
education, 28*p*
Brown v. *Board of Education of Topeka,* 198–199, 198*p,* 530
citizenship and, 63*c,* 64
equality in, 22*p*

exit exams, 328
Grutter v. *Bollinger* (2003), 200, 200*p*
local government expenditures and, 328, 503
need for, 38
No Child Left Behind Act (2002), 338*c*–339*c*, 339
occupations and, 38*c*
Puritans and, 87
Regents of the University of California v. *Bakke* (1978), 200–201
school voucher programs, 40
as a social institution, 32–33, 32*p*, 38–39
state government and, 308, 328
Education, Department of, 252*c*
Eighteenth Amendment, 187*c*, 523
Eighth Amendment, 162*c*–163*c*, 169
Eisenhower, Dwight D., 239, 284*c*
elastic clause, 220
Eldred, Eric, 439
Eldred v. *Ashcroft* (2003), 439
elections, 117–118
of 1800, 635
of 1912, 596
of 1932, 596
of 1960, 629*p*
of 1976, 635
of 1980, 632, 635
of 1992, 597, 635*p*
of 1996, 597
of 1998, 634
of 2000, 597, 603, 618–619, 620, 621, 623, 637
of 2002, 617, 635
citizens and, 66
general, 616–619, 617*p*, 618*c*, 619*p*
opinion polls, 628
primary, 606, 617
reported by the media, 627–629, 628*p*, 629*p*
winning, 635
See also campaigns; voting
Electoral College, 117, 636–637, 636*m*, 637*p*
electors, 636
electric services, 330
Eleventh Amendment, 187*c*
Elizabeth II, Queen of England, 48*p*
Elkin Act (1903), 234
Ellis Island, 16
embezzlement, 537
eminent domain, 167
empires, 86*m*–87*m*
employment
age and, 42*c*
discrimination and, 432
employers and, 420–421
full, 482–483
Employment Act (1946), 482–483, 483*p*
Energy, Department of, 252*c*
England
Bill of Rights, 93
colonial government and, 84–87, 85*p*, 86*m*–87*m*
French and Indian War, 95
immigrants from, 11, 12*c*, 12*m*
laws from, 519–520
Magna Carta, 92, 92*p*, 93
mayor-council plan, 324
Parliament, 93, 95, 96
revolt against, 95–98, 95*p*, 96*p*, 97*p*, 98*p*
trade and, 100
See also Great Britain
English language, 204
Enron Corporation, 435
entitlement programs, 501
entrepreneurship, 367*c*, 382–384, 382*p*
environmental laws, 432, 432*p*, 434*p*, 442, 442*p*, 515*p*

Environmental Protection Agency (EPA), 253, 432*p*, 442, 442*p*
EOP. *See* Executive Office of the President
EPA. *See* Environmental Protection Agency
equal opportunity, value of, 20
Equal Pay Act (1963), 21
equal protection, 197, 201, 203
Equal Rights Amendment, 194*p*
equality, value of, 19, 23*c*
affirmative action and, 199*p*, 200*p*, 201–202
in education, 22*p*
segregation and, 197–199, 197*p*, 198*p*
women and, 201–202, 201*p*
in the work place, 21
equity, 563, 564, 567, 571
Ethiopia, 682
ethnic groups, 8
European Americans, 11–13, 12*c*, 12*m*, 16, 76*c*
European Union, 663, 683
evidence, obtaining, 570, 572
ex post facto laws, 221
excise tax, 302, 448
exclusion laws, 16
executive agencies, 253
executive agreements, 244
executive branch, 112, 114, 240–247
appointments to, 243
checks and balances, 130*c*
creation of, 94
executive departments, 251–253, 252*c*
Executive Office of the President, 249–251, 250*c*
foreign policy and, 651–652, 651*p*, 652*p*
independent agencies of, 253–254, 253*p*, 254*p*
organization of, 249–254, 250*c*, 252*c*
political parties and, 591
powers of, 126, 126*p*
purpose of, 117
state constitutions and, 99
Supreme Court and, 284, 284*c*
See also President, U.S.
executive departments, 251–253, 252*c*
Executive Office of the President (EOP), 249–251, 250*c*
executive orders, 243
executive privilege, 256, 258
expansion policy, 658

F

factors of production, 351–352, 383, 383*c*
Fair Labor Standards Act (1938), 217, 229, 390, 438
Fair Minimum Wage Act (1998), 233
faith-based social services, 180
family
child custody, 566, 573
domestic relations cases, 566
rules and, 35
as a social institution, 32–33, 32*p*, 35
structure of, 34, 34*p*, 35*c*
farming, 5, 356–357, 356*p*
FBI. *See* Federal Bureau of Investigation
FCC. *See* Federal Communications Commission
FDIC. *See* Federal Deposit Insurance Corporation
federal budget, 445, 445*c*, 448, 448*c*
Federal Bureau of Investigation (FBI), 249*p*, 340, 536
Federal Communications Commission (FCC), 253
federal court
Congress and, 220
judges of, 274
organization of, 271–274, 273*m*, 289
role of, 266–270, 266*p*, 267*p*, 268*p*, 269*c*
special, 273
state courts and, 269–270, 269*c*
types of cases in, 270

Federal Deposit Insurance Corporation (FDIC), 254*p*, 470
Federal Election Commission, 634
Federal Emergency Management Agency (FEMA), 46*p*
federal funds, 303
federal government
    budgets and the, 498–499, 499*c*
    in circular flow, 485
    economic regulations, 433–434
    fiscal policy, 441–442
    income, 446–448, 446*c*–447*c*, 448*c*
    local government and, 333, 338*c*, 339–341
    monetary policy, 444
    national debt, 501, 501*c*
    spending policies, 500–501, 500*p*, 501*c*
    tax revenues and, 497–498
federal law, 128, 310, 519
Federal Reserve, 507
Federal Reserve Act, 234
Federal Reserve Board, 470
Federal Reserve System
    bonds, 474
    control of money supply, 474
    discount rate, 474
    districts, 470, 471*m*
    functions of, 470–474
    history of, 469, 469*p*
    loans to banks, 474
    monetary policy, 441
    organization of, 470
    regulation of banks, 473
federal statute, 519
Federal Trade Commission, 437
federalism, 129, 295–297, 313
The Federalist, 114, 122, 281
Federalists, 120, 121, 160, 595. *See also* Anti-Federalists
Feingold, Russell, 125*p*
felony, 526, 544
FEMA. *See* Federal Emergency Management Agency
Fifteenth Amendment, 187*c*, 190, 194, 617
Fifth Amendment, 162*c*–163*c*, 166, 167, 168
filibuster, 231, 231*p*
Fillmore, Millard, 250*c*, 284*c*
financial choices, 405
    insurance, 415, 415*c*
    savings decisions, 412–414, 413*c*
    spending decisions, 409–411, 411*c*
    See also economic choices
financial institutions, 466*c*, 467. *See also* banks and banking
fire codes, 329
fire department, 329, 329*p*
First Amendment, 162*c*–163*c*, 163, 164, 165, 268, 439
    court cases about, 173–178
    PACs and, 625
First Continental Congress, 96
fiscal policy, 441–442
fixed expenses, 406, 406*p*
flags, 670*p*
floor leaders, 225, 591
Florida, 321*p*
    2000 election in, 618–619, 620, 621
    congressional representatives, 216*c*
    education in, 328
    Electoral College electors, 636*m*
    Gideon v. *Wainwright* (1963), 544
    Hispanic Americans in, 14
    prison population, 549*c*
    state constitution, 296*m*
    in the Sunbelt, 5
Food and Drug Administration (FDA), 438
food safety, 387
Ford, Gerald, 250*c*, 250*p*, 284*c*, 635
Ford, Henry, 360*p*
foreign aid, 649, 649*p*, 684

foreign policy, 244, 251
    businesses and, 654, 654*p*
    challenges to, 663–665
    containment, 659
    creating, 651–655
    debates regarding, 656
    definition of, 646
    détente, 660
    expansion policy, 658
    goals of, 646–647, 647*c*
    isolationism, 657, 658, 659
    terrorism, 665, 669*p*
    tools of, 648–650, 648*m*, 648*p*, 649*p*, 650*p*
foreign service officers, 652
Foreman, Michele, 39*p*
foster care, 34
Fourteenth Amendment, 187*c*, 189, 194, 197–198, 404, 617
Fourth Amendment, 162*c*–163*c*, 166, 167
fractional reserve banking, 466
France, 658
    colonies of, 86*m*–87*m*
    French and Indian War, 95
    immigrants from, 12, 12*c*, 12*m*
    in United Nations, 687
Franklin, Benjamin
    Constitutional Convention, 111, 118, 123
    Declaration of Independence and, 97
    letter of, 119
Franklin, Shirley, 340, 340*p*, 498*p*
free enterprise, 367, 369
    business cycle, 440–442
    common good and, 431
    supply and demand, 378–381, 380*c*
freedoms
    protecting, 515
    value of, 21, 23*c*
French and Indian War, 95
fringe benefits, 404
fundraising, 625, 625*c*, 634

G

gambling, 538
garbage collection, 330
Garfield, James A., 250*c*, 284*c*
Garner, James A., 336*p*
gas services, 330
GDP. *See* gross domestic product
General Assembly, United Nations, 687
general welfare, 218
genetic modification, 387
George, King of England, 126
Georgia, 498*p*
    Electoral College electors, 636*m*
    ratification of the Constitution and, 123*c*
    state constitution, 296*m*
    in the Sunbelt, 5
Germany, 660*p*, 661
    government of, 47
    immigrants from, 12, 12*c*, 12*m*
Gerry, Elbridge, 117
Gideon, Clarence, 544, 544*p*
***Gideon* v. *Wainwright* (1963),** 544
Ginsburg, Ruth Bader, 243*p*, 272*p*, 278, 284, 439
global democracy, 676
goals and values, 361
    careers and, 418
    financial choices and, 405
gold, 16, 461, 461*p*, 470
Goldberg, Jack, 404
***Goldberg* v. *Kelly* (1970),** 404
Golding, William, 511
Gompers, Samuel, 390

Goode, Wilson, 345
goods, 41, 44
    circular flow of economic activity and, 376–377, 378c–379c
goods and services, 359–360
Gorbachev, Mikhail, 660
Gore, Al, 597, 620, 623, 637, 637p
government
    of ancient Greece and Rome, 91, 91p, 92
    circular flow, 484–486, 484c–485c, 486p
    crimes against, 538
    forms of, 47–48, 48p
    goals of, 124–125
    influences on, 67, 91–93, 93c
    limited, 129–131, 130c
    role of, 45–46, 45p, 46p
    rules of, 48
    running for office, 66, 74
    as a social institution, 32–33, 32p
    trade and, 95, 95p
government agencies, 521
government corporations, 254
governors
    budgets of, 301, 306
    colonial, 84, 85
    judges and, 307, 311
    legislatures and, 301
    length of term, 99
    roles of, 305–307
grand jury, 168, 545
Grant, Ulysses S., 284c
grants, 333, 340
Great Britain, 658
    government of, 48, 48p
    in United Nations, 687
    See also England
Great Compromise, 115p, 116–117
Great Depression, 450, 482
Greece, 522
    government of, 91, 93c
    immigrants from, 12, 12c, 12m
Green Party, 597, 599c
Greenspan, Alan, 470, 474, 474p, 507
gross domestic product, 444, 444c
gross domestic product (GDP), 487–488, 488c, 489, 499, 499c, 500
groups, 30–31, 30p, 31p, 33. See also social institutions
Grutter, Barbara, 200, 200p
Grutter v. Bollinger (2003), 200, 200p
Guardian Angels, 550p
gun ownership, 166

H

halfway houses, 551
Hamilton, Alexander, 88, 89p, 114, 122, 595, 595p
Hammurabi, 522, 522p
Hanna, Mark, 600, 600p
Harding, Warren G., 250c, 284c
Harrison, Benjamin, 284c
Harrison, William Henry, 250c, 284c
Hastert, Dennis, 213p
Hatch, Orrin, 231, 231p
Havel, Vaclav, 682p
Hawaii, 658
    Electoral College electors, 636m
    state constitution, 296m
Hayes, Rutherford B., 284c
health
    services, 328
    state government and, 308
Health and Human Resources, Department of, 252c
health insurance, 414, 415, 415c

hearings, 554
Henry, Patrick, 85, 85p, 97, 122
high schools, 328
highways, 129p
Hispanic Americans, 12c, 12m, 14, 14p
    affirmative action and, 199
    in Congress, 237c
    population, 17
Hitler, Adolf, 47
Holland, 86m–87m
Holmes, Oliver Wendell, 177, 178
Homeland Security, Department of, 252c, 253, 650, 650p
homicide, 537
Hoover, Herbert, 241p, 284c
hopper, 225, 225p
House of Representatives, U.S., 114, 116, 223p
    amendment process, 160–161, 161c
    benefits, 217
    bills become laws, 225–226, 227c, 229–233
    congressional districts and, 215–216, 216c
    Constitution and, 125–126
    International Relations Committee, 653
    requirements, 217
    salaries, 217
    Speaker of the House, 224
    taxes and, 219
    See also Congress, U.S.; legislative branch
housing, 4–5, 4p, 252c, 566, 566p
Housing and Urban Development, Department of, 252c
Hughes, Charles Evans, 276
human rights, 647, 656
Humphrey, Hubert, 597
hung jury, 547
Hungary, 661, 681
Hussein, Saddam, 47

I

Iceland, 652, 654, 655
Idaho
    Electoral College electors, 636m
    state constitution, 296m
Illinois
    congressional representatives, 216
    death penalty in, 169
    Electoral College electors, 636m
    Skokie case, 175–178, 175p
    state constitution, 296m
    state government in, 338
immigrants, 10–11, 10p
    diversity and, 13
    European Americans, 11–13, 12c, 12m
    Hispanic Americans, 12c, 12m, 14, 14p
    illegal, 335
    naturalization process, 54p, 56–57, 57c
    population, 76c, 335
    time line, 16
impeachment, 131, 220, 282, 301
income, 402
    disposable, 405
    earned, 403
    of federal government, 446–448, 446c–447c, 448c
    fringe benefits, 404
    from savings, 412, 413c
    stock dividends, 404, 412, 413c, 414
    types of, 403c
income tax, 302, 332, 333c, 377, 446–447, 446c–447c, 486, 493–494, 494c, 499, 503
incumbents, 635
independent agencies, 253–254, 253p, 254p
Independent Party, 599c
independent voters, 603
India, 676p

Indiana
   Electoral College electors, 636*m*
   state constitution, 296*m*
indictment, 545
indirect tax, 495
industrial economy, 395
industrial unions, 393. *See also* labor unions
industrialization, 386, 389
inflation, 443–444, 489, 499
initiative, 300
injunction, 563
insurance, 414, 415, 415*c*
interest groups, 213, 624–625, 624*p*, 625*c*
interest payments, 377
intergovernmental revenue, 333
Interior, Department of the, 167, 252*c*
International Court of Justice, 689, 689*p*
International Whaling Commission, 651, 652, 655
Internet
   evaluating sources on, 275
   political campaigns and, 623
   privacy and, 222
   taxing purchases made on, 493
internment camps, 60
Interstate Commerce Act (1887), 234
Iowa
   caucus, 608
   Electoral College electors, 636*m*
   state constitution, 296*m*
   Tinker case, 174–175, 174*p*
Iran, 684
Iraq, 47
Iraq War, 219, 219*p*, 656, 671
Ireland, 11, 12*c*, 12*m*
isolationism, 657, 658, 659
Israel, 664, 685
Italy, 12, 12*c*, 12*m*
item veto, 307

J

Jackson, Andrew, 284*c*, 568, 568*p*
Jackson-Lee, Shirley, 224*p*
Jamestown, Virginia, 361*p*
Japan, 658, 663
   farming in, 356–357, 356*p*
   government of, 48
   immigration from, 16
   World War II and, 219, 244, 659, 659*p*
Japanese Americans, 60
Jay, John, 113, 122
Jefferson, Thomas, 134, 257, 257*p*, 284*c*, 595, 595*p*, 635, 666
   and bicameral legislature, 116
   Declaration of Independence and, 97, 98, 98*p*, 113
Jeffords, Jim, 233, 233*p*, 601*p*
Jews, 12
job interviewing, 68
job-training programs, 551, 551*p*
John, King of England, 92, 92*p*
Johnson, Andrew, 220, 221*p*, 250*c*, 284*c*
Johnson, Lyndon B., 10, 250*c*, 284*c*
joint committees, 226
judges, 173
   appointment of, 278, 307, 310, 311
   civil laws and, 527–529, 527*p*
   decisions of, 519–520
   federal court, 274
   impeachment of, 220
   nomination of, 126, 127
   private, 576, 576*p*
   role of, 268
   state court, 311
   terms of service, 312

judicial action committee, 312
judicial activism, 283
judicial branch, 112, 114
   checks and balances, 130*c*
   creation of, 94
   federal courts, 266–270, 266*p*, 267*p*, 268*p*, 269*c*, 274
   powers of, 127
   purpose of, 117
   state levels, 310
   See also courts; Supreme Court, U.S.
judicial restraint, 283
judicial review, 276–277, 277
Judiciary Act (1789), 271, 277, 289
***The Jungle* (Sinclair),** 438
jurisdiction, 269–270
jury duty, 62, 63*c*
jury of peers, 62, 63*c*
jury trials, 169, 268, 268*p*, 271, 546–548, 546*c*–547*c*
   civil laws and, 527–529, 527*p*
   in civil trials, 570–571
Justice, Department of, 252*c*
justice, value of, 22, 23*c*
Justinian Code, 522
juvenile courts, 269–270, 552–554
juvenile justice system, 552–554, 554–555, 555*p*

K

Kalahari, Africa, 364*p*
Kansas
   Electoral College electors, 636*m*
   state constitution, 296*m*
Kazakhstan, 664
Keating-Owen Child Act (1916), 570
Kelly, John, 404
Kennedy, Anthony M., 183, 272*p*, 284
Kennedy, Edward, 230, 232, 233, 237
Kennedy, John F., 239, 250*c*, 260, 284*c*, 629*p*, 681
Kentucky
   elections in, 603
   Electoral College electors, 636*m*
   state constitution, 296*m*
   state senators, 298*p*
Kerry, John, 607*p*
Khrushchev, Nikita, 260
King, Martin Luther, Jr., 14, 21*p*, 184*p*, 207*p*
Korean War, 653*p*, 659, 682
Korematsu, Toyosaburo, 60
***Korematsu v. United States* (1944),** 60
Kulongoski, Ted, 602

L

labor, 351, 484
   changes in, 394–395
   circular flow of economic activity and, 376–377, 378*c*–379*c*
   as factor of production, 383, 383*c*
   women and, 394, 394*p*
Labor, Department of, 252*c*, 392
labor groups, 654, 654*p*
Labor Party, 599*c*
labor unions, 432
   accomplishments of, 394
   child labor, 388*p*, 389, 390, 431*p*
   collective bargaining and, 390
   history of, 389–390, 393–395, 393*c*, 394*p*, 396*c*, 396*c*
   methods of, 390–391, 391, 391*c*, 391*p*, 392, 392*p*
   See also industrial unions
land, 352, 484
   as factor of production, 383, 383*c*
land use, local government and, 331–332, 331*p*
Landrum-Griffin Act (1959), 393

Language, English, 204
larceny, 537, 543*c*
Latin America, 658, 664, 675
Latinos, 12*c*, 12*m*, 14, 14*p*
law, due process of, 168, 169, 404
law enforcement, 45*p*, 46
    USA Patriot Act and, 49
    See also criminal justice system; police
laws, 125
    changing, 48, 523
    citizens' duties and, 61, 62*c*
    civil, 527–529, 527*p*, 562–567
    civil cases, 564–567
    Congress and, 212–213
    courts and, 266
    criminal, 525–526, 525*p*, 526*p*, 529
    ex post facto, 221
    global democracy, 676
    of government agencies, 521
    how bills become, 225–226, 227*c*, 229–233, 300–301, 300*p*
    interpreting, 268
    kinds of, 524–529
    legal codes, 522
    legislative, 518–519
    local, 321
    morals and, 516
    organization of, 521–522
    property and, 514
    punishment and the, 48
    purpose of, 511, 512–516
    state and federal, 128
    state government and, 295
    survey about, 519
    See also Constitution, U.S.
Laws and Liberties of Massachusetts, 522
lawsuits, 562
lawyers, 543, 545, 548*p*, 573
League of Nations, 658
League of Women Voters, 620
legal codes, 522, 527
legislative branch, 112
    checks and balances, 130*c*
    creation of, 94
    laws made by the, 518–519
    number of representatives, 115–117, 116
    parts of, 114
    powers of, 125–126
    state constitutions and, 99
    See also Congress, U.S.; House of Representatives, U.S.; Senate, U.S.
legislatures, 84
    state, 298–303, 298*p*, 299*p*, 300*p*
Leland, Mickey, 14, 14*p*
lemon laws, 410
letters to the editor, 304
libel, 165
Libertarian Party, 599*c*
libraries
    local government and, 337*p*
    Supreme Court decisions regarding, 279
lieutenant governor, 309
limited government, 129–131, 130*c*
limited resources, 356–357, 356*p*
Lincoln, Abraham, 58, 240*p*, 250*c*, 284*c*, 596
liquidity, 412, 414
loans, 464–465, 465
lobbyists, 213
local government
    borrowing by, 333
    in circular flow, 485
    cities, 323–326, 323*p*, 324*c*, 325*p*
    direct expenditures, 502
    economic regulations, 433–434
    education and, 328
    federal government and, 338*c*, 339–341
    federalism and, 295–297
    health and welfare services, 328
    intergovernmental revenue, 333
    land use and, 331–332, 331*p*
    laws and, 319, 519
    policy decisions in, 327
    political parties and, 592–593
    public policy, 294–292
    public safety and, 329, 329*p*
    relations between, 336–337
    revenues, 332–334, 333*c*
    service charges, 333
    services of, 327–332, 333*c*
    special districts, 323
    spending by, 502–503
    state government and, 337–338, 338*c*, 339–341
    taxes and, 332, 333*c*, 486, 502–503
    types of, 320–326
    utilites and, 330, 330*p*, 333
Locke, John, 93*c*, 94, 94*p*, 97, 131
lockouts, 391, 391*c*, 392
Lord of the Flies **(Golding),** 511
Los Angeles, California, 331*p*
lottery tickets, 302
Louisiana, 129*p*
    Electoral College electors, 636*m*
    Hispanic Americans in, 14
    state constitution, 296*m*
Louisiana Purchase, 257, 257*p*, 666
Louisiana Territory, 257

M

Madison, James, 122, 134, 160, 277, 284*c*
    Bill of Rights and, 160–162
    Constitutional Convention, 111, 114–115, 114*p*
    Ninth Amendment and, 170
    as Secretary of State, 257
Magna Carta, 92, 92*p*, 93, 93*c*, 162
Maine
    Electoral College electors, 636*m*
    prison population, 549*c*
    state constitution, 296*m*
majority opinion, 280
majority party, 224, 591
mandatory sentencing, 550
Mandela, Nelson, 685
manslaughter, 537
manufacturing sector, 395, 418*c*–419*c*
Marbury, William, 277
Marbury* v. *Madison, 277
March on Washington, 184*p*, 207*p*
market, 42
market economy, 366–367, 366*p*, 367*c*
    principles of, 376–381
    rules for, 483
market price, 381
market sector, 485
markets, 366
Marshall, John, 277, 277*p*
Marshall, Thurgood, 198–199, 278, 278*p*, 554, 554*p*
Marshall Plan, 656
Maryland
    death penalty in, 169
    Electoral College electors, 636*m*
    ratification of the Constitution and, 123*c*
    state constitution, 296*m*
Mason, George, 162*p*
Massachusetts
    Big Dig, 340*p*
    Electoral College electors, 636*m*

farming in, 5
ratification of the Constitution and, 123*c*
revolt against England, 97
Shays' Rebellion, 100–101, 101*p*
state constitution, 296*m*
Massachusetts Bay Colony, 88
Mayflower Compact, 83, 99
Mayflower (**ship**), 83, 88, 99
mayor-council plan, 324–325, 324*c*
McCain, John, 125*p*, 634*p*
McCulloch **v.** *Maryland* (**1819**), 570
McGovern, George, 282
McKinley, William, 250*c*, 284*c*
Meat Inspection Act, 234
media
campaigns use of, 624, 632–633
election reporting by the, 627–629, 628*p*, 629*p*
violence in the, 540, 540*p*
mediation, 575, 576*p*
Medicaid, 501
Medicare, 501
melting pot, 11
Menino, Thomas M., 336*p*
Mexico, 658, 673*p*, 683
Michigan
Electoral College electors, 636*m*
prison population, 549*c*
state constitution, 296*m*
Middle East, 663, 664, 675, 685
Midler, Bette, 67*p*
migration, 5
military
President and, 242*p*, 244
serving in the, 61, 61*p*, 62*c*
See also Defense, Department of
Milosevic, Slobodan, 689*p*
minimum wage law, 217, 218, 225, 229–233, 229*p*, 231*c*, 231*p*, 232*p*, 233*p*, 237, 394
Minimum Wage Restoration Act, 230
Minnesota
Electoral College electors, 636*m*
state constitution, 296*m*
minority party, 224, 591
Miranda **v.** *Arizona,* 283, 530
Miranda warning, 168, 168*p*, 542
misdemeanor, 526, 544, 548
Mississippi
congressional representatives, 216*c*
Electoral College electors, 636*m*
state constitution, 296*m*
Missouri
Electoral College electors, 636*m*
First Amendment laws in, 268
state constitution, 296*m*
Missouri Compromise, 188, 189*m*
Missouri Plan, 311
mixed economy, 368–369, 485
mock trials, 577, 577*p*
monarchy, 47, 48*p*, 84, 257
monetary policy, 441, 444
money, 42
characteristics of, 458–459, 458*p*, 459*p*
circular flow of economic activity and, 376–377, 378*c*–379*c*
counterfeit, 455
facts about, 455
functions of, 456–457, 456*p*, 457*p*
kinds of, 462–463, 462*p*, 463*c*
regulating supply of, 441
supply of, 474, 475
value of, 459
See also capital

money management
budgeting, 406–406
financial choices, 405–407
income, 402–405, 403*c*
money supply, 462–463, 463*c*
monopolies
controlling, 437
definition of, 436
legal, 437
Monroe, James, 284*c*, 657, 657*p*
Monroe Doctrine, 657, 658
Montana
Electoral College electors, 636*m*
state constitution, 296*m*
taxes in, 496
Montesquieu, Baron de, 93*c*, 94, 99, 112, 131
Montreal Protocol, 687
morals, 516, 519
motor voter registration, 617, 617*p*
movement, 5
Muhlenberg, Frederick, 224*p*
municipal courts, 269–270
municipality, 323
Mural Arts Program, 345
murder, 537, 543*c*
mutual funds, 413, 413*c*
mutual savings banks, 466*c*, 467
Myanmar, 683

N

NAACP. *See* National Association for the Advancement of Colored People
Nader, Ralph, 597
NAFTA. *See* North American Free Trade Agreement
Napoleon, 257
NASA. *See* National Aeronautics and Space Administration
Nast, Thomas, 325*p*
National Aeronautics and Space Administration (NASA), 253, 253*p*, 256
National Association for the Advancement of Colored People (NAACP), 198
National Constitution Center, 110*p*
national convention, 161, 588*p*, 600
delegates at, 608, 608*p*
purpose of, 609, 609*p*
national debt, 501, 501*c*
National Foreign Trade Council, 683
national government, 99, 115
concurrent powers, 129
federalism and, 129, 295–297
powers of, 127*c*, 297
reserved powers, 129
shared powers, 127*c*, 295
state government and, 296
National Guard, 305
national income accounting, 487–488, 487*c*, 488*c*
National Labor Relations Act (1935), 393, 438
national security, 646
National Security Council (NSC), 251, 251*p*, 645, 652
nationalism, 673
nations
characteristics of, 673
competition among, 680
conflicts and, 679, 680*c*, 681–682
cooperation among, 683–685, 683*p*, 684*p*, 685*p*
definition of, 672
economic development in, 676–677, 677*p*
histories of, 673–675
United Nations, 686–689, 687*p*, 688*p*, 689*p*, 691
Native Americans
affirmative action and, 199

colonial rule and, 674
disease and, 16
Europeans and, 16
population of, 15*c*
NATO. *See* North Atlantic Treaty Organization
natural disasters, 46, 46*p*
natural rights, 94
naturalization process, 54*p*, 56–57, 57*c*
Nazi Party, 175–178, 175*p*
Nebraska
    Electoral College electors, 636*m*
    state constitution, 296*m*
    state legislature, 299
neighborhood watch programs, 534*p*, 550, 550*p*
neutrality, 657
Nevada
    education in, 328
    Electoral College electors, 636*m*
    state constitution, 296*m*
New Deal, 246, 440, 440*p*, 450
New England, 4*p*, 322, 322*p*
New Hampshire
    Electoral College electors, 636*m*
    primaries in, 608
    prison population, 549*c*
    ratification of the Constitution and, 123*c*
    state constitution, 296*m*
New Jersey
    conservation in, 293
    at Constitutional Convention, 115
    Electoral College electors, 636*m*
    ratification of the Constitution and, 123*c*
    state constitution, 296*m*
New Jersey Plan, 115–117
New Mexico
    Electoral College electors, 636*m*
    Hispanic Americans in, 14
    housing in, 4*p*
    state constitution, 296*m*
New York, 318*p*
    Electoral College electors, 636*m*
    health agencies, 308
    laws of, 127
    prison population, 549*c*
    ratification of the Constitution and, 123*c*
    state constitution, 296*m*
    Zenger trial, 88–89, 89*p*
New York City, 195*p*
news programs, 517
newspapers, 50, 362, 568
NGOs. *See* nongovernmental organizations
Nicaragua, 682
Nineteenth Amendment, 187*c*, 192, 617
Ninth Amendment, 162*c*–163*c*, 170
Nixon, Richard M., 242*p*, 250*c*, 250*p*, 284*c*, 597, 629*p*
    Watergate scandal and, 258, 258*p*, 262, 282, 282*p*
No Child Left Behind Act (2002), 338*c*–339*c*, 339
no-fault insurance, 580
Noble Order of the Knights of Labor, 390
nongovernmental organizations, 690
nonpartisan, 591
Norman conquest, 322*p*
North, migration from, 5
North American Free Trade Agreement (NAFTA), 654*p*, 683
North Atlantic Treaty Organization (NATO), 648, 648*m*, 661, 681, 691, 692*m*
North Carolina
    Electoral College electors, 636*m*
    ratification of the Constitution and, 123*c*
    state constitution, 296*m*
North Dakota
    Electoral College electors, 636*m*

prison population, 549*c*
state constitution, 296*m*
North Korea, 664*p*, 680, 682, 684
NSC. *See* National Security Council
nuclear weapons, 653, 671, 684, 692*m*

O

OAS. *See* Organization of American States
Occupational Outlook Handbook, 420, 420*p*
Occupational Safety and Health Administration (OSHA), 438, 438*p*
O'Connor, Sandra Day, 272*p*, 278, 279*p*, 284
Office of Management and Budget (OMB), 251
Ohio
    Electoral College electors, 636*m*
    state constitution, 296*m*
Oklahoma
    Electoral College electors, 636*m*
    state constitution, 296*m*
Oklahoma City, Oklahoma, 538
older Americans, 6
OMB. *See* Office of Management and Budget
O'Neill, Tip, 634
open primary, 606
opinion polls, 280, 628
opportunity cost, 356
ordinances, 321, 519
Oregon
    court cases and, 313
    elections in, 624
    Electoral College electors, 636*m*
    state constitution, 296*m*
    taxes in, 503*p*
Organization for Economic Cooperation and Development (OECD), 648
Organization of African Unity, 683, 691
Organization of American States (OAS), 648, 683
original jurisdiction, 269–270, 270, 271, 273, 279
Ottoman Empire, 86*m*–87*m*

P

PACs. *See* political action committees
Paine, Thomas, 97, 97*p*
Palau, 689
Palestinians, 664, 685
Papua New Guinea, 689
pardons, 246
Parliament, 93, 95, 96, 519–520
parole, 548, 549*p*
partnerships, business, 384–385, 384*c*
passport, 59*p*
Pataki, George, 603*p*
patents, 514
Paterson, William, 115
Patriot Act (2002), 570
patriotism, 49
patronage, 601
peace, 647, 684
peace Corps, 655*p*
peacekeepers, United Nations, 687, 691*p*
Pearl Harbor, 659, 659*p*
Pelosi, Nancy, 214*p*
Penn, William, 322*p*
Pennsylvania, 66*p*
    Electoral College electors, 636*m*
    ratification of the Constitution and, 123*c*
    state constitution, 296*m*
Pentagon, 538
People's Republic of China, 368
Perot, Ross, 597

personal injury cases, 573
personal recognizance, 544
petition, freedom of, 165, 300
Philadelphia, 110*p*, 337, 345
    Constitutional Convention, 111, 113–114, 113*p*
    First Continental Congress, 96
Phillips, Ida, 202
Phillips v. *Martin Marietta Corporation* (1971), 202
photographs, 195*p*
Pierce, Franklin, 284*c*
Pilgrims, 88
plaintiff, 267, 562, 569, 571, 573
planks, 591
planning commission, 331–332
platforms, party, 591, 609, 610
plea bargaining, 545
Pledge of Allegiance, 49, 55
Plessy, Homer, 198
Plessy v. *Ferguson* (1896), 197–198, 199
pocket veto, 228
point of view, 50, 166*p*
Poland, 661, 681
police, 45*p*, 46, 329, 510*p*
    crime and, 540
    See also criminal justice system; law enforcement
policy making, 327
political action committees (PACs), 624–625, 624*p*, 625*c*, 634
political cartoons, 20*p*, 47*p*, 65*p*, 96*p*, 121*p*, 166*p*, 190*p*, 226*p*,
    246*p*, 277*p*, 299*p*, 325*p*, 365*p*, 392*p*, 412*p*, 437*p*, 456*p*, 496*p*,
    514*p*, 538*p*, 565*p*, 606*p*, 613*p*, 627*p*, 653*p*, 688*p*
political parties, 247
    campaigns and, 601, 634
    candidates and, 591, 591*p*, 605–609, 607*p*, 608*p*, 609*p*
    changes in, 601–603
    citizens and, 592–594
    Congress and, 213
    definition of, 590
    executive branch and, 591
    history of, 595–596
    identification with, 602*c*
    lawmaking and, 213
    local government and, 592–593
    national convention, 600, 609, 609*p*
    patronage, 601
    platforms, 609, 610
    role of, 590–594
    supporting, 600
    third parties, 596–597, 599*c*
    two-party system, 595–603
    voter loyalty and, 602
    voting and, 602–603
    See also Democratic Party; Republican Party
political socialization, 49
Polk, James K., 239, 284*c*
poll tax, 190, 190*p*
polling place, 614*p*, 617–618, 618*p*
population, 24*c*, 255
    African Americans, 15*c*, 17
    ages of Americans, 6–7
    Asian Americans, 15*c*
    baby boomers, 7
    census, 17, 129
    distribution of, 4
    districts and, 299
    diverse, 2*p*, 8, 10–11, 13, 17
    Hispanic Americans, 15*c*, 17
    immigrant, 76*c*, 335
    Native Americans, 15*c*
    prison, 525, 549, 549*c*
Portman, Christopher, 66*p*
Portugal, 86*m*–87*m*
Postal Service, U.S., 254

poverty, 539, 550
Powell, Colin, 66, 649*p*
pre-trial process, 543–545, 546*c*–547*c*
Preamble, 124–125, 218, 515
precedent, 268, 281
precincts, 599
preference primary, 608
preliminary hearings, 543
prepaid legal plans, 578
prescription drugs, 496
President, U.S.
    bills become laws, 225–226, 227*c*, 228
    budget and, 246, 251
    Cabinet, 253
    candidates for, 607–609, 607*p*
    as chief diplomat, 242*p*, 244
    as chief executive, 243
    as chief of state, 247
    as commander in chief, 242*p*, 244
    Congress and, 241, 243, 245, 255–256
    creating the office of, 240–241
    domestic policy, 245
    duties of, 240
    Economic Report, 500
    Electoral College and, 117, 636–637, 636*m*, 637*p*
    executive departments, 251–253, 252*c*
    Executive Office of the President, 249–251, 250*c*
    executive privilege, 256, 258
    foreign policy and, 244, 251, 651–652, 651*p*, 652*p*
    impeachment of, 131, 220, 282, 301
    independent agencies, 253–254, 253*p*, 254*p*
    judicial powers, 246, 274, 278, 284, 284*c*
    National Security Council, 645
    as party leader, 247
    powers of, 126, 126*p*, 241, 255–259, 255*p*, 257*p*, 258*p*, 259*p*
    qualifications of, 241
    role of, 242–247, 242*c*–243*c*, 244*c*, 245*p*, 246*p*
    salary of, 241
    State of the Union Address, 242*p*, 245
    Supreme Court and, 257, 258
    term of office, 128*p*, 241
    veto and, 228, 228*p*, 245
president pro tempore, 224, 225
press, freedom of the, 88–89, 89*p*, 164–165, 172, 173*p*
pretrial motions, 545
price, 42
    stability, 482–483, 489
primary elections, 606, 617
primary sources, 176, 183, 191, 257, 296
    appeals court, 571
    bias in, 556
    campaign brochures, 632
    Code of Hammurabi, 522, 522*p*
    Colin Powell, 66
    Koffi Annan speech, 689, 695
    Occupational Outlook Handbook, 420, 420*p*
prisons, 525, 548, 549, 549*c*
privacy issues, 222
private judges, 577, 577*p*
private sector, 485
probable cause, 542
probate cases, 567
probation, 554
product-liability cases, 579, 580
product safety, 432, 438
production, 352–354, 352*p*, 353, 353*p*
    technology and, 360, 360*p*
profit, 367, 382
Progressive Party, 596, 597
progressive tax, 493
Prohibition, 523, 523*p*
propaganda, 490, 490*p*, 626, 626*c*

Index

property, crimes against, 537
property cases, 564
property rights, 167, 514
property taxes, 321, 332, 333*c*, 486, 503
proportional tax, 493
prosecution, 267, 543
Protestants, 12
public assistance, 328, 440, 450
public defenders, 543
public documents, 119
public health, 328
public opinion, 248, 285, 517
public policy, 294–292
public safety, 329, 329*p*, 513, 513*p*
public sector, 485, 497
public utilities, 437
Puerto Rico, 214*p*
Pure Food and Drug Act (1906), 234
Puritans, 83, 87, 88

Q

Qing Empire, 86*m*–87*m*
quotas, 649

R

racism, 14, 22, 199
rape, 543*c*
ratification, 100, 120, 121*p*, 123, 123*c*, 128
reading skills
    analyze word parts, 184, 186, 190, 194, 491, 493, 496
    ask questions, 41, 428, 430, 434, 631, 637
    clarifying meaning, 2, 238, 400, 588
    comparison and contrast, 210, 229, 233, 318, 320, 325, 326, 510, 518, 523
    identify cause and effect, 91, 374, 388, 395, 560, 574, 581
    identify contrasts, 223, 512, 516, 670, 672, 677, 686
    identify implied main ideas, 69, 75, 298, 657, 665
    identify main idea, 54, 56, 58, 292, 294
    identify signal words, 212, 215, 217
    identify stated main idea, 644, 646, 650
    identify supporting details, 59, 67, 305, 310, 651, 655
    interpret nonliteral meanings, 120, 122, 271, 274, 460, 467
    make comparisons, 218, 221, 334, 336, 524, 529, 679
    paraphrasing, 18, 20, 23, 249, 253, 254, 409, 415, 595, 603
    predict, 34, 443, 449, 622
    preview, 41, 622, 631, 637
    read ahead, 4, 6, 8, 240, 245, 247, 402, 407, 590, 594
    reading process, 28
    recognize multiple causes, 84, 376, 381, 562, 567
    recognize word origins, 196, 198, 203, 480, 482, 483, 487, 489, 497, 503
    recognize words that signal sequence, 175, 350, 363, 542, 551, 552, 555
    recognizing cause and effect, 82
    rereading, 10, 11, 17, 255, 258, 259, 590, 594
    sequence, 158, 160, 162, 163, 170, 353
    set a purpose, 30, 614, 616, 621
    summarize, 416, 421, 605, 609
    support a point of view, 540
    understand effects, 95, 386, 569, 573
    understand sequence, 358, 534, 536
    use context clues, 110, 112, 124, 126, 264, 266, 270, 276, 285, 454, 456, 459, 469, 475
    use prior knowledge, 45, 436, 442
    use signal words, 327, 341
Reagan, Ronald, 284*c*, 285, 632, 635
recall, 300–301, 300*p*
recession, 440, 442, 448, 475
Red Cross, 690
referees, 577, 577*p*

referendum, 300
Reform Party, 597
Regents of the University of California v. *Bakke* **(1978),** 200–201
regressive tax, 494, 494*c*
regulatory commissions, 253
rehabilitation programs, 551, 551*p*
Rehnquist, William, 272*p*, 283, 283*p*
Reich, Robert, 257
religion, 12
    affiliation in the United States, 36, 36*c*
    conflicts regarding, 37
    as a social institution, 32–33, 32*p*, 37, 37*p*
        freedom of, 37, 46, 88, 164
Reno, Janet, 312, 312*p*
Reno, Nevada, 332, 332*p*
Reno v. *Condon* **(2000),** 312
representative democracy, 58, 248
representative government, 84, 94
republic, 91, 92, 124
Republican Party, 247
    balance of power and, 601*p*
    characteristics of, 597–600, 598*c*
    history of, 596
    platform of, 610
    symbol of, 596
    voter loyalty and, 602–603
reserved powers, 129
revenue, 302, 333*c*, 334
reverse discrimination, 200–201
Revolutionary War, 82*p*, 99, 166
    economy after the, 100–101
Reynolds v. *Sims* **(1964),** 299
Rhode Island
    Articles of Confederation and, 99
    Electoral College electors, 636*m*
    founding of, 88
    judges in, 312
    ratification of the Constitution and, 123*c*
    state constitution, 296*m*
Rice, Condoleeza, 652*p*
Richardson, Elliot, 262
Ridge, Tom, 650
robbery, 537, 543*c*
Roe v. *Wade,* 283
Romania, 681
Rome, 91, 91*p*, 92, 93*c*, 519, 522
Roosevelt, Franklin Delano, 128*p*, 242*p*, 246, 250*c*, 259, 284*c*, 286, 450, 450*p*, 596, 659*p*
Roosevelt, Theodore, 239, 250*c*, 284*c*, 596, 597
rule of law, 61
rules, 31, 512
    education and, 39
    family, 35
    government, 48
    religion and, 36
    See also laws
Rumsfeld, Donald, 652*p*
Russia, 658, 661
    colonies of, 86*m*–87*m*
    foreign aid to, 684
    immigrants from, 12, 12*c*, 12*m*
    in United Nations, 687
Rwanda, 664, 684, 689

S

sales taxes, 302, 332, 333*c*, 486, 491, 493, 503
Sanchez, Linda and Loretta, 213*p*
sanctions, 650
Saudi Arabia, 47
savings accounts, 464

savings-and-loan companies, 414, 466c, 467
savings plans, 412–414, 413c
scabs, 391, 391c
Scalia, Antonin, 272p, 284
scarcity, 356
school voucher programs, 40
Schwarzeneggar, Arnold, 301
Scotland, 11, 12c, 12m
Scott, Dred, 188, 188p
search and seizure, 167, 167p
search warrant, 167
Sears, Roebuck and Co., 386p
Seattle, Washington, 644
Second Amendment, 162c–163c, 166
Second Continental Congress, 97, 99
Secret Service, U.S., 455
Secretariat, United Nations, 688
Security Council, United Nations, 687
segregation, 197–199, 197p, 198p
select committees, 226
self-government, 84
self-nomination, 605
sellers, 378–381, 380c
Senate, U.S., 114, 116, 125p, 215, 216
    amendment process, 160–161, 161c
    benefits, 217
    bills become laws, 225–226, 227c, 229–233
    Constitution and, 125–126
    filibusters in, 231
    foreign policy and, 653
    Foreign Relations Committee, 653
    judicial appointments and, 274, 278, 285
    president pro tempore, 224, 225
    requirements, 217
    salaries, 217
    Vice President and, 224, 225
    See also Congress, U.S.; legislative branch
Seneca Falls Convention, 191
sentencing guidelines, 548, 550
separate but equal, 198–199, 530
separation of church and state, 164
separation of powers, 94, 99, 112, 129, 131, 241
September 11 attacks, 49, 166, 253, 297, 433p, 448, 538, 665
Serbia, 664
service charges, 333
service economy, 395
service learning, 7, 64, 202, 230, 256, 330, 502, 575
service sector, 6, 6c, 395, 418c–419c
services, 41, 44
    circular flow of economic activity and, 376–377, 378c–379c
    government, 46
Seventeenth Amendment, 187c
Seventh Amendment, 162c–163c, 169
shared powers, 127c, 295
Sharon, Ariel, 664
Shays, Daniel, 101, 101p
Shays' Rebellion, 100–101, 101p, 112
sheriff, 321, 321p
Sherman, Roger, 116, 117
Sherman Anti-Trust Act (1890), 234, 437
Sinclair, Upton, 438, 438p
sit-down strikes, 390, 391c, 392
Sixteenth Amendment, 187c
Sixth Amendment, 162c–163c, 169, 544
skateboarding, 327, 327p, 337
Skokie case, 175–178, 175p
slander, 164
slave trade, 115
    Constitutional Convention and, 115
    history of, 117p
    Three-Fifths Compromise and, 117
slaves and slavery, 14

abolishing, 186–189, 188p, 189m, 196
    Republican Party and, 596
    status of, 86
slowdowns, work, 390, 391c, 392
Small Business Job Protection Act (1996), 232
small claims court, 578
Smith, Gordon, 602
social institutions, 32–33, 33p
    See also groups
social roles, 69–70, 70c
    expected behaviors of, 71–72, 71c, 71p, 72p
    level of participation, 73
    volunteers, 73c, 74
    See also citizens
Social Security Act (1935), 7, 394, 440, 447, 450, 486, 501
social security tax, 446–447
social services, 180
    agency, 553
    illegal immigrants and, 335
socialization, 31
society
    education and, 38–39
    family and, 35
        religion and, 37, 37p
soldiers, housing of, 167
sole proprietorship, 384, 384c, 386
Somalia, 689
Souter, David, 272p, 284
South
    migration to, 5
    slavery in, 187–188, 189m
South Africa, 664, 685, 685p
South America, 364, 658
South Carolina
    Electoral College electors, 636m
    ratification of the Constitution and, 123c
    state constitution, 296m
South Dakota
    Electoral College electors, 636m
    state constitution, 296m
South Korea, 677, 677p, 682
sovereignty, 673
Soviet Union, 680
    Cold War, 681–682, 681p, 682p
    collapse of, 660–661, 682, 682p
    communism in, 659, 681
    in United Nations, 687
space program, 252, 253p
Spain, 14, 86m–87m, 658
Spanish-American War, 658p
Speaker of the House, 224
special districts, 323
speech
    court cases about free, 173–178
    freedom of, 37, 164, 172, 173p
    laws and free, 268
spending policies, 497–498, 497p
    federal, 500–501, 500p, 501c
Spitzer, Eliot, 603p
split ticket, 602, 603p
standard of living, 676, 677p, 688
standing committees, 225–226
State, Department of, 251, 252c, 652
state convention, 608
state court systems, 173, 310
    appeals court, 310
    federal courts and, 269–270, 269c
    federalism and, 313
    function of, 311
    judges in, 311
    supreme court, 270, 310
    trial courts, 310

state government, 115
    attorney general, 309
    budgets, 309
    in circular flow, 485
    comptroller, 309
    concurrent powers, 129
    constitutions, 99, 296*m*, 313
    direct expenditures, 502
    district boundaries and, 215
    economic regulations, 433–434
    education and, 308, 328
    executive agencies, 308
    executive branch, 305–309
    federal funds and, 303
    federalism and, 129, 295–297
    financing, 302–303, 302*c*, 303*p*
    impeachment and, 301
    judicial branch, 310
    laws and, 295, 300–301, 300*p*, 519
    legislatures, 298–303, 298*p*, 299*p*, 300*p*, 301
    local government and, 333, 337–338, 338*c*, 339–341
    national government and, 296
    powers of, 127, 127*c*, 170, 295, 296
    public policy, 294–292
    reserved powers, 129
    secretary of state, 309
    shared powers, 127*c*, 295
    spending by, 502–503, 503*p*
    taxes and, 486, 497, 502–503
    transportation agency, 308
    treasurer, 309
    U.S. Constitution and, 127
state law, 128, 310
State of the Union Address, 242*p*, 245
states' rights, 127, 161, 297
Statue of Freedom, 186*p*
status offender, 552
statutes, 519, 527
steel mills, 257
stele, 522, 522*p*
Stevens, John Paul, 272*p*
stock market, 42, 470, 507
    corporations and, 385
    dividends, 404, 412, 413*c*, 414
storefront law offices, 578–579, 579*p*
straight ticket, 602
strikebreakers, 391, 391*c*, 392
strikes, labor, 390, 391, 391*c*, 391*p*, 392
strong-mayor plan, 324–325
subpoena, 570
Sudan, 664
suffrage. *See* voting rights
suffragists, 190, 191, 191*p*, 192, 195, 195*p*
summit meeting, 649
summons, 569*p*
Sunbelt, 5
supervisors, county, 321
supply and demand, law of, 378–381, 380*c*, 436
Supreme Court, U.S., 158*p*, 264, 265, 272*p*, 273, 312, 313
    affirmative action and, 199–202, 200*p*
    appealing to the, 280*c*–281*c*
    appointments to the, 246, 278, 285
    changes in, 283
    checks and balances, 284
    Chief Justice, 279, 283
    creation of, 127
    death penalty and, 550
    Dred Scott case, 188, 188*p*, 196
    First Amendment cases, 173–178
    hearing arguments, 279
    influences on, 281–282
    judicial review, 276–277, 277

    President and, 257, 258, 284, 284*c*
    role of, 196–197
    segregation and, 197–199, 197*p*, 198*p*
    selecting cases, 279
    term limits debate, 286
    work of, 278–280
    writing opinions, 280
    See also judicial branch
Supreme Court cases
    Brown v. *Board of Education of Topeka,* 198–199, 198*p*, 268, 530
    Bush v. *Gore* (2000), 620
    Crosby v. *National Foreign Trade Council* (2000), 683
    Eldred v. *Ashcroft* (2003), 439
    Gideon v. *Wainwright* (1963), 544
    Goldberg v. *Kelly* (1970), 404
    Grutter v. *Bollinger* (2003), 200, 200*p*
    Korematsu v. *United States* (1944), 60
    Marbury v. *Madison,* 277
    McCulloch v. *Maryland* (1819), 570
    Miranda v. *Arizona,* 283, 530
    Phillips v. *Martin Marietta Corporation* (1971), 202
    Plessy v. *Ferguson* (1896), 197–198, 199
    Regents of the University of California v. *Bakke* (1978), 200–201
    Roe v. *Wade,* 283
    Skokie case, 175–178, 175*p*
    Tinker case, 174–175, 174*p*
    United States v. *Nixon* (1974), 282, 282*p*
surplus budget, 448, 448*c*, 499, 499*c*
surveys, 248

T

Taft, William Howard, 263, 284*c*, 597
Taft-Hartley Act (1947), 393
Tammany Hall, 325*p*
tariff, 448, 649
Tax Court, 273
tax revenues, 486
    budgets and, 498–499, 499*c*
    federal, 497–498
    local government, 502–503
    spending policies, 497–498, 497*p*
    state, 497, 502–503
taxes
    ability-to-pay principle, 493
    benefits-received principle, 492, 492*c*, 492*p*
    businesses and, 486, 496
    characteristics of good, 492, 492*c*
    citizenship and, 63*c*, 64
    colonists and, 95*p*, 96, 96*p*
    Congress and, 219
    cuts to, 500, 504
    direct and indirect, 495
    economic activity and, 433, 434
    effects of, 495–496, 496*p*
    excise, 302, 448
    fairness of, 491–493, 491*p*, 492*c*
    income, 302, 332, 333*c*, 377, 446–447, 446*c*–447*c*, 486, 493–494, 494*c*, 499, 503
    on Internet purchases, 493
    local, 332, 333*c*
    poll, 190, 190*p*
    progressive, 493
    property, 321, 332, 333*c*, 486, 503
    proportional, 493
    regressive, 494, 494*c*
    sales, 302, 332, 333*c*, 486, 491, 493, 503
    state, 302
Taylor, Zachary, 250*c*, 284*c*
tea, 95*p*

nnology, 360, 360*p*
    careers and, 417, 417*p*
television, 629, 629*p*
Tennessee
    Electoral College electors, 636*m*
    state constitution, 296*m*
Tenth Amendment, 162*c*–163*c*, 170, 170*p*, 295
terrorism, 166, 253, 538, 646, 646*p*, 650, 665, 669*p*
Texas
    Electoral College electors, 636*m*
    Hispanic Americans in, 14
    prison population, 549*c*
    state constitution, 296*m*
    in the Sunbelt, 5
Third Amendment, 162*c*–163*c*, 166, 167
third parties, 596–597, 599*c*
Thirteenth Amendment, 187*c*, 188, 194, 196, 617
Thomas, Clarence, 272*p*, 278, 284, 285
Three-Fifths Compromise, 117
Thurmond, Strom, 597
Tiananmen Square, 662
time deposits, 413, 413*c*
time lines
    banking, 470
    Cold War, 681
    foreign policy, 662–663
    immigration, 16
    labor unions, 390
    law, 570
    local government, 322
    political parties, 597
    voting, 192–193
    wars, 244
Tinker, Mary Beth, 174–175, 174*p*
Tinker case, 174–175, 174*p*
town clerk, 322
town meeting, 75*p*, 322
towns and townships, 320, 321, 322, 322*p*, 323
trade
    agreements, 649
    Crosby v. *National Foreign Trade Council* (2000), 683
    deficit, 654
    England and, 100
    foreign policy and, 647, 649–650
    government and, 95, 95*p*
    international, 654, 683
    North American Free Trade Agreement (NAFTA), 683
    slave, 115
trademark, 514
traditional economies, 363–364, 363*p*, 364*p*
traffic courts, 269–270
traffic laws, 512, 512*p*, 522
Trans-Alaska pipeline, 434*p*
transfer payments, 500–501
transportation, 308
Transportation, Department of, 252*c*
Transportation Security Administration, 433*p*
traveler's checks, 462
treason, 538
treasurer, county, 321
treasurer, state, 309
treaties, 126, 255, 649, 653
trespassing, 564, 564*p*
trial by jury. *See* jury trials
trial courts, 270
trials, 168
Truckee River, 332, 332*p*
Truman, Harry S, 239, 244, 250*c*, 257, 284*c*, 592*p*, 597, 659
trust, 436
Trusteeship Council, United Nations, 689
Truth in Lending Law, 473

Twelfth Amendment, 187*c*
Twentieth Amendment, 187*c*
Twenty-fifth Amendment, 187*c*
Twenty-first Amendment, 187*c*
Twenty-fourth Amendment, 187*c*, 190
Twenty-second Amendment, 187*c*
Twenty-seventh Amendment, 187*c*, 194
Twenty-sixth Amendment, 187*c*, 193
Twenty-third Amendment, 187*c*
Tyler, John, 250*c*, 284*c*
tyranny, 89, 92, 96

U

Ukraine, 664
unemployment, 394, 539
UNESCO, 688
UNICEF, 688
Uniform Commercial Code, 565
unitary system, 295
United Nations, 659, 671, 686–689, 687*p*, 688*p*, 689*p*, 691
United States Conference of Mayors, 336, 336*p*
***United States* v. *Nixon* (1974),** 282, 282*p*
University of Michigan, 200
USA Patriot Act, 49
Utah
    Electoral College electors, 636*m*
    state constitution, 296*m*
utilities, 330, 330*p*, 333, 437

V

values, 18, 19–22, 23*c*, 31, 519
    careers and, 418
    crime and, 538, 539
    economic goals and, 430–431
    finanancial choices and, 405, 409–410
Van Buren, Martin, 284*c*
vandalism, 537
variable expenses, 406, 406*p*
verdicts, 570–571
Vermont
    congressional representatives, 215
    Electoral College electors, 636*m*
    prison population, 549*c*
    state constitution, 296*m*
Veterans Affairs, Department of, 252*c*
veto, 228, 228*p*, 245, 307
Vice President, U.S., 250, 250*c*, 250*p*
    as president of the Senate, 224, 225
victimless crime, 538
Vietnam War, 219, 659, 682
villages, 323
Virginia, 361*p*
    Articles of Confederation and, 99
      burgesses, 84, 85, 85*p*
    Declaration of Rights, 162*p*
    Electoral College electors, 636*m*
    farming in, 5
    ratification of the Constitution and, 122, 122*p*, 123*c*
    state constitution, 296*m*
Virginia Plan, 114, 115–116
volunteers, 9, 73*c*, 74
voting
    age, 193, 617
    basics of, 617–619, 618*c*, 619*p*
    districts, 599
    Electoral College, 636–637, 636*m*, 637*p*
    influences on, 622–629
    information about, 620–621
    political parties and, 602–603
    purpose of, 621

registration, 617, 617*p*
as responsibility of citizens, 65–66
See also elections
voting rights, 190, 194
of African Americans, 189–190, 189*p*, 190*p*, 617
age, 589, 617
time line, 192–193
voting age and, 193
of women, 191–192, 191*p*, 192*p*, 195, 195*p*, 523, 617
Voting Rights Act, 193

W

wage labor, 388–390
Wagner Act (1935), 390, 393
Wallace, George C., 597
wants, 350–351, 351*p*, 353
War Powers Resolution, 219, 244
warrant, 542
warranties, 410
Warren, Earl, 283, 283*p*, 530
wars, 244. *See also* conflicts; individual wars
Warsaw Pact, 681, 682, 692*m*
Washington
Electoral College electors, 636*m*
state constitution, 296*m*
Washington, D.C., 184*p*, 207*p*, 636*m*
Washington, George, 242, 284*c*, 595
Articles of Confederation and, 101
on bicameral legislature, 116
Constitutional Convention, 111, 113, 113*p*, 123
in Revolutionary War, 100
water and sewage treatment, 330
Watergate scandal, 258, 258*p*, 262, 282, 282*p*
weak-mayor plan, 324–325
Web sites. *See* Internet
Webster, Daniel, 250
welfare, 180, 328, 440, 450, 503
Welfare Reform Act (1996), 180
West
land rush in, 322*p*
migration to, 5
West Germany, 660*p*, 661
West Virginia
Electoral College electors, 636*m*
state constitution, 296*m*
whaling, 651, 652, 654, 655
Whig Party, 595, 596
whips, 225, 591
white-collar crime, 537
White House, 238*p*, 250
Whitman, Christine Todd, 293
Whitman, Meg, 203*p*
wilderness programs, 555
Williams, Roger, 88
wills, 567
Wilson, Woodrow, 241*p*, 284*c*, 597, 658
Wisconsin, 432*p*
Electoral College electors, 636*m*
state constitution, 296*m*
witchcraft, 519
witnesses, 63, 63*c*, 547, 573*p*
women
affirmative action and, 199–202, 200*p*
business owners, 464
in Congress, 219*p*, 224*p*, 237*c*
earnings of, 199
equality and, 201–202, 201*p*
in government, 498*p*
mayors, 340, 340*p*
Phillips v. *Martin Marietta Corporation* (1971), 202

on Supreme Court, 278, 279*p*
voting rights of, 191–192, 191*p*, 192*p*, 195, 195*p*, 523, 617
in the workforce, 201*p*, 202–202, 203*p*, 394, 394*p*
work force, 5–6, 6*c*, 394, 394*p*
full employment, 482–483
service jobs, 6, 6*c*
work place
equality in, 21
safety, 431, 431*p*, 433*p*, 438, 438*p*
Works Progress Administration (WPA), 440*p*
World Court, 689, 689*p*
World Trade Center, 49, 538
World War I, 490, 490*p*, 658
World War II, 219, 244, 659
writ of habeus corpus, 221
write-in candidate, 605
Wyoming
Electoral College electors, 636*m*
prison population, 549*c*
state constitution, 296*m*

X

X Games, 337

Y

yellow-dog contracts, 391, 391*c*, 392
Yeltsin, Boris, 682*p*

Z

Zakim Bridge, 480*p*
Zenger, Peter, 88–89, 89*p*, 164
zoning, 331

Acknowledgements

Cover Design

Staff Designer: Nancy Smith
Vendor: Studio Montage; Seann Dwyer

Team Credits

The people who made up the Civics: Government and Economics in Action team—representing editorial, design services, market research, on-line services/multimedia development, product marketing, and production services—are listed below.

Suzanne Biron, Ellen Bowler, Dan Breslin, Lance Hatch, Deb Levheim, Grace Massey, Tim McDonald, Elizabeth Pearson, Nancy Smith, Mark Staloff, Tom Starbranch, Patricia Williams, Tracy Wilson, Sarah Yezzi

Program Development, Design, and Production

Editorial and Design, Project Management: Pearson Education Development Group
Production: Argosy Publishing

Maps

Argosy Publishing: 105,189, 263, 273, 296, 314, 399, 471, 618, 619, 636, 641, 648, 694 **Colin Hayes:** 35, 36, 71, 161, 216, 220, 231, 252, 383, 475

Tech Art

Argosy Publishing: 42, 51, 62, 76, 77, 103, 133, 181, 205, 235, 237, 243, 261, 275, 287, 302, 314, 315, 333, 343, 371, 380, 385, 393, 396, 397, 405, 411, 423, 424, 425, 444, 445, 446, 446–447, 448, 452, 471, 477, 488, 492, 498, 499, 501, 505, 531, 533, 543, 577, 584, 611, 613, 618, 625, 636, 639, 647, 666, 667, 692, 693, 695 **Mike Hortens:** 35, 36, 71, 161, 216, 220, 231, 252, 383, 475

Illustration

Jim Starr: 32 **Ken Batelman:** 280–281, 306–307 **John Bleck:** 322, 338–339, 378–379, 626 **Susan Poulakis:** 528

Photography

Cover: tl, Syracuse Newspapers/Dick Blume/The Image Works; tml, Wally McNamee/Corbis; tm, Alex Wong/Getty Images, Inc.; tmr, Joseph Sohm/ChromoSohm Inc/Corbis; tr, AP/Wide World Photos; m, Steven W. Jones/Getty Images, Inc.; b, Tom Collicott/Masterfile Corporation

Unit 1: 1 Scott Barrow, Inc./SuperStock

Chapter 1: 7 Pearson Eduction Development Group PEDG; 10 Corbis/Bettmann, David Young-Wolff PhotoEdit Bonnie Kamin, PhotoEdit Derek Cole, Index Stock Imagery Inc., Omni-Photo Communications, Inc. Skjold Photographs; David Kelly Crow, PhotoEdit; Rudolph Vetter, National Archives and Records Administration/Presidential Library; The Granger Collection; 19 David McNew Getty Images, Inc - Liaison; 23 David Young-Wolff, Getty Images Inc. - Stone Allstock; 21 Harvey Finkle, Harvey Finkle; 22 Jose L. Pelaez, Corbis/Stock Market; 25 Will Hart, PhotoEdit

Chapter 2: 28–29 Felicia Martinez, PhotoEdit; 30 Bill Market, PictureQuest; 30–31 David Young-Wolff, PhotoEdit; 30–31 Corbis Digital Stock; 32 David Mager, Pearson Learning; 34 Guy Cali, PictureQuest; 37 The Image Works; 38 EyeWire Collection, Getty Images – Photodisc; 38 Tom & Dee Ann McCarthy, PictureQuest; 39 Kevin Lamarque, Corbis/Bettmann; 40 Tom Stewert, Corbis/Bettmann; 41 Doug Menuez, Getty Images Inc. – PhotoDisc; 42 Joe Sohm, The Image Works; 42 Steve Skjold, PhotoEdit; 43 Andre Jenny, Alamy.com;

43 Lou Jacobs Jr., Grant Heilman Photography, Inc.; 45 Ron Chapple, Getty Images, Inc. - Taxi ; 46 Adam DuBrowa, FEMA; 47 Copley News Service; 48 John Stillwell, AP/Wide World Photos; 48 Max Nash, AP/Wide World Photos; 53 Chuck Savage, Corbis/Bettmann; Ariel Skelley Corbis/Bettmann; Bob Daemmrich/Stock Boston, Inc., PictureQuest; Charles Gupton, Corbis/Bettmann; Reuters/Dan Chung, Corbis/Bettmann; Spencer Platt, Getty Images, Inc - Liaison; PictureQuest; 208–209; Steve Gottlieb, PictureQuest; 54–55 Morton Beebe, Corbis/Bettmann; 56 Frank Siteman, PictureQuest; 58 Spencer Grant, PhotoEdit; 59 Ryan McVay, Getty Images – Photodisc

Chapter 3: 60 Corbis/Bettmann; 61 Mario Villafuerte, Getty Images; 62 Dave Bartruff; Corbis/Bettmann; 62 Robert Brenner, PhotoEdit; 63 Will Hart, PhotoEdit; 63 Corbis RF; 64 CM Studio, Pearson Education Development Group PEDG; 65 Kirk Anderson; 65 AP/Wide World Photos; 67 Mitchell Gerber, Corbis/Bettmann; 68 Pearson Learning; 69 Michael J. Doolittle, The Image Works; 71 Tracy Frankel, Getty Images Inc. - Image Bank; 72 Tanya Constantine, Brand X Pictures; 73 John Eastcott, Stock Boston; 75 Najlah Feanny, Corbis/Bettmann

Unit 2: 80–81 Jack Zehrt

Chapter 4: 100 Corbis/Bettmann; 101 Corbis/Bettmann; 104 Bettmann, Corbis/Bettmann; 82 Corbis/Bettmann; 82 The Granger Collection; 84 Library of Congress; 89 North Wind Picture Archives; 90 Corbis/Bettmann; 91 Dagli Orti, Picture Desk, Inc./Kobal Collection; 92 Mary Evans Picture Library Ltd; 93 The Granger Collection; 93 The Granger Collection; 94 The Granger Collection; 95 American Antiquarian Society; 96 The Granger Collection, The Granger Collection, 96 The Granger Collection; 96 Corbis/Bettmann; 96 The Granger Collection; 97 National Gallery of Art, Washington D.C.; 97 Getty Images Inc., Hulton Archive Photos; 98 Bettmann, Corbis/Bettmann; 99 The Granger Collection

Chapter 5: 110–111 National Constitution Center; 113 The Granger Collection; 114 Jack Zehrt, Getty Images, Inc. - Taxi; 117 The Granger Collection; 117 The Granger Collection; 117 Bettmann, Corbis/Bettmann; 117 Getty Images Inc., Hulton Archive Photos; 117 Corbis/Bettmann; 117 The Granger Collection; 118 Corbis/Bettmann; 118 Independence National Historical Park; 120 Getty Images Inc., Hulton Archive Photos; 121 Bettmann, Corbis/Bettmann; 121 Susan Walsh, AP/Wide World Photos; 122 Art Resource, N.Y.; 122 Patrick Henry Memorial Foundation, Red Hill; 125 Kenneth Lambert, AP/Wide World Photos; 129 Philip Gould, Corbis/Bettmann; 130 Peter Gridley, Getty Images, Inc. - Taxi; 130 Corbis Digital Stock; 130 Corbis Digital Stock; 157 Independence Hall Interior. First floor. Assembly Room, View from center doorway. Photograph by Robin Miller, 2001. Independence National Historical Park Corbis/Bettmann158 Corbis/Bettmann

Chapter 6: 158–159 Dennis Breck, Stockphoto.com; 162 Stephen J. Boitano, AP/Wide World Photos; 163 Amy Etra, PhotoEdit; 166 Christian Science Monitor; 167 Mikael Karlsson, 167 911 Pictures; 168 AP/Wide World Photos; 169 David Young Wolff, PhotoEdit; 170 Reuters New Media, Corbis/Bettmann; 172–173 Tony Freeman PhotoEdit; 174 Corbis/Bettmann; 174 AP/Wide World Photos; 175 Bettmann, Corbis/Bettmann; 177 Pearson Eduction Development Group PEDG; 178 Michael Newman, PhotoEdit; 178 Robin Sachs, PhotoEdit; 179 Bettmann, Corbis/Bettmann; 180 Skjold, The Image Works; 183 Jacques M. Chenet, Corbis/Bettmann; 186 Sandra Baker, Getty Images, Inc - Liaison; 187 Bob Daemmrich, Bob Daemmrich Photography, Inc.; 188 AP/Wide World Photos; 188 The Granger Collection; 188 Getty Images Inc., Hulton Archive Photos; 189 Culver Pictures, Inc.; 189 Corbis/Bettmann

Chapter 7: 190 Library of Congress; 191 The Granger Collection; 193 David Young-Wolff, PhotoEdit; 193 Tony Freeman, PhotoEdit, 194 Bettmann, Corbis/Bettmann; 194 Stephen Frisch Stock Boston; 195 Library of Congress; 197 Hulton Archive Getty Images Inc. - Hulton

Archive Photos; 198 AP/Wide World Photos; 199 NASA/Johnson Space Center; 200 AP/Wide World Photos; 201 Andersen Ross, Getty Images Inc. – PhotoDisc; 202 Laima Druskis, Pearson Education/PH College; 202 Pearson Eduction Development Group PEDG; 203 David McNew, Getty Images; 204 Wolfgang Kaehler, Corbis/Bettmann; 207 Corbis/Bettmann

Unit 3: 208–209 Steve Gottlieb/ Stock Connection / PictureQuest

Chapter 8: 210–211 AP/Wide World Photos; 213 Michael Geissinger, The Image Works; 213 AP/Wide World Photos; 214 Reuters New Media, Corbis/Bettmann; 214 AP/Wide World Photos; 214 Lawrence Jackson, AP/Wide World Photos; 215 AP/Wide World Photos; 216 Dave Martin, AP/Wide World Photos; 218–219 B.M Sobhani, ZUMA Press; 219 Ken Stewart, ZUMA Press; 219 Getty Images Inc. - Hulton Archive Photos; 219 AP/Wide World Photos; 220 The Granger Collection; 220 The Granger Collection; 222 Steve Cole, Getty Images, Inc.- Photodisc.; 224 Dennis Cook, AP/Wide World Photos; 224 Wally McNamee, ZUMA Press; 224 Art Resource, N.Y.; 225 U.S. House of Representatives; 226 The Cartoon Bank; 227 Joseph Sohm/Visions of America, LLC, PictureQuest; 227 Corbis Digital Stock; 229 Michael Newman, PhotoEdit; 230 Pearson Eduction Development Group PEDG; 231 William Philpott, Getty Images; 232 AP/Wide World Photos; 233 Dennis Brack, Stockphoto.com

Chapter 9: 238–239 Dennis O'Clair/Stone, Getty Images Inc. - Stone Allstock; 240 Stock Montage/Hulton|Archive, Getty Images Inc. - Hulton Archive Photos; 241 Corbis Digital Stock; 241 The Granger Collection; 241 Corbis/Bettmann; 241 Corbis/Bettmann; 241 Stock Montage, Inc./Historical Pictures Collection; 241 The Granger Collection; 241 The Granger Collection; 242 AP/Wide World Photos; 242 AP/Wide World Photos; 243 AFP, Corbis/Bettmann; 243 AP/Wide World Photos; 244 Bill Gentile, Corbis/Bettmann; 244 AP/Wide World Photos; 244 Corbis/Bettmann; 245 AP/Wide World Photos; 246 The Detroit News; 247 Bettmann, Corbis/Bettmann; 247 AP/Wide World Photos; 249 Richard T Nowitz, Corbis/Bettmann; 250 AP/Wide World Photos; 251 Eric Draper, The White House Photo Office; 253 NASA/John F. Kennedy Space Center; 254 James Leynse, Corbis/Bettmann; 255 Reuters New Media, Corbis/Bettmann; 256 Pearson Eduction Development Group PEDG; 257 The Granger Collection; 258 Hulton Archive, Getty Images Inc. - Hulton Archive Photos; 258 Corbis/Bettmann; 272 Pearson Learning; 264–265 Corbis RF

Chapter 10: 266 Joe Sohm/Pictor, ImageState/International Stock Photography Ltd.; 266 SuperStock, Inc.; 267 Bonnie Kamin, PhotoEdit; 268 David Young Wolff, Getty Images; 269 John Blanding, AP/Wide World Photos; 270 Mike Mergen, AP/Wide World Photos; 272 Reuters New Media, Corbis/Bettmann; 272 Corbis/Bettmann; 274 Corbis/Bettmann; 277 Ankers Photographers Supreme Court Historical Society; 278 Corbis/Bettmann; 278 Corbis/Bettmann; 281 Reuters NewMedia Inc., Corbis/Bettmann; 282 Corbis/Bettmann; 283 AP/Wide World Photos; 283 AP/Wide World Photos; 284 The Granger Collection; 286 Bettmann, Corbis/Bettmann

Unit 4: 290–291 Eric Fowke / PhotoEdit

Chapter 11: 292–293 Joseph Sohm/ChromoSohm Inc., Corbis/Bettmann; 295 Randy Wells, Getty Images Inc. - Stone Allstock; 297 Reuters, Corbis/Bettmann; 299 Nebraska Game and Parks Commission Nebraska Land Magazine; 299 Steve Greenberg; 300 Kim Kulish, Corbis/SABA Press Photos, Inc.; 300 Paul Sakuma, AP/Wide World Photos; 301 Pearson Eduction Development Group PEDG; 302 Spencer Grant, PhotoEdit; 303 Michael Newman, PhotoEdit; 304 Pearson Learning; 306 AP/Wide World Photos; 307 Jack Kurtz, The Image Works; 307 AP/Wide World Photos; 307 AP/Wide World Photos; 308 Tina Fineberg, AP/Wide World Photos; 310 Gary C. Knapp, AP/Wide World Photos

Chapter 12: 318–319 Alan Schein Photography, Corbis/Bettmann, 320 Philip Gould Corbis/Bettmann; 321 Carl J. Single/Syracuse Newspapers, The Image Works; 321 Geoff Brightling, Dorling Kindersley Media Library; 321 Luis Alvarez, AP/Wide World Photos; 322 EyeWire Collection, Getty Images - Photodisc; 323 EyeWire Collection, Getty Images - Photodisc; 325 Prentice Hall School Division; 326 Corbis/Bettmann; 327 Dale Atkins, AP/Wide World Photos; 329 Arnulf Husmo, Getty Images Inc. - Stone Allstock; 329 Gilles Mingasson/Liaison, Getty Images, Inc - Liaison; 330 Joseph Sohm, Photo Researchers, Inc.; 330 Pearson Eduction Development Group PEDG; 331 Doulas Slone, Corbis/Bettmann; 332 Larry Prosor, SuperStock Inc.; 332 Phil Schermeister, Corbis/Bettmann; 334 EyeWire, Collection Getty Images - Photodisc; 334 Rich Pedroncelli, AP/Wide World Photos; 335 Kevin Horan, Getty Images Inc. - Stone Allstock; 336 Glen Martin The Denver Post; 337 Donald Dietz Stock Boston; 337 Tim Boyle, Getty Images; 339 Susan Farley, Getty Images, Inc - Liaison; 340 Michael Busselle, Getty Images Inc. - Stone Allstock; 340–341 Michael Dwyer, Stock Boston; 341 Michael Mulvey, Corbis/Bettmann

Unit 5: 346–347 Joseph Sohm; Visions of America / Corbis.

Chapter 13: 348–349 James Lemass Index Stock Imagery, Inc.; 350 Izzy Schwartz Getty Images - Photodisc; 350–351 Eddie Hironaka, Getty Images Inc. - Image Bank; 351 Steve Dunwell, Getty Images Inc. - Image Bank; 352–353 Randy Wells, Corbis/Bettmann; 352–353 Vittoriano Rastelli, Corbis/Bettmann; 353 Rhoda Sidney, The Image Works; 356 Garry D. McMichael, Photo Researchers, Inc.; 356 Hiroshi Harada, Photo Researchers, Inc.; 357 Latin Focus, Photo Agency; 358 Richard Cummins, Corbis/Bettmann; 358 StockFood, America; 359 Michael Newman. PhotoEdit; 359 Reuters New Media, Corbis/Bettmann; 360 Adam Lubroth, Getty Images Inc. - Stone Allstock; 360 Bettmann, Corbis/Bettmann; 361 Hulton Archive, Getty Images Inc. - Hulton Archive Photos; 362 Dwayne Newton, PhotoEdit; 363 Jeff Greenberg Unicorn, Stock Photos; 364 Jason Laure, Laure' Communications; 366 David Buffington, Corbis/Bettmann; 367 Gerry McMichael, Photo Researchers, Inc.; 367 Richard Pasley, Stock Boston; 368 Pearson Eduction Development Group PEDG; 369 Hisham Ibrahim/Photographer's Choice, Getty Images, Inc.; 372 Bob Daemmrich, Photography, Inc.

Chapter 14: 380 Bill Aron, PhotoEdit; 380 Mark Richards, PhotoEdit; 381 Frank Siteman, PhotoEdit; 382 Corbis Royalty Free; 384 Tom & Dee Ann McCarthy, Corbis/Bettmann; 386 The Granger Collection; 388 Corbis/Bettmann; 389 Pearson Eduction Development Group PEDG; 390 Private Collection, The Bridgeman Art Library International Ltd.; 390 Corbis/Bettmann; 390 Corbis/Bettmann; 391 Hekimian Julien Corbis/Sygma; 391 Jonathan Nourok PhotoEdit; 391 AP/Wide World Photos; 392 The Cartoon Bank; 394 Chris Ryan Getty Images; 394 Corbis/Bettmann; 395 Chuck Savage, Corbis/Bettmann; 395 Reuters NewMedia Inc., Corbis/Bettmann

Chapter 15: 402 Comstock Images; 402 Comstock Images; 405 Gary Conner, PhotoEdit; 405 Comstock Images; 406 Barbara Peacock, Getty Images, Inc. - Taxi; 406 Ron Kimball, Ron Kimball Photography; 406 Yang Liu. Corbis/Bettmann; 406 Comstock Images; 406 Corbis RF; 408 Ron Kimball, Ron Kimball Photography; 409 Bill Aron, PhotoEdit; 411 Cydney Conger, Corbis/Bettmann; 412 The Cartoon Bank; 413 David Young Wolff, PhotoEdit; 415 Getty Images – Photodisc; 417 David Young, Wolff PhotoEdit; 417 Underwood & Underwood, Corbis/Bettmann; 420 David Young Wolff, PhotoEdit; 420 U.S. Department of Labor; 423 Bob Krist, Corbis/Bettmann

Unit 6: 426–427 Getty Images / Getty Images Editorial.

Chapter 16: 428–429 Bill Varie, Corbis/Bettmann; 431 Lewis Hine, Corbis/Bettmann; 432 Pam Gallichio, U.S. Environmental Protection Agency Headquarters; 432 Richard T Nowitz, Corbis/Bettmann; 433 AP/Wide World Photos; 434 Corbis Royalty Free; 436 Nancy P. Alexander, PhotoEdit; 438 Tom Carter, PhotoEdit; 439 AP/Wide World Photos; 440 Detail of street scene from City Life Mural by Victor Arnautoff/Richard Cummins/Corbis; 441 Pearson Eduction Development Group PEDG; 442 Tim Wright, Corbis/Bettmann; 445 D. Boone Corbis/Bettmann; 445 David Young-Wolff, PhotoEdit

Chapter 17: 454–455 David Young-Wolff, PhotoEdit; 456 Brian Pieters, Masterfile Corporation; 457 G.K. & Vikki Hart/Image Bank, Getty Images Inc. - Image Bank; 457 Vincent Hobbs, SuperStock, Inc.; 458

Acknowledgements

...au of Engraving, AP/Wide World Photos; 458 Treasury ...artment, AP/Wide World Photos; 459 Corbis/Bettmann; 461 Culver Pictures, Inc.; 462 Spencer Grant, PhotoEdit; 462 Comstock, Royalty Free Division; 463 C Squared Studios, Getty Images - Photodisc; 465 The Cartoon Bank; 466 Susan Van Etten, PhotoEdit; 467 Tony Freeman, PhotoEdit; 468 Bonnie Kamin, PhotoEdit; 469 Ron Sherman, Photographer; 472 Amy Etra, PhotoEdit; 473 Butch Dill; 474 Reuters NewMedia Inc., Corbis/Bettmann

Chapter 18: 480–481 AP/Wide World Photos; 482 AP/Wide World Photos; 486 AFP Corbis/Bettmann; 487 Glenn Paulina, Transtock, Inc; 487 Jules T. Allen, Corbis/Bettmann; 489 Susan Van Etten, PhotoEdit; 491 AP/Wide World Photos; 492 Mug Shots/Stock Market, Corbis/Stock Market; 494 Eric Larrayadieu/Stone, Getty Images Inc. - Stone Allstock; 494 Mitch Wojnarowicz, The Image Works; 495 The Cartoon Bank; 496 Getty Images Inc. - PhotoDisc; 496 Corbis/Bettmann; 497 Richard Laird/Taxi, Getty Images, Inc. - Taxi; 499 AP/Wide World Photos; 500 Townsend P. Dickinson, The Image Works; 501 Susan Van Etten, PhotoEdit; 502 Pearson Eduction Development Group PEDG; 503 AP/Wide World Photos

Unit 7: 508–509 Royalty-Free / Corbis.

Chapter 19: 510–511 Geri Engberg, The Image Works; 512 Mark C. Burnett, Stock Boston; 512; Getty Images; 512 Getty Images - Photodisc; 513 Tim Wright, Corbis/Bettmann; 514 United Media/United Feature Syndicate, Inc.; 515 Frank Oberle Getty Images Inc. – Stone, Allstock; 515 Peter Adams, Getty Images, Inc. - Taxi; 516 University of Pennsylvania Philadelphia; 518 David Stoecklein, Corbis/Bettmann; 520 Micael Newman, PhotoEdit; 521 The Granger Collection; 522 David Mendelsohn, Masterfile Corporation; 522 U.S. Department of Agriculture; 523 The Granger Collection; 525 Joe Sohm, Alamy.com; 526 Jeff Greenberg, PhotoEdit; 527 Ryan McVay, Getty Images - Photodisc; 527 Getty Images Inc. – Stone, Allstock

Chapter 20: 534–535 Leslye Borden, PhotoEdit; 537 Sandy Huffaker/Getty Images News Services, Getty Images, Inc - Liaison; 538 The Cartoon Bank; 539 Corbis Royalty Free; 540 HIRB, Index Stock Imagery, Inc. 542; Alan Youngblood, Silver Image Photo Agency, Inc. 543; Siede Peis, Getty Images - Photodisc- 544; Bettmann Corbis/Bettmann; 545 Bob Daemmrich, Bob Daemmrich Photography, Inc. 546; Bob Daemmrich Photography, Inc. 546; Bob Daemmrich Photography, Inc. 547; Michael Newman, PhotoEdit; 548 John Neubauer, PhotoEdit 549; Mikael Karlsson, Alamy.com 550; Bob Daemmrich, The Image Works 550; Spencer Platt/Getty Images News Service, Getty Images, Inc - Liaison; 553 Jeff Greenberg, PhotoEdit 553; Pearson Eduction Development Group PEDG; 554 James Shaffer, PhotoEdit 555; Bob Daemmrich, The Image Works

Chapter 21: 560–561 Alan Klehr/Stone Getty Images Inc. - Stone Allstock; 564 AP/Wide World Photos; 565 CartoonStock Ltd. CSL; 566 A. Ramey, PhotoEdit; 566 Steve Warmowski/Journal-Courier, The Image Works; 568 Corbis/Bettmann; 569 Bonnie Kamin, PhotoEdit; 571 Jeff Cadge/Image Bank, Getty Images Inc. - Image Bank; 573 AP/Wide World Photos; 574 Robert Llewellyn ImageState/International, Stock Photography Ltd.; 575 Pearson Eduction Development Group PEDG; 576 AP/Wide World Photos; 577 Michael Newman, PhotoEdit; 578 Bill Fritsch/Brand X Pictures, Alamy.com; 579 Andre Jenny, Alamy.com; 579 V.C.L./Tipp Howell/Taxi, Getty Images, Inc. - Taxi; 581 Frank Herholdt/Stone, Getty Images Inc. - Stone Allstock

Unit 8: 586–587 David Butow / Corbis/SABA.

Chapter 22: CS Getty Images, Inc. – Photodisc; 588–589 David Butow, Corbis/Bettmann; 590 VictoryStore.com; 590 VictoryStore.com; 591 Mark Kegans, Getty Images; 592 Bettmann, Corbis/Bettmann; 592 AP/Wide World Photos; 593 Pearson Eduction Development Group PEDG; 594 AP/Wide World Photos; 595 The Granger Collection; 595 Corbis/Bettmann; 596 The Granger Collection; 601 Alden Pellett, Getty Images; 602 David J. & Janice L. Frent Collection, Corbis/Bettmann; 602 Wally McNamee, Corbis/Bettmann; 602 Walter P. Calahan, Folio, Inc.; 602 Walter P. Calahan, Folio, Inc.; 602

Corbis/Bettmann; 603 AP/Wide World Photos; 604 Pearson Learning; 606 The Cartoon Bank; 607 Chris Hondros, Getty Images; 608 AP/Wide World Photos; 608 Corbis/Bettmann; 609 Wally McNamee, Corbis/Bettmann; 611 Bob Daemmrich Photography, Inc.

Chapter 23: 614–615 Getty Images Editorial, Getty Images, Inc - Liaison; 616 Rob Crandall, The Image Works; 617 NOVASTOCK, PhotoEdit; 618 Jonathan Nourok, PhotoEdit; 618 AP/Wide World Photos; 619 Joseph Sohm/ChromoSohm Inc. Corbis/Bettmann; 619 AP/Wide World Photos; 619 AP/Wide World Photos; 620 Robert King, Getty Images, Inc - Liaison; 622 Jonathan Nourok, PhotoEdit; 623 Eric Fowke, PhotoEdit; 623 The Granger Collection; 624 Rachel Epstein, PhotoEdit; 625 AP/Wide World Photos; 627 The Cartoon Bank; 628 Laura Kleinhenz, Corbis/Bettmann; 628 Mark Richards, PhotoEdit; 629 Bettmann, Corbis/Bettmann; 631 VictoryStore.com; 632 Michael Newman, PhotoEdit; 633 Pearson Eduction Development Group PEDG; 634 AP/Wide World Photos; 635 Joseph Sohm/ChromoSohm Inc., Corbis/Bettmann; 635 Najlah Feanny/Saba, Corbis/SABA Press Photos, Inc.; 637 AP/Wide World Photos; CS Bob Daemmrich Bob Daemmrich Photography, Inc.

Unit 9: 642–643 Jeff Christensen / Getty Images Editorial

Chapter 24: CS Michael Newman PhotoEdit; 494 AP/Wide World Photos; 642–643 Morton Beebe, Corbis/Bettmann; 647 Airman Jonathan M. Cirino, U.S. Navy News Photo; 649 Sean Gallup, Getty Images, Inc - Liaison; 651 Reuters NewMedia Inc., Corbis/Bettmann; 652 AP/Wide World Photos; 653 "Three Men in a Tub" by Fred Seibel. Reprinted by permission of the Richmond Times-Dispatch/Corbis; 654 AP/Wide World Photos; 654 AP/Wide World Photos; 655 Ernest Manewal, SuperStock, Inc.; 657 Photri-Microstock, Inc.; 658 Corbis/Bettmann; 659 The Granger Collection; 659 AP/Wide World Photos; 660 David & Peter Turnley, Corbis/Bettmann; 660 Peter Turnley, Corbis/Bettmann; 661 Pearson Eduction Development Group PEDG; 664 AP/Wide World Photos; 665 AP/Wide World Photos

Chapter 25: 670–671 Jon Bradley/Stone, Getty Images Inc. - Stone Allstock; 672 Morton Beebe, Corbis/Bettmann; 673 Lynsey Addario, Corbis/Bettmann; 676 Harald Sund/Getty Images Editorial, Getty Images, Inc - Liaison; 677 Paul Chesley/Stone, Getty Images Inc. - Stone Allstock; 679 Christopher Morris/Stock Photo, Black Star; 680 AFP, Corbis/Bettmann; 680 European Press Photo Agency, EPA, AP/Wide World Photos; 680 AP/Wide World Photos; 682 Owen Franken, Corbis/Bettmann; 682 Peter Turnley, Corbis/Bettmann; 683 Ren Norton/Stephen P. Crosby, The Boston Herald; 684 Reuters NewMedia Inc., Corbis/Bettmann; 685 Peter Turnley, Corbis/Bettmann; 687 AFP, Corbis/Bettmann; 687 Henry Kaiser, eStock Photography LLC; 688 The Cartoon Bank; 689 AFP, Corbis/Bettmann; 690 Pearson Eduction Development Group PEDG; 691 Francoise de Mulder, Corbis/Bettmann; UO 346–347 Erik Freeland, Corbis/Bettmann UO 426–427 Getty Images Editorial Getty Images, Inc - Liaison; UO 508–509 Alan Schein Photography Corbis/Bettmann; David Young-Wolff/PhotoEdit, PictureQuest

Note: Every effort has been made to locate the copyright owner of material used in this textbook. Omissions brought to our attention will be corrected in subsequent editions.